The Deep Roots of Moder.

MW00795592

This book explores the deep roots of modern democracy, focusing on geography and long-term patterns of global diffusion. Its geographic argument centers on access to the sea, afforded by natural harbors which enhance the mobility of people, goods, capital, and ideas. The extraordinary connectivity of harbor regions thereby affected economic development, the structure of the military, statebuilding, and openness to the world – and, through these pathways, the development of representative democracy. The authors' second argument focuses on the global diffusion of representative democracy. Beginning around 1500, Europeans started to populate distant places abroad. Where Europeans were numerous they established some form of representative democracy, often with restrictions limiting suffrage to those of European heritage. Where they were in the minority, Europeans were more reticent about popular rule and often actively resisted democratization. Where Europeans were entirely absent, the concept of representative democracy was unfamiliar and its practice undeveloped.

John Gerring is Professor of Government at the University of Texas at Austin.

Brendan Apfeld is a data scientist at CVS Health.

Tore Wig is a professor of Political Science at the University of Oslo.

Andreas Forø Tollefsen is a Senior Researcher at the Peace Research Institute Oslo (PRIO).

The Deep Roots of Modern Democracy

Geography and the Diffusion of Political Institutions

John Gerring

University of Texas, Austin

Brendan Apfeld

CVS Health

Tore Wig

University of Oslo

Andreas Forø Tollefsen

Peace Research Institute Oslo (PRIO)

CAMBRIDGE
UNIVERSITY PRESS

CAMBRIDGE
UNIVERSITY PRESS

University Printing House, Cambridge CB2 8BS, United Kingdom

One Liberty Plaza, 20th Floor, New York, NY 10006, USA

477 Williamstown Road, Port Melbourne, VIC 3207, Australia

314–321, 3rd Floor, Plot 3, Splendor Forum, Jasola District Centre,
New Delhi – 110025, India

103 Penang Road, #05–06/07, Visioncrest Commercial, Singapore 238467

Cambridge University Press is part of the University of Cambridge.

It furthers the University's mission by disseminating knowledge in the pursuit of
education, learning, and research at the highest international levels of excellence.

www.cambridge.org
Information on this title: www.cambridge.org/9781009100373
DOI: 10.1017/9781009115223

© John Gerring, Brendan Apfeld, Tore Wig, and Andreas Forø Tollefsen 2022

First published 2022

A catalogue record for this publication is available from the British Library.

ISBN 978-1-009-10037-3 Hardback
ISBN 978-1-009-11489-9 Paperback

To Larry Ceplair, Jim Gregory, Martin Jay, and Michael Rogin, who got me excited about history so many decades ago that it seems like history, but still lives with me.

J.G.

To my grandparents, Burns and JoAnne.

B.A.

To my parents, for teaching me the value of history, and to Sirianne, for making the years working on this project bright.

T.W.

To Jan Ketil Rød, Halvard Buhaug, and Håvard Strand, who sparked my interest in GIS and spatial thinking, and to Mette, Elise, and Ida, for patience, love, and support.

A.F.T.

Contents

List of Figures   *page* xiii
List of Maps   xiv
List of Tables   xv
Acknowledgments   xvii

Part I   Introduction

1   Deep Roots   3

2   Democracy   19

Part II   Maritime Geography

3   Harbors and Democracy   47

4   Harbors   68

5   Regional Comparisons   105

6   Global Analyses   165

7   Mechanisms   183

Part III   European Diffusion

8   Democracy As a European Club   211

9   European Ancestry   224

10 Colonial and Post-colonial Eras   246

11 Global Analyses   287

Part IV   Alternate Explanations

12 Modalities of Geography   307

13 Modalities of European Diffusion   322

14 Economics, Institutions, Culture   340

Part V   Conclusions

15 A Summary View   371

16 Connectedness   379

   Appendix A: Variables   398
   Glossary   408
   Bibliography   410
   Index   507

   Online Appendices
   B Ports in History
   C Overall Governance
   D European Ancestry
   E Sources

Detailed Contents

List of Figures   *page* xiii
List of Maps   xiv
List of Tables   xv
Acknowledgments   xvii

I Introduction

1 Deep Roots   3
   Extant Work   7
   In Search of Distal Causes   10
   Key Terms   14
   A Roadmap   17

2 Democracy   19
   Intellectual History   20
   Definition   23
   Origins   27
   Evolution   33
   Measurement   35
   The Study of Democracy   42

II Maritime Geography

3 Harbors and Democracy   47
   Economic Development   48
   Military Organization   52
   Statebuilding   55
   Openness   59
   By Land or by Sea   65

4 Harbors   68
   Maritime History   69
   Ports   76
   Natural Harbors   84
   Natural Harbor Distance   93

Alternate Measures   97
Units of Analysis   100
Other Modes of Transport   101

5   Regional Comparisons   105
Europe   109
North Eurasia   118
Middle East and North Africa   124
Sub-Saharan Africa   132
East Asia   138
Southeast Asia   151
South Asia   157
Conclusions   163

6   Global Analyses   165
The Early Modern Era   166
Grid-cell Tests   168
Specification Tests   171
Port/Harbor Distance   174
Democracy Indices   176
Samples   177
Impact   179
Conclusions   182

7   Mechanisms   183
Economic Development (Including Urbanization)   183
State Size   191
Diversity   199
Democratic Values   200
Crossnational Tests   202
Mediation Analyses   203
Conclusions   207

III European Diffusion

8   Democracy As a European Club   211
European Democracy for Europeans   213
Democracy As a Club   216
Gaining Entrance to the Club   218
Summary, Caveats, and Implications   219

9   European Ancestry   224
Imperialism as a Maritime Enterprise   225
Diaspora   230
Demography   231
Europe   233
European-ness   237
Counting Europeans   238
Demography and Colonialism   243

10 Colonial and Post-colonial Eras   246
    The British Empire   249
    The French Empire   267
    The Spanish Empire   270
    The Portuguese Empire   276
    Democracy and Oppression   277
    Statistical Tests   281

11 Global Analyses   287
    Specification Tests   287
    Measures of Democracy   289
    Measures of European Ancestry   289
    Sub-sample Analyses   293
    Replications   295
    Instrumental Variables   298
    Impact   300
    Conclusions   301

IV **Alternate Explanations**

12 Modalities of Geography   307
    Climate   308
    Irrigation   309
    Agriculture   310
    Mountains   312
    Islands   313
    Tests   315
    Impact   319
    Conclusions   321

13 Modalities of European Diffusion   322
    Colonialism   322
    Religion   325
    Language   328
    All Together Now   330
    Conclusions   337

14 Economics, Institutions, Culture   340
    Agricultural Transitions   340
    Modernization   342
    Inequality   345
    Labor Scarcity   346
    Marriage and Family   347
    Feudalism   350
    Parliaments   352
    Christianity   353
    Catholicism   355
    State Size   357
    State–Society Relationships   359

Ideas   361
Conclusions   364

V Conclusions

15 A Summary View   371
   The Evidence Reviewed   371
   Determinism?   374

16 Connectedness   379
   The Changing Relevance of Connectedness   380
   Globalization and Democracy   392
   From National to International Democracy?   395

   Appendix A: Variables   398
   Glossary   408
   Bibliography   410
   Index   507

   Online Appendices
   B: Descriptive Statistics
   C: Ports in History
   D: Overall Governance
   E: European Ancestry
   F: Sources
      Part I   Cited in the Appendices
      Part II   Maritime History
      Part III   European Diffusion

Figures

1.1 A historical model of modern democracy   *page* 6
2.1 The salience of "democracy" and "republic" through
    the ages   21
2.2 Two dimensions of democracy   26
2.3 Polyarchy through time   39
3.1 Harbors and democracy   67
4.1 Three maritime terms   69
4.2 Histograms of natural harbor distance   97
6.1 Varying grid-cells   170
6.2 Natural harbors and democracy, predicted values for the
    contemporary era   180
6.3 The impact of natural harbors on democracy
    through time   181
7.1 City foundings and port status through history   189
7.2 Harbor distance and population density   190
7.3 Harbor distance and state size (grid-cells)   195
7.4 State size and democracy through time (grid-cells)   196
8.1 European ancestry and representative democracy   220
9.1 A speculative model of European ancestry   233
9.2 Histogram of European ancestry   242
9.3 Colonial duration and European ancestry   244
11.1 Predicted values from benchmark model, 1960–2019   301
11.2 The impact of European ancestry on democracy
     through time   302
13.1 European influence on democracy through time   338
16.1 Mountains and democracy through the modern era   381
16.2 Globalization and democracy   393

Maps

2.1 Succession among ethnic groups in the premodern era   *page* 37
2.2 Polyarchy around the world, 2019   40
4.1 Ports in antiquity   77
4.2 Ports in 1890   80
4.3 Ports in 1953   81
4.4 The Sicilian coastline   87
4.5 Distance from predicted port to actual port   92
4.6 Natural harbors   92
9.1 European ancestry over time   241

Tables

2.1	Ethnographic Atlas polity types	*page* 36
4.1	The European maritime revolution	72
4.2	The global maritime revolution	74
4.3	Port datasets and their correspondences	82
4.4	Port types	88
4.5	Prediction models and their fit	90
4.6	Natural harbour distance scores	95
4.7	Distance variables	98
5.1	Cross- and within-region comparisons	108
5.2	European parliaments, 1200–1700	119
6.1	Democracy prior to the modern era	167
6.2	Specification tests (grid-cells)	169
6.3	Specification tests	172
6.4	Measures of port/harbor distance	175
6.5	Democracy indices	177
6.6	Sample restrictions	178
7.1	Cities and ports	187
7.2	Natural harbors and economic development (grid-cell)	192
7.3	Lagged state size and democracy (grid-cells)	198
7.4	Diversity in inland and coastal cities	201
7.5	Democratic values	202
7.6	Mechanisms: first-order tests	204
7.7	Mediation analysis	206
7.8	Factor analysis of mediation variables	207
9.1	Colonial capitals and their ports	228
9.2	Alternate indices of European ancestry	242
10.1	Legislative activity across British colonies in the Americas	252
10.2	History of representation in the British Caribbean	254
10.3	Elective colonial assemblies	282
10.4	The legacy of European ancestry within empires	283
10.5	Independence	285
11.1	Specification tests	288

11.2	Democracy indices	290
11.3	Measures of European ancestry	291
11.4	Sample restrictions	294
11.5	Replications	297
11.6	Instrumental variable analyses	299
12.1	Geographic factors, intercorrelations	317
12.2	Geographic factors, specification tests	318
12.3	Geographic factors, predictive power in the contemporary era	319
13.1	Colonialism	324
13.2	Religion	328
13.3	Language	329
13.4	Intercorrelations among European pathways	331
13.5	"Horse races"	332
13.6	Major pathways from Europe, predictive power	333
14.1	Agricultural transition	342
14.2	Economic development	344
14.3	Labor scarcity	345
14.4	Kinship intensity	349
14.5	State history	362
A.1	State-level variables	398
A.2	Grid-cell level variables	404
A.3	Bespoke datasets	407

Acknowledgments

This book has deep roots. What follows is a partial accounting.

For data, assistance finding sources, and answers to our incessant queries we are grateful to Scott Abramson, David Altman, Quamrol Ashraf, Peter Bang, Jeanet Bentzen, Ulba Bosma, Andrew Brooks, Bruce Campbell, Larry Ceplair, Fred Cooper, Paulo Teodoro de Matos, Cesar Ducruet, Peter Emmer, Bouda Etemad, Gary Feinman, Steve Friesen, Michael Gibbs, Steven Gray, Sumit Guha, Ken Hall, Dominik Hangartner, Richard Hardack, Rob Harrison, John Hattendorf, Allen Hicken, Wayne Hughes, Dave Kang, Morgan Kelly, Edgar Kiser, Ubo Kooijinga, Charlie Kurzman, Matt Lange, Vic Lieberman, David Ludden, Patti Maclachlan, Jim Mahoney, Juraj Medzihorsky, Sankar Muthu, Nathan Nunn, Jari Ojala, Olukunle Owolabi, Louis Putterman, Mark Ravina, Glenn Robinson, Alex Sanmark, Walter Scheidel, Jonathan Schulz, Humphrey Southall, Sanjay Subrahmanyam, Julian Swann, Nick Tackett, Marjolein t'Hart, Geoff Uttmark, Michiel van Groesen, Jan Willem Veluwenkamp, David Weil, Chris Welzel, and Tiffanesha Williams.

Portions of the project were presented to seminars held at American University, Gothenburg University (as part of the annual V-Dem conference), Griffith University, the Massachusetts Institute of Technology, and University of Oslo. We are grateful to seminar participants.

Essential feedback on the manuscript was received from Michael Bernhard, Alexandra Cirone, Adam Clulow, Lee Cojocaru, Michael Coppedge, Scott Gates, Jacob Hariri, Vanya Krieckhaus, Evan Lieberman, Raul Madrid, Pat Manning, Lachlan McNamee, Jørgen Møller, Lee Morgenbesser, Jack Paine, Glenn Robinson, Svend-Erik Skaaning, David Stasavage, Arun Swamy, Nick Tackett, Richard Unger, David Waldner, Kurt Weyland, from members of a graduate seminar on democracy at University of Texas, Austin, spring 2020, and from two anonymous reviewers for the Press.

In the painstaking process of collecting and coding data we are grateful to Lee Cojocaru. For research assistance, we are grateful to Vlad

Ciobanu, Ingvild Leren Stensrud, Sindre Haugen, and Christian Gladman Gundersen.

We are grateful, finally, for the upswelling of interest in history among social scientists, from whom we have learned so much. This includes Daron Acemoglu, Lisa Blaydes, Carles Boix, Mark Dincecco, Stephen Haber, Andrej Kokkonen, Alex Lee, Nathan Nunn, Ola Olsson, Jim Robinson, Jim Scott, Dan Smith, Adam Storeygard, Anders Sundell, Jan Teorell, Charles Tilly, Bob Woodberry, and Daniel Ziblatt – as well as those listed above who contributed directly to this book.

Historians, anthropologists, and archeologists are much too numerous to list. The Bibliography will give the reader some idea of our heavy debts.

I

Introduction

1 Deep Roots

The past is never dead. It's not even past.

William Faulkner (2011 [1951])

Why are leaders chosen in free and fair elections in some countries while in others they inherit power, seize power, or engineer victory in rigged elections? Why is political speech unregulated in some countries and tightly controlled in others? Why are opposition leaders free to express their views in some countries while in others they languish in jails, are subject to harassment or assassination, or go into exile?

There are many possible answers to the question of regimes and a great deal of work has accumulated on the subject.[1] Yet, for all its richness and sophistication this body of work is narrowly circumscribed in time. Most studies focus on the postwar era. A few peer into the nineteenth century. Prior to that, work is thin and tends to be focused on particular historical and regional contexts.

As a point of departure, we assert that patterns of democracy and dictatorship observable across the world today are not simply the product of recent history. They have deeper roots.

In this book, we concern ourselves with those distal causes. This means that we will be dealing with factors that are structural rather than eventful. Causes and effects are separated by centuries, in some cases by millennia. And the pathways from X to Y are long and tortuous. Some time will be required before we can hope to unravel them.

Without further ado let us lay out our arguments, which center on geography and long-term patterns of diffusion. Following that, we shall review alternate explanations, introduce our data and methodology, and define key terms. By way of conclusion, we provide a roadmap of the book.

---

[1] For surveys of the literature see Coppedge (2012), Coppedge et al. (2022b), Møller, Skaaning (2013), Teorell (2010).

Harbors

Our geographic argument centers on access to the sea. This is afforded by natural harbors, which may be located on the coast or on navigable rivers that flow, unimpeded, to the coast. Harbors enhance mobility – of people, goods, capital, and ideas.

The extraordinary connectivity of harbor regions affects economic development (nurturing trade, urbanization, human capital, and economic growth), the structure of the military (away from standing armies and toward naval power), statebuilding (toward smaller states, confederations, or overseas empires with semi-autonomous colonies), and openness to the world (through trade, migration, tourism, religious pilgrimages, and conquest).

Each of these developments shifts the balance of power between rulers and citizens. As a result, areas situated close to harbors are more likely to evolve in a democratic direction than areas surrounded by large landmasses or inaccessible coasts.

As is the case with most geographic arguments, there is no identifiable point of onset. We surmise that the importance of harbors increased as shipping technology improved and ships displaced overland travel as the dominant mode of communication, travel, and trade. This was a long process, occurring at different speeds in different parts of the world. In Asia, it was well underway in the premodern era; in many parts of the New World it is a comparatively recent phenomenon. Accordingly, we expect that the influence of harbors on political institutions unfolded over a very long period of time in regions of the world where shipping has a long history, and over a shorter period of time in regions where shipping is a more recent technological development. Everywhere, we expect some attenuation as other forms of transport, travel, and communication supplant the primacy of shipping at the end of the twentieth century.

European Ancestry

Although there was considerable variety in political institutions throughout the premodern world, only one area developed systems of representation through parliaments. Defined in this fashion, democracy (i.e., representative democracy) was invented in Europe.

Beginning about 1500, with the advent of sailing vessels capable of circumnavigating the globe, Europeans began to populate the distant abroad, often in the shadow of colonial conquest. By 1900, they could be found virtually everywhere, in varying proportions. We argue that the resulting ratio of Europeans to non-Europeans – which we call *European ancestry* – structured the fate of regimes around the world.

Larger numbers of Europeans meant greater *exposure* to the idea of democracy for non-Europeans, transmitted through schools, churches, newspapers, radio, direct contact with settlers, settler societies abroad (such as the new hegemon, the United States), and the metropole. Larger numbers of Europeans brought additional features that we refer to as the *infrastructure* of democracy including education, advanced transport and communications, urbanization, a nation-state form of political organization, property rights, capitalism, and wealth. Larger numbers of Europeans, finally, changed *incentives*. For Europeans, it meant that they were likely to control political outcomes under democratic rules. Consequently, they had an incentive to invest in democratic institutions and were more likely to respond positively to claims by slaves and indigenes for inclusion.

It is important to appreciate that democracy in the first instance meant democracy *for Europeans*. Where they were numerous they established some form of representative democracy, usually with restrictions (de jure or de facto) limiting suffrage and officeholding to those of European descent. Where they were in the minority they were more reticent about popular rule and often actively resisted democratization. And where Europeans were entirely absent, the concept of representative democracy was unfamiliar and the practice undeveloped. In this fashion, Europeans served as agents of diffusion as well as agents of constraint.

We expect that the impact of European ancestry on democracy applied with increasing force as European influence over the world grew, reaching its apogee during the twentieth century – at which point most of the world was directly controlled by, or under the regional hegemony of, a European power or transplanted European settlers. By the turn of the twenty-first century, the influence of Europe and various "neo-Europes" across the world was declining and the concept of representative democracy no longer a European preserve. Thus, we conjecture that the impact of European demography on regimes increased monotonically across the early modern and modern eras with some attenuation in recent decades (and expected further attenuation in the future).

Synthesis

These two arguments are interconnected. That representative democracy developed on the European continent is, in part, a product of its aqueous geography. And that Europe discovered the world, rather than the reverse, was also a product of an aqueous geography. Harbors foster

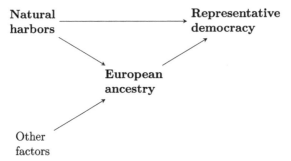

Figure 1.1 **A historical model of modern democracy**
The overall framework of the book, tying together Part II (on harbors)
and Part III (on Europeans).

an outward orientation, as trade and seafaring come naturally to civilizations bordering the sea. From this perspective, it is not surprising that the
age of globalization was led by Europeans rather than Asians or Africans.
Finally, we must make allowances for how Europe traversed the world. It
was of course through ships. And this means that areas (outside Europe)
well endowed with natural harbors were the first to be discovered, the
most likely destinations for European migrants, and the areas most
closely linked to Europe through trade and cultural exchange. Harbors
connect.

To summarize, we argue that natural harbors serve as a prime mover of
political institutions in the modern era, having a direct effect on the
development of representative democracy as well as an indirect effect
through the European diaspora. This historical model is illustrated sche-
matically in Figure 1.1.

Although the schema is admirably compact, it is important to signal
that the *mechanisms* at work in our framework – represented by the solid
arrows in Figure 1.1 – are quite complex. We are hard put to identify a
parsimonious theory, one that reduces to a few fundamental precepts
that operate consistently across millennia on a global scale. So far as we
can tell, natural harbors and European ancestry mattered for *many*
reasons.[2]

---

[2] These connecting threads are elaborated briefly in the passages above and at length in
Chapter 3 (with respect to natural harbors) and Chapter 8 (with respect to European
ancestry). In the concluding chapter, we offer some ideas about the role of connectedness
in fostering democracy in the modern era, integrating ideas from these chapters into a
broader theory.

Extant Work

Big arguments about big subjects do not materialize out of thin air. They arise from an ongoing conversation with the scholarly literature. In this case, the conversation extends beyond disciplinary boundaries, encompassing work by historians, archeologists, classicists, as well as historically inclined social scientists. The Bibliography includes nearly two thousand articles and books, with additional sources on related subjects listed in Appendix E (online at Dataverse). Here, one will find precedents for nearly every claim made in this long book.

Yet, the schema represented in Figure 1.1 is not simply a restatement of accepted wisdom. Indeed, most of the secondary studies cited in this book are not focused on democracy per se but rather on the histories of specific regions or adjacent subjects such as maritime history or colonial history.

To our knowledge, no study of democracy has identified a causal role for natural harbors, though a few historical studies emphasize the liberating role of the sea and of maritime culture more generally (e.g., Abulafia 2019; Lambert 2018). Likewise, no study has systematically explored the role of European ancestry as a conditioning factor in modern regimes, though the idea is presented briefly in Hariri (2012) and the impact of European settlement on *economic* development outside Europe is widely acknowledged.[3] In these respects, our arguments may claim novelty.

Alternate Explanations

When one paints on a large canvas, as we do in this book, there may be an unspoken expectation that everything about the topic will be revealed. That is not the case here. The schema presented in Figure 1.1 is far-reaching but by no means comprehensive. Democracy is affected by myriad factors, many of which have nothing to do with natural harbors or European ancestry. Lots of things are going on.

How do these other causal factors fit with our own explanation? This is important as a matter of clarity and also as an issue in causal inference. Note that when dealing with observational data (where the treatment of theoretical interest is not randomized) every rival hypothesis poses a potential problem of confounding.

---

[3] See Acemoglu, Johnson, Robinson (2001, 2002), Easterly, Levine (2016), Engerman, Sokoloff (2000).

Even if rival explanations are orthogonal (non-confounding), we still want to know something about their relative impact and robustness. Some factors are trivial and others substantial. Some are robust to a wide variety of measures, specifications, and estimators; others are more delicate, depending upon stronger assumptions. Unless we test alternate causal factors together with our own, and unless these tests are directly comparable, we cannot assess these issues. Cumulation requires standardization.

For the narrow reason of reaching causal inference, and the broader rationale of building general knowledge, we take an inclusive approach to alternate explanations. These are introduced briefly and tested against available evidence from the modern era, wherever possible. Of course, we do not have the space to discuss each theory at great length or to conduct extensive tests of every possible hypothesis, and many theories have never been operationalized on a global scale. Accordingly, these tests – summarized in the next section – should be regarded as probative.

A Brief Survey

From extant work on *geography* we can identify numerous factors that might influence institutional development. These include climate, irrigation, agricultural potential, mountains, and islands.[4] Each can be operationalized in a variety of ways, leading to a large number of testable hypotheses. Our analyses show that distance from the equator is a strong predictor of democracy in the modern era, though it should be noted that this geographic factor appears to operate almost entirely through European ancestry. Other geographic factors are not as robust. These theoretical and empirical questions are vetted in Chapter 12.

Extant work on *European diffusion* has focused on several pathways from Europe to the world. Principal among these are colonialism and Protestantism.[5] These factors can be measured in a variety of ways, offering a variety of testable hypotheses. Our analyses confirm that

---

[4] On climate, see Elis, Haber, Horrillo (2017). On irrigation, see Bentzen, Kaarsen, Wingender (2016), Wittfogel (1957). On agriculture, see Ang, Fredriksson, Gupta (2020), Mayshar, Moav, Neeman (2017), Scott (2017), Stasavage (2020). On mountains, see Braudel (1972[1949]: 38–9), Korotayev (1995), Scott (2009). On islands, see Anckar (2008), Congdon Fors (2014), Srebrnik (2004). Naturally, these topics are not as compartmentalized as the references suggest; a fuller discussion can be found in Chapter 12.

[5] On colonialism, see Lange (2004), Olsson (2009), Owolabi (2015). On Protestantism, see Anderson (2004), Bollen, Jackman (1985), Brown (1944), Bruce (2004), Hadenius (1992), Lankina, Getachew (2012), Tusalem (2009), Woodberry (2012). For further discussion see Chapter 13.

Protestantism is a strong predictor of democracy in the modern era, though questions may be raised about its causal status. These issues are discussed in Chapter 13.

In addition, there is a large residual category of potential causal factors that might be described as *economic*, *institutional*, or *cultural*. This includes the timing of transitions to sedentary agriculture, modernization, inequality, labor scarcity, patterns of marriage and family, feudalism, parliaments, Christianity, Catholicism, state size, state–society relations, and ideas. Our global analyses (which, of necessity, leave aside Europe-specific causes) show some evidence in favor of agricultural transitions, kinship intensity, and state history, though the relationship of these factors to democracy is sensitive to choices in specification. In any case, most of these factors are downstream from our framework, illustrated in Figure 1.1. Indeed, some of these factors are identified as causal mechanisms in our framework. These issues are discussed in Chapter 14.

Of course, this does not exhaust the panoply of potential causes of democracy. A short tour of recent work would include additional factors such as civil society (e.g., popular protest, civil organizations, trust), constitutional rules (e.g., presidentialism, electoral systems, federalism, decentralization), elites (e.g., divisions, alliances, pacts, leadership succession), macroeconomics (e.g., inflation, unemployment, per capita GDP growth, trade), human capital (e.g., education, health, the age distribution of the population), social diversity (ethnic, linguistic, or religious), and international influences (e.g., international organizations, foreign aid, foreign intervention, short-term diffusion).[6] We regard these factors as proximal and thus downstream from our argument.

To conclude, our empirical tests – presented in Part IV of the book – suggest that one geographic factor (equator distance) has an effect on modern democracy comparable to the impact of natural harbors and that one alternate pathway from Europe (Protestantism) is as strongly correlated with modern democracy as European ancestry. Other factors do not seem to be robust predictors of democracy in the modern era or are downstream from the factors of theoretical interest in this study. Accordingly, our two-part theoretical framework (if true) adds substantially to what is currently known about the long-term causes of democracy.

---

[6] These factors, and many others, are reviewed in synthetic works on democracy, cited above.

In Search of Distal Causes

We turn now to methodological considerations. How can one test non-manipulable causes that operate slowly, almost imperceptibly, over the course of centuries?

Let us begin with the most common species of explanation for the rise of democracy. This sort of explanation focuses on features specific to Europe, e.g., classical Greece, the Roman Empire and its dissolution, feudalism, the Catholic Church, family and marriage patterns, a culture of individualism, a spirit of liberty, and so forth.[7] These sorts of explanations generally offer limited variability within Europe, or none that could be regarded as the basis for a strong empirical test given the interdependent relationship of European states and cultures. Beyond Europe, one is left with a binary contrast between Europe and everywhere else, which is not very revealing given that Europe is different from other regions in many ways, each of which constitutes a potential confounder. Explanations that feature something distinctive about Europe are therefore not very tractable.

Our theory is more falsifiable. All three nodes of theoretical interest – natural harbors, European ancestry, and democracy – are measurable on a global scale across the modern era and offer considerable variability across regions and within regions. This facilitates a wide variety of empirical tests.

Of course, these tests are not as conclusive as experimental tests, where the treatment of theoretical interest is manipulated by the researcher. By way of entrée, it may be helpful to identify the hard and soft points of the empirical analyses to come.

As a feature of geography, natural harbors are causally exogenous. There is no risk that the outcome could impact the cause, or that other causes could affect both. However, there is a risk that any association found between harbors and democracy might be spurious if the former serves as a proxy for some (unmeasured) factor; hence the importance of specification tests that include all geographic factors that could plausibly impact the long-term development of political institutions. Doubts would be further eased if one could trace the impact of harbors on democracy through a set of observable mechanisms. Unfortunately, a long and tortuous route connects geography to regimes in the modern era. Some of these putative pathways can be measured and tested. But since natural harbors are static, and affect social relations slowly over

---

[7] Citations to this voluminous literature can be found in Chapters 2 and 14.

the course of millennia, we cannot process-trace their relationship to democracy.

European ancestry changes over time and bears a more proximal relationship to the outcome; as such, the mechanisms are less mysterious. However, there are questions about the exogeneity of this causal factor that resist easy answers, despite our attempts to model the relationship with instrumental variables.

These are the problems of causal inference that we wrestle with in subsequent chapters. In this section, we review our general approach. This is complicated ground and we cannot hope to cover it in any detail. Nonetheless, it is important to foreshadow the evidence that lies ahead.

Data

Data for this project is gathered from a variety of sources. Port locations in the ancient world are drawn from *The Catalogue of Ancient Ports and Harbours* compiled by Arthur de Graauw (2017), who culls from the Barrington Atlas, the Pleiades project, the Digital Atlas of the Roman Empire, and many other primary and secondary sources. In the modern era, we rely on *Lloyd's List* (Ducruet et al. 2018) and several editions of the *World Port Index* (US Navy 1953; NGIA 2017). Helpfully, all of these sources provide the precise GIS location of ports, allowing for fine-grained analyses. We note parenthetically that this project makes extensive use of maps, all of which employ a standard WGS 84 geographic coordinate system (EPSG 4326).

Maritime history is tracked through inland transport rates, Soundtoll traffic, trade, ship departures from Europe to Asia, ship tonnage and speed, number of mariners, and migration rates – for which we draw on a wide variety of historical sources. We explore the relationship of ports to early cities, city foundings, contemporary megalopolises, urbanization, colonial capitals, state size, ethnic diversity, and democratic values (the latter with data drawn from the latest round of the World Values Survey, which provides the GIS location of each interview). We also construct a ratio measure of the degree to which states relied on naval or land forces. And we collect original data on the share of Europeans in colonies and countries around the world from 1600 to the present, the largest database of its kind.

We devote special care to the outcome of interest. To measure democracy in the early modern era we enlist data on legislatures in British North America (Graham 2018), the British Caribbean (from various sources), and across all European colonies (Paine 2019). Within Europe, we enlist data on parliaments extending back to the Middle

Ages (Abramson, Boix 2019). And across ethnic groups we utilize the Ethnographic Atlas (Murdock 1967), from which a simple measure of democracy is derived from procedures used to select headmen in bands, tribes, and small states.

Even so, data sources on political institutions in the premodern era are quite limited. Consequently, our analysis of democracy during this period rests primarily upon traditional historical materials of a qualitative nature – the vast secondary literature produced by historians, archeologists, anthropologists, classicists, and a few historically minded social scientists. Here, we adopt a case study approach focused on within-region comparisons (e.g., across Europe or across South Asia) or within-colonizer comparisons (e.g., across British colonies or across Spanish colonies).

In the modern era, it is possible to measure democracy on a global scale with greater precision and nuance. Our benchmark measure is the Polyarchy index from the Varieties of Democracy (V-Dem) project (Coppedge, Gerring, Glynn, et al. 2020; Teorell et al. 2018). Although V-Dem stretches back to 1789 and extends to all sizeable countries and some colonies, it omits micro-states and many colonies. To generate more comprehensive coverage we interpolate missing data with other sources.

As secondary measures of democracy in the modern era we enlist the Polity2 index from the Polity IV project (Marshall, Monty, Jaggers 2016) and the Lexical index of electoral democracy (Skaaning et al. 2015) Occasionally, we home in on specific aspects of democracy like male suffrage (measured by V-Dem for the twentieth century and Bilinski 2015 for the nineteenth century).

Statistical Tests

Methods of analysis follow from what is plausible with the data that is available. In many cases, it is possible to conduct statistical tests of hypotheses using colonies, countries, cities, grid-cells, or individuals as units of analysis.

A cross-sectional research design is preferred, as the predictors of theoretical interest are static (in the case of natural harbors) or sluggish (in the case of European ancestry). In the latter setting, we supplement cross-sectional models with fixed-effect models.

To control for time-effects across the observed period we include time dummies and cluster standard errors according to the unit of observation. As an additional test we focus on a single point in time close to the present (2000 CE), eliminating the problem of temporal autocorrelation but with considerable information loss (since all other years are dropped). Potential problems of causal identification are probed with instrumental variables that attempt to model assignment to treatment. Myriad specification tests are enlisted in order to probe different assumptions about the data-generating process. Descriptions of each variable and its source are placed in Appendix A and descriptive statistics in Appendix B (online at Dataverse).

Our approach to causal identification is eclectic. We recognize that there is rarely a single "correct" approach to the analysis of observational data. At the same time, there are a limited number of *plausible* approaches, each of which rests on a somewhat different set of assumptions about the data-generating process. If the results of these tests are relatively stable, one can justify greater confidence that the relationship might be causal. But we should not kid ourselves. Macro-level causal relationships occurring across centuries can never be estimated precisely and always require supporting theory and assumptions.

Assuming that a factor plays a causal role, its impact on democracy may be understood along several dimensions. First, we present graphs of estimated values for the outcome as the variable of theoretical interest varies. Second, we examine changes in impact over time using rolling regressions. Where possible, we examine the impact of a factor when grid-cells are aggregated differently, which helps to address potential problems posed by interference across units (stable unit treatment assumption, aka SUTVA) as well as the modifiable area unit problem.

In comparing the strength of relationships across rival predictors we employ several techniques. First, we take note of what is called (loosely) "statistical significance," as registered in p values and t statistics. While prone to abuse, these statistics are informative if we bear in mind their assumptions and their limitations. Second, we compare the impact of a set of variables on total model fit, understood in linear models with the R^2 statistic. None of these approaches is sufficient on its own. However, taken together, they give us a fairly nuanced sense of how valuable different predictors might be in explaining regime types in the modern era.

Qualitative and Quantitative Evidence

Not all our arguments can be subjected to formal statistical tests. This is perhaps true for any large project but it is especially true for the present project. Because of the nature of the available evidence, chapters focused on the premodern era incline towards qualitative data while chapters focused on the modern era incline towards quantitative data. Let us briefly review the strengths and weaknesses of these rather different styles of evidence as they pertain to the present study.[8]

Large-N cross-case analyses in this book rely on variables that are either objective in nature or coded by others, reducing the scope of potential authorial bias. Large-N models are also capable of handling stochastic error. Finally, findings are apt to be generalizable since our global samples contain nearly all the sizeable polities in the world, functioning more like a census than a sample.

Small-N comparisons of a most-similar variety eliminate many background factors that might serve as confounders in a large-N analysis. They also allow us to look closely at the development of those cases through time, which may reveal processes (i.e., causal mechanisms) that are not visible in statistical analyses. However, they are subject to biases in the secondary literature, upon which we are reliant. It should be noted that the sources consulted for this project are mostly English-language, which limits our reach. Material of this nature also requires greater authorial judgment and is subject to questions about generalizability.

Ideally, these methodologies complement each other, shedding light on different aspects of our research question and invoking different assumptions. In this instance, neither is very solid without the other.

Key Terms

As a final act of theoretical exposition, we must define several key terms that recur in this chapter and the chapters that follow. This includes *democracy*, the *state*, and various *historical periods* (premodern, modern, etc.).

Our proposed definitions are not unusual. However, because these concepts are understood in many ways it is important to define them formally so that readers know what we have in mind. Doing so will also help to clarify the meaning and scope-conditions of our theory.

Democracy

Generally understood, democracy means rule by the people. In ascertaining the degree to which people rule we distinguish two dimensions: *membership* (the number of people living within a polity who are granted

---

[8] For general discussion of the vices and virtues of case study and large-N cross-case research see Gerring (2017).

citizenship rights) and *accountability* (the control they have over policy-making). Membership varies, in principle, from one (only the ruler is empowered) to all (full citizenship rights are granted to all permanent residents). Accountability varies from none (there is no accountability whatsoever) to full (whatever that might mean). Democracy is thus a matter of degrees.

When we characterize a polity as democratic we mean that the polity in question was more democratic (autocratic) than other contemporaneous polities. We realize that no sizeable polity in antiquity bestowed full membership on all permanent adult residents, and thus none would be considered a democracy today. Nonetheless, to say that ancient Athens was a democracy is meaningful if this statement is understood relative to polities existing at that time. Similar caveats apply to our use of the term democracy prior to the twentieth century, a period when suffrage was generally restricted along gender and/or racial lines.

We recognize, finally, that two quite different forms of popular rule qualify as democratic.

Direct democracy means that citizens make policy decisions themselves, usually through popular assemblies or consultative bodies. From what we can tell, these mechanisms were widespread in the premodern era. Although classical Athens is the best-known example there is no reason to suppose that it was unique. Citizens probably played important deliberative and decision-making roles in other city-states, as well as in bands and tribes without statelike forms of political organization. We show in Chapter 2 that this sort of democracy was widespread throughout the premodern world, and by no means limited to Europe.

Representative democracy means that citizens rule through representatives who are accountable to them. This entails a representative assembly (a parliament), regular elections to that body, and a constitution prescribing formal rules of operation and perhaps specific rights reserved for citizens. Here, Europe played a leading role. During the Middle Ages, the concept and practice of representative democracy developed in various places across the European subcontinent. In the modern era, it spread throughout the world and is now considered to be essential for the achievement of democracy in statelike political organizations. Since our theoretical objective is primarily focused on the modern era and on statelike entities, in the chapters that follow we usually refer to democracy as a set of representative institutions.

Further discussion of the conceptualization and measurement of democracy, and its applicability to regimes past and present, can be found in Chapter 2.

States

The framework illustrated in Figure 1.1 applies to statelike political organizations. These organizations have a single locus of power (a capital), sovereignty or semisovereignty (some degree of self-rule, as enjoyed by most overseas European colonies), a recognized territory that the government controls, and a governmental apparatus that persists from one ruler to the next.

This definition may be regarded as an ideal-type, which existing polities reflect to varying degrees. Inevitably, there are problems of operationalization. When does a chiefdom take on the attributes of a state? When does a state lose that designation, due to deficits in one or more of the foregoing attributes? There are plenty of borderline cases that would be difficult to code even with full information. As one moves back in time, information becomes scarcer and details are even harder to resolve.

Nonetheless, the distinction between states and non-state or pre-state entities such as bands, tribes, and small chiefdoms is crucial. Our framework does not purport to explain modes of organization or degrees of democracy within the latter.[9]

Periods

Because we are examining vast stretches of history it is important to make some distinctions among periods. Although these distinctions are arbitrary, and much blurrier around the edges than the following dates imply, they are nonetheless indispensable. Accordingly, we adopt the following conventions:

- *Premodern:* from the first civilizations to 1789 or first European contact
  - *Ancient:* from the first civilizations to 800
  - *Medieval:* from 800 to 1500
  - *Early modern:* from 1500 to 1789 or first European contact
- *Modern:* from 1789 (or first European contact) to the present
- *Contemporary:* from 1960 to the present

Note that the dividing line between modern and premodern is sometimes defined by the French Revolution (1789) and sometimes by the cataclysmic encounter between Europeans and other peoples (which occurred in different places at different times and with varying severity).

---

[9] We do attempt to offer a preliminary *description* of regimes across all polities – state and non-state – in Chapter 2. But when we turn to the task of *explanation* our purview narrows.

In the latter instance, "premodern" refers to societies as they existed, or were thought to exist, prior to European contact. We trust that these varying usages will be clear from context.

A Roadmap

Chapter 2 explores the meaning and measurement of democracy through the ages and offers a brief survey of its manifestations. As such, it sets the stage for arguments to follow.

Part II of the book focuses on maritime geography. In Chapter 3, we explain how the presence of natural harbors might affect the long-run prospects of democracy. In Chapter 4, we discuss maritime history, the history of ports, and our strategy for identifying natural harbors, culminating in our key empirical variable – natural harbor distance. The final section discusses an obstinate units-of-analysis problem. Chapter 5 explores the role of ocean exposure on the long-run development of political institutions by looking at each of the major regions of the world with statelike polities in the premodern era. Chapter 6 probes the relationship of natural harbors to democracy in a series of crossnational tests, focused mostly on the modern era. Chapter 7 offers an empirical exploration of possible mechanisms at work in the relationship between harbors and democracy.

Part III focuses on the diffusion of democracy from Europe. Chapter 8 lays out our argument for how European ancestry influenced regime types around the world. Chapter 9 discusses issues of conceptualization and measurement – who qualifies as European and how their numbers can be estimated in colonies and countries around the world and through time. Chapter 10 explores the colonial and post-colonial era, focusing on particular colonizers and regions. Chapter 11 analyzes the relationship between European demography and democracy in a global context.

Note that Parts II and III are organized in a parallel fashion. The first chapters (3 and 8) introduce each theoretical framework and are relatively short. Readers wishing to know about our arguments can head straight to these chapters. Later chapters deal with conceptualization and measurement (Chapters 4 and 9), case studies (Chapters 5 and 10), and crossnational empirics (Chapters 6 and 11).

Part IV explores alternate explanations for the deep history of modern democracy. Chapter 12 focuses on geographic factors including climate, irrigation, agriculture, mountains, and islands. Chapter 13 considers alternate pathways of European influence including colonialism (especially English), religion (especially Protestant), and language (understood as including any European language). Chapter 14 explores a wide variety of causal factors centered on economics, institutions, and culture.

Part V is the concluding section of the book. Chapter 15 summarizes the arguments and evidence presented in preceding chapters. Following that, we come to terms with an issue looming over these arguments, which may be viewed by some readers as "deterministic." Chapter 16 moves beyond the arguments and evidence of the book, sketching a broader vision. There, we argue that democracy is advanced when human *connectedness* is enhanced. This process includes many forms of transport and communications (not just shipping) and involves migration and travel on everyone's part (not just Europeans).

Appendices offer further details. Appendix A defines all variables used in the book and their sources. Appendix B provides descriptive statistics. Appendix C provides extensive lists of early cities and their port status, European colonies and their relationship to ports, and coastal and inland cities and their assumed levels of diversity. Appendix D explores additional outcomes connected to the quality of governance that might be affected by natural harbors and European ancestry. Appendix E shows data sources and historical coding of European ancestry for each country, colony, or dependency from 1600 to 2019. Appendix F lists sources cited in the previous appendices and also additional sources – not cited in the Bibliography – that provide background information pertaining to various sections of the book. Because of their ungainly size Appendices B–F are posted online in Dataverse, along with replication materials.

2   Democracy

Democracy is commonly described as having an inherent superiority over every other form of government. It is supposed to advance with an irresistible and pre-ordained movement. It is thought to be full of the promise of blessings to mankind; yet if it fails to bring with it these blessings, or even proves to be prolific of the heaviest calamities, it is not held to deserve condemnation. These are the familiar marks of a theory which claims to be independent of experience and observation on the plea that it bears the credentials of a golden age, non-historical and unverifiable.   Henry Sumner Maine (1886: vii–viii)

What is democracy and how can we chart its history? Although it is not our mission to settle these difficult questions it is important to offer a provisional map of our subject.

We begin with a brief discussion of the history of the idea of democracy. By this, we mean the history of the term itself as well as other terms that dance around the periphery – liberty, freedom, representation, and so forth – and thus express various elements of democracy's core meaning, which we take to be *rule by the people*.

In the second section, we propose a definition that we believe is suitable for a broad, historical inquiry. This definition involves two dimensions: membership and accountability, each understood as a matter of degree.

In the third section we turn to the institutional history of democracy. Where did democracy originate? We show that when defined in a broad fashion, elements of democracy were present everywhere in the premodern world.

In the fourth section, we follow the evolution of democracy in early modern and modern eras, as it progressed from "direct" to "representative" modes appropriate to larger political units (e.g., nation-states). Here, the leading edge was European.

The fifth section of the chapter focuses on the problem of measurement. We begin with indicators available in the premodern era and proceed to the – much more extensive – indicators available for the modern era.

The final section of the chapter makes a case for why we should focus on the distant past in order to better understand democracy in the twenty-first century – the importance of the *longue durée*.

Intellectual History

Although our primary interest is in democracy as a set of institutions, it is important to understand a little bit about the intellectual history of this key concept. Institutional history and intellectual history, while separate objects of study, inform each other in revealing ways. And yet, as we shall see, the intellectual history of this topic is rather difficult to grasp.[1]

Let us begin with the term itself. Through most of recorded history "democracy" was not a salient term. It existed in all European languages but it didn't register very often in the written record. This is evident in a Google Ngram showing the share of published work (in English) in the Google Books database with the term "democracy." Figure 2.1 shows that the term was vanishingly rare in the seventeenth century, growing somewhat more common in the eighteenth and nineteenth century, and becoming quite popular in the twentieth century. By contrast, "republic" was much more commonly invoked before the twentieth century (leaving aside a momentary drought around 1700).

Not only was "democracy" low-profile prior to the twentieth century, it also bespoke a lowly status. Historical texts generally equate democracy with mob rule. To say someone was a democrat was disparaging. Only recently has the term become widely valorized.[2]

Because of its paucity and negative valence, the concept of democracy cannot be approached solely through its terminological history. The intellectual history of this concept is obliged to incorporate neighboring terms that conveyed aspects of popular rule but were more commonly used and carried a positive valence. These include liberty, freedom, constitutional rule, rule of law, natural rights, equal rights,

---

[1] Aspects of this intellectual history may be gleaned from many works, e.g., Cartledge (2016), DeWiel (2000), Dunn (1992, 2005), Israel (2010, 2013), Keane (2009), Kloppenberg (2016), Kurunmäki, Nevers, Te Velde (2018), Markoff (1999), Meier (2011), Miller (2018), Morgan (1989), Muller (1966), Osborne (2012), Pocock (1975; 1980), Siedentop (2014), Skinner (1978), Stromberg (1996), Tuck (2016). Works focused on the term itself include Christophersen (1966), Naess (1956), Palmer (1953), Rosanvallon (1995), Shoemaker (1966).

[2] Granted, we have only the record of literate people, who enjoyed elite status of one sort or another. Since these writers did not self-identify as members of the demos it should not be surprising that they viewed popular power with circumspection. As for the common people, we cannot say for sure how they regarded the idea, or whether they thought much about it.

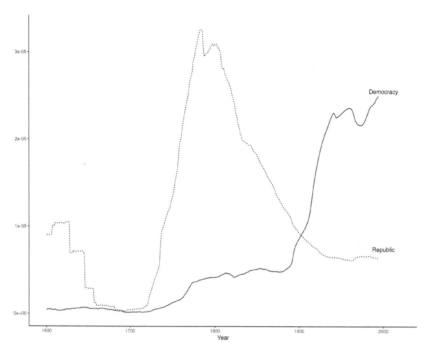

Figure 2.1 **The salience of "democracy" and "republic" through the ages**
The relative frequency of each 1-gram (word) as a fraction of all 1-grams published (in English) within a given year, averaged across a fifty-year moving window. Terms are matched using case-sensitive search on the first letter and case-insensitive search on subsequent letters. Data provided by Google Ngram (Michel et al. 2011).

limited government, responsible government, and republic (included by way of reference in Figure 2.1). One must also consider popular slogans such as "what touches all should be approved by all," "the rights of Englishmen," "the rights of man," "no taxation without representation," and *"liberté, égalité, fraternité."* Often, democratic sentiment was framed in terms of evils to be avoided – tyranny, corruption, oppression, power, feudalism, slavery, the Slave Power, aristocracy, the Norman yoke, communism, and so forth. Each of these terms and expressions has a complex history.

Complicating matters further, democracy has no well-established classic text or set of texts. The western political tradition – from the Greeks to the Romans to the Enlightenment – might be regarded as a canon. However, this is a diffuse and heterogeneous collection of texts.

Extracting a democratic lineage from this body of work requires considerable effort and interpretation.[3]

Moreover, democracy has no founding figure, someone who embodies the ideal in popular thought – a Moses, Buddha, Confucius, Christ, Muhammad, or Marx. The names of the foremost protagonists of democracy in ancient Greece, in Rome, or in the republics of early modern Europe, are often obscure. We do not know who should be credited for the Magna Carta, for example. Accordingly, the history of democracy cannot be told through biographies of great men and women, their deeds, and their ideas. This is understandable when one considers that the capacity for self-rule cannot be won by a hero or granted as a gift. Moses could lead his people to freedom; but no individual can lead a people to democracy. It doesn't work that way.

This does not mean that leaders and ideas are irrelevant. After all, the idea that a group without power deserves a share of power is a powerful idea. But it should be understood that democracy's history is a piecemeal one, in which each struggle has a very specific focus.

When excluded groups fought for rights they often had a rather limited view of who should wield power – namely, themselves. Nobles fought for privileges that would grant them autonomy and security from the vicissitudes of the king. Merchants fought for property rights. Serfs fought for freedom of movement. Imperial subjects fought for independence from colonial rule. Slaves and indigenous people fought for civil liberty. Working men – and somewhat later, women – fought for suffrage. And so forth.

Democratic struggles tend to have a local meaning and application. For every group that is granted democratic rights there is another group that is excluded from those rights. This feature of democratic advance is understandable, as none of these struggles would have succeeded if they had been overly ambitious. One can rarely see beyond the next hill; nor would it make strategic sense to do so.

From the present vantage point all of these struggles could be seen as democratic struggles, and some were in fact interconnected. But few of the participants conceptualized it that way. Their sights were set on

---

[3] By way of contrast, "liberty" is an ideal that stretches back in time, has always been valorized, at least by those who fought for it, and boasts a widely recognized pantheon of heroes – Cicero, Machiavelli, More, Locke, Sidney, Bolingbroke, Jefferson, Constant, Mill, and so forth. This intellectual history is more readily apparent, though of course subject to interpretation. See De Ruggiero (1927), Eliot (1853), Manent (1996), Rosenblatt (2018), Schmidtz, Brennan (2010), Skinner (2012). For a glimpse of the complexities, one might contemplate attempts to apply the concept to parts of the world where the concept of liberty/freedom is not well defined (e.g., Kelly, Reid 1998).

immediate goals. Until the mid-nineteenth century, few leaders appealed to the general ideal of *democracy*.

This brings us to a central point: democracy is a constructed concept and does not (at least until very recently) reflect the conscious ideas or ideologies of the protagonists. In this light, our use of the term to cover historical developments across millennia of recorded human history is an outrageous anachronism.

Yet, if we wish to make systematic comparisons across different time periods we must employ a systematic vocabulary. We cannot adopt different terms in every period just to stay contemporary. Virtually any attempt to deal with the distant past involves the use of abstract terms (e.g., feudalism, republicanism) that were not understood, or were differently understood, by contemporaries. "Democracy" is an arbitrary choice, to be sure. But it is perhaps somewhat less arbitrary than other possible choices.

Definition

How, then, should the concept of democracy be defined (for present purposes)?

As a general definition, everyone seems to agree that democracy means *rule by the people*. This meaning extends back to ancient Greece and thus unites ancient and contemporary uses of the term. However, what it means to rule, and who the people are, is a matter of dispute. Here, one finds considerable variation.

The Varieties of Democracy ("V-Dem") project identifies seven conceptions of democracy – electoral, liberal, consensus, majoritarian, participatory, deliberative, and egalitarian (Coppedge, Gerring, Glynn, et al. 2020). David Held (2006) offers an even wider array of democratic models – classical, republican, liberal, Marxist, competitive elitist, pluralist, legal, participatory, and deliberative – each of which takes different forms.

We see no end to this debate. Nor should there be. Democracy means different things in different contexts because there are different ways in which people can rule. Moreover, these factors change from time to time and place to place, and are almost never directly observable. Small wonder that democracy is a contested concept.

Nonetheless, in the interest of clarity we must define our terms. Our operating hypothesis is that democracy has deep roots, which means we must craft a concept that takes cognizance of those roots. If our definition focuses only on elections with mass suffrage no trace of democracy will be found before the nineteenth century and we will have closed off the past for any clues into the present. Our chosen definition thus reflects the extraordinarily broad context of this project, which encompasses polities across the world and throughout history.

Granted, we might have adopted other concepts – oligarchy, republicanism, etc. – to represent democracy's prehistory. However, that approach presupposes a clean typology that sorts polities from ancient times to the present into categories that are mutually exclusive and exhaustive. We cannot envision such a framework. Thus, although the reader will encounter other terms periodically in the text, they are employed only for aesthetic relief. Our theoretical focus throughout this book is on democracy.

In conceptualizing this concept we distinguish two dimensions: *membership* in the body politic (aka citizenship) and *accountability*.[4]

Membership

The body politic, or political community, refers to those members of a society who enjoy rights and privileges allowing them to participate meaningfully (freely) in politics (Tussman 1968). At one extreme, only one or several individuals enjoy full rights of political participation. This body politic is composed of an individual (a personal dictatorship), or a family who pass down power in a hereditary fashion (a monarchy). In other polities, effective participation is extended to a privileged social class, e.g., to aristocrats (an oligarchy), merchants (a plutocracy), priests (a theocracy), or army officers (a stratocracy). Rights of participation may also be shared broadly, e.g., among all free (non-enslaved) men, all men, or all adults. This sort of polity may be called a democracy if one is only focused on issues of membership.

For present purposes, what is important is that membership in a body politic may be exclusive or inclusive. Sometimes, the line separating members and non-members is easy to draw, as when certain classes of people are explicitly excluded (by law or constitutional provision) from participation. Sometimes, it is more opaque, as when practices diverge from formal procedures, when there are no formal procedures, or when different sorts of rights are reserved for different types of citizens. These empirical issues are often difficult to sort out but nonetheless central to determining a polity's democratic status.

---

[4] This follows Dahl's (1971) influential conceptualization. Since Dahl was focused on the modern era, it made sense to view elections as the central mechanisms of accountability, and qualifications for participation in elections (suffrage) as the criterion of membership in the body politic. In our context, with a much longer historical perspective, it makes sense to define these dimensions in a broader fashion.

Accountability

In any sizeable polity there must be a single person or a small body charged with executing decisions. Whether organizing a hunt or supervising the implementation of a health reform bill, there must be someone in charge. Let us call this individual (or small body) the *executive*.

In some cases, the executive is not accountable to anyone. It is, effectively, a body politic of one, as discussed above. In other cases, the executive responds to cues from a group of citizens who compose the body politic. He or she is accountable to them. This moves the polity in a more democratic direction.

In order to determine how much accountability exists we must understand the nature of this relationship. To what extent is the principal (the body politic) able to monitor the behavior of the agent (the executive) and sanction poor performance? How much control does the principal have over the agent?

There are many ways to establish a principal–agent relationship, and many ways to subvert it, so this is not an easy matter to assess. Presumably, one would want to know how the executive is chosen and under what circumstances s/he can be removed. Of equal importance is whether members of the body politic are able to effectively coordinate with each other. In a very small circle of members, coordination should be fairly easy to achieve. As the circle widens, this task becomes more complex. We shall assume that effective coordination – independent of the executive – involves the ability to speak freely, a flow of information ("news") that is not controlled by the executive, and independent organizations (e.g., guilds, firms, interest groups, clubs, associations, political parties).

As with the question of membership, there are many details to consider and they are not easy to measure. Indeed, they are generally not directly observable. Even so, they are essential to determining whether, or to what extent, the members of the body politic rule.

A Two-Dimensional Schema

Having introduced two key dimensions of democracy let us put them together. To do so, we present a diagram in which membership is represented on the X axis and accountability on the Y axis, as shown in Figure 2.2.[5]

---

[5] This schema is reminiscent of Dahl (1971: 6) and, more recently, of Ferejohn and Rosenbluth (2016: 308).

MEMBERSHIP

Figure 2.2 **Two dimensions of democracy**
The concept of democracy, understood across two dimensions, along
with several exemplars.

In this schema, an ideal-type *autocracy* occupies the lower-left quadrant (low/low), where membership is effectively limited to one individual
(and his/her family or clique) and there is no accountability to a larger
group. An ideal-type *democracy* occupies the upper-right quadrant (high/
high), where all (adult) inhabitants are members of the body politic and
where the executive is fully accountable to them. Well-known polities are
placed within the schema where they seem, in our judgment, to belong
(very approximately).

Several points about the schema illustrated in Figure 2.2 deserve
comment.

First, the two dimensions of democracy *vary independently*. A polity may have narrow membership but high accountability, a combination found in ancient Athens, where citizenship was limited to free men native to the city but where those men were able to govern themselves with little delegation of power (and hence, one supposes, few problems of accountability). Likewise, a polity may be characterized by broad membership but weak accountability, a combination found in regimes such as contemporary Russia and sometimes referred to as "electoral authoritarian" (Schedler 2006) or "competitive authoritarian" (Levitsky, Way 2010).

Second, and relatedly, the two dimensions are in considerable *tension* with each other. The more inclusive a regime, the harder it generally is to assure that the people who are sovereign in principle are sovereign in practice, i.e., that they actually exercise accountability over the executive. Where numbers increase so do coordination problems. Masses of people are hard put to deliberate, reach decisions, and oversee complex tasks of implementation. Moreover, as a regime becomes more inclusive it is likely to encounter citizens who are ill-equipped to engage meaningfully in politics. They may not have resources or free time for leisure activities such as debating the pros and cons of government health care or immigration policy. And some people are simply uninterested in politics. This is one reason why the ideal-type democracy – combining full membership and perfect accountability – is unlikely ever to be achieved.

Third, the two criteria must be judged across *different levels* of government. A regime that is autocratic at the top may be more democratic at the bottom. This is not an easy matter to ascertain, especially in the premodern era. However, we often have a general sense of how centralized polities were, which is a clue to whether citizens may have enjoyed some powers at local levels.

Fourth, regime types are *matters of degree*, with autocracy at one end and democracy at the other. Historical and contemporary polities exhibit a range of variation along this continuum. Arguably, no real existing polity has ever fully instantiated either extreme: there are no pure autocracies or pure democracies. There is always something more that could be done to improve – or mitigate – the ideal of popular rule. Describing these differences of degree is what this chapter is about. Explaining these differences of degree is what the rest of this book is about.

Origins

According to a traditional view, democracy has its origins in Europe, a region associated with liberty since its invention (Wilson, van der Dussen

2005: 13). This history may be traced back to ancient Greece and Rome, to Germanic tribes that inherited lands abandoned by the western empire, to the western branch of Christianity, to the medieval and Renaissance-era city-states of northern Italy and the Hanse, to the parliaments that grew up across the continent, or to the English and French revolutions. Whatever the point of origin, the point of geographic contrast is usually Asia.[6]

Posed in this fashion, the debate over democracy's origins is complicated by an implicit *orientalism* (Said 1978). For centuries, European writers – including Aristotle, Hippocrates, Montesquieu, Marx, and Weber – have presented a stylized vision of polities in the East as "Asiatic (or Oriental) despotism."[7] These descriptions were usually based loosely on accounts provided by European travelers who had wandered to distant lands and returned to tell their stories. Tales featuring stories of absolutist excess – inevitably tinged with sexual innuendo – attracted more attention back home than tales of negotiation or decentralized governance. The orientalist trope was hard to resist.[8]

There were also organizational reasons to view polities outside Europe through autocratic lenses. In order to establish hegemony in regions where they were vastly outnumbered, European imperial powers needed local rulers whom they could negotiate with, coopt, and coerce. Where centralized forms of rule existed, indirect rule was possible. Given existing constraints of manpower and revenue this was usually preferable to direct rule, which required greater investment and greater risk.[9] Accordingly, in non-settler colonies Europeans – and especially the British and the Dutch – looked for leaders who embodied monarchical power. Where such leaders did not exist they were sometimes invented – which is to say, someone with regal bearing was promoted to chief (a "warrant chief") and treated as if he possessed all the authority of a monarch. By contrast, societies without any semblance of monarchy

---

[6] See Acton (1919: ch. 1), Capen (1875), Clayton (1911), Eliot (1853), Guizot (2002 [1851]), Hattersley (1930), Maine (1886), May (1877), Muller (1966), Norcross (1883), Sidgwick (1903). More recent accounts, also highlighting the central role of Europe, include Canfora (2006), Cartledge (2016), Congleton (2010), Dunn (1992, 2005), Farrar (1988), Keane (2009), Kloppenberg (2016), Meier (2011), Miller (2018), Patterson (1991), Siedentop (2014), Stromberg (1996), Treadgold (1990). Reviews of the literature can be found in Gray, Smith (2019) and Knutsen, Møller, Skaaning (2016).

[7] See Gunn (2003: ch. 6), Hobson (2004), Sinopoli (2003: ch. 3).

[8] Recently, the pendulum seems to have swung back in the other direction, towards an appreciation of the insights and complexity to be found in European views of the east (Curtis 2009; Osterhammel 2018; Rubiés 2005).

[9] Gerring, Ziblatt, Van Gorp, Arevalo (2011), Phillips, Sharman (2020), Sharman (2019).

were viewed as stateless, i.e., anarchic and presumably uncivilized. Many European colonists did not care to observe, or perhaps did not have the tools to observe, democratic forms of governance in the societies they came into contact with. Consequently, we can expect that accounts from the colonial era overplay the authoritarian qualities of non-European societies and underplay their democratic qualities (Legesse 2000: ch. 1).

Europeans were not alone in portraying distant polities through autocratic lenses. A similar pattern is found when consulting Chinese sources (essential to the reconstruction of political history in Central and Southeast Asia). Reports prepared for the emperor were "pervaded by the Chinese conception of their own centralized State" (Kulke 1986: 2; see also Wolters 1982: 16). Accordingly, Chinese observers inferred a degree of power consolidation that may not have existed in neighboring regions. Like European imperialists, the Chinese also had good reasons to exaggerate the power of local potentates. (Of what value was a tribute if the tributary was weak?)

One must also consider the motives of rulers everywhere, who had an incentive to magnify their own power and influence. Since written accounts came primarily from court insiders – with a goal to flatter the prince by emphasizing his wisdom and power – it is not surprising that local accounts accentuated the autocratic nature of premodern politics.

To be sure, many non-European polities were manifestly undemocratic, even by the standards of the day. The orientalist vision was not entirely false. If one compares European polities with empires in Egypt, China, Persia, the Mughal Empire, the Ottoman Empire, and the Inca Empire one must conclude that power in European polities was generally more dispersed.

However, these well-known exemplars were not very representative of polities outside Europe, most of which were small or highly decentralized and contained elements of consultation. This is recognized by a panoply of descriptive labels assigned by modern historians to premodern states – "contest," "feudal," "galactic," "mandala," "oligarchic," "patrimonial," "prebendal," "segmentary," "solar," "theatre," "tributary," and so forth. Premodern and early modern states were, on the whole, fissiparous. Rulers could not govern their subjects in an autocratic fashion even if they wanted to. Away from the center, and where most of the population resided, local governance was often grounded in assemblies or in informal practices of popular consultation.

Outside statelike political organizations, e.g., among bands, tribes, and many chiefdoms, anthropological and archeological evidence suggests that political power was widely diffused and leaders were likely to be highly constrained in what they could do. In the premodern era, non-state polities were preeminent in most regions of the world.[10]

Putting these pieces together, we are able to assemble a strong prima facie case that Europe was *not* the sole repository of democratic institutions. Instead, there appears to have been considerable variation in governing arrangements across the globe.[11] It is not a binary story of *Europe versus the rest.*

All of this suggests that we must be wary of what one might call an "absolutist bias" in the historical record. Historians, archeologists, and anthropologists are cognizant of this bias, and most recent studies present a more nuanced picture, balancing the reports of contemporaries against other evidence. Several recent accounts portray examples of premodern democracy (or proto-democracy) outside of the European context.[12] As an entrée to our study let us briefly explore this evidence.

Scattered Accounts from outside Europe

In Central Asia, despite a popular perception of despotic power wielded by marauding khans such as Temujin (1162–1227), Tom Barfield (2010: 59–60) writes,

strong group solidarity was undermined by a number of structural political weaknesses ... The first was that these descent or locality groups were necessarily of small size. Second, because such groups had a strong cultural predisposition toward equality, it was difficult for a leader to consolidate power. In such a system every man and every group could at least imagine the possibility of becoming dominant, and resented being placed in a subordinate position. Anyone in a leadership position was therefore plagued by jealous rivals who would be happy to replace him or at least throw obstacles in his way if they could not ... Third, even if a man succeeded in surmounting this rivalry, the position of leader itself was structurally weak. It lacked the right of command and so depended on the ability to persuade others to follow.

---

[10] See Barfield (1989, 1993, 2010), Bicchieri (1972), Boehm (1984, 2009), Cashdan (1980), Flannery, Marcus (2012), Kelly (2013), Knauft (1991), Lee (1979), Lee, DeVore (1968), Middleton, Tait (2013), Roberts (2014), Salzman (2004), Scheidel (2017: Kindle locations 761–88), Weir (2007).

[11] See Berman (2007), Canfora (2006), Posada-Carbó (2016).

[12] See Acemoglu, Robinson (2019), Bentzen, Hariri, Robinson (2019), Blanton (2016), Giuliano, Nunn (2013), Isakhan, Stockwell (2011, 2015), Jacobsen (1943), Kaviraj, Khilnani (2001), Manglapus (1987), Muhlberger, Paine (1993), Sen (2003), Stasavage (2020), Taylor (2002), Vlassopoulos (2007). Traces of this alternative account can be found in earlier studies including Capen (1875), Hattersley (1930) – and, of course, Rousseau (1994[1762]).

Other specialists on the region often comment on the fissiparous nature of clan and tribal leadership, the voluntary nature of larger confederations that arose periodically, and the use of councils as a mechanism to reach consensus.[13]

In South Asia, there is considerable evidence of village-level accountability, which sometimes featured regular elections.[14] There were also small states where political power was highly deconcentrated – variously described as republics, clan states, gana-sanghas, oligarchies, or democracies.[15] Charles Drekmeier (1962: 277–80) summarizes:

> The republics of India were about the size of the Greek city-states, averaging perhaps several thousand square miles. The need for quick action or for security often resulted in the delegation of power. Executive authority was usually vested in a council of elders, a cabinet, or an assembly ... The small size of these states facilitated popular government where it would never have been practicable in a state of imperial dimensions. But probably only nobles were eligible for election to these offices. The power structure of nonmonarchical states can best be described as aristocratic.

> The assembly was of considerable size: there are records of 5,000 and 7,707 'rajas' – usually of the Kshatriya caste. The prevalence of factions was the chief weakness of such states. When parties formed, their members sat in separate groups. Assemblies of republican states exercised relatively complete control over the executive council; council members, as well as officers of the military, were chosen by the central assembly. The executive group of these republics may have had as many as twenty or thirty members or as few as four. The assembly controlled foreign relations, but the need for secrecy eventually shifted this control from the assembly to the executive.

In Korea, during much of the Silla dynasty (57 BCE – 935 CE), "the dominant center of political power ... was the aristocratic Hwabaek Council, which exercised a broad range of powers, including choosing kings, deliberating on major policy questions, and executing policy decisions" (Duncan 2000: 15–16). Monarchical power in successive eras, after unification of the Korean peninsula, was by no means absolute, and by many accounts politics was highly consensual and consultative, albeit limited to a small elite.[16]

---

[13] See Fletcher (1986), Golden (1992), Khodarkovsky (2002), Manz (1989), Rossabi (1998).

[14] See Drekmeier (1962: 270–80), Mookerji (1919: 150–60), Sastri (1955[1935]: 486–519; 1975: 278), Sircar (1989: 240–1).

[15] See Alktekar (1984), Avari (2007: 88–90), Keay (2010), J.P. Sharma (1968), R.S. Sharma (2005: 129), Thapar (2002: 147–50).

[16] See Jae-Woo (2011), Kim (2012: 60, 193), Seth (2010: 38–52), Shon (1998).

In Southeast Asia, Anthony Reid (1993a: 253) reports,

the conciliar principle was well established at some port-states the Dutch visited around 1600. At Banten (then under its regency), at Banda, and in Ternate they found that no important commercial or political decision could be made without an assembly of many notables, each having a say. A form of oligarchy was institutionalized in eighteenth-century Sule, long after the high tide of absolutism had retreated. [Here], government was in the hands of a council of the sultan and fifteen datu. "The Sultan has two votes in this assembly, and each datoo has one. The heir apparent ... if he sided with the Sultan has two votes; but if against him, only one. There are two representatives of the people, called Manteries, like the military tribunes of the Romans."

Further confirmation can be found in other historical work focused on Southeast Asia in the premodern era (e.g., Hall 2011: 337; Ricklefs 2008: 32). Sometimes, the vehicle for democracy was an immigrant group such as the Chinese, who organized self-governing communities in various locations throughout the region (Yuan 2000).

In Africa, one finds a good deal of variation in political organization, e.g., between the more centralized states and "acephalous" societies.[17] However, the most common form of organization, according to many historical and anthropological accounts, was the age-grade system. John Reader (1997: 265-7) summarizes,

Chiefs had status, but little authority or power over the community in general, beyond the respect they may have earned in their everyday dealings. Indeed, as though to counter the frictions likely to arise if authority and power were vested in certain chiefs and lineages and thus flowed vertically, from the few at the top to the majority at the bottom, a system emerged whereby authority and power were spread horizontally throughout the group as a whole, touching every lineage and family ... The age-grade system divided all males into groups, each of which included all individuals within a particular range of ages (the range often covered five, seven, or fourteen years). Each group was allocated a standard set of social and political duties. As individuals advanced in years they changed duties until those surviving had progressed through the complete set. Thus the system sustained no permanent or hereditary rulers or office-holders ... With its respect for the wisdom and judgements of the oldest members in a group, the age-group system established gerontocracy as the dominant form of political organization in sub-Saharan Africa. Since it was mutually recognizable among different groups, regardless of their origin or present status, the age-group system deposed the vertical authority of family lines, transcended the divisive nature of ethnic boundaries, and even provided a basis for compatible interaction between groups speaking different languages ...

---

[17] See Ayittey (2006), Richards (1959: 14–15), Tymowski (2009), Vansina (1962: 331–3).

Reader (1997: 267) concludes, "the abiding strength of the gerontocratic system was that it functioned on a basis of compromise not coercion, and was disseminated by a process of consent, not conquest." Even in more centralized states such as the Sokoto Fulani Empire, kings were elected from among surviving members of a very extended royal family and ruled in a consultative fashion (Johnston 1967: 170–2).

Of indigenous peoples of western North America, Joseph Jorgensen's (1980) extensive survey concludes, "on the whole they were simple and the authority invested in leaders was nominal. Indeed, it was not so much clearly acknowledged authority as it was suasion, which leaders exercised because of the prestige and respect accorded to them, that characterized the leadership of most groups in western North America" (209). Jorgensen notes a strongly collaborative style of leadership:

> The chiefs of all California tribelets practically always received advice from the heads of the leading families, or from sodality leaders, or from powerful shamans. As a matter of fact a single shaman, either as a leader in a sodality organization, or simply as an independent operator, very frequently exercised authority nearly equal to that of the chief, and many of their decisions were announced jointly. (221)

Leadership succession was generally based on achievement, sometimes with an admixture of inheritance – as when potential leaders were chosen from a single family or group of families (Jorgensen 1980: 233).

Among the Plains Indians, Maurice Smith (1925: ch. 3) notes that councils, rather than chiefs, were sovereign. Generally composed of elders or accomplished warriors, councils did not tend to follow well-developed protocols, for none were needed. They met frequently, were the ultimate source of policy decisions, declared war and negotiated peace, elected chiefs or secured their inheritance (if the office was hereditary), and seem to have imposed their will over chiefs in many circumstances. Instead, they reflected considered opinion among leaders of the tribe. "The council was the most important political institution among the Plains tribes," Smith (1925: 73) concludes.

Evolution

Having demonstrated that many premodern polities contained strong elements of democracy, it is important to say something about *how* the people ruled. Prior to the modern era, popular rule (to the extent that it existed) was exercised in a fairly "direct" fashion, i.e., through popular assemblies or consultative bodies.

This, in turn, was partly a product of size. In small societies, power could be exercised by assemblies of citizens who gathered together to debate policies, choose leaders, or execute specific actions (e.g., hunting expeditions, public works, warfare).

Democracy in the premodern era was a predominantly local affair. Power was exercised in a largely informal fashion, relying on norms and practices ("tradition") rather than written laws and constitutions ("rational-legal" authority, in Weberian terms). Relationships tended to be personal rather than bureaucratic. This does not mean that small-scale societies are always democratic; the point is simply that face-to-face contact offers a potential mechanism of popular control. Moreover, the threat of exit from a small society is ever-present, and this presumably imposes constraints on what leaders can get away with.

In large-scale societies, exit is more complicated and popular rule more difficult to arrange, requiring well-defined institutions. Specifically, there must be an assembly that represents the interests of a larger body of people who are not present. The concept of representation is therefore critical (Pitkin 1967). And there must be a mechanism for selecting those representatives – e.g., by election or by lot – that ensures accountability to the group they purport to represent.

Stipulatively, direct democracy is workable in small societies but not in large societies, and representative institutions are not needed in small societies but are required in large societies if the people are to rule. Scale matters (Gerring, Veenendaal 2020).

If this assumption is correct it stands to reason that as polities increased in size (through population growth or conquest), and state forms of political organization displaced pre-state forms of political organization, opportunities for direct democracy diminished. Direct democracy survives today at local levels (Bryan 2010), in specialized institutions such as the popular initiative and referendum (Altman 2010), and in other venues (Fung, Wright 2003). However, these mechanisms are probably not viable without the supporting architecture of representative institutions (Macpherson 1977: 112). Accordingly, in considering democracy in the modern era – the primary goal of this book – we focus on its *representative* aspects.

Here, Europe played a leading role. Representative bodies, with members chosen through elections and constitutional (explicit, written) limitations on executive power, seem to have developed first in that region. The parliaments that arose in Europe during the medieval and early modern eras were virtually unique at the time. They operated under different principles than earlier small-scale examples of democracy. Generalizing broadly, they were representative rather than direct, formal rather than informal, structured by constitutional law, and eventually elective. In this respect, the conventional account of democracy's history, which traces its origins to Europe in the Middle Ages, is correct.

Measurement

Having constructed a sketch of democracy through the ages based largely on secondary accounts, the reader is probably wondering whether this ground could be covered in a more systematic fashion. Can we *measure* the various differences we have vaguely alluded to?

The Premodern Era

According to a tacit division of labor, anything that happened before 1789 is the province of historians, anthropologists, archeologists, and classicists. These scholars have produced libraries of specialized studies focused on particular regions and eras upon which we draw in formulating the preceding account. However, synthetic work is rare, and generally does not aim for systematic measurement or testing of theoretical propositions.

There are a few important exceptions.

Several recent datasets track the organization of assemblies in Europe beginning in the Middle Ages.[18] Another tracks legislatures in European colonies beginning in 1600 (Paine 2019). These datasets have vastly enhanced our understanding of politics in the premodern era, and we exploit them in our own analysis (see Chapters 5 and 10).

However, several limitations should be noted. First, these data collection efforts are not global in reach. Second, they do not have much to say about the extent of membership in the body politic (e.g., who was entitled to citizenship), the method of selection (e.g., how many members were elected, who was eligible to serve, who was eligible to vote), and the power of the assembly vis-à-vis the executive (who was generally unelected). Nor do these datasets inform us about governing practices at local levels, where much of the power resided and where mechanisms of governance were often more democratic.

Another systematic resource relevant to our topic is the Ethnographic Atlas, an anthropological database originally compiled by George Murdock (1967) from numerous ethnographies conducted mostly in the late nineteenth and early twentieth centuries. The Atlas, part of the

---

[18] See Abramson, Boix (2019), Kokkonen, Møller (2020), Stasavage (2010), Van Zanden, Buringh, Bosker (2012).

Human Relations Area Files (HRAF) project, observes societies at a single point in time, a nonspecific period vaguely defined as existing prior to the influx of Europeans. HRAF includes 1,265 ethnic groups.

Of these, a subset of 186, known as the Standard Cross-Cultural Sample (SCCS), is coded in a more thoroughgoing fashion (Murdock, White 1969). Although much smaller, the SCCS is chosen with the aim of being representative of the larger Atlas. One variable from the SCCS records the existence of councils, or other collective decisionmaking bodies, which Stasavage (2020) treats as a signal of local democracy. Since the SCCS sample is small we do not make use of it.

One variable from the Atlas records the traditional form of succession for the headman of each ethnic group. If chosen by election or consensus the polity is commonly regarded as democratic, at least at local levels (Greenbaum 1977). Coding categories and the distribution of data are shown in the first section of Table 2.1.

The limitations of the Ethnographic Atlas as a measure of democracy are probably already apparent. First, it focuses primarily on non-state entities – bands, tribes, and small chiefdoms. This is evident from the

Table 2.1 *Ethnographic Atlas polity types*

Variable	Code	Definition	N	%
Selection of headman (v72)	1–5, 8	Patrilineal heir, matrilineal heir, appointment by a higher authority, informal consensus, personal influence, or age, influence, wealth, or social status, absence of any such office	1401	85
	6–7	Election or formal consensus or informal consensus (non-hereditary)	238	15
Jurisdictional hierarchy (v33)	0	Missing data	181	11
	1	No political authority beyond the local community	703	43
	2	One level above the local community (e.g., petty chiefdoms)	447	27
	3	Two levels above the local community (e.g., larger chiefdoms)	194	12
	4	Three levels above the local community (e.g., states)	85	5
	5	Four levels above the local community (e.g., large states)	29	2

Variables drawn from the Ethnographic Atlas (Murdock 1967). Total number of ethnic groups = 1,639.

Jurisdictional hierarchy variable, which distinguishes levels of centralization above the village, as shown in the lower section of Table 2.1.

Second, the Atlas codes only a single point in time, understood as the "ethnographic present," i.e., a nonspecific period vaguely defined (outside Europe) as existing prior to the influx of Europeans. This point in time ranges from several thousand years BCE to 1960, though most of the data points lie in the late nineteenth or early twentieth centuries. Needless to say, it is difficult to make comparisons across such disparate time periods.

Finally, only one indicator of democracy with decent coverage can be extracted from the Atlas, and it is rather difficult to interpret. Most writers do not distinguish election from formal or informal consensus, probably because elections were not very formal affairs and may not even have been recorded. Where elections occur, we do not know how broad the electorate is. Where selection is by informal consensus, we do not know whether or to what extent this consensus is conditioned or coerced. We know nothing about tenure in office and whether there were formal or informal term limits.

Even so, the Ethnographic Atlas is the most systematic source on regimes in the premodern era. To visualize this information globally, we produce a map of the world in which ethnic groups where headmen are selected by election or informal consensus are distinguished from the

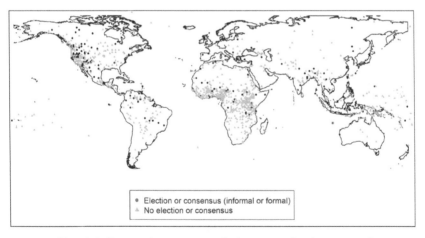

Map 2.1 **Succession among ethnic groups in the premodern era**
Succession to office as local headman or chief based on original coding from the Ethnographic Atlas (Murdock 1967), as described in the text and in Table 2.1.

rest. Map 2.1 shows that, by this measure, democratic mechanisms of leadership selection were dispersed throughout the world. Democracy in the premodern era was by no means the exclusive preserve of Europe.

The Modern Era

In the modern era, states become the dominant forms of political organization and most polities are quite large. (Only a few, like Tuvalu, are small enough so that a substantial share of the citizenry could assemble in one place.) In this setting, direct democracy is probably not workable, or at best serves only as an adjunct to representative democracy, for reasons discussed. Accordingly, in measuring democracy in the modern era we privilege measures of representative democracy – centered on elections, parliaments, and constitutional constraints on the exercise of power.

Within this broad ambit, there are many indicators to choose from.

As a principal measure we employ the Polyarchy index of electoral democracy (Teorell, Coppedge, Lindberg, Skaaning 2018). Conceptually, this index follows in the footsteps of Robert Dahl's (1971) influential framework. Empirically, it draws on data from the Varieties of Democracy ("V-Dem") project, a survey employing the judgments of more than 3,000 country experts from around the world (Coppedge, Gerring, Glynn, et al. 2020). An average of five experts rate each territory-year-indicator. These indicators form the basis of various mid-level indices, five of which are combined in the Polyarchy index: (a) elected officials, (b) clean elections, (c) associational autonomy, (d) inclusive citizenship, and (e) freedom of expression and alternative sources of information.

The V-Dem project extends from 1789 to the present, offering the longest time-series of any extant dataset. However, it omits some historical states, most micro-states, and many semisovereign states, producing a truncated and somewhat unrepresentative sample. To remedy this problem of potential bias and to maximize empirical leverage we linearly interpolate missing data using the Lexical index of electoral democracy and the Contestation index (both of which are introduced below). These additional indices are highly correlated with Polyarchy (Pearson's r = 0.88 for Lexical and 0.80 for Contestation), so a linear interpolation seems sensible.

About 10,000 observations – out of a total 35,000 – are interpolated in this fashion. Although this may seem like a lot it is important to bear in mind that the interpolated data points are much less likely to appear in regression analyses due to missingness on predictors. Consequently, the vast majority of data points in most of the analyses that follow are not interpolated. In any case, we conduct robustness tests with the core

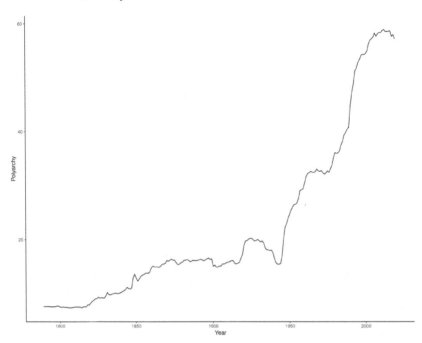

Figure 2.3 **Polyarchy through time**
Mean value of the Polyarchy index (augmented) from 1789 to 2019.

Polyarchy index. (Relationships of theoretical interest are generally stronger in this smaller sample – without interpolated data.)

To get a sense of variation over time in this key index we plot the mean value across all states in the sample over the 1789–2019 period. Figure 2.3 demonstrates that the value of Polyarchy climbs slowly through the nineteenth century, drops during World War II, and then ascends spectacularly in the late twentieth century, with a small reversal in the past decade.

Next, we provide a map of the world showing each country and its democracy score in 2019, visualized in Map 2.2. There is nothing especially noteworthy about this map that would not be familiar to those who follow the topic, though naturally one might quarrel with the shadings assigned to particular countries. To ensure that our findings are not idiosyncratic to a particular index of democracy, we offer several additional measures of this key concept.

As a secondary measure we employ the Polity2 index from the Polity IV project (Marshall, Monty, Jaggers 2016). Polity2, still the most commonly employed index of democracy in the social sciences, utilizes a

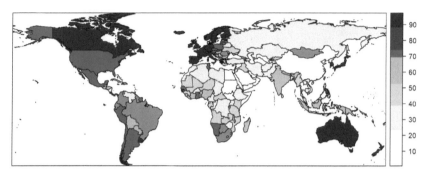

Map 2.2 **Polyarchy around the world, 2019**
Map of countries and their Polyarchy index scores (augmented) in
2019. Darker shades indicate a higher democracy score.

weighted additive aggregation procedure across five sub-components:
competitiveness and openness of executive recruitment, competitiveness
and regulation of political participation, and constraints on the chief
executive. Since it is familiar to many readers we will not spend time
discussing its rather complicated construction.

A third overall measure of democracy is provided by the Lexical index
of electoral democracy (Skaaning et al. 2015). This index rests on the
identification of core features of (electoral) democracy, which are priori-
tized according to their relative importance to the concept. The lowest
level is the absence of elections. Subsequent levels are created by the
addition of a single attribute, each of which brings the regime closer to
the democratic ideal. Seven levels are recognized on this ordinal scale:

0: No elections.
1: No-party or one-party elections.
2: Multiparty elections for legislature.
3: Multiparty elections for legislature and executive.
4: Minimally competitive, multiparty elections for legislature and
   executive.
5: Minimally competitive, multiparty elections with full male or female
   suffrage for legislature and executive.
6: Minimally competitive, multiparty elections with universal suffrage
   for legislature and executive.

An advantage of the Lexical index is that coding decisions are relatively
factual in nature, requiring less judgment on the part of the coder than
most other indices. A second advantage is that the coding procedure is
also a method of aggregation. Scores increase as a state satisfies more

attributes, so the knotty problem of aggregation is solved (if one is willing to accept the rather demanding assumptions underlying lexical aggregation).

We generally avoid binary measures of democracy such as the Democracy–Dictatorship index (Cheibub, Gandhi, Vreeland 2010) or the "BMR" index (Boix, Miller, Rosato 2013). In a binary index, all aspects of democracy must be reduced to 0s or 1s. This means that North Korea receives the same code as Russia or Turkey (autocratic, in most binary datasets), and Sweden receives the same code as Papua New Guinea (democratic, in most binary datasets). While for some purposes it may be reasonable to code democracy in a categorical fashion, for most purposes it is important to register differences of degree.

We also ignore indices whose coverage is limited to the twentieth century such as Freedom House indices of Political rights and Civil liberties (Freedom House 2015) or the Unified Democracy Scores (Pemstein et al. 2010). These indices are highly correlated with the Polyarchy index, in any case, so we have no reason to think that their inclusion would alter any of the findings reported here.

Occasionally, we move from composite indices down the ladder of abstraction to specific dimensions of electoral democracy. Three variables of this sort appear in the following chapters.

Male suffrage is understood as the approximate percentage of enfranchised male adults older than the minimal voting age, as measured by V-Dem (Coppedge, Gerring, Glynn, et al. 2020) for the twentieth century and by Bilinski (2015) for the nineteenth century.

Elections is a binary variable coded as 1 wherever regularly scheduled national elections are on course, as stipulated by election law or well-established precedent (Coppedge, Gerring, Glynn, et al. 2020).

Contestation is calculated as the share of votes or seats earned by the previous winner (the highest vote-getter, P) in the current election minus the share of votes or seats obtained by the challenger (C) in the current election, subtracted from 100:

$$100 - (\text{Share}_p - \text{Share}_c) \qquad [2.1]$$

A value of 0 indicates the absence of contestation: there are no elections or the previous winner gains all the votes/seats. Values between 0 and 100 indicate that the previous winner is again the highest vote-getter, though they face competition from a challenger, with values nearer 100 signifying closer electoral contests. Values above 100 indicate turnover in the top position, i.e., the previous winner is bested by the challenger, again, with values nearer 100 representing greater competitiveness (Gerring, Hicken, Weitzel, Cojocaru 2018).

A significant advantage of this contestation index is its superior coverage: nearly 36,000 state-years from 1789 to the present. Of course, many of those observations are composed of zeroes: no elections, or elections where one party wins all votes. The distribution is stacked up at the left end of the scale. Nonetheless, this is a meaningful zero with respect to the concept of representative democracy.

The Study of Democracy

The immense scholarly oeuvre devoted to democracy is focused largely on the contemporary era. This means that there is only a short window of time within which to observe the development of regimes. Longer-term trends are obscured. Relatedly, most academic work focuses on proximal relationships. In a case-study format, researchers process-trace events leading to regime change in a country, which may be compared to other countries sharing similar background characteristics (Bogaards 2019). In a large-N cross-country format, an indicator of regime change is regressed against an independent variable of theoretical interest, usually accompanied by country and year fixed effects and perhaps a lagged dependent variable (Coppedge 2012: ch. 9; Seawright 2019). Whether approached qualitatively or quantitatively, the researcher's focus is on short-term relationships between a change in X (a putative cause) and a change in Y (regime status).

Of course, there is nothing wrong with focusing on proximal causes if they offer a satisfactory explanation of an outcome. However, this does not appear to be the case for regimes. In panel regressions, 95–99 percent of the through-time variance in regime type is "explained" by a lagged dependent variable, with some small additional increment accorded to an independent variable of theoretical interest.[19] There is not much oomph to these regressions.[20]

One possible explanation is that the event known as regime change is largely stochastic. A recent paper alleges that many episodes of democratization are the product of elite miscalculations – democracy "by mistake" (Treisman 2020a).

---

[19] In the case of our chosen indicator of democracy, the Polyarchy index, a lagged regression model produces an R^2 of 0.98.

[20] Even the master predictor, per capita GDP, explains only a small proportion of the variability in regime type in panel regressions. Some studies conclude that its effect is limited to democratic stabilization rather than democratic transition (Knutsen, Gerring, Skaaning et al. 2019; Przeworski, Limongi 1997). Others question its causal status altogether (Acemoglu, Johnson, Robinson, Yared 2008).

Another reason that it is difficult to predict transitions is that they are rare. To get a sense of this, let us temporarily adopt a binary view of the world in which all regimes are categorized as democracies or autocracies. Employing a dataset provided by Boix, Miller, and Rosato (2013), we count the number of transitions (from autocracy to democracy or democracy to autocracy) occurring within each country from 1800 (or year of independence) to 2015. It turns out that of the 222 countries in the dataset, 123 have experienced no transitions, 56 have experienced one transition, 20 have experienced two transitions, 12 have experienced three transitions, 10 have experienced four or five transitions, and one country – Greece – has experienced seven. Note that over half of all countries register no change in regime and 80 percent have transitioned only once or not at all. Regime stability is clearly the modal value according to this dichotomous measure. Once countries get on a democratic or autocratic track they tend to remain there for a long period of time.

If we adopt a more fine-grained measure of democracy (such as the Polyarchy index, introduced above) we can see that the *relative positions* of countries around the world are also highly durable. Regional patterns are striking. Europe, North America, and Australasia are the most democratic regions of the world; the Middle East, Central and North Africa, and the Asian heartland are the least democratic regions; and Latin America is somewhere in between. This pattern has held steady for several centuries.

The persistence of regime types over the modern era helps to explain why regression models focused on changes through time offer little explanatory power. We do not mean to suggest that the analysis of democracy's proximal causes is doomed. The point is simply that it misses a good deal of the action and therefore needs to be supplemented by a longer-range perspective. Deeper causes are at work. These distal causes operate across centuries, making it more or less likely that a given country will experience a regime transition at some point in its history and – if a transition occurs – that it will endure. In the following sections of the book we explore the role of two structural factors that have been operative for centuries: maritime geography (Part II) and European diffusion (Part III).

II

Maritime Geography

> Brothels and colonies are two extreme types of heterotopia, and if we
> think, after all, that the boat is a floating piece of space, a place without a
> place, that exists by itself, that is closed in on itself and at the same time is
> given over to the infinity of the sea and that, from port to port, from tack
> to tack, from brothel to brothel, it goes as far as the colonies in search of
> the most precious treasures they conceal in their gardens, you will
> understand why the boat has not only been for our civilization, from
> the sixteenth century until the present, the great instrument of economic
> development ..., but has been simultaneously the greatest reserve of the
> imagination. The ship is the heterotopia par excellence. In civilizations
> without boats, dreams dry up, espionage takes the place of adventure,
> and the police take the place of pirates.   Michel Foucault (1986: 27)

Water formed the world's first highways. Consequently, territories with
ocean access were more likely to develop links to other parts of the world.
During much of human history, one could plausibly assert that "the land
separates and the sea connects" (Malkin 2011: 15).

The commercial, technological, demographic, cultural, and geopolitical implications of these connections have been plumbed by an extensive
literature on maritime history, trade, and imperialism. But little attention
has been paid to the implications of water transport – and, more specifically, of natural harbors – for the development of democracy.

Chapter 3 lays out our theory. In Chapter 4, we discuss the measurement of natural harbors, show their placement around the world in a series
of maps, lay out our construction of the key variable of theoretical interest
(distance from nearest natural harbor), and discuss a knotty units-of-
analysis problem. Chapter 5 explores the impact of ocean exposure on
the development of political institutions by looking in a synoptic fashion at
the political history of major regions of the world, approached in a case
study fashion. Chapter 6 probes the relationship of natural harbors to
democracy in a series of global statistical tests. Chapter 7 explores possible
mechanisms at work in the relationship between harbors and democracy.

3   Harbors and Democracy

> If there were no sea, man would be the most savage and destitute of all creatures. But as it is, the sea brought the Greeks the vine from India, from Greece transmitted the use of grain across the sea, from Phoenicia imported letters as a memorial against forgetfulness, thus preventing the greater part of mankind from being wineless, grainless and unlettered.   Plutarch, *Moralia, Aquane an ignis sit utilior*, section 7 (1957: 299)

Prior to the development of motorized transport long-distance travel was laborious, and overland routes especially so. It was costly and slow to convey persons and goods across territory, especially if the ground was rugged, heavily forested, or prone to flooding. Consequently, most lives and livelihoods were local, contained within the compass of a small area.

Rivers and oceans offered an escape from this circumscribed existence, opening up the world to travel, trade, and conquest on a larger scale. Geography structured mobility. Where people lived in close proximity to navigable rivers and oceans they could transport themselves, and their goods, further and more efficiently than those constrained to move across overland routes. Not surprisingly, waterways were the preferred mode of carrying goods and people from place to place for most of recorded history.

Over time, oceans gained preeminence over rivers. While riverine systems could connect markets within a landmass, only oceans could connect those markets with the rest of the world. In the early modern and modern eras, oceans enhanced global connectivity.

However, having an ocean nearby does not mean that large ships carrying heavy freight have easy access to that turbulent body of water. Docking is possible only if there is a working port, and working ports are difficult to construct unless there is a natural harbor. Thus, as ships increased in size – and as oceangoing travel increased in importance – so did the importance of natural harbors. These points of embarkation enjoyed a central location in international networks.

In the contemporary era, ships were partially displaced by other modes of transport (e.g., rail, road, and air) and in time they were entirely displaced as a mode of communication. However, harbors and their hinterlands tended to retain a high level of connectivity. The history of Amsterdam is illustrative. Founded on a natural harbor, Amsterdam established itself as a port city in the fourteenth century and developed gradually into a rail, road, and airway hub in subsequent centuries. Although shipping plays a minor role in the city's economy today, the investments required to establish and maintain other forms of transport arose (in part) because of the city's initial geographic advantage – its central location along the waterways of Holland. In this fashion, natural harbors carry a powerful legacy effect, a prime example of path dependence.[1]

We argue that harbors enhance mobility – of people, goods, capital, and ideas – and this, in turn, affects (a) economic development, (b) military organization, (c) statebuilding, and (d) openness to the world. Each of these factors shifted the balance of power from rulers toward citizens. As a result, areas situated close to harbors are more likely to evolve in a democratic direction than areas surrounded by large land-masses or inaccessible coasts.

In this chapter we introduce each of these factors. Readers should be aware that our treatment will be brief. Further illustrations and more extensive referencing of the scholarly literature on these subjects are postponed for subsequent chapters. Chapter 7 focuses specifically on mechanisms that can be measured and tested. Here, we throw down the gauntlet, in the hope that some of our points will seem evident and that others can be proven subsequently.

Economic Development

Adam Smith was one of the first to discern a connection between waterways and commerce.

As by means of water-carriage a more extensive market is opened to every sort of industry than what land-carriage alone can afford it, so it is upon the sea-coast, and along the banks of navigable rivers, that industry of every kind naturally begins to subdivide and improve itself, and it is frequently not till a long time after that those improvements extend themselves to the inland parts of the country. (Smith 1976 [1776]: 36)

The point is valid, a fortiori, for long-distance trade. "What goods could bear the expense of land-carriage between London and Calcutta?," Smith (1976: 36) wonders.

---

[1] Our argument runs parallel to earlier work on path-dependent sequences building from initial geographic advantages. For example, Bleakley & Lin (2012) note the path-dependent nature of portage sites, which lead to the growth of urban areas.

In a similar vein, Max Weber (1922: 354) writes,

The external conditions for the development of capitalism are ..., first, geographical in character. In China and India the enormous costs of transportation, connected with the decisively inland commerce of the regions, necessarily formed serious obstructions for the classes who were in a position to make profits through trade and to use trading capital in the construction of a capitalistic system, while in the west the position of the Mediterranean as an inland sea, and the abundant interconnections through the rivers favored the opposite development of international commerce.

There seems to be general agreement that oceans nurture long-distance commerce.[2] And commerce tends to flow through port cities, which attract new residents – initially fishermen, then merchants, later longshoremen and manufacturers, and finally highly educated white-collar workers and entrepreneurs who form the backbone of post-industrial economies (Bakker et al. 2020; Lawton, Lee 2002). Of particular interest is the concentration of human capital in port cities and their hinterlands. Ports serve as conveyor belts for migration (Feys et al. 2007) and migrants are often highly skilled or in search of skills. Port cities encourage the clustering of occupations that prize human capital, and facilitate spillover from person to person and industry to industry in an environment of dense settlement and regular inter-action (Audretsch, Feldman 1996). Human capital, in turn, has a recursive effect on city development, serving to attract investment and in-migration (Glaeser 2000). As port cities grow, they are well positioned to realize gains from agglomeration,[3] making them central nodes in the global economy, connecting hinterlands with coastal areas and with the world abroad.[4]

Thus, from the birth of oceanic transport to the present day. harbors have nurtured trade, urbanization, human capital, and economic growth, features that we treat together as components of economic development.[5] The importance of ports to their hinterlands is attested by the custom, common in some parts of the world until recent times, of referencing a region by the name of its principal port (Sengupta 2011: ch. 1). Here, the gateway quite literally defines the hinterland.

---

[2] See Acemoglu, Johnson, Robinson (2005), Daudin (2017), Pascali (2017), Tracy (1990).
[3] See Fujita, Mori (1996), Krugman (1991, 1993).
[4] See Bosker, Buringh (2017), Parkins, Smith (1998).
[5] See Alvarez-Villa, Guardado (2020), Ducruet, Cuyala, El Hosni (2018), Fujita, Mori (1996), Jia (2014). Estimating the short-term impacts of ports in the contemporary era is somewhat more difficult, as discussed in Santos, Salvador, Soares (2018).

Implications for Democracy

We can now consider the impact of harbor-driven economic development on democracy.

The rise of trade is likely to enhance the political power of those who benefit (directly and indirectly) from trade, namely the bourgeoisie. If political power follows economic power, this social class, residing largely in urban centers (note the derivation of "bourgeois" from "burg"), will play a central role in politics and will be accorded a status befitting a wealthy social class (Isaacs, Prak 1996; Spufford 2002).

Merchants, traders, and manufacturers, and the professional classes that arise to service their businesses, have a strong incentive to establish and defend property rights and rule of law. Their power is commercial, not military. Accordingly, they must limit arbitrary actions by rulers to expropriate wealth and they must develop institutions that help to enforce contracts. Failure to do so would jeopardize their line of work. From there, it is a short step to civil liberties like freedom of speech and assembly.

Capitalist activities thrust merchants into contact with others who are quite different from themselves. In the search to maximize profits capitalists are encouraged to adopt an agnostic view of rituals and belief systems. Dogmatism hinders profits. Of the London stock exchange, Voltaire (2007: 20) observed,

> you will see representatives from all nations gathered together for the utility of men. Here Jew, Mohammedan and Christian deal with each other as though they were all of the same faith, and only apply the word infidel to people who go bankrupt. Here the Presbyterian trusts the Anabaptist and the Anglican accepts a promise from the Quaker. On leaving these peaceful and free assemblies some go to the Synagogue and others for a drink, this one goes to be baptized in a great bath in the name of Father, Son and Holy Ghost, that one has his son's foreskin cut and has some Hebrew words he doesn't understand mumbled over the child, others go to their church and await the inspiration of God with their hats on, and everybody is happy.

In this respect, capitalism fosters meritocracy and tolerance, which augurs well for the ideal of liberty.[6]

The rise of the bourgeoisie has a fragmenting effect on the social order, as the wealth of this new class is largely independent of the clergy, of agriculture, and of government. Accordingly, the bourgeoisie is a countervailing power wherever it is not dominant (which is to say, in most places).

---

[6] For further work on the *doux commerce* thesis see Becker (1971), Hirschman (1977), Montesquieu (1989 [1748]).

In the modern era, education begins to play a significant role in business enterprise, and professional classes arise (lawyers, doctors, accountants, managers, engineers, and the like). Here, we can speak of education, and educational centers (schools and universities), as elements of development.

In all these respects, it seems fair to regard development – encompassing urbanization, the bourgeoisie, and education – as a harbinger of democracy in the premodern world.[7] In the modern era, where studies generally focus on gross domestic product (GDP) as a proxy for economic development, a similar conclusion is generally drawn (see Chapter 14). In light of this considerable body of research, the case for economic development as a proximal factor in democratization seems quite strong. One cannot help but recall Barrington Moore's (1966) famous dictum: "no bourgeoisie, no democracy."

To be sure, not all cities were cradles of democracy. In some empires they served as bureaucratic arms of the state (Norena 2015: 197). This was often the case when, due to a dearth of natural harbors, population centers were located inland. Rhoads Murphey (1969: 68) writes:

Traditional Asia, before the eighteenth century, was composed primarily of inward-facing states and empires. The great cities, and indeed nearly all of the important urban centers, were inland, related to internal rather than external concerns. Without exception in any of the traditional states, the largest city was the political capital. These capitals were intended as cosmic creations, substantive and symbolic pinnacles of and resplendent thrones for the Great Tradition, enshriners as well as administrators of a relatively homogeneous and particularistic culture, to which the market towns and the peasant villages of the Little Tradition also belonged. Their planned, monumental urban forms reaffirmed their role as the head pieces of unitary civilizations centered on their own cultural worlds. They were predominantly political and cultural rather than economic phenomena, functioning as microcosms of the national polity, symbols of authority, legitimacy, and power, creators and molders of literate culture, and seats of the dominant ideology. Commercial functions, both in the capitals and in the other traditional Asian cities, were for the most part secondary, and were in any case under varying degrees of control or manipulation by the state, whose chief monument was the city itself.

Similar conclusions might be drawn with respect to urban centers in other regions where ocean transport was not well developed.

Likewise, not all bourgeois classes played their historic role. Some remained dependent on the state or served as appendages to the

---

[7] See Abramson, Boix (2019), Acemoglu, Johnson, Robinson (2005), Ansell, Samuels (2010, 2014), Dahlum, Wig (2021), Fox (1977: ch. 5), Fukuyama (2014), Mauro (1990), Moore (1966), Pirenne (1925, 1963).

aristocracy. However, these failures usually arose from weakness. Where trade and manufactures formed a small portion of a society's economy, bourgeois classes were generally parasitic, playing a subsidiary political role and accorded a lowly social status. Where only a few were well educated these elites cozied up to power, looking to the state for status and remuneration. More development usually entails a stronger and more independent role for these classes.

The point is clearer when one contrasts the bourgeois class with its main competitors, which we shall define loosely as whatever social stratum is dominant in the countryside. In rural areas, ordinary citizens are generally less educated, less wealthy, and less interconnected (because diffusely settled and distant from transport networks). Here, power is likely to be monopolized by a landlord, chief, priest, boss, or cacique. This dynamic is often exacerbated by the presence of economic disparities rooted in control of land or divisions of caste, race, or ethnicity, which are characteristic of rural societies under conditions of sedentary agriculture. As a result, it is difficult to develop and maintain civil and political institutions that constrain the use of power, allowing common people a voice in government. The countryside is not generally regarded as fertile ground for representative democracy.[8] Moreover, the immobile character of agriculture means that surplus is more easily taxed and elites are less capable of retaining independence. The political economy of an agrarian state is not propitious for democracy (an issue discussed in Chapter 12).

Military Organization

Any state with an abundance of natural harbors is exposed to attack from the seas and must therefore worry about defending its shoreline. Insofar as port cities become wealthy from trade they form an especially attractive and accessible target. Mahan (1890: 35) writes,

Numerous and deep harbors are a source of strength and wealth, and doubly so if they are the outlets of navigable streams, which facilitate the concentration in them of a country's internal trade; but by their very accessibility they become a source of weakness in war, if not properly defended.

Harbor-rich areas needed strong navies, not just to protect themselves but also to protect their access to ocean trade. For Venice, "there was no real distinction between trade and defence when it came to maritime

---

[8] See Albertus (2017), Blinkhorn, Gibson (1991), Huber, Safford (1995).

matters. Venice lived by sea-borne trade and thus the defence of the Republic was almost coterminous with the defence of trade" (Rose 2020: 41).

Because naval power depends more on technology and skill than on sheer manpower it was possible for even the smallest states to protect themselves against external threats and even to project power abroad. This might include the establishment of strategic outposts, trade entrepôts, or overseas colonies.[9] Examples of thalassocracies (sea powers) in the premodern and early modern eras include Minos, Phoenicia, Carthage, Athens, the Vikings, Venice, Genoa, Portugal, the Netherlands, England, Oman/Muscat, Brunei, Srivijaya, Malacca, Johor, and Aceh.[10]

By contrast, states without harbors are less exposed to ocean attack and also less dependent upon ocean-borne trade. Military and economic threats, as well as military and economic opportunities, are centered on the control of territory rather than water. The ideal military vehicle for territorial defense and conquest is a standing army, a large permanent force directly accountable to the ruler. Examples of great land empires featuring large armies can be found in Persia, China, Russia, and along the Indo-Gangetic plain.

In this fashion, geography structures military investments. "Each nation tends to orient its political, economic and military life around the advantages of its geographical position vis-à-vis other nations. And history reveals that this orientation has usually favored either the ocean-maritime element or the continental," writes Reynolds (1984: 2; see also Padfield 2000: introduction).

Before proceeding we must take note of what these terms meant through the premodern era. At a time when military organization was fairly primitive the notion of a state possessing a "navy" or "army" may seem anachronistic. Naval power might consist of merchant ships and privateers it could retain or direct in the event of an attack. A land army might consist of troops raised in an ad hoc fashion from landed aristocrats, who served simultaneously as captains in the field. Thus, when we refer to navies and armies in the premodern era we draw a distinction that must be regarded as a matter of degree. Over time, military bureaucracies grew, becoming more regularized and professional, and the distinction becomes clearer.

---

[9] See Glete (1993). "Overseas" is understood here in a minimal sense, i.e., separated by a body of saltwater.

[10] See Abulafia (2010, 2014), Lambert (2018), Reynolds (1974).

Implications for Democracy

What are the implications of these varied military structures for democracy?

For centuries, a standing army – i.e., a permanent army staffed by professionals at the beck and call of the ruler – was regarded in republican circles as a tool of oppression.[11] Examples of army-backed coups and interference in politics stretch from ancient Rome to the modern era.[12] John Trenchard (1662–1723), a leader of the Country (or Commonwealth) tradition of the British Whigs, and coauthor of *Cato's Letters*, writes:

> If we inquire how these unhappy nations have lost that precious jewel *liberty*, and we have as yet preserved it, we shall find their miseries and our happiness proceed from this, that their necessities or indiscretions have permitted a standing army to be kept amongst them, and our situation rather than our prudence, hath as yet defended us from it, otherwise we had long since lost what is the most valuable thing under heaven. (Trenchard 1697: 4)

Accordingly, the Whig solution to the problem of defense was to develop a navy, wherever natural circumstances allow. We elaborate the logic as follows.

Navies are closely tied to trade. In Venice, "the crews of the merchant marine and the navy were the same people" (Lane 1973: 48). Accordingly, navies followed the course of trade and generally served the cause of traders, the bourgeois actors associated with the growth of early democratic institutions, as noted in the previous section. In the contemporary era, navies remain closely tied to the urban middle classes (Böhmelt, Pilster, Tago 2017). They may also have a more liberal political outlook. Heginbotham (2002: 87) argues that "naval officers generally ally with liberal political leaders in domestic political battles over the organization of the state, whereas army officers form alliances with integral nationalist leaders."

Navies require less manpower than armies, so a smaller number of troops is available to would-be tyrants. By contrast, armies offer vast numbers of troops, in whom discipline and hierarchy are instilled. Reynolds (1984: 8) argues that "the effect has been a general tendency toward authoritarian government, national regimentation and a servile population."

---

[11] See Humphrey, Hansen (2010), Schwoerer (1974). Granted, a professional army may be more propitious for democracy than a poorly trained militia or presidential guard (Madrid 2020). However, we argue that it is not as propitious as a (professional) navy.

[12] See Hebblewhite (2016), Kennedy (2013), Rommelse, Downing (2015: 400), Singh (2014).

Navies also generally require a higher level of specialized training (Heginbotham 2004: 78), which may lead to a professionalization of the armed forces, sufficient to discourage them from meddling in politics. Reynolds (1984: 6) observes,

Sailors learn their professional skills at sea among a small ship's company, where administrative and political considerations are minimal. They are technical experts, skilled in the technology of service at sea and sensitive to the inherent fragility of their machines. And seamanship knows no politics. By contrast, land-oriented officers deal with vast administrative organizations of many men and large tracts of territory and are in constant physical association with the political organs of government.

It is easy to see why generals have often assumed political power while admirals have rarely seen fit to enter politics.

Finally, and perhaps most importantly, the military technology of a navy is not well designed for domestic use. Because ships cannot be deployed across the countryside, rulers are not likely to employ the navy to crush internal dissent or to rally forces – unless they happen to be located in or near port cities. It is the army that is generally employed to put down rebellions and fight civil wars. Accordingly, wayward admirals with a taste for power are in a less favorable position to stage a coup than wayward generals with similar ambitions.[13]

For all these reasons, it is not surprising that naval power is commonly associated with democratic rule and land-based armies with autocracy. Reynolds (1984: 6) concludes: "A vital component of the democratic spirit, navies have remained a pillar in the support of free institutions, socially as well as strategically."[14] A modern example can be found in the case of Chile during the 1891 civil war when the navy sided with the opposition, helping to defeat the army and setting Chile on the path to democracy (Collier, Sater 2004).[15]

Statebuilding

In the premodern era, regions with high ocean exposure tended to nurture smaller states than areas situated away from the coast. For corroboration, one may contrast coastal Europe with inland Europe, coastal East Asia with inland Asia, mainland Southeast Asia with

---

[13] See Moore (2004), Pilster, Bohmelt (2012: 360), Singh (2014: 86).

[14] Gestures in a similar direction can be found in Aristotle (1932), Downing (1992), Gibler (2007), Hintze (1975), Lambert (2018), Moore (1966: 32), Padfield (2000: Introduction), Rodger (2017), Russett, Antholis (1993), Zolberg (1980).

[15] We are indebted to Raul Madrid for this example.

"island" Southeast Asia, and inland Africa with coastal Africa. Several factors may explain this relationship between littoral geography and statebuilding.[16]

In aqueous regions, the proliferation of cities (discussed above) makes it difficult for would-be expansionists to conquer and hold territory. Cities are centers of wealth and population and are likely to be stoutly defended.

Cities located in close proximity can also band together for self-preservation when confronted with a more powerful adversary. Coordination problems are easier to solve when multiple cities inhabit the same region. This may account for the prevalence of confederations and alliances in areas where independent cities thrived, such as ancient Greece (e.g., Delian League, Peloponnesian League), northern Italy (e.g., Lombard League), and northern Europe (e.g., Kalmar Union, Livonian Confederation, United Provinces of the Netherlands, Hanseatic League, Swabian League).

Finally, one might consider the impact of sea borders on political legitimacy.[17] Legitimacy stems, in part, from a feeling of shared identity and shared fate. This poses a challenge for would-be rulers who hail from overseas. Even if their intentions are benevolent they are likely to be viewed by indigenes as foreign, alien. Perhaps, they are more likely to nurture exclusionist views themselves, cultivating invidious distinctions and proscribing acts of miscegenation. Remaining apart, it is more difficult for overseas rulers to establish and maintain control. This may help to explain why contiguous (territorial) empires tend to endure longer than noncontiguous (overseas) empires. Statebuilders were ultimately successful in uniting England, Wales, and Scotland, but they were unable to hold on to Normandy and Brittany and struggled to vanquish Ireland, just across the Irish Sea. In various respects, sea borders provide "stopping power" (Mearsheimer, 2001). Over time, this dynamic structures national identities and states.

For all these reasons, oceanic areas tend to foster smaller states. By contrast, in areas *without* natural harbors, sea borders, and dense urban networks, territorial expansion is difficult to stop. Whatever state is militarily dominant in a region is likely to expand its control across

---

[16] Geography has often been cited as a factor in the territorial size of states, in particular, the fragmentation of Europe and the comparative unity of mainland East Asia. For further discussion and citations to the literature see the section on Europe in Chapter 5. There, we explain why we think harbors might play a more important role than other geographic features such as mountains.

[17] For an in-depth treatment of legitimacy and its connection to perceived identity, see Hechter (2013).

adjacent territories. Expansion neutralizes potential threats from neigh-boring states, enhances revenue sources, and offers booty to leaders of the armed forces, who can be compensated with expropriated land. In this light, it is no surprise that the largest and longest-lasting empires in world history were usually situated in non-oceanic areas, e.g., along the Nile, the Yellow River, the Indus River, the Deccan plateau, the Iranian/Persian plateau, the steppes of Central Asia, and the Ethiopian highlands.

Granted, maritime empires have existed since antiquity, and in the early modern and modern eras great oceanic empires encompassed distant entrepôts and colonies (Strootman et al. 2020). The largest of these, the British Empire, consisted of a minuscule metropole and vast holdings overseas. In this situation, however, the authority of the metro-pole is often attenuated. Due to the difficulty of governing territories across bodies of water, and the clear distinction between "us" and "them" imposed by ocean borders, these territories were more likely to be governed in an indirect fashion. Although the point should not be pushed too far, it is possible to discern a divergent pattern of expansion according to which maritime statebuilders relied on forms of cooperation and cooptation to establish hegemony among subjugated populations, while territorial statebuilders relied on military coercion and a more direct style of rule.[18]

Implications for Democracy

What are the implications for democracy of states that are differently sized and structured?

In premodern times, when transport and communications technology was primitive, there are good reasons to suppose that territorial expanse was in tension with popular control.[19] A larger territory meant that it was more difficult for people to assemble in one place and to coordinate with one another. Indeed, arguments in favor of monarchical rule often hinged on the impossibility of popular rule across a large territory (Gerring, Wig et al. 2020).

Territorial size matters even if (as is often the case) that territory is sparsely settled. All large states include areas of diffuse settlement, e.g., the desert regions of Egypt, the desert and mountain regions of China,

---

[18] Strootman (2020: 1) remarks, "Relying on naval power rather than land armies, and availing themselves of (pre-existing) trade networks, maritime empires often were less centralized and state-like than land-based empires."

[19] Blockmans (1978, 1994), Hansen (2000: 611–12), Stasavage (2010, 2011).

the Andean region of the Inca, the steppe regions of the Mongol Empire, and the Siberian region of Russia. Although few people inhabit these regions, they must still be governed. Otherwise, they are likely to become seedbeds of unrest and revolt or points of entrée for foreign incursions.

Thassalocracies also sometimes include vast territories (as noted), and thus are subject to the same logistical difficulties that beset land empires. However, because distant colonies separated by water were apt to be governed indirectly they might enjoy some measure of self-government, and might even be governed in a democratic fashion. Likewise, the clear distinction between metropole and colony imprinted by oceanic borders means that the former could be governed democratically even if the latter was not. In this fashion, Athens (in the classical age) and England (in the early modern and modern eras) were capable of maintaining democratic institutions. Not so for Rome as it expanded from republic to empire, for its territory was mostly contiguous, making it difficult to separate (logistically, politically, and culturally) the republican metropole from "foreign" colonies.

A final implication of state size involves patterns of military conflict. We assume that conflict arises from propinquity.[20] If a state has many immediate neighbors, wars are likely to be more frequent, particularly in the premodern era. Insofar as an aqueous environment fosters political fragmentation we can anticipate continual military contestation. Because states are small we can also anticipate that many of those conflicts will have fatal consequences. Losing a major battle may entail losing a realm. Europe, a continent in perpetual turmoil with states rising and falling at a torrid pace, offers a case in point.[21]

By contrast, in a region dominated territorially by a single hegemon smaller states or tribes are not in a position to mount an effective challenge, except in the occasional circumstance of imperial involution. From the hegemon's perspective, most wars will be regarded as peripheral conflicts, waged far from the capital and of less consequence to the current ruler, who can afford to lose battles and territories without sacrificing the realm. The existence of a regional hegemon also reduces conflict for smaller – client or tributary – states in the region. East Asia, a continent that has generally been at peace since the rise of a unified Chinese empire, offers a case in point (Kang 2010).

Thus, rulers of large states did not face the desperate straits of rulers of small states, where war was incessant and posed an existential threat, instigating a desperate search for revenue, arms, and fighting men. Note

[20] See Bremer (1992), Gibler (2007, 2012), Gleditsch (2009), Most, Starr (1980).
[21] See Dincecco, Onorato (2018), Scheidel (2019), Tilly (1992).

also that in a region composed of small states, citizens had more exit options and therefore could exact a higher price for loyalty. This may help to explain why leaders of small states in Europe were more likely to treat their citizens with diffidence, offering constitutional rights and representative assemblies in exchange for cooperation (Bates, Lien 1985; Levi 1989). It may also help to explain why wars offered an occasion for rulers to call parliaments into session, an implicit acknowledgment of their limited prerogative.[22] Leaders of small states negotiated from a position of weakness, while leaders of large states often did not have to negotiate at all.

For all these reasons, we do not find it surprising that city-states have been linked to democratic rule and empires to autocratic rule since time immemorial.[23] Likewise, instances of imperial expansion seem to have been accompanied by a dimunition of popular control over government. Examples of this dynamic can be found when the Roman Republic expanded beyond Italy into Europe and the Mediterranean, when the Mongols expanded across Eurasia, and when Russia expanded to the East.

Before quitting this subject we must interject an important caveat. The role of statebuilding in structuring power relations applies primarily to periods prior to the twentieth century. In the contemporary era, the development of superior transport and communications means that size is less of a barrier to citizen coordination. Thus, we expect the negative relationship between size and democracy to attenuate over time. However, there may be an important legacy effect: the size of polities in a region during the early modern era may predict the regime status of polities in that region in the modern era.

Openness

We have observed that states with many natural harbors face economic inducements to develop trade. The role of trade is accentuated if the state is also small, for trade dependence varies inversely with size (Gerring, Veenendaal 2020: 310–12). Once foreign trade is in place the state is apt to depend upon this lucrative revenue source, instituting an incentive for state actors to protect and extend merchant activities wherever possible.

---

[22] See Abramson, Boix (2019), Cox, Dincecco, Onorato (2020), Stasavage (2011), Van Zanden, Buringh, Bosker (2012). For qualifications of this classic argument see Kenkel, Paine (2020).

[23] See Griffeth, Thomas (1981), Hansen (2000), Jacobsen (1943), Molho, Raaflaub, Emlen (1991), Nichols, Charlton (1997), Parker (2004).

This, in turn, structures its stance toward the world. While economies centered on terrestrial commerce can afford to shut their gates, as China did during the fifteenth century, economies centered on long-distance trade can ill afford to turn their backs on a major source of income (Pomeranz, Topik 2014).

Where harbors abound, one can also expect a high rate of migration (Curtin 1984; Feys 2012; Feys et al. 2007). This is a feature of available technology (the ability to hop on and off seagoing vessels) and also of extensive social networks. Diaspora communities lower barriers to migration, spurring chain-migration. And this means that port cities are likely to be more diverse than inland cities, and a lot more diverse than the countryside.[24]

Although we do not have space to elaborate on all the avenues of influence and exchange, it should be clear that harbor regions were open to a wide variety of international forces, serving as gateways for trade, migration, tourism, religious pilgrimages, conquest, and colonization.[25]

Implications for Democracy

What implications does openness have for democracy?

Through waves of migration, port cities came to host an astounding diversity of peoples – merchants, mariners, pirates, naval recruits, renegades, exiles, gamblers, revolutionaries, and other adventurers of polyglot origin. Of particular note are the diaspora communities who played a key role in international commerce as merchants and mariners. Prominent examples in the ancient world include Assyrians, Phoenicians, and Greeks. In the early modern and modern eras one may cite the Cantonese, Malays, Lebanese, Jews, Basques, Bretons, Huguenots, Maghribi (Maghrebi), Greeks, Portuguese, Genoese, French-Canadian *coureurs de bois*, Armenians, Parsees (Parsis), Gujarati, Swahili, and Arabs (often Omani) hailing from the Persian Gulf.[26]

Diversity was not simply a by-product of port activity; it was also a cause, stimulating the growth of new markets and the exchange of new

---

[24] See Basu (1985), Broeze (1989, 1997a), Darwin (2020), Fawaz, Bayly (2002), Floor (2006), Gilchrist (1967), Gipouloux (2011), Graf, Huat (2008), Hein (2011), Jarvis, Lee (2008), Knight, Liss (1991), Lawton, Lee (2002), Lockard (2010), O'Flanagan (2008), Pearson (1998), Reid (1980, 1993a, 1999), Subramanian (2008), Tan (2007), Wink (2002).

[25] Appropriately, a recent book on the history of port cities is entitled *Vanguards of Globalization* (Mukherjee 2014). See also Darwin (2020).

[26] See Cohen (1971), Curtin (1984), Greif (2006b), Kagan, Morgan (2009), Mauro (1990), McCabe et al. (2005), Poettering (2018), Studnicki-Gizbert (2007), Subrahmanyam (1996).

ideas. "A sign of prosperity in any port city was the size and variety of its foreign population," remarks John Darwin (2020: xxvii).

This extraordinary diversity undercut gradations of status and power that were firmly entrenched in more homogeneous terrestrial zones. Port cities seemed to nurture a democratic culture, a culture that promoted hard work, merit, and a spirit of fraternity.[27] In this vein, Herman Melville (1850: 120) describes life on the open sea.

[W]e sailors sail not in vain. We expatriate ourselves to nationalize with the universe; and in all our voyages round the world, we are still accompanied by those old circumnavigators, the stars, who are ship mates and fellow-sailors of ours – sailing in heaven's blue, as we on the azure main. Let genteel generations scoff at our hardened hands, and finger-nails tipped with tar – did they ever clasp truer palms than ours? Let them feel of our sturdy hearts, beating like sledge hammers in those hot smithies, our bosoms; with their amber-headed canes, let them feel of our generous pulses, and swear that they go off like thirty-twopounders.[28]

Mariners moved freely, or comparatively freely, through the world, inhabiting a liminal space where hierarchies were less defined. Authority on a ship is tight but does not extend to the shore. Accordingly, port cities are often described as libidinal, anarchic locations where persons of every description intermingled, and illicit behavior thrived. Plato remarks,

the sea is, in very truth, a right briny and bitter neighbour ... for by filling the markets of the city with foreign merchandise and retail trading, and breeding in men's souls knavish and tricky ways, it renders the city faithless and loveless, not to itself only, but to the rest of the world as well. (*The Laws*, quoted in Van Oss 1985: 33)

Accounts by historians, ethnographers, authors of fiction, and world travelers up to the present day echo themes of corruption and licentiousness. Oceans are more often associated with vice than with virtue. But they are also, for the same reasons, zones of comparative freedom.[29]

"The oceans have always been the vector for radical and dangerous ideas," observes Andrew Lambert (2018: 329). In this light, it is perhaps unsurprising that oceans and waterfronts were often at the forefront of movements for greater social liberty, political freedom, and cosmopolitanism.[30] Osterhammel (2014: 281) notes,

---

[27] See Davis (2003), Lane (1997: ch. 3), Mah (2014), Van der Walt (2011).

[28] We are indebted to Richard Hardack for identifying this passage.

[29] See Beaven, Bell, James (2016), Gunda (1984), Horden, Purcell (2000), Howell, Twomey (1991), Mah (2014), Paine (2013), Redford (2013), Rediker (1987), Wink (2020: 66 Kindle ed.).

[30] See Alavi (2015), Anderson, Frykman, van Voss, Rediker (2013), Gilje (2007), Lemisch (2015), Linebaugh, Rediker (2000), Magra (2009), Nash (1986). Gdansk, the birthplace of a popular groundswell for democracy and self-determination in Poland as the Soviet regime crumbled, offers a contemporary example.

Security forces of every kind view port cities as breeding grounds for crime and civil commotion – a reputation that was borne out in the twentieth century even more than in the nineteenth. In Germany the revolution of 1918 started with a naval mutiny; in Russia, sailors rose up in 1921 against a revolution that had betrayed its principles. Dockworkers stood in the forefront of the struggle against colonialism and foreign interests, whether in China (Hong Kong and Canton), India (Madras), Vietnam (Haiphong), or Kenya (Mombasa).

Of course, diversity may hinder the development of democracy if groups have trouble communicating, regard each other with suspicion or enmity, or are in violent conflict. Throughout history, those branded "foreigners" have been excluded from participation in politics or provided targets for active repression. Yet, over the longer run, exposure to diversity may lead to greater acceptance of innovation and greater tolerance of difference (ideological, ethnic, linguistic, or religious).[31] These attitudes, in turn, should be conducive to democracy, where differences of opinion and identity are intrinsic.

One particularly important type of port-migrant is the dissident – who, by virtue of religious or political beliefs or personal practices is not welcome in his or her native land. Accessible oceans serve as mechanisms for the transport of dissidents as well as dissenting views. Persons, weapons, and written material are easy to slip on and off an oceangoing vessel. Although most smuggling is undertaken for economic gain, some may be motivated by political or religious objectives.

One must also consider the *content* of ideas that have diffused across the world. While hierarchy may have held sway through the premodern era, in the modern era democracy and associated concepts such as equality, rule of law, and personal rights came to the fore. According to one version of the story, these ideas developed in Europe, from whence they diffused to the rest of the world, as discussed in Part III of this book. Because harbors served as contact points for Europeans, they were subject to the earliest and most intensive European influence. Insofar as democratic ideals spread by diffusion (Brinks, Coppedge 2006), we can anticipate that citizens living in the vicinity of harbors are likely to adopt democratic norms.

Finally, one must consider the impact of openness on the balance of power between ruler and ruled. We have observed that migration played a larger role in aqueous regions because long-distance transport was

---

[31] See Driessen (2005: 131), Gipouloux (2011: ch. 11), Hall (2011: 340), LaViolette (2008). Jha (2013) argues that communities with active trading ports develop high levels of economic specialization and complementarities, which reduce zero-sum competition between social and ethnic groups, leading to greater harmony among diverse populations.

readily available and would-be migrants could tap into ethnic or religious networks to facilitate their next move. Since states in oceanic areas tended to be small, in- and out-migration involved a non-trivial portion of the population. And since oceanic states were dependent upon highly mobile factors such as capital and trade, the prospect of entrance – and the corresponding threat of exit – was especially consequential.[32]

Rulers of small states in oceanic regions worked hard to retain the citizens they had and to attract new citizens from the many prospects who continually washed up on their shores. In 1747, the ruler of Palembang (Sumatra) remarked, "It is very easy for a subject to find a lord, but it is much more difficult for a lord to find a subject" (quoted in Andaya 1992: 97).

In order to attract capital and human capital in a region with multiple harbors a port needed to maintain an open and tolerant attitude toward foreigners (including foreign religions); it needed to provide an effective guarantee of property rights; and it needed to limit resource extraction by revenue-hungry rulers. A port without these features would attract little business, prompting merchants to move elsewhere. Ports regularly rose and fell according to this dynamic. Frederic Lane (1973: 3) comments, "A king who destroyed his merchants, lessened his power to compete with other kings" (quoted in Lambert 2018: 35).

Accordingly, port cities were often granted special privileges, establishing a sanctuary where markets could operate with limited interference from the state. In eighth-century China, a government representative commented on the governance of the lucrative port city, Guangzhou:

The merchants of distant kingdoms only seek profit. If they are treated fairly they will come; if they are troubled, they will go. Formerly, [Guangzhou] was a gathering place for merchant vessels; now, suddenly they have changed to Annam. If there has been oppressive misappropriation over a long period of time, then those who have gone elsewhere must be persuaded to return; this is not a matter of litigation, but of changing the attitudes of officials. (Quoted in Paine 2013: 304)

In early modern Europe, Hoffman and Norberg (1994: 308) judge that "even a grasping despot would be better off negotiating with merchants

---

[32] Arguments about mobility and good governance are commonly associated with the work of Charles Tiebout (1956), who treated citizens as voters who vote with their feet by choosing the locality whose policy preferences align with their own. This may affect the behavior of local governments, who wish to maximize their tax base by attracting citizens to their jurisdiction. This, in turn, may be achieved by providing public goods at a reasonable cost. Frankly, we are not sure whether the Tiebout model offers an accurate description of the behavior of citizens and politicians across localities in the contemporary era. However, there are good reasons to suppose it may have applied across countries prior to the contemporary era, especially in coastal areas.

over taxes rather than imposing levies by force and then watching their assets slip away." Other examples of this bargaining dynamic can be found in the Aztec and Maya civilizations (Chapman 1957: 116), the Mediterranean (Revere 1957), the Persian Gulf (Floor 2006), the Indian Ocean (Hasan 2004; Wink 2002), West Africa (Arnold 1957; Curtin 1984: 42), Southeast Asia (Blussé 2013; Reid 1980: 248; Reid 1993a: 246–7), and Asia at large (Broeze 1989, 1997a; Gipouloux 2011).[33] An echo of this ancient pattern persists today in the form of free ports and free trade zones (MacElwee 1925: ch. xvii).

Assurances of property rights for traders were especially important. To this end, rulers sometimes devolved political power to merchants, giving them a degree of self-governance not enjoyed by other classes. Alternatively, the entire structure of government might be controlled by merchants, or constrained by constitutional rules, giving credence to the idea that only those institutional changes that are secure from arbitrary decisions by the sovereign offer credible commitment into the future (North 1990; North, Weingast 1989).

Of course, rulers of coastal states were not always friendly to trade and amenable to compromise and constitutional rule. They might choose to exact heavy tariffs, quotas, or other barriers on the passage of goods and they might control in- and out-migration, using harbors as points of interdiction. However, where ocean access was plentiful such regulations were apt to be met by piracy and smuggling, becoming counterproductive in the long run.[34] Islands, peninsulas, fjords, deltas, beaches, and saltwater swamps have long served as conveyors of contraband and sanctuaries for pirates (Eklof 2006; Murphy 2007). And the more harbors are available in a given region the more opportunities traders have to unload their goods. In the eastern Mediterranean, along the North and Baltic Seas, along the eastern seaboard of North America, and across the Indonesian and Philippine archipelagos, merchants could navigate among hundreds, if not thousands, of suitable harbors. If one was unfriendly, others would be chosen.

Thus, for a variety of reasons arising from their open borders, states built around harbors were incentivized to reap the benefits of affluence without resorting to expropriation. Sometimes, there was an explicit exchange of revenue for representation, paving the way for constitutional governance.[35] Importantly, revenue raised through negotiation generally

---

[33] For general discussion see Pearson (1991), Polanyi (1968: 239).

[34] See Alvarez-Villa, Guardado (2020), Amirell, Müller (2014), Anderson (1995), McDonald (2015), Pennell (2001), Rediker (1987).

[35] See Bates, Lien (1985), Kiser, Barzel (1991), Moore (2004).

offered a higher yield than revenue raised from coercion,[36] reinforcing a dynamic of bargaining and consent.

By contrast, in regions distant from harbors wealth took the form of land, an inherently immobile form of capital. A territorial state has less incentive to cater to landholders, for they cannot take their means of production with them. The peasantry is also tied to the land and there are no readily accessible modes of long-distance transport, so there is little threat of exit on the part of common laborers. It might be desirable to attract more peasants to enhance the productivity of the land; however, this prospect is unlikely given that an inland territory is off the beaten track and working the land offers little pecuniary reward (relative to maritime or urban occupations). For these reasons, rulers of large states located away from the coast had less hope of attracting new inhabitants and less fear of losing the ones they had. Consequently, they were incentivized to develop a coercive apparatus for collecting revenue, one that heightened state control over property and people.[37]

By Land or by Sea

The explanatory framework introduced in this chapter integrates familiar themes from a vast secondary literature, some of which is cited above and some of which is reviewed in Chapter 14. One theme is so central to our argument that it deserves special mention.

Many historical studies rest on a focal contrast between two polity types, variously labeled trading/agrarian, merchant/aristocratic, capital-intensive/coercion-intensive, city-state/territorial state, coastal/continental, sea/land, maritime/terrestrial, or thalassocracy/tellurocracy. Although the emphasis of each paired term is somewhat different, there are strong similarities across these polar types.[38] David Armitage (2007: 28) explains,

The opposition of land powers and sea-powers – behemoths and leviathans, elephants and whales – is fundamental both chronologically and ontologically to western historiography. Indeed, it can be seen to arise simultaneously with historical thinking itself in the works of Herodotus, Thucydides, Xenophon and later, Polybius, where it is connected to such basic oppositions as that emerging

[36] See Dincecco (2009), Hoffman, Norberg (1994), Kiser, Barzel (1991).
[37] See Ringrose (1989), Tilly (1992).
[38] See Benda (1962), Clark (1995), Fleck, Hanssen (2006), Fox (1971), Guizot (1877 [1838]), Hearnshaw (1940), Kautsky (1982), Lambert (2018), Leur (1955), Mackinder (1919), Oppenheimer (1975[1914]: ch. 4), Parker (2004), Pirenne (1925), Rosecrance (1986), Schmitt (1997[1954], 2003[1950]), Sidgwick (1903), Stasavage (2011), Tilly (1992), Weber (1922).

between the 'East' (Asia) and the 'West' (Europe), and the opposed axes of tyranny (associated with monarchy) and liberty (exemplified by democracy). That opposition was emblematized in the contention between the Persian land-empire and the Athenian thalassocracy, with lasting consequences for the figuration of such empires. In this typology, Athens itself stood at the end of a series of sea-powers, just as it would stand at the head of such a sequence of empires for later observers of the *translatio imperii*.

Polities are often well described by their geography, and the contrast between "land" and "sea" is a recurring theme. We take comfort from the fact that writers through the ages have drawn conclusions similar to our own.

Our contribution is to synthesize this work into a general argument about how littoral geography structures regimes. We argue that areas with an abundance of natural harbors were more likely to develop ports, and this meant that they developed differently than landlocked areas or areas where a good deal of investment and technology was required in order to construct a working port. In particular, ports enhanced mobility – of people, goods, capital, and ideas – and this affected economic development, military organization, statebuilding, and openness to the outside world. Each of these factors played a role in shifting the balance of power between citizens and their rulers, accounting for movements in a democratic direction.

This complex set of relationships is summarized in Figure 3.1. We list four of these causal mechanisms together because we assume that there are many interconnections among them. Indeed, they are rather difficult to prize apart.

Finally, we must address the temporal component of our argument. Some evidence suggests that the association between liberty and the open seas extends back to ancient times. Of the Mediterranean world during the Bronze Age, Lambert (2018: 23) observes,

> maritime societies were noticeably more inclusive than landed contemporaries, often involving women and non-royals. In these trade-based polities political power was shared. Free-standing sea states run by 'consortia of sea-trading families accumulated a degree of wealth belied by their diminutive size'. Archives from Ugarit (Ras Sharma) reveal a merchant class with real political power and a thriving maritime culture.

It is difficult to say for sure.

In any case, our theoretical argument suggests that the impact of harbors on political institutions should follow the development of shipping. Seagoing vessels developed at different times in different places, so each region follows a somewhat different timeline, as indicated in the following chapter. Since seagoing vessels developed earlier in the

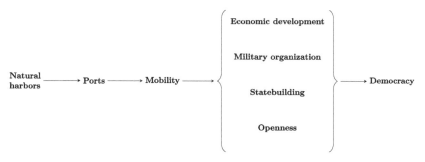

Figure 3.1 **Harbors and democracy**
Diagram of the posited causal chain from natural harbors to democracy.

Mediterranean than in most other regions, it stands to reason that this relationship might have a longer history in that enclosed sea, characterized by relatively calm waters. Globally, shipping did not reach a crescendo until the late nineteenth century. In the twentieth century, its role in transport continued to rise but its role in travel was quickly displaced by airplanes and its role in communications was entirely supplanted by modern telecommunications. Accounting for some institutional overhang, we anticipate that the impact of harbors on democracy culminated in the mid- to late twentieth century.

In summary, the arguments set forth in this chapter include one main hypothesis and two ancillary hypotheses:

H_1 Distance from the nearest natural harbor predicts the rise of democracy.

H_a The relationship between harbors and democracy is mediated by four factors: economic development, military organization, statebuilding, and openness.

H_b The relationship between harbors and democracy rises to a peak in the twentieth century, declining thereafter.

These hypotheses will be explored empirically in subsequent chapters. Most of our attention will be on the main effect (H_1). Questions about mechanisms are addressed peripherally in our historical discussion of different regions in Chapter 5 and explicitly in crossnational tests shown in Chapter 7.

4   Harbors

> When we had come thither into the goodly harbour, about which on both sides a sheer cliff runs continuously, and projecting headlands opposite to one another stretch out at the mouth, and the entrance is narrow, then all the rest steered their curved ships in, and the ships were moored within the hollow harbour close together; for therein no wave ever swelled, great or small, but all about was a bright calm.
>
> Homer, *Odyssey*, Book 10: 87–97 (Murray 1919: 351)

In the previous chapter we presented a theory about the potential impact of harbors on ocean access and from thence on political development. In this chapter, we examine the concept of a harbor, its implications for maritime history, and its operationalization as a measurable indicator.

We begin with a brief survey of maritime history. In the second section, we review what is known about the construction of ports in the premodern and modern eras, as well as various data sources that identify the location of ports historically. In the third section, we introduce our approach to identifying natural harbors. In the fourth section, we introduce the key variable, *natural harbor distance*, which forms the basis for later analyses. In the fifth section, we discuss alternate measures. In the sixth section we tackle a complicated but crucial methodological issue: the units of analysis upon which our geographic argument is based. The final section discusses alternate modes of transport – rivers, roads, railroads, and airplanes – and their possible implications for democracy.

Before diving in (so to speak), it is important to distinguish between three closely related terms that assume specialized meanings in the book. For present purposes, a *port* is anywhere boats traveling long distances habitually come to shore. Ports are usually fitted out with some sort of artificial enhancements such as a dock. A *natural harbor* is a location which, by virtue of the geomorphic features of its coastline, is conducive to the development of a working port. A *harbor* is a natural harbor that has become a working port. These interrelationships are clarified in the Venn diagram shown in Figure 4.1.

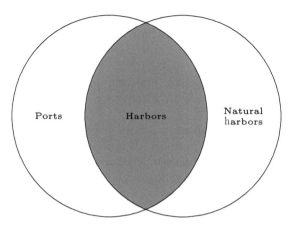

Figure 4.1 **Three maritime terms**
Venn diagram showing the interrelationship among three closely related terms, as employed in this book.

Maritime History

Maritime history is a long-standing arena of historical research. To reconstruct the distant past, researchers have examined early recorded histories, ethnohistorical observations, computer simulations, satellite-tracked buoys, historical linguistics, sunken ships, naval architecture, population genetics, and historical artifacts that presumably crossed bodies of water. They have also conducted replication experiments, where voyages are undertaken with historical shipping technology to see how far (and in what direction) they will go.[1]

---

[1] For *general* maritime histories see Abulafia (2019), Anderson, Peters (2014), Armitage, Bashford, Sivasundaram (2017), Balard (2017), Bentley, Bridenthal, Wigen (2007), Benton, Perl-Rosenthal (2020), Buchet, Le Bouëdec (2017), Casson (1984, 1994a, 1994b, 1995), Catsambis, Ford (2011), Darwin (2020), De Souza (2002), De Souza, Arnaud (2017), Ducruet (2016), Finamore (2004), Gillis (2012), Gould (2011), Griffiths (1997), Hamilton-Paterson (2011), Harlaftis, Valdaliso, Tenold (2012), Hattendorf (2007), Haws, Hurst (1985), Hérubel (1936), Höghammer (2017), Howell, Twomey (1991), Hutchinson (1994), Johnstone (1980), Jowitt, Lambert, Mentz (2020), Klein, Mackenthun (2004), Lambert, Martins, Ogborn (2006), Lindsay (2013[1874–76]), Mancall, Shammas (2015), Mance, Wheeler (1945), Mathew (1995), Mathieson (2016), McGowan (1980), Mukherjee (2013), Paine (2013), Parry (1981), Peters, Anderson (2016), Redford (2013), Runyan (1987), Stein (2017), Steinberg (2001), Zumerchik, Danver (2010), as well as the *International Journal of Maritime History*. On the maritime history of *Europe and the Mediterranean* see Abulafia (2010), Blockmans, Krom, Wubs-Mrozewicz (2017), Braudel (1972[1949]), Casson (1991), Cunliffe (2008), du Jourdin (1993), Hohlfelder (2008), Horden, Purcell (2000), Kingsley (2004), Kirby,

Some archeologists see a central role for the sea in the original peopling of the world, according to which early humans crossed discrete landmasses in boats, rather than terrestrial connections between continents (Erlandson 2010; Kaifu et al. 2020). While the thesis remains speculative, everyone agrees that seafaring has an ancient history extending back at least to the Early Pleistocene era (Bednarik 2014: 1; Boyle, Anderson 2010).

Our interest is not in occasional journeys or one-time migrations but rather in regular round-trip journeys that allowed for trade, circular migration, and an ongoing exchange of ideas and technology. One recent synthesis offers the following timeline for this sort of regularized oceanic travel:[2]

> 5500 BCE: Mesopotamia
> 4500 BCE: Persian Gulf, Egypt, eastern Mediterranean
> 4000 BCE: Indian Ocean, southern Mediterranean
> 3000 BCE: northern Mediterranean, Southeast Asia
> 2000 BCE: Asia-Pacific, Iberian peninsula
> 1000 BCE: Oceania, western South America, North Atlantic

The earliest travels referenced in this timeline were probably not very extensive. As seafaring technology advanced it was possible to make longer journeys, on rougher waters, with improvements in speed, cargo

Hinkkanen (2000), Lambert (2018), Lewis, Runyan (1985), Manning (2018), McGrail (2004, 2014, 2015), Miller (2012), Norwich (2007), Pryor (1992), Semple (1931), Seymour (2004), Simmons (2014), Starr (1989), Tartaron (2013), Tilley (2004), Unger (1980, 1997, 2006, 2011). On the *Arabian seas and the Persian Gulf* see Barendse (2000, 2016), Potter (2009, 2014a), Sheriff (2010), Sheriff, Ho (2014). On *Africa*, see Harris (2016), Hilling (1969, 1970), Hoyle (1967b), Kea (1982). On *Asia* see Alpers (2014), Andrade, Hang, Yang, Matteson (2016), Arasaratnam (1994), Begley, De Puma (1991), Boomgaard (2007), Bose (2006), Bowen, McAleer, Blyth (2011), Broeze (1996), Bruijn, Gaastra (1993), Chaudhuri (1978, 1985, 1991), Das Gupta (1994, 2004), Das Gupta, Pearson (1987), Deng (1997, 1999), Emmerson (1980), Hall (1985, 2011), Hourani (1975), Lombard, Aubin (2000), Machado (2014), Manguin (1991, 2004), Margariti (2008), McPherson (1993), Meilink-Roelofsz (1962), Mukherjee, Subramanian (1998), O'Connor, Veth (2000), Panikkar (1945), Pearson (2003, 2005), Ptak, Rothermund (1991), Ray (1999), Reade (1996), Reid (1980, 1993a, 1993b, 1997), Schottenhammer (2005, 2008), Shaffer (1995), Steensgaard (1975), Sutherland (2003, 2007), Villiers (1952), Wink (2002), Wolters (1967). On the *Atlantic*, see Butel (1999), Cañizares-Esguerra, Seeman (2016), Cassidy (1968), Cunliffe (2001), Karras, McNeill (1992), Kupperman (2012), Morris (1992), Outhwaite (1957). On the *Caribbean*, see Andrews (1978). On the *Pacific*, see Armitage, Bashford (2014), Couper (2009), D'Arcy (2006), Denoon, Meleisea (1997), Feinberg (1995), Freeman (2010), Howe (1984), Irwin (1994), Kirch (2017), Matsuda (2012).

[2] See Anderson (2010: 10), and also Bentley (1999: 218).

bulk and weight, reliability, and regularity.[3] By 1000 CE, sailing vessels plied most of the world's archipelagos and seas, generally hugging close to the shore (Manning 2005: 101). After 1500, long-distance voyages from Europe reached regularly across the Atlantic, opening up the Americas and Australasia to seagoing travel and inaugurating direct interconnections on a global scale (Butel 1999).

Ocean travel not only made new lands accessible, it also reduced the cost of transport. Estimates suggest that water transport was ten to fifteen times cheaper than land transport in ancient and medieval Europe,[4] and possibly twenty-eight times cheaper in South Asia (Mukherjee 2010: 31). According to Diocletian's Edict on Prices (McCormick 2001: 83), it cost less "to ship grain from one end of the Mediterranean to the other than to cart it 75 miles." Even today, one study concludes that "the overall cost efficiency (price per ton-mile) of short-sea shipping seems to be some 25 times higher than that of long-trader trucking" (Kaukiainen 2012: 65).

Global shipping, centered largely on Europe, accelerated in the early modern and modern eras.[5] In the sixteenth century, there were an estimated 770 voyages from seven European countries to Asia. In the seventeenth century, this number rose to 3,161. And in the eighteenth century it rose again to 6,661 – a constant stream of traffic, carrying men (and a few women), goods, technology, and ideas (Maddison 2001: 63).

Table 4.1 tracks several dimensions of maritime progress in Europe during the early modern and modern eras. This includes the number of ships passing through the Danish Soundtoll, foreign trade shipped through British ports, trade between Europe and Asia, the total weight of all ships, the number of mariners, the number of people with experience on the high seas, shipping productivity, total migrants, and migration rates (the share of Europeans who shifted their primary residence, temporarily or permanently). These dimensions of maritime activity show fairly consistent increases during the observed period, with a marked acceleration across many indicators in the late nineteenth century. Here, it seems reasonable to speak of a maritime revolution.

---

[3] See Casson (1995), Leighton (1972), Lewis, Runyan (1985), McGrail (2015), Pryor (1992).

[4] For various estimates, see Jones (2000), Leighton (1972: 157–65), Pounds (1973: 414–17), Skempton (1953: 25), Smith (1976[1776]: 15–16).

[5] For work on periods prior to 1500 see Phillips (1998), Scammell (1981, 1995, 2003), Tracy (1990, 1991). For work on the early modern and modern periods see Armitage (2007), Banga (1992), Bankoff (2017), Bose (2006), Emmer, Gaastra (1996), Mancke (1999), Smith (2018), Steel (2011), Unger (2006, 2011).

Table 4.1 *The European maritime revolution*

	Soundtoll traffic (*ships*)	Trade shipped thro' UK (*tonnage, 000s*)	Departing Europe for Asia (*tonnage, 000s*)	Ships (*tonnage, 000s*)	Mariners (*000s*)	Persons w/ maritime experience (*000s*)	Productivity (*tonnage/ manpower*)	Migrants, Europe & abroad (*millions*)	Migration rate (%)
1501–50	1205		205	1000	145	580	3	9	11
1551–1600	3902		260		180	720	7	11	13
1601–50	36 442	219	708	1000	170	680	9	14	14
1651–1700	30 216	452	1038	1500	230	920	9	16	16
1701–50	35 335	897	1897		260	1040	10	21	18
1751–1800	80 523	2812	2624	3500	348	1392	11	24	16
1801–50	121 158	21 760			472	1888	13	45	21
1851–1900					565	2260	26	119	35
Source	*A*	*B*	*E*	*C*	*C*	*C*	*D*	*C*	*C*

Statistics represent the average annual value within the specified 50-year window, as near as can be determined. (Often only one or several years are available.) Numbers rounded to nearest integer. *Sources: A* (Ojala 2011: 172), *B* (Usher 1928: table 2), *C* (Lucassen, Unger 2000: table 1), *D* (Lucassen, Lucassen 2009: tables 3, 5), *E* (de Vries 2010: table 1).

While Europeans dominated international shipping lanes from (roughly) 1500 to 1900, they were not the only players. Global statistics are measured according to a number of parameters in Table 4.2.

The first section of this table shows total carrying capacity for the world's fleets, disaggregated by mode of locomotion. Sailing ships continued to carry a sizeable portion of the world's goods through the early twentieth century.[6] However, their role was increasingly displaced by steamships, which offered greater reliability, making fixed schedules possible even over long distances. They were also capable of carrying much heavier loads, which meant that it was economical to transport cheap and bulky commodities from one continent to another, exploiting comparative advantage.[7]

The second section of Table 4.2 examines ships that were widely used over the past seven centuries. These oceangoing vessels are assessed according to their weight, speed, and capacity (measured in tons or cubic meters).[8] If ships are introduced during the same period they generally have different purposes, so it is to be expected that changes along these dimensions are not entirely monotonic. However, the general trend is toward greater size, speed, and capacity.[9] Bear in mind that "metric tons" is calculated somewhat differently in the early and later parts of our time series, so these comparisons are inexact.

The fourth section looks at the cost of ocean shipping relative to a benchmark year (1910). It will be seen that costs begin to plummet around the turn of the nineteenth century, reaching what appears to be a fairly stable equilibrium in the late twentieth century.

The final section of Table 4.2 examines merchandise exports as a share of overall production (GDP). Here, the increase is generally monotonic, though with a dip in the interwar years reflecting an era of protectionism and war. Since most commodities and manufactures were transported by ship, this is a reliable signal of shipping's importance in the global economy.[10]

---

[6] See Graham (1956), Kelly, Ó Gráda (2019), McGowan (1980), Ronnback (2012), Solar, Hens (2016).

[7] See Darwin (2020), Griffiths (1997), Pascali (2017), Smith (2018), Steel (2011).

[8] A similar account, focused on warships, can be found in Hugill (1995: 122).

[9] There were also dramatic improvements in safety, especially around the turn of the nineteenth century and associated with "greatly improved charts, the growing availability of affordable manuals teaching basic navigational techniques, and improved navigational aids such as lighthouses and channel markings" (Kelly, Ó Gráda, Solar 2021).

[10] On the connections between shipping and trade see Harlaftis, Valdaliso, Tenold (2012), Hugill (1995: ch. 3), Jacks, Pendakur (2010), North (1958, 1965, 1968), O'Rourke, Williamson (1999: ch. 3), Pascali (2017), Unger (2011). Note that the debate over whether advances in shipping *technology* were critical to increases in trade is ancillary to our concerns.

Table 4.2 The global maritime revolution

| | Carrying capacity Tonnage (000s) | | | | Ships | | Capacity | | Cost | Exports/GDP* |
	Sail	Steam	Total	Name	Deadweight metric tons	Speed knots	metric tons	cubic m.	1910 = 100	%
1310s				Venetian			110			
1330s				Genoese			115			
1350s				Venetian			170			
1420s				Venetian			170			
1470s	320		320							
1480s				Venetian merchant galley			260			
1500s				Venetian merchant galley			280			
1520s				Venetian merchant galley			260			
1540s				Venetian merchant galley			280			
1570s	730	0	730							
1670s	1450	0	1450							
1750s									298	
1780s	3950	0	3950							
1790s									376	
1820s	5800	20	5880							1
1830s									287	
1850s	11 400	800	14 600							
1870s				Sailing bulk carrier	1500	4	1500		196	5
				China clipper	1500	5		2500		
1880s				Handysize steamer	1425	9	1000	1700		

Decade				Ship type						
1900s	6500	22 400	96 100							
1910s	4200	41 700	171 000							
				Two-deck steam liner	7350	12	5100	10 900	100	8
				Steel four-mast bark	4100	6	4100	6400		9
1920s				Ore carrier	20 600	11	16 500		107	
1930s				Oil tanker	14 200	13	11 300			
1940s				Liberty ship	10 850	11	8700	15 700		
				T2 tanker	16 610	14	13 300			
1950s				Cargo liner	13 400	20	10 700	24 000		7
1960s				First-gen. container ship	24 820	22		46 520	47	
1970s				Panamax bulk carrier	66 000	14	55 000			11
				Ultra-large crude tanker	300 000	15	250 000			
				Capemax bulk carrier	180 000	14	150 000		51	14
1990s				Ro-ro cargo ship	11 750	20		36 100		
2000s				Container feeder	11 500	20		27 000		
				Post-Panamax container ship	156 300	22		368 500		

Source Maddison (2001: 95) | | | | *Before 1550:* Lane (1964: 231), total commercial cargo *After 1870:* Kaukiainen (2012: 66, table 4.1) | | | | | Crafts, Venables (2003: 329) | Maddison (1995: 233) |

*Includes Western Europe, North America, Australia, and New Zealand.

In the twenty-first century, oceans continue as a medium of transport, with container ships carrying an ever greater share of the world's goods.[11] Currently, approximately 90 percent of world trade (by volume) is ocean-borne (Bretagnolle 2016: 32), leading to the well-worn phrase "90 percent of everything." However, oceans no longer serve as a common mode of transcontinental travel (having been displaced by airplanes) or communication (having been displaced by telegraph, telephone, and then the Internet). In these respects, the role of oceans as global connectors has diminished.

Ports

The ocean is not much use unless one has a way to access it – hence, the crucial role of ports situated directly on the sea or on a large river or lake with navigable access to the sea. (Inland ports with no ocean access also perform useful functions but are probably less propitious for democracy, for reasons explained at the end of this chapter.) In this section, we review what is known about the placement and development of ports, beginning with ancient times and proceeding to the modern era.

The Premodern Era

The oldest known port in the world, along the Red Sea, dates back some 4,500 years (Lorenzi 2013). Historical studies focused on ports, littoral zones, and port cities are legion,[12] and yet there has been no systematic

---

[11] See Broeze (2002), Hummels (2007), Levinson (2016).

[12] General treatments include Alexandersson, Norström (1963), Beaven, Bell, James (2016), Beerbühl, Schulte, Vögele (2004), Bosa (2014), Darwin (2020), Ducruet (2006), Fisher, Jarvis (1999), Fujita, Mori (1996), Graf, Huat (2008), Hein (2011), Inman (1975), Jackson (1983), Jarvis, Lee (2008), MacElwee (1925), Mah (2014), Morgan (1952), Mukherjee (2014), Ng, Ducruet (2014), Polanyi (1963), Rudolf (1980), Salomon et al. (2016), Sargent (1938), Shaler (1894), Vernon-Harcourt (1885), Weigend (1958). Many studies have a regional focus, e.g., on *Europe and the Mediterranean* (Blackman 2008; de Graauw 2017; Driessen 2005; Eser et al. 2018; Fuhrmann 2020; Gugliuzzo 2015; Hoyle, Pinder 1992; Höghammer 2017; Keyder, Özveren, Quataert 1993; Kovietz 1978; Lawton, Lee 2002; Lee 1998; Marnot 2011; Oleson, Hohlfelder 2011; Preiser-Kapeller, Daim 2015; Revere 1957), the *Persian Gulf* (Floor 2006; Potter 2014a), the Atlantic (Bosa 2014; Gilchrist 1967; Knight, Liss 1991; Morgan 2017; Nash 1986; O'Flanagan 2008), *Africa* (Chittick 1980; Deasy 1942; Harris 2016; Hilling 1969; Hilling, Hoyle 1970; Hoyle 1967b; Pollard, Ichumbaki 2017), *India and the Indian Ocean* (Banga 1992; Blussé 2013; Boussac, Salles, Yon 2016; Broeze, Reeves, McPherson 1986; Deloche 1983; Kosambi, Brush 1988; Macmillan 1928; McPherson 2002; Pearson 1998; A. Subramanian 2009; L. Subramanian 2008), or *Asia and Southeast Asia* (Basu 1985; Broeze 1989, 1996, 1997a; Gipouloux 2011; Kathirithamby-Wells, Villiers (1990), Lee, Song, Ducruet 2008; Lockard 2010; Macmillan 1926). Beyond this, there are countless histories of specific ports and port cities.

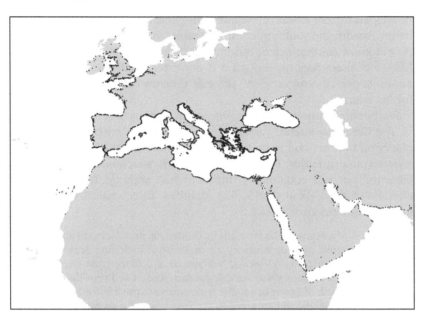

Map 4.1 **Ports in antiquity**
All ports listed in *The Catalogue of Ancient Ports and Harbours* (de
Graauw 2017), excluding eastern Africa below the Horn ($N = 13$),
western Africa below the Bight of Benin ($N = 1$), and northern Norway
($N = 4$). Total: 5,069.

attempt to identify these features of littoral geography through time on a
global scale.

The most far-reaching effort to date focuses on Europe, the
Mediterranean, and the Middle East in antiquity. Drawing clues from
ancient and modern writings along with data from the Barrington Atlas,
the Pleiades project, and the Digital Atlas of the Roman Empire, Arthur
de Graauw compiled *The Catalogue of Ancient Ports and Harbours* (hereafter *The Catalogue*) – a seemingly comprehensive list of over 5,000 ports
(including several hundred *potential* ports) located directly on the coast
or along rivers that could be reached by oceangoing vessels. For a subset
of about 3,500, founding dates can be established. These range from
30,000 BCE to 551 CE, with most falling after 750 BCE.

Ports included in *The Catalogue* are represented in Map 4.1. The
Mediterranean, the Iberian peninsula, northern France, and the British
Isles are populated by so many ports that they form a virtually continuous
line along the coast. By comparison, the frequency of portages is somewhat attenuated in the Red Sea and the Persian Gulf, and much less

developed further north (in Scandinavia) and further south (East Africa below Agadir, the southern coast of Arabia, and the Indian Ocean). We do not know to what extent this map accurately represents the maritime history of these regions, though it is consistent with standard historical accounts (which is no accident, since de Graauw relies on those accounts for his dataset).

Harborage requirements were limited in ancient times. Ports included in *The Catalogue* offered various forms of shelter: "anchorages, landing places on beaches and ports with structures like access channels, breakwaters (moles), jetties, landing stages, quays, warehouses for storage of commodities and equipment, shipsheds and slipways for ships."[13] In another study, Veikou (2015: 42) identifies three critical geomorphological requirements:

(1) Presence of a sandy beach for loading, unloading, and dockyard activities; (2) Protection offered by a promontory or rocky area, including protection from marine currents and coastal winds, but also as a defence from enemy attack, because a hilly promontory was suitable for fortification and provided a lookout; and (3) The mouth of a river or smaller watercourse to provide fresh water for the settlement and sailors and to serve as an easy route for communication with the interior.

As time went on, the size of ships increased, requiring greater depth. Since big ships cannot be dragged onshore during a storm they also require greater protection from the raging seas. And since bulky cargo needs to be loaded and unloaded they require tranquil waters. As seagoing travel developed, therefore, the problem of harborage became more acute. Nathaniel Shaler (1894: 101) estimates that larger vessels, requiring secure ports, evolved in the Mediterranean two millennia ago – though they had not entirely displaced smaller vessels at that time.

Tracking ports through premodern history is difficult. *The Catalogue*'s data does not reveal which ports in Europe, the Mediterranean, and the Middle East were fully operational, or how much business they conducted. In other regions of the world we know even less about the placement and role of ports in the premodern era. It is one thing to establish the point that ports have been around for a long while. It is another to establish exactly which ports were in business over which periods of time.

One must also bear in mind that geomorphic changes over long periods of time are likely to affect the development and demise of ports. This includes sea-level changes, sedimentation, marine erosion, tectonics, and the displacement of rivers or river deltas. Ports situated at the

---

[13] De Graauw (2017). For more information, see www.ancientportsantiques.com.

mouth or border of a river may shift over time as a river realigns, silt accumulates, or new docks are constructed. This pattern is especially evident in South and Southeast Asia, where rivers regularly relocated.[14] Accordingly, we cannot always infer the harborage provided by a coastal location three thousand years ago from its characteristics today. For this reason, the early history of ports is obscure, and likely to remain so.

The Modern Era

Fortunately, our primary theoretical interest is in the modern era, when evidence of ports and their activities is more abundant. During this shorter time period, geomorphic changes are also more limited, allowing one to infer the characteristics of the coastline a few centuries ago from its characteristics today. In this time period, finally, there are many fewer ports suitable for oceangoing vessels – a product of the increasingly demanding requirements of modern portage.

For all these reasons, it is a much simpler task to identify ports in the modern era than to identify those that may have existed in the premodern era, when ports were more numerous, more transient, and less well-defined. Given that global maritime activity accelerates in the eighteenth and nineteenth centuries (as shown in the previous section), the modern era is also a plausible point of focus for our theory. If ocean access matters for democracy it should matter most in the modern era – the era of ocean transit, par excellence.

A number of sources shed light on the location of ports in the early modern and modern eras.

The *Soundtoll Registers* tabulates information on ships passing through the Baltic from 1497 to 1857, a total of about 1.8 million passages (Gøbel 2010). This is a remarkable resource for those studying the development of shipping in Northern Europe. However, it does not shed much light on the location of ports globally.

Lloyd's List began in the late seventeenth century as the publication of a coffee house in London where shipmasters and insurers assembled to hammer out deals and get news of arrivals and departures. Early issues listed the name of the vessels arriving and departing London, their captain, and their origin or destination. In the eighteenth century, the publication developed into a premier source of information on shipping throughout the world and it is now one of the oldest continuously published journals in existence.[15] César Ducruet and collaborators have

---

[14] See Arasaratnam (1994), Wink (2002: 416–19; 2020: ch. 1).
[15] See Fayle, Wright (1928), Martin (1876), McCusker (1991).

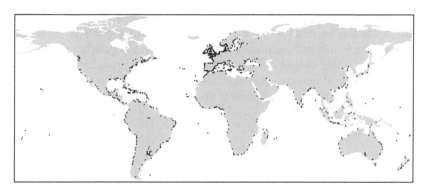

Map 4.2 **Ports in 1890**
Ports included in *Lloyd's List* (compiled by Ducruet et al. 2018) in 1890
(*N* = 897).

transcribed data contained in these historic publications as part of the
World Seastems project,[16] providing an incomparable historical dataset
showing (among other things) the location of working ports across the
world from the late nineteenth century to the present. The world's ports
in 1890 according to Lloyd's are shown in Map 4.2, offering evidence of
the degree to which shipping had extended to the far corners of the world
by the end of the nineteenth century.

In the mid-twentieth century, the *World Port Index* (WPI) becomes an
authoritative source for data on shipping throughout the world.
Originally published by the Hydrographic Office of the US Navy, this
database is now the responsibility of the National Geospatial-Intelligence
Agency (NGIA). Along with precise locations (latitude/longitude), the
WPI offers information about each port, which is regularly updated. The
ports from the first edition of the WPI (1953) appear in Map 4.3, at
which point 5,455 working seaports could be identified.

In the twenty-first century, a number of additional sources have arisen.
The *World Port Source* includes nearly 5,000 ports across the world, with
GIS markers and a coding of their size.[17] *Navigocorpus* includes a smaller
collection of 790 ports, along with information about specific ships, their
captains, and their passages.[18] For our purposes, these sources are
redundant (though for other purposes they may be quite useful).

In summary, we are able to identify four non-redundant datasets that
sample the universe of ports at different points in time: (a) antiquity (*The
Catalogue*), (b) the late nineteenth and twentieth centuries (Lloyd's),

---

[16] See world-seastems.cnrs.fr.   [17] See www.worldportsource.com/index.php.
[18] See Dedieu et al. (2011) and navigocorpus.org.

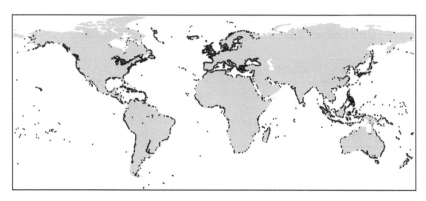

Map 4.3 **Ports in 1953**
Ports included in the *World Port Index* (WPI) 1953 (*N* = 5,455).

(c) the mid-twentieth century (WPI 1953), and (d) the twenty-first century (WPI 2017). Key features of these data sources are noted in the top portion of Table 4.3.

The largest global dataset is offered by Lloyd's. However, this dataset is compiled over a century-long period. At any given point in time (after 1953), the WPI offers a considerably larger collection of ports. Accordingly, we regard this as our primary source.

Some information about the development of ports through time can be gleaned from these various datasets. Ports appear to have been most numerous across the Mediterranean and adjoining seas during antiquity. *The Catalogue* identifies over 5,000 ports in this one region of the world. Of course, many of these landing sites were little more than beaches or creeks and a few are hypothetical (they may or may not have been in use). Over time, the number of locations along the Mediterranean where ships could dock became more limited. As ships grew in size demands on ports and port infrastructure grew, and fewer could offer satisfactory docking. Additionally, inland infrastructure improved so that a single port could service a large hinterland. Just as a smaller number of large ships displaced many small ships we expect that a smaller number of large facilities displaced a larger number of smaller, less formal facilities.

The process of winnowing appears to continue in the contemporary era, as evident in the reduced number of ports covered by the WPI from 1953 to 2017. At the same time, we note that the number of ports in *Lloyd's List* grows dramatically from 1890 to 2009. This may reflect a growth in ports or improvements in Lloyd's data collection procedures. It is difficult to say.

Table 4.3 *Port datasets and their correspondences*

		Datasets		
	Period	*Region*	*N*	*Reference*
1	Antiquity	Europe, MENA	5087	The Catalogue (de Graauw 2017)
2	1890–2009	Global	7034	Lloyd's (Ducruet et al. 2018)
3	1953	Global	5455	WPI (US Navy 1953)
4	2017	Global	3669	WPI (NGIA 2017)

			Correspondences				
	Mean	*Median*		*Mean*	*Median*	*Mean*	*Median*
1 → 2:	22.53	12.98	2 → 1:	80.00	13.58	1 → 3:	23.38	12.52
3 → 1:	74.37	10.60	1 → 4:	28.06	18.34	4 → 1:	82.66	12.55
2 → 3:	26.62	3.32	3 → 2:	30.23	5.31	3 → 4:	28.11	3.01
4 → 3:	16.28	0.00					

Correspondences: For each port listed in a source dataset, we calculate the distance (in km) to the nearest port in the target dataset. From these distances, we calculate the arithmetic mean and median to produce summary measures of fit. For example, 1→2 refers to the mean and median distance between all ports in #1 (*The Catalogue*) and the nearest ports in #2 (Lloyd's). Since #1 is limited to the Mediterranean region, we consider only this region when making comparisons with other sources.

The problem is that there is no established definition or measure of what qualifies as a port. Different datasets presumably define the subject differently, and it is not even clear that they maintain a constant definition through time, making it difficult to interpret time trends.

What we can evaluate is the *correspondence* between ports listed in different datasets. This is recorded in the bottom portion of Table 4.3, where we show the mean and median distance between ports in each dataset. These are treated as directed dyads in which one is the "source" and the other the "target," generating two measures for each dyad.

It will be seen that mean distances are considerably greater than median distances, attesting to the right-skew of the distribution: a few ports lying far apart drag the mean away from the median. Accordingly, we regard the median as somewhat more informative. By this measure, there is a fairly close fit between ports located in our four datasets. Where time periods are closer, that correspondence is higher. And where the source itself is also the same – as for WPI measured in 1953 and 2017 – it is closest of all, rendering a median distance of zero.

Path Dependence

The high correspondence between ports datasets collected at different points in time attests to an important feature of our topic: *path dependence.*

Granted, the traffic received by a port responds to many factors that are likely to change from decade to decade, e.g., the growth or decline of the local and regional economy serviced by a port, the population of the adjoining port city, transport connections to the hinterland, operating costs and fees, security, investments in port infrastructure, trade taxes and embargoes, and so forth.[19] Ships, and shipping lines, can easily redirect their course from one port to another if there are good reasons to do so, especially if there are multiple ports within the same coastal region. Over the past several centuries, the dominant port along the continental border of the North Sea has shifted from Lubeck to Hamburg to Bruges to Antwerp to Amsterdam and most recently to Rotterdam, with many other ports playing important roles at various times. Similar shifts have been noted in Europe at large (Bretagnolle 2016: 31), in the Persian Gulf (Potter 2014b), in Kerala (Malekandathil 2010), in East Africa (Hoyle 1967a, 1968), in Southeast Asia (Blussé 2013), and in China (Wang, Ducruet 2013). Ports across any oceanic region experience shifts in traffic over time.[20]

However, once a sizeable port is established in the modern era it tends to stay in business in some capacity. In the rare circumstance of closure its replacement is likely to be located in the same region, which means that the hinterland will still have ready access to a working port. Accordingly, there is strong path dependency in the general location of ports across the modern era. A port in 1800 is likely to be a port, or near a port, today. Of twenty-seven Spanish ports observed from 1880 to the present, none have subsequently gone out of business, despite the considerable political and economic turmoil occurring in Spain over that period (Castillo, Valdaliso 2017). We expect that the same pattern of persistence characterizes other oceanic regions.[21]

Path dependency in port location is a product of the huge fixed costs associated with the creation of a working port – including associated transport networks (railroads, roads) that link a port to its hinterland, aggregations of human capital that occur in the hinterlands, and all the

---

[19] See Ducruet, Lee, Ng (2010), Harlaftis, Valdaliso, Tenold (2012).
[20] For general discussion and statistics pertaining to the rise and fall of major ports globally see Alexandersson, Norström (1963), Ducruet et al. (2016).
[21] Long-term persistence in network position can be found across African ports over the past century, for example (Hidalgo, Ducruet (2020).

infrastructure associated with a port city. In the age of steamships, a port was required to provide "lights, buoys, and breakwaters; a minimum depth at dockside of 9.75 meters; dry docks and repair shops; cranes and warehouses; and supplies of food, water, and naval stores" (Headrick 1981: 32–3). In the age of container ships, infrastructural requirements of a suitable ocean port have multiplied severalfold. Accordingly, it is usually more cost-effective to improve an existing port than to found a new one, de novo. And once initial investments have been made it is fairly cheap to maintain a port, even if that port is no longer sufficient to accommodate the largest vessels.

Because ports are "sticky" – once established they tend to be retained (at least one in each major region) – the placement of a port can be expected to impact the long-term development of a region. This brings us to the question of port location.

Natural Harbors

The placement of ports is to some extent contingent on natural features of the coastline. This does not mean that there are no artificial enhancements. No port, even in ancient times, was entirely pristine. At the very least, there were usually man-made docks. The point is that some areas are more suitable than others, and therefore more likely to be chosen as a port for oceangoing traffic. In this respect, the geomorphology of a coastline affects its maritime activity.

Of the Mediterranean region during the ancient era, Blackman (2008: 642) observes,

The indented coastline of the Aegean provided many good natural harbors, so many cities needed to build no more than a shoreline quay or jetty against which even large merchant ships could berth. But some cities lay on exposed coasts and required a different solution. A feature of certain harbors on exposed coastlines in Greece and Sicily may show Phoenician influence: an artificial harbor basin (*cothon*) excavated landward of the coastline. This technique was particularly important along Phoenician trade routes on the North African coast. The basin sometimes made use of existing low-lying ground or a lagoon, perhaps joined to the sea by one or more channels.

Ancient harbors required "cozy, well-protected refuges, with no great depth," for the ships were small (Blackman 2008: 645). The absence of tidal ranges and large waves in the Mediterranean obviated a major problem encountered in other areas. Beaches provided an alternative – good enough for small boats in the ancient and medieval eras – where proper harbors were unavailable. (This of course was true everywhere, not just in the Mediterranean region, much of which is rather rocky.)

Since some coastlines are better suited than others to harvest the fruits of seaborne commerce this geographic feature of the landscape probably shaped the civilizations that arose. Taking a long view, Shaler (1894: 101; see also Broodbank 2006) writes,

The ... first lessons in seamanship seem to have been acquired in tolerably sheltered waters where bays or islands favored tentative experiments in navigation. Wherever any of the shores of the Old World abound in inlets or are beset with islands ... we almost invariably find that the maritime spirit was developed in a measure quite up to the progress in other arts. On the other hand, wherever the shore was not deeply embayed or fringed with islands the folk seem never to have acquired the mariner's craft, however far they have advanced in other constructive arts ... We thus perceive that natural harbors, or rather the conditions of a shore line affording ... a gradual passage from the conditions of the land to those of the wide ocean, favor the development of sailors.

As the size of ships increased so did harborage requirements. Accordingly, ports suitable for large oceangoing vessels were generally located in areas that afforded some natural protection from the high seas.[22]

To be clear, ports could be constructed almost anywhere. However, the cost of doing so might be high. Accordingly, it made little sense for builders to ignore features of littoral geography. Like any large-scale infrastructure project, ports are enormously expensive (Headrick 1981: 32–3), and the more alterations of the natural landscape are required, the greater the expense. Note also that the harborage requirements of ships become more demanding as they grow in size, and there is no end in sight for the ever-advancing lengths, girths, and depths of ocean vehicles (see Table 4.2).

It is no surprise, therefore, that geographic features of the coastline have impacted the placement of ports throughout history, a pattern continuing to the present day. Naturally, other factors also influenced the decision to

---

[22] This was especially the case outside Europe. Advanced harbor construction methods, offering artificial enhancements to the natural landscape, were developed first in Europe, which means that harbors elsewhere were more likely to build on natural features. Adrian Jarvis (1998: xviii) notes, "Large parts of the world did not have indigenous shipping industries, and only needed the capability to handle ships rather than boats after the arrival on the scene of European traders or colonists. As a result, ports tended to grow up in places which offered such advantages as a sheltered natural harbour or access to major rivers for transhipment of goods to or from rivercraft ... For this reason, we could travel the coast of Africa from the Straits of Gibraltar to the Red Sea and never encounter a fully-impounded dock with an entrance lock, and a circumnavigation of Australia would yield a similar result. Those places which, like India, had substantial sea-borne trade before European involvement, had often developed that trade before their civil engineering skills had reached the point they could ignore natural disadvantages, with the result that they too depended heavily on tidal harbours with relatively little engineering input. As a result, Indian maritime historians have concentrated on the trade rather than the engineering. This does not mean that there is no dock or harbour engineering in Africa or Australia, but it does mean that there is much less of it."

invest in a working port. This includes the characteristics of the hinterland (its population, wealth, agricultural productivity, sources of fresh water, mineral deposits, climate, disease vectors), the military defensibility of the potential port, as well as local politics and inland infrastructure. We need some method of identifying the purely *geomorphic* features of coastlines that make them more or less conducive to the development of ports. Only in this fashion can we treat harbors as causally exogenous.

A Prediction Model

We shall assume that coastlines that are jagged should be propitious for the development of a modern port. Accordingly, we create a high-resolution measure of the complexity of the coastline, normalizing the vector length of the coastline within each 50 × 50 km grid-cell. For each grid-cell that contains a coastline, we count the number of nodes required to represent the line. A perfectly straight line has no nodes, while a very curvy line requires lots of nodes. So, the number of nodes offers a pretty good estimation of how uneven the coastline is – so long as this number is discounted by the length of the coastline falling within a grid-cell. Our measure of squiggliness (S) is derived from the expression,

$$S = \text{Nodes } (N)/\text{Distance } (km) \qquad [4.1]$$

For a concrete example let us examine the coastline of Sicily, which is divided into grid-cells in Map 4.4. The western edge of the island offers an example of a coastline that is especially squiggly: 57 nodes across a distance of roughly 75 kilometers, rendering a squiggliness score of 0.761. By contrast, the neighboring cell – just to the east – is straighter, with only 17 nodes across 53 kilometers, rendering a modest squiggliness score of 0.324. This procedure is repeated across every coastal grid-cell of the world (excluding Antarctica).

Although "squiggliness" is a matter of degrees, for our purposes it is essential to impose a cutoff so that each grid-cell can be coded in a binary fashion – as a natural harbor, or not. To find this threshold, we estimate regression models in which characteristics of the coastline predict the existence of ports or harbors existing in the world today.

Our measures of the latter are drawn from the first edition of the WPI, published in 1953. This captures the world of shipping at its historical apex. Still dominant as a mode of transporting goods over long distances, ships were losing their preeminence as a mode of long-distance travel as air travel became more convenient and affordable. They had already lost their preeminence as a mode of communications with the advent of telegraphs and telephones.

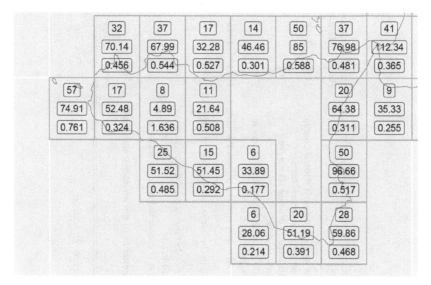

Map 4.4 **The Sicilian coastline**
Contours of the coastline of Sicily, Italy. Within each grid-cell, the top
row indicates the number of nodes necessary to construct the line. The
middle row indicates the length of the line. The bottom row indicates
the product – nodes divided by length – our standardized measure of
coastline squiggliness.

At this point in time, the WPI reports 5,455 ports with connections to
the global shipping industry. These ports are classified into eight types, as
described in Table 4.4. We regard two of these types – (A) coastal natural
and (D) river natural – as *harbors*, i.e., ports situated along a coastline
that provides shelter and anchorage without need for additional breakwaters, thus favoring the eventual development of a working port.
Historical studies suggest these geographic characteristics were usually
critical to the establishment of working ports sufficient to load and
unload merchandise from oceangoing vessels.[23] There were 3,484 such
harbors in 1953, constituting over half of the total sample.

The next step is to identify the measure of squiggliness that best
predicts the existence of (a) ports or (b) harbors around the world. To

---

[23] For historical studies, see Morgan (2017), Shaler (1894), Weigend (1958). For examples
of recent papers using natural harbors as exogenous predictors see Alvarez-Villa and
Guardado (2020), focused on Mexico, and Henderson, Squires, Storeygard and Weil
(2016), which encompasses the entire globe. Our classification of natural harbors follows
Henderson et al.

Table 4.4 *Port types*

	Type	Definition	Ports	Harbors
A	Coastal natural	Coastal harbor sheltered from wind and sea by virtue of its location within a natural coastal indentation or in the protective lee of an island, cape, reef or other natural barrier.	2431	2431
B	Coastal breakwater	Coastal harbor lying behind a man-made breakwater constructed to provide shelter, or supplement inadequate shelter already provided by natural sources.	764	
C	Coastal tide gates	Coastal harbor, the waters of which are constrained by locks or other mechanical devices in order to provide sufficient water to float vessels at all stages of the tide.	33	
D	River natural	Harbor located on a river, the waters of which are not retained by any artificial means. Facilities may include quays, wharves, piers, or jetties.	1053	1053
E	River basin	River harbor in which slips for vessels have been excavated in the banks, obliquely or at right angles to the axis of the stream.	80	
F	River tide gates	River harbor, the waters of which are constrained by locks or other mechanical devices in order to provide sufficient water to float vessels at all stages of the tide.	60	
G	Canal or lake	Harbor located in the interior portion of a canal or lake that is connected with the sea by a navigable waterway.	267	
H	Open roadstead	Port which has no natural or artificial barrier to provide shelter from the wind, sea, and swell.	767	
	Total		5455	3484

Ports listed in the WPI (1953) and their classifications. Types A and D qualify as harbors in our lexicon.

do so, we iterate the following procedure. First, we experiment with different transformations of the squiggliness variable, e.g., linear and logged, different polynomials, and so forth. Second, we estimate a range of different models. For example, our simplest model would be one with only a linear squiggliness term and a linear length term, while our most complex model is one with ten polynomials of the squiggliness measure. The polynomial measures are in line with our expectation that there will be some non-linear relationship between squiggliness and having a port. At any rate, we let the data decide, resolving our quest when we find the model that yields the best prediction of port or harbor locations. Specifically, we first estimate a number of models and take a sample of those with the highest R^2 and lowest out-of-sample prediction error. In this first stage we select three models. Then, we take the predicted values from each model and use them to create dichotomous indicators for "predicted port" or "predicted harbor," according to different predicted-value thresholds and see which of these binary indicators offer the best prediction. Using this iterative procedure, we settle on a model with four polynomials:

$$P(Port) = b_0 + L(s) + L(s)^2 + L(s)^3 + L(s)^4 + L(s)^5 \qquad [4.2]$$

where $L(s)$ is the log of squiggliness and b_0 is the intercept. This model has the lowest out-of-sample classification error and the highest R^2 when predicting whether cells have ports or harbors.

This protocol is followed for all ports and then for all harbors listed in the WPI 1953, generating two sets of predictions, one focused on ports and the other on harbors. The predictive success of these models is shown in Table 4.5.[24]

As it happens, our approach is about as successful predicting ports (section 1) as it is predicting harbors (section 2). And the two models issue predictions that are extremely close to each other (section 3). There is not much difference between these two approaches, which is perhaps not surprising since harbors compose most of the ports listed in the WPI (see Table 4.4). Both models are much better at predicting the absence of ports (75 percent) and harbors (78 percent) than their presence (54–59 percent), which is also to be expected.

As a benchmark measure of natural harbors we employ estimates from the first prediction model, based on *all* ports in the WPI 1953. The second prediction model, based on ports classified as harbors, will be regarded as a robustness check. Our rationale is that the distinction

[24] When compared with other binary prediction models for unbalanced outcomes (e.g., Ward, Greenhill, Bakke 2010) these models offer a pretty strong fit.

Table 4.5 Prediction models and their fit

1.

Source: Model 1

	Target: WPI ports	
	No (8958)	Yes (2804)
No (7986)	6711	1275
Yes (3776)	2247	1529
Correct	75%	54%

Distance (km)	
Mean	93.26
Median	37.70

2.

Source: Model 2

	Target: WPI harbors	
	No (9798)	Yes (1964)
No (8415)	7604	811
Yes (3347)	2194	1153
Correct	78%	59%

Distance (km)	
Mean	100.13
Median	48.14

3.

Source: Model 1

	Target: Model 2	
	No (8415)	Yes (3347)
No (7986)	7961	25
Yes (3776)	454	3322
Correct	95%	99%

Distance (km)	
Mean	10.09
Median	0

The fit between (1) Model 1 and actual ports in the WPI 1953, (2) Model 2 and actual harbors in the WPI 1953, and (3) Model 1 and Model 2. Correspondence is calculated, first, in a binary fashion according to whether a predicted port can be found in the same grid-cell in the target dataset. It is calculated, second, by the distance (in km) from each port grid-cell in the source dataset to the nearest port grid-cell in the target dataset, from which we report the arithmetic mean and median across the sample. Sample: all coastal grid-cells, excluding Antarctica ($N = 11,762$). Note that the number of port/harbor grid-cells listed in parentheses is smaller than the number of ports/harbors listed in Table 4.3 because some grid-cells contain more than one port or harbor.

between artificial and natural ports ("harbors") is somewhat arbitrary and thus open to bias. These two measures are in any case highly correlated. Model 1 predicts results from Model 2 with 95–99 percent accuracy, as shown in Table 4.5. Not surprisingly, results from regression models are virtually indistinguishable (see Table 6.4). Henceforth, unless otherwise qualified, the term "natural harbor" refers to coastal grid-cells whose geomorphic conditions suggest that they are propitious for the development of a working port, based on the first prediction model.

Importantly, our two models predict a larger number of ports and harbors than appear in the WPI. This is consistent with the idea that some coastlines suitable for a modern port were, for one reason or another, never developed, or only partially developed (falling short of the threshold for inclusion in the WPI). This is what one would expect in regions of the world blessed with a great many natural harbors. No purpose would be served by constructing modern ports, with their expensive infrastructural requirements, in every fjord of Norway or along every island shore of the Indonesian archipelago. This sort of slippage between natural harbor and port scarcely affects our estimates so long as the port-suitable coastline that remains undeveloped lies close to a port-suitable coastline that *is* developed into a modern port, as appears to be the case in Norway and the Indonesian archipelago. Our natural harbor distance variable, introduced below, reports a low score for all areas that lie close to a port-suitable location. (All of Norway and nearly all of the Indonesian archipelago receives a low score.)

It is of course possible that there are regions of the world with port-suitable locations but no working ports (or none that meet the threshold of inclusion to the WPI). To explore this possibility, we generate a map of the world showing the distance between natural harbors (predicted ports) and actual ports in the WPI. Map 4.5 demonstrates that the greatest error (predicted ports that are a long way from actual ports) is in the Arctic, where squiggly coastlines (which under normal circumstances would be conducive to port development) are iced over for much of the year. This affects the scoring of only two countries – Canada and Russia – and is therefore inconsequential in state-level analyses.

In any case, it is important to emphasize that our theory is geographic, not infrastructural. Accordingly, we expect some slippage between natural harbors and working ports and harbors. Not every natural harbor will become a port and not every working port will be located in a natural harbor. This was true in ancient times and it is true today. We want to measure the natural features of coastlines that are conducive to ports. So long as our model achieves this we needn't worry too much about how tight the fit to actual ports or harbors is. A loose fit will presumably

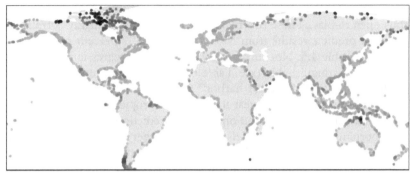

Distance (km)   [0,69]   (69,172]   (172,342]   (342,590]   (590,1737]

Map 4.5 **Distance from predicted port to actual port**
Distance (km) from each predicted port (Model 1) to the nearest
actual port in the WPI 1953. Darker hues represent greater distance.
Numbers within brackets indicate the range (in kilometers)
encompassed by each color.

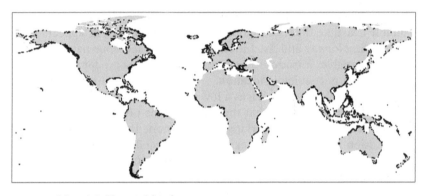

Map 4.6 **Natural harbors**
Location of natural harbors as predicted by Model 1, where all ports
in the WPI (1953) are the outcome to be predicted. Dots represent a
grid-cell with a natural harbor (N = 3,775).

attenuate our estimates of the causal impact of geography on democracy.
As such, our approach to measurement is a conservative one.

The locations of natural harbors around the world, as identified by the
first prediction model, are shown in Map 4.6. The coasts of Europe, the
Americas, Southeast Asia, and East Asia are for the most part well
provisioned. By contrast, the coastlines in Africa and the Middle East (with
the exception of the Red Sea and Persian Gulf) have fewer natural indentations and thus a lower frequency of natural harbors along their coasts.

The global Map 4.6 also reveals substantial variability *within* regions. Northern Europe has more natural harbors than Southern Europe (outside of the Aegean and Adriatic). The northern Mediterranean has many more natural harbors than the southern Mediterranean. Most natural harbors in Africa are clustered in a few locations on the west and east coasts. Most of the natural harbors in Asia are located in Southeast and East Asia. And so forth. We shall have much more to say about the location of natural harbors in the next chapter, but now we must think about how they relate to the hinterland.

Natural Harbor Distance

We expect the impact of natural harbors on political development to attenuate with distance. The greater the distance, the less impact a port is likely to have on the hinterland, for the ocean is less accessible. This was especially the case before the advent of modern transport systems, and remains true today. Accordingly, our measure of natural harbors is transformed into a *distance* variable.

By this measure, what counts is not simply the perforations of a coastline but the depth of the interior. Southeast Asia and Europe receive very low scores because most areas of these aqueous subcontinents are close to a natural harbor. Asia and Africa, by contrast, receive higher scores because even where the coastline is corrugated the hinterland is a long way off.

To measure natural harbor distance on a global scale we build on the PRIO grid-cell database, which divides the world into uniformly sized squares, each of which is 0.5 × 0.5 decimal degrees, i.e., approximately 50 × 50 km at the equator (Tollefsen et al. 2012). This produces 259,200 grid-cells across the entire world and 64,818 across the terrestrial world (excluding Antarctica). For each of these (terrestrial) grid-cells, we measure the geodesic (great-circle) distance (in kilometers) from the centroid to the nearest natural harbor, as defined in the previous section.

To construct a *state-level* measure of natural harbor distance, we begin by gathering GIS polygons for colonies, dependencies, and countries across the world back to 1789. We rely on *Cshapes* (Weidmann et al. 2010) for the 1946–2015 period. From 1789 to 1945 we rely on *Euratlas* (www.Euratlas.com) for Europe and the digitization of existing maps from sources such as *GeaCron* (geacron.com/the-geacron-project) for states outside Europe. Combining these sources, we are able to generate a set of polygons for sovereign and semisovereign states from 1789 to the present. Next, we take the arithmetic mean of natural harbor distance calculated for all grid-cells falling within a state's polygon. This provides a state-level measure of natural harbor distance.

Note that when state boundaries change so does a state's natural harbor distance score. The United States had a lower score in 1789 than it did in 1860, for example, a product of its incorporation of the continental landmass of North America north of the Rio Grande and south of the 49th parallel. A list of all states and their scores in 2000 on this key variable is displayed in Table 4.6.

We have now developed two measures of natural harbor distance, one centered on grid-cells and the other on states. Histograms of these variables are shown in Figure 4.2. Both variables reveal a strong right skew, with many areas having low scores (close proximity to a natural harbor) and a few registering very high scores. This is a concern if extreme values serve as high-leverage cases or if there is reason to believe that the relationship is non-linear. Tests show that the relationship between natural harbor distance and democracy is robust when the former is transformed by the natural logarithm, though there is no improvement in model-fit. The relationship is also robust when states with very high scores are removed (see Table 6.6). Thus, we see no theoretical or empirical reason to abandon the assumption of linearity in our benchmark model.

A related concern is potential collinearity with other geographic predictors of long-run economic and political development. Collinearity leads to fragile estimates or to potential confounding if the collinear variable is excluded from the model.

Fortuitously, intercorrelations with other variables commonly employed to measure the influence of geography on long-term economic and political development are weak. Natural harbor distance is empirically distinct from most other commonly used geographic variables (see Table 12.1). This is apparent in the stability of estimates across different specifications (see Table 6.3).

Two partial exceptions should be noted. Distance from natural harbors is modestly correlated with distance from nearest ocean or sea (Pearson's $r = 0.47$ across grid-cells and 0.77 across states). This is to be expected given that one is a necessary condition of the other: no ocean, no harbor. It is not a very strong correlation because not all shorelines have natural harbors (as shown in Map 4.6). Indeed, some islands have no natural harbors at all, accounting for moderately high scores on the natural harbor distance variable for Bermuda, Micronesia, and Maldives (see Table 4.6).

Distance from natural harbors is also modestly correlated with a dummy variable measuring whether a state is landlocked or not

Table 4.6 *Natural harbor distance scores*

Country	Score	Country	Score	Country	Score	Country	Score
Bahrain	0.00	Portugal	0.73	Mexico	1.93	United States	5.02
Hong Kong	0.00	Indonesia	0.73	Thailand	1.95	Republic of Congo	5.15
Dominica	0.00	Seychelles	0.75	Senegal	1.97	Malawi	5.30
Singapore	0.00	Brunei	0.75	Tonga	2.03	Slovakia	5.36
St. Kitts/Nevis	0.00	São Tomé	0.77	Gabon	2.09	Zimbabwe	5.39
Trinidad/Tobago	0.16	Honduras	0.79	Mozambique	2.13	Angola	5.40
Antigua	0.18	Papua New Guinea	0.80	Guyana	2.16	Namibia	5.49
Haiti	0.19	Slovenia	0.84	Luxembourg	2.19	Ethiopia	5.59
Belize	0.24	Croatia	0.84	Germany	2.24	Georgia	5.72
Gambia	0.26	Saint Lucia	0.85	Serbia	2.36	Mauritania	5.79
Grenada	0.28	Belgium	0.86	Austria	2.37	Russia	6.00
Grenadines	0.28	Sweden	0.92	Jordan	2.45	Pakistan	6.03
Greece	0.29	Malaysia	0.93	Syria	2.54	Bermuda	6.04
Ireland	0.30	Nicaragua	0.96	Guinea	2.67	Brazil	6.52
Comoros	0.33	Vietnam	0.96	Canada	2.67	Micronesia	6.56
Philippines	0.34	Italy	0.97	Poland	2.80	Libya	7.08
Cuba	0.35	Sierra Leone	0.98	Turkey	2.82	Maldives	7.41
Cabo Verde	0.36	Palau	1.00	Laos	2.85	Burkina Faso	7.58
Guinea Bissau	0.36	Piedmont-Sardinia	1.05	Ukraine	2.87	Bolivia	7.87
Samoa	0.37	Liberia	1.07	Côte d'Ivoire	2.88	Nepal	8.06
Panama	0.38	Bangladesh	1.08	Myanmar	2.92	Armenia	8.10
Iceland	0.38	Tunisia	1.09	Venezuela	2.94	Algeria	8.14
Norway	0.38	Fiji	1.10	Lesotho	2.97	Botswana	8.55
Costa Rica	0.39	Eritrea	1.11	Morocco	2.99	Afghanistan	9.21
Vanuatu	0.41	Bosnia & Herzegovina	1.19	Romania	3.12	Paraguay	9.37
Taiwan	0.41	Chile	1.20	Saudi Arabia	3.20	Azerbaijan	9.69
Djibouti	0.42	Finland	1.22	Somaliland	3.33	Uganda	9.88

Table 4.6 (*cont.*)

Qatar	0.42	Swaziland	1.34	Egypt	3.42	China	9.88
Jamaica	0.42	Mauritius	1.36	Switzerland	3.43	Zambia	9.94
Solomon Islands	0.42	Uruguay	1.40	Argentina	3.45	Sudan	10.03
Bahamas	0.45	Ecuador	1.40	Ghana	3.49	Tuvalu	10.06
United Kingdom	0.47	Spain	1.42	Australia	3.58	Burundi	10.58
Denmark	0.49	Palestine-West Bank	1.46	Togo	3.59	Rwanda	10.72
Japan	0.51	Guatemala	1.49	Benin	3.63	Mali	10.80
Cyprus	0.52	Madagascar	1.53	South Africa	3.67	Nauru	10.85
Kuwait	0.54	Bulgaria	1.53	Somalia	3.84	DRC	11.62
El Salvador	0.54	Israel	1.58	Colombia	3.92	Kiribati	11.85
Netherlands	0.54	Latvia	1.58	Peru	4.07	Marshall Islands	12.11
Dominican Rep.	0.54	N. Macedonia	1.64	Cameroon	4.14	Central African Rep.	12.16
Timor-Leste	0.57	Malta	1.68	Czechia	4.19	Niger	12.36
Lebanon	0.59	Cambodia	1.72	India	4.22	Turkmenistan	12.95
Sri Lanka	0.60	Suriname	1.76	Hungary	4.26	Aruba	13.32
New Zealand	0.63	Lithuania	1.76	France	4.28	Chad	14.04
South Korea	0.63	East Germany	1.76	Kenya	4.43	Tajikistan	14.97
Montenegro	0.64	Kosovo	1.79	Bhutan	4.74	Mongolia	15.28
UAE	0.64	South Yemen	1.87	Belarus	4.80	Uzbekistan	16.23
Estonia	0.64	Oman	1.87	Nigeria	4.80	Kazakhstan	17.30
Equatorial Guinea	0.65	Yemen	1.88	Iraq	4.88	Kyrgyzstan	19.21
North Korea	0.65	Barbados	1.90	Tanzania	4.88		
Albania	0.72	Moldova	1.91	Iran	4.96		

Distance to nearest natural harbor (100 kilometers), averaged across all grid-cells in a state in 2000 CE. States = 198. Mean = 3.53. Median = 1.90. Standard deviation = 3.94.

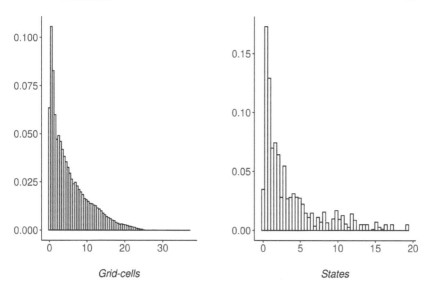

Figure 4.2 **Histograms of natural harbor distance**
Histograms of natural harbor distance (kilometers), measured across
grid-cells and states.

(Pearson's r = 0.53 across states). The fit is modest because some
landlocked nations such as Kosovo, Moldova, and Switzerland are nonetheless fairly close to a natural harbor while some states with ocean access
have very large hinterlands (e.g., China) or coasts with few natural
harbors (e.g., Algeria, Morocco).

As it happens, natural harbors are a much stronger predictor of democracy than other water-related geographic features. When tested in the same
specification with natural harbor distance, a variable measuring distance
from nearest ocean bears the "wrong" (unexpected) sign and a variable
measuring the landlocked status of a state registers a coefficient close to
zero. At the same time, the inclusion or exclusion of these variables has
virtually no impact on estimates for natural harbor distance (Table 6.3).
On this basis, we feel confident in asserting that the placement of harbors
is not serving as a proxy for other geographic factors.

Alternate Measures

We believe that our approach to measurement is defensible. But it is
certainly not the only approach that might be taken. Accordingly, a
variety of alternate measures are developed and tested.

We have already introduced a second prediction model, centered on harbors rather than ports and represented in Table 4.5. In addition, we construct a number of variables that do not rely on prediction models at all. Specifically, we measure distance to *actual* ports listed in WPI 1953, in WPI 2017, and in Lloyd's (at various points in time). We also measure distance to *harbors* as classified by the WPI 1953 and the WPI 2017 (port types *A* or *D* in Table 4.4).

Distance variables constructed from these measures of ports and harbors are very highly correlated, as shown in Table 4.7. The one partial outlier is Lloyd's in the grid-cell analysis. This is partly a product of the fact that Lloyd's stretches back to 1890. If one limits the analysis to a comparison between ports listed in the WPI and Lloyd's centered on the same years the grid-cell correlations improve to 0.72 in the 1950s and 0.78 in the 2000s. Correlations are higher, in any case, in the state-level analyses.

Table 4.7 *Distance variables*

Grid-cell level correlations						
Distance to nearest …	1.	2.	3.	4.	5.	6.
1. Natural harbor, as predicted by model 1: ports (WPI 1953)	1.00					
2. Natural harbor, as predicted by model 2: harbors (WPI 1953)	0.99	1.00				
3. Port (WPI 1953)	0.90	0.89	1.00			
4. Harbor (WPI 1953)	0.90	0.89	0.99	1.00		
5. Port (WPI 2017)	0.90	0.90	0.97	0.96	1.00	
6. Harbor (WPI 2017)	0.89	0.89	0.95	0.96	0.98	1.00
7. Port (Lloyd's)	0.47	0.46	0.61	0.60	0.60	0.57
State-level correlations						
Distance to …	1.	2.	3.	4.	5.	6.
1. Natural harbor, as predicted by model 1: ports (WPI 1953)	1.00					
2. Natural harbor, as predicted by model 2: harbors (WPI 1953)	0.99	1.00				
3. Port (WPI 1953)	0.89	0.89	1.00			
4. Harbor (WPI 1953)	0.92	0.93	0.97	1.00		
5. Port (WPI 2017)	0.90	0.90	0.99	0.96	1.00	
6. Harbor (WPI 2017)	0.93	0.93	0.93	0.95	0.95	1.00
7. Port (Lloyd's)	0.85	0.85	0.80	0.84	0.82	0.83

Correlations (Pearson's r) among variables measuring distance to nearest port, harbor, or natural harbor.

A somewhat different approach to estimation treats the actual location of ports (based on the WPI 1953) as the regressor of theoretical interest. This may be instrumented by exogenous factors in a two-stage analysis. Chosen instruments (used in separate models) include (a) distance from predicted ports (from our first prediction model) and (b) ocean distance.

The concept of a natural harbor also demands further scrutiny. For example, one might judge that areas prone to freezing-over in the winter are not terribly useful as ports, as they are serviceable only part of the year. Accordingly, we eliminate from consideration natural harbors in areas of the Arctic that are icebound for much of the winter.

One must also interrogate the concept of "distance." Our measure calculates distance as the crow flies. Another approach takes account of the topography of the hinterland (its ups and downs), measuring distance as a person walks. This constitutes another robustness test.

Ports do not operate in isolation from each other. Some are more tightly networked than others, a feature that probably mattered quite a lot in the premodern era when most trips were local. Accordingly, we adopt a number of approaches to estimate the centrality of each natural harbor within broader networks of natural harbors. Centrality then serves as a weighting device in the calculation of natural harbor distance.

A very different approach to measurement calculates the *total number* of ports, harbors, or natural harbors in a country. This number may be understood in a linear or logarithmic functional form, or may be calculated as a share of that country's total area. (Landlocked countries receive a score of zero across all these measures.) It should be clear why this approach is less than ideal insofar as it treats country borders as exogenous. It also takes no notice of how accessible the ports are to various regions of a country. (It is not a "distance" measure.)

All of these approaches to measurement are plausible, though perhaps not equally plausible. In any case, results from regression tests based on these various measures are very close. Regardless of whether we are using actual ports, actual harbors, predicted ports, predicted harbors, instruments, ice-free natural harbors, distance adjusted for topography, or total number of ports, harbors, or natural harbors the estimates hold steady. (See Table 6.4 for results from most of these options; others are available upon request.)

Thus, while operationalizing the concept of a natural harbor involves many choices, they turn out not to be very consequential. Every path in the "garden of forking paths" (Gelman, Loken 2014) leads to the same exit.

Units of Analysis

Before concluding, we need to address a knotty methodological problem concerning the units of analysis employed in Part II of the book. Recall that we measure natural harbor distance at the grid-cell level *and* the state level, introducing some redundancy. There is a reason for this.

Grid-cells are properly regarded as the "treated" units in our study. By virtue of being closer to (further from) a natural harbor, we surmise that a democratic form of rule is more (less) likely to develop on that territory. Grid-cells are also stable over time, which is important for a causal process that unfolds over centuries. By contrast, people and states come and go, and their comings and goings are presumably conditioned by geography, which means that they are partly endogenous.

Grid-cells are subject to several problems, however. First, they are arbitrary, and hence susceptible to the modifiable areal unit problem (Openshaw 1984: 3). It is possible that a different mapping of grid-cells to the earth's surface would result in a different relationship between natural harbors and democracy.

Second, the treatment status of one unit may affect other units, violating SUTVA (Rubin 1986). Democracy does not evolve autonomously within each grid-cell. This is not simply because ideas diffuse (passively) but also because states actively intervene to affect the regimes of those within their hegemonic purview (Owen 2010).

To mitigate these concerns, we conduct sensitivity tests in which the size of grid-cells is adjusted so that robustness under various assumptions can be assessed (see Figure 6.1). If results are consistent, the modifiable areal root problem is mitigated. Since bigger units are less susceptible to SUTVA problems (being further apart they are presumably more independent), estimates from large grid-cells may also be regarded as less biased, though at the cost of considerable information loss.

For these purposes, grid-cells are a logical choice of unit. However, they suffer from a clustering problem. All grid-cells located within a state receive the same democracy score (since democracy is a state-level attribute), which means they are not fully independent. This may incline one to regard *states* as the appropriate unit of analysis.

Since there is no simple solution to the unit-of-analysis problem we approach the issue in a multimethod fashion. Tests in Chapter 6 enlist both grid-cells and states as spatial units. Since each unit of analysis is subject to a different sort of bias they serve a complementary role.

To make this a trifle more concrete, let us consider the largest and smallest states (by territory) in the world at the present time: Russia and Tuvalu. Where PRIO grid-cells are the units of analysis Russia carries

600,000 times the weight of Tuvalu. Where states are units of analysis they receive precisely the same weight. Since it is not clear, a priori, which is more appropriate, we present both grid-cell and state-level analyses. As it happens, estimates produced from these very different units of analysis are quite close.

Other Modes of Transport

Ocean travel is not the only way to get around. Inland waterways, roads, railroads, and airplanes also served (and continue to serve) as global connectors, and a good deal of evidence suggests that they enhance economic development and overall mobility.[25] The invention of the term "air-port" was intended to suggest that connections by air would serve similar functions as existing connections by ship. It is reasonable to imagine that these alternate modes of transport might also enhance democracy, and to some extent we embrace this reading (see Chapter 16). However, non-oceanic modes of transport are also easier for state actors to control. As such, they bear ambivalently on democracy and in some instances may serve as handmaidens of autocracy.

Let us begin with lake and river navigation, which preceded ocean travel in most parts of the world by virtue of greater safety and ease of transit. Inland waterways formed, and still form, a backbone of transport and commerce, which means that many of the virtues we have associated with ocean access could also be attributed to river access. However, a single fort or armed ship at the mouth of a river or at the junction of two rivers offers a point of surveillance and control over all traffic that passes along that artery, allowing officials to exact taxes, interdict contraband, and prevent the movement of dissidents, slaves, or foreigners. In a river valley, where the river is central to transport and to economic life generally and where much of the population lives along the banks of a major artery and its tributaries, governments can easily project their power. They may even organize vast irrigation projects, further entrenching their authority (see Chapter 12).

As a rule, the fewer interconnections there are within a riverine system, and the fewer independent outlets to the sea, the easier it will be for a state to exercise control. Where rivers and oceans fail to connect, or where a river is broken by cataracts, it is necessary to haul goods from one waterway to the next. Because there is usually just one plausible path

---

[25] On railroads see Donaldson (2018). On postal services see Rogowski et al. (2021). On rivers and canals see Hornell (2015[1946]), Smith (2020), Tvedt, Coopey (2010). On transport generally see Farhadi (2015).

between adjacent waterways, these portages attract a great deal of traffic and generally become places of settlement, points of taxation, and junctures of state control.

Europe's rivers fit the mobility ideal insofar as most of them are navigable (without extensive alterations), they often connect with one another, and – most importantly – they have separate outlets to the sea. There is no single chokepoint. By contrast, Africa's rivers are rare, do not interconnect, and are often interrupted by cataracts. Russia's rivers flow to the north, where they are icebound for much of the year, or to the south into the Caspian, which has no ocean access. They also come together at a single node near the Valdai Hills. In these respects, they are ripe for centralized control (see Chapter 5).

To be sure, breaks in a riverine system can sometimes be mended through the construction of canals, and navigability along existing rivers can be enhanced through dikes, dams, dredging, bank reinforcements, perhaps even by diverting or redirecting rivers along a different path. While this enhances transport options, it is unlikely to enhance citizens' freedom to move about as they choose. These are massive projects, requiring substantial initial investments and ongoing maintenance. As such, sovereigns or local potentates are in a better position than private citizens to undertake them – raising capital, impressing laborers, and reaping the long-term benefits via taxes on travel and commerce. Engineering also tends to make water passageways narrower, more consistent, more predictable, and hence easier to control, especially if bureaucrats are strategically placed at canals, dams, locks, and other chokepoints.

Evidence of the ways in which riverine transport assisted state control may be found in the history of tariffs. Adam Smith (1976 [1776]: 40) observed, "The commerce ... which any nation can carry on by means of a river which does not break itself into any great number of branches or canals, and which runs into another territory before it reaches the sea, can never be very considerable; because it is always in the power of the nations who possess that other territory to obstruct the communication between the upper country and the sea." One estimate suggests there were a total of 60 toll stations on the Rhine, 80 on the upper Danube, and 130 on the Loire in the Middle Ages (Postan 1987: 183–4; quoted in Nilsson 2017: 36).

In light of these points, we should expect to see the development of centralized, autocratic polities in the premodern era wherever a single riverine system traverses an extensive territory with only one or two outlets to the sea.[26] This pattern may be discerned along the Nile

---

[26] See Benda (1962), Feinman (2017), Feinman, Marcus (1999), Hall (2011: ch. 1), Trigger (2003).

(Egypt), the Tigris and Euphrates (Mesopotamia, contemporary Iraq), the Niger (West Africa), the Indus and Ganges (the northern portion of South Asia), the Yellow and Yangtze (China), the Mekong (China, Laos, Cambodia, Vietnam), the Chao Phraya (Thailand), and the Volga (Russia). By contrast, territories with abundant sea access but few navigable rivers (such as characterized most regions of the Mediterranean and "island" Southeast Asia) or areas rich in both seas and rivers (such as northern Europe) tended to develop more democratic forms of rule, and for the most part retain those institutions today.[27]

What we have said about rivers also applies to transportation networks that arose around roads, railroads, and airplanes. Because of their scarcity, their expense, and their visibility these infrastructural developments generally served a centralizing function. Governments are needed to create and maintain them, and government employees – police, military, and bureaucrats – can easily survey, control, and tax whatever moves along their arteries. Alcock, Bodel, and Talbert (2012: 4) note,

in China, the grand imperial highways ... were reserved for the sole use of the emperor (and were often hidden from view by walls or palisades erected on either side). On other highways in China during the Classical Era, official checkpoints regulated travelers so as "to control the flow of people, things, and ideas as much as possible, lest too much commerce and too much movement disrupt subject populations engaged in sedentary agriculture, the basis of stable rule within civil society."

Royal roads and imperial highways were not freeways.

Simplifying matters, we assert that rivers promise freedom only insofar as they offer untrammeled access to the ocean, while roads, railroads, and airports are usually prone to state control. For this reason, our theoretical focus is on oceans rather than these other forms of transit.

We recognize that saltwater sometimes passes through narrow straits, which form chokepoints at which states can interdict and tax marine traffic. Examples include the Sound Toll (controlled by Denmark through most of its history), the Malacca Straits (controlled by a series of local states including Srivijaya, the Malacca Sultanate, the Johor Sultanate, and Singapore), the Strait of Bosporus (controlled by the Byzantine Empire, the Ottoman Empire, and now the modern state of Turkey), the Suez Canal (controlled initially by Britain and then by Egypt), and the Panama Canal (controlled initially by the US and then by Panama).

---

[27] On the relative prevalence of rivers and seas in Asia and the Mediterranean see Wink (2004: ch. 1).

However, these narrow passageways are exceptional. When contrasted with rivers, roads, railroads, and airports, oceans are wide open and hard to contain, even in an era of advanced technology. In this light, the term *freeway* is more appropriate for the high seas than for any other mode of transport, aqueous or terrestrial. Grotius's famous tract *Mare Liberum* (Grotius 2012 [1609]), claiming the principle of freedom on the high seas, was perhaps truer as a matter of fact than as a matter of international law when he wrote. Even today, the high seas remain a realm of comparative freedom. Try as they might, it is difficult for states to control what goes on beyond their territorial waters (or even within them).

It follows that the greater a region's exposure to that ocean, the greater the freedom of movement enjoyed by its inhabitants. Andaya (1992: 97) notes that although a seventeenth-century ruler of Java tried to constrain foreign travel, this edict was unlikely to have been successful as it would have involved surveillance over a coastline stretching across hundreds of miles and including countless nearby islands in the Indonesian archipelago. In this environment, rulers are hard put to restrict the movement of peoples and goods. This is why we anticipate that oceans have emancipatory potential while other modes of transport bear ambivalently on democracy.

5   Regional Comparisons

> The nations that ... appear to have been first civilised, were those that
> dwelt round the coast of the Mediterranean Sea. That sea, by far the
> greatest inlet that is known in the world, having no tides, nor
> consequently any waves except such as are caused by the wind only,
> was, by the smoothness of its surface, as well as by the multitude of its
> islands, and the proximity of its neighbouring shores, extremely
> favourable to the infant navigation of the world; when, from their
> ignorance of the compass, men were afraid to quit the view of the
> coast, and from the imperfection of the art of shipbuilding, to abandon
> themselves to the boisterous waves of the ocean. To pass beyond the
> pillars of Hercules, that is, to sail out of the Straits of Gibraltar, was, in
> the ancient world, long considered as a most wonderful and dangerous
> exploit of navigation. It was late before even the Phoenicians and
> Carthaginians, the most skilful navigators and ship-builders of those
> old times, attempted it, and they were for a long time the only nations
> that did attempt it.   Adam Smith (1976 [1776]: 38)

Having laid out our theory (Chapter 3) and having offered background
information on maritime history and the measurement of natural harbors
(Chapter 4), we begin our presentation of evidence. In this chapter, we
examine the histories of specific regions for clues into the relationship of
harbors to democracy.

We take a long historical view, with the knowledge that humans have
been plying the seas for millennia. Of course, ocean travel developed at
different times in different places. During most of the premodern era,
saltwater was a dangerous mode of transport and regular travel was
limited to a narrow band hugging the coastline or sheltered seas, and to
specific times of the year when winds were favorable. Over time, shipping
and navigational technology advanced and these restrictions eased. The
rhythm of progress was different in each part of the world. And because
progress was slow and uneven there is no prospect of identifying a
specific point of onset at which the dynamic between oceans and democracy begins. Nonetheless, we can anticipate that the social, economic,
and political impact of natural harbors is likely to keep pace with the

advance of ocean travel in a region. If we have some sense of the latter we ought to be able to make predictions about the former.

In general, we expect that rivers (with access to the sea) played a more important role as sources of harborage in earlier times, when ships were small and could navigate shallow waters and narrow passages. Likewise, requirements for harborage along the coast were less demanding. Small vessels could be pulled up onto the beach or into a stream. As ships increased in size, ports tended to move from rivers to the coast and their depth and breadth increased. Since this chapter reaches back to ancient and medieval times, rivers and makeshift ports play a larger role in our story than in Chapter 6, which is focused primarily on deep water harbors in the modern era.

Readers should also appreciate that we cannot hope to cover the history of all regions of the world in a single chapter, even with our restricted theoretical lens. Some choices must be made about where to focus.

Since the story of globalization outside Europe is told in Part III of the book, we reserve our attention in this chapter to Europe and to the *pre-*colonial world outside Europe – including parts of the world that never succumbed to direct European control. Since our theory pertains to states (rather than bands, tribes, or chiefdoms) we leave aside regions of the world such as Australasia and the Americas where state forms of political organization were rare (prior to the arrival of Europeans).[1]

This leaves seven major regions of the world, each with a distinctive history: Europe, North Eurasia, the Middle East and North Africa (MENA), sub-Saharan Africa, East Asia, Southeast Asia, and South Asia. Each composes a section of this chapter.

Comparisons will be drawn across these regions and also – more importantly – *within* these regions, utilizing a "most-similar" style of analysis (Gerring 2017). Because neighboring areas within the same region generally share similar histories and cultures they are subject to similar forces, which means that there are probably fewer confounders lurking in the background. For example, it may be more revealing to compare coastal and inland regions of Europe than to compare Europe to Asia. Of course, limiting ourselves to within-region variation also minimizes variation in inputs and outputs of theoretical interest,

---

[1] We realize that a few statelike polities developed in the Americas prior to European colonization, e.g., the Aztec, Mayan, and Inca civilizations. However, most of the land in the Americas was lightly populated by bands, tribes, and chiefdoms. Moreover, information about the few statelike polities is scarce, making it difficult to reach firm conclusions about our subject.

attenuating causal leverage. However, there is substantial variability in harbor distance within most regions of the world, and whatever patterns are discernible should be less susceptible to confounding.

Additionally, a case-centered mode of analysis should make it possible to study some of the mechanisms identified in our theoretical exposition. This is helpful even in a situation where the independent variable of interest is static and cannot be "process-traced" in the usual sense.

To summarize our comparisons across and within regions, and to structure the following discussion, we list all geographical areas in Table 5.1. For convenience, we use current names to designate these areas in the table, even though our concern is with the history of these geographic areas. "France" means the history of the area currently occupied by France. (In our discussion, we shall also have occasion to speak about the *polity* of France as it existed through history. We trust that this distinction will be clear.)

For each designated area, we indicate mean distance (kilometers) to the nearest natural harbor (as described in the previous chapter) across all grid-cells within that area. Naturally, these statistics depend upon how one chooses to define regions and the more or less aqueous areas within each region. Different choices would result in different statistics. But not *that* different. Europe is more aqueous than MENA under any possible definition of these regions. Readers may find it helpful to glance back at Map 4.6, which shows the location of coastlines suitable for natural harbors throughout the world and gives a more nuanced sense of ocean access across regions and sub-regions of the world.

Our expectation is that areas with intensive ocean exposure will develop more democratic institutions than areas further away from natural harbors. To address this point we draw on the secondary literature for each region. Evidently, these materials are richer for some regions than for others, and none are designed for systematic comparison through time and space. Unfortunately, there are no global datasets at present that can be enlisted to measure differences in democracy in a comprehensive fashion prior to the modern era, as discussed in Chapter 2. These are limitations we must accept.

Specialists will have their own opinions, and we regret that we do not have the space to elaborate on various historical debates pertaining to each region. All we can do is indicate how a region's history fits our theoretical account – or, on occasion, how it diverges from that account. For the most part, we shall be rearranging standard features of these regional histories to show how geography – in particular, natural harbors and navigable rivers with ocean access – might have served as a prime mover.

Table 5.1 *Cross- and within-region comparisons*

Regions	Sub-regions	Natural harbor distance
Europe		173
Less aqueous:	Austria, Czech Rep./Slovakia, France, Hungary, Germany, Poland	342
More aqueous:	Balkans, British Isles, Finland, Italy, Low Countries, Scandinavia	77
North Eurasia		544
Less aqueous:	Russia	600
More aqueous:	Eastern Europe	194
MENA		477
Less aqueous:	Afghanistan, Algeria, Egypt, Iran, Iraq, Jordan, Libya, Saudi Arabia, Sudan, Syria	655
More aqueous:	Israel/Palestine, Lebanon, Morocco, Persian Gulf, Tunisia, Turkey, Yemen	242
Africa		717
Less aqueous:	Great Lakes region, Sahel, Congo, Ethiopia, Great Zimbabwe	914
More aqueous:	Niger Delta/Yorubaland, Swahili Coast	110
East Asia		897
Less aqueous:	China	989
More aqueous:	Japan, Korea, Taiwan	55
Southeast Asia		120
Less aqueous:	Burma, Cambodia, Laos, Thailand, Vietnam	219
More aqueous:	Malay peninsula, Indonesian and Philippine archipelagos	69
South Asia		457
Less aqueous:	Bhutan, Nepal, Pakistan, Indian states: Bihar, Madhya Pradesh, Punjab, Rajasthan, Uttar Pradesh	627
More aqueous:	Bangladesh, Maldives, Sri Lanka, Indian states: West Bengal, Gujarat, Kerala, Tamil Nadu	148
World		542

Natural harbor distance: mean distance (kilometers) to nearest natural harbor of all grid-cells within each designated area, as defined today. *Hypothesis:* greater ocean access generates more democratic outcomes.

To be clear, this is not a "total" history. We are not attempting to offer a complete account of the political histories of these large and diverse regions. If we were, we would need many more pages to cover the countless *non*-aquatic factors that also affected each region's political history. In our synoptic account, these are relegated to the background. Our goal is to offer a focused, theoretically informed interpretation of how the histories of these regions relate to their aquatic, or non-aquatic, geographies.

Europe

A glance at a map is sufficient to demonstrate that Europe is the most oceanic region of the world. (The only potential rivals are archipelagos like the Caribbean or the South Pacific, which do not contain nearly as much territory or as many people.) It is also blessed with a great many natural harbors. The mean distance from a natural harbor across the European continent is 173 kilometers, well below the global mean of 542 kilometers.

Not surprisingly, European civilization hinged to a greater extent than most on aquatic connections. This is reflected in maritime technology, where Europe was often on the leading edge. By way of illustration, Deng (2011: 210) offers a short list of innovative shipping designs including "the Roman trireme (third century BCE–second century), the Viking Dragon ship (eighth–twelfth centuries), the Baltic cog (twelfth–thirteenth centuries), the Venetian great galley (fourteenth century), the Portuguese/Spanish caravel (fifteenth century), the full-rigged ship (fifteenth–seventeenth centuries), the Dutch fluyt (sixteenth–seventeenth centuries), the Spanish galleon (sixteenth–seventeenth centuries), the man-of-war (seventeenth century), the ship-of-the-line (eighteenth century), to the clipper (nineteenth century), ... the tall ship (nineteenth–twentieth centuries), [and] ... the paddle steamer (early nineteenth century)." He concludes that China's technological prowess, while superior to Europe's in many areas, was no match for European maritime technology through most of the premodern era.

Here, we attempt to show the various ways in which Europe's intimate connection to water and water transport might be related to the development of representative democracy.

Statebuilding

One aspect of our story centers on the diminutive size of polities occupying the European continent (Abulafia 2003, 2010). After the fall of the Roman Empire, these states were small in territory relative to statelike entities elsewhere in the world. It was not only their diminutive size but also the diversity of these units that differentiated Europe from other parts of the world in the medieval and early modern eras. Wim Blockmans (2009: 284–5) offers the following typology, from smallest to largest:[2]

---

[2] The Ottoman Empire is omitted from this list as it lies outside our definition of Europe.

- Free peasant communities joined in a loose federation (East Friesland, Graubünden);
- Autonomous towns with a more or less extensive agrarian hinterland (German free imperial cities such as Nuremberg and Hamburg; Genoa, Novgorod, Ragusa/Dubrovnik);
- Local lordships which may at some point have been elevated to a higher status such as a duchy or principality (Mechelen, Salins, Liechtenstein, Monaco, San Marino, Andorra);
- Federations of autonomous towns and peasant communities (Swiss Confederation, Friesland);
- Leagues of towns, sometimes including feudal lords (the German Hanse, the Swabian League);
- Regional states dominated by one large city which subordinated other towns, lordships and communities to it (Venice, Florence, Milan);
- Ecclesiastical principalities (the papal state, the states of the German Order in Prussia and the states of the Maltese Order, the territorial temporalities of the archbishop of Cologne, the bishop of Liège);
- Effectively autonomous (secular) territorial principalities (the duchies of Brittany, Saxony and Ferrara and the County of Toulouse before 1271);
- Personal unions of territorial principalities in which each of the constituent entities kept its own institutions, but the prince determined a common policy (Hainault, Holland and Zeeland under the houses of Hainault and Bavaria; the Low Countries under the houses of Burgundy and Habsburg; Jülich, Marck and Berg);
- Integrated kingdoms (England, France, Portugal, Scotland, Sweden);
- Personal unions of one or more kingdoms and/or territorial principalities (Poland–Lithuania; Bohemia–Moravia–Lausitz; the Crown of Aragón, comprising Aragón–Catalonia–Mallorca–Valencia (1412), later also Sicily, Naples and Sardinia, all united in 1479 with the Crown of León–Castile); Denmark–Sweden–Norway in the Union of Kalmar (1397–1523);
- Empires (Holy Roman Empire).

Note that although the Holy Roman Empire encompassed a sizeable territory this loosely strung entity was ruled in a highly decentralized manner and effective power was wielded at the principality level (Wilson 2016). Arguably, it is better classified as a confederation than an empire. In this light, the typical European state was considerably smaller than the typical state in most other regions of the world.

One might regard the fragmentation of Europe as an accident of fate, the product of the strange collapse of the Roman Empire, a collapse which was not preordained (Hui 2005; Stasavage 2016). From our perspective, however, it is not the fall of Rome that is strange but the inability of its successors to put the pieces back together. Note that few of the great empires in China, Persia, Egypt, and northern India lasted as long as the Roman Empire. However, after they fell they were reconstituted, in some cases after only a brief hiatus (e.g., in the guise of a new dynasty). Not so for Europe, despite repeated attempts – by the Holy Roman Empire, the Austro-Hungarian Empire, France under Napoleon, and Germany under Hitler. All significant states in Europe aspired to rule the continent and Rome was the primordial model. The idea, and the ambition, stood before every European statebuilder. The fact that none of these initiatives succeeded suggests that this task faced some formidable structural obstacles.

In looking to explain this failure many writers emphasize the distinctive geographic traits of Europe.[3] Some credit Europe's rugged terrain, its several mountain ranges, its historically dense forests, or its absence of a centrally located, highly productive agricultural region. While these factors may provide a useful contrast to China, they are not unique in a global context.

What really distinguishes Europe globally are its aquatic features: a heavily indented coastline, many sizeable islands (e.g., Britain, Ireland, Mallorca, Corsica, Sardinia, Sicily) and several archipelagos, myriad peninsulas (Europe, it is sometimes said, is a "peninsula of peninsulas"), and many criss-crossing rivers with navigable access to the sea. These features offered plentiful opportunities for harborage, and this in turn set in motion a dynamic of continent-wide urbanization that made it difficult for would-be emperors to conquer the territory, and, if they were successful in that venture, to sustain their conquered territories (Blockmans 1994; Tilly 1992).

Eventually, rulers resigned themselves to this fact, establishing an international order that respected the sovereignty of states with well-defined borders, formalized in a series of treaties now referred to as the Westphalian state system. In Spruyt's (2020: 1–2) reading, "the claims of Charles V, the Holy Roman Emperor, to rule all of Christendom in the early sixteenth century constituted some of the last claims of universalist rule in Europe." By contrast, imperial powers in other parts of the world were not obliged to recognize the sovereignty of neighboring states, as they were militarily inferior and perhaps not even statelike in organization. Accordingly, these empires claimed universal sovereignty (Pines,

<hr>

[3] See Braudel (1972[1949]: 161–2, 191–2), Chirot (1985: 183), Diamond (1992, 1998), Dincecco (2010), Epstein (2002), Jones (1981), Lagerhof (2014), Pounds, Ball (1964), Scheidel (2019: ch. 1), Van Evera (1998).

Biran, Rüpke 2021). While France, Austria, Spain and Prussia were forced to acknowledge limitations to their expansionist quest, the Chinese, Mugal, and Ottoman empires were not – at least, not until a much later date, and then with reference to European powers rather than neighboring states (see, e.g., Fairbank 1968; Kang 2010).

Military competition may well have spurred the development of state capacity, as argued by Charles Tilly (1992) and many others. However, "Weberian" military and tax bureaucracies did not spur the consolidation of power in the hands of a single governing group. Indeed, political fragmentation and consequent incessant warfare probably helps to account for the weakness of rulers relative to other actors. Leaders were desperate for funds to defend and extend their borders, their trading networks, and their colonies, and thus not in a strong position vis-à-vis merchants, landed aristocrats, and the church. They were forced to bargain continually with their adversaries, a dynamic that many writers believe was critical to the development of proto-democratic institutions such as parliaments and constitutions.

Urbanization

Another factor that distinguished medieval and early modern Europe from most other regions of the world was its high level of urbanization. While other regions also developed large cities, Europe had more cities and their reach extended to every part of the continent. The urban network was denser in Europe than anywhere else in the premodern world, a feature often linked to the abundance of waterborne commerce. Cities grew up along navigable rivers and coastlines, especially where natural harbors were available.[4]

Cities, in turn, seem to have played a key role in the development of democracy, and especially in developing concepts of citizenship and freedom.[5] The etymological evidence inscribed in Latin and Germanic languages supports this thesis: *citizen* derives from *city* (Latin: *civitas*), and terms for middle class in French and German (*bourgeois*, *Burger*) originally referred to denizens of a city. Freedom within a European city had a very specific meaning insofar as citizens were free of feudal ties and direct subjugation to a lord (Friedrichs 2000: 4) – hence the well-worn medieval phrase, *Stadtluft macht frei* ("city air makes one free").

---

[4] See Blockmans, Krom, Wubs-Mrozewicz (2017), Bosker, Buringh (2017), Bosker, Buringh, van Zanden (2013), Tilly, Blockmans (1994).

[5] See Angelucci, Meraglia, Voigtländer (2017), Clark (2009: 13), Ertman (1997), Pirenne (1925), Weber (1922).

Among cities, those with ocean ports or easy access (through navigable waterways) to the ocean were distinguished by "the predominance of trade and commerce and the ideology of merchant capital" (Lee 1998: 167). Here, links between water, trade, and liberty were most visible.

Within-Region Comparisons

Of course, Europe was not all of one piece. Some areas are more exposed to the ocean than others, and thus (according to our theory) should trend in a more democratic direction.

The northernmost areas include the British Isles, the Low Countries, and Scandinavia. These areas have a long and intimate relationship with the sea, and probably deserve to be regarded as the most democratic regions of the continent if one considers the entirety of their recorded history. Moving further south and east, in lands that would become France, Prussia/Germany, Poland, Austria, Czechia, Slovakia, and Hungary, the presence of the ocean is weaker, as are democratic institutions over the course of early modern and modern history.

Prior to the development of motorized transport, access to the ocean depended upon navigable rivers, which were more plentiful in some regions than others. In the Low Countries, Blondé, Boone, and Van Bruaene (2018: 10) note,

the geography exhibits a multiplicity of large rivers (Rhine, Maas, Scheldt) and small ones which, as a consequence of the minor fall in topography, run a diffuse course over an expansive territory. This pattern is entirely different from that of one dominant, very long waterway like the Rhône or the Danube: those have delineated valleys that sometimes formed a narrow corridor of towns but frequently penetrated less deeply or broadly into the hinterland. Formulated in political terms: though it was still possible to control shipping along the valleys from a few strategic points because there was no other way through, in the Low Countries many options to evade such controls existed; controlling people and levying tolls on shipping – or practising outright extortion – were a lot more difficult. Moreover, the rivers did not form any outer boundaries of the Low Countries, and only on certain trajectories did they function as boundaries between principalities. Thanks to the lower cost of river transport, large groups of people were able to take part directly or indirectly in movement and exchange between towns.

As a secondary consequence, the Low Countries gave birth to one of the most urbanized regions of Europe, and one without a dominant capital.

Brabant had four chief towns – Leuven, Brussels, Antwerp and 's-Hertogenbosch – each of which was the largest town and the judicial capital of one of the districts into which the duchy had been subdivided. In twelfth-century Flanders the seven largest towns dominated, of which Arras and Saint-Omer were absorbed in stages by the county of Artois formed at the end of that century. At the beginning of the fourteenth century, Walloon Flanders was placed directly under the French crown, as a result of which Douai and Lille were also separated from the three remaining chief towns of Dutch-speaking Flanders, namely, Ghent, Bruges and Ypres. They, too, exercised diverse forms of administrative and judicial dominance within their districts. When Walloon Flanders reverted as a dowry to the counts of Flanders from the Burgundian dynasty in 1384, it nevertheless retained its separate administrative status, in which Lille was the capital. In the county of Holland, Dordrecht was indeed the oldest town, but it still did not enjoy the position of a capital, in part on account of its location outside the centre of the county; yet for that chief position Leiden and Haarlem stood too much on an equal footing in size and significance, above all from the fourteenth century onwards. In practice Amsterdam, Delft and Gouda also proved to be frequently consulted in government affairs, such that there were de facto six relatively major towns, (Blondé, Boone, Van Bruaene 2018: 10–11)

To the south, France was slower to develop parliamentary institutions and constitutional rule. It is notable that Île-de-France, the core of what would become the French state, was distant from the coast, both geographically and geopolitically. David Loades (2000: 1–2) points out, "Brittany was an independent duchy, and English control of Gascony meant that direct access to the Atlantic was denied. Picardy and Normandy, when these were in French hands, offered reasonable outlets to the North Sea and the Channel, but direct royal control was never strong." In the south, access to the Mediterranean was unreliable, as states and provinces in the Midi enjoyed considerable autonomy.

Within the territory now called France one may compare coastal regions with regions in the interior. Surveying the activity of regional parliaments in the Renaissance period, Major (1980) distinguishes those that regularly voted and collected taxes from those that did so only rarely or not at all. He finds that coastal regions in the north (e.g., Brittany, Normandy), west (e.g., Guyenne), and south (e.g., Languedoc, Provence) were generally in the former camp while those in the center (e.g., Paris, Marche, Limousin) were more often in the latter camp.[6] A similar pattern is discernible in a more detailed analysis conducted by Kiser and Linton (2002).

---

[6] See Major (1980: xv), where provinces refer to boundaries in 1601, and explanations on p. 46. Additional studies address the role of assemblies in Languedoc (Beik 1985; Bisson 1964).

In similar fashion, one may compare coastal areas along the Iberian peninsula such as Andalusia, the Basque country, Aragón/Catalonia, and Valencia with inland regions such as Castile. Across most periods, democracy – in the form of city governments and regional parliaments – was more active, and monarchs more constrained, in regions situated near the coast and near to harbors.[7]

Thus, across most regions of Europe ocean exposure correlates with democracy. We are not the first to notice this salient feature of European history. According to a venerable theory, whose first formal statement was probably by Edward Whiting Fox (1971), the history of the European continent can be divided into commercial zones along the coast and navigable rivers, and inland zones. The former gave birth to independent ("free") cities, where a dynamic bourgeoisie fought against the depredations of lords and monarchs. The latter gave birth to continental empires based on the wealth provided by landed estates (Clark 1995: 7–8). Hence the time-honored contrast between England, where constitutional governance and representative institutions got an early start and were for the most part maintained, and France, where representative institutions were weaker and where "absolutism" (by European standards) flourished in the seventeenth and eighteenth centuries.

Ringrose (1996: 221–2) views the matter through the lens of transport costs.

Towns with cheap waterborne transport could respond to market forces over long distances, allowing them to integrate many localized comparative advantages. Since land transport was expensive, trading cities had less to gain from control of large areas of land and tended to have modest territorial empires and small armies. Consequently, they were controlled by commercial oligarchies that governed by committee and consensus. Their most urgent political problems reflected their dependence on distant trading partners and on reciprocal recognition of business practices and contracts.

By contrast, inland states lived with high-cost transport that made it difficult to concentrate bulky food, fuel and raw materials. To sustain a governing elite, inland governments relied on force, corvée labour and arbitrary authority in order to concentrate the necessary resources. This reliance on force pushed inland polities in the direction of authoritarian government, militarization and cultural values that emphasized hierarchy and military skills.

Charles Tilly's well-known distinction between capital-intensive regions and coercion-intensive regions is also germane. Tilly (1992: 30) explains,

---

[7] See Møller (2017), Nader (1990), O'Callaghan (1989), Payne (1973: 105–6).

In the coercion-intensive mode, rulers squeezed the means of war from their own populations and others they conquered, building massive structures of extraction in the process. Brandenburg and Russia ... illustrate the coercion-intensive mode ... In the capital-intensive mode, rulers relied on compacts with capitalists – whose interests they served with care – to rent or purchase military force, and thereby warred without building vast permanent state structures. City-states, city-empires, urban federations, and other forms of fragmented sovereignty commonly fall into this path of change.

Importantly, Tilly's examples of coercion-intensive states are "continental" (inland) states while his examples of capital-intensive states lie along the edges of Europe in the aqueous zones, fitting our geographic framework.

Central to our argument is the idea that oceanic states lean more heavily on naval forces than on land-based forces ("the army"). Of course, regular ("standing") armed forces emerged slowly through European history. Indeed, their tardy development, and the reliance on irregular troops provided by feudal lords or mercenary companies, was one of the proximal causes of the weak European state (by the standards of empires elsewhere in Eurasia). Yet, even in their irregular form, states with extensive coastlines like England, Norway, Sweden, and those situated along the Iberian and Italian coasts were the leading naval powers of Europe.

David Loades (2000) narrates the slow, halting, but ultimately crucial rise of England to naval mastery over the North Atlantic, showing how English monarchs, initially oblivious, came to realize the economic and political importance of investing in a permanent navy. Loades also shows how direct ties between the Crown and early foreign trade companies (e.g., the Levant Company, the Merchant Adventurers, and the East India Company) fostered a naval orientation that permeated the highest rungs of British politics. The Crown depended upon revenues provided by these merchant companies. The companies depended upon England to defend its ships against pirates, privateers, and foreign navies, and to maintain access to maritime markets across Europe and (later) across the world. Since the companies took the form of joint stock enterprises, they enlisted capital from the landed aristocracy, providing an economic and political link between city and country which would play a critical role in British history as a counterweight to the Crown.

Across Europe, capital-intensive states rested on a social class composed of merchants who conducted overseas trade and artisans who fabricated products to be sold on international markets. These bourgeois classes generally played a dominant role in politics, limiting the prerogatives of the executive (generally a monarch) and helping to secure the independence of parliament or assemblies of elites and the stability of constitutional rule.[8]

Switzerland

One region of Europe fits poorly into our framework. Switzerland sits in the middle of the continent, landlocked, while boasting perhaps the oldest continuous democratic history anywhere in the world, extending back to the Middle Ages.[9] While this history does not bear out our prediction, several points bear emphasis.

First, the area now occupied by Switzerland is not nearly so remote as is often thought. Seven rivers – Rhine, Aare, Rhone, Reuss, Linth/Limmat, Saane, and Thur – provide ready access to the North Sea (via the Rhine), the Mediterranean (via the Rhone), the Adriatic (via the Po and the Adige), and the Black Sea (via the Danube). Moreover, despite the vertiginous heights of the Alps there are many points of entry and exit. Finally, because of its central location – between Italy and Central Europe – Switzerland has long served as a transit point across the continent.

All of these factors served to keep Switzerland well connected. Its apparent isolation – and its vaunted neutrality – is actually a fairly recent development. Of course, it is true that Switzerland is more distant from the ocean than other parts of the continent, so our theory cannot claim any credit for the sturdy democratic heritage of this mountainous region.

On this point, we would point out that Switzerland's democratic history diverges from the European norm in one crucial respect. To this day, institutions of democratic governance are predominantly direct rather than representative (a distinction introduced in Chapter 2). Power is centered on the canton, where popular assemblies still deliberate and vote on specific initiatives as they have for hundreds of years. Because of the extreme decentralization of power in the Swiss confederation, representative institutions at the center do not wield nearly as much power as they do in other European states, or for that matter across the world. This is relevant because our theory is centered on representative institutions and on governance at the state level. We pointed out that direct democracy was probably widespread in bands, tribes, and city-states in many parts of the world in the premodern world (Chapter 2), a

---

[8] See Acemoglu, Johnson, Robinson (2005), Brenner (2003), Gauci (2001), Israel (1995), Pincus (2009), Pincus, Robinson (2011).

[9] See Barber (1974), Brady (1985), Head (2002), Steinberg (1996).

feature that owes nothing to ocean access. From this perspective, the unique features of Swiss democracy fall outside our theory.

Parliaments

For most regions of the world we are unable to measure the character of democratic (or proto-democratic) institutions in a systematic fashion prior to the modern era – an issue discussed in Chapter 2. Europe is different, thanks to the efforts of scholars who have traced the rise of parliaments through the medieval, Renaissance, and early modern eras.[10]

Our analysis draws on the most recent and comprehensive effort of this nature. Abramson and Boix (2019) measure the existence of parliaments throughout Europe and the number of times each parliament was convened in each century from 1200 to 1700. Along with this painstaking coding, the authors list the locations of each parliament. We use these place-names to determine their GIS locations (latitude/longitude). Each PRIO grid-cell within Europe is then coded at century intervals according to whether it did, or did not, have a working parliament (one that met at least once during the century). This forms our dependent variable in a grid-cell analysis in which natural harbor distance is the predictor of theoretical interest, shown in Table 5.2.

Model 1 includes only the regressor of interest, along with dummies for each century. Model 2 adds several covariates that can be expected to affect the location of parliaments – population (log) and city (a binary code). These demographic factors may also be affected by natural harbors, in which case they must be considered downstream from the variable of theoretical interest. In any case, there is not much variation in the estimated relationship of natural harbors to parliamentary activity across the two specifications. In both models, distance from harbors is negatively correlated with parliamentary activity, corroborating our theory.

North Eurasia

Stretching across Eastern Europe and Russia is an immense territory we shall call North Eurasia.[11] We realize that this is not a common term, and in some respects arbitrary (Bassin 1991). However, we need some way to designate two adjoining areas that for many years shared a common history, and then diverged.

---

[10] See Kokkonen, Møller (2020), Stasavage (2010), Van Zanden, Buringh, Bosker (2012).
[11] This section benefitted from close readings by Michael Bernhard and Lee Cojocaru.

Table 5.2 *European parliaments, 1200–1700*

Model	1	2
Natural harbor distance	−0.06***	−0.05***
	(−3.61)	(−2.75)
Population (log)		0.001***
		(7.2)
City (binary)		0.068***
		(69.2)
Centuries	6	6
Grid-cells	11 756	11 756
Observations	72 342	71 118
R^2	0.049	0.111

Outcome: functioning parliament, coded 1 if it meets at least once during a century (Abramson, Boix 2019). *Spatial units:* PRIO grid-cells. *Temporal units:* centuries. *Not shown:* Century dummies, Constant. *Estimator:* ordinary least squares, standard errors clustered by grid-cell, t statistics in parentheses. *p<.10 **p<.05 ***p<.01

In the medieval era, observers of polities west of the Urals would have had difficulty locating any political-institutional differences between the territory now controlled by Russia and the territory now understood as Eastern Europe (including the present-day countries of Finland, Sweden, Norway, the Baltic republics, Belarus, Ukraine, Poland, Czechia, Slovakia, Hungary, Romania, Moldova, Bulgaria, and Serbia).

Cities in this region, many of which enjoyed a high degree of autonomy, included Budapest, Kiev (Franklin, Shepard 1996; Vernadsky 1948), Lithuania (Stone 2014), Lublin, Moscow, Novgorod (Birnbaum 1981; Crummey 1987: 32–4; Lukin 2017), Prague, Pskov, Smolensk, and Trakai. Institutions of governance were fairly similar by most accounts (Franklin, Shepard 1996: 342–3; Riasanovsky 1963).

Beginning in the early modern era the area centered on Moscow – known as Muscovite Rus', Muscovy, and later Russia (and, for a time, the Soviet Union) – swallowed up the surrounding city-states and then went on to conquer diffusely settled territories to the east, forming a gigantic land-based empire. While states in Eastern Europe continued their evolution toward representative democracy – interrupted briefly by Soviet occupation – Russia moved in an authoritarian direction, a contrast that persists to this day.

Scholars argue over when, precisely, the divergence began. Critical junctures might be identified during the reign of various Russian czars including Vasilii II, who ruled from 1425 to 1462 (Blum 1961: 135), Ivan the Great, who ruled from 1462 to 1505 (Bendix 1978: 111–15),

Alexis, who ruled from 1645 to 1676 (Longworth (1990: 175–6), and
Peter the Great, who ruled from 1782 to 1825.

Likewise, there are many possible explanations for Russia's authoritarian turn. One answer is found in "the forceful leadership of rulers from
Ivan III to Ivan IV and in their methods of subjugating the elite, including disgrace, confiscation of property, abolition of a servitor's right to
move freely to a new place of service, the use of informers, and the taking
of loyalty oaths that imposed collective responsibility on the elite"
(Kollmann 1987: 1–2). The weakness of the Russian aristocracy (the
boyars), which posed little resistance to the growing strength of the
monarchy (Alef 1970), is often ascribed to its divisions. This, in turn,
may have been a product of "partible inheritance, a postulated impover-
ishment of the landed service class, the ravages of warfare, and the system
of precedence (*mestnichestvo*)" (Kollmann 1987: 3). One may also point
to the weakness of feudalism (Pipes 1974); the weakness of a legal-
constitutional tradition (Madariaga 1995: 272–3); the persistence of
patrimonial rule; the influence of the Golden Horde, which controlled
Muscovy as a tributary state (de Hartog 1996); the influence of the
Byzantine Empire, which may have provided a template for the Russian
state; the Russian Orthodox church, which was closely allied with the
state; the small and largely rural population; the dependence of cities and
the bourgeoisie on the Crown (Hittle 1979); and imperial conquest to the
east, incorporating new lands, providing new revenue, and thus
empowering the monarchy (Khodarkovsky 2002).[12]

There are many possible reasons, and we do not mean to discount any
of them except to note that geography may have played a role beneath the
surface.

Water and North Eurasia

Eastern Europe, though not quite as aqueous as Western Europe, is well
served by ports along the Baltic and by a host of navigable rivers that run
north to the Atlantic or south to the Black Sea, offering connections to
the Mediterranean. This suite of rivers includes the Elbe, Oder, Vistula,
Danube, Neva, and Dnieper. Accordingly, Eastern Europe was an integral part of the Hanseatic League, whose trade connected Germanic
lands with the Atlantic states (England, the Low Countries,
Scandinavia) to the north and Italian city-states to the south.

[12] For further discussion see Halecki (1952), Szűcs, Parti (1983).

However, as one moves further east rivers become scarcer, and are generally navigable only part of the year. "During the winter for 2–7 months the rivers are covered with ice and in spring they are flooded," observes Evgenij Nosov (1996: 175). Locations otherwise suitable for harbors along the Arctic are not very useful, as their seasons of operation are limited (though global warming may be changing that).[13] The largest waterway, the Volga – often viewed as the artery of Russian history (Hartley 2021) – empties into the Caspian Sea, which is more accurately labeled a lake since it offers no natural access to the ocean.

This was a closed riverine system until the construction of a system of canals, most of which are of fairly recent vintage, e.g., Volga–Baltic Waterway (begun in the nineteenth century and subsequently expanded), the White Sea–Baltic Canal (1931–3), the Moscow Canal (1932–7), the Volga–Don Canal (1952), and so forth (Allin 1981; Zeisler-Vralsted 2015). Previously, it was possible to reach the interior from the north only by traversing an arduous series of portages (Westerdahl 2015). The interior was therefore insulated from European trade through most of its history. There is no Russian equivalent of the Hans. Accordingly, Russia scores poorly on our measure of ocean exposure, well above the global mean (see Table 5.1).

To be sure, there are river systems and they formed the lifeblood of medieval states throughout the region now occupied by Russia, as they did in Eastern Europe. However, these rivers are scarce and largely isolated from one another. As such, they were easy for states to tax and control. Westerdahl (2015) reports that in the medieval era "the chiefdoms of the ancient 'Rus were designed to control the water traffic from the Baltic to the Black Sea by way of overland portages across the watersheds between the river systems." In a similar manner, Nosov (1996: 176) describes Kiev and Novgorod as "locks on the neck of two large funnels, pulling in all the threads of communication of the East Slavic territories … [giving them] administrative control of the area." This was possible because there were few passages across this vast territory. Rulers could place a chokehold on trade by controlling key portages, using that leverage to master larger and larger domains. The secret of the Russian state, concludes Kerner (1942: 5), is in "the domination of

---

[13] To avoid unnecessary complexities, our benchmark measure of natural harbors does not take account of climatic circumstances such as frozen waterways. However, a secondary measure of natural harbor distance, discussed in Chapter 4, counts only harbors that are open most of the year. When tested in a crossnational framework this measure is also robust.

river systems and the control of portages between them by means of ostrogs (blockhouses) or of fortified monasteries."

Another feature of riverine systems in the lands of the 'Rus is that portages come together at a central node. Kerner (1942: 1) alleges that Moscow's centrality in Russian political life is owed to its geographic location, near the Valdai Hills, "a small upland region in northwestern Russia, less than one hundred miles square and not much more than one thousand feet above sea level at its highest point, from which rise great rivers that, either by themselves or by easy portages to others, lead through two continents to give access to all the seas in the world." From this inland perch, it was possible to control trade across the heartland of Russia.

This conclusion is validated by a formal network analysis of river transport. In this study, Pitts (1978) maps rivers and their interconnections in order to determine the most likely location for the capital of a Russian state. Echoing Kerner, Pitts finds that Moscow is the most likely location because of its centrality within the northern Asian riverine system.

The paucity of harbors and rivers east of St. Petersburg also meant that there were fewer urban agglomerations, and fewer interconnections between them. Nosov (1996: 178) comments,

Due to the geographical position of Russia the towns in its northern part were scattered over large distances. It is impossible to speak about one network of towns covering this part of the country. This picture differs greatly from the distribution of towns in Western Europe. On the territory of the Novgorod land, which in the 12th century covered approximately 350,000 square km, there were only seven towns ... Ladoga was situated 200 km from Novgorod which was the centre of the region, Rusa 55 km, Pskov 200 km, Izborsk 230 km, Novy Torg 300 km. The towns were small islands in a forest sea, connected to each other by threads of rivers.[14]

Unencumbered by obstreperous cities, the Muscovy/Russian state was able to expand rapidly (Hittle 1979). As it grew, it overwhelmed the power of the landed aristocrats, the boyars, who were domesticated in the service of the state to a greater degree than in Europe.[15] Gustave Alef (1970: 16–17) comments,

An important ... element contributing to the rapid evolution of a strong Muscovite monarchy was the absence of serious opposition by the aristocracy. By the fifteenth century, at the very time the grand princes moved to consolidate

---

[14] See also Rozman (1976).   [15] See Blum (1961), Crummey (1987), Kivelson (1996).

their power, the East Russian nobles concerned themselves primarily with their economic well being, with social privileges and with vying for state positions they considered in keeping with their aristocratic station. Unlike their counterparts in neighbouring Lithuania, they could not force conditions upon the ruling prince; the aristocracy in East Russia came largely as petitioners, seeking employment commensurate with their social station or their previous political importance. As petitioners they were hardly capable of guarding their previous rights; as supplicants, vying with others of similar condition and previous position, they were unable to stand as a class against the continuing inroads made into their former prerogatives by the growing royal power.

Continual territorial expansion meant that the Russian state was able to draw on vast resources, allowing it to control the terms upon which tenure would be resolved and to pay off servitors of the state without additional tax instruments (Longworth 1990: 175–6).

The size of the growing Russian empire also meant that it was difficult for nobles to coordinate with one another, to act as a class "for itself," in Marxian terminology. Alef (1970: 18–19) notes,

The conquests ... compounded the problems of the old aristocracy, for former rulers of the annexed regions and their servitors began to clamor for significant military and administrative positions in the enlarged realm. Descendants of the old untitled Muscovite aristocracy and the princes who had recently enrolled in service found themselves in competition for the influential posts at court and in the army. The animosities that developed over family seniority and personal position caused constant strife and thereby prevented any possibility of a coalescence of interest to resist the growing powers of the crown.

Contrasts

In our view, many of the time-honored explanations for Russia's divergence from Europe (listed at the outset) may be traced back to the differing geographies of the two regions. Eastern Europe is closely linked to the Baltic in the north and the Black Sea and Mediterranean in the south. By contrast, Russia was distanced from the ocean insofar as its major river terminates in a lake and its Arctic ports and north-flowing rivers are iced-over through much of the year. The current riverine system, assisted by an extensive system of canals, is more integrated into ocean trade but these connections are of very recent vintage, and remain highly centralized insofar as cargo must float through the capital region and is thus easy to survey and control. Russia is a lot less oceanic than Eastern Europe, and this may have contributed to its autocratic political culture, exacerbating tendencies long associated with Asia.

Middle East and North Africa

For centuries, territories bordering the Mediterranean shared a common history, leading many historians to regard it as a single cultural unit.[16] However, beginning sometime in the Middle Ages, the northern and southern coasts of this sea began to diverge economically and politically, a pattern that persists today.

To explain this divergence, scholars have pointed to the influence of Islam, its special characteristics (Lewis 2001), and its possible impact on trade (Pirenne 2013), structures of rule (Blaydes, Chaney 2013; Cox 2017; Crone 1980; Greif 2006a, 2006b), local governance (Bosker, Buringh, van Zanden 2013), legal systems (Kuran 2012), and other factors that we do not have space to review. In work focused on the contemporary period, the influence of oil has been a major theme (e.g., Crystal 1990).

Here, we shall highlight the possible role of geography as a prime mover in the MENA region (the Middle East and North Africa). For the most part, our attention will focus on the period prior to the discovery of oil, as this factor dislocates the history of many states and falls outside our theory.

Water and the MENA Region

The MENA region hugs the water. Moving east from Morocco on a map one finds the southern coast of the Mediterranean, the Red Sea, the Gulf of Aden, the Arabian Sea, the Persian Gulf, and to the north, the Black Sea. No current state except Jordan is landlocked. However, there are few natural harbors, as shown in Map 4.6. The average distance to the nearest natural harbor across the MENA region is 477 kilometers, just under the global average, despite abundant coastlines.

Commenting on the geographic circumstances of Arabia and their impact on the history of the region, Hourani (1975: 5–6) notes,

It has no navigable rivers and few first-class harbors. The Red Sea, stretching for some 1,200 miles, had in early times the effect of isolating rather than uniting Egypt with Southwest Arabia. The northern half of this sea in particular presented severe obstacles. It is flanked on both sides by hundreds of miles of waterless desert. Immense coral reefs skirt both coasts and in places extend far out into the sea; considerable knowledge and skill were required to avoid being wrecked on them. The coral islands favored piracy, to which the hungry nomads

---

[16] E.g., Abulafia (2003, 2010), Braudel (1972[1949]), Broodbank (2013), Horden, Purcell (2000), Norwich (2007).

on both sides were all too prone, regarding it as a simple extension of their desert raids. Good harbors are almost wanting here, so that there was no safe refuge from the dangers of storms or pirates. The northward passage was especially hard to early seafarers, because northerly winds blow down this part of the sea the whole year round. Rather than face the terrors of the Red Sea, the Arabs developed camel routes along the whole western side of their peninsula. Conditions in the Persian Gulf were more favorable; but here too there is a lack of fresh water on both sides, and piracy is encouraged by the number of the islands and the poverty of the coastal peoples. As a result, 'Uman was in none too close contact with Mesopotamia and Iran.

Wink (2002: 422) echoes these observations, noting "the coasts of the Arabian peninsula have no major indentations anywhere. The paucity of shelters here is unparalleled in the Indian Ocean. The one good natural harbor along the southern coast is Aden." The Red Sea, conclude Curtin, Feierman, Thompson, and Vansina (1995: 33), was "usable in connection with camel caravans, but it never played the same historical role as the Mediterranean in uniting peoples and cultures around its fringes."

Many studies recognize a divergence in transport networks, with Europe tending to waterborne commerce and the Middle East adopting caravans through the desert as the main form of transit (Bulliet 1975). These transport choices were not illogical; they built on geographic foundations that distinguished the northern and southern borders of the Mediterranean and undoubtedly made good sense at the time. However, they made less sense for the MENA region in later years as maritime technology evolved and became more efficient than land travel. Some writers see this as a key to Europe's enhanced productivity in the early modern and modern eras (Bosker, Buringh, van Zanden 2013).

Since major transport networks in the MENA region followed desert routes or the Nile, large cities were generally located at some remove from the coast – e.g., Baghdad, Damascus, Fez, Marrakesh, and Fustat/Cairo – reinforcing the "territorial" identity of these polities (Bosker, Buringh, van Zanden 2013: 1425). Although the Islamic world in medieval times was highly urbanized, Udovitch (1977: 144) notes that "no major political or administrative center was located on the seacoast. Furthermore, even though there were numerous Islamic coastal towns of some economic and commercial importance, the major entrepôts of trade and economic life were invariably located some distance inland."

More generally, Udovitch (1977: 144) perceives "a consistent ambivalence, if not wariness, of the ... sea." Coastal areas in the MENA region were regarded as frontier outposts, exposed to attack – a fairly common occurrence. The Mamluk rulers of Egypt went so far as to destroy fortifications along the Mediterranean so as to deprive hostile forces of a foothold on their territory (Petersen 2005: ch. 10; Udovitch 1977: 144–7). The Crusades, although ultimately unsuccessful, were destructive. And at the time Islamic states did not have the capacity to control the seas along their coasts, or they did not choose to invest the resources that would have been necessary to muster a naval force. This dynamic changed with the expansion of the Ottoman Empire in the sixteenth century (Imber 2002: ch. 8). However, long-established patterns of inland settlement, overland transport, and ambivalence toward the sea remained (Soucek 2008).

The paucity of ports along the Mediterranean, the Persian Gulf, and the Arabian Sea had an additional implication: cities, located inland, were (with a few exceptions) located at some remove from each other and were not well connected. Inland territories, we observed, do not generally sustain continuous urban agglomerations. Indeed, the only regions with a continuous string of cities in the premodern era lay along the highly indented coasts of upper Anatolia and the Levant. These regions resemble the northern Mediterranean more than the southern Mediterranean, both in their littoral geography and to some extent in their politics.

Because the MENA region did not possess a dense array of cities it would have been difficult to create and sustain trading networks and military alliances along the model of the Hanse. Accordingly, it was possible for a single army to sweep through the region without meeting much organized resistance. Barbara Jelavich (1983: 127–8) offers a revealing comparison between the Ottoman and Habsburg empires, neighbors and competitors for many centuries.

The Ottoman lands had been collected by victorious sultans at the head of conquering armies. It had not been necessary to make concessions to the local nobility; they were annihilated unless they surrendered and converted to Islam. They were then the subjects of the sultan. In contrast, the Habsburg territories were assembled primarily through alliances and marriages; guarantees often had to be given to the local estates that their historic rights and individuality would be protected.

It is true that the two empires were both highly decentralized. But beyond that, their governance structures were quite different, with parliaments being the norm in Habsburg lands and the exception in Ottoman lands (Imber 2002). One possible explanation is that empire-building by conquest leaves the ruler in a stronger position than empire-building by marriage. The sultan had no reason to cede representative institutions to recalcitrant nobles and burgers.

Relatedly, states in the MENA region have been quite extensive and amazingly long-lived. The Byzantine Empire endured from 395 to 1453. The Ottoman Empire, which eventually displaced it, lasted from 1299 to 1922. Through most of this time Egypt was under the nominal control of one of these empires. If regarded as a quasi-independent polity Egypt boasts an even more impressive record of continuity extending from the first pharaohs to the present day. Another series of empires with considerable historical continuity arose in Persia.[17] In Europe, the only rival is the Roman Empire, whose tenure was long but restricted to the ancient period.

We have already reviewed the reasons why extensive land empires make it difficult to create and sustain democratic institutions. It is possible that imperial longevity also imposes barriers to democratization. Bureaucratic structures are likely to become entrenched, as are norms of hierarchy and deference.

Thus, despite the geographic proximity and shared history of societies along the banks of the Mediterranean, the divergence of political institutions that appeared in the early Middle Ages may have geographic sources. The northern portion was a lot more accessible to the sea than the southern portion.

Inland MENA

Within the MENA region there is considerable variability in ocean access. Present-day countries lying furthest from natural harbors include Afghanistan, Algeria, Egypt, Iran, Iraq, Jordan, Libya, Saudi Arabia, Sudan, and Syria. These are inland states insofar as most of their territory is located at some remove from the coast, or at least from natural harbors (see Table 5.1). Their territories are quite large and populations are diffusely settled, fitting our expectation about the interplay of harbors and state development. In the Maghreb much of the population is situated along the Mediterranean, while elsewhere population centers are generally located inland.

Most of these states do not profit from navigable rivers offering easy access from the interior to the coast. Egypt, situated along the Nile, and Iraq, situated along the Tigris and Euphrates, are exceptions to this rule. However, we have observed that where a single riverine system bisects a territory it often facilitates centralized control (see Chapter 3). Such would appear to be the case here.

---

[17] An authoritative multivolume history can be found in the *Cambridge History of Iran* series.

All of these inland states have strong autocratic histories, which for the most part continue to the present day. The core components of these histories follow the gross outlines laid out in our theory (Chapter 3). States with long, continuous histories such as Egypt and Persia/Iran drew on sedentary societies and agricultural resources, following the pattern of agrarian states. Other states, with shorter histories and more fissiparous societies, built on tribal structures that may have been somewhat democratic when operating at a local level but did not scale up into institutional forms conducive to democracy in a large nation-state. Charles Lindholm (1996) notes a long-standing contrast in the Middle East between "local democracies" and "national despotisms."

Coastal MENA

Elsewhere in the MENA region we find better coastal access, as judged by distance to the nearest natural harbor (see Table 5.1). This includes the current states of Israel/Palestine, Lebanon, Morocco, Tunisia, Turkey, Yemen, and several micro-states in the Persian Gulf.

The ancient thalassocracy of Carthage (the site of contemporary Tunis) exemplifies a political structure that was typical of sea-states in the Mediterranean region, according to Lambert (2018: 37). After about 650 BC, this evolving structure "privileged merchants, while enhancing the political role of the middling order," meaning that rulers were obliged to gain consent from their subjects. In stark contrast to continental powers of the same epoch, "Carthage was ruled by a Senate and two annually elected magistrates, or suffetes, drawn from the elite" (Lambert 2018: 37).

At the western edge of the Mediterranean, the Anatolian coast is indistinguishable from Greece, with which it has a shared history. This region's geography and political history bears more than a passing resemblance to Europe, which is not surprising given their ongoing interplay. In the ancient Phoenician cities, politics reflected a commercial and maritime orientation. Lambert (2018: 32–33) writes,

Their kings may have held the political initiative, and some religious significance, but they shared power with the mercantile elite through a Council of Elders and a People's Assembly. Enfranchising commercial wealth tied policy to economic interests, ensured the king did not forget the overriding importance of the sea, and offered a voice to those who owned the ships that made Phoenician cities significant. The people of these small cities needed to be political realists: they spent much of their existence as subjects, direct or indirect, of great powers, securing economic interests by timely concessions, support or tribute.

The Byzantine Empire, with its capital in the natural harbor of Constantinople (currently, Istanbul), is a more ambiguous case. Kaldellis (2015: xii) argues that the eastern wing of the Roman Empire embodied a "continuation of the Roman res publica; and its politics, despite changes in institutions, continued to be dominated by the ideological modes and orders of the republican tradition." As such, there were important limitations on the exercise of power. As such, there was no dichotomy between western freedom and eastern despotism. But the Byzantine Empire was no democracy, by any stretch of the term.

The Ottoman Empire may be regarded as the geographic successor to the Byzantine Empire since it also was headquartered in Istanbul. Of course, the territories of the Empire extended far and wide, and many of those territories stretched into regions distant from the coast. However, regardless of which configuration one considers, the Empire has a natural harbor distance score that is lower than that of the region overall, and on this account must be considered part of "coastal" MENA.

Although the Ottoman Empire was not very democratic, ascriptive differences – religious, linguistic, racial – were tolerated (Barkey 2008). This policy was eventually formalized in the millet system recognizing separate administrative and judicial systems for each major group, which broke down largely according to religion (Muslim, Christian Orthodox, Catholic, and Jewish).

Relatedly, Ottoman rule was considerably decentralized, which meant that whatever forms of government existed were allowed to function in a semi-autonomous fashion. By the nineteenth century, a number of autonomous regions could boast representative institutions, including Egypt, Montenegro, Romania, Samos (currently part of Greece), Serbia, and Tunisia (Hanioğlu 2010: 118)

In the nineteenth century, during the Tanzimat period, Ottoman rulers embraced a host of liberalizing reforms including the extension of civil liberties and greater equality for non-Muslims and a secularization of the legal code. In the 1860s, partially elective millet assemblies were established. Briefly in the 1870s, and continuously beginning in 1908, elections were held for the Chamber of Deputies, the elected lower house of the Ottoman parliament (Kayali 1995). On the eve of World War I, it would have been difficult to distinguish levels of democracy in the Ottoman and Austro-Hungarian empires, as both combined an elective legislature with a hereditary monarch, who retained most of the power. After the fall of the Ottoman Empire, its successor state, Turkey, followed a path that is considerably more democratic than that of most states in the region (Zürcher 2017).

For states bordering the Persian (Arabian) Gulf, the ocean is also ubiquitous. As a result, the Gulf was quite different from inland territories in the Middle East, being outward-oriented, highly mobile, diverse in race, religion, ethnicity, and language, and actively engaged in long-distance trade. Potter (2014b: 134) concludes that port cities along the Gulf "probably maintained more regular ties with trading partners in the Indian Ocean region than with capital cities such as Tehran or Baghdad." In these respects, the Persian Gulf constituted a mini-Mediterranean, with a great deal of intermixing across peoples of Arabian, Persian, and African descent who were engaged in fishing, pearling, and dhow trade.

These differences extended to political organization. Robert Landen (1967: 47–9) reports on the selection of leaders in the coastal state of Oman prior to the arrival of the British, when members of the Ibadi community of Islam played a guiding role.

The election of an imam followed a set pattern. The leading political and religious shaykhs of the Ibadi community gathered at a central spot … under the presidency of a respected, learned shaykh to discuss the candidates. If the members of this distinguished conclave agreed on a choice they gave the nominee their allegiance. This acceptance of a nominee by the notables was the first part of the bay'ah (investiture) ceremony. The second half of the bay'ah was preceded by the elector's choice being proclaimed to the people. The mass of the people could then indicate their acceptance or rejection of the imam elect. The part played by the people in the bay'ah was not an empty formality, for many of those nominated in the conclave of the notables failed to receive the necessary public accolade and so never took office. An interesting feature of Omani Ibadism was the fact that an imam might have to agree to abide by certain conditions or restrictions at the time of his election. This went as far as the designation of some imams as "weak imams" who had to rule in close consultation with the sect's religious and political leaders. Other imams were not encumbered by such restrictions and ruled with more self-discretion. If an imam failed to perform his duties he could be deposed. In addition, since the imam's office was dependent upon the goodwill and elective mandate of the faithful, there was no hard rule that the community had to have an imam at all times. What was important to the community was that "God's law" must be enforced; it was possible that a group of notables acting in consultation and concert with one another could rule in place of an imam although such a body was not empowered to pronounce judgments that would appreciably add or change anything in the body of Ibadi law. The presence of an imam in the Ibadi community depended, in the final analysis, on the need for central direction at a given time.

In this account, the *ulema* were fully capable of removing an imam who had failed to uphold his duties. "An imam or ruler who deviated from the norms imposed by the ulema was branded a malik (king), and it was an article of belief among the Ibadis that "we do not allow kings" (Landen 1967: 49; see also Wilkinson 1972: 78).

Much later, in the late eighteenth century, elections designed to select the most qualified candidate gave way to elections that generally anointed a dynastic successor, a monarchic pattern that persists to the present (Bathurst 1972: 101–2). However, this was not the historic system of leadership selection, and judging from the frequently contested successions and civil wars that followed, the monarchic solution does not seem to have been entirely legitimate.

At the northern edge of the Persian Gulf, Kuwait Town also claimed a superb natural harbor, which served as the foundation for fishing, pearling, shipping, shipbuilding, and trade since the eighteenth century (Al-Nakib 2014: 201; Broeze 1997b). As the population grew, so did the need for an institutionalized system of rule, one that went beyond the informal customs brought by the Utbi tribe from the desert. Al-Nakib (2014: 202) relates:

the heads of the main families decided that a leader needed to be chosen from among themselves to settle all problems and disputes in the town and to protect it from external attack. In 1752 Sabah I (r. 1752–1756) was selected for this position and entered into a social pact with the urban families: he would ensure the safety and stability of the town so that its inhabitants could live and work comfortably and peacefully, while the townspeople would carry on earning their income through trading and pearling.

From the very start, merchant families dominated the local economy, occupying a special position in Kuwaiti society and politics, sharing power with the hereditary office of the shaikh. Crystal (1990: 4) explains, "Their political power grew from the social institutions of marriage (intermarriage between merchants and the ruling family ...) and *majlis* (regular social councils for airing grievances and concerns) which gave them informal but daily access to the rulers." In her reading, the merchant's clout lay with the revenue they provided to the shaikh and the ever-present threat of departure. Since the Gulf was a highly integrated economic area, with many ports of call, merchants could quite easily decamp if their interests were not respected. The exit threat was potent, leading to considerable political power in the day-to-day governing of the small territory throughout the eighteenth and nineteenth centuries. This culminated in the establishment of parliamentary representation, a product of the Majlis movement of 1938 led by the merchant community in defense of their economic interests, and following closely the script of the growth of parliamentary power in early modern Europe (Crystal 1990: ch. 3).

When oil was discovered in the early twentieth century this delicate balance between bourgeoisie and royalty was upset, as the shaikh was able to monopolize revenue drawn from this new resource. With that economic clout, Kuwait developed into a fairly strong monarchy. Even so, the legacy of its past persists in the form of an elective legislature that is strong by MENA standards, and in a position to challenge the reigning monarch (Herb 2014).

Similar patterns of political development can be seen elsewhere in the Gulf. In the early twentieth century, these emirates – under the nominal control of Britain – seemed poised for a domestic political transition based on the power of merchants and institutionalized in limited-suffrage assemblies that would share power with the sovereign. However, the discovery of oil displaced this trajectory, reinforcing the power of hereditary rulers who were able to control the flow of rents (Zahlan 2016).

In these various respects, the history of coastal MENA is considerably more democratic – offering numerous parallels to polities located along the northern coasts of the Mediterranean – than the history of inland MENA.

Sub-Saharan Africa

Although sub-Saharan Africa (hereafter, "Africa") is geographically close to Europe its history was quite separate until the modern era.[18] Trade routes across the Mediterranean, the Red Sea, and the Indian Ocean tied some parts of Africa to the rest of Eurasia, but these parts were coastal or along the Nile. Trade with the interior of sub-Saharan Africa was less common, as it required traversing the Sahara.

The long history of slave trading might be regarded as an exception to this dictum. From 1400 to 1900, an estimated 18 million people were forcibly removed from their natal land (Nunn 2008: 141–2; see also Eltis et al. 1999; Manning 1990). While this signifies a thriving transoceanic trade, it is nonetheless the case that trading partners were usually local, or depended upon intermediaries such as Arabs in the north or Jahanke (Diahkanke) in Senegambia (Curtin et al. 1978: 229). There was little direct contact between those in the interior and inter-oceanic trade, testifying to the isolation of the former.

Many obstacles stood in the way of increased contact. Arid deserts and dense jungles posed a barrier to overland travel, as did the tsetse fly, the prevalence of malaria and other disease vectors, and the absence of

---

[18] This section benefitted from a close reading by Pat Manning.

valued commodities (other than people) or large population centers that might have served as markets for European goods. Another obstacle was the huge expanse of the continent, which encompasses 18 percent of the world's surface area (sufficient to hold the United States, Western Europe, China, India, and Argentina).

Of particular interest to our study is the general absence of navigable rivers (Marsh, Kingsnorth 1972: 48) and natural harbors (Table 5.1). Hilling and Hoyle (1970: 7) note that "Africa's coasts are not well endowed with natural harbours of adequate depth and ease of access for modern navigation, and the problems of creating artificial ports are great ... [including] the surf barrier and littoral sand movement in West Africa and ... the coral hazard along the ... coastline of eastern Africa." Of the western seaboard, White (1970: 13–14) explains:

Under natural conditions [the coastline] functions more as a barrier than as a zone of contact between land and sea. This coast, extending for some 3,840 km between Cape Verde and Mount Cameroun, is for the most part fault-guided and generally lacks major indentations. The contrast with the coast of Atlantic Europe or of Japan is extreme. Throughout the year the Atlantic swell breaks on the shore as a very heavy surf ... Unless protection can be given from the swell, ships cannot tie up to a quay, but most lie offshore and transfer their cargoes to small boats of special design and limited capacity operated by skilled crews ... Eastward from Cape Palmas, the south-westerly swell breaks at an angle to the beach, giving rise to a longshore drift, which has been estimated to move beach sand past a fixed point at the rate of 1 to 1½ million tons per annum. This creates an almost continuous offshore bar, behind which are longitudinal and transverse lagoons, the latter being the drowned valleys. Breaks in the bar are rare and the surf makes passage extremely dangerous. Even if the sheltered waters of the lagoons can be reached, they are rarely deep enough for ocean-going ships. The rivers are generally small in volume and flow is restricted during the dry season. Even if there is no coastal dune, rivers fail to prevent formidable bars which may be up to 5.6 km wide. Even where ships can occasionally enter estuaries, these are normally lined with mangrove swamps. These are in themselves formidable barriers, which can be penetrated neither by vessels nor by vehicles. Natural causeways are few and artificial ones costly.

White (1970: 14) concludes, "in the whole of West Africa there are only two good natural harbours, the Dakar Roads and the Sierra Leone river, but both of these are at the western end of the coast" (see also Connah 1987: 98–9). To this, one might add Abidjan harbor, the Senegal and Gambia rivers, which served as ports of call in the pre-colonial era, as well as multiple islands and inlets along the Upper Guinea coast (Brooks 2003: ch. 1). Further south, one might note the Congo River estuary, Luanda, and Cape Town – though one may quibble over whether they qualify as excellent natural harbors.

The east coast of the African continent is somewhat more accessible to oceangoing vessels (Connah 1987: 153), and has a long history of (mostly Arab) voyagers. The Swahili Coast is discussed at length below. To the north of the Swahili Coast, one finds the harbors of Asmara, Djibouti, and others at the juncture of the Red Sea and the Arabian Sea. To the south, suitable portage could be found at Beira, Maputo, and Durban. However, there is no easy river access into the interior, meaning that the coasts are cut off from developments within the vast continent.

The disjuncture between coastal and inland areas is accentuated by a persistent disparity in climate. Along the coast, the air is frequently hot, humid, and filled with insects, while land in the interior is often elevated and therefore more moderate in temperature and less prone to malaria. For all these reasons, population centers were more frequently located in the middle of the continent than along the coasts.

The geographic contrast between Europe and Africa is thus fairly stark. Following our theoretical framework, this may help to explain why democracy within statelike entities was much more common in the former than the latter during the premodern era. (Recall that our theory is not concerned with pre-state entities.)

Inland Africa

We turn now to comparisons across the African continent (below the Sahara). Unfortunately, it is difficult to observe the development of political institutions in Africa prior to European colonization. Knowledge of premodern polities in the region is not extensive. Since these were not literate cultures our understanding rests on surviving oral histories, archeological remains (which do not weather well in the tropics), accounts by European explorers, administrators, or missionaries (often grossly biased), or ethnographies carried out in the modern era. Even so, a few observations about states in Africa during the pre-colonial era can be hazarded – and more attention to the topic than has been possible here is most definitely warranted.[19]

To begin with, larger states were more likely to be governed in an autocratic fashion in the premodern era. Areas of population concentration and political authority could be found in the Great Lakes region, including the Nkore/Ankole, Bunyoro, Buganda, Burundi, Busoga/Soga,

---

[19] For general surveys see Connah (1987), Curtin, Feierman, Thompson, Vansina (1995), Fortes, Evans-Pritchard (1940), Murdock (1959), Tymowski (2009), and Vansina (1962, 2004). Recent work is surveyed in Manning (2015), and Manning, Miller (2019).

Ruanda/Rwanda, and Toro kingdoms and lesser-known predecessors (Beattie 1960; Reid 2002; Wrigley 1996); the Sahel, including the Ghana, Songhai/Songhay, Fulani, Hausa, Kanem-Bornu, Kangaba, Mali, and Sokoto states (Connah 1981; Fisher 1975; Ford, Kaberry 1967; Hogben, Kirk-Greene 1966; Johnston 1967; Levtzion 1973; Smaldone 1976; Vansina 1966); the Congo, including the Bemba, Kongo, Luba, and Lunda states (Vansina 1990); Ethiopia, probably the longest-lived African empire (Marcus 2002); and the Great Zimbabwe Empire (Garlake 1973).

These states, described variously as empires, kingdoms, or caliphates, were located inland from the coast. They often benefitted from trading networks, which they could control from strategic locations along a caravan route or a river that was navigable inland if not all the way to the ocean. But the main source of revenue was agriculture, so rich soil and plentiful rainfall generally contributed to strong states.

The aforenamed states were generally governed in a monarchic fashion, though sometimes the king was elected and the position occasionally alternated between different royal houses. Sometimes, as in Ghana and Mali, rulers employed slaves as bureaucrats, which we can assume exerted a centralizing effect (Levtzion 1973: 112–13). All in all, it was a fairly autocratic political environment.

Niger Delta and Yorubaland

Coastal areas in Africa tended to be less developed, for reasons already noted. However, a few exceptions deserve notice. One such locale was the Niger Delta, including the many rivers and streams that lead from this major transport route to the sea along the southern coast of present-day Nigeria. We shall consider this territory along with Yorubaland, which extends further north and west through the coastal areas of western Nigeria (including present-day Lagos), Benin, and Togo.

In the Niger Delta, waterborne trade formed a major component of the economy (Alagoa 1970). Walter Rodney (1975: 253) explains,

The terrain was a major determinant of the size of the political entities on the coast, most of which were fishing villages. Seldom did the political writ of a village extend beyond its own boundaries; and family and clan allegiances led to the division of political power and authority – often expressed in religious terms. Such was the sociopolitical pattern on the littoral among the Ijo, Ibibio and Efik. Inland, too, segmentary lineages and small-scale political organization were the norm in the region south of the Benue and east of the Niger ... Their agriculture allowed major trade in surpluses; they were proficient in iron-working; their commercial activity extended throughout this region; and they had devised judicial and religious institutions which partially transcended the boundaries of their village governments. Over a wide area, large numbers of people spoke the various dialects of the Ibo language.

In these respects, Iboland, home of the Ibo (or Igbo), is redolent of many European coastal areas. These villages – or, arguably, city-states (Princewill 2000) – also cultivated a participatory form of governance (Ejiofor 1981; Jones 1963). Nwabara (1977: 19) writes,

All laws were debated and passed by the *Oha* – the congregation of all the adults of the village. As in the ancient Greek *polis*, every adult participated in the deliberation. Each law passed by the *Oha* was debated first in the *Unu nna* assembly, which also consisted of all male adults. The laws so passed became the laws of the land – *iwu ala* – and an infringement of the law was punished accordingly.

Neighboring Yorubaland was governed in a more centralized fashion. The oba was a king of divine status who played an important spiritual role (Smith 1988: 91). Yet, extensive spiritual powers did not necessarily go hand in hand with extensive secular powers. Indeed, quite the reverse, according to Robert Smith's (1988: 91–2) account.

Not only was he [the oba] bound by rules and precedents in his personal life but these also required him to submit all business to councils of chiefs and officers, and only after consultation and deliberation by these bodies could a policy be decided upon and proclaimed in the oba's name. Every oba had at least one council of chiefs who formed a powerful, usually hereditary, cabinet, and in most kingdoms there were lesser councils for the regulation of the different aspects of government. Moreover, the chieftaincies were hereditary within the 'descent groups' or extended families which made up the population of the town. Thus, the chiefs were representatives of their family groups as well as being officials of the king and kingdom. Although the oba's authority expanded and contracted according to his personality and to the political, economic, and other conditions obtaining during his reign, he still seems normally to have been subject to many restraints. It was these restraints which most sharply distinguished the Yoruba kingdom from the authoritarian monarchies of, for example, Benin and Dahomey, and from those based on conquest, like the Fulani emirates of northern Nigeria.

Smith (1988: 95) concludes that "Yoruba society was in practice surprisingly democratic. Distinctions of rank and wealth were offset by the obligations and benefits of the family and by common ownership of the land; opportunities to acquire high office and wealth were many, and no freeman was without a protector among the chiefs of his town."

Swahili Coast

Another part of the African continent with easy access to the ocean lies upon the eastern shore in the region now occupied by southern Somalia,

Kenya, Tanzania, and northern Mozambique. Because of multiple natural harbors – including Dar es Salaam, Kilwa, Lamu, Mafia, Malindi, Mikindani/Mtwara, Mogadishu, Mombasa, Pemba, Tanga, and Zanzibar (Hoyle 1967a) – and favorable trade winds, the Swahili Coast has been engaged in trade across the Indian Ocean for a millennium or more.[20]

As in other harbor-rich coastal areas, traders – generally Swahili-speaking but hailing from anywhere along the coast of the Indian Ocean – formed a ruling class. And as in other coastal areas, there was an abundance of micro-states, most of which are not much larger than a single town or city. As in Europe (but different from the pattern common in sub-Saharan Africa), towns along the coast tended to be walled and the larger establishments were constructed similarly of stone (Winters 1983: 18). Each enjoyed considerable autonomy (Horton, Middleton 2000: 157–8), warranting the term *city-state* (Sinclair, Håkansson 2000)

Some of these city-states appear to have been ruled in a republican fashion. Marguerite Ylvisaker (1979: 67) describes the government of Lamu in the nineteenth century as follows:

The town was divided into two halves called Zaina and Suudi, and all of the noble families were affiliated with one or the other. The halves elected leaders from the heads of their constituent families and, alternately, the elected leaders from the two sections ruled the whole town for four-year periods. Even though the elders of the leading families acted as advisers to the … ruler …, this form of government also leaned toward division. That the military regiments were also drawn from the two halves did not lessen this tendency.

Nearby Rasini, on Patu Island in the Lamu archipelago, is also described as "a rather loose political structure …, where there was neither a sultan nor a single ruling family" (Ylvisaker 1979: 85).

In their overview of governing institutions up and down the Swahili Coast, Horton and Middleton (2000: 158) note that although many had a ruling family, republican (non-monarchical) regimes were not uncommon (see also Hull 1976: 10; Mathew 1956: 65–7). "Coastal East Africa differs from many other areas of the continent by the absence of highly developed systems of kingship" (Horton and Middleton 2000: 175). In most towns, patricians who were high-ranking Swahili governed.

---

[20] Wide-ranging works on the history of East Africa or Swahili culture include Chittick (1980), Horton, Middleton (2000), Marsh, Kingsnorth (1972), Mathew (1956), Middleton (2004), Nicholls (1971), Pearson (1998), Pollard, Ichumbaki (2017).

Virtually every patricians' town has had what is often described as a 'Council of Elders,' and this has most probably comprised the heads of the patrician lineage groups. Even when the town had a king, this council seems to have had particular importance, especially in relation to economic activity and in dealing with disputes over succession. In some towns, the influence of the patrician lineage heads was such that kings were not deemed necessary. This was the case for much of the history of Lamu, Siyu, Faza, Barawa, Merca and Mogadishu, but may well also have been so for many of the towns that are known only archaeologically and about which nothing survives of their governance. (Horton and Middleton 2000: 159)

Frequently, towns were divided into moieties who alternated in power, as described by Ylvisaker (above). All in all, governance structures along the Swahili Coast prior to colonial seizure seem to have been fairly democratic.[21]

Contrasts

Conclusions about Africa during the premodern era must be hedged with caveats. Sources are scarce and often difficult to interpret. Many do not reflect on the topic of political institutions. And since most of the political units were small there are inevitable disagreements over which ones qualify as "states," and hence are relevant to our inquiry.

With these caveats, it is nonetheless possible to discern a contrast between inland states, which tended to be larger and be ruled in a more autocratic fashion, and coastal states, which tended to be smaller and more democratic. Indeed, the only areas of sub-Saharan Africa with a concentration of natural harbors – in the west along the Niger Delta and in the east along the Swahili Coast – were also the areas with the most democratic institutions prior to the influx of Europeans.

East Asia

We define East Asia narrowly, including the three historic states – China, Korea (north and south), and Japan – with sidelong glances at Taiwan.[22] Across all of these states (as presently configured) we find an average

---

[21] In smaller towns, governance was even more democratic than in the cities. In rural Zanzibar, Middleton (2004: 64) writes, "Each town still has its council, known as Watu Wanne, 'The Four men,' together with an elected headman, a central-government-appointed representative known as the *sheha*, and the ritual leader (separate from local mosque controllers) known as *mzale* or *mvyale*, almost always a woman, whose task is to control the evil spirits of the neighborhood."

[22] This section benefitted from a close reading by Adam Clulow.

distance of 897 kilometers to the nearest natural harbor (Table 5.1). This is considerably higher than the global mean, signaling that East Asia is less aqueous than other regions of the world.

Within this region geographic contrasts are stark. Japan and Korea stand at the aquatic end of the spectrum while China is at the other extreme. Indeed, Table 4.6 reveals that only a handful of countries are more removed from natural harbors than China.

As it happens, these three ancient polities were in fairly close contact with each other through most of the premodern era and borrowed extensively from each other. Granted, most of the borrowing was from China, which usually occupied a dominant position. We can expect that these borrowings, as well as the coercive influence of the hegemon (China) on its neighbors (Kang 2010), attenuated differences that might have arisen if the three states had developed in greater isolation from each other. Under the circumstances, whatever differences in political institutions do appear may be attributable to some underlying factor that exerts centrifugal pressure. In the present instance, our focus is on geography – specifically, ocean access.

Before we begin we must return to the recalcitrant units-of-analysis problem, introduced in Chapter 4. It may seem that in treating China, Korea, and Japan as fundamental units in our discussion we are reifying concepts. All three states changed shape over time, China most dramatically. And it is unclear that their evolution was a foregone conclusion, just as the division of the Korean peninsula – which we ignore, for the most part, since it occurs outside the time period of immediate concern – is not a foregone conclusion.

To repeat a central point from Chapter 4, grid-cells are the treated units in this study; states (i.e., city-states, countries, empires, or colonies) are simply aggregations of grid-cells. And yet, we have also argued that geography structures the shape of states. In particular, ocean exposure has a mitigating effect on the tendency of states to enlarge their borders. East Asia offers a prime example of this dynamic at work.

From a core area along the Yellow River, Chinese civilization expanded in all directions until it met geographic barriers posed by desert/steppe, mountains, tropical forest, or ocean. Try as they might, Chinese emperors could do little to control these outlying regions in a direct fashion, resorting to indirect, tributary relationships. Korean and Japanese states also had expansionist ambitions but faced tighter geographic obstacles – the sea, and for Korea the mountains to the north – that both protected them from China and from the tribesmen of Central Asia, and also inhibited expansion. In short, it seems plausible to regard geography as part of the explanation for why three ancient states arose in

East Asia and managed to maintain their political autonomy (for the most part) over the millennia. We turn now to a more detailed discussion of each state's history.

China

The period of state formation in China occurred so early that it is difficult to say much about its circumstances.[23] What we know is that after a period when several states fought for preeminence, known as the Warring States period (475–221 BCE), the plains of North China were united under the Qin. This is understood as the watershed between ancient and imperial eras of Chinese history. From this point onward, the main territory of North China was usually united under a single dynasty. Despite periodic dynastic failures, a centralized system of rule was regenerated time and again. Thus, unlike Europe, and indeed to an extent unknown anywhere else in the premodern world, an extremely large tract of territory achieved political unity and retained it (with a few interruptions) up to the present day.

Of significance is not merely how China managed to unify but how it managed to erect and maintain a centralized system of rule in which imperial power stretched across a vast domain, governing in a fairly direct fashion (by the standards of the day).

Nicolas Tackett (2018: 7) highlights, among other things, the role of Chinese "technologies of governance":

Regimes based in China Proper enjoyed access to a provincial bureaucratic infrastructure that facilitated the collection of taxes and the conscription of military troops across a vast territory. Moreover, government administrators possessed a technocratic expertise made possible by an accumulated written historical tradition, and by the continuity of bureaucratic practice across over two millennia of history, traditions preserved even during periods of disunity. Periodic bureaucratic innovations, if determined to be effective, were maintained in subsequent dynasties as part of the accumulation of tools available to state planners. At the heart of the Chinese provincial bureaucracy was a hierarchy of prefectures (or commanderies) and subordinate counties, first established in the Qin Dynasty at the dawn of the imperial period. Although regional kingdoms were reestablished in the first decades of the Han Dynasty, these were ultimately abolished in the late 2nd century BCE, so that all of China Proper thereafter fell under the prefecture-county system. To this day, one finds in many regions of China counties that were first established in the Qin, a remarkable example of the long-term continuity of the Chinese bureaucratic system.

---

[23] This section benefitted from a close reading by Nick Tackett.

With respect to appointment and promotion, Tackett (2018: 8–9) notes a variety of initiatives that served "to ensure that local administrators remained loyal agents of the central government."

One might add to this the role of Confucian/Legalist ideology, which seems to have legitimated centralized, dynastic rule. Zhao (2015: 14) explains,

In the Confucian-Legalist state, the emperors accepted Confucianism as a ruling ideology and subjected themselves to the control of a Confucian bureaucracy, while Confucian scholars both in and out of the bureaucracy supported the regime and supplied meritocratically selected officials who administrated the country using an amalgam of Confucian ethics and Legalist regulations and techniques. This symbiotic relationship between the ruling house and Confucian scholars gave birth to what is by premodern standards a powerful political system – a system so resilient and adaptive that it survived numerous challenges and persisted up until the Republican Revolution in 1911.

Another important piece of this puzzle lies with the social structure of China. Comparing classes in China with Europe, Bin Wong (1997: 107) notes:

Late imperial China had no estates, and notions of class did not matter to the construction of political order as they did in Europe. In China, the same ideological vision perceived local and central order to be of one piece. The units of social order were not estates but families, lineages, and villages. Elite families spanned different economic and social functions, but the vision of social order did not privilege those functional differences. While Chinese thought recognized functional differentiation into scholars, peasants, merchants, and tradesmen, these did not become the primary units for organizing social order. They were never accorded institutionally distinct corporate status. Elite families were those that managed to diversify the pursuits of their sons into government service, management of family lands, and commerce. At any point in time the basis of elite status for a particular family could be possession of a civil service degree and official post, wealth made from trade, or major landholdings. Some families were more likely to reproduce their success in one kind of elite activity than another. In general, there was a continuum of possibilities without any sharp distinctions among elite members that were reproduced over time. In Europe as well there was social mobility among aristocrats and men of commercial wealth, but these European elites possessed institutionalized voices which Chinese elites lacked. European elites also possessed military forces of their own; towns lost their own forces before aristocrats, who fielded independent armies in France as late as the Fronde rebellion of the mid-seventeenth century. Chinese elites lacked both military force to organize revolts and civilian voice to express their interests against those of the state. While European elites had institutionalized voices that circumscribed the limits of the ruler's authority, Chinese elites participated in extending the reach of state power and authority by sharing a common Confucian agenda for promoting social order.

These persistent features of Chinese society and politics could be exogenous, which is to say, they could have become established at an early stage of Chinese history and then perpetuated themselves. But it is also possible that they owe their provenance – or at least their persistence – to geographic features that set China apart from most other states.

The first Chinese states arose along the banks of the Yellow River, in the northern portion of what is now China. Later, people moved southward, along the banks of the Yangtze River and to the Pacific coast. But most imperial and post-imperial capitals, and the center of population in China's period of state formation, were in the north and at some remove from the coastline (Tackett 2018: 2–3). In this sense, China was a territorial empire.

It has, to be sure, a nautical history,[24] and areas lying along the coast bear resemblance to coastal areas elsewhere in Eurasia.[25] In the fourteenth and early fifteenth centuries, Schottenhammer (2019: 192) calls China "*the* political and military maritime power of the world." This brief episode of primacy culminated in the remarkable voyages of Admiral Zheng He to various points in Southeast and South Asia (Levathes 1994), events that occurred a half century *prior* to Columbus's visit to the New World.

Yet, the Ming dynasty also instituted a series of Seabans (restrictions on maritime activity) and, shortly after Zheng He's triumphant voyages, limited official contact with the outside world. This was followed somewhat later by the Qing dynasty coastal depopulation policies (1661–83). To be sure, private trade continued in port cities such as Fujian (Ho 2011) and in the semi-autonomous territory of Taiwan (Hang 2015), and there was a modest reopening after 1684 (Zhao 2013). China was never entirely isolated from the world. But there seems no doubt that its official stance affected economic contacts with the world and constrained the development of China as a global economic force and as a sea power.

Why China forsook its oceanic opportunity is the subject of much commentary (Schottenhammer 2019; Suryadinata 2005). In Ho's (2011: 17) judgment, the Seabans were designed "to monopolize foreign contacts and trade under state control by prohibiting private activity and increasing surveillance of the coast." It is possible that opening up new markets and a new locus of spending threatened the position of powerful members of the court. It may even have been viewed as a threat to the Ming dynasty. Perhaps Zheng He's voyages, the pinnacle of Chinese

---

[24] See Deng (1997, 1999), Lo Jung-Pang (2012), Ng (2017), Po (2018), Yangwen (2011).
[25] See Sze Hang Choi (2017), Clark (1991). But see also So (2000).

naval exploration, constituted an elaborate form of exile, motivated by internal palace politics (Deng 2011: 217).

We will never know for sure. What we do know is that Chinese emperors were able to outlaw long-distance oceangoing travel for a period of time, reinforcing an economic system weighted toward agriculture and a foreign policy that was isolationist by European standards. The ocean was looked upon as a defensive barrier, rather than an opportunity for expansion as it was for European empires (Ng 2017: 99).

We assume that the official closing of China would have been less likely, as well as more difficult to achieve, if the empire's population had been concentrated along the coast and heavily engaged in ocean fishing and commerce. In this light, it is notable that during the periods of fragmentation those polities that were centered on the ocean-exposed southwestern territory such as the state of Min (910–46) in Fujian, the Kingdom of Wu-Yue (907–78), the Southern Tang dynasty (937–75), the Southern Han dynasty (917–71), and the Southern Song empire (1127–1279) adopted many traits commonly associated with thalassocracies (Schottenhammer 2019). Lo Jung-Pang (2012: 24) remarks that denizens of the south "were progressive in thought and restless in action, imaginative and enterprising, quick-witted and adventurous, adapted by nature to commerce and nautical pursuits." He further notes that "the words 'Guangzhou' and 'merchant,' 'Ningbo' and 'sailor,' 'Fujian' and 'navy,' are commonly associated" (Lo Jung-Pang 2012: 24). A polity's attitude toward the sea is thus structured in important respects by its physical proximity to the sea.

Yet, despite China's extensive coastline its interior is even more expansive, stretching all the way to inner Asia, where the rich loess soil gives way to sand, mountains, or steppe. Because the coastal and inland areas are contiguous, and existing mountains are insufficient to provide defense, the brief tenure of the foregoing states along the coast proved to be exceptions to the general rule according to which the vast expanse of mainland East Asia is governed by a single polity.

Accordingly, most of the productive land within the Chinese state lies far from the coast. So long as China remained predominantly agricultural, most of its population would also lie in the interior. Deng (2011: 216) reports that in 1900, at the tail end of the imperial era, the agricultural sector employed over 80 percent of the labor force. Likewise, taxes from trade never constituted a major portion of the Chinese imperial budget (Schottenhammer 2019: 209–10).

Although China's interior gains access to the coast through two major river systems – along the Yellow and Yangtze – this is fairly limited access given the size of the territory. Moreover, these rivers were easy for imperial troops to police and control. It seems likely that they served the state more than they served the cause of individual liberty. It is hard to imagine merchants navigating hundreds of miles of river without encountering government taxes and without submitting to regulatory regimes such as the Ming dynasty's prohibition on foreign travel.

Although China became fairly urbanized it did not develop a system of independent cities, capable of resisting the imprecations of the imperial state. Commercial relationships tended to be bounded within river valleys: Beijing in North China, Sian (Xi'an) in Northwest China, Chungking (Chongqing) in the Upper Yangtze, Wuhan in the Middle Yangtze, Shanghai in the Lower Yangtze, Foochow (Fuzhou) in the Southeast Coast, and Canton (Guangzhou) in Lingnan. In each case, Skinner (1977: 282–3) reports, "the major commercial cities of the region had stronger economic links with one another than any had with cities outside the region, and the densest interurban trade was almost wholly contained within the regional core. Moreover, the densely populated and urbanized core areas were closely associated with riverine lowlands." By all appearances, merchant capital played a secondary role to agriculture in China's economy, and merchants had low social and political status. China, Skinner (1977: 102) observes, "did not sustain a self-identifying and self-perpetuating urban elite as a component of the population." This, too, could be chalked up to China's status as a non-oceanic state.

There is, to be sure, much more that could be said about the role of geography in structuring the development of political institutions (Skinner 1977; Tackett 2018). However, we must content ourselves with a brief review of those aspects of central theoretical concern.

Korea

From 57 BCE to AD 668, the Korean peninsula (including part of Manchuria) was divided among three main kingdoms: Baekje, Silla, and Goguryeo (aka Koguryo, Goryeo).[26] Kim (2012: 60) describes these polities, as follows:

The most peculiar feature of the political process in each of the Three Kingdoms was the councils for political decision making, which demonstrates that each of the Three Kingdoms was a union of the aristocracy. In Koguryŏ, in the reign of King Sindae (165–179), the post of *kuksang* (prime minister) was established. Unlimited in tenure, *kuksang* headed Koguryŏ's council of the high aristocracy.

---

[26] Our account of Korean history draws on Duncan (2000), Jae-Woo (2011), Kim (2012), Seth (2010), and Shon (1998).

Later *kuksang* was replaced by the position of *taedaero* with a three-year term of office. In the sixth and seventh centuries, when the aristocracy regained strength, *taedaero* was elected by the high aristocracy, but sometimes the most powerful aristocrat took it by force. When the aristocracy could not reach an agreement on the right person for the position, the contestants would resort to arms. The king, unable to control them, would be forced to close his palace gates to protect himself from the struggle. Also, the high aristocracy of the 5th rank and above assembled in council to discuss and decide important affairs of state.

In Paekche high aristocratic officials met and elected the chief minister on a large rock called *chŏngsaam*. In Silla a council of the high aristocracy, termed the Hwabaek, consisted of aristocrats called *taedŭng*. Headed by a top aristocrat called sangdaedŭng, the Hwabaek council decided the most important state affairs, such as succession to the throne and declarations of war. Both *taedŭng* and *sangdaedŭng* were members of true-bone lineage. The principle of unanimity governed Hwabaek decisions, and council meetings were convened at one of the four sacred sites – Mt. Ch'ŏngsong to the east of the capital, P'ijŏn field to the west, Mt. Uji to the south, or Mt. Kŭmgang to the north. This council institution of the Three Kingdoms implies that political decision making at the time took the form of an "aristocratic democracy." The Ŭijŏngbu, or State Council, system of the later Chosŏn dynasty seems to have followed the tradition of these earlier council institutions.

These features persisted after the peninsula was united by the Silla dynasty and later by the Koryo dynasty. Political and economic power remained a monopoly of an aristocratic caste – those of the Holy or True Bone rank within the Bone Rank system. They were also the paramount force at local levels (Duncan 2000: 13). Only members of this caste were eligible for the throne and for the aristocratic assembly, the Hwabaek Council.

Meanwhile, the key executive office during the Koryo period, the Security Council, was staffed by regular bureaucrats through most of the Koryo period. Although Korean rulers attempted to establish a meritocratic bureaucracy, including eunuchs on the Chinese model that would be accountable solely to them, they were hamstrung by aristocratic opposition. Importantly, the Korean exam system was limited to those of aristocratic blood. Key offices thus remained in the hands of hereditary castes, whose interests and loyalties were often opposed to the king. Unlike China, where "a family's prestige ... seems to have stemmed from its history of central office holding, status in Koryo, while enhanced by central office holding, ultimately derived from a tradition of local autonomy." The Bone castes were not a service aristocracy.

In the Choson period (1392–1897), one sees persistence in the basic social and political institutions, which again feature a rivalry between throne and aristocracy. However, the balance of power seems to have swung toward the former (Kim 2012: 193).

Thus, over the course of Korean history one witnesses a continual jostling for power between monarchy and aristocracy, which seesaws back and forth over the centuries but is, overall, rather evenly balanced. While the king's supreme authority is unchallenged, his ability to rule is constrained. Arbitrary power is fettered and some collective accountability, via the Haebeck Assembly and the Bone aristocracy more generally, exists. Seth (2010: 40) concludes that "Throughout Korean history, the position of the monarch was more humble than in many premodern Asian societies ... [R]ulers shared power with aristocratic families who governed through various councils or committees."

What might account for the aristocracy's ability to resist centralizing pressures that had long since overwhelmed local opposition in China? Duncan (2000: 49) identifies the diminutive status of Korea – especially as contrasted with the local hegemon, China – as a factor weakening imperial power.

The Koryo kings' recognition of Chinese suzerainty and their acceptance of letters of investiture from the emperor may have provided them with external sanction, but at the same time it consequently undermined any claims to ultimate authority deriving from Heaven. The Koryo rulers had no choice but to seek additional legitimization in traditional ideologies such as Buddhism and geomancy, which were closely linked to landed Silla aristocratic and local warlord interests.

Size matters, and it was difficult for kings of modest Korean kingdoms to claim the legitimacy accorded to a grand empire like China. Likewise, the modest size of Korea limited the revenue sources available to Korean monarchs, which meant they were more dependent upon landed aristocrats to carry out tasks of governance, and to defend the state from periodic threats (from China, from Mongols, from Japan, or from European powers). In this light, it is not surprising to find features of Korean political history that mimic the struggles for power between monarchs and aristocratic (or commercial) classes in Europe, with the aristocratic assembly, the Hwabaek Council, playing the role of a medieval parliament.

Japan

Japanese political history exhibits features that should be familiar to Korean specialists. Here, too, one finds an ongoing joust for power between monarchs and the noble class – which, as in Korea, shifts back and forth from period to period.

During the classical period (538–1185), the aristocracy often held the upper hand. Of the Nara state (672–784), Naoki Kojiro (1993: 237–41) writes,

The highest officials of the state made up a select group from Yamato and Kawachi that included the emperor, members of his household, and leaders of such old and powerful clans as the Fujiwara, Otomo, Isonokami (formerly Mononobe), and Abe (a Fuse branch). The total number of individuals in this elite group (fifth rank or higher) probably came to no more than 125. Provisions of the Taiho code ... protected the exclusiveness of this group by allowing their high ranks and offices to be passed on to their sons and grandsons.

The authority of the emperor at the top of this select group was great but not unlimited. He could issue an edict ordering the appointment of a crown prince or minister, but his edict had to be countersigned by the chancellor, minister of the left, or minister of the right. On the other hand, the following matters could not be acted on by the Council of State until its recommendations had been reported to the emperor and approved by him: (1) scheduling important state ceremonies like the Great Feast of the Enthronement (Daijosai), (2) increasing or decreasing the government's operating costs, (3) altering the number of officials, (4) inflicting punishments by death or exile, and (5) forming or abolishing districts. The emperor could approve or disapprove a recommendation but could not make amendments. Usually he approved. In principle, then, the emperor had dictatorial power, but in practice, his power was limited by the consultative authority of the Council of State.

As in Korea (and Europe), the principal instruments of power in Japan were assemblies, most importantly the Council of State (Daijō-kan or Dajō-kan), the highest organ of the Imperial government, but also the Council of Kami Affairs (mentioned above). During the Heian period (794–1185) this Council of State seems to have reached its apogee (Hurst 1999: 586–7). Later, in the tenth and eleventh centuries, it declines in importance, losing its status and independence to the Fujiwara clan.

While comparisons with Korea are informative, so are contrasts with the regional hegemon, China. Naoki Kojiro (1993: 237–41) reflects on differences between the Korean emperor and the Council of State, on the one hand, and the T'ang emperor and various state organs – the Secretariat (Chung-shu sheng), the Chancellery (Men-hsia sheng), and the Department of State Affairs (Shang-shu sheng) – on the other.

The heads of these Chinese bodies were the state's highest administrators, but they were no more than instruments of inquiry and did not have complete authority over their own departments. The Secretariat's highest officer would draft imperial edicts after receiving instructions from the emperor, and officials of the Chancellery would examine the draft and make revisions.

Other departmental heads could see memorials and report their views to the throne. The Secretariat, which administered the six boards, would see that an edict was implemented after it had been examined and revised by the Chancellery. But the Chancellery did little more than look for textual deficiencies and usually did not consider the edict's contents. China's highest state officials, therefore, did not have nearly as much authority as did their counterparts in Japan.

Heads of Chinese aristocratic clans were also relatively weak, as we can see when comparing the ranks given to the sons and grandsons of high-ranking officeholders with those received by their Japanese counterparts. Chinese law stated that the heirs of first-rank officers were entitled to senior seventh rank lower grade, whereas in Japan they would receive fifth rank lower grade. A study of the ranks bestowed on the sons of officials at lower levels of the aristocracy also shows that the Japanese were treated better.

But what made the Japanese bureaucratic structure quite different from that of China was the Council of Kami Affairs, which was placed under the emperor at a position equal to that of the Council of State. The compilers of the Taiho code, though giving close attention to Chinese law, were obviously intent on preserving and using traditional sources of sacral authority. Because the Japanese law provided crucial support for the emperor's spiritual and secular authority, historians commonly think of these years as the high point of the 'administrative and penal law (*ritsuryo*)' order.

Similar contrasts could be drawn at other points in history. Throughout, Japanese governance was considerably less centralized than Chinese.

Comparisons *within* Japan are also relevant to our question. Coastal regions were naturally more dependent upon foreign trade than inland regions, which were often cut off from direct contact with the outside world. John Whitney Hall (1955: 41) notes that in the sixteenth century, due to the weakness of the Ashikaga shogunate,

Sakai, Hirano, Hakata, and a few other port cities of central Japan won a degree of freedom from feudal control. Sakai in particular, the "Venice of Japan" to the Jesuits of the late sixteenth century, took on the form made familiar by free cities of Europe: a port governed by its chief burghers, protected by walls and moats, and by its own militia.

Wakita (1999: 39) clarifies that the city was not – or at least not continuously – free from outside control. Nonetheless, the city council "was empowered to negotiate ... imposts [on trade] and to apportion them among the city's residents ... [They also] maintained law and order ..., [and] oversaw the conduct of local shrine festivals and religious celebrations." Wakita also notes the appearance of councils in nearby communities in the Osaka region (see also Morris 1981).

Over time, these free cities, which seemed destined to follow a route similar to the Hanseatic League, gave way to the superior military force of the *daimyo* (feudal lords). There were too few of them to form a counterweight to agriculture, and their commercial development was not so great relative to the resources provided by wet rice agriculture and other commodities, which remained the mainstay of Japan's economy.

Under the Tokugawa regime, foreign trade was tightly controlled. After 1633, trade was limited to a few domains (principally, Nagasaki, Tsushima, and Kagoshima) and a few trading partners. Since trade was allowed with China (even without formal relations), Korea, and the Dutch (the dominant European power in the region), it was not as constrained in practice as it was in theory (Hellyer 2009). Still, international trade was limited after the late seventeenth century, and the development of free cities on the European model was prevented.

We do not mean to imply that Japan developed into an autocracy. Summarizing the political institutions of the Tokugawa (aka Edo) period (1603–1868), Ravina (1995: 1000–1) writes:

In the eighteenth century the shogunate, or *bakufu*, exerted direct control over land assessed at over four million koku, roughly 15 percent of Japan. Another 10 percent was entrusted to liege vassals (hatamoto), who staffed the shogunate's administration. The imperial family and various religious orders held roughly one-half million koku. The remaining three-quarters of Japan was ruled by some 250 *daimyo*, whose domains ranged in size from ten thousand koku to over one million. A political map of early modern Japan thus reveals an intricate patchwork of distinct governments, with broad areas of ambiguous and overlapping authority …

This spatial fragmentation of authority was paralleled by a vertical division of political rights. The shogun was effectively the supreme political authority in Japan, but the title referred to a military appointment by the emperor. The *daimyo* were, in theory, invested vassals of the shogun, and their fiefs could be revoked for infractions of shogunal edicts. Within their domains, however, *daimyo* held formidable political power. The *daimyo* maintained independent standing armies, wrote their own legal codes, set and collected their own taxes, controlled and policed their own borders. The shogunate maintained a monopoly on foreign policy, but the domains were entrusted with the management of their own domestic affairs. The authority of the shogunate was, of course, an important part of the Tokugawa system. The *sankin kjtai* system, for example, wherein *daimyo* were required to spend alternate periods of time in Edo, the shogun's capital, served as a constant reminder of the primacy of the Tokugawa house. The shogunate also issued laws regulating the personal conduct of *daimyo* and retained the right to oversee *daimyo* marriages and adoptions. But the authority of the shogunate focused on *daimyo*: it claimed only limited and indirect suzerainty over the commoner population of *daimyo* domains. The shogunate never asserted a right to tax commoners outside its direct holdings.

This system of fragmented power has been likened to European feudalism, where vassals owed formal allegiance to a suzerain who did not – and effectively could not – control them, except to the extent of deterring acts of overt betrayal. Japan featured an elaborate and well-defined social system, with a small ceremonial class of nobles at the top, the shogun and *daimyo* in the next tier (wielding actual political and economic power), followed by the samurai (warriors). Below them were castes of peasants, craftsmen, and merchants. As in Europe, these corporate entities served as a brake on state power.

Mary Elizabeth Berry (1986: 240) comments on the weakness of the national state in the early modern era, which operated without a police force, direct taxes, conscription, a public treasury, judiciary (though a supreme court was established in 1722), an extensive bureaucracy, or office of public works. "Power was concentrated," she admits, "but in the collective body of the *daimyo* who retained control over local taxation and military force." In these respects, Japan was highly decentralized and constitutionally constrained.

Contrasts

In the passages above we have tried to describe political institutions governing the three dominant and long-standing states in East Asia – China, Korea, and Japan – during the premodern era. It will be obvious to all readers that these states have very long histories and that many things changed over the course of several millennia. We have focused on those elements that seem most persistent.

We concluded that China was the most autocratic of the three states during most of the premodern era, a pattern that is even more accentuated at the present time. In Korea, a monarch with hereditary rights to the throne ruled through most of Korean history. However, that monarch was forced to share power with a well-organized aristocratic class, who populated an aristocratic assembly (Hwabaek), whose approval the king required for all major initiatives and who also enjoyed a monopoly over bureaucratic offices. In Japan, there were no formal institutions of powersharing. Nonetheless, the Tokugawa regime was so decentralized that it functioned, de facto, in much the same way. *Daimyo* governed the countryside, with minimal interference from the ritual center of power (Heian, modern-day Kyoto) or the actual center of power (Edo, modern-day Tokyo). This meant that there were severe constraints on what the ruler could do.

This three-part comparison fits neatly with our geographic theory. China was a gigantic land-based empire, with its capital and the major portion of its population and economy located away from the coast and just two major rivers offering navigable access to the coast. Korea is a peninsula, with a wealth of navigable rivers and natural harbors. No portion of its land is very far from the coast – though it is worth pointing out that the mainland portion of Korea (in the North) is today a supreme autocracy while the peninsular portion (in the South) is highly democratic. Japan is an island, and one with a great many natural harbors. Sajima and Tachikawa (2009) regard it as a maritime state. As such, it fits our expectations for democratic rule, and indeed has developed into one of the world's most democratic countries.

One part of this story is perplexing. Given their abundance of natural harbors and extensive coastlines, our theory would suggest that Korea and Japan should have maintained their maritime engagements – military and economic – throughout the early modern era rather than shutting them down, following China's lead (Andrade 2014).

To understand these outcomes, we must step back from the particulars of each state to examine the region as a whole, as the behavior of states is necessarily strategic, and in the early modern era the threats were regional rather than global. In a region with a single hegemon (China), whose status was not in doubt and which had shut down trade except through a few highly controlled entry and exit points, Japan and Korea had little to gain from maintaining open trade with the rest of the world (Clulow 2010: 28). After all, much of the trade undertaken by these two states was with China (Hellyer 2009: 16), so it behooved them to keep their main trading partner happy. Opening trade with Southeast Asia, South Asia, and Europe would have jeopardized trade with their most important market. It might also have invited violent reprisals, forcing these smaller states to seek protection from European powers and thereby sacrificing their autonomy.

Indeed, there was much to be lost by deeper engagement with the west. By this time, the Portuguese were taking over global trade routes, soon to be displaced by the Dutch and then the English. These were threatening forces, militarily and culturally (as they were attached to Christian missionary activity). The way to stop them was to close borders. And this isolationist strategy worked, at least for a while (Reid 1997, 2004). East Asia is one of the few regions of the world to effectively resist European influence, and these three states retained their sovereignty, for the most part, throughout the age of imperialism. Before the west forcibly opened East Asia to the world, it helped to shut down transoceanic contact.

Southeast Asia

Southeast Asia is one of the most oceanic regions of the world, as demonstrated in Table 5.1. If our geographic theory of institutions is correct, democracy should thrive in this aqueous environment. As it happens, the empirical record is mixed. But this mixed status is, we will argue, a product of a central geographic distinction within the region – between inland and oceanic Southeast Asia.[27]

Exactly where the inland region ends and the aquatic region begins is a matter that cannot be determined with any exactitude. Inland regions are connected to a coastal region, and the coastal regions tend to exhibit many of the traits we will associate with island Southeast Asia. For example, one may contrast "upper" Burma, the historic center of Burmese culture, centered on rice agriculture, with "lower" Burma, an aquatic zone depending centrally upon trade across the Bay of Bengal and the Indian Ocean (Gommans, Leider 2002). Similar contrasts could be made with respect to inland and coastal regions of Thailand and Cambodia.

The contrast we wish to draw is clearer, and more accentuated, if we define inland as referring to *continental* Southeast Asia, which may be counterposed to "island" (or archipelago) portions of the subcontinent.

Inland Southeast Asia

Inland Southeast Asia refers to the continental portion of the region, including present-day Burma, Cambodia, Laos, Thailand, and Vietnam. (One might add the Yunnan province of China, though we shall exclude it in deference to traditional usage.) Here, natural harbors are infrequent and large territories have minimal access to the sea.

Granted, several magnificent rivers including the Irrawaddy, Salween, Chao Phraya, and Mekong, extend deep into the interior of the continent. However, these aquatic zones were isolated from each other and thus did not form an interlocking series of rivers. There is generally only one access route to the coast.

Burma is an interesting case insofar as it has plentiful coastline along the Bay of Bengal and thus might be expected to have ample access to the sea. However, the Rakhine coast is separated from the main population center along the Irrawaddy river valley by the Arakan Mountains to the west. Consequently, only the south, where the Irrawaddy discharges, has good ocean access. This is a good example of why distance to the nearest harbor, rather than distance to the coast, forms our variable of theoretical interest.

---

[27] This section benefitted from a close read by Arun Swamy. For further discussion of the inland/island contrast, see Andaya, Andaya (2015), Blussé (2013), Reid (1989).

Accordingly, inland Southeast Asia provided sequestered river valleys that were fairly easy to control and to exploit, as all traffic up and down these central arteries could be taxed from a single location – often, a capital city.

It is not surprising to discover that these river valleys formed the economic and geopolitical backbone of successive empires: Pagan (present-day Burma), Angkor/Khmer (present-day Cambodia), Lan Na (present-day northern Thailand), and Ayudhya/Siam (present-day southern Thailand). Most were reliant on agriculture, and specifically on grains such as rice, which are highly productive and provide an easily extractable resource for statebuilding – though foreign trade was also pursued.

Barbara Andaya (1992: 64–5) stresses the personalistic nature of power in the great inland states of Southeast Asia. Though tied together by family bonds and clientelistic networks, these bonds were fragile and did not lend themselves to as high a degree of centralized control as in China. As an example, Andaya (1992: 65) offers Ayutthaya.

The territory under Ayutthaya's control ... was divided into a number of graduated *muang* or settlements, each under its own governor. The latter might acknowledge the overlordship of Ayutthaya and drink the sanctified water of allegiance to show their loyalty, but as royal relatives and *muang* lords their status could be almost equivalent to that of the ruler. The governor of Kamphaengpet ... was "like a king" inside his own territory. Independence naturally increased with distance from the centre, and although a law of 1468–9 claims that twenty kings paid Ayutthaya homage, its hold sat lightly on distant Malay Muslim tributaries such as Pahang, Kelantan, Terengganu, and Pattani. These areas essentially acted as autonomous states and as long as appropriate gifts were sent regularly to Ayutthaya there was little interference in their affairs.

A wealth of near-synonyms have been proposed to describe the fissiparous nature of Southeast Asian polities including *galactic* (Tambiah 1976), *mandala* (Wolters 1982), *segmentary* (Southall 1988), *solar* (Lieberman 2003), or feudal (ubiquitous). Although decentralized, it is important to remind ourselves that there were no independent parliaments or assemblies, no elections, no written constitutions limiting the power of monarchs, no widely used language of "rights," and no formal institutions for decentralizing power (as in premodern Korea and Japan). In these respects, the inland states of Southeast Asia do not appear very democratic at all, even by the standards of the time.

Island Southeast Asia

Island Southeast Asia includes the Malay peninsula, the Indonesian archipelago (with an estimated 17,000 islands), and the Philippine archipelago (with an estimated 7,000 islands). A glance at Map 4.6 shows that natural harbors are ubiquitous throughout these aqueous regions. Only the large islands – Sumatra, Borneo, and New Guinea – have significant portions of territory located at a distance from the coast, and most of the inland territory is diffusely populated. With the partial exception of Java, which is densely populated and where capital cities have sometimes been stationed away from the coast, population centers in "island" Southeast Asia tend to lie near the coast, either directly on the water or at a short remove along a navigable river. This pattern of settlement describes Aceh, Banda, Banjarmasin, Banten, Brunei, Demak, Grisek/Surabaya, Johor, Makassar, Manila, Melaka, Palembang, Pasai, Patani, Srivijaya, Ternate, and many other city-states or "harbor-cities," as they are sometimes called (Manguin 1991; Reid 1989: 55).

It is a platitude to say that the culture and society of island Southeast Asia is entangled with the sea (Boomgaard 2007; Emmerson 1980). Examining the ancient history of the region, Pierre-Yves Manguin (1986) finds that boats are the dominant metaphor by which organized social units are represented.

Likewise, the economy of Southeast Asia is intimately connected to its ocean setting. Located in between major civilizations – with India and Europe to the west and China to the east – long-distance trade was almost unavoidable. Over time, as maritime activity expanded, Andre Wink (2002: 436–7) describes "a decisive shift of power toward trade-based coastal centers, and an increase in urbanization on the maritime frontier" of the Indian Ocean during the early modern era. These cities "were open in physical and economic terms, while pluralistic in political terms ... [and] characterized by a high degree of unregulated and even lawless competition."

Another consequence of island geography is that polities in Southeast Asian archipelagos tended to be small and decentralized (prior to the twentieth century). Andaya (1992: 95) notes, "a kingdom made up of a scattering of islands is far less amenable to central control than is the floodplain of a large river basin such as the Irrawaddy or the Menam." Prior to the colonial era, island Southeast Asia was populated primarily by city-states (Reid 2000).

Monarchies were common in these small polities, especially after the conversion of the region to Islam. Villiers (1990a: 95) notes that "Islamic concepts of monarchy gave to those rulers who were converted to Islam a means of legitimizing their position and thereby of enhancing their claim to hereditary, absolute rule."

There is no hint of democracy in Srivijaya, the leading maritime kingdom during the medieval era (Nik Hassan Shuhaimi 1990). However, we don't know much about this polity; some even question its existence (Kelley 2020). For those who believe it existed, Srivijaya was different from inland empires. Kulke (2016: 49) describes "a powerful confederation of autonomous harbour cities with shifting centres" – an "amorphous polity" (80). He characterizes the power of early rulers as "precarious" even at the center of the polity (54). "In contrast to agrarian based polities," Kulke (2016: 80) points out that "state power was not based on territorial control only, but on the formation and control of strong riverine networks. The inland people were not subjects of Śrīvijaya. They were engaged in a mutual contract relationship, renewed on a regular basis by ritual gift exchange and by ceremonial oath taking." Kulke (2016: 81) credits this quality for Srivijaya endurance, which outlasted most inland empires. "Its polycentric nature enabled it to maintain beyond its core area peculiar, often inconsistent relations of dominance and dependency with such important autonomous port cities and polities like Malayu-Jambi and Kedah."

Everywhere in island Southeast Asia, rulers were compelled to maintain a tolerant and welcoming attitude toward foreigners and foreign trade. In 1615, the Sultan of Makassar declared his own version of the principle of *mare liberum*:

God made the land and the sea; the land He divided among men and the sea He gave in common. It is unheard of that anyone should be forbidden to sail the seas. If you seek to do that, you will take the bread from the mouths of my people. (Quoted in Villiers 1990b: 154)

Accordingly, Villiers (1990b: 154) reports that "any foreigner who wished was permitted to settle freely, to practice his own religion and to trade without any restriction beyond the payment of light dues and the giving of presents to the rulers."

Rulers also had to contend with rich and well-organized merchants, ready to withhold funds or decamp for another port if their interests were not respected. Anthony Reid (2000: 422) describes the situation as follows:

Almost every *negeri* [polity] had an hereditary ruler (*raja*). The most influential Melaka-derived Malay texts make much of the loyalty of the Malay to the *raja*, even in a situation of profound provocation ... Nevertheless, this emphasis on loyalty should be read as a novel attempt to build up the institution of monarchy where it had shallow and fragile roots and was constantly under threat ... The Malay *negeri* which arose there were essentially built by merchants, and their monarchs rule either in a conciliar fashion which incorporated a diversity of interests, or they ruled rather briefly.

On many occasions, a queen was chosen to symbolize sovereignty. This is widely viewed by historians as a device to maintain power among the *orangkaya* [merchant] oligarchy. Queens were "the best guarantee against arbitrary tyranny and vainglorious warfare" (Reid 2000: 423). Reid lists an extraordinary number of instances in which women occupied thrones in city-states across the archipelago: Pasai, Sumatra (1405–34), Majapahit, Java (1427–47), Palembang, Sumatra (1430–40), Ternate, North Maluku (1521–35), Japara, Java (1550–75), Patani, North Maluku (1584–1700), Banten, Java (1600–5), Sukadana, Borneo (1608–22), Jambi, Sumatra (1630–55), Kelantan, Malaya (1610–71), Aceh, Sumatra (1641–99), and Solor, Lesser Sundas (1650–70). He also points out that "periods of female rule coincided with cosmopolitan trade-friendly regimes," lending credence to the idea that security of property was associated with female rule (Reid 2000: 423).

A few polities went further, governing themselves without the services of any hereditary ruler at the helm. Of these, one has attracted considerable attention among historians. The Banda Islands, located between Timor and New Guinea, were the principal source of nutmeg and mace in the early modern era. With a virtual monopoly over production of these valued commodities, they held an enviable position in international markets. A thriving trade resulted, which empowered the merchant class.

Trade was centered on the island of Banda, which possessed four harbors (Villiers 1981: 737–8). (The other islands offered poor harborage and thus transported their spices to Banda by small boats for shipment abroad.) Lape (2000: 40) comments on the ongoing significance of harborage, "one of the factors that have made the town of Naira, with its harbor protected year round, the largest settlement in the Bandas today and its center of trade and government."

From trade came wealth, and from wealth came a distribution of power that sounds familiar to those versed in early modern European history. Villiers (1981: 729) relates:

authority in the Banda Islands seems to have derived from wealth (hence the term orang kaya – rich man), which in turn was partly determined by the number of people whom an orang kaya had at his command to cultivate the communal land on his behalf. As commercial activity increased in the Banda Islands and the price of nutmeg and mace rose in overseas markets, so the orang kaya developed into a kind of mercantile aristocracy collectively controlling a group of very small but prosperous coastal communities.

Historians agree that Banda had no hereditary ruler, or that this ruler – if he existed – was accountable to the *orangkaya*. Although existing sources do not describe the institutions of rule in any detail, Clulow

(2016: 27) surmises, "Lacking a single ruler or any sort of overarching state structures, the Banda Islands were administered by a loose confederation of elders," the *orangkaya*. Villiers (1990a: 95) states that the *orangkaya* were "dependent upon election by their peers."

The reason we know so little about Banda is that the entire society was wiped out – exterminated – by the Dutch in what was perhaps the worst atrocity of colonial rule in the Dutch Indies. In any case, Villiers (1981: 728–9) is pretty sure that their system of rule was not so different from that found elsewhere in island Southeast Asia.

All sixteenth-century sources agree that the Bandanese had no king but were ruled by an oligarchy of elders or orang kaya. Castanheda says each village had a governor (regedor) whom the inhabitants called Shahbandar (Xabandar) but whom, however, they only obeyed out of friendship or respect. This system of government by oligarchies of petty chiefs seems to have been very much like that prevailing in the Philippines at the time the Spanish first arrived there. The Filipino units of settlement or barangays were ruled over by a council of elders headed by a datu or raha. A similar political system obtained on Ambon and also in the Moluccas before the creation of the four sultanates of Ternate, Tidore, Bacan and Gilolo (Halmahera) as a result of Moslem influence and the introduction of Moslem ideas of monarchy. In the Historia das Molucas, written about 1544, we are told that formerly "each place had its own lordship, territory and boundaries (senhdrio, camarqua e demarquafao) in which the people lived in common, each of his own free will and governed themselves by the votes of the elders". The Suma Oriental says that in Motir, which at the time Pires wrote had not yet been subjected to any Islamic influences, "each part supports its own lord". In 1534, Tristao de Ataide wrote that neither Motir, which was, at least in theory, under the joint control of the sultans of Ternate and Tidore, nor Makian had a king but both were ruled by governadores. Makian possessed seven or eight chiefs and 400 warriors and Motir ten or twelve chiefs and 200 warriors.

Following Villiers, we regard Banda as typical of politics in island Southeast Asia. If this picture is correct, or substantially so, then this region qualifies as one of the few areas of the world where statelike organizations persisted without the continuity and coherence provided by hereditary rule.

South Asia

We shall define South Asia in an inclusive fashion, including the present-day states of Bangladesh, Bhutan, India, Maldives, Nepal, Pakistan, and Sri Lanka. So defined, the region registers a natural harbor distance score that is slightly below the global average, but a marked contrast to aqueous

Southeast Asia. As in Southeast Asia, we find many contrasts between regions, which we designate broadly as inland or coastal.[28]

Inland South Asia

Inland South Asia is traversed by rivers. This is especially so in the north, where the Ganges, Indus, and Brahmaputra river systems connect territories to the Arabian Sea in the west and the Indian Ocean in the east. These river systems gave birth to the Indus or Harappa civilization (3000–1500 BCE) and somewhat later to a variety of republics with democratic characteristics (JP Sharma 1968). However, these small polities do not seem to have survived into the early modern era. Leaving aside the diffusely settled mountains, deserts, and forests – where small polities survived – political power across the Indo-Gangetic plain became the preserve of much larger, and considerably less democratic, states. This includes (in rough chronological order) the Magadha Empire, the Maurya Empire, Imperial Kannauj, the Delhi Sultanate, and the Mughal Empire. Along the Deccan plateau this includes the Tondaiman, Satavahana, Vakataka, Kadamba, Chalukya, Rashtrakuta, Western Chalukya, and Maratha empires.

All of these imperial constellations may be classified geographically as "inland" insofar as their population centers, including most of the capital cities, were located at some remove from the coast. Although rivers served as a principal means of transport these societies were not heavily engaged in foreign trade, and economic resources and tax bases were primarily agricultural. Inland states in South Asia did not shut out the world, on the model of East Asian states in the early modern era, but neither did they extend outward. Traders exercised little power and held positions of low social status, while cities enjoyed little independence (Wink 2002: 431–2), and foreigners from the distant abroad were rarely encountered (except in case of invasion). The riverine basis of mobility and trade, and the limited access points available to the coasts, meant that large states had no trouble controlling ingress and egress. Inland trade was state-controlled (Subrahmanyam 1990: 89–90).

In these respects, the experience of inland South Asia fits our theoretical model of autocratic rule. Helmut Scharfe (1989: 26) confirms,

Until very recent times monarchy was almost the exclusive form of government in India, though the form and content of monarchical rule varied greatly over the times. From the point of view of the royal family, the kingdom was family

---

[28] This section benefitted from a close reading by Arun Swamy.

property of which the king served as manager. The rule passed on principally through the male line of descent in most dynasties [in the North].

Granted, elements of democracy probably survived at the village (*panchayat*) level, where some leaders seem to have been elected and in any case tended to be highly accountable (at least to the dominant caste), from what we can tell. However, local governance had little impact on imperial government.

Coastal South Asia

Coastal South Asia refers, first of all, to "peninsular" India. This includes present-day Kerala, home to the historic Chera/Cera kingdom and various statelets; Karnataka, home to the historic Vijaynagara kingdom; and Tamil Nadu/Andhra Pradesh, home to the historic Cola/Chola/Choda and Pallavas kingdoms. In addition, we include the coastal region of Gujarat, which boasts its own peninsula and multiple harbors, including the historic port of Surat. Bengal, on the eastern edge of South Asia, is another area with plentiful access to the ocean.

All of these regions had well-developed trading relationships extending back to antiquity or the early modern era. However, the role of harbors and inland rivers in this trade differed by region.

In peninsular India, rivers are not easily navigable which meant that trade was coastal rather than inland (Subrahmanyam 1990). Although the area is not blessed with many natural harbors (Subrahmanyam 1990: 12–14), ships in the early modern era docked on beaches or in seaports at the mouths of rivers. Wink (2002: 416–17) reports, "there was an almost infinite number of minuscule anchoring points and maritime establishments on India's peninsular coasts, either on the seaboard itself or in small bays and inlets, at the mouths of rivers and in lagunas" (see also Arasaratnam 1986; Seshan 2012). As in Bengal, maritime options were plentiful and no central node was able to maintain a stranglehold on trade.

Gujarat is well endowed with natural harbors, and partly as a consequence has an ancient history of local and long-distance trade (Pearson 1976).

In Bengal, rivers are ubiquitous and generally navigable. Accordingly, inland transport was well developed from an early date (Mukherjee 2010). Because there were multiple outlets to the shore and multiple riverine networks no single juncture held a chokehold on trade. "Below the pulsating quartet of Dhada, Musharidabad, Calcutta and Patna, lay a string of towns dispersed all over the region," notes Mukherjee (2010: 33).

Ports could be constructed anywhere, though they would have to follow the changing course of the river system.

States across coastal South Asia tended to be smaller and less centralized than states in inland regions. Yazdani (2017: 527) describes the Gujarati state in the eighteenth and nineteenth centuries (as the Mughal Empire declined) as "complex and poly-centric." "Power was divided between the nobles, merchants (especially Banias, Muslims and, Marathas), British, Portuguese, local potentates, landlords and piratical petty chiefs."

The present-day state of Kerala, located further south on the eastern seaboard near the tip of the Indian peninsula, also offers a history of decentralized rule and diffuse power. In the medieval era (800–1124), local councils enjoyed considerable autonomy but were probably controlled by a Brahmin elite – "caste councils," according to Narayanan (1996: 73), who describes the state as an oligarchy, on the model of feudal Europe. There were four great temples in the capital, each of which was the seat of a representative from the chief settlements in the countryside (Narayanan 1996: 77). These temples also provided representatives to the king's council (Narayanan 1996: 85). In this fashion, the Brahmins seem to have been able to constrain the king and to rule in a collective fashion across the small state. Narayanan (1996: 73) concludes,

In appearance, [the king, or Perumal] resembled any other regular hereditary monarch but in effect he was largely influenced if not controlled by an oligarchy of Aryan Brahmin settlers who commanded the agricultural wealth and dominated the realm of religion and culture.

The distinct social groups (*jati*) that defined so much of Indian life also provided the basis for self-rule. Accordingly, caste councils were common at local levels throughout southern India, providing a degree of democracy that presumably constrained rulers at the top.[29]

The much-studied Cola/Chola state had a well-developed and intricate system of elections at local levels (Chandra 2007: 29–32; Hall 1980: 5–20). Mookerji (1919: 154) explains,

The village was divided for purposes of the selection into thirty wards or electoral units. There was a meeting of each ward at which the residents were to assemble, and each of them was required to write down on a ticket the name of the person he voted for after consideration of his eligibility for membership of the committee as defined by the regulations framed by the assembly. The tickets were then to be arranged in separate packets corresponding to the thirty wards. Each packet bore

[29] Arun Swamy (personal communication, 2021).

the name of the ward it represented on its "covering ticket". The packets were put into a pot. Then the pot was placed before "a full meeting of the great assembly, including the young and old (members), as also all the temple priests who happened to be in the village on the day 'without any exception whatever' in the inner hall (where) the great assembly (meets). In the midst of the temple priests, one of them who happens to be the eldest shall stand up and lift that pot, looking upwards so as to be seen by all people." One of the young boys who did not know what was inside was then called to pick out one of the packets. The tickets in this packet were then "transferred to another (empty) pot and shaken", i.e. shuffled thoroughly. The boy then drew one ticket out of the pot and made it over to the arbitrator (madhyastha). "While taking charge of the ticket thus given (to him), the arbitrator shall receive it on the palm of his hand with the five fingers open. He shall read out (the name on) the ticket thus received. The ticket read (by him) shall also be read out by all the priests present in the inner hall. The name thus read out shall be put down (and accepted)." Thirty names were thus to be chosen, representing each of the wards.

The system thus combined elements of election by choice and by lot. Apparently, suffrage was wide, though there were restrictions on who could serve, and supervision by Brahmin priests suggests that they had considerable influence over the process. Even so, one would be hard pressed to find an example of elections that were as democratic as these anywhere in the ancient or medieval world, with the possible exception of Greece.

Of course, our theoretical concern is primarily with state-level governance rather than local governance. To that point, Hall (1980: 19–20) notes the existence of higher-level bodies within the Chola dynasty that seem to offer political representation.

At the regional level were the *nadu* and *cittirameli-periyanadu* assemblies, while the *nagaram*, merchant assemblies located in market towns, interacted with all four. Contemporary epigraphy records the multi-functioning character of these institutions. Each collected taxes from local inhabitants, exercised varying degrees of land control, and assumed certain judicial powers, all functions which contributed to the appearance of local autonomy.

The literature on southern India in the medieval era is immense and difficult to summarize. Burton Stein (1980, 1989) views the Cola/Chola/Choda and Vijayanagara kingdoms as considerably less centralized than the typical northern kingdoms. In the south, the king is thought to have played a largely symbolic role, leaving smaller states in a tributary role, free to govern themselves with respect to domestic affairs. In some instances, such as those reviewed above, this has led to considerable diffusion of power in a direction that must be viewed as more democratic. Others disagree (for a recent review see Sinopoli 2003: 85–8), so we cannot say that this contrast is entirely clear-cut. Nonetheless, the inland/coastal contrast is a common motif among works of South Asian history and politics.

What seems clear is that the coastal regions of South Asia fostered a great variety of medium to small states with decentralized structures of power. Subrahmanyam (1986: 359) writes: "[North India appears to have] all the characteristics of a glittering patrimonial-bureaucratic empire while, once south of the Godavari, state forms become segmentary, diffuse and decentralized." This follows from the coastal environment, its many ports (albeit some of them makeshift), and thriving trade relationships – some of it local and some extending into Arabia, the Mediterranean, and Southeast Asia. Although we cannot say very much about the power of traders and merchants, it seems obvious that they wielded more power than they did in the inland empires, and that they were given some autonomy to run their businesses (often through ethnic or religiously based networks). They were also extraordinarily diverse, with populations of Jews, Christians, Muslims, and Hindus and a wide variety of ethnicities. In these respects, coastal South Asia follows the pattern of ocean-exposed areas in other parts of the world. Indeed, a sizeable literature treats the Indian Ocean – from Gujarat to Aceh – as part of a coherent cultural zone, interlocked by trade.[30]

Although our primary interest is in political institutions, we cannot ignore the social institutions that presumably undergird and reinforce the political order. The salient feature of South Asia is its caste system, which Wink (2020: 49) traces back to the medieval era (but not as far back as the classical era). The caste system was predominant in inland, agricultural areas – "settled" societies (Wink 2020: 51). By contrast, "the seaboard always remained beyond the pale of the Hindu caste system" (Wink 2020: 50). Here, as elsewhere, ports were regarded as areas subject to mixing and corruption. As a result, "women of both the Nayar and sacerdotal Brahman castes were expressly prohibited from entering the seaports for fear of ritual pollution" (Wink 2020: 50). South Asia thus confirms a pattern found elsewhere in the world, where aquatic regions seem to foster greater diversity and a more egalitarian culture.

---

[30] See Alpers (2014), Andrade, Hang, Yang, Matteson (2016), Arasaratnam (1994), Begley, De Puma (1991), Boomgaard (2007), Bose (2006), Bowen, McAleer, Blyth (2011), Broeze (1996), Bruijn, Gaastra (1993), Chaudhuri (1978, 1985, 1991), Das Gupta (1994, 2004), Das Gupta, Pearson (1987), Deng (1997, 1999), Emmerson (1980), Hall (1985, 2011), Hourani (1975), Lombard, Aubin (2000), Manguin (1991, 2004), Margariti (2008), McPherson (1993), Meilink-Roelofsz (1962), Mukherjee, Subramanian (1998), O'Connor, Veth (2000), Panikkar (1945), Pearson (2003, 2005), Ptak, Rothermund (1991), Ray (1999), Reade (1996), Reid (1980, 1993a, 1993b, 1997), Schottenhammer (2005, 2008), Shaffer (1995), Steensgaard (1975), Sutherland (2003, 2007), Villiers (1952), Wink (2002), Wolters (1967).

Contrasts

Despite the many contrasts between inland and coastal South Asia one must bear in mind that the latter was subordinate to the former in most historical periods. By comparison with Europe and Southeast Asia, South Asia is a region where the land dominates the sea. Accordingly, long-distance trade never displaced agriculture to the extent that it did in some parts of Europe and Southeast Asia, and in this light it is not surprising that merchants never enjoyed the political and social prominence they did in those regions. Nor is it surprising to find ritualistic prohibitions against seafaring in the region's dominant religion. Wink (2020: 66) reports,

medieval Hindu law ... imposed severe restrictions ... on sea travel, even prohibiting it for certain high castes, and warned against the interaction with overseas *mlecchas* and the ritual neglect and defilement that such interaction inevitably entailed. These restrictions were taken seriously by many high-caste Hindus, especially Brahmans, and from early medieval times onward, deeply entrenched maritime taboos and thalassophobia are in evidence.

What India did not possess is an empire sufficiently strong and centralized to prohibit foreign travel, as the Ming Empire did in China. Its extensive coastline would have made such a prohibition difficult to enforce, in any case.

Conclusions

In this chapter we have examined the histories of specific regions for clues into the relationship between natural harbors and democracy. Some of the comparisons are cross-regional. Here, the most oceanic regions – Europe and Southeast Asia – are compared with other regions whose exposure to the ocean is less intense.

Yet, it is difficult to reach firm conclusions based on comparisons across subcontinents, as the available cases are few and myriad potential confounders loom. Hence, most of our energy was expended on finer, within-region contrasts – between areas more and less exposed to the ocean, summarized in Table 5.1.

Our discussion encompasses a very long time frame extending back into the premodern era. As there is no systematic measure of institutional differences prior to the modern era we draw on an extensive library of secondary work (produced mostly by historians along with a few historically minded social scientists).

The strength of this secondary literature is its detailed description of particular polities and eras. However, this tight focus makes it difficult to piece together a comprehensive picture of regimes around the world. Studies usually aim to elucidate distinctions through time and space: how period A differs from period B, or region A from region B. Vocabulary is honed for contrast, not comparison.

There is also a problem of sample selection. We have not dealt with all regions of the world (for reasons explained at the outset) or all statelike polities within those regions. Our intention was to generate sensible most-similar comparisons. But it is possible that in selecting good comparison cases we unintentionally ignored polities that do not exhibit the theorized relationship. Case studies are prone to problems of generalizability (Gerring 2017).

Finally, there is a problem of evidence. We have relied on a secondary literature that is vast and ill-defined. Our canvas of this literature may have missed some important facts or historiographic debates, and our presentation of the evidence has been, perforce, schematic. We expect specialists to quarrel with some of the conclusions we have drawn.

Nonetheless, by focusing on polities within the same region or neighboring regions we hope to have sharpened comparisons so that there are fewer potential confounders to worry about. Likewise, we have had occasion to identify some of the mechanisms that may be at work in connecting geography to institutions, elaborating on points laid out in a cursory fashion in Chapter 3.

In the next chapter we switch gears, adopting a global and statistical approach to hypothesis-testing, one that incorporates an extremely large sample of polities (practically a census) – but one that, due to data limitations, focuses primarily on the modern era.

6   Global Analyses

> The ocean is a wilderness reaching round the globe, wilder than a
> Belgian jungle, and fuller of monsters, washing the very wharves of
> our cities and the gardens of our sea-side residences. Serpents, bears,
> hyenas, tigers rapidly vanish as civilization advances, but the most
> populous and civilized city cannot scare a shark far from its
> wharves.   Henry David Thoreau, *Cape Cod* (1906: 188)

Having explored the relationship of ocean access to political institutions
within specific regions, stretching back through the premodern era, we
turn now to empirical tests that encompass the world, focusing mostly on
the modern era.

Readers should bear in mind that establishing causality for distal
causes and outcomes measurable only at a highly aggregated level is a
complicated business. General methodological issues were discussed
briefly in Chapter 1. Issues pertaining to the conceptualization and
measurement of democracy were discussed in Chapter 2. The measurement of our key independent variable, as well as the aggravating unit-of-
analysis problem, were discussed in Chapter 4.

Recall that "natural harbor distance" refers to the distance of each
grid-cell to the nearest port-suitable location, as determined by the shape
of the coastline. Scores for grid-cells are aggregated to provide scores for
polities, taking the mean value of all grid-cells that fall within the boundaries of a polity at a particular point in time. Unless otherwise indicated,
units of analysis in the following tests are polities rather than grid-cells.

We begin the chapter with a test focused on the early modern era,
where democracy is measured with data from the Ethnographic Atlas.
Next, we turn to the modern era, where measures are abundant and offer
much better coverage across sovereign and semisovereign units. Our
general strategy will be to test as many assumptions about the data-
generating process as possible. In this spirit, subsequent sections offer
(a) tests using grid-cells as units of analysis, (b) varying model specifications, (c) varying measures of harbors and harbor distance, (d) varying
measures of democracy, and (e) varying samples. A final section

examines the predicted impact of harbors on democracy and how that impact may have varied over time.

The Early Modern Era

The Ethnographic Atlas, introduced in Chapter 2, allows for a proxy measure of democracy based on the mechanism of selection for the headman of an ethnic group. If chosen by election or formal consensus (non-hereditary), or by informal consensus (non-hereditary), this is regarded as a signal of a more democratic polity.

While previous studies have attempted to show that these facets of premodern polities are related to modern democracy (Bentzen, Hariri, Robinson 2019; Giuliano, Nunn 2013), our goal will be to see whether natural harbors help to explain patterns of democracy in the early modern era. Unlike previous studies, local democracy is on the left side of our causal model.

Regrettably, the Atlas is focused primarily on non-state entities – bands, tribes, and small chiefdoms – which lie outside the ambit of our theory, as discussed in Chapter 1. Helpfully, the Jurisdictional Hierarchy variable (v33) from the Atlas distinguishes various levels of political organization, classified within a six-part index (0–5), as explained in Chapter 2.

Table 6.1 tests different thresholds, allowing us to gauge the degree to which stateness serves as a scope-condition for our theory. Model 1 is unrestricted (all levels), Model 2 focuses on Jurisdictional Hierarchy levels 2–5, Model 3 on levels 3–5, and the remaining models on levels 4–5. The most restrictive sample (levels 4–5) is viewed as the benchmark as it is most consistent with the scope-conditions of our theory. Even so, this variable omits many larger states and empires that existed in the premodern era so it is by no means a comprehensive test of statelike polities. In Model 5, we add a vector of regional dummies. In Model 6, we include other geographic factors that might plausibly impact political institutions.

Natural harbor distance bears a negative relationship to local democracy in all these tests, corroborating our theory. The estimated effect increases as the sample is restricted to statelike entities, which conforms more closely to the scope-conditions of our theory but also truncates the sample. Although the relationship is not always statistically significant (at standard thresholds), these analyses suggest that proximity to natural harbors may have had some impact on political institutions in the early modern era. Stronger tests will have to await stronger evidence, i.e., more sensitive measures of democracy that offer better coverage of states in the premodern era.

Table 6.1 *Democracy prior to the modern era*

Jurisdictional hierarchy	0–5	2–5	3–5	4–5	4–5	4–5
	1	2	3	4	5	6
Natural harbor distance	−0.0069***	−0.0100***	−0.0152***	−0.0271***	−0.0138	−0.0249**
	(−2.677)	(−2.847)	(−2.707)	(−2.877)	(−1.469)	(−1.997)
Region dummies						✓
Geographic covariates					✓	✓
States (contemporary)	129	114	94	66	65	64
Years	1	1	1	1	1	1
Obs (ethnic groups)	1014	503	240	102	100	99
R^2	0.00703	0.0159	0.0299	0.0764	0.240	0.222

Outcome: Democratic selection of headman as coded by the Ethnographic Atlas (Murdock 1967). *Spatial units:* ethnic groups. Jurisdictional hierarchy: 0 = missing data, 1 = no political authority beyond the local community (e.g., petty chiefdoms), 2 = one level above the local community (e.g., larger chiefdoms), 3 = two levels above the local community (e.g., states), 4 = three levels above the local community (e.g., states), 5 = four levels above the local community (e.g., large states). *Geographic covariates:* Crop, Pasture, Forest, Grass, Shrub, Savanna, Barren, Water, Mountains, Temperature, Irrigation potential, River distance, Ocean distance. *Not shown:* Constant. *Estimator:* ordinary least squares, t statistics in parentheses. *p<.10 **p<.05 ***p<.01

Grid-cell Tests

Having looked briefly at the relationship of harbors to democracy in the early modern era, we turn to the modern era. This is the centerpiece of our theory, which rests on the development of shipping technology, a process that occurred slowly over many centuries and did not achieve full force until the advent of steamships in the mid-nineteenth century. Accordingly, the remainder of the chapter focuses on the period beginning in 1789, for which we use our benchmark measure of democracy, the Polyarchy index (introduced in Chapter 2).

We begin with a series of tests focused on PRIO grid-cells (50 × 50 km) as spatial units, shown in Table 6.2. Model 1, the benchmark, regresses democracy against natural harbor distance with no additional covariates aside from annual dummies. Model 2 is limited to a single cross-section centered on the year 2000.

Tests that follow introduce a variety of geographic factors that might serve as confounders. This includes geographic factors that could have a direct impact on democracy as well as those whose effects are likely to be indirect, via economic development (for further discussion see Chapter 12).

Model 3 includes distance from the equator, transformed by the natural logarithm. Model 4 includes precipitation, measured as average annual rainfall and its quadratic (as suggested by Elis, Haber, Horrillo 2017). Model 5 includes an index measuring the distance of each grid-cell from the nearest navigable river. Model 6 includes a measure of irrigation potential. Model 7 includes a measure of mean temperature. Model 8 includes a vector of agricultural zones measuring the portion of a state that is classified as boreal, temperate desert, tropical and sub-tropical desert, dry temperature, polar, subtropics, tropics, water, or wet temperature. The final model combines all of the foregoing variables in a single specification.

Estimates for harbor distance are remarkably consistent across these analyses and are highly significant. (t statistics range from ~87 to ~116, which is to be expected given the gargantuan sample.)

Varying Grid-cells

Evidently, 50 × 50 km grid-cells cannot be regarded as entirely independent of each other; there is bound to be considerable spatial endogeneity (a violation of SUTVA). There may also be an areal-root problem. Both issues are discussed at length in Chapter 4.

Table 6.2 Specification tests (grid-cells)

Time period	All	2000	All	All	All	All	All	All	All
	1	2	3	4	5	6	7	8	9
Natural harbor distance	-1.450***	-2.022***	-1.418***	-1.482***	-1.456***	-1.488***	-1.487***	-1.512***	-1.309***
	(-104.349)	(-101.553)	(-103.151)	(-110.519)	(-104.296)	(-116.970)	(-115.081)	(-110.556)	(-86.665)
Covariate(s)			Equator distance	Precipit-ation^2	River distance	Irrigation potential	Temp-erature	Agricultural zones	All previous
States	196	186	196	196	196	196	184	173	173
Grid-cells	65 026	64 842	65 026	64 612	65 026	64 669	62 410	59 949	59 783
Years	228	1	228	228	228	228	228	228	228
Observations	10 710 181	64 842	10 710 181	10 648 118	10 710 181	10 657 788	10 399 277	10 056 647	10 032 772
R^2	0.331	0.116	0.337	0.336	0.332	0.334	0.333	0.355	0.380

Outcome: Polyarchy index of electoral democracy, augmented. Spatial units: PRIO grid-cells. Agricultural zones: share classified as crop, pasture, forest, grass, shrub, savanna, barren, water, or mountains. Not shown: Year dummies, Constant. Estimator: ordinary least squares, standard errors clustered by grid-cell, t statistics in parentheses. *p<.10 **p<.05 ***p<.01

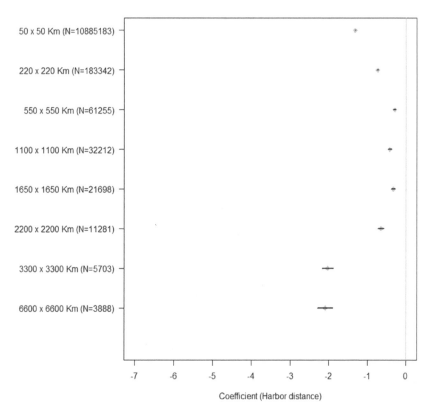

Figure 6.1 **Varying grid-cells**
Outcome: Polyarchy index of electoral democracy, augmented.
Displayed: coefficients for natural harbor distance, surrounded by 95%
confidence intervals, from the benchmark model (Model 1, Table 6.2)
when re-estimated across grid-cells of different sizes. Grid-cell sizes
(in kilometers) and total number of grid-cells (*N*) in each analysis are
shown on the *Y* axis. *Sample period:* 1789–2019.

In Figure 6.1, we probe possible spillover and areal-root effects by
varying the size of grid-cells. Specifically, we create eight sets of grid-cells
corresponding to different sizes. For each unit of analysis, the benchmark
model (Model 1, Table 6.2) is re-estimated. Figure 6.1 plots the coefficients, surrounded by confidence intervals, for natural harbor distance,
with the size of the cells and the number of observations listed on the
Y-axis. The larger the cells, the fewer the observations, meaning that the

precision of the resulting estimates is likely to attenuate (reflected in larger confidence intervals).

This exercise demonstrates that our results are robust in the face of potential areal-root problems. There is some variation in effect size across the analyses, with the largest cells generating the largest effect sizes. This may be interpreted as a signal that spillover problems attenuate with the size of the chosen units, as one would expect. Tiny grid-cells located next to one another are likely to share many background characteristics and influence each other's political institutions. As such, the impact of the treatment of theoretical interest – natural harbor distance – is blunted. As grid-cells become larger, and hence further apart, they exhibit greater independence, allowing for a more accurate estimate of the full impact of natural harbors on regimes. If this reasoning is correct, one should have greater confidence in the bottom estimates than the top estimates in Figure 6.1. However, the relationship between grid-cell size and effect size is not monotonic so these patterns are hard to interpret, and may be stochastic.

The main takeaway is that the negative effect of natural harbor distance on democracy persists even when dramatic changes in the size of units under observation are introduced. This suggests that our results do not reflect arbitrary choices in spatial units.

Specification Tests

The remainder of this chapter focuses on states rather than grid-cells as units of analysis. A state might be semisovereign (e.g., a colony or dependency) or fully sovereign (e.g., a country or empire). As it happens, most of our data is of the latter type so readers may sub-vocalize "countries" as they interpret the following regressions. (In Table 6.6 we test sovereign and semisovereign states side by side.)

Tests in Table 6.3 mirror those in Table 6.2 but contain a larger set of covariates for the simple reason that more data is available and relevant at state levels than at grid-cell levels.

In Model 1, the benchmark, the Polyarchy index is regressed against natural harbor distance and annual dummies. Remarkably, this estimate is extremely close to that obtained from our previous analyses, where grid-cells served as units of analysis (see Model 1, Table 6.2). This offers reassurance that our findings are not the product of a particular set of boundaries imposed by modern states. Consider that Russia provides roughly one-third of the data points in our grid-cell analysis while it is only one state out of 180 or so in our state-level analysis. Apparently, it matters little which way one slices the cake as the estimated impact of natural harbor distance on democracy is virtually identical.

Table 6.3 Specification tests

	1	2	3	4	5	6	7	8	9	10	11
Natural harbor distance	-1.275*** (-5.198)	-1.859*** (-5.869)	-1.244*** (-4.441)	-1.026*** (-3.530)	-1.281*** (-5.278)	-1.701*** (-3.261)	-1.304*** (-4.161)	-1.282*** (-4.712)	-0.970*** (-3.637)	-1.514*** (-5.397)	-1.184*** (-5.424)
Covariate(s)		Area	Precipit-ation^2	Irrigation potential	River distance	Ocean distance	Landlocked	Island	Fish	Oil resources	Equator distance
States	196	190	196	178	196	196	196	188	188	196	196
Years	231	231	231	231	231	231	231	231	231	231	231
Observations	32324	31711	32322	29934	32322	32322	32322	31411	31602	32324	32324
R^2	0.395	0.416	0.403	0.405	0.395	0.396	0.395	0.395	0.445	0.404	0.487

	12	13	14	15	16	17	18	19	20	21	22
Natural harbor distance	-1.888*** (-6.136)	-1.558*** (-6.163)	-1.930*** (-7.056)	-1.375*** (-4.490)	-1.334*** (-4.881)	-1.377*** (-4.576)	-1.537*** (-5.658)	-1.516*** (-4.569)	-1.012** (-2.498)	-1.007*** (-3.162)	-0.943*** (-3.987)
Covariate(s)	Tropical	Temp-erature	Frost days	Soil	Desert	Elevation	Rugged-ness	Agric. suitability	All previous	Agric. zones	Regions
States	173	186	146	173	173	173	173	164	142	172	196
Years	231	231	231	231	231	231	231	231	231	221	231
Observations	29013	31088	24168	29013	29013	29013	29013	27335	23543	26399	32322
R^2	0.429	0.486	0.465	0.399	0.405	0.395	0.395	0.382	0.581	0.394	0.518

Outcome: Polyarchy index of electoral democracy, augmented. *Not shown:* Year dummies, Constant. *Estimator:* ordinary least squares, standard errors clustered by state, t statistics in parentheses. *p<.10 **p<.05 ***p<.01

Subsequent tests focus on a wide variety of geographic covariates that are conceptually – and perhaps empirically – related to natural harbors and might also be expected to affect democracy, either directly or indirectly (through their impact on economic development). This includes area (square kilometers, log), precipitation (average annual rainfall and its quadratic), irrigation potential, distance to the nearest navigable river (averaged across grid-cells in a state), distance to the nearest ocean or sea (averaged across grid-cells), landlock (a dummy indicating whether the state has no direct access to the sea), island (a dummy indicating whether a state is separated by water from a major continent), fish stock, resource curse (total income per capita drawn from oil resources, with missing values coded as zero so as to avoid sample truncation), distance from the equator (log), tropical (share of territory that is classified as tropical), temperature (average annual temperature), frost (number of days per annum that the temperature dips below 0 Celsius, averaged across a state), fertile soil (share of territory), desert (share of territory), elevation (average), ruggedness (terrain ruggedness index), agricultural suitability (taking into account a variety of climatic, topographic, and soil-related features). These tests are displayed in Models 2–19.

Model 20 includes all previous variables in a single specification. Model 21 includes a vector of agricultural zones: crop, pasture, forest, grass, shrub, savanna, barren, water, and mountains. Model 22 includes a vector of regions (dummies for each region of the world). Of course, regions have no clear theoretical justification and may be defined in a variety of ways. Nonetheless, insofar as unmeasurable geographic factors are likely to be related by distance, regional dummies may help to identify them.

Results from these tests are encouraging, as natural harbor distance maintains its negative and highly significant relationship to democracy in all specifications. Remarkably, the estimates are also fairly close, suggesting that the relationship is not likely to be sensitive to further specification tests. This can be explained by the fact that most widely recognized geographic factors are not highly correlated with natural harbor distance (see Table 14.2).

One result bears a more extended discussion. Model 6 includes a covariate measuring the distance of a state to the nearest sea or ocean, calculated in the same fashion as the harbor distance variable. One would expect estimates for the latter to attenuate in this model, as the two variables are fairly highly correlated (Pearson's r = 0.77). However, the estimate for natural harbor distance is actually stronger than in the benchmark (Model 1), even though the samples are nearly identical. Additionally, we should note that ocean distance is a very poor predictor of democracy in this model, where it bears the wrong sign (positive, rather than negative) and is nowhere near standard thresholds of statistical significance. Granted, in a bivariate model – including only ocean distance and year dummies on the right side – the former is negatively correlated with democracy, bearing out our general theory about ocean exposure. But the relationship is not nearly as strong, or as robust, as that between natural harbors and democracy. Evidently, having a coastline is not very useful unless easy access is afforded to that turbulent body of water. This is what distinguishes the northern and southern shores of the Mediterranean, and what distinguishes Europe from Africa and the MENA region, as discussed in Chapter 5.

Port/Harbor Distance

The definition and operationalization of the key predictor, natural harbor distance, was discussed at length in Chapter 4. In Table 6.4, this key concept is tested in our benchmark specification with different operationalizations.

Model 1 presents the benchmark index, which uses the contours of the coastline to predict the existence of a port based on all ports listed in the first edition of the *World Port Index* (1953).

Model 2 transforms this variable by the natural logarithm. The model-fit of this specification is not improved over the linear benchmark model and the t statistic is somewhat reduced. Accordingly, there seems to be no empirical justification for adopting a more complex (and more difficult to interpret) functional form.

Model 3 returns to the benchmark index which is now supplemented by a quadratic term to test for non-linearity. There is no evidence of non-monotonicity, as the quadratic term registers a coefficient close to zero.

Model 4 uses the contours of the coastline to predict the existence of a port classified as a *harbor* in the first edition of the WPI, as discussed in Chapter 4.

The next set of tests focus on actual ports that exist today or existed at some point in the past. (There are no prediction models.) This includes all ports in WPI 1953 (Model 5), harbors in WPI 1953 (Model 6), all ports in WPI 2017 (Model 7), and harbors in WPI 2017 (Model 8).

Model 9 is based on all ports listed in Lloyd's (Ducruet et al. 2018), a source that stretches back to 1890 and offers data for states observed at irregular intervals. Missing data within a time series is linearly interpolated to generate annual observations from 1890 to 2008.

The final models in Table 6.4 take a different approach to measurement. Here, the regressor of theoretical interest – actual distance to

Table 6.4 Measures of port/harbor distance

Regressor	Predicted distance to nearest …				Actual distance to nearest …					Instrumented distance to nearest …	
Facility	Port	Port	Port	Harbor	Port	Harbor	Port	Harbor	Port	Port	Port
Year	1953	1953	1953	1953	1953	1953	2017	2017	1890–2009	1953	1953
Source	WPI	WPI	WPI	WPI	WPI	WPI	WPI	WPI	Lloyd's	WPI	WPI
Estimator	OLS	OLS	OLS	OLS	OLS	OLS	OLS	OLS	OLS	2SLS	2SLS
Instrument										Predicted distance	Ocean distance
	1	**2**	**3**	**4**	**5**	**6**	**7**	**8**	**9**	**10**	**11**
Functional form											
Linear	−1.275***		−1.418	−1.292***	−1.618***	−1.652***	−1.588***	−1.676***	−1.752***	−1.566***	−1.000***
	(−5.198)		(−1.599)	(−5.141)	(−6.136)	(−6.141)	(−5.945)	(−5.840)	(−4.227)	(−5.190)	(−2.779)
Logarithmic		−5.544***									
		(−4.027)									
Quadratic			0.012								
			(0.187)								
Year dummies	✓	✓	✓	✓	✓	✓	✓	✓		✓	✓
Year + Year²									✓		
States	196	196	196	196	196	196	196	197	195	196	196
Years	231	231	231	231	231	231	231	231	119	231	231
Observations	32 324	32 324	32 324	32 324	32 324	32 324	32 324	32 537	18 885	32 324	32 322
F-stat. (1st stage)										129.74	77.70
R²	0.395	0.391	0.395	0.395	0.403	0.406	0.402	0.405	0.279	0.383	0.378

Outcome: Polyarchy index of electoral democracy, augmented. *Not shown:* Constant. *Estimator:* OLS (ordinary least squares) or 2SLS (two-stage least squares), standard errors clustered by state, t statistics in parentheses. *p<.10 **p<.05 ***p<.01

nearest port (WPI 1953) – is instrumented by factors assumed to be exogenous. In Model 10, the chosen instrument is distance from a coastline whose geomorphic conditions are conducive to the development of a port, following the prediction model described in Chapter 4. In Model 11, the chosen instrument is distance from the nearest ocean or sea. These two instruments presuppose different assumptions about the data-generating process. In Model 10, we suppose that the nature of the coastline conditions the probability of a port. In Model 11, we suppose that having a coastline (of any sort) conditions the probability of a port. Both instruments provide a good fit for the regressor of theoretical interest, as demonstrated by F-statistics from the first-stage model.

Estimated coefficients for port/harbor distance are very close across all the linear models displayed in Table 6.4. (Since these variables are measured in distance to nearest port or harbor, coefficients are directly comparable.) This is not surprising given that our various measures of port/harbor distance are highly correlated. Pearson's r correlations range from 0.80 to 0.96, and a principal components analysis shows that the first factor explains 90 percent of the variance across the six variables.

It is worth mentioning that alternative measures of harbor and port distance are generally stronger than the benchmark (Model 1). But the important takeaway is that regardless of how we measure this concept, distance from port or harbor bears a strong, monotonic negative relationship to democracy.

There are, of course, many other ways in which distance to ports and natural harbors might be measured, as discussed in Chapter 4 ("Alternate Measures"). We explore these options empirically and find that results are robust and also highly correlated. For reasons of space, we do not include these tests in Table 6.4.

Democracy Indices

In Table 6.5, we explore the relationship of natural harbor distance to different indices of democracy, each of which was introduced in Chapter 2. All measures are rescaled to a 0–100 scale so that coefficients are comparable.

Model 1 is the benchmark measure, Polyarchy with missing data interpolated. Model 2 utilizes the same Polyarchy index with no interpolated data. Model 3 employs the Lexical index. Model 4 adopts the Polity2 index. Model 5 focuses on the index of electoral Contestation.

Estimates of the impact of natural harbor distance on democracy vary somewhat across these outcomes, which are not perfectly correlated and cover different samples (N ranges from just under 17,000 to nearly

Table 6.5 *Democracy indices*

Outcome	Polyarchy, augmented	Polyarchy	Lexical	Polity2	Contestation
estimator	OLS	OLS	OLS	OLS	Tobit
	1	2	3	4	5
Natural harbor	−1.275***	−1.779***	−2.462***	−2.456***	−2.157***
distance	(−5.198)	(−5.709)	(−5.340)	(−5.476)	(−3.961)
States	196	179	193	168	195
Years	231	231	231	219	229
Observations	32 324	24 096	18 866	16 684	34 860
R^2 *(pseudo-likelihood)*	0.395	0.346	0.297	0.194	(−59937)

Democracy, variously measured, regressed on harbor distance. *Not shown:* Year dummies, Constant. Standard errors clustered by state, t statistics in parentheses. *p<.10 **p<.05 ***p<.01

35,000). Nonetheless, all estimates are highly robust. Importantly, the weakest estimate is for the benchmark. Estimates of the causal effect of natural harbor distance on democracy are roughly twice as strong when we adopt the Lexical index, Polity2, or Contestation as the chosen indicator of regime type. This is partly a sample effect, which brings us to our next topic.

Samples

Sometimes, the composition of a sample affects the results of a statistical analysis. In our case, the sample is fairly comprehensive – including most statelike polities that existed from 1789 to the present. But this is a polyglot population, and may hide a good deal of causal heterogeneity. To get a sense of this issue, Table 6.6 offers a series of analyses in which specific units are excluded.

Model 1 focuses on a single year in the contemporary era, 2000. This obviates the problem of repeated observations for the same unit that are not fully independent, a violation of SUTVA. The cost is the loss of a good deal of information: all years except one are dropped.

Models 2 and 3 distinguish sovereign and non-sovereign territories. In coding this complex concept we rely primarily on a formal, juridical conception of sovereignty – recognition by European states, ability to sign treaties, and membership in international bodies such as the League

Table 6.6 *Sample restrictions*

Excluded	All years but 2000	Non-sovereign states	Sovereign states	Europe, North & Central Asia	Americas	MENA	Sub-Saharan Africa	Asia: East, Southeast, South, Pacific	Natural harbor distance <3	Natural harbor distance >10
	1	2	3	4	5	6	7	8	9	10
Natural harbor distance	-1.893***	-1.890***	-0.373***	-0.624***	-1.328***	-1.436***	-1.209***	-1.556***	-1.444***	-1.422***
	(-4.330)	(-5.720)	(-3.238)	(-2.762)	(-4.661)	(-5.487)	(-3.988)	(-5.264)	(-2.899)	(-3.509)
States	193	193	156	145	161	174	147	159	84	180
Years	1	231	231	231	231	231	231	231	231	231
Observations	193	19 566	12 758	25 275	25 414	28 710	24 493	25 406	11 701	30 125
R^2	0.0644	0.345	0.193	0.415	0.364	0.425	0.399	0.405	0.393	0.387

Outcome: Polyarchy index of electoral democracy, augmented. Polities excluded from each analysis listed across the top row. *Not shown:* Year dummies, Constant. *Estimator:* ordinary least squares, standard errors clustered by state, t statistics in parentheses. *p<.10 **p<.05 ***p<.01

of Nations and the United Nations. It will be seen that the relationship between natural harbors and democracy is considerably stronger for sovereign territories (Model 2) than for non-sovereign territories (Model 3). This may be because there is greater variance across sovereign states, because the sample is larger, or because the sample is weighted toward the contemporary era.

The next set of tests exclude particular regions of the world. One can anticipate some attenuation of the causal effect when specific regions are excluded as the sample is smaller and variation on X and Y is truncated. Still, it is a useful exercise. (Note that although we include regional dummies in some of the previous specification tests this does not tell us which regions are especially influential.) These tests demonstrate that the relationship between natural harbors and democracy is virtually unaffected by the exclusion of the Americas (Model 5), MENA (Model 6), sub-Saharan Africa (Model 7), and Asia (Model 8). It *is* strongly attenuated when Europe, North Eurasia, and Central Asia are excluded (Model 4), as is perhaps to be expected given the leading role of harbors and democracy in European history and the sheer size of this region (fifty-four states). In any case, the main effect persists.

The final tests in Table 6.6 remove states that receive a low score (Model 9) or high score (Model 10) on the harbor distance variable (which varies from 0 to 19.2). These extreme cases often play an influential role in linear models and are especially worrisome where values are not equally distributed, as is the case here (see Map 4.6). Despite truncated values for the predictor, estimates of the relationship between harbor distance and democracy remain strong, and consistent with the benchmark, confirming that our finding is not attributable to a small set of influential cases lying at the extremes of the distribution.

Impact

Assuming natural harbors have a causal effect on democracy we want to know how big that effect might be. To get a sense of causal impact as estimated by the benchmark analysis we plot predicted values for democracy as natural harbor distance varies, holding other factors (in this case, year dummies) at their means. The sample is restricted to the contemporary era, where subsequent analyses show the relationship is likely to be strongest.

Figure 6.2 shows that an increase in harbor distance from minimum to maximum values translates into a drop of over thirty points on the Polyarchy index, a non-trivial effect. In Chapter 12, this effect is compared to other geographic predictors, where we show that there

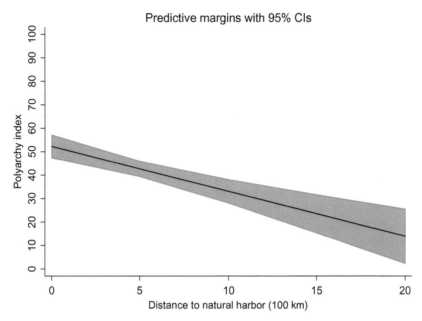

Figure 6.2 **Natural harbors and democracy, predicted values for the contemporary era**
Estimated impact of a change in distance to natural harbor (100 km) on the Polyarchy index of electoral democracy, augmented, based on the benchmark specification (Model 1, Table 6.3), surrounded by 95% confidence intervals. *Years:* 1960–2019.

is only one potential rival, judged by various specification tests and measures of impact.

Changes through Time

It is implausible to suppose that the influence of harbors on democracy is entirely constant across two and a half centuries. To probe changes through time we run consecutive models on a moving three-decade window beginning in 1789–1838 and ending in 1970–2019. Coefficients for natural harbor distance, flanked by 95 percent confidence intervals, are graphed for each time period in Figure 6.3. Note that the sample is changing over this period so different cross-sections sometimes include different states.

The coefficient estimates in Figure 6.3 reveal that natural harbor distance is associated with less democracy in all periods of the modern

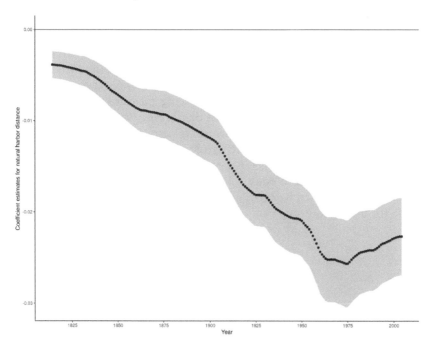

Figure 6.3 **The impact of natural harbors on democracy through time**
Rolling regressions in which the Polyarchy index of electoral democracy (augmented) is regressed against natural harbor distance and annual dummies in a moving 30-year window from 1789 to 2019. Estimated coefficients for natural harbor distance, flanked by 95% confidence intervals, are graphed for the midpoint of each 30-year window.

era. However, there is a substantial shift toward greater influence across the observed period, with some attenuation in the final decades. It would appear that the influence of harbors on democracy has deepened over time, though this trend may have peaked in recent decades. This would make sense in light of the displacement of ships by other modes of transport (railroads, roads, airplanes) and communication (telephone, radio, television, Internet).

And yet, we have also noted that these other elements of infrastructure often follow in the geographic path of earlier investments. Cities originally founded on natural harbors are now likely to be central nodes within new infrastructural networks. In this light, one might expect the long-run implications of natural harbors to continue indefinitely via path dependence. It is too soon to tell.

Conclusions

This chapter has demonstrated a robust link between natural harbors and democracy. We have shown that this relationship obtains in tests that utilize varying units of analysis (grid-cells of varying sizes as well as states), varying model specifications, varying measures of harbors and harbor distance, varying measures of democracy, varying samples, and varying time periods. This extensive set of tests, and the stability of the estimates generated by these tests, give us confidence that the relationship might be causal. Aqueous geography seems to be conducive to democratic structures of power.

In the next chapter, we focus on the mechanisms that might be responsible for this relationship.

7 Mechanisms

Statistical tests presented in the previous chapter, and narrative evidence presented in Chapter 5 indicate a robust association between natural harbor distance and democracy. Areas close to harbors are more likely to be democratic than areas situated far away. In this chapter, we probe for evidence of the causal mechanisms laid out in Chapter 3.

Unfortunately, many of the factors referenced in our theoretical discussion are not measurable on a global scale, especially in periods prior to the contemporary era. And those factors that are measurable are diffuse, overlapping, and probably mutually reinforcing. We should not imagine a set of distinct pathways that might be measured and tested in isolation. Nonetheless, some attempt at verification is better than none at all. In this spirit, we enlist a variety of evidence.

The first section of the chapter is focused on the relationship between harbors and economic development. The second section focuses on state size. The third section focuses on social diversity. The fourth section focuses on democratic values. The fifth section brings together all factors that are thought to have a monotonic relationship to democracy and are measurable across the modern era. The final section enlists these same factors in a formal mediation analysis.

Economic Development (Including Urbanization)

If harbors mattered for travel and trade, and shipping mattered for economic development, then we should see a positive association between harbors and economic development. This association should become stronger over time as oceangoing shipping grows in volume and importance. In the late twentieth and early twenty-first centuries we anticipate a slight attenuation as shipping is displaced by other modes of travel and communications.

In the modern era, economic development is usually measured by per capita GDP. Prior to the modern era, in periods when aggregate output cannot be reliably estimated, scholars often rely on demographic indicators such as population, population density, and urbanization (proxied by the growth of cities).

One must bear in mind that demographic signals of economic development are not indicative of *human* development in the premodern era. Indeed, the evidence suggests that urban locations were less healthful than rural locations prior to the twentieth century (Scott 2017). However, as a measure of aggregate wealth (surplus), technological sophistication, and the complexity of economic organization, demography is a useful guide.

Ports and Cities

We begin by considering the evolving relationship between ports and cities. This relationship was more intimate in the past than it is in the present era. Taking a long view, we can identify several historical epochs in the port–city relationship.[1]

Originally, ports and cities were close companions with little or no separation between denizens of the water and denizens of the land. This was a function of the small size of ancient and medieval cities, primitive ground transport options (making proximity a virtue), and (in many parts of the world) security concerns that gave everyone an incentive to locate within city walls. For a variety of reasons, all urban activities – maritime, manufacturing, entertainment, lodging – generally occurred within a small ambit. If cities were segregated it was by "nation" (language, religion, race); even so, ethnic neighborhoods were cheek-by-jowl.

In the modern era, cities expanded, transport options improved, and security was less of a concern. Accordingly, ports became a distinctive urban zone, segregated from other municipal functions. Likewise, sailors and dockworkers came to be viewed as a distinctive social class – generally, not a very respectable one. In addition to docks, the harbor area tended to host flop houses and entertainment geared for a rough class of customers.

Late in the twentieth century, harbors were often relocated at some remove from the city center. This opened up more space for city development and often improved accommodations for docks and ships, which required more and more space and deeper and deeper waters. Connections with rail and road networks became more important than proximity to urban dwellers or local manufacturing. Oil tankers required their own special facilities. The port enterprise moved into an industrial phase.

---

[1] See Hoyle (1989), Konvitz (1978), Murphey (1989).

In the final era, efforts were (and are) often made to reintegrate port areas into cities – removing physical separation, adopting mixed-use zoning, and pursuing beautification. Since the human labor required for port operations has shrunk dramatically, and ports now enlist a variety of highly skilled and less-skilled workers, the class of maritime workers is smaller and less well defined. They no longer occupy a significant niche within most national labor movements.

These changes are dramatic, and ports today often bear few visible signs of their origins. However, if we want to understand why cities appeared in some places rather than others we need to take a long view of our subject. Ports were critical to city formation in most parts of the world and in most historical eras. And they seem to have become more critical as time went on. Summarizing the history of port-led urbanization in Europe, Robert Lee (1998: 148) relates,

In Spain urbanization was essentially a coastal phenomenon: apart from the capital, Madrid, all the large cities (Barcelona, Cadiz, Malaga, Seville and Valencia) were on or near the coast. French ports – such as Bordeaux, Marseille, Nantes and Rouen – were also important regional capitals; many of the new towns of the late seventeenth century, including Brest, Lorient, Cherbourg and Rochefort, were created explicitly for naval purposes; and during the eighteenth century maritime ports, particularly on the Atlantic coast, registered substantial growth. In the Netherlands the port cities of Amsterdam and Rotterdam dominated the urban landscape and ports were among the fastest growing urban communities in nineteenth-century Italy. Gothenburg was and remains the chief port and second city of Sweden; and in Norway towns were invariably coastal. In Britain, a period of almost perpetual naval warfare in the eighteenth century, the increasing competitiveness of manufactured products, and the rapid expansion of maritime trading, meant that many port cities (including dockyard towns and fleet stations) registered substantial growth: by 1801 21 of the 54 largest towns with more than 10,000 inhabitants were seaports.[2]

Lee (1998: 147) reports that 40 percent of large cities (with populations greater than 100,000) across the world in 1850 were located in seaports.

To grapple with these issues in a systematic fashion we produce two datasets. The first is a compilation of the oldest continuously inhabited cities in each region of the world, contained in Table C.1 (online at Dataverse). This set of 261 cities is by no means comprehensive, and the concept of "old" is in any case a matter of degree. One can imagine a longer list for each region that includes more cities, most of which would be of a more recent vintage. But even a non-systematic compendium should be sufficient to establish some basic facts about the history of cities

---

[2] See also Acemoglu, Johnson, Robinson (2005), Lawton, Lee (2002).

and ports. Along with a city's original name, historical location, and current location, we offer an approximate date of founding – which in most cases represents the oldest record of existence, or archeological projections of the dates at which city walls or other artifacts were in use. For each city, we then code whether it was located on or very near a port with ocean access at the time the city was founded.

To get a sense for the demographic role of ports at the present time, we next survey the hundred largest cities in the world today, shown in Table C.2 (online at Dataverse). Collectively, these giant metropolises comprise roughly one-sixth of the world's population. As in Table C.1, each city is coded according to its port status. One additional modification is introduced. If a city served as a river port historically but not in the contemporary era, it is given a special code.

A casual glance at these tables suggests that ports have played an enduring role in the life of cities from earliest times. A majority of the world's largest cities initially served as ocean ports and many still function as avenues to the sea, even if other transport infrastructure has partially displaced oceangoing vessels. Many were developed by European colonialists, as we shall see in Chapter 9.

In Table 7.1, we extract the most salient bits of information from these tables to offer a more precise depiction of the port–city relationship. Among early cities, nearly two-thirds (63 percent) appear to have functioned as ports. Among contemporary megalopolises this figure remains stable, rising slightly (to 68 percent) if we count the status of these cities as ports during their founding period. However, the association between ports and cities is not uniform across regions.

Oceania has the most ocean ports, and virtually no old cities are without ports (only 7 percent of the sample). Of course, these cities are rather new by comparison with other regions, with an average founding date centered on 1913.

In the MENA region, old cities are quite old indeed, and most (75 percent) were founded along waterways. This suggests that the movement away from the coast, which we discuss in Chapter 5, occurred at a later date. Indeed, the most recent of the old cities listed in Table C.1 (online) – Fes (789) and Marrakesh (1070) – were located at some considerable remove from the ocean and did not function as port cities.

In North America, most old cities (74 percent) were founded along a river (22 percent) or an ocean (52 percent). With an average founding date of 1650 CE, they are also comparatively recent.

In Europe, the most oceanic region of the world, we are not surprised to find that even the oldest cities are likely to be founded along rivers (20 percent) or oceans (47 percent). The same is true for waterborne

Table 7.1 Cities and ports

	No port		River port		Ocean port		Total	
	%	Founding	%	Founding	%	Founding	N	Founding
Early cities	37	−175	20	95	43	249	262	63
Oceania	7	1913	20	1820	73	1824	15	1829
MENA	25	215	13	−1550	63	−291	16	−322
North America	26	920	22	1650	52	1590	27	1429
Europe	33	−498	20	−349	47	−774	85	−598
Southeast Asia	33	968	46	967	21	1143	24	1048
East Asia	35	−216	48	−818	17	−18	23	−470
South America	38	1342	15	1534	46	1539	13	1463
Africa	42	627	0		58	1146	19	927
Central & South Asia	60	−374	40	−52	0		15	−245
West Asia	72	−1468	0		28	−2062	25	−1635
Contemporary megalopolises	32		32		36		100	

River port: rivers with direct (navigable) ocean access. Contemporary megalopolises are counted as river ports if they served as a river port either currently or historically. *Founding*: founding date, mean across sample. Negative numbers indicate years BCE. *Sources*: early cities (Table C.1 online), contemporary megalopolises (Table C.2 online).

Southeast Asia, whose cities are much newer (average founding date = 968 CE).

East Asia is not far behind these oceanic areas, with 65 percent of its old cities located along rivers or oceans and presumably serving as ports, at least in their early years. Like Europe, these cities are for the most part ancient (average founding date = 216 BCE). As in the MENA region, we can discern a historical movement away from the coast in the premodern era: cities with a later founding date were more likely to be founded inland.

Old cities in South America lie mostly along rivers or oceans (62 percent), and in this respect are not so different from other regions. These are comparatively new cities, with founding dates averaging around 1342 CE.

Africa is unusual insofar as old cities are either located on the ocean (58 percent) or inland without river access to the ocean (42 percent). This bespeaks the general absence of navigable rivers with ocean access in the continent.

In Central and South Asia, a majority (60 percent) of old cities have neither river access to the ocean nor direct ocean access. Many lie far from the coast. In West Asia, similarly, cities are located primarily inland without river access to the coast (72 percent), and thus do not function as ports. In this respect, these regions follow a pattern that is quite different from the global norm.

To probe these relationships through time, Figure 7.1 focuses on the founding dates of early cities (from Table C.1 online) from 2000 BCE to 2000 CE. (We leave aside earlier years as there are very few data points.) For each 200-year interval, we calculate the share of foundings that occurred in cities located on a river (with ocean access) or ocean, and thus presumably served as ports. Cities with no port serve as the omitted category.

Figure 7.1 shows that cities founded on the shores of an ocean (or sea) outnumber cities founded on rivers during all but one period – around 0 CE. The ocean/river advantage seems to increase over time, with ocean port cities vastly outnumbering river port cities across the past millennium. This reflects our general observation that oceans began to overshadow rivers as points of transit and centers of population in the early modern and modern eras (Chapter 4). One can also see that the number of port city foundings overwhelms the number of non-port city foundings (nearly 100 percent) over the past 200 years, confirming the dominant role of water transport in the modern era.

Another approach to this question leaves aside the somewhat arbitrary concept of "cities" (which, as we have observed, can be defined in

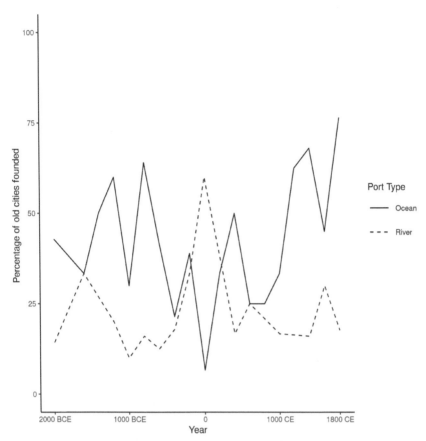

Figure 7.1 **City foundings and port status through history**
City founding dates by port type: (a) ocean or (b) river, calculated as a
share (%) of all ports listed in Table C.1 (online at Dataverse) founded
during each 200-year period. *Omitted:* cities that have neither ocean nor
river ports. The earliest years (3500 BCE to 2000 BCE) in our dataset are
omitted by reason of scarce data.

different ways), focusing instead on population density. The ISAM-
Hyde dataset provides population estimates for each terrestrial grid-cell
back to AD 0. To gauge the impact of ports on population agglomeration,
we employ our familiar natural harbor distance variable as a predictor in
a series of regression tests conducted at century intervals from AD 0 to
2000. Figure 7.2 plots the regression coefficients from these analyses
surrounded by a 95 percent confidence interval.

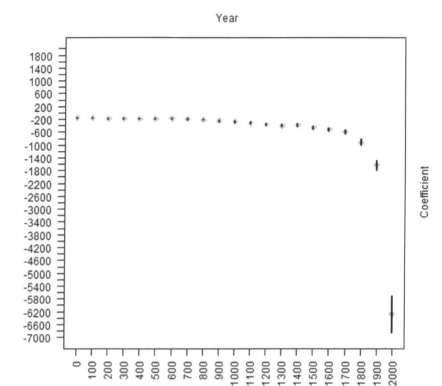

Figure 7.2 **Harbor distance and population density**
X-axis: year (CE). *Y-axis:* average change in population within a
grid-cell associated with a 100-km increase in distance to the nearest
natural harbor. Data on population from the HYDE database (Klein
Goldewijk et al. 2011). *Units of analysis:* grid-cells (*N* = 65,061).

It will be seen that harbor distance is negatively associated with population density in all periods. However, the relationship becomes much
stronger in the modern era and especially in the twentieth century, when
humanity takes a headlong rush toward regions located in the vicinity of
natural harbors.

The Modern Era

We turn now to the modern era, again relying on data at the grid-cell level.
Here, we can measure population (effectively, population density), urbanization (the share of people within a grid-cell living in a city), and, for the
last several decades, gross cell product, a grid-cell measure of GDP.

For each outcome we present two tests in Table 7.2. The first is a bivariate specification with only the regressor of theoretical interest along with a trend variable and its quadratic. (Most of these models do not converge when annual dummies are employed so we model time-effects in a more parsimonious fashion.) Tests that follow incorporate additional geographic factors that may serve as confounders, including region and state dummies. Note that although state boundaries are to some extent endogenous to the treatment (an issue discussed in Chapter 4), they are also a potential confounder. (Model 4 includes a smaller set of covariates because of problems of collinearity.)

These tests show a strong geographic effect. Grid-cells further away from a natural harbor are less populated, less urban, and less economically productive in the modern era.

State Size

In Chapter 3 we offered a number of arguments about state size. We argued, first, that the existence of natural harbors constrains the territorial size of states in the premodern era.

In antiquity, a glimpse of this relationship can be found in the location of city-states and empires, the two dominant statelike political organizations of the era. Mogens Hansen's (2000) survey of city-states throughout the world suggests that most were in close proximity to the sea via a harbor or navigable river. Regions with extensive city-state cultures include Northern Europe (e.g., the Vikings, the Dutch Republic), the Mediterranean (e.g., Sumerians, Babylonians, Phoenicians, Greeks, Etruscans, Romans [prior to the empire], Venice, Milan, Florence, Genoa, Ragusa), West Africa (e.g., the Fante, Yorubaland, various states along the Niger Delta), East Africa (e.g., the Swahili), Southeast Asia (e.g., Aceh, Brunei, Melaka, Srivijaya), and the Yucatan peninsula (the Mayan civilization). There were of course exceptions. However, city-states located away from the coast such as those in pre-dynastic China, Central Asia (along the Silk Road), and Arabia (along the caravan route), did not usually endure into the early modern era. Meanwhile, most empires were centered on interior continental zones.

In modern times, the Persian Gulf provides an excellent example of the dynamic by which geography structures the size of states. Along the northeastern coast, where there are few natural harbors, the territory has been monopolized by Persia/Iran, for centuries one of the larger polities in the Middle East (628,000 square miles). Along the southwestern coast, where the geomorphology is strongly indented – generating a number of superb natural harbors – one finds an abundance of smaller states. This

Table 7.2 *Natural harbors and economic development (grid-cell)*

Outcome	Population		Urbanization		Gross cell product	
	1	2	3	4	5	6
Natural harbor distance	−2618.349***	−2627.752***	−0.008***	−0.006***	−0.072***	−0.052***
	(−31.873)	(−22.659)	(−18.061)	(−8.443)	(−25.427)	(−13.957)
Equator distance		✓		✓		✓
Ocean distance		✓		✓		✓
River distance		✓		✓		✓
Temperature		✓		✓		✓
Irrigation potential		✓		✓		✓
Rainfall + Rainfall²		✓		✓		✓
Crop		✓				✓
Pasture		✓				✓
Forest		✓				✓
Grass		✓				✓
Shrub		✓				✓
Savanna		✓				✓
Barren		✓				✓
Water		✓				✓
Mountains		✓				✓
Region dummies		✓		✓		✓
State dummies		✓		✓		✓
States	200	170	176	170	181	171
Grid-cells	65 059	59 783	59 949	59 783	64 708	62 169
Years	228	228	228	228	4	4
Observations	10 882 821	10 134 218	10 181 524	10 134 218	249 862	240 010
R²	0.0179	0.441	0.0127	0.0634	0.00889	0.160

Spatial units: PRIO grid-cells. *Not shown:* Year, Year², Constant. *Estimator:* ordinary least squares, standard errors clustered by grid-cell, t statistics in parentheses. * p<.10 ** p<.05 *** p<.01

included the so-called Trucial states (many of which regrouped as part of the United Arab Emirates) – Abu Dhabi (26,000 square miles), Dubai (1,500), Sharjah (1,000), Ras al-Khaimah (650), Fujairah (450), Umm al-Qaiwain (300), Ajman (100) – along with Muscat/Oman (82,000), Kuwait (6,200), Qatar (4,000), and Bahrain (213). Southward, away from the Persian Gulf, Saudi Arabia (927,000 square miles) unites the rest of the Arabian peninsula, whose other shores – along the Red Sea and the Arabian Sea – are comparatively straight-edged and have not spawned independent kingdoms or countries.[3]

The same phenomenon appears in East Asia, where smaller states such as Korea, Taiwan, and Japan hover along the coast while the interior was controlled by various manifestations of the Chinese Empire. In Southeast Asia, micro-states dotted the Indonesian archipelago until the advent of the Dutch, while larger states dominated the continental landmass. In Europe, a coterie of smaller states still cluster along the indented coast-line of the North Sea including (at the present time) Belgium, the Netherlands, Denmark, Sweden, Norway, Finland, Estonia, Lithuania, and Latvia. In previous eras, much smaller units predominated, creating what was undoubtedly the most fragmented agglomeration of states ever recorded in human history (see Chapter 5). Further south, in the interior of the continent, larger states such as France, Prussia, and Austria-Hungary came together. Southern Germany and Switzerland, the home of countless principalities, serve as a partial exception to this pattern, as they were highly fragmented (prior to the unification of Germany) and at some distance from the coast (though directly tied to the coast through numerous navigable rivers).[4]

Our explanation for these patterns, set forth in Chapter 3, centers on the role of natural harbors. Briefly, pixelated coastlines give rise to numerous ports, which in turn provide access to ocean trade, forming the basis for urban agglomerations. With fiscal and demographic resources at their disposal, these territories are in a position to stake sovereign (or at least semisovereign) claims. In the interior, or where coastlines offer infrequent harborage, states tend to encompass larger territories, for there is little to impede the dominant state in each region from conquering adjacent territories.

In the modern era, under the influence of European imperialism and advanced technology, the impact of harbors on state size is less marked.

---

[3] All territory sizes are drawn from Abu-Hakima (1972: 47–8) and represent these states as they existed circa 1972.

[4] Special factors such as the late arrival of primogeniture may explain the German exception (Fichtner 1989).

Note that colonial borders, which often became the basis for modern states, were formed by European powers with little attention to local factors on the ground, so there is less reason to suppose that coastlines exerted a strong influence on statemaking.

To test this thesis, we assemble a dataset with all statelike entities and their geographic domains from the Middle Ages to the present. Principal sources included EurAtlas (for Europe) and GeaCron (for regions outside Europe). Of course, the borders of states in the premodern era were not precisely defined. Still, our data sources offer a general idea of the borders of large empires like China and Persia, as well as smaller states such as England and Venice, and this is sufficient for present purposes. We know which ones were large and which were small. Importantly, GeaCron treats contiguous empires as a single unit and overseas empires as separate units. This means that the Russian Empire is very large while the British Empire is represented by the metropole and by its various colonies, each of which is treated as a separate state with its own boundaries.

For each grid-cell, we record the size of the state that it belongs to at each point in historical time. (Grid-cells governed by non-state entities such as bands or tribes are excluded.) This outcome is regressed on our principal predictor, distance from nearest natural harbor. The analysis is repeated at century intervals from 1300 to 2000. Coefficients from these regressions are reported in Figure 7.3, surrounded by 95 percent confidence intervals.

These iterated analyses show that there is a strong positive relationship between harbor distance and state size. We are also able to show that this relationship attenuates over time, with a precipitous decline in the twentieth century, coincident with the arrival of new states in Africa and South Asia that were colonial creations and thus bore little relationship to the natural landscape. We conclude that harbors structured geopolitics so as to favor the survival of small states prior to the contemporary era.

Our second argument concerns the impact of state size on democracy. We argued that this effect was quite strong in the premodern era. Hansen (2000: 611–12) summarizes,

Throughout history and until the second half of the eighteenth century all the large so-called 'territorial' states were monarchies. Many city-states, perhaps even the majority, were monarchies too, but due to the small size of city-states quite a few became republics, i.e., states ruled by councils and assemblies in which decisions were made by vote after a debate. And even in monarchic city-states there is not infrequently evidence of debating and voting [in] councils and assemblies. The republican city-states were mostly oligarchies but sometimes democracies. The oligarchies were ruled by councils and magistrates elected

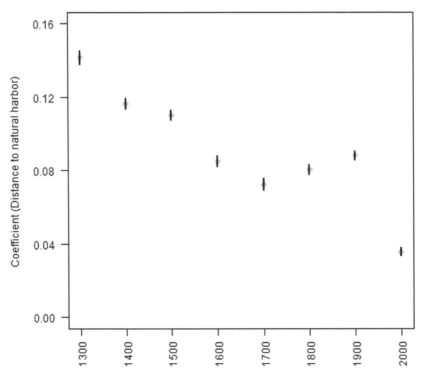

Figure 7.3 **Harbor distance and state size (grid-cells)**
Results from analyses in which the size (the log of 100 km square) of the
state that incorporates a grid-cell is regressed against that grid-cell's
distance from the nearest natural harbor. This analysis is repeated at
100-year intervals from 1300 to 2000. Dots represent point estimates
for natural harbor distance, and black segments represent 95%
confidence intervals (which are very small due to the large sample).

from among the well-to-do citizens; in democracies the principal political
institution was often a popular assembly. The essential characteristic common
to both types of constitution is that decisions were made in meetings, by majority
verdict, and after a debate among the participants.

This apparently strong relationship between polity size and governing
institutions attenuated in the modern era, we believe, because of the
development of sophisticated communications and transport infrastructure that helped to solve coordination problems posed by territorial size.

To test the time-varying impact of state size on regimes we regress
democracy on the territory of states (log) along with equator distance and
annual dummies in a rolling regression stretching from 1789 to 2019.

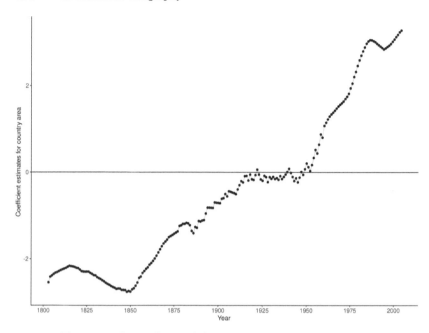

Figure 7.4 **State size and democracy through time (grid-cells)**
Rolling regressions in which the Polyarchy index of electoral democracy
(augmented) is regressed against state size (territory, logged) along with
harbor distance and annual dummies in a moving 30-year window from
1789 to 2019. Coefficients for state size, flanked by 95% confidence
intervals (which are tiny, due to the enormous size of the sample), are
graphed for the midpoint of each 30-year window. *Units of analysis:*
PRIO grid-cells.

Figure 7.4 reports the estimated coefficient from each regression, flanked
by its confidence interval. This set of analyses indicates a dramatic
transformation. In the first period, extending up to the First World
War, territory size is negatively associated with democracy. In the latter
period, beginning at the end of the Second World War, it is
positively associated.

We are unable to explain why a larger territory might enhance the
prospects of democracy so we do not propose a causal interpretation of
the coefficients in the contemporary period. However, we have given
many reasons to suppose that size may have exerted a negative effect
on democracy in the premodern era (see Chapter 3), so we are comfort-
able offering a causal interpretation of the relationship in the nineteenth
century, which we believe is indicative of a long-standing relationship

extending back through the premodern era, a relationship noted by many others (see Chapter 3 for citations to the literature).

In the next set of analyses, we probe whether the size of states in an earlier era might affect the status of democracy in a later period. The logic is one of institutional overhang. If the impact of harbors on the size of states is limited to periods prior to the twentieth century (as suggested by Figure 7.3), and if this has the effect of fostering democracy in that period (as suggested by Figure 7.4), it is plausible to suppose that those institutional features might survive into the contemporary era. Political institutions, and the political cultures that support them, are often durable.

This hypothesis is tested in analyses displayed in Table 7.3. For each grid-cell, we measure the area of the state to which it belongs during each period. State size is measured at century intervals from 1300 to 1700 and annually after 1789. In each period, we exclude territories without state-like organization. Since the latter were common in the premodern era, these analyses do not employ the full set of terrestrial grid-cells. Democracy, the outcome of interest, is measured in the contemporary era (1950–2019).

Models 1–5 are bivariate models in which contemporary democracy is regressed against state size in previous historical eras along with annual dummies. Models 6–8 measure state size with a 200-year lag. Model 7 includes a variable measuring state size contemporaneously with the outcome. Model 8 adds geographic covariates measuring natural harbor distance, equator distance, along with a vector of regional dummies.

Effects are generally larger when state size is measured further back in time. However, these estimates are rather unstable, reflecting smaller sample sizes. (The further back in history we travel, the fewer grid-cells were governed in a statelike fashion.) In the modern era, where the sample is larger, coefficients are smaller but more precisely estimated.

In any case, all analyses show a negative relationship. Grid-cells that were incorporated into smaller states in the past are more democratic today than grid-cells that were previously incorporated into larger states (most of which deserve the appellation *empire*).

The importance of state history is reinforced by the inclusion of a contemporary measure of state size in Models 7–8, which shows a *positive* relationship to state size. Again, we do not infer a causal relationship from this result (which is in any case rather weak). But it underlines the point that historic state size and contemporary state size bear different relationships to democracy.

The fact that Southeast Asia and Europe, the most aqueous regions of the world, were broken into small governing units through most of the

Table 7.3 Lagged state size and democracy (grid-cells)

State size in	1300	1400	1500	1600	1700	t-200	t-200	t-200
	1	2	3	4	5	6	7	8
State size, historic	-3.157***	-12.833***	-16.479***	-5.514***	-2.029***	-1.731***	-1.973***	-1.878***
	(-41889)	(-46219)	(-53483)	(-24666)	(-57776)	(-103733)	(-88120)	(-78055)
State size, contemporaneous							0.616***	0.217***
							(20850)	(8284)
Natural harbor distance								✓
Equator distance								✓
Region dummies								✓
States	36	37	40	55	62	105	101	100
Grid-cells	3242	3666	4434	5574	14802	27917	27765	27760
Years	67	67	67	67	67	28	21	21
Observations	210710	238278	287212	360920	960597	633264	510657	510553
R^2	0.243	0.294	0.345	0.222	0.543	0.332	0.325	0.622

Outcome: Polyarchy index of electoral democracy, augmented. *Estimator:* ordinary least squares, standard errors clustered by grid-cell. *Not shown:* Year dummies, Constant. * $p<.10$ ** $p<.05$ *** $p<.01$. Sample limited to the contemporary era (1950–2019). State size measured in millions of square kilometers.

premodern era may have bequeathed a democratic legacy. The fact that governing units in both regions are larger in the contemporary era probably does not impede their democratic achievements. In this instance, the past matters more than the present, as there is little reason to suppose that territorial size affects regime type in the late twentieth century.

Diversity

We argued in Chapter 3 that natural harbors spur social diversity. Prior to the arrival of air travel in the mid-twentieth century, all overseas visitors would pass through ports, which served as gateways to the interior. Many would stay, generating a diverse population (relative to the hinterland). Moreover, demand for labor would attract migrants from the countryside, with diverse social backgrounds, further stimulating the diversity of port cities.

To get an empirical handle on these differences we collect a sample of major inland and coastal cities in countries around the world. (Rural areas, we assume, are generally less diverse and less cosmopolitan, regardless of their geographic location.) We assume that most of the coastal cities possess a working port of some sort; for present purposes it matters little if the harbor is natural or artificial. Landlocked countries, and countries that are too small to register any significant differences between "inland" and "coastal" (e.g., Singapore) are omitted. We focus on the largest cities in each country so that the comparisons are cleaner. In a large country with many cities we omit those with ambiguous coastal/inland locations (i.e., midway to the coast). The resulting list, shown in Table C.4 (online at Dataverse), includes 95 countries and 470 cities, of which 245 are classified as inland and 225 as coastal.

Evidently, we have not followed a strict set of rules for case selection and the resulting sample is therefore difficult to evaluate. Nonetheless, the extensive set of comparisons offered in Table C.4 serves an illustrative function. We believe that if readers consult countries they are familiar with they will find a fairly consistent pattern: cities by the coast are more diverse than cities located at some remove from the coast. We suspect that this pattern was considerably stronger prior to the advent of railroad, road, and air travel. Nonetheless, remnants of this ancient demographic pattern should still be visible today.

To test this thesis, we undertake a further analysis on a subset of countries for which suitable demographic data (disaggregated by ethnicity) is available. These thirty-nine countries are accompanied by an asterisk in Table C.4. Most are located in the Organization for Economic Cooperation and Development (OECD), so this is by no means a representative sample. However, any biases in our sample probably run against our thesis insofar as more-developed countries are likely to have more-developed transportation infrastructure, lessening the historic role of ships and hence the advantage of coastal locations in attracting migrants.

Each of the thirty-nine countries is represented by several cities (two to five), whose ethnic populations are measured at some point in the past decade. To gauge diversity we construct a Herfindahl index of ethnic heterogeneity, understood as the probability that two randomly chosen persons living in a city are members of different ethnic groups. This comprises our dependent variable in Table 7.4. Model 1 includes only the regressor of interest, a binary classification of whether a city is coastal or inland (as coded in Table C.4). Model 2 includes a measure of population. Both models include country fixed effects, allowing us to focus the comparison on cities within the same country. This is important, given that the identification of ethnic groups is highly contextual but likely to be consistent within a given country at a particular point in time (especially as the data is usually drawn from the same source, i.e., a national survey or census).

Results of both analyses are consistent, and estimates virtually identical. Coastal cities are more ethnically diverse than inland cities. Although the effect is not overwhelming, we suspect that it was more marked in earlier periods – prior to the development of effective road, railroad, and air travel – when water transport was dominant.

Democratic Values

If our theorizing about the long-term impact of harbors on democracy is true, it should be reflected in widely held values and norms. Areas located close to natural harbors should be supportive of democracy as a normative ideal, at least in the modern era when democracy comes to be widely valorized and is no longer a term of abuse.

To explore this possibility, we construct a measure of democratic values based on questions from the World Values Survey (WVS) registering respondents' approval or disapproval of the following regimes: (a) democracy, (b) army rule, (c) rule by experts, (d) theocracy, and (e) rule by a strong leader. Each is scaled such that positive scores indicate more democratic attitudes; then, they are summed together into a composite index.

Table 7.4 *Diversity in inland and coastal cities*

	1	2
Coastal (dummy)	0.047*	0.049*
	(1.893)	(1.945)
Population (log)		✓
Countries	39	39
Observations (cities)	107	107
R^2	0.776	0.779

Coastal/inland status of cities as predictor of ethnic diversity. *Outcome:* ethnic fractionalization index. *Estimator:* ordinary least squares, t statistics in parentheses. *Not shown:* Country dummies, Constant. * p<.10 ** p<.05 *** p<.01. The country sample is identified in Table C.4 (online). Cities included in this analysis are also listed in Table C.4, though not all cities in Table C.4 are included in this analysis by reason of missing data. Data on ethnicity for each city drawn from Wikipedia entries, which report data from recent surveys or censuses.

Conveniently, the latest round of the WVS (2020) includes latitude–longitude coordinates indicating the approximate location where respondents were surveyed (presumably, where most of them reside). With this information, we construct a natural harbor distance variable for each respondent. Country fixed effects are included in all models, which narrows the comparison to citizens located in the same country, mitigating many potential confounders. Model 2 adds a measure of urbanization at the grid-cell level. Model 3 adds a vector of individual-level attributes including income, age, education, and gender.

Results, displayed in Table 7.5, show that as harbor distance increases people become more skeptical of democracy and more favorably disposed toward undemocratic forms of government such as theocracy or army rule. Remarkably, the relationship is stable across all three models, despite the fact that added covariates lie downstream from the factor of theoretical interest. We also conduct disaggregated tests on each component of the index (not shown). There, we find broadly similar results, suggesting that the results are generalizable across questions that capture a range of dimensions pertaining to democracy.

The relationship between harbors and democratic values displayed in Table 7.5 may be a product of the influence of harbors on the attitudes of citizens living in those regions and/or the influence of harbors on migration patterns (with the assumption that people with more democratic attitudes may migrate to harbor areas). In both scenarios, the observed relationship is supportive of our theory.

Table 7.5 *Democratic values*

	1	2	3
Natural harbor distance	−0.029***	−0.026***	−0.026***
	(5.630)	(4.502)	(4.344)
Grid-cell covariates			
Urban		✓	✓
Individual-level covariates			
Income			✓
Age			✓
Education			✓
Gender			✓
Country dummies	✓	✓	✓
Countries	36	36	36
Observations (respondents)	42 790	38 963	37 975
R^2	0.966	0.964	0.965

Outcome: democratic values index based on the World Values Survey (WVS) 2020, as explained in the text. Individual-level covariates are also drawn from the WVS 2020. *Estimator:* ordinary least squares, t statistics in parentheses. Standard errors clustered on grid-cells. *Not shown:* constant. * p<.10 ** p<.05 *** p<.01.

Crossnational Tests

While economic development is measurable at the grid-cell level, most other stipulated mechanisms in our theory are not. Accordingly, the next set of tests enlist state-level indicators.

Here, our primary measure of economic development is the traditional metric of per capita GDP (log). To capture capital mobility, we measure imports as share of GDP (log), which may also be regarded as a measure of development.

To capture long-run human capital we track the development of universities through time (Apfeld 2019). Specifically, for each grid-cell year from 1789 to the present we measure distance from the nearest university. This is aggregated by taking the average value across all grid-cells within a state. The resulting statistic is transformed by the natural logarithm and then calculated as a stock variable with 1 percent annual depreciation.

To measure the character of defense forces we examine the relative strength of naval-to-land forces. Naval strength is proxied by naval tonnage (Crisher, Souva 2014) and land forces by total military personnel (National Material Capabilities, COW v 5.0; Singer 1987). As a first step, we replace missing values for both variables with minimum values on each scale (under the assumption that sizeable naval and land forces have been captured by these indices, leaving only minimal forces as missing). In the second step, both variables are transformed by the natural logarithm. In the third step, a ratio is calculated from the two variables: naval forces/land forces.

To capture the long-term process of diffusion, we measure the European diaspora – specifically, the share of population in states around the world who are of European ancestry, as described in Chapter 9.

Tests presented in Table 7.6 represent the estimated coefficient for natural harbor distance across these outcomes in three specifications. The first specification includes only the regressor of interest along with year dummies. The second specification includes distance from the equator and a vector of region dummies. The third specification includes a large panel of geographic covariates, as listed.

Most of these relationships are robust (at conventional thresholds of statistical significance), and also fairly stable across the various specifications. We conclude that the existence of a natural harbor is an important long-term predictor of per capita GDP, trade, human capital, naval defense forces, and the diffusion of Europeans.

Of particular note is the impact of natural harbors on per capita GDP, the most widely used measure of economic development. In a bivariate regression of per capita GDP on natural harbor distance centered on one year (2000), the latter accounts for about 16 percent of the variability in the outcome. Moreover, the impact of natural harbors on GDP is stronger (judging by standardized coefficients) and more robust (in various specification tests) than most of the other geographic variables tested.

We also note that the impact of harbors on globalization is robust across a wide variety of indicators. This includes alternate measures of trade drawn from World Development Indicators and Penn World Tables as well as more subjective measures of trade openness constructed by the Heritage Foundation. We also tested an index of social globalization produced by the KOF Swiss Economic Institute intended to measure the spread of ideas, information, images and people. Across all these measures we find that greater distance from a natural harbor is associated with reduced exposure to outside influences.

Mediation Analyses

Having satisfied ourselves that the five chosen mediators are likely to be affected by natural harbors, we turn to a formal mediation analysis, following the procedure developed by Imai et al. (2011).

Table 7.6 *Mechanisms: first-order tests*

Outcome		Specification		Specification		Specification
GDP per capita (log)	1.	−0.082***	2.	−0.071***	3.	−0.079***
		(−6.294)		(−7.282)		(−3.981)
Trade openness:	4.	−0.079*	5.	−0.025	6.	−0.114***
imports/GDP		(−1.911)		(−0.625)		(−2.700)
University distance	7.	13.784***	8.	12.468***	9.	11.561**
		(4.901)		(4.461)		(2.132)
Naval/land forces	10.	−0.067***	11.	−0.041**	12.	−0.101***
		(−3.249)		(−2.025)		(−2.922)
European ancestry (%)	13.	−2.260***	14.	−2.675***	15.	−2.235***
		(−5.257)		(−4.923)		(−2.841)
Covariates						
Equator distance				✓		✓
Island						✓
Landlock						✓
Territory (log)						✓
Precipitation + Precipitation^2						✓
River distance						✓
Irrigation potential						✓
Tropical						✓
Temperature						✓
Frost days						✓
Soil quality						✓
Desert						✓
Elevation						✓
Rugged						✓
Agricultural suitability						✓
Fish						✓
Region dummies				✓		
Year dummies		✓		✓		✓

Five outcomes tested across three specifications, generating fifteen models. *Displayed:* results for the predictor of theoretical interest: natural harbor distance. *Estimator:* ordinary least squares, standard errors clustered by state, t statistics in parentheses. * p<.10 ** p<.05 *** p<.01

This approach, grounded in the potential outcomes framework, decomposes the total average treatment effect (ATE) into the average direct effect (ADE), which yields the portion of the ATE that is not mediated via the mediator, and the average causal mediation effect (ACME), which represents the portion of the ATE that is attributed to mediation. Analyses are conducted on states rather than grid-cells as most of the mediators are measurable only at the state level. Specifications follow the benchmark (Model 1, Table 6.3) except that decade dummies are substituted for annual dummies in order to render the analysis tractable.

Table 7.7 reports estimates for each of the five mediators, as shown in Models 1–5. Because mediators overlap, these analyses are likely to overestimate the impact of each variable. There is no easy way around this problem. A conservative approach is to generate a single factor that measures the common latent dimension of these mediators, as determined by a principal components analysis, shown in Table 7.8. Estimates from this variable are shown in Model 6 of Table 7.7, though it should be noted that this protocol probably *under*estimates the combined impact of the five mediators.

It will be seen that all the ACMEs are in the expected direction (negative) and fairly precisely estimated. This suggests that a significant portion of the ATE runs through our five specified mediators. Second, we find strong and "correctly" signed coefficients for the ADE in all of our mediation analyses. In two analyses – focused on imports and universities, respectively – the ADE is considerably stronger than the ACME. As the table makes clear, the common factor produces the largest mediation effect, accounting for roughly 86 percent of the total effect of natural harbor distance on democracy, suggesting that the proposed mechanisms can account for a significant portion of the relationship between harbor distance and democracy.

Since the mediators are correlated it is hard to disentangle their relative contributions. Nonetheless, some clues can be drawn from the proportion mediated by each factor, as shown in Table 7.7.

GDP is a substantial mediator, as one might expect. However, the harbors–democracy relationship is not just a story about economic development. Moreover, if democracy fosters growth this mediation effect is greatly overestimated.[5]

The factor showing the largest proportion mediated is European ancestry, the centerpiece of Part III of the book. It is also worth noting that European ancestry is, by most accounts, exogenous to economic development (Easterly, Levine 2016).

We conclude that although the relationship between port distance and democracy is not fully explained by the five chosen mediators, our analyses provide some corroboration for the mechanisms proposed in Chapter 3. Of course, this does not exclude the possibility that other – as

---

[5] Studies indicating a democratic growth effect include Gerring et al. (2005) and Acemoglu, Naidu et al. (2019).

Table 7.7 *Mediation analysis*

Mediator	GDP pc	University distance	European ancestry	Trade openness	Naval/ land power	Common factor
	1	2	3	4	5	6
Average causal mediation effect (ACME)	−0.932***	−0.535***	−0.817***	−1.226***	−0.458***	−2.041***
Average direct effect (ADE)	−0.570***	−0.708***	−0.409***	−2.137***	−1.866***	−0.325***
Average total effect (ATE)	−1.502***	−1.243***	−1.226***	−2.546***	−2.324***	−2.366***
Proportion mediated (ACME/ATE)	0.62	0.29	0.66	0.16	0.187	0.864
Years	210	210	210	140	145	145
States	193	189	187	182	168	168
Observations	22 622	31 509	31 762	12 146	11 484	10 514

Outcome: Polyarchy index of electoral democracy, augmented. *Exogenous cause*: natural harbor distance. *Mediators*: (1) GDP per capita (log), (2) distance from nearest university (log, stock), (3) European ancestry (%), (4) trade (imports as a share of GDP), (5) naval/land power index, (6) common factor from principal components analysis. *Specification*: Model 1, Table 6.3, where decade dummies replace annual dummies. *Estimator*: Imai et al. (2011), standard errors clustered by state. * p<.10 ** p<.05 *** p<.01. *Not reported*: Decade dummies (all models).

Table 7.8 *Factor analysis of mediation variables*

	Factor loadings
Trade openness	0.696***
Naval/land power	0.380***
European ancestry	0.511***
University distance	−0.544***
GDP pc	0.905***
Explained variance	.397

Factor analysis estimated using varimax rotation.

yet unidentified – mechanisms may also be at work in explaining the distal relationship between natural harbor distance and democracy.

Conclusions

In this chapter, we have explored a variety of mechanisms that might help to explain the strong relationship between natural harbor distance and democracy discovered in Chapters 5 and 6.

The first section is focused on the relationship between harbors and economic development. As measures of the latter we examined cities, population density, urbanization, and per capita GDP. Employing a diverse set of research designs – including grid-cell and state level tests – we find that each measure of economic development is negatively correlated to natural harbor distance and that this relationship becomes stronger over time.

The second section focuses on state size. There, we find that natural harbor distance is positively correlated with the territorial size of states, though the relationship attenuates in the twentieth century – presumably because most of the new states that arrive in the contemporary era are the product of European machinations that have little to do with natural features of the landscape. This confirms our argument that natural harbors served as a brake on territorial aggrandizement in the premodern era. We also find that state size is negatively correlated with democracy in the nineteenth century, a result that we believe can be extended back into the premodern era. If so, this confirms our argument about the role of territory in constraining options for democratic rule prior to the contemporary era. Finally, we show that the size of states at the dawn of the modern era presages regime types in the contemporary era: states whose progenitors were small are more likely to be democratic today.

The third section focuses on social diversity. There, we find that cities located along the coast of a country are more ethnically diverse than cities located in the interior of a country.

The fourth section focuses on democratic values, as measured by the World Values Survey. There, we find that natural harbor distance is associated with less support for democracy and greater support for army rule, rule by experts, theocracy, or rule by a strong leader. This relationship holds even when controlling for country, urbanization, and various background characteristics of respondents.

The fifth section brings together all factors that are thought to have a monotonic (non-time-dependent) relationship to democracy and are measurable across the modern era. This includes economic development (proxied by per capita GDP), capital mobility (proxied by trade openness), human capital (proxied by distance from nearest university), naval power (proxied by the ratio of naval to land forces), and European-led globalization (proxied by European ancestry). The final section enlists these same factors in a formal mediation analysis. Both sets of analyses corroborate our assertion (in Chapter 3) that these serve as important mediators.

III

European Diffusion

We now turn to the second causal factor in our argument about democracy's deep roots.

Due to advances in shipping technology (see Chapter 4), Europeans were at last able to circumnavigate the world. One may date the onset of this age of global exploration to Columbus's discovery of the New World (1492), Vasco da Gama's ocean voyage to India (1497–9), or Magellan's trip round the world (completed in 1522). We shall use the year 1500 as our watershed, signaling the beginning of the early modern era.

From this point onward, humans located all across the globe began to interact with each other on a regular basis. The age of globalization had begun. Sometimes, this interaction was peaceful and often it was violent. Always, it was consequential.[1]

Before beginning, we must take note of the atrocities we are about to narrate. This includes the violent conquest of vast portions of the world, the forcible removal and enslavement of African populations, and the extermination of indigenous peoples.

In attempting to deal with these subjects in a dispassionate, "scientific" manner there is a danger of normalizing what is abhorrent. We do not wish to contribute to a loss of moral perspective. To understand does not mean to excuse.

In any case, the vestiges of this brutal process persist in the present. This is why it matters. We must cope with the consequences of the first truly global encounter among humans, begun in 1500 and continuing in some attenuated form today.

---

[1] Wide-ranging studies include Abernethy (2000), Albertini, Wirz (1982), Canny (1994), Crosby (1972), Curtin (1989, 1998, 2002), Engerman, Sokoloff (2012), Etemad (2007), Fieldhouse (1966), Kohli (2020), Krieckhaus (2006), Mahoney (2010), Zwart, van Zanden (2018).

Despite the horrors of European imperialism some of the long-term effects might be counted as positive.[2] One of these is the legacy of democracy, which we explore in the following chapters.

Chapter 8 lays out an argument explaining how European demography (the share of Europeans in a territory) may have influenced regimes around the world. Chapter 9 discusses issues of conceptualization and measurement – who qualifies as European and how their numbers can be counted in colonies and countries through history. Chapter 10 explores the colonial and post-colonial era, focusing on particular colonizers and regions, for which we rely primarily on the voluminous secondary literature. Chapter 11 analyzes the relationship between European demography and democracy in a global context with the use of crossnational statistical tests.

---

[2] For example, a number of studies find a positive association between colonialism and growth (Easterly, Levine 2016; Feyrer, Sacerdote 2009; Grier 1999). But see also Kohli (2020).

It is now a fixed principle of the policy of Great Britain ... that her colonies of European race, equally with the parent country, possess the fullest measure of internal self-government ... But there are others which have not attained that state, and which, if held at all, must be governed by the dominant country, or by persons delegated for that purpose by it. This mode of government is as legitimate as any other, if it is the one which in the existing state of civilization of the subject people most facilitates their transition to a higher stage of improvement. There are, as we have already seen, conditions of society in which a vigorous despotism is in itself the best mode of government for training the people in what is specifically wanting to render them capable of a higher civilization ... The ruling country ought to be able to do for its subjects all that could be done by a succession of absolute monarchs, guaranteed by irresistible force against the precariousness of tenure attendant on barbarous despotisms, and qualified by their genius to anticipate all that experience has taught to the more advanced nation. Such is the ideal rule of a free people over a barbarous or semi-barbarous one.   John Stuart Mill (1862)

Suppose one takes a broad view of the concept of democracy (see Chapter 2), and suppose one were able to measure this concept comprehensively outside Europe and across polities of all sorts (bands, tribes, chiefdoms, city-states, empires) at two points in time – (a) just prior to the arrival of Europeans and (b) just after their arrival.

It seems evident that the immediate impact of Europeans on democracy was starkly negative. Existing systems of governance, many of which were probably quite democratic (as argued in Chapter 2), were disrupted and displaced by new systems of governance that systematically disenfranchised indigenous inhabitants. Not only were indigenes prohibited from participating in politics; they also enjoyed few civil rights or property rights and were often placed in positions of servitude. From this perspective, the initial wave of European globalization was clearly bad for democracy. Indeed, it is difficult to imagine a more undemocratic outcome.

Now, let us redefine the outcome. Instead of a broad definition of democracy, let us adopt a narrower one focused on competitive elections, representative assemblies, and written constitutions. Let us also focus on state forms of political organization rather than bands, tribes, and chiefdoms. This way of thinking about democracy is consistent with how the concept is usually understood in the modern era, and comports with crossnational indicators such as Polyarchy and Polity2. With this perspective on our topic, the influx of Europeans may be viewed in a more positive light. Here, a case can be made for Europeans as progenitors of global democracy.

For those who doubt the efficacy of elections and representative institutions as instruments of popular rule and who bemoan the loss of communal decisionmaking this may seem like a poor choice of concepts.[1] But for those who view large states as inevitable, and who regard representative democracy as the only way of harnessing leaders to popular demands within the context of these ungainly political units, it may seem like a reasonable choice. Representative democracy may not be ideal but perhaps it is the least-worst alternative, as Churchill suggested.

We shall not attempt to resolve this debate. But it is important to emphasize that any claims for a positive European effect on democracy is premised on a particular definition of democracy. Instead of saying that Europeans brought democracy to the world it might be more correct to say that they replaced one vision of democracy ("direct") with another ("representative").

Exactly why representative democracy arose in Europe and not elsewhere is a question with many possible answers. Natural harbors may have played a role, as argued in Part II. But other factors surely also contributed (see Part IV). In any case, arguments set forth in Part III of the book do not presume any particular answer to the question of *why* Europe became the incubator of representative institutions.[2]

What is important for present purposes is that representative democracy was invented only once. Its existence throughout the non-European world may therefore be considered a product of diffusion. Outside Europe, representative democracy was imported.

Accordingly, a plausible approach to explanation (outside Europe) focuses on factors conducive to, or impeding, the diffusion process. We argue that a primary mechanism of European influence was

---

[1] See Barber (2003), Pateman (1970).
[2] We shall probably never understand the original invention itself; and even if we were to do so that factor might, or might not, help us to understand its diffusion. After all, invention and diffusion are quite different processes.

demographic. The probability of developing representative democracy hinged on the ratio of Europeans to non-Europeans within a colony or country.

Where Europeans were numerous they established some form of representative democracy, though often with restrictions limiting suffrage or officeholding to those of European heritage. This became the accepted rule by which leaders were selected.

Where they were in the minority they were more reticent about popular rule and often actively resisted democratization. Nonetheless, the idea of democracy diffused through educational systems, churches, newspapers and other media, economic contacts, and through the example set by the colonial government (at least at local levels), the metropole, and in Europe more generally.

Where Europeans were entirely absent, the concept of representative democracy was unfamiliar and the practice undeveloped.

We argue that this demographic mechanism was the most powerful pathway of democratic diffusion from Europe to the world and one of the more enduring causes of political institutions in the modern era. The first sections of the chapter lay out our theoretical framework. The final section offers a brief summary and specifies a set of hypotheses to be tested in later chapters.

European Democracy for Europeans

As Europeans conquered the world they brought their ideas about political organization with them. Wherever they were situated, Europeans tended to view themselves as rights-bearers – inheritors of the legacy of the classical age, of the Enlightenment, and of the age of revolution.[3]

Europeans also developed and carried with them other features that formed the *infrastructure* of democracy, e.g., written languages, educational systems, advanced transport and communication systems, urban patterns of settlement, nuclear family structures, nation-states, property rights, capitalist economies, and wealth. We do not know which of these features is most important for democracy. But we do know that they developed in tandem and were closely interconnected.

Because democracy (in its representative form) was valued by Europeans, and because they possessed the infrastructure required for sustaining democratic forms of government, it is not surprising that democracy arose first in areas settled by Europeans. In this respect, as

---

[3] See Armitage, Subrahmanyam (2009), Simon (2017).

in many others, colonies in the New World were a continuation of the Old World, "Neo-Europes" (Crosby 1986).

However, democracy was not viewed by Europeans as a nostrum suitable for all peoples everywhere. Even within Europe, there were limitations on who could participate in politics based, e.g., on social class and sex (Goldstein 2013). Outside Europe, it was generally assumed that non-whites, non-property holders, and women were incapable of self-government, or that they would need many years of apprenticeship before developing that capacity.[4]

This assumption had a number of underpinnings. It drew on a vision of democracy in which citizens must possess property (signaling their independence) and education (signaling their capacity for rational thought). It drew on a Eurocentric vision of the world in which non-Europeans were savage (uncivilized, ungodly) or servile (in thrall to despots or masters), and hence unable to govern themselves in a responsible manner. In a much-quoted passage, which serves as this chapter's epigraph, John Stuart Mill articulated the enlightened opinion of the day, in which abstract considerations of political theory intermingled with what one can only describe as racism.[5]

We must also consider how defining democratic capacities in this exclusive fashion served the interests of Europeans. "Democracy" (along with associated ideals of equality, representation, and so forth) provided a convenient mechanism for binding together members of the European community, overcoming class antagonisms and monopolizing power in heterogeneous societies around the world. While the economic interests of a European worker and large landowner might differ, they were both usually granted civil and political rights, in this fashion differentiating themselves from those who fell on the wrong side of the color line (Morgan 1975). Insofar as the exercise of democratic rights was reserved for Europeans it also served as a mechanism of political control – for the passage of discriminatory property rights laws and measures of "self-defense" that displaced indigenous peoples and made room for European settlers.[6]

Thus did values and interests combine to make democracy (for Europeans) a popular ideal (among Europeans). Avid proselytizers of property rights and Christianity, Europeans were not keen to spread the

---

[4] See Fieldhouse (1966), Fradera (2018), Huttenback (1976), Lynch (1973), Paine (2019), Reinsch (1902: 197), Ross (1982), Ward (1976), Waterhouse (2010: 240–5), Wight (1946, 1952).
[5] For a review of recent work on liberalism and empire see Sartori (2006).
[6] See Albertini, Wirz (1982: 259), Lützelschwab (2013), Woollacott (2015: 99).

gospel of democracy among indigenes, transplanted migrant workers, and slaves. Political freedom meant freedom for whites – initially, white men.[7]

To be sure, Europeans *sometimes* extended civil and political rights to non-Europeans. However, emancipation, enfranchisement, and qualification for public office for non-Europeans came about with greatest alacrity in places where Europeans predominated. Here, the extension of rights posed little threat to European hegemony. In England, three members of the tiny Parsee community were elected from various London constituencies to the House of Commons: Dadabhai Naoroji, a Liberal representing Finsbury Central (1892–5), Mancherjee Bhownagree, a Conservative representing Bethnal Green North East (1895–1900), and Shapurji Saklatvala, representing Battersea North for Labour (1922–4) and then for the Communist party (1924–9). These foreign-born MPs were curiosities, but they were granted full participation in their parties and in activities of the Commons (Anwar 2001: 533).

By contrast, where Europeans were in the minority, fear of popular rule prompted them to resist democratization and also to resist independence from the metropole wherever that seemed destined to inaugurate mass democracy.[8] India, the crown jewel of the British Empire, offers a classic example. Few Indians could vote and electoral institutions were limited to municipalities and legislative councils, neither of which enjoyed much power. Britishers resisted moves toward independence, not to mention moves toward greater democracy. So it was that members of the Parsi community could vote and even attain entrance to the most powerful office in the land in a country where Indians were a tiny minority, but they could not vote or attain office in their country of origin.

At the high point of the British Raj, the Earl of Elgin (governor-general of India, 1893–8) wrote to Lord Curzon (viceroy of India, 1899–1905), expressing the view that "we could only govern by maintaining the fact that we are the dominant race – though Indians in services should be encouraged, there is a point at which we must reserve the control to ourselves, if we are to remain at all" (quoted in Sarkar 1983: 23). Here, racial distinction serves as an explicit rationale for depriving Indians of political rights.

One must bear in mind that where Europeans were scarce, they occupied a precarious race-based hierarchy, depending upon fragile coalitions and acquiescence from those who constituted a clear majority

---

[7] See Foner (1994), Greene (2010), Huttenback (1976), Lake (2012), Morgan (1975), Paine (2019).
[8] See Albertini, Wirz (1982: 139, 332), Carvalho, Dippel (2020), Greene (2010: 76), Lynch (1973: 20, 51, 127, 158, 163, 190, 265, 325), Williams (1970: ch. 22).

of the population. Revolts by indigenes or slaves were common and often costly (Domingos et al. 2019; Dubois 2004; Maddox 1993), as was the case for the Indian rebellion of 1857, which culminated in the deaths of an estimated 6,000 British soldiers and civilians, roughly one of seven Britishers then living in India (Peers 2013: 64). In making sense of Europeans' actions we must reckon with their fear and foreboding in the face of determined resistance.

Democracy As a Club

The foregoing narrative suggests a historical model in which democracy serves as a coordinating device for group interests. To appreciate this angle on the history of democracy – how it made sense and resonated with contemporaries – we need to consider its origins in Europe as a narrowly defined *club*.

Voluntary associations have a long and varied history in Europe (Clark 2000; Kloppenborg, Wilson 1996). Beginning in the medieval period, cities, guilds, parties, fraternities, companies, churches, and universities in Europe were often formally incorporated based on models drawn from Roman and/or canon law. John Najemy (1979: 49–50) explains,

Each corporation was in essence the product of collective self-government by a body of equals. Many were based on some social, professional, or voluntary principle of selective inclusion. The legal principles used by the canon lawyers to explain the nature of ecclesiastical corporations in the thirteenth century were also applicable to the experience of the many secular corporations of late medieval Italy. A corporation was inherently the free creation of its members, acting voluntarily and in concert. The powers exercised in the name of the corporation were held to reside in the community of the members. The membership of the corporation, or a council representing the same, delegated those powers to elected heads, who served for limited terms and with the specific mandate to preside over the corporation, or to represent it, within the limits of its written constitution, according to the will of the majority, and for the common good of the community.

Each corporation developed methods of governance – consultative and decisionmaking bodies, judicial bodies, formal limits on the exercise of executive power, methods of leadership selection and deselection, protected rights for all members, and so forth – that presage contemporary democratic institutions.[9] Over time, these oligarchic corporations

---

[9] See Berman (1983), Bilder (2006), Black (1984), Ciepley (2017), Gierke 1900[1881], Greif (2006b), Maitland (2003), McLaughlin (1932: 50), Post (1943, 1964), Runciman (2000), Tierney (1982).

acquired a legal personality and began to perform functions of a semi-public nature. Many of them, especially the communes and some organizations of merchants, also gained the power to make and enforce their own laws. Self-regulation and limited but increasing legislative power and jurisdiction were the first steps toward the assumption by medieval corporations of an autonomous political existence. To this point the development was principally internal and common to a variety of different corporations and organized societies. (Najemy 1979: 49–50)

These corporate bodies retained strictly limited memberships whose purpose was oriented toward advancing the interests of their members. It is not surprising, therefore, that when forming new political communities Europeans regarded themselves as owners of corporations that performed acts of governance, primarily for their own benefit. The Mayflower Compact is one prominent example. Although it seems strange to us today to see democracy working in a highly exclusivist fashion, to Europeans of the early modern era this was entirely normal and expected.

The legacy of this corporatist history can be found in colonial charters (Lutz 1998) and municipal charters (Weinbaum 2010). Indeed, municipalities continued to function as the property of their shareholders, i.e., ratepayers, into the twentieth century in cities like Chicago (Einhorn 2001).

Of course, the governance of a political community involved spillover effects to the rest of society since some policies are non-excludable. However, the distinction between members (citizens) and non-members (slaves, subjects, savages) assured that only some residents enjoyed full civil rights and property rights. Membership criteria, along with most of the benefits of membership, were excludable, forming "club goods" (Buchanan 1965; Marciano 2021).

From this perspective, democracy began as a club and only gradually extended its membership to include all those residing in a sovereign territory. Since club membership was defined primarily by race (a convenient marker of European origin), the extent to which this club was inclusive or exclusive (relative to the community in which it was situated) depended upon the demographic heritage of a society. Where the population was predominantly non-European, club membership was restrictive and democracy accordingly limited. Where the population was predominantly European, membership was expansive and the club was indistinguishable from the community at large. Here, we can expect high-quality democracy (by the standards of the time). In this fashion, demography structured regime outcomes.[10]

---

[10] This schema bears resemblance to selectorate theory (Bueno de Mesquita et al. 2003). However, the latter framework is intended to explain the quality of governance while our goal is to explain regime types.

Gaining Entrance to the Club

One might have supposed that non-Europeans, excluded from the demo-cratic club and in many ways oppressed by the institutions of representative democracy, would react negatively to the ideal. However, this does not appear to have been the case. Rather than rejecting democracy non-Europeans fought for inclusion – for civil rights, for political rights, and for parties and policies that served their interests. We have already mentioned the struggle for citizenship in India. Similar struggles occurred in Latin America (between indigenes and the favored mestizos), in Africa (between blacks and whites), in Northern Africa (between Arabs and Europeans), and pretty much everywhere that Europeans attempted to rule over. The American Civil Rights movement in the latter half of the twentieth century is one of hundreds of episodes in which non-Europeans struggled for civil and political rights against privileged elites of European descent. This ongoing struggle constitutes a critical stage in the advance of democracy around the world. It is what makes democracy a global, rather than purely European, phenomenon.

In this respect, the diffusion of the idea of democracy is similar to the diffusion of the national idea – also commonly attributed to Europe.[11] European powers proclaimed an exclusivist regime, one dominated by Europeans in which others were relegated to the status of subordinate subjects. Non-Europeans responded by claiming equality and autonomy, based on an idea of nationality drawn from the European experience. Indian nationalists insisted that, rather than subjects of the Crown, India was an independent nation whose rights and claims stood equal to the British nation.

For our purposes, what bears emphasis is that democratic ideals (and to some extent nationalist ideals) were likely to be most firmly planted where Europeans were most numerous: the three historic Presidencies (Madras, Bombay, and Calcutta) in South Asia; along the coasts and especially in the port cities of East and Southeast Asia; in southern Africa; the Southern Cone of Latin America; the Bahamas, Barbados, Bermuda, and the Cayman Islands in the Caribbean; and throughout North America and Australasia.

One can suppose that commercial ties, intermarriage, schools, universities, churches, newspapers, and other media served important roles in the diffusion process. Universities may have served an especially important function in spreading the gospel of democracy among non-European

---

[11] See Bendix (1978), Breuilly (1993), Gellner (1983), Hobsbawm, Ranger (1983), Kedourie (1960), Kohn (1944), A. Smith (1978).

elites. Wherever they went, Europeans established universities (Newton 1924), and those who attained university education were often in the vanguard of movements for independence and democratization (Kurzman, Leahey 2004).

Through these avenues, facilitated by the adoption of European languages and global trade, familiarity with democracy and its accoutrements grew. Democracy, linked closely to concepts of republicanism, nationalism, liberalism, cosmopolitanism, equality, and revolution, was an international movement. The international popularity of Giuseppe Mazzini – in Argentina, Chile, Brazil, India, and throughout Europe – is testament to the contagiousness of these ideas in the nineteenth century.[12] And there was the practical example of democracy at work – in many of the Europe colonies, in metropoles (to varying degrees at various times), in Europe at large, and in European settler societies like the United States.

For all these reasons, where Europeans were numerous the ideal of democracy was likely to be firmly implanted. It was the only game in town. Gaining power, for non-Europeans, meant gaining power through democratic institutions, and the rules of the game were well understood.

Where Europeans were less numerous, familiarity with democratic principles was apt to be less widespread. Likewise, democratic institutions were weaker, perhaps only a polite fiction or perhaps entirely absent. Moreover, European resistance to the inclusion of non-Europeans was greater, as discussed. In this environment, it is understandable that non-Europeans would regard the democratic ideal more skeptically and seek to gain power through other means. And because of their demographic superiority the extraparliamentary route to power was also more availing.

In this fashion, demography left its imprint on political institutions long after independence was declared and colonial authority evaporated. The logic of our argument extends, as well, to societies that were never brought under European control.

Summary, Caveats, and Implications

In summary, the demographic balance between Europeans and non-Europeans changed the dynamic in three important ways.

First, larger numbers of Europeans meant greater *exposure* to the idea of democracy for non-Europeans, transmitted through schools, churches,

---

[12] See Bayly, Biagini (2008), and more generally Palmer (2014), Polasky (2015).

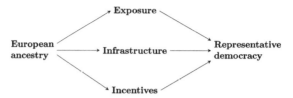

Figure 8.1 **European ancestry and representative democracy**
A sketch of the mechanisms presumed to be at work in the relationship
between demography and democracy.

newspapers, radio, direct contact with settlers, settler societies abroad
(such as the new hegemon, the United States), and the metropole.

Second, larger numbers of Europeans brought additional features that
we have referred to as the *infrastructure* of democracy (aka "modernization"): education, advanced transport and communications, urbanization,
a nation-state form of political organization, property rights, capitalism,
and wealth.

Third, larger numbers of Europeans changed *incentives*. For Europeans,
larger numbers meant that they were likely to control political outcomes
under democratic rules. Consequently, they had an incentive to invest in
democratic institutions and were more likely to respond positively to
claims by slaves and indigenes for inclusion. This, in turn, meant that
non-Europeans had a stake in democracy. It also meant that extraconsti-
tutional protest was unlikely to succeed, except perhaps as a point of
leverage to gain access to the democratic system. Numbers did not favor
a coercive route to power.

Precedents and Caveats

The various pieces of the theory set forth in this chapter have been lying
about for some time. Indeed, there is nothing especially novel in what we
have argued, as we build on a prodigious body of secondary work by
historians and historically inclined social scientists who have studied the
impact of Europeans on the modern world. We endeavor to reference
this work here and in subsequent chapters, though we can do no more
than scratch the surface of a very large oeuvre.

One intellectual tradition bears special mention. According to this
view, geographic factors, reflected in differential European mortality
rates across the world, stimulated European colonists to establish good
institutions (e.g., property rights) in some places and bad institutions in
others. These institutional legacies led to differential rates of economic
development over the long run, accounting for disparities in wealth and
poverty found across the world today. The thesis arises from the work of

many historians and from economists who built on that corpus,[13] attaining its canonical form in two companion studies by Acemoglu, Johnson, and Robinson (2001, 2002), of which there are many subsequent elaborations (e.g., Easterly, Levine 2016). Our work builds on this framework with a focus on democracy, a more specific explanation (European ancestry), and a broader purview (extending to the entire world, not just the colonial world). We also emphasize the explicitly racial aspects of this history, which are not reducible to an economic calculus.

At this point, three important caveats must be inserted.

First, we have applied the term "democracy" to a wide range of practices that contemporaries would have called by other names. Our rationale for engaging in this historical anachronism is laid out in Chapter 2. Briefly, it would be time-consuming and confusing to use a panoply of different terms in varying contexts; moreover, there was no single term that was widely used to represent phenomena that today would be classified as elements of representative democracy.

Second, there is a long history of democratic development within Europe that lies outside our theoretical scope.[14] We do not mean to suggest that representative democracy was fully achieved in its natal land, or that it is complete today. Reversals such as those of the interwar era (Skaaning 2011) were not uncommon, and challenges in the form of anti-democratic populist movements persist (Gora, de Wilde 2020). Nonetheless, Europe has generally registered a higher level of democracy than other regions of the world, and other high achievers (e.g., New Zealand, the United States, Uruguay) are apt to be populated largely by European immigrants. In this sense, it is reasonable to regard Europe as a source of democratic diffusion.

Third, in arguing that prospects for democracy in the modern era vary with the share of Europeans in a society we do not mean to imply that regime types are *solely* a product of the beliefs and actions of Europeans. Evidently, many other factors come into play. These factors lie in the background of our explanation. Demography is important, but it is not destiny (see Chapter 15).

Hypotheses

With these caveats, we argue that there is good reason to imagine that European ancestry has had considerable influence on the course of

---

[13] See Engerman (1981), Engerman, Sokoloff (1997, 2000), Hall, Jones (1999), North (1990).

[14] See also Canfora (2006), Cartledge (2016), Congleton (2010), Dunn (1992, 2005), Farrar (1988), Keane (2009), Kloppenberg (2016), Meier (2011), Miller (2018), Patterson (1991), Siedentop (2014), Stromberg (1996), Treadgold (1990). Reviews of the literature can be found in Gray, Smith (2019) and Knutsen, Møller, Skaaning (2016).

democracy over the past two centuries. Several more specific arguments flow from this central thesis.

First, limitations on democratic development were manifested by the exclusion of non-Europeans from the franchise and from the privilege of holding public office. The racial line dividing Europeans and non-Europeans was reflected in the institutions Europeans created.

Second, non-Europeans were more likely to be included as full (or partial) members of the political community where they were few in number – and hence, less threatening to European hegemony.

Third, Europeans employed the institutions of representative democracy to further entrench their rule. Those excluded from citizenship, or deprived of full civil and political rights, could not defend their interests, which meant that democracy was an instrument of oppression against slaves and indigenes.

Fourth, European settlers' desire to retain control over territories outside Europe conditioned their attitudes toward independence. Where they were a majority, they agitated for independence from the mother country. Where they were a minority, they preferred continued association with, and subordination to, the metropole.

Fifth, territories subject to direct rule by a European power were constrained in their political development, usually in a non-democratic direction. This was especially the case for non-English colonies. Once independence was achieved, political institutions were allowed to develop more freely. At this point, the influence of demography exerted itself even more strongly. Accordingly, we expect a stronger relationship between European ancestry and democracy in the colonized world *after* independence.

Sixth, the relationship between European demography and regime type changed over time. The relationship was strongest at a point in history (a) when the ideal of democracy was widely embraced by Europeans but not widely diffused among non-Europeans, (b) when racial distinctions between Europeans and non-Europeans were pervasive and invidious, and (c) when Europeans exercised greatest influence across the world. It seems plausible that these factors reached their apogee sometime in the twentieth century. By the end of that century, ideas and practices associated with representative democracy diffused to such an extent that it could no longer be regarded as a European patrimony. Additionally, ideas about national identity and race evolved such that the color line separating Europeans and non-Europeans blurred or became less consequential. Finally, the global hegemony of Europeans waned such that Europeans could no longer impose their preferred political institutions on the rest of the world. These trends seem likely to continue. Thus, although the legacy of the European era persists, its effects are likely to weaken as time goes on.

Finally, although demography was not the only avenue of European influence it probably had greater impact on the course of democracy in the modern era than other pathways from Europe such as religion (where Protestantism is often granted a leading role) or colonialism (where English tutelage is often granted a leading role).

These arguments can be summarized in a main hypothesis and several ancillary hypotheses as follows:

H_1 European ancestry is a distal cause of democracy.

H_a European settlers imported the idea of representative democracy to other parts of the world.

H_b Civil and political rights were allocated so as to exclude non-Europeans, de jure or de facto.

H_c The inclusion of non-Europeans was more likely where they were fewer in number.

H_d Institutions of representative democracy allowed Europeans to coordinate their interests, which often ran against the interests of excluded groups.

H_e For former European colonies, the date of independence varies inversely with European ancestry. (Colonies with more Europeans gain independence earlier.)

H_f The relationship between European demography and democracy is stronger in the post-independence era than in the colonial era.

H_g The relationship between European demography and democracy peaks in the mid-twentieth century, declining thereafter.

H_h European demography has a bigger impact on democracy in the modern era than other pathways from Europe such as religion (e.g., Protestantism) and colonialism (e.g., English colonialism).

These propositions will be explored empirically in subsequent chapters. We do not intend to demonstrate the causal mechanisms at work in this explanatory sketch as these factors are hard to measure and difficult to distinguish – though gestures in this direction may be found in Chapter 10, where we examine the colonial and post-colonial experience.

The old river in its broad reach rested unruffled at the decline of day, after ages of good service done to the race that peopled its banks, spread out in the tranquil dignity of a waterway leading to the uttermost ends of the earth. We looked at the venerable stream not in the vivid flush of a short day that comes and departs for ever, but in the august light of abiding memories. And indeed nothing is easier for a man who has, as the phrase goes, "followed the sea" with reverence and affection, than to evoke the great spirit of the past upon the lower reaches of the Thames. The tidal current runs to and fro in its unceasing service, crowded with memories of men and ships it had borne to the rest of home or to the battles of the sea. It had known and served all the men of whom the nation is proud, from Sir Francis Drake to Sir John Franklin, knights all, titled and untitled – the great knights-errant of the sea. It had borne all the ships whose names are like jewels flashing in the night of time, from the GOLDEN HIND returning with her rotund flanks full of treasure, to be visited by the Queen's Highness and thus pass out of the gigantic tale, to the EREBUS and TERROR, bound on other conquests – and that never returned. It had known the ships and the men. They had sailed from Deptford, from Greenwich, from Erith – the adventurers and the settlers; kings' ships and the ships of men on 'Change; captains, admirals, the dark "interlopers" of the Eastern trade, and the commissioned "generals" of East India fleets. Hunters for gold or pursuers of fame, they all had gone out on that stream, bearing the sword, and often the torch, messengers of the might within the land, bearers of a spark from the sacred fire. What greatness had not floated on the ebb of that river into the mystery of an unknown earth! ... The dreams of men, the seed of commonwealths, the germs of empires.   Joseph Conrad, *Heart of Darkness*

The age of globalization inaugurated a historic encounter between Europeans and non-Europeans. Out of that crucible, many things were born and many things (and people) died. Among the births, one might count representative democracy, an idea that spread round the world on European ships. Where Europeans settled in large numbers, and where the local population was small, or was eviscerated by disease, slaughter, and dislocation, democracy was likely to arise. Where Europeans were outnumbered democracy arose more slowly, if at all.

In the previous chapter, we laid out the general argument. In this chapter, we focus on the demographic story. The first section discusses imperialism as a maritime enterprise, linking Parts II and III of the book. The second section focuses on the European diaspora. The third section turns to other factors affecting the demographic balance between Europeans and non-Europeans, e.g., fertility rates among European settlers, survival rates among non-Europeans exposed to European diseases and firepower, and preexisting population density. The fourth section focuses on how "Europe" should be defined. The fifth section tackles the problem of how to identify Europeans and their ancestors around the world over the past four centuries – a challenging task, to say the least. The sixth section lays out our strategy for measurement. The final section compares our measure of European ancestry with extant measures of colonialism, demonstrating that these are quite separate concepts.[1]

Imperialism as a Maritime Enterprise

Empires extended back to the earliest states, i.e., to Egypt, Mesopotamia, and China. What was new, or at least comparatively new, in the early modern era was the idea of an empire that extended across oceans. As far back as Athens, colonies could be found scattered across the eastern Mediterranean, and dynastic conglomerates often incorporated dispersed territories on the European subcontinent. But, before 1500, empires tended to be relatively compact, encompassing contiguous territories or non-contiguous territories a short distance away. After 1500, all this changed, opening an era of global imperialism and colonization – first Portugal, then Spain, the Netherlands, England, and France, followed by Belgium, Germany, and Italy. Europeans were not the first empire-builders, but they were the first *overseas* empire-builders.

In this venture they did not always possess overwhelming military superiority. Sometimes, Europeans suffered losses, and often they avoided military conflict in situations where the outcome was uncertain (Sharman 2019). Local alliances and arrangements of mutual

---

[1] This chapter draws on a large body of work on European migration and colonialism, e.g., Abernethy (2000), Belich (2009), Canny (1994), Curtin (1989, 1998, 2002), Easterly, Levine (2016), Engerman, Sokoloff (2012), Etemad (2007), Fieldhouse (1966), Hatton, Williamson (2005), Hoerder, Moch (1996), Lange, Mahoney, Vom Hau (2006), Mahoney (2010), Moch (2003), Nugent (1989), Ringrose (2018), Zwart, van Zanden (2018).

convenience may have been as important as military conquest in paving the way for imperial expansion.[2] And the self-imposed isolationism of powerful states such as China, Japan, and Korea was a precondition for establishing European dominance across Asia (Andrade 2010, 2014).

In one area, however, Europeans enjoyed clear supremacy. By 1500, after the grounding of the Chinese navy, the maritime powers of Europe ruled the high seas. Likewise, long-distance trade was "carried out almost entirely on European ships, largely manned by European shippers, and managed by European entrepreneurs and/or state officials" (Zwart, van Zanden 2018: 20).

Whatever its proximal causes, European dominance of the ocean in the early modern and modern eras was a long-term product of that continent's extraordinary exposure to the ocean and the fragmented sovereignty of states on that continent, as argued in Part II of the book. Most Asian states did not aspire to rule the seas or to develop far-flung colonial enterprises, as their political and economic roots were in the land (Andrade 2014; Pearson 1991). But every European state with an ocean border and ambitions to trade needed to develop and maintain its own navy. Failure to do so would threaten its survival and its economic wellbeing, as navies secured effective rights to the sea. Sir Walter Raleigh commented, "Whosoever commands the sea commands the trade; whosoever commands the trade of the world commands the riches of the world, and consequently the world itself."[3]

Without naval supremacy, it is difficult to imagine that European powers would have been able to build and defend their global empires. European imperialism was, first and foremost, a naval enterprise. Maritime history and imperial history are therefore inseparable.[4] Through their maritime exploits a tiny continent, comprising only 8 percent of the world's landmass, managed to control 24 percent of the world by 1800 and 84 percent on the eve of World War I (Zwart, van Zanden 2018: 23).

Harbors afforded a point of initial contact and subsequent development for European colonial enterprises.[5] Harbors were needed to replenish supplies of food, water, and (after the advent of coal-powered steamships) fuel, and served as a refuge from inclement weather and

---

[2] See Bayly (2016), Ringrose (2018), Wills (1993).   [3] Quoted in Spence (2015: 9).

[4] See Andrade (2011), Andrews (1984), Cipolla (1965), Headrick (1981), Hearnshaw (1940), Kinkel (2018), Modelski, Thompson (1988), Paquette (2019), Raudzens (1999). We use the term "naval" loosely since permanent government-funded navies were not established until well into the early modern era.

[5] See Basu (1985), Bosa (2014), Darwin (2020), Gaikwad (2014), Garcia (2017), Kosambi, Brush (1988), Ricart-Huguet (2021), Seshan (2017).

attacks from pirates or hostile powers. Many harbors served an entrepôt role, offering an entrée to local markets. Where colonial powers elected not to establish formal colonies they might establish "treaty ports" offering Europeans extraterritorial rights, as happened in China and Japan.[6] Or they might insist upon "free trade" agreements designed to open markets to European companies, as occurred in Siam, the Ottoman Empire, and elsewhere (Horowitz 2004; Lynn 1999). In either case, colonial port cities played a key role. "Port cities were the gateways through which Western economic and political influence penetrated the non-European world," observe Broeze, Reeves and McPherson (1986: 1; see also Murphey 1969).

To explore this feature of colonialism in greater depth we assemble a list of all sizeable European colonies – including protectorates, mandates, and the like but excluding treaty ports and concessions – where a European power, or several powers, claimed sovereignty for at least a century. Colonial holdings without a designated administrative unit – i.e., no governor, no capital, as in many tiny Pacific islands – are not included. Colonial jurisdictions follow those laid out by the colonizer. Thus, New England colonies are listed separately, for this is how the English Crown divvied up its holdings. Where a territory had multiple capitals at various points during its tenure as a colony (e.g., Canada), only the capital with longest duration is included. In cases where a territory was colonized by multiple countries, only the colonizer with the longest tenure is listed.

The resulting compilation contains 231 colonies. For each colony, we note the colonizer, whether the colony was landlocked, and whether the colonial capital (the administrative headquarters of the colony) was situated on an ocean port, a river port (a river or lake with navigable access to the sea), or neither. The results of this coding exercise are displayed in Table C.3 (online at Dataverse).

In Table 9.1, the information contained in this table is reduced to a few key dimensions. We count the share of colonial capitals that had access to the ocean, either directly (because the capital lay in close proximity to a sea or ocean) or indirectly (because it lay upon a navigable river that discharged into the ocean or a lake that discharged into a navigable river with ocean access).[7] The startling feature of this table is in the first row. Eighty-two percent of colonial capitals enjoyed access to

---

[6] See Bickers, Jackson (2016), Hoare (1995), Mayers, Dennys (1867), Nield (2015).

[7] Prior to the nineteenth century, river harbors were almost as useful as harbors that lay directly on the ocean as most ships did not require deep clearance and thus could navigate shallow rivers.

Table 9.1 *Colonial capitals and their ports*

	Ocean (%)	River (%)	Neither (%)	Total (N)
Colonies				
All	68	14	18	231
Landlocked	0	9	91	22
Regions				
Africa	64	11	25	112
Asia-Pacific	85	15	0	48
Caribbean	94	6	0	18
America, Mexico	36	0	65	14
North America	52	48	0	21
South America	56	17	28	18
Colonizers				
Australia	100	0	0	2
Belgium	0	50	50	2
Denmark	75	0	25	8
Spain	50	3	47	30
France	57	24	19	37
Italy	67	0	33	3
Netherlands	83	17	0	12
New Zealand	100	0	0	1
Portugal	94	6	0	36
England/United Kingdom	65	18	17	100

Units of analysis: colonies, disaggregated by region and colonizer. Statistics aggregated from Table C.3 (online).

the ocean, most through a harbor that lay directly on the ocean. Only twenty-two capitals had no access at all and the reason for most of these cases is easily explained: most were in landlocked colonies.

Europeans leaving their home continent did not choose their destinations randomly. Where a natural harbor or navigable river existed, Europeans could dock their ships safely and disembark heavy equipment including war materiel. This was a decisive advantage for establishing military preeminence, for maintaining colonies, once established, and for linking them to a global trade network. Consequently, most colonies were coastal.

For example, in India the directly ruled Presidencies – Madras, Bombay, and Calcutta – occupied the coastal areas of the subcontinent, instituting a historic reversal from the previous pattern, in which power and people were located inland, primarily along the Indus and Ganges river valleys. Even where a European power claimed a substantial hinterland, as Britain eventually did in India (taking control gradually from princely states), European settlers and their industries tended to cluster in cities along the coast (Andrade 2014; Ross, Telkamp 1985).

There is, however, substantial variation across regions, as shown in the second section of Table 9.1. In Asia-Pacific, the Caribbean, and North America *all* colonial capitals enjoyed ocean access. Colonial capitals in Africa and South America are less favored though still predominantly oceanic: 75 percent and 72 percent, respectively. Mesoamerica is by far the least oceanic, with only 35 percent of its colonial capitals situated on the coast or along navigable rivers with access to the coast.

The final section of Table 9.1 differentiates among various colonial powers. It will be seen that all European colonizers generally chose coasts or navigable rivers as sites for their capitals. For most of its history, the Portuguese Empire was a coastal empire, centered on trading ports along the coast of Africa and Asia. Late in the day, Portuguese entrepôts began to extend into the hinterlands of Africa and South America, though European settlers tended to remain near the coast.[8] The Dutch Empire was also a maritime empire, centered on entrepôt colonies along the coasts of Asia, the Americas, Africa, and, most extensively, Southeast Asia.[9] The French Empire extended deep into the interior of Africa and North America; even so, a majority of settlers from the metropole congregated in watery zones along the coast of Quebec, Cochinchina, and Algeria, and on various islands of the Caribbean. Thus, the demographic and political center of the empire remained coastal (Southworth 1931). The British Empire, finally, was emphatically an oceanic empire. Despite its reach and territorial claims over a quarter of the world's land area (at the conclusion of World War I), the vast majority of its settlers, administrators, wealth, and infrastructure were centered on coastal regions across the world.[10]

Of the major colonizers (those with more than three colonies), Spain is the odd case: nearly half of its colonial capitals were blocked from the ocean. Although the empire began on the seas, exploiting ports along the coasts of Asia, Africa, and the Americas (Goodman 1997), in the Americas the empire extended inland and colonial administrators sought higher ground. This pattern was especially marked in the northern portion of South America, Central America, and Mexico (Van Oss 1985). The inland character of New Spain may reflect Spain's mercantilist orientation (Mahoney 2010). It was also presumably a response to existing demographic and organizational patterns. Pre-colonial empires

---

[8] See Bethencourt, Curto (2007), Boxer (1969), Newitt (2004).
[9] See à Campo (2002), Boxer (1965a), Parthesius (2009).
[10] See Andrews (1984), Black (2004), Bowen, Mancke, Reid (2012), Cannadine (2007), Metcalf (2008).

in this region were often located inland, and the conquistadors found it easiest to appropriate these capitals as their own, concentrating their commercial and religious activities where human capital and mineral riches were most abundant.

Nuances notwithstanding, we should not lose sight of the big picture. Table 9.1 demonstrates that as Europeans cast their eyes across the globe, deciding where to focus their power, their financial investments, and their people, access to the ocean was a principal desideratum. If a region was blessed with natural harbors it was likely to be blessed – or cursed, one might say – with Europeans.

Diaspora

Although imperialism paved the way for a European diaspora in the early modern and modern eras, it was not the only factor at work. Some colonies received a great many European settlers, while others attracted very few. So we must separate imperialism from emigration (an issue we return to at the conclusion of the chapter).

The European diaspora began with the age of exploration and continued on a sizeable scale through the early twentieth century. During this period, an estimated sixty or sixty-five million left the continent for points abroad (Etemad 2007: 18). This dramatic shift of population from one small subcontinent to the rest of the world peaked in the mid- to late nineteenth century, coincident with the arrival of the steamship, which dramatically lowered the time and cost required for an ocean voyage, as well as the health risks. After World War I, migration slowed considerably due to decelerating population growth in Europe as well as (eventually) improvements in European economies and the rise of welfare states, relieving pressure on potential emigrants.

Later migrants generally followed in the footsteps of their predecessors, typically, members of their family or village, a process known as chain migration. They were also responsive to economic and demographic realities that earlier settlers had established. Hence, the following discussion focuses on the era of mass European migration, circa 1500–1900, and especially on early waves of emigration (prior to 1850), which instituted path-dependent patterns.

Although migrants emigrated from all parts of Europe, regions with the largest volume of emigrants at any given time were characterized by industrialization (which displaced farmers), the absence of serfdom (making it possible for agricultural classes to relocate), limited availability of cheap and arable land, high fertility rates (hence, population pressure), and a significant wage gap between home state and destination state

(Hatton, Williamson 2005). Another important feature, in our estimation, was easy access to ocean transit via natural harbors. Not only did steamships make emigration affordable, they also stimulated migration by actively recruiting passengers in the hinterland of ocean ports (Feys et al. 2007; Feys 2012).

These features coalesced at various historical junctures in all areas of Western Europe with the notable exception of France, whose fertility rates dropped earlier and more precipitously than in other regions of Europe. The leading "donors" from 1851 to 1910 were Austria-Hungary, the British Isles, Denmark, Finland, Germany, Ireland, Italy, the Netherlands, Norway, Portugal, Spain, Sweden, and Switzerland, with smaller numbers emanating from Belgium and France.[11]

For these migrants, some destinations were preferred to others. Distance (from Europe) appears to have been a minor factor in this decision. To be sure, North America was closer to Europe than South America, and ocean passage was accordingly cheaper and less onerous. This may account for the higher rate of immigration to the US (especially among poor emigrants) relative to other destinations in the Americas. These are marginal differences, however. Russia, Central Asia, the southern coast of the Mediterranean, and Africa, the areas closest to Western Europe, received few emigrants, while New Zealand and Australia, at the other end of the world, were inundated.

Factors other than distance generally structured choices about where to migrate. Healthful climates were generally located away from the equatorial zone, where malaria and other dangers lurked (Curtin 1989, 1998). Of equal importance was the ready availability of land that was fertile and available for exploitation via planting, trapping, timber, and other agricultural pursuits.[12] Mineral wealth sparked gold rushes and other speculative booms but not large-scale permanent migration as Europeans were not keen on hard labor under dangerous conditions for little pay.

Demography

Migration from Europe is just one part of our story. We must also consider fertility rates among those who emigrated. Where settlers

---

[11] See Hatton, Williamson (2005: 53), as well as Nugent (1995: 30). Russia, which sits outside Europe in our classification, was a comparatively small donor. Unfortunately, exact figures are unavailable for earlier periods of European migration. We suspect that Scandinavia, the Low Countries, and the Iberian peninsula would be more strongly represented while the UK would hold its position near the top.

[12] See Adelman (1994), Bhandar (2018), McLaren, Buck, Wright (2005), Weaver (2003), Webb (1986).

traveled as families there was a mix of males and females, leading to a normal reproductive pattern. Under circumstances of plenty, this translated into high fertility and impressive population growth (Carter, Sutch 2013: 43). Where settlers traveled in small numbers to areas perceived to be dangerous or otherwise unfit for European women, reproductive rates were slower as settlers were likely to serve a term of duty and then return home to the metropole, where their family (current or future) awaited. In the interim, they might couple with members of the native population, but these offspring were of uncertain identity – an issue discussed at length below.

Of even greater importance to the resulting demographic balance was the density of indigenous populations. Where indigenes were densely settled they were unlikely to lose their demographic predominance, regardless of the number of Europeans who entered the territory. This describes much of Asia, some parts of Africa, and the equatorial region of the Americas (from southern Mexico to Peru). Indigenous demography played an especially important role in the New World, where native peoples were susceptible to the scourge of European diseases (smallpox, influenza etc.). Where populations were densely settled they tended to recover as resistances built up; where populations were diffusely settled, they might never recover and were easy to displace.

A second factor affecting demographic balance was the commodities encouraged by a region's geography. Family farming was not as remunerative as labor-intensive cash crops (sugar, tobacco, cotton, coffee, tea, cocoa, sisal, oil seeds, oil palms, rubber, or fruit) or mining (e.g., for gold or silver). Thus, where soil and climate resources allowed, or where natural resources were discovered underground (alluvial deposits could be harvested by individual miners working for themselves on the model of the California and Alaska gold rushes), these industries proliferated. To be profitable in a low-technology environment, plantations and mines required a large labor force that would do hard and dangerous work under close supervision for little or no remuneration. Europeans would not submit to these conditions (except under temporary arrangements of indentured servitude), presumably because they had better options. Consequently, plantation and mining economies came to be dominated by non-European workers – indigenes, slaves imported from Africa, or migrant workers from Asia (Engerman, Sokoloff 2012).

In summary, where climate and soil were suitable for European emigration and the establishment of family farms and where indigenous populations were diffuse, Europeans usually became a sizeable ethnic group. This describes the Americas away from the equator, Australasia, and the southern tip of Africa. Where geographic and demographic

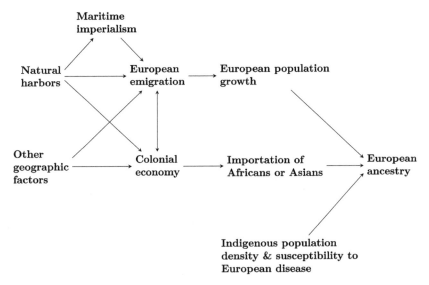

Figure 9.1 **A speculative model of European ancestry**
Causal diagram reconstructing various influences on European
ancestry (outside Europe).

conditions were not propitious, Europeans may have operated trading
posts, mines, plantations, or missions; they might have also controlled
the levers of political, military, and economic power; and they might have
established colonies that endured for centuries. However, their demographic presence remained slight.

The intricacies of this process are hard to reproduce with a series of
nodes and arrows. Still, it may be useful to lay out the most important
elements of this story in a causal diagram, as shown in Figure 9.1.[13] The
outcome of this interplay of causal factors – listed on the far right – is the
quantity of interest in Part III of the book: European ancestry.

Europe

Having addressed the causal factors at work in the European diaspora,
we turn to issues of conceptualization and measurement. The region
known today as Europe is a cultural construction, open to varying
interpretations that change over time (Hay 1966; Pagden 2002). There

---

[13] For an alternative account of European settlement focused exclusively on Africa see
Frankema, Green, Hillbom (2016).

is a long etymology. Indeed, the identity of three continents – Asia, Africa ("Libya") and Europe – and their association with women, goes back at least as far as Herodotus (Wilson, van der Dussen 2005: 14–15).

Our geographic theory, presented in Part II of the book, suggests that what was most distinctive about Europe was its watery environment. Accordingly, we define Europe as the regions west of the Urals lying closest to a natural harbor. So defined, the complete list of European states, including now-defunct states that make a cameo appearance in a few of our analyses, is as follows: Albania, Andorra, Austria, Baden, Bavaria, Belgium, Bosnia, Brunswick, Bulgaria, Croatia, Czechia, Denmark, East Germany, Estonia, Finland, France, Germany, Greece, Hamburg, Hanover, Hesse-Darmstadt, Hesse-Kassel, Hungary, Iceland, Ireland, Italy, Latvia, Liechtenstein, Lithuania, Luxembourg, Macedonia, Mecklenburg Schwerin, Modena, Moldova, Montenegro, Nassau, Netherlands, Norway, Oldenburg, Papal States, Parma, Piedmont-Sardinia, Poland, Portugal, Romania, San Marino, Saxe-Weimar-Eisenach, Saxony, Serbia, Slovenia, Spain, Sweden, Switzerland, Tuscany, Two Sicilies, Ukraine, United Kingdom, Vatican City, and Württemberg. For present purposes, "Europeans" are people whose ancestors lived in these regions in 1500.

Alternate Definitions

We prefer to define Europe in a geographic fashion as this fits with our previous argument (in Part II of the book) and also lends greater exogeneity to the concept. By contrast, definitions of Europe that hinge on political or cultural properties may be endogenous to other features that could serve as confounders.

Even so, we readily acknowledge that Europe could be defined differently. One might mark its territory by the furthest extent of the Roman Empire or by the spread of Christianity. One might extend its borders to include more of Central Europe or Southern Europe, or shrink its borders to exclude the Celtic fringe. The eastern borders of Europe are notoriously ambiguous, as there are no clear-cut geographical boundaries separating Europe from Asia (Wolff 1994).

As a secondary definition, we propose that a state is part of the European cultural zone if its principal or official language was Latinate or Germanic in the modern era. This decision-rule generates a list of contemporary states including Andorra, Austria, Belgium, Denmark, France, Germany, Iceland, Ireland, Italy, Liechtenstein, Luxembourg, Malta, Moldova, Monaco, Netherlands, Norway, Portugal, Romania, San Marino, Spain, Sweden, Switzerland, and the United Kingdom.

We use this secondary definition in robustness tests (see Chapter 11). As it happens, this coding adjustment has negligible impact on our findings.

We conclude that although Europe is impossible to define in an authoritative fashion, it is unlikely that a different definition would affect the findings reported in subsequent chapters. Most emigrants hailed from the western portions of the continent. There is little doubt about the European status of the leading exporters. Whether Europe is extended further east or south matters little because the demographic impact of these areas was relatively small – and in any case migration patterns tended to follow those established by earlier waves of migration from Western Europe, as noted.

A Common Identity

In treating Europeans as a single cultural group we do not mean to suggest that all Europeans were the same. Differences in cultures and institutional practices across the subcontinent were considerable, and we assume that this mattered for economic development and the development of democracy, both within Europe and abroad.[14]

Yet, national differences attenuated over time. This is evident within Europe, and is even more marked outside Europe as settlers from different states began to think of themselves as inheriting a common European (aka Christian, civilized, or white) culture rather than a specifically British, Dutch, French, etc. culture. In the Cape colony, Giliomee and Elphick (1979: 359–60) report that from 1652 to 1820,

colonial society was dominated by a group whose members variously described themselves as "colonists," "inhabitants," "Africaners," "Christians," "whites," or "Europeans." This group was larger than an ethnic group as usually defined, for it embraced people of different languages (Dutch, German, French, etc.), different religious denominations (Dutch Reformed, Lutheran, etc.), and different cultures. Despite its diversity the European group remained distinct from other groups in the colony (blacks, Khoikhoi and Bastaards) ... [T]here was a comparatively favourable sex ratio among the European population; thus a rather small number of Cape marriages were mixed and children of extramarital miscegenation were not usually regarded as European ... This high rate of endogamy confirms the impression we have gained from the documents that the European group was decidedly aware of its identity and distinctiveness from other groups. It retained this identity throughout our period, adding to its members chiefly from further European immigration and internal generation ... We call the European group a "race" because membership of it was almost always

---

[14] See Bernhard et al. (2004), Lange, Mahoney, Vom Hau (2006), Olsson (2009), Paine (2019).

determined by birth rather than choice, because it embraced many European nationalities, and because physical appearance (which entailed more than mere skin colour) was an important badge of group membership.

In a similar fashion, French Algeria drew migrants from throughout Europe (especially Spain, Italy, and Malta); over time, they began to form an identifiable community of "colons," later understood as "pieds noir" (Prochaska 1990: 25). Likewise, the first settlers to North America considered themselves English, Dutch, German, and so forth. But over time these national identities lapsed, to be replaced by a generic identity – in this case, "white" or "American" (read: American of European descent).

The melting-pot metaphor is more clearly applicable to Europeans than to non-Europeans. Accordingly, we treat Europeans within each state as a unitary group, overlooking cleavages based on country of origin, language, religion, and ideology.

We recognize that every European settlement generated its own intra-European conflicts, and these gradations of status and power were consequential. However, when it came to establishing basic rules and norms about who could vote, hold office, or enjoy civil rights, distinctions among Europeans were less relevant than distinctions between Europeans and non-Europeans. In constitutional matters, race trumped nationality, ethnicity, language, religion, and party.[15] In the United States, the Irish became white, as the phrase goes (Ignatiev 2012), and quickly mastered the art of politics (Erie 1990). So did other Catholics, whom the predominantly Protestant population initially mistrusted. By contrast, it took another century for blacks to attain the juridical rights accorded to white Americans, a struggle that continues to the present day. In this respect, we feel justified in treating Europeans as a unitary category.

Precisely *why* race came to predominate over other identities is a question that we leave in abeyance, though we presume that the encounter between Europeans and the wider world that occurred during the age of imperialism was of some importance (Schwartz 1994). In an age before passports, distinctive skin pigmentation allowed Europeans to readily distinguish themselves from natives, migrant laborers, and slaves, facilitating the formation of a social order that was egalitarian in some respects (among whites) and hierarchical in other respects (across the color line).[16]

---

[15] See Fredrickson (2002: 68), Gann, Duignan (1962: 69), Giliomee, Elphick (1979: 359–60), Mills (1997).

[16] See Allen (1994), Belich (2009: 5), Bethencourt (2015), Eliav-Feldon, Isaac, Ziegler (2009), Fanon (1970), Fradera (2018), Kennedy (1987), Mohanram (2007), Pagden (2009), Ross (1982).

European-ness

The variable of theoretical interest in this study is the share of people living in a society who are European *by ancestry*. This is not a matter that modern demographers have attended to, though it was a concern for demographers in the early twentieth century (Ittmann 2013). In any case, there is no standard database that one might draw upon.

There is also a serious problem of definition. Who, exactly, is European? The same general problem besets any study of ethnicity and race.[17] Lines are drawn differently at different times and places, and where populations intermix over long periods these lines are especially blurry.

In the face of these obstacles we adopt a constructivist definition of ancestry. A European is what people – specifically, surveyors and enumerators – understood to be a European. This understanding was likely to change over time and was especially elastic in places with high rates of miscegenation such as Latin America and many parts of Asia.[18]

Since racial mixing has a direct effect on our outcome it is worth contemplating this dynamic within colonial society. Bender (1978: 34) takes a structural perspective:

The experience of European colonization shows that white attitudes towards miscegenation and mesticos were strongly influenced, if not actually determined, by the interplay of two demographic factors: ratio of European men to women and the proportion of whites in relation to non-whites. Whenever Indians and/or blacks comprised a majority of the population and most of the whites were single males, a significant mestico group developed (usually equal to the size of the European population) which was racially and social distinguished from both blacks and whites. It is almost axiomatic that where these demographic conditions obtained there was a noticeable absence of any stigma against sexual intercourse between white men and non-white women; on the contrary, it was normal and expected. This was as true for the English in the Caribbean, the Spanish from Chile to Mexico, the French in Martinique, the Dutch in Brazil and the West Indies, as it was for the Portuguese and other Europeans in Brazil.

If a smaller European:indigene ratio leads to higher rates of miscegenation and to greater acceptability of the practice, thus softening racial lines, then over time a larger group of citizens are likely to be granted status as European (McNamee 2020). "Mestizo" merges with "white."

---

[17] See Lieberman, Singh (2012), Simon, Piché, Gagnon (2015).
[18] For Latin America, see Carvalho et al. (2004), Loveman (2014), McNamee (2020). For Asia, see Ringrose (2018). For general surveys see Edwards, Caballero, Song (2012), Rocha, Aspinall (2020), Simon, Piché, Gagnon (2015).

In any case, our constructivist approach to category definition suggests that a European is whatever a European is considered to be. Flexibility in the category is acknowledged by our theory. Since the value of European-ness in our theory has nothing to do with genetics (it is not as if Europeans are genetically predisposed to democracy) and everything to do with sociology, it is the latter that matters. With this in mind, let us turn to the enumeration problem.

Counting Europeans

Europeans were responsible for most surveys and censuses during the colonial period and one can be fairly confident that they counted them-selves, as they were acutely conscious of their separate status. Surveys often classified respondents by country (e.g., "English"), by continent (e.g., "European"), or by race (e.g., "white"), so we have a good sense of how many shared a European heritage (by whatever standards were applied at that time and place).[19]

To deal with heterogeneity in how Europeans were defined we include regional dummies in our main analysis and conduct sub-sample analyses focused on specific colonizers – British, Spanish, and French – where definitions were likely to be more consistent. We also conduct time-series analyses with state (country or colony) fixed effects. To deal with cross-temporal heterogeneity we include year dummies in our main analysis and conduct sub-sample analyses limited to particular eras.

At the same time, we do not want to overplay the fluidity of these boundary lines. Racial categories were constructed, but they were not constructed out of whole cloth. Prior to the twentieth century, the color line was strictly monitored and policed in most societies throughout the world. At any given time, most people had a clear sense of where they stood and could do little about it (Twinam 2015). The rigidity of race – which was assumed to reflect far-reaching genetic differences between human populations – makes it a harder, more exogenous category than it is today. Indeed, race-consciousness undergirds our statistics. One may assume that a primary purpose for gathering demographic data in which people are classified by origin or pigmentation was to reinforce those invidious distinctions (Loveman 2009; Nobles 2000). Thus, despite the weaknesses of census and survey methodology in times past, we have greater confidence in data drawn from historical eras – when it had a clearer meaning – than in data from the contemporary era, when its

---

[19] For work on censuses as they developed over time see Kertzer, Arel (2002), Loveman (2009, 2014), Rocha, Aspinall (2020).

meaning seems increasingly ambiguous, when the categories sometimes disappear entirely from censuses and surveys, or when categories fragment into dozens of mixed-race identities, which are variously understood by surveyors and survey respondents (Rocha, Aspinall 2020).

Historians and social scientists – not to mention, contemporaries – discuss the European (aka white) identity as if it was real. Likewise, studies of ethnicity, religion, and other ascriptive categories assume that these categories were, and are, meaningful. We shall do the same, with the usual caveats.

To maximize coverage, minimize stochastic error, and to get a sense of convergent validity, we collect data from as many sources as possible. Over fifty secondary sources are included. These cull innumerable primary sources, i.e., censuses, surveys, and informal estimates, as detailed in Appendix F (online at Dataverse). Our efforts build on a previous dataset collected by Easterly and Levine (2016), which provides 23 percent of our data points.

Statistics of interest include (a) number of Europeans, (b) total population, and (c) European share of population. Where only one of these elements is missing it is calculated by the authors. Where total population is missing we draw upon Fariss et al. (2017), which aggregates a number of primary datasets. From these sources, we assemble 2,193 data points drawn from 237 states (countries and colonies) from 1600 to 2019.

To aggregate estimates across multiple sources and to generate a continuous dataset with annual estimates for each state back to 1600 we take several additional steps. For states outside Europe, we mark the date of the first recorded European settlement or (if the latter is unknown) the first European contact. This is coded as zero (no Europeans), forming the first data point in the series. For states within Europe, we record the number of Europeans as 100 percent in 1950. This estimate is extended back to 1600 under the assumption that the share of Europeans within that state did not change greatly during a period when in-migration (from outside Europe) was limited.

For the remaining time period (after the point of first European contact for non-European territories and after 1950 for European territories), we estimate yearly data points across available data using a loess smoother that regresses population on year with a smoothing parameter ($\alpha = 0.85$). The quadratic function is appropriate for data patterns with a single curvature, as is the case for most territories under observation – where the share of Europeans increases to a peak and then decreases, forming an inverted-U shape. For European countries, the share of Europeans tends to decrease in a monotonic fashion after 1950, also nicely captured by the quadratic function. With this aggregation procedure we generate estimates of European ancestry for 99,067 state-years, representing the demographic histories of 237 states from 1600 to 2019.

One particular nuance of our measure of European ancestry is the unit-of-analysis problem. Our calculations focus on states, however they might be defined through history. Since these definitions changed we must consider the impact of these changes. In particular, European colonies tended to start small, often in port cities that served as European enclaves. As they grew, taking control (or at least claiming formal sovereignty) over the hinterland, the share of Europeans dropped as a function of changing boundaries. Angola and Mozambique became less Portuguese as they absorbed their hinterlands, just as the US became less European as its borders moved west toward the Pacific.

Fortuitously, these historical changes in borders capture what is relevant to our theory. Note that the formal boundaries of a political unit define the relevant population, and thus the probable impact of European ancestry on its political institutions. A unit that is defined narrowly, to include only (or primarily) Europeans, is apt to democratize. A unit that is defined broadly, including a swath of territory with many indigenes, is less likely to democratize – for all the reasons laid out in Chapter 8. This seemingly arbitrary aspect of state borders is therefore well suited to our theoretical question.

While the crossnational regression analyses in Chapter 11 are limited to sovereign and semisovereign units, in the qualitative analyses undertaken in Chapter 10 we occasionally survey the governance of cities within states. Here, the relevant calculation of European ancestry is urban. And because there was enormous variation across cities and regions of a state in the density of European settlers, this provides some additional leverage on our question, albeit one that cannot be undertaken in a systematic fashion due to the absence of historical demographic data covering municipalities or subnational regions on a large scale.

To give readers a sense of the data, our sources, and our method of interpolating missing values, we produce graphs for each territory, shown in Appendix E (online at Dataverse). We also produce maps of the world at century-long intervals, shown in Map 9.1.

Reassuringly, our measure of European ancestry is highly correlated with other attempts to measure this concept, as shown in Table 9.2. Helpfully, it has much better coverage than these other measures – nearly 100,000 polity-year observations from 1600 to 2019.

A histogram of the European ancestry variable, in Figure 9.2, shows bimodal peaks located at each end of the scale. Most polities have very

1600
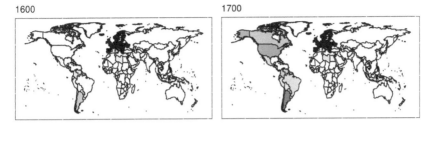

1700

1800
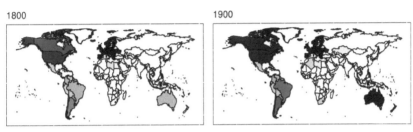

1900

1950
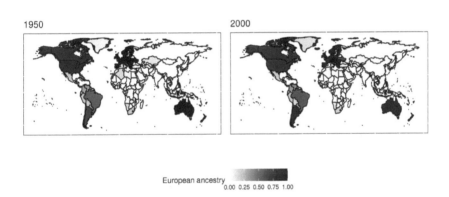

2000

European ancestry
0.00 0.25 0.50 0.75 1.00

Map 9.1 **European ancestry over time**

few people from the European subcontinent, a handful are composed
primarily of Europeans, and the remainder fall somewhere in between.
Note that measurement error at the extremes is less likely than measurement error in the messy middle. Since extreme values provide the most
influential data points in a regression analysis, problems of causal identification stemming from measurement error are mitigated.

Table 9.2 *Alternate indices of European ancestry*

Index	Years	States	Obs	Pearson's r
Acemoglu, Johnson, Robinson (2001)	1900	157	157	0.66
Easterly, Levine (2016)	1600–1800	12	132	0.74
Easterly, Levine (2016)	1800–1900	32	3232	0.84
Putterman, Weil (2010)	2000	164	164	0.86
Authors	1600–2019	237	99 067	

Correlation (Pearson's r) of the authors' index of European ancestry with alternate indices. Note that the primary sources for all of these indices overlap, so these indices are not independent of each other.

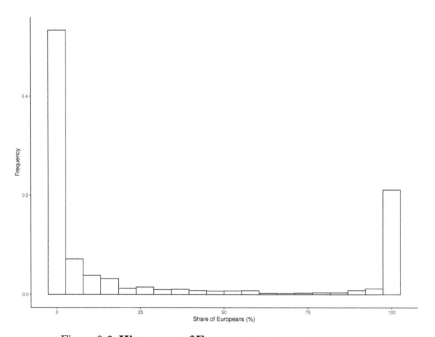

Figure 9.2 **Histogram of European ancestry**
Histogram of European ancestry variable, showing the share of Europeans in 237 states from 1600 to 2018. Not all states are observed continuously across the period so this is an unbalanced panel.

Although the distribution illustrated in Figure 9.2 hugs the two extremities of the scale, we do not regard European ancestry as a binary variable in disguise. Indeed, we show that the relationship of theoretical interest is robust even when each mode is excluded from the analysis (see Table 11.4).

Demography and Colonialism

Since the distinction between European demography and European colonialism is central to our theory let us dwell for a moment on the contrast between these two concepts.

Colonialism denotes formal control (but not full integration) of a territory by a metropole (generally overseas). It covers cases like British India, where a tiny British contingent attempted to control an entire subcontinent, and protectorates like Bechuanaland where there were scarcely any settlers, as well as cases like New England, where settlers fairly quickly displaced indigenes.

It stands to reason that the longer a European power is in control of a foreign territory the more Europeans are likely to migrate to that territory. However, one should not expect a one-to-one correspondence. Cape Verde, Mozambique, and Belize have colonial histories stretching for over 400 years but experienced very little European settlement. By contrast, Australia and Uruguay had relatively brief colonial histories (roughly a century, depending on how one marks the point of onset) but a great many Europeans migrated there, making them prime examples of settler colonies. In Latin America, the centers of Spanish colonial government were in Mexico and Peru, while the center of Spanish (and other European) demography was in the Southern Cone, which was lightly governed in the colonial era.

Accordingly, European ancestry and European colonialism are quite different concepts. To illustrate the point, we graph the intersection of these two variables in Figure 9.3. European ancestry is the share of persons in a state whose ancestors migrated from Europe, as laid out above. Colonialism is measured by the duration of colonial rule (Olsson 2009).

It will be apparent that these two variables are weakly correlated (Pearson's $r = 0.23$). Even if colonialism is measured differently, e.g., as direct/indirect rule (Lange 2004), or as the intensity of governance structures, one will find only a fair to middling correlation with European ancestry.

In the chapters that follow we shall endeavor to show that formal control over a territory (colonialism) is much less important for the fate of democracy than who lives in that territory, i.e., the demographic balance between Europeans and non-Europeans. Later, in Chapter 13, we test the two theories of democracy side-by-side. There, we show that the duration of colonial rule is a weak predictor of modern democracy when European ancestry is included in the same model.

This is not to say that colonialism is irrelevant to democracy. We concur with others who have argued that there was a difference in

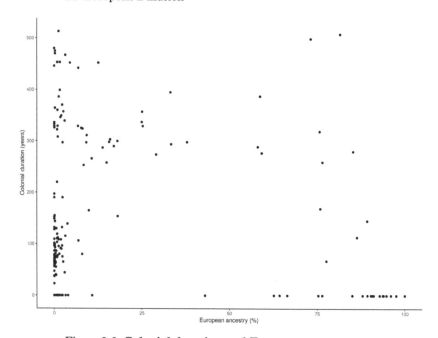

Figure 9.3 **Colonial duration and European ancestry**
The intersection of colonial duration and European ancestry for the
non-European world in 2000. Pearson's r: 0.229.

governance and in regime legacies between the English and other
European colonizers, and there may be a difference between territories
that were intensively colonized and those that were colonized lightly or
not colonized at all. However, in our view the principal mechanism
by which colonialism affected the post-colonial fates of states was
demographic.

While colonial rulers exercised formal control over their holdings they
lost that control after independence. This does not mean that the colonial experience ceased to influence politics in the post-colonial era; but it
was certainly a more diffuse sort of influence. By contrast, influence
channeled through settlers was bound to persist in the post-colonial era
as those settlers (or their descendants) generally remained, wherever they
were a more than token presence. The demographic channel of influence
thus changed very little pre- and post-independence.

Moreover, this mechanism was not simply a response to the establishment of a colony or the length of time a colony remained under control of
the metropole. Many factors affected the flow of European migration, as
summarized in Figure 9.1, and most of these factors were independent of

the colonial power. In most cases, migrants arrived before a formal declaration of European sovereignty and continued arriving long after the colonial tie was sundered. Very few Americans of European descent living today can trace their ancestors to settlers who arrived prior to 1776. Sometimes, European settlement was completely independent of colonial control. For example, Israel was settled initially by European Jews fleeing persecution. A protectorate followed from 1923 to 1948 but this had little impact on patterns of migration or the long-term development of the Jewish state.

Importantly, migrants did not restrict their migration choices to colonies of the metropole. "Spanish" America received many Portuguese, Italians, and Irish. "English" America received Europeans from everywhere on the subcontinent. There were more Dutch in South Africa than English, even though the English government controlled more of the territory prior to independence. And so forth.

Finally, it is important to note that the interests of settlers were not always in sync with those of the metropole. Settlers tended to be motivated, first and foremost, by land, and secondarily by control over labor (often coerced). Establishing property rights over land and people meant conflict, and conflict entailed costs for the metropole, whose primary interest was in maintaining order. Thus, colonial officers often sought to restrict the incursions of settlers and the mistreatment of slaves and indigenes while settlers frequently ignored these restrictions or fought to remove them (McNamee 2023).

Our perspective on the era of European globalization thus sheds a different light on the colonial experience. In contrast to the prevailing legal-bureaucratic approach (tracking issues of formal, jurisdictional sovereignty), we adopt an approach rooted in demography.

10   Colonial and Post-colonial Eras

> Since I know that you will be pleased at the great success with which the Lord has crowned my voyage, I write to inform you how in thirty-three days I crossed from the Canary Islands to the Indies, with the fleet which our most illustrious sovereigns gave me ... When I reached Cuba, I followed its north coast westwards, and found it so extensive that I thought this must be the mainland, the province of Cathay ... From there I saw another island eighteen leagues eastwards which I then named "Hispaniola" ... In this island of Hispaniola I have taken possession of a large town which is most conveniently situated for the goldfields and for communications with the mainland both here, and there in the territories of the Grand Khan, with which there will be very profitable trade.   Christopher Columbus, 1493[1]

If Europeans affected the rise of representative democracy around the world we ought to see this relationship manifested during the colonial and post-colonial eras, when European power was at its zenith.[2]

In this chapter, we turn our attention to sets of colonies that were under the control of a single colonizer. We focus on the four largest European empires – British, French, Spanish, and Portuguese – as they offer the most extensive historical literatures and the greatest within-empire variation. (Following convention, we spend more time on the British Empire than on the others, which may be justified by the greater territory and greater colonial variations afforded by the world's greatest empire.)

Each empire had its own timeline, its own peculiar institutions, and its own culture. Each was also centered on a different geographic region, or regions. It would not be surprising, therefore, if each empire bore a different relationship to our topic. British colonialism, for example, is generally regarded as more propitious for democratic rule than other European colonialisms (see Chapter 13).

---

[1] Cohen (1969: 115–16, 120), requoted in Phillips (1994: 24–5).
[2] This chapter benefitted from close readings by Charlie Kurzman and Kurt Weyland.

We do not need to settle this question, which lies in the background of our argument. The point is, by focusing on particular colonizers we are able to hold constant some important background features that might otherwise serve as confounders. By scoping down – from the entire world to specific subsets of states that experienced similar colonial histories – we may be able to generate stronger causal inferences. More important, we are able to delve into causal mechanisms that remain obscure in global analyses.[3]

We shall try to establish four central points.

First, when Europeans transported themselves, their languages, their religions, their technology, and their way of life they also brought along their norms and practices of self-governance. This included institutions of political representation, which were usually applied at local levels even if not at national (colony-wide) levels (Russell-Wood 1999). Note that what we are calling democracy usually went by other names during the colonial period, as discussed in Chapter 2. Whatever its appellation, elections and representative bodies were the accustomed mode of resolving disputes and holding leaders in check, and Europeans expected to utilize those institutions in their new abode. Perhaps, colonists coming from England had a more democratic heritage to draw upon than colonists from other European countries (at least in the modern era). And certainly, the political institutions of each European power evolved over time, so the legacy of colonialism was not fixed.

Nonetheless, political institutions were mostly inherited, with some innovations on the ground in response to the unique circumstances of each colonization experience. Although the mythology of settler societies often highlights a struggle for freedom against the colonial power – and national autonomy was, in many cases, a serious and costly struggle – the institutions that governed domestic affairs were not invented of whole cloth. Americans fought for independence; this they can claim credit for. But it is a stretch to say that they created their own institutions of self-governance, as these were largely English in origin. Likewise, for other

---

[3] To be sure, in choosing to focus on colonialism we necessarily exclude regions that managed to escape the ordeal, or experienced a weaker version of it, i.e., the Near East, Central Asia, the Far East, and selected countries in other regions such as Thailand, Ethiopia, and Liberia. For countries with a continuously independent history there is very little activity to observe, for prior to the twentieth century there were few Europeans and very little progress toward the goal of democracy. In other words, there was little change on the inputs and outputs of theoretical interest. Case study methods are of little avail in these settings. However, this does not mean that these regions lie outside our theoretical framework. Indeed, these facts fit neatly into our theory and inform the global analyses that follow in the next chapter.

former European colonies, who drew inspiration from the metropole and from other European countries or settler societies.

"Frontier" democracy was not so different from "metropole" democracy, even though the class structure was different – and this, itself, had important ramifications for which Europeans could participate. On this account, frontier democracies might be considered more democratic than the metropole whose ideals inspired them. Bonvini and Jacobson (2022: 92–3) note that frontiersmen often saw themselves as radical democrats.

By the 1850s, many volunteers and intellectuals came to view conquest and colonization as part and parcel of the struggle of democracy against despotism, obscurantism and barbarism. Such ideas were particularly prevalent on frontiers, or, at least, in places regarded as "frontiers", but they also reverberated in and emanated from central polities. In Algeria, European settlers were resolute republicans. They equated civilization with settlement and opposed the assimilationist policies of Napoleon III as representative of big business, large landholding and native rights. In a like manner, Buenos Aires liberals promised to implant European smallholding in the "desert" and, by so doing, sought to undo agreements between Indian caciques and the large cattle export interests of the caudillos. To some republicans on both sides of the Atlantic and Mediterranean, universal suffrage, freedom of press and association, free trade, abolition, judicial rights and the cult of liberty went hand in hand with White settlement, smallholding agriculture, and bringing civilization to savage lands from North Africa to Patagonia.

Our second argument relates to settler attitudes to democracy. We argue that Europeans worked to establish democratic institutions (mostly for Europeans) in contexts where they formed a numeric majority, or where they were a sufficiently large minority that they could control politics through patronage, clientelism, or exclusive suffrage laws. Where Europeans were a small minority, they favored undemocratic institutions of governance, e.g., direct rule by a centrally appointed colonial governor, perhaps in consultation with a Legislative Council (on which Europeans usually managed to maintain a controlling interest). Bluntly stated, Europeans were considered worthy and capable of self-governance; natives and slaves were not. Racism and representative democracy were intimately conjoined.

Third, democracy – where it existed – often served as a tool of white supremacy. Through the mechanism of elections and assemblies Europeans deliberated on their shared goals and interests and reached a consensus, which then became the law of the land (except in the rare circumstance of intervention by the metropole). Because non-Europeans were generally excluded from participation in democratic bodies their interests were not given expression, much less formal representation.

Not surprisingly, the result was often prejudicial – reserving the best land, full property rights, civil rights, and other benefits for Europeans and their descendants. If there was any defense of slave or indigenous rights it came more often from the metropole (far away in Europe) than from the elective assembly nearby. Manumission, forced upon British colonies by the metropole in the nineteenth century, is one example of this dynamic. Thus, democracy often worked against the interests of racial justice, and sometimes furthered the elimination of indigenes (Adhikari 2015, 2021; Wolfe 2006). The evangelizing fervor with which the democratic ideal – closely associated with the civilizing ideal – was spread across the world inspires the label "democratic imperialism" (Bonvini, Jacobson 2022).

Finally, we argue that where Europeans found themselves a small minority they despaired of making democracy work for them. Under these circumstances, they usually supported a continuation of direct rule by the metropole, as this avoided the unpleasant question of popular rule and also afforded some protection against native or slave rebellions. Thus, European ancestry should predict the alacrity with which Europeans advocated for independence and the willingness of the metropole to grant it.

In making these arguments we draw on a large literature devoted to European colonialism and post-colonialism. Most of this literature is focused on a particular colonial power, as referenced below. But a few wide-ranging treatments inform our account. Of particular interest are histories focused on the experiences and perspectives of European settlers, the central protagonists in our theory.[4] After reviewing the histories of the four chosen empires, we turn to general considerations about the association of democracy and colonial oppression. The final section of the chapter enlists several large-sample statistical tests to corroborate our arguments.

The British Empire

The British Empire was the largest empire in world history. At its apex, in 1920, it encompassed 36 million square kilometers – one-quarter of the

[4] See, e.g., Adelman (1994), Adhikari (2015, 2021), Albertini, Wirz (1982), Bateman, Pilkington (2011), Belich (2009), Cavanagh, Veracini (2017), Denoon (1983), Elkins, Pedersen (2005), Evans, Grimshaw, Phillips, Swain (2003), Fieldhouse (1966), Findlay, Lundahl (2017), Gann, Duignan (1962), Harper, Constantine (2010), Huttenback (1976), Kennedy (1987), Laidlaw, Lester (2015), Lamar, Thompson (1981), Lloyd, Metzer, Sutch (2013), McNamee (2023), Reinsch (1902), Russell (2001), Veracini (2010), Woollacott (2015).

world's land area, spread across every region of the globe. Leaving aside the long history of "internal colonialism" across the Celtic fringe of England (Hechter 1975), one might mark the beginning of overseas British colonialism with the exploration and subsequent settlement of the eastern seaboard of North America, beginning with the shortlived Roanoke colony in 1585. But permanent colonies did not get established until the seventeenth century and large-scale emigration began in the eighteenth century.

From the beginning, governance in the English colonies was viewed by the (predominantly English) colonists as an extension of rights enjoyed at home in the metropole. Insofar as colonists possessed political and civil rights in England, there was no reason to suppose that they should sacrifice those rights when undertaking the arduous task of establishing colonies abroad, especially as their actions would presumably enhance the power, wealth, and prestige of the mother country. Likewise, whatever standards for the possession of rights obtained back home ought to obtain in the New World. If the main criterion for suffrage and officeholding in England was the possession of property, and a higher share of colonists possessed property than did citizens back home, this meant that suffrage would be more extensive in the New World than the old. It was a matter of extending principles already in use (Ward 1976).

The thesis of intellectual diffusion – the transplanting of the "rights of Englishmen" to the English colonies – is probably the oldest and most venerable theory of American political institutions and political culture. There are of course many versions, of which the most famous is the "liberal tradition" synthesis by Louis Hartz (1955).[5] Later, Hartz (1969) applied the same basic thesis to other (mostly British) settler societies – but with a twist. Each society in the New World – the United States, New Zealand, Australia, Canada, South Africa, and Latin America – began as a fragment of the Old World, bringing a somewhat different political culture to the new context in which they found themselves.

While we would not deny that colonists heading out to these remote areas were different from each other in some respects, we believe that the most important conditioning factor was not a difference of ideals but rather the different demographic circumstances they faced.

---

[5] For later work on the intellectual history of politics in North America and the Caribbean see Bailyn (1967), Greene (1986, 1988, 2010), Kammen (1969), Pole (1966), Ward (1976).

The Americas

Let us begin with the Americas, where English settlers generally won limited rights of self-government, thereby establishing some of the oldest legislatures in the world. Vibrant assemblies were soon founded throughout the region, e.g., in Virginia (1619), Bermuda (1620), Massachusetts Bay (1634), Connecticut (1637), Maryland (1638), Plymouth (1639), New Haven (1639), Barbados (1639), St. Kitts (1642), Antigua (1644), Rhode Island (1647), Montserrat (1654), Nevis (1658), Jamaica (1664), North Carolina (1665), South Carolina (1671), East Jersey (1668), West Jersey (1681), New Hampshire (1680), Pennsylvania (1682), and New York (1683) (Kammen 1969: 11–12). Somewhat later, European settlers further north gained elective councils, in Nova Scotia (1758), Prince Edward Island (1773), New Brunswick (1785), and Lower and Upper Canada (1791) (Evans et al. 2003: 44). These assemblies offered some of the earliest examples of contested elections outside Europe, and they were clearly modeled on the experience of the metropole and on the mother of all parliaments, the House of Commons.[6]

However, colonial assemblies were not of equal importance across the Americas. And since the health of the legislature is often regarded as a signal of the health of democracy, it is worth looking closely at this indicator. Graham (2018) has produced a dataset counting the number of bills passed in colonial assemblies across the Americas from 1692 to 1800 observed at decadal intervals (with varying coverage). We exclude Canadian colonies because we lack data on European ancestry, leaving twenty-three colonies in North America and the Caribbean ("West Indies"), most of which are observed over the better part of a century. Bills per annum range from 0.6 to 43.4, with a mean of about 10 and a median of about 8.

In Table 10.1, we offer two regression models. One is a bivariate specification in which the number of bills is regressed against European ancestry along with year dummies. The second adds the population of the colony. (Changes in functional form such as transforming inputs or the output by the natural logarithm does not affect these results.) In both models, we observe that a larger share of Europeans is associated with a more active legislature, corroborating our general theory.

This impression is reinforced when examining the entire history of representation within these colonies. Where the white population expanded its demographic dominance, parliamentary institutions survived and prospered. This describes the history of mainland

---

[6] See Allen (1981), Jordan (2002), Paine (2019).

Table 10.1 *Legislative activity across British colonies in the Americas*

	1	2
European ancestry (%)	0.103**	0.067**
	(2.604)	(2.639)
Population		✓
Colonies	23	23
Years	11	11
Observations	185	185
R^2	0.205	0.549

Outcome: Number of bills passed per annum. *Not shown:* Year dummies, Constant. *Estimator:* ordinary least squares, standard errors clustered by colony, t statistics in parentheses. ***p<.01 **p<.05 *p<.10 *Source:* Graham (2018).

North America under British tutelage and after independence. Where, on the other hand, indigenous and transplanted African populations outstripped the European population, threatening revolt or majority rule, Europeans and their descendants generally resisted independence or relinquished rights to self-governance by transitioning to a Crown colony.[7]

The Caribbean

The point is clearest when comparing the fate of representative institutions within the British Caribbean. These island colonies shared a history of British rule, plantation agriculture (mainly sugar, along with some cotton and tobacco), and extensive slavery. Most also possessed a substantial degree of self-rule centered on an elective legislature.[8]

However, they diverged sharply in their domestic political institutions in the late nineteenth century. The instigating factor was the emancipation of slaves throughout the British Empire in 1834, and somewhat later (at the conclusion of the Civil War), in the neighboring United States. In succeeding decades, elective assemblies were retained in four colonies: the Bahamas, Barbados, Bermuda, and the Cayman Islands. All other British colonies in the Caribbean – a total of thirteen – either relinquished popularly elected legislatures, transitioned to a mostly nominated

---

[7] For further discussion of the reticence of English colonists to extend suffrage and other political rights to indigenes see Paine (2019).

[8] See Craton (2003), Gragg (2003), Lewis (1968), Rogers (1970), Spurdle (1962), Swinfen (1970), Wrong (1923).

legislative assembly, or never developed a legislature in the first place (Swinfen 1970: 98). Details are contained in Table 10.2.[9]

Although one can devise ad hoc explanations for this pattern based on the varied histories of these diverse colonies,[10] the salient fact is that the only colonies to maintain elective institutions of self-governance were those with substantial numbers of European settlers. To illustrate the point, Table 10.2 shows European ancestry in 1870, about the time when these colonies – more specifically, their white inhabitants – were making their fateful choices.

Only the Bahamas, Barbados, Bermuda, and the Caymans contained substantial numbers of Europeans. Although nowhere near a majority (except in Bermuda), we surmise that their numbers were sufficient to maintain political control, in collaboration with colored elites (an issue we return to below). With respect to Barbados, Rogers (1970: 315) explains: "Despite a franchise which was no more restrictive than elsewhere, the upper classes were able to perpetuate their dominance in the assembly through extraordinarily high property qualifications which excluded many proprietors as well as members of the middle and lower orders." With respect to the Bahamas, a contemporary described the system in the late nineteenth century in the following terms:

This mockery of representation is the greatest farce in the world. The coloured people have the suffrage, subject to a small property qualification, but have no idea how to use it. The elections are by open voting, and bribery, corruption and intimidation are carried on in the most unblushing manner, under the very noses of the officers presiding over the polling booths. Nobody takes any notice, and as the coloured people have not yet learnt the art of political organization, they are powerless to defend themselves. The result is that the House of Assembly is little less than a family gathering of Nassau whites, nearly all of whom are related to each other, whilst the coloured people are ground down and oppressed in a manner that is a disgrace to the British flag. (L. D. Powles, quoted in Lewis 1968: 314)

---

[9] Guyana (British Guiana) is a complicated case but its regressive constitutional reform in 1928 is interpreted here as an interruption in legislative continuity. Mitchell (1973: 141) writes: "A new constitution was forced through in 1928 in which the Court of Policy was abolished in favour of a legislative council comprising the [unelected] Governor, Colonial Secretary, Attorney General, 8 nominated officials, 5 nominated unofficial members, and 14 elected members. In addition to having a government majority in the legislative council, the Governor was also given powers to override it. An executive council of 12 was set up, composed of officials, 3 nominated unofficial members, and 2 of the elected members of the legislative council, who were also nominated by the Governor. Apart from extending the franchise to women, the highly restrictive voting qualifications were retained."

[10] See Lewis (1968), Rogers (1970), Wrong (1923).

Table 10.2 *History of representation in the British Caribbean*

Colony/country	Settlement or seizure by UK (ca.)	Assembly		Independence	European ancestry (%), 1870
		Elective	Nominated		
Antigua	1632	1644–1898, 1936–	1866–98	1968	4
*Bahamas	1635	1729–		1973	16
*Barbados	1626	1639–		1966	12
Belize (British Honduras)	1660	1854–69, 1936–		1981	6
*Bermuda	1612	1684–	1870	–	45
*Cayman Is.	1660	1831–		–	38
Dominica	1763	1771–1897, 1924–	1865–98	1978	1
Grenada	1763	1766–1877, 1924–	1875–77	1974	>1
Guyana (British Guiana)	1831	1739–	1928–66	1966	3
Jamaica	1655	1664–1866, 1884–	1886	1962	4
Montserrat	1628	1663–1866	1866	–	1
St. Kitts/Nevis	1624	1642–1878, 1936–	1866–78	1983	4
St. Lucia	1803	1924–	1803	1979	2
St. Vincent/Grenadines	1763	1776–1877, 1924–	1868–77	1979	2
Trinidad/Tobago	1797,1803	1763–1876, 1925–		1962	5
Turks & Caicos Is.	1670		1848–73	–	5
Virgin Is.	1666	1773–1859	1859–67	–	3

Elective: a majority of members of at least one chamber of the legislature are selected through popular elections (generally with severe suffrage restrictions). *Nominated*: a majority of members of the legislature are nominated, usually by a colonial governor. *Continuous history of elective assembly from seventeenth or eighteenth century to the present. Adapted from Craton (2003: 98), Lewis (1968: 95), Mitchell (1973: ch. 14), Paine (2019), Rogers (1970: 1–3), Wight (1946), Wrong (1923: 80–1).

While one may decry these abuses, it is nonetheless the case that there was more representative democracy (for Europeans) in the Bahamas, Barbados, Bermuda, and the Caymans than elsewhere in the British Caribbean. Where Europeans composed a minuscule proportion of the population it would have been impossible to retain control of an election-based system of rule – even one with plenty of room for manipulation, as described above – once slaves were manumitted, a condition imposed by the metropole. The masses of non-Europeans were too numerous to bribe, intimidate, and/or otherwise coerce. Under the circumstances, the abandonment of elective institutions and forfeiture of governing responsibilities to the Crown was the only operable strategy for Europeans seeking to retain dominance over society and their hold on property in these highly profitable outposts.[11]

Granted, whites had accomplices within the colored population who also benefitted from rents accruing from a plantation economy and often supported the move from self-governance to Crown status (Carvalho, Dippel 2020). This accords with a pattern of coalition-building or clientelism (depending upon one's perspective) that we see elsewhere in the colonial and post-colonial world, where in situations of scarcity Europeans reach out to members of the mixed-blood (colored, mestizo, etc.) community for support, sharing the proceeds of an exploitive regime in order to secure their dominance. In this fashion, whites and their colored allies were able to secure the dissolution of a political system that no longer served their interests.

European-Dominated Settler Societies

Elsewhere in the British Empire, attitudes toward democracy also hinged on demographic realities, specifically, the size of the European population relative to the indigenous population. Where this ratio was unfavorable (to Europeans), there was great reluctance to extend the franchise. Through time, as the European/indigene ratio increased, attitudes became more liberal. In both instances, it seems that demographic realities conditioned political realities. Liberality was a function of demographic superiority.

In the Canadian provinces, suffrage laws were fiercely debated in British Columbia in the late 1860s. Opponents of an unrestricted law warned,

---

[11] See Ashdown (1979: 34), Froude (1888), Lewis (1968: 106).

Some ten thousand whites would have to contend at the polls with fifty thousand painted, whiskey-drinking "red-skin" voters … peradventure to sit in a Legislature in which the savage element largely predominated. (Quoted in Evans et al. 2003: 54–5)

Accordingly, suffrage was restricted to property holders or subject to a literacy test, both of which had the effect of disenfranchising indigenes.

In other Canadian provinces, where whites enjoyed demographic predominance, there was no need to erect restrictive suffrage requirements and voting laws tended to be more liberal. Evans and colleagues (2003: 58), observe: "Each of the Canadian colonies that entered into the Confederation (Ontario, Quebec, New Brunswick and Nova Scotia in 1867; British Columbia in 1871; and Prince Edward Island in 1873) retained its distinctive franchise, crafted in order to safeguard settler hegemony in their particular historical circumstances" (see also Bartlett 1979–80).

In Australia, support for the inclusion of indigenous people came from European enclaves in the East (New South Wales and Victoria), while opposition was stiffest in the lightly settled western provinces (Queensland, South Australia, and Western Australia), where aboriginal numbers were highest (relative to European settlers). Thus, in 1902, a law for universal suffrage – treating indigenes and Europeans on equal terms – was introduced by a senator from New South Wales (where most Europeans were concentrated). In opposition, one Queensland senator complained,

It is all very well for honorable senators [in the East] to be benevolently inclined towards aboriginals and coloured aliens, but that policy means letting loose a large number of persons who will be able to affect our elections in Queensland in a manner that will be detrimental to the interests of that State and of the whole Commonwealth. (Quoted in Evans et al. 2003: 146)

The point was echoed by a senator from Western Australia, who declaimed that a liberal suffrage bill

would be all right for Tasmania, where there are no blacks, and probably all right for such States as New South Wales or Victoria; but to give the vote to most of the aboriginals in Western Australia would be a very serious matter indeed. (Quoted in Evans et al. 2003: 147)

Those who defended liberal suffrage laws appealed to what they viewed as demographic realities, pointing out that the Aborigines were a "failing race" and therefore did not constitute a viable threat to "White Australia" (Evans et al. 2003: 148). In the event, the conservatives won. The Commonwealth Franchise Act of 1902 decreed: "No aboriginal native of Australia, Asia, Africa or the Islands of the Pacific, except New Zealand, shall be entitled to have his name placed on an Electoral Roll unless so entitled under section forty-one of the Constitution" (quoted in Evans et al. 2003: 149).

In the United States, the development of political institutions occurred within the context of several European/non-European cleavages. The first racial division was between Europeans ("whites") and native Americans ("Indians"). Here, democracy played a critical role in establishing and extending European power, as Indians were not eligible to vote (de jure or de facto). Likewise, colonies were generally formed at a point in time when the first inhabitants of the land had been chased away, slaughtered, or forced onto reservations. This separate constitutional status, while in principle offering a modicum of self-government, also served to disenfranchise the indigenous inhabitants of the land. In this respect, Indian reservations served the same function as Bantustans in South Africa, a century later. White-dominated democracy was the instrument by which Indian removal policies were carried out, opening up land for new settlers and offering a legitimation device for extermination (Rogin 1975; Satz 1975).

The second racial division in the United States was between white and black inhabitants of the land (Myrdal 1944). Although the Indian population atrophied, a substantial African American population of slaves, and then freed slaves, survived. Consistent with our theory, African Americans generally enjoyed greater civil and political rights in parts of the country where they were least numerous as a share of the general population, i.e., in the north and west. In the south, where African Americans were numerous – and in some counties, the majority – successive institutions of exclusion (slavery, Jim Crow, and then the "white primary") effectively maintained white power for a century after manumission.[12]

Numerous historians have commented on the strange marriage between democracy and racial exclusion (Morgan 1975; Vickery 1974). The Jacksonian movement, writes George Fredrickson (1971: 70),

carried the rhetoric of popular democracy to an extreme almost unparalleled in American political history, while at the same time condoning a form of anti-Negro demagoguery that anticipated the Southern race baiters of a later era ... Even the most radical spokesmen for "the common man" ... went out of their way to emphasize that their "democracy" was for whites.

---

[12] For various aspects of this history see Acharya, Blackwell, Sen (2018), Key (1949), Klinkner, Smith (1999), Mickey (2015).

After the Civil War, this dynamic continued. Woodward (1951: 211) comments,

The barriers of racial discrimination mounted in direct ratio with the tide of political democracy among whites. In fact, an increase of Jim Crow laws upon the statute books of a state is almost an accurate index of the decline of the reactionary regimes of the Redeemers and the triumph of white democratic movements.

In this fashion, egalitarian ideals that applied only to whites – through the medium of a *Herrenvolk* democracy – were employed to head off determined cross-racial, class-based challenges from the Populist movement in the 1890s (Goodwyn 1976) and at other points in American history.

Southern Africa

In southern Africa, British settlers never gained the demographic hegemony they enjoyed in North America or Australasia. However, the demographic balance was different across their disparate holdings.

In particular, Europeans were a much higher share of the population in Cape Colony than in other colonies (Curtin et al. 1995: 293). And within the city of Cape Town, Europeans composed a majority by the mid-nineteenth century (Ross 1985: 109). Consistent with our expectations, Cape Colony established the most liberal suffrage laws, a (formally) race-blind policy that was maintained for several decades after independence within the federal rubric of the Union of South Africa.[13]

By contrast, other colonies – including the Transvaal and the Orange Free State – established legislatures whose electorate was limited to whites, a pattern that would remain constant during their history (Evans et al. 2003: 90). Of course, the white population of Transvaal and Orange Free State was dominated by Boers, descendants of Dutch settlers, and one might argue that the exclusivist policies adopted in those colonies were a product of an illiberal political philosophy shared by these settlers, insulated from liberal Protestant missionary movements such as Methodism (then popular in Britain).

In this respect, Natal offers a better comparison case. After annexation in 1843, Boers deserted Natal and the colony's white population was subsequently almost exclusively British in origin. Henceforth, what distinguished Natal from the Cape was racial demography, not intra-European demography. While whites composed a significant minority in the Cape, they were outnumbered 15 to 1 in Natal, even after

---

[13] See Curtin et al. (1995: 437–8), Edgecombe (1978), McCracken (1967).

aggressive resettlement programs (Evans et al. 2003: 102). This fact had direct political repercussions. Evans and colleagues (2003: 101) explain,

The extent of the demographic imbalance between European and non-European in Natal was much greater and starker than in the Cape. This was reflected, almost from the start of representative government in 1856, in settler determination not to allow the Indigenous population the political power which would follow from the free grant of a nonracial franchise on genuinely non-racial terms.

Thus, although the Colonial Office forced Natal to adopt a color-blind suffrage law (as in the Cape), they found ways to manipulate elections so that non-white residents were effectively excluded. The solution was a separate Native Law ("Shepstone") system, which segregated blacks from participation in white institutions – akin to what would later be called Bantustans. Accordingly, "an African wanting to register for the vote would first have to apply to be formally exempted from 'Native Law' on the grounds that he could show that he was 'civilised' and should become a colonial citizen" (Evans et al. 2003: 104). Later, even more stringent criteria were added to this restrictive law, effectively removing the franchise from all but the most determined black applicants, who were required to present three white witnesses to testify on their behalf. According to a colonial commission, in 1907 only seven Africans qualified to vote in Natal out of an electorate of 24,000 (Evans et al. 2003: 106).

In South Africa, as in the US, blacks were allowed to play a role in politics only where their role was subordinate, and this, in turn, was a product of demography. Where blacks were scarcest (relative to whites) they could participate, albeit on unequal terms.

As Cape Colony evolved, demographic realities changed. This, in turn, was the product of the discovery of gold in the interior of the continent and the consequent decision to annex neighboring territories – the Ciskei (1866) and then the Transkei (1885). These increases in territory brought in a great many Africans and very few whites. Thus, in 1860 there were roughly 180,000 whites and 314,000 Africans and by 1891 there were 376,000 whites and 1.148 million Africans. The corresponding statistics representing European ancestry shifted from 57 percent to 33 percent, meaning that Europeans went from majority to minority status. Moreover, there were movements afoot to register large numbers of these new citizens, especially among the mission-educated elite (Evans et al. 2003: 161).

In response to these changing demographic realities, the Parliamentary Voters' Registration Act (1887), stiffened barriers to registration for

Africans in the Cape. Cecil Rhodes, then serving on the Cape parliament, explained:

> We have got to treat natives, where they are in a state of barbarism, in a different way to ourselves. We are to be lords over them ... The native is to be treated as a child and denied the franchise. (Quoted in Evans et al. 2003: 162)

Subsequently, the Franchise and Ballot Act (1892) erected further barriers to black participation (Evans et al. 2003: 163). All told, these restrictions entailed "the trebling of the property qualification from £25 to £75 a year, plus a literacy test; the disqualification of communal tenure as a means of satisfying the property qualification; and the disqualification of even individual tenure as a means of satisfying the property qualification if the land was held in the Glen Grey district," where many Africans lived (Evans et al. 2003: 164).

Despite these many restrictions, participation and elective office in the Cape was still nominally nonracial and some Africans managed to vote. One even managed to gain entrance to the Cape Provincial Council in 1914 (Evans et al. 2003: 165). This qualifies the Cape as more demo-cratic – by a few degrees – than the rest of the colonies-cum-states in this apartheid regime, corroborating our theory.

India

After the loss of North America, India became Britain's most valued possession. Initially, this growing territory was governed by the East India Company via a charter from the British government. Later, after the 1857 Mutiny, it was governed directly through the India Office in London in collaboration with the governor-general, though the princely states still enjoyed a good deal of autonomy. Little thought was given to institutions of representative government (Seal 1971: ch. 1).

The question of what rights English and other European settlers would be granted in these territories arose gradually. Initially, most expats were stationed there on a temporary basis, either as employees of the East India Company or of the British government (civil servants or troops). As such, there was no call for representation; Britishers were on a job. Over time, the class of "unofficials" grew and began to chafe under the arbitrary rule of the East India Company, and – in some areas – subjec-tion to local laws (Marshall 1990).

In 1861, British settlers were granted seats on legislative councils. Although these bodies were by no means sovereign it was a position of strategic importance as it gave them a regularized channel by which to register their voice before appointed decisionmakers in colonial capitals, i.e., in Bombay, Madras, and Calcutta. From this perch, they served as a highly influential pressure group (Marshall 1990: 41). Thus far, it seemed that colonial settlers were on a well-established trajectory toward greater self-government and democracy, achieved in the New World English colonies in the eighteenth century. However, settlers were not alone in pressing their claims for representation. Marshall (1990: 41) notes, "as Indian claims became increasingly assertive, the ambitions of the unofficial Whites became more and more defensive." The problem was simple: the more power was devolved to assemblies the more difficult it would be to exclude the vast majority of the inhabitants.

For a time, such considerations halted the advance of democracy. However, the British colonies (those administered directly by British governors) were in dire need of funds. To that end, steps were taken in 1840–1 to assess municipal taxes in Calcutta and Madras, where a concession would be made for the provision of local councils with some powers of legislation over each city. A few years later (in 1847) another act created a board of commissioners in Calcutta, with three appointed members and four elective members – to be chosen by ratepayers from each of four wards (Misra 1970: 569). Similar developments occurred in Bombay about the same time (Misra 1970: 571). Although briefly withdrawn in the next decade, the principle of elective municipal bodies was reinstated in these three municipalities in the 1870s, and later extended to other municipalities throughout India. Although suffrage restrictions were extremely high, limiting participation to those with money and education, Indians eventually gained a majority – at least of the elective seats – and these seats slowly (with some reversals) came to surpass the appointed seats (Misra 1970: ch. 8). The dynamic was a familiar one: "The various stages in the growth of the [municipal] Corporation's popular character exhibit this clash of interests between the native population demanding more democratic rights and the Local Government temporizing for as long as possible" (Choudhuri 1973: 308).

Each proposed advance of democracy was met with a howl of protest, and the loudest protesters were those with the most to lose – namely, European settlers, who originally enjoyed a monopoly of power over local authorities. In 1882, the government of Bengal considered, at the insistence of a local Bengali, an amendment "to give Indian district magistrates and sessions judges the same powers as their European counterparts" (Seal 1971: 164). After receiving approval from the viceroy (Lord Ripon) and the Viceroy's Council, it was put before the British secretary of state and a bill was formulated for debate in the Commons. Then, the outcry began. Seal (1971: 165) relates,

It united the entire unofficial European community – the planters and merchants of eastern India, and the Calcutta bench and bar in particular – into an hysterical condemnation of the Viceroy and an unrestrained attack on the educated Indians whose fitness to sit in judgement over white men and women in the mofussil the bill had dared to suggest. A European and Anglo-Indian Defence Association was formed ... There was wild talk of a white mutiny, of packing the Viceroy off to England by force, of getting the European Volunteer Corps to disband. These attacks on Indians rapidly undid the gradual improvement in race relations since Canning's time; the cry of "our women in danger" revived fears and passions latent since the Mutiny. They were not confined to India. In England, too, the controversy evoked an outspoken attack on liberal policy towards India and an uncompromising assertion of the doctrine of racial superiority. The Times took the lead. The case was put bluntly by Fitzjames Stephen. It was not the bill alone, but the entire tenor of Ripon's policy that he found disturbing: "it is impossible to imagine any policy more fearfully dangerous and more certain, in case of failure, to lead to results to which the Mutiny would be child's play than the policy of shifting the foundations on which the British Government of India rests. It is essentially an absolute government founded, not on consent, but on conquest." [Opponents fulminated against] "the *d—d nigger party".

In this vein, *The Englishman*, the leading English-owned paper in Calcutta, declared the bill,

nothing more than the first instalment of a series of laws to enable the Government to pursue its plan of rapidly Indianising the entire administration of the country ... In fighting against [the] Bill ... the European community are fighting against their own ruin and the destruction of British rule in India. (Quoted in Seal 1971: 166)

Despite the openly racist opposition, it is nonetheless significant that the leading edges of liberal reform in the subcontinent were located in the three coastal territories most heavily populated by Europeans: Bombay, Madras, and Calcutta (Bayly 2012; McPherson 2002: 91).[14] The explosive potential of representative democracy, once introduced to Calcutta and other leading cities, is the theme of Choudhuri's (1973: 6) detailed account.

The representative character of the Calcutta municipality under the Act of 1863 enabled the town authority to have adequate funds and this fact, coupled with the wide publicity of the proceedings of meetings of the Justices in the newspapers and periodicals of the town, revolutionized the life of municipal Calcutta ... As the middle-class people were imbued with western knowledge and ideas, they longed for the western mode of government for the protection of

---

[14] According to the Census of British India in 1871–2 (cited in Charlton-Stevens 2020: 677), 80 percent of all Europeans (including those classified as Indo-Portuguese) were in Madras, Bombay, and Bengal (of which Calcutta was the leading city).

their liberties and advancement of their welfare. Naturally enough the people of Calcutta, who were admittedly in the van of intelligence and enlightenment, were at this time urging for a further extension of municipal privileges.

Not only were these cities the spearhead of municipal reform, they were also springboards for the movement of self-rule, as many of the early leaders of the Congress party were drawn from municipal-level representative bodies (Johnson 2005). The ideals of democracy and independence coincided. In Choudhury's (1973: 308) estimation, the "demand for the Indianisation of the [municipal] Corporation was as much a concomitant as a causative factor underlying the nationalist struggle for self-government."

In addition to the institutional story, there is an intellectual story centering on the transmigration, and transmogrification, of ideas. Chris Bayly (2012: 346) summarizes:

Liberalism ... achieved a loose and long-lived hegemony over Indian political thought in part because of the Anglicisation of public life. The political arguments of Mill, Spencer and Comte were spread to the educated classes through English and later vernacular newspapers, books and pamphlets ... But this was no simple case of diffusion ... British liberal ideas were deconstructed and reassembled to reflect Indian conditions and structures of thought ... [and] they changed greatly over time from an early stage of constitutional liberalism in the 1830s to the quasi-socialistic communitarian liberalism of 1900 and after.

Of principal importance to this diffusion of democratic ideas were the universities in Britain and India that offered positions to a growing Indian elite, hungry for western-style education and the opportunities that flowed therefrom. These institutions were, likewise, concentrated in the three coastal Presidencies. Graduates of these institutions became leaders in the independence movement and founders of India as an independent, and resolutely democratic, nation (Seal 1971). European immigrants and ideas thus played a key role in the intellectual ferment that was to define India's history in the twentieth century.

East Asia

Although we do not have space to pursue the subject in great detail, it is worthwhile recounting how the demography of British imperialism affected the development of political institutions in other territories under their (formal or informal) control

In East Asia, the Treaty of Nanjing (1842) forced the Imperial Chinese government to recognize five treaty ports along the coast. Of these, Shanghai was the largest and also attracted the largest congregation of Britons (Bickers 1998: 166).

Britons and other Europeans never comprised more than a small minority of the population in treaty port cities such as Shanghai, let alone their hinterlands. However, the governance structure devised by the Treaty and subsequent agreements meant that Britons were sovereign only over their own communities. In Shanghai, this meant the English – later, International – Settlement. Within the circumference of the Settlement, Britons were numerous enough (roughly 1 percent of the population) to control the arms of elective government.

The vehicle of quasi-democratic governance was the Shanghai Municipal Council (SMC), annually elected by an electorate constructed with severe suffrage restrictions. Bickers (1998: 168) explains: "The SMC was annually elected on a property-based franchise that excluded most Britons from voting, and even more from standing for election, while others held multiple votes depending on the number of properties they represented." The purpose of these restrictions, coupled with rampant gerrymandering, was to maintain power in British hands even as the non-British population (comprising Japanese, White Russians, and a preponderance of Chinese) grew. Nonetheless, elective government was established shortly after the establishment of the English/ International Settlement, and remained in force until the end of its period of autonomy.

Contrast this situation with that faced by British settlers in India. There is no appreciable difference in numbers if one takes into account the population of British India and the population encompassed by imperial China. Europeans composed an infinitesimal portion of these large populations. However, in India the British aspired to govern an entire continent. As such, they were specks in a vast ocean. That is why democratic governing structures developed extremely slowly under the British Raj. There was no way, even with the assistance of severe suffrage restrictions, that they could conceivably govern a continent democratically. In Shanghai, their ambitions were much more limited, and that is why an elective system of government was allowed – and, indeed, encouraged – there.

The Middle East

As in Asia, British presence was light in the Middle East.[15] Some lands within the British sphere of influence retained formal independence (e.g., Ethiopia, the Ottoman Empire/Turkey, Persia/Iran). Others were

---

[15] This section benefitted from extensive feedback from Glenn Robinson, to whom we are grateful.

granted protectorate status (e.g., Egypt, Sudan). Only one attracted significant numbers of European migrants. This was the land of Palestine, viewed as the ancestral homeland of the Jewish people.

The territory now known as Israel was settled by Ashkenazi Jews beginning in the late nineteenth century. Most settlers originated in Central Europe, forming the social base of what would become a British Mandate (from 1922) and eventually a Jewish state (from 1948) (Shafir 1996, 2017).

Initially, no European power sponsored this population movement. In this respect, the settlement of Palestine was different from other European settlements around the world. However, when the Ottoman Empire came out on the losing side of World War I and was forced to divest itself of territories outside the metropole (which was known hence-forth as Turkey), Britain assumed responsibility for Palestine under the terms of a League of Nations mandate. From the very beginning, the Balfour Declaration made clear Britain's intention to establish a Jewish homeland (Migdal 2012: 56). In this respect, British actions were consistent with their actions elsewhere, giving preference to European migrants over indigenes.

This preference became clear as a system of government was established in the new mandate. Attempts were made to include representatives from the principal social groups living in the territory in an elective legislature. However, Jewish settlers, who constituted a minority of the population (about 10 percent of the total population of Palestine at the time of the Balfour Declaration in 1917, and about 30 percent at the time of Israel's independence in 1948), resisted any solution granting representation to Arabs in proportion to their numbers, and Arabs quite naturally resisted any solution that arbitrarily imposed parity across the two groups (Horowitz, Lissak 1979; Sager 1985: 9). No attempt was made to impose a democratic settlement. Accordingly, the mandate was governed in much the same fashion as a Crown colony (Sager 1985: 8).

Lacking representation at the protectorate level, the two groups organized internally. Jewish settlers built on a foundation of representative government developed through the Zionist Congress. From its first meeting in Basle, Switzerland, in 1897, this international congress was elected by proportional representation, nurturing the growth of political parties and possessing "most of the attributes of a parliament" (Sager 1985: 3). The Zionist Congress seems to have been especially important as a model for self-governance among the Jewish settlers of Palestine (Sager 1985: ch. 1), who quickly established an Elected Assembly (Assefat Hanivharim), which served as the highest governing body of the Knesset Israel. Elections to this body (in 1920, 1925, 1931, and

1944) also employed proportional representation and were dominated by the same political parties who got their start in the Zionist Congress. Needless to say, the electorate was limited to Jews (Horowitz, Lissak 1979: 24).

No analogous system of representation by election arose among the Arab population, partly because they did not accept the terms of the Balfour Declaration and refused to sanction the idea of a Jewish home on their natal land (Horowitz, Lissak 1979: 21; Migdal 2012: 56).

In the event, democracy within the Jewish community – the Yishuv – served as a successful coordinating device. Meanwhile, the Arab population remained fragmented across numerous rural localities, led by local notables who were hard put to coordinate on a national strategy or to mobilize their constituencies in a more than episodic fashion (Robinson 1997).

In another parallel to settler/indigene politics elsewhere, the main constraint on further Jewish immigration and land appropriation was the British colonial authorities, who were sensitive to Arab sensibilities – at least, more sensitive than the democratically elected body representing Jewish settlers (Migdal 2012: ch. 3).

At the end of an increasingly ineffective British mandate, the 1948 war resulted in the mass expulsion of the Arab population, whose postwar population in the new state of Israel was about one-tenth its former strength (Migdal 2012: 76). Conveniently, Jewish settlers could now extend the system of democracy that they had been practicing among themselves to the entire population without jeopardizing their control.

In subsequent years, and through subsequent wars, the area claimed by Israel and its Jewish settlers expanded, sometimes in the special form of West Bank settlements in which Jews enjoy full citizenship while Arabs (known eventually as Palestinians) have no political rights and limited civil rights (Yiftachel 2006). By the careful construction of boundaries and the delineation of citizens and non-citizens, and by cultivating immigration among Jews throughout the world, the state retains its Jewish majority and its European-style democracy. Sammy Smooha (quoted in Yiftachel 2006: 87) comments, "Israel defines itself as a state of and for Jews, that is, the homeland of the Jews only … The state extends preferential treatment to Jews who wish to preserve the embedded Jewishness and Zionism of the state." The demographic balancing act is delicate, and increasingly precarious (Lustick 2019).

So constituted, the mandate of Palestine and, from 1948, the independent state of Israel has been the most democratic polity in the Middle East, despite the exclusion of most of the original inhabitants. Thus, the story of European democracy for Europeans is replicated, once again.

The French Empire

The French overseas empire began, concomitant with the English, in the early sixteenth century, and was also targeted initially on the Americas. While the first colonies were unsuccessful, by the early seventeenth century the colony of Quebec had been established. This would become the most important and most enduring French colony in the New World.

As our theory predicts, it was also the site of the first democratic experiment in the French colonial world. In 1657, by order of the Crown, a council was created, consisting of the governor and the director of trade, both of whom were appointed, and four councillors, who were elected. The council did not enjoy total sovereignty, but it operated by majority vote and held sway in most policymaking decisions. Lanctot (1934: 132) remarks, "at a time of complete royal autocracy in France the two thousand colonists of Canada were enjoying a sort of system of popular representation, and were electing representatives empowered to regulate and administer the most important activities of government in the fields of trade and public finance."

Although the government of Louis XIV was not as authoritarian as it pretended, it was certainly a good deal less democratic than England. Accordingly, colonial ventures were controlled by the Crown, which did not generally countenance popular assemblies in the New World, notwithstanding the Sovereign Council of New France (discussed above) and assemblies of settlers in Martinique and Saint-Domingue (Pritchard 2004: 256–8).

After the Revolution, France turned (fitfully) in a democratic direction, and its newer colonies in Africa were given opportunities to participate. In contrast to British colonialism, the French approach to governance featured direct rule, which prohibited self-government. However, those colonies with the highest concentrations of French settlers were generally integrated into the metropole as departments with full rights of suffrage and representation – at least, for those with French citizenship, which in practice was bestowed preferentially upon those with European heritage (white or mixed-race).

Democracy in French colonies was thus directly linked to France insofar as *colonnes* participated in elections to the Assemblée Nationale and viewed themselves as children of the French Revolution – Republicans, to a man. (Women were not granted the franchise in France until 1945.) This was briefly the case in Saint-Domingue, where those of French descent and some free Black men enjoyed suffrage prior to the Haitian revolution (Dubois 2004: 162–70). It also became the norm in Algeria (Choi 2017), Cochinchina (Albertini, Wirz 1982: 199), French Guiana, French India, Guadeloupe, Martinique, Reunion, and the four historic communes of Senegal (Johnson 1971). Although the method of allocating legislative seats across colonies was never formalized, areas where French settlers and their descendants were more numerous such as Algeria obtained greater representation.[16]

In Indochina, an elected Colonial Council was established in 1880 "with representation accorded to both the natives and to Europeans, though by different systems for each" (Roberts 1967 [1929]: 85). In this fashion, Europeans (largely French) were able to maintain control.

Likewise, in the historic communes of Senegal, whites did not compose a majority of the electorate but were nonetheless able to monopolize power through most of the colonial period with the assistance of Creole allies (Johnson 1971).

The dilemma facing European settlers, Prochaska (1990: 24) notes, was "how to coerce the colonial administration into granting them representative government while at the same time denying it to the indigenous population." This trick was achieved – at least for a while – by the development of parallel institutions. Prochaska (1990: 24) continues, "The main example of such parallel structures in the political sphere is two-college institutions which keep the indigenous people separate from and unequal to the European settlers."

Prochaska's research centers on Bône, a French seaside enclave in Algeria, where "duly elected Algerian municipal council members formed the official Algerian political elite," accompanied by "the adjoint indigène (appointed Muslim representative) who wielded real power in the Algerian community by virtue of his position as a broker, a liaison between the Muslim and European communities" (Prochaska 1990: 24). Sung Choi (2017: 203) reports,

While all of Algeria was French, only Europeans were governed under "common law", which granted full citizenship rights since 1848, while colonized subjects were relegated to a customary local jurisdiction that answered only indirectly to French authorities. These subjects were initially classified as indigènes, a category that had no legal definition or identity beyond what it was not: French national with full rights. And although indigènes could not benefit from French laws, they were nevertheless subject to French rules and governance if charged with crimes against Europeans.

---

[16] For general discussion see Roberts (1967[1929]), Southworth (1931), Winnacker (1938).

Although elections were regular in Bône, openly contested by two well-organized machine-style political parties ("Opportunists" and "Radicals") and the winners fully vested with political power, they were limited-franchise events.

Since legislative power rested in France, French colonists directed their efforts toward policies emanating from Paris. It was a well-organized and persistent initiative on behalf of a mobilized constituency with clear interests at stake. By all appearances, it was highly successful. "Throughout Algeria local settler power was linked to and cemented by an influential settler lobby in Paris, comprised largely of the *élus algériens*, the French representatives of Algeria who sat in the Assemblée Nationale. In turn, these *élus algériens* played a major role in the *parti colonial*, the foremost interest group lobbying for colonial expansion during the Third Republic" (Prochaska 1990: 190).

Democracy worked nicely for French settlers, who enjoyed full citizenship rights in France. They could effectively control most aspects of colonial policy by exerting political pressure in Paris, where the non-enfranchised subjects of their rule had no voice. What this meant, in specific terms, was expulsion of the Berbers and Arabs from their ancestral lands in favor of recent migrants from France and elsewhere in Europe, who expropriated the most productive agricultural land and secluded themselves in the toniest urban neighorhoods. In addition, subjects of French colonies were routinely subject to forced labor (Cooper 2014: 7). Jules Ferry, a critic of French colonialism, remarked "The commune *de pleine exercice* is the exploitation of the native in broad daylight *à ciel ouvert*" (quoted in Prochaska 1990: 183).

If we examine governance at the *municipal* level, a similar picture emerges. In cities where French and other European settlers composed a majority or large minority, elected councils were often allowed, albeit limited to whites and their allies. For example, in Saigon, after the lapse of military rule in Indochina (1867), an administrative council was established that included "leading citizens" (who we shall assume were predominantly white). In 1869, a majority of these councilors were elected through a franchise limited to French citizens. In 1870, all councilors were elected, of whom a few were Vietnamese. This situation endured until 1931, when a more centralized style of governance was imposed (Guillaume 1985: 184; see also Tai 1984).

As time went on, suffrage laws were liberalized. And yet, French settlers found ways of manipulating the results. Reinsch (1902: 204) summarizes the situation across the empire at the turn of the twentieth century:

There are in French India 500 European to 76,000 native electors, but the latter usually do not even take the trouble to vote, as they well know that their votes are powerless to influence the course of the election [as a result of ballot fraud]. In Senegal the electoral body comprises about 700 whites, 400 mulattoes, and 8000 blacks. The latter are controlled entirely by their chiefs, with whom arrangements concerning the purchase of their votes in large blocks can readily be made ... In the three Algerian provincial councils the native element is represented only by a few appointed delegates, who, for practical purposes, have absolutely no power. The representatives of the French colonists may be said virtually to compose these councils.

After World War II, French policy toward citizenship in the colonies became more inclusive, at least on paper, as demanding stipulations had the effect of excluding most non-white beneficiaries. Fred Cooper (2014: 6) explains,

In 1945, the demand for an inclusive citizenship in empire was revolutionary. The overwhelming majority of Africans – like Algerians – were then considered French nationals and French subjects but not French citizens. They could become French citizens only if they gave up their personal status under Islamic or "customary" law, accepted the rules of the French civil code over marriage and inheritance, and convinced administrators that they had fully accepted French social norms. Few chose to do so; fewer still were accepted.

All of this notwithstanding, one must acknowledge that the pockets of French colonists in Algeria, Cochinchina, French Guiana, French India, Guadeloupe, Martinique, Reunion, and the four historic communes of Senegal experienced a good deal more democracy in the Third Republic than areas of French control where *colons* were scarcer such as French Morocco, French Tunisia, Côte d'Ivoire, French Dahomey, French Sudan, Senegambia, Niger, Mauritania, French Upper Volta, French Togoland, Chad, Oubangui-Chari, French Congo, Gabon, French Cameroon, Madagascar, French Somaliland, or Comoros. Democracy existed, to the extent that it could be said to exist, where Europeans lived. It was democracy for Europeans. Only occasionally did non-Europeans manage to gain control of electorally based systems of selection prior to World War II (Reinsch 1901; Winnacker 1938).

The Spanish Empire

The Spanish Empire began earlier than the British and French, and was focused on the New World.[17] Columbus's voyage (1492) was the opening bell, after which colonies were founded at Santo Domingo

---

[17] This section benefitted from a close reading by Raul Madrid.

(1496), Cuba (1515), Mexico (1521), Peru (1537), and elsewhere in Latin America west of the territory reserved for Portugal by the Treaty of Tordesillas, as well as in the Philippines (1571). Our discussion will focus on Latin America.

In Spanish colonies with small European populations we find a repetition of a theme encountered among English colonies, namely, a reluctance to separate from the metropole due to worries about violent insurrection or majoritarian democracy. The shadow of the bloody – and successful – Haitian revolution loomed large. "In parts of Spanish America slave revolt was so haunting a prospect that the creoles would not lightly leave the shelter of imperial government," writes Lynch (1973: 20).

Elsewhere, where slaves were scarce but indigenes numerous, the prospect of Indian revolts was equally worrisome. Lynch (1973: 164) points out that there were thirteen Indian rebellions in one province of Peru in the late eighteenth century. The largest of these, the Tupac Amaru uprising, vowed to systematically extirpate Europeans. This far-reaching rebellion overwhelmed local militias, constituting the greatest threat to colonial control since the invasion of the continent (Serulnikov 2013: 2–3). It is estimated that ten thousand Spaniards, creoles, and mestizos lost their lives during the course of the conflict. This was nowhere near the number of fatalities sustained by Indians, estimated to be on the order of one hundred thousand. But this did not take anything away from the horror of the event for those with white skin.

Consequently, elites in Cuba, Peru, Venezuela, and wherever there were large numbers of slave or indigenous populations resisted the call for independence (Lynch 1973: 20, 170, 190). Although "ideas of liberty, equality, and fraternity appealed to prominent creoles in many parts of the empire, ... it was unlikely that Peruvian creoles, cognizant of the huge Indian population and the dire consequences of class warfare, would travel far or quickly along the danger path," John Preston Moore (1966: 174) notes.

Governance in New Spain

Having discussed the issue of independence (which of course bears on democracy since self-rule is one of the precepts of representative democracy), we turn to the question of how Spanish colonies were governed, pre- and post-independence.

In the earliest years of conquest, Spanish settlers enjoyed many of the same rights of self-governance they enjoyed back home through regional courts (the *audiencia*) and municipal councils (the *cabildo*). The *audiencia* granted representation to creole elites, giving colonists experience in self-government and providing a template for governance after independence (Burkholder, Chandler 1977). The more important vehicle of governance was the *cabildo*, which was elected on a regular schedule by those with requisite Spanish blood (J. P. Moore 1954). However, by the end of the sixteenth century many of these rights were withdrawn and the integrity of the electoral process damaged by the Crown's (or its appointee's) ability to sell offices or appoint its own officers. Habsburg, and especially Bourbon, monarchs did not countenance representative institutions across their domains (J. P. Moore 1966: ch. 1). Much later, during the waning years of the colonial era, *cabildos* were granted greater freedom.[18] A liberal era in Spanish history opened in the 1820s, but by this time most of Spain's holdings in the Americas had gained independence. So, most of the variation one might have found within the Spanish Empire appears in the post-independence period, to which we now turn.

According to the traditional view, Latin America inherited from Spain (and Portugal) an authoritarian or "centralist" political culture (Hanson 1974; Veliz 1980). While there is no doubt that Castile was less democratic than England through most of the early modern and modern eras, one should not overplay the distinction. After all, Spain also had a long history of local government (*cabildos*) and regional assemblies in formerly independent states such as Aragón, Catalonia, Castile-León, and the Basque country.[19] The founders of independent states in Latin America looked to recover this long-standing tradition.

Moreover, liberal episodes in Spanish history (1812, 1820–3) were contemporaneous with independence movements and the formation of new constitutions in the Americas. The Spanish Cadiz constitution of 1812 offered equal representation to Americans, established three branches of government with the legislature dominant, and granted suffrage to all adult males (except blacks). Local government enjoyed an efflorescence of popular sovereignty. "Cities and towns were to have councils, composed of elective alcaldes, procurators, and regidores," with most offices elected annually (J. P. Moore 1966: 212–13). It was, in short, a considerably more democratic document than obtained in other republics at the time (Drake 2009: 60), and immensely influential across Spanish America (Chust 2017).

Latin American liberalism drew not just from Spain but also from other cultural currents emanating from Europe. This included the ancient exemplars, Greece and Rome, as well as Renaissance Italy,

---

[18] See Halperin (1981: 51–5, 84–92), Haring (1999), J. P. Moore (1966).
[19] See Møller (2017), Nader (1990), O'Callaghan (1989).

contemporary England, revolutionary France, the Netherlands, and the former British colony to the north, the United States.[20] There were many republican examples to choose from. Drake (2009: 58) emphasizes, "Whatever the doubts, debates, and disasters, Latin America – from independence throughout the rest of the nineteenth century – generally subscribed to a classic 'liberal' model of development, similar to that of the United States" (see also Jorrin, Martz 1970).

In this light, it is no surprise that once the heavy hand of the Spanish Crown was lifted – allowing Latin Americans to establish political institutions of their choice – there arose a strong association between European ancestry and democracy. Those areas with strong links to Europe were quicker to adopt democratic innovations and more likely to keep them.

Within Argentina, Buenos Aires was the province with the heaviest concentration of European settlers (Moya 1998), who composed nearly 70–80 percent of the city's population in the late eighteenth and early nineteenth centuries.[21] Bonvini and Jacobson (2022: 91) remark, "In the State of Buenos Aires, the definition of 'civilization' became so equated with a 'republicanized' and idealized vision of Europe that it was arguably more 'European' than Europe itself." This was also the province that pioneered the use of popular elections for offices such as the *cabildo* (local government), governor, and deputies to various juntas, assemblies, or congresses between 1810 and 1820 (Drake 2009: 79). Most rural provinces of Argentina did not develop electoral institutions until later, as was the case elsewhere in Latin America. In 1821, Buenos Aires was the only province to recognize universal male suffrage and to maintain that practice in subsequent decades.[22] In Chile, a similar story unfolded. Santiago, the province with the greatest concentration of European settlers, initiated the first electoral contests (Drake 2009: 80).

Across the states of Spanish America, Argentina, one of the most European in demographic composition, was the first to adopt lasting universal male suffrage (in 1853), preempting other states in the region by many decades (though Colombia briefly recognized the practice from 1853 to 1886). We do not mean to suggest that nineteenth-century Argentina was a model democracy. Restrictive naturalization procedures disqualified recent immigrants from suffrage, and elections were by no means free and fair (James 1995). In the twentieth century, democracy

---

[20] See Demélas-Bohy, Guerra (1996), Garner, Smith (2017), Graham (1994: 73), Guerra (1994), Rodríguez O. (1998), Sabato (2018: 5).
[21] See Socolow (1982: 25), and also Geler, Rodriguez (2020: 182).
[22] See Alonso (1996: 182), Drake (2009: 112), Sabato (2001).

was interrupted on multiple occasions by military coups. Nonetheless, Argentina's political institutions have surpassed the mean value of democracy within Latin America through most of the last two centuries. "Despite illicit procedures and voter disenchantment," Drake (2009: 113) writes, "majoritarian national elections took place on a regular basis from 1862 until the military coup of 1930." Argentina, Drake concludes, "compiled one of the most stable electoral histories in Latin America" (Drake 2009: 113; see also Zimmermann 2009).

Chile established perhaps the most democratic history of any country in Latin America during the nineteenth century. Valenzuela (1996: 223) notes, "At least once every three years, beginning in 1823 and unfailingly except for the 1891 presidential contest, Chilean voters were summoned to the polls for presidential, congressional, and/or municipal elections throughout the nineteenth century." Despite statutory restrictions on suffrage, Valenzuela (1996: 224) judges that these criteria "could be met by artisans, most if not all adult male salaried workers and miners, and petty merchants." This, in turn, stems from the fact that Chile was wealthier than most other Latin American nations. Most important, the opposition was allowed to organize and compete in each election, if not on entirely equal terms. This fertile ground led to the formation of the major Chilean parties, which endured through most of the subsequent century (Scully 1992).

As a general rule, democracy has found more favorable footing in the European-dominated Southern Cone (Argentina, Chile, Uruguay) and in the one state in Central America with a sizeable European inheritance (Costa Rica). By contrast, states with demographic profiles that are predominantly non-European (indigenous, mestizo, or black) such as Bolivia, Ecuador, Paraguay, and Peru in South America and Guatemala, El Salvador, and Honduras in Central America have more authoritarian regime histories.

If one opens the aperture slightly, to admit the one large Portuguese colony in Latin America into our comparative frame, the picture is reinforced. Brazil, too, has a higher than average share of Europeans (concentrated mostly in the south) and a better than average history of democracy when compared with other polities in the region.

Of course, we are talking about differences of degree. And, of course, the democratic histories of each state waxed and waned. All experienced multiple reversals. But, overall, the picture is consistent with our theory.

We are by no means the first to notice this association. However, other commentators usually view the issue through the lens of heterogeneity, with the idea that more diverse states, or states with greater inequality, are at a disadvantage in developing democratic institutions (Drake 2009:

14; Engerman, Sokoloff 2005). We show, in Chapter 11, that there is no attenuation in the relationship between European ancestry and democracy when measures of ethnic, religious, and linguistic fractionalization or income inequality are introduced into a regression model. Nor, for that matter, is it clear that ethnic heterogeneity discourages democracy (Gerring, Hoffman, Zarecki 2018) or that inequality discourages democracy (see Chapter 14).

What hindered the development of democracy in Spanish America was not heterogeneity or inequality per se. Differences among Europeans, for example, did not serve as a hindrance to the establishment of broad suffrage rights and free and fair elections. Rather, it was a particular type of heterogeneity – differences based on race. While racial differences between whites, blacks, and indigenes in Latin America and their implications for politics and society have been explored by many writers, the connection to democracy is often missed.[23]

The simple point is that white elites of European descent were apprehensive about extending power to masses who were racially distinct. Drake (2009: 84) writes,

They believed the common people should not participate in electoral decisions until they became more educated, cultured, and indeed leavened with immigrants from Europe. Until then, the elites intended to govern in the name of the people. This assumption conditioned not only suffrage requirements but also the even higher property and income qualifications for holding office.

For many Latin American elites, the viability of democracy hinged explicitly on demography. Juan Bautista Alberdi (1810–84), an Argentine diplomat and writer, was known for his motto, "To govern is to populate," by which he meant the encouragement of further immigration from Europe (quoted in Drake 2009: 95). It was the same logic that prompted whites in the United States such as Thomas Jefferson to advocate the emigration of former slaves back to Africa.

Where Europeans were scarcer, elites took a harsher tone. Simón Bolívar declared,

I am convinced to the very marrow of my bones that America can only be ruled by an able despotism ... We are the vile offspring of the predatory Spaniards who came to America to bleed her white and to breed with their victims. Later the illegitimate offspring of these unions joined with the offspring of slaves transported from Africa. With such racial mixture and such a moral record, can we afford to place laws above leaders and principles above men? (Quoted in Lynch 1973: 249)

---

[23] See Andrews (2016), Appelbaum et al. (2003), Fisher, O'Hara (2009), Graham (2010), Loveman (2014), Telles (2014), Twinam (2015), Wade (2017).

The abridgment of democracy was a natural, and seemingly inevitable, solution to this race problem.

What this meant, in practical terms, is that the institutions of democracy in Latin America were adapted so as to exclude elements of the population deemed unworthy or incapable of exercising political power in a responsible fashion. Tools of disenfranchisement centered on property, profession, literacy, and relationships of dependency (including slaves and servants), and were maintained in many countries well into the twentieth century (Engerman, Sokoloff 2005; Kellam 2013). They fell disproportionately on citizens of indigenous or African heritage. For countries composed of predominantly European stock these laws were of less import, as more citizens cleared the bar. For countries with large indigenous or Afro-Latino populations, these laws had the effect of disenfranchising a majority of the citizenry, seriously compromising the quality of democracy.

The Portuguese Empire

Portuguese imperial rule was more centralized than the British Empire but less centralized than the Spanish. As such, Portuguese colonies enjoyed considerable autonomy when it came to governing themselves.[24]

That autonomy was greater where there was a larger collection of Europeans. Where colonists were scarce, as in many Asian colonies, they were often under direct military rule. Where colonists were more numerous, they were subject to viceroyalty systems with elaborate bureaucracies and advisory councils, which provided some informal representation for prominent (white) citizens (Diffie, Winius 1977: 322–9).

Within the latter structure, municipal councils (aka *consilium, consejo, concelho, ayuntamiento, cabildo, senado da camara*) were formed where there was a concentration of European settlers. Albertini and Wirz (1982: 422) report that "wherever there was a white colonial population of any size, it was organized as a council, having representative organs and some administrative autonomy." Councils were duly formed in Goa (1510), Bahia (1549), Luanda (1575), Macao (1586), São Tomé (by 1528), Massangano, Angola (1676), Cachoeira (1698), and various white enclaves in Mozambique including Mozambique island, Quelimane, Sena, Tete, Sofala, Inhambane, Zumbo, and Manica (ca. 1763).[25]

---

[24] See Boxer (1965b), Diffie, Winius (1977: 329–31).
[25] See Bethencourt (2007), Boxer (1965b, 1969: 278), Disney (2009), Wills (2011: 42–3).

These bodies were modeled directly on Portuguese municipal councils – "usually with the same responsibilities, rights and privileges as equivalent bodies in Portugal" (Disney 2009: 164) – and often held charters from Portuguese cities (Boxer 1969: ch. 12). Detailed rules governed the construction of voter lists, the selection of electors, and their nomination of officials, several of whom were chosen randomly to serve fixed terms of office (Boxer 1965b: introduction).

Though controlled by elites, working-class whites also enjoyed limited representation (Boxer 1965b, 1969: ch. 12). However, rights of participation were generally reserved for whites, with concessions to mestizos where those of pure European extraction were scarce,[26] and officeholding was "predominantly by men of European birth, or at any rate by men with a relatively small admixture of indigenous blood. ... [I]f there was not always a rigid colour-bar, there was a definite, and, in the circumstances, a natural and inevitable prejudice in favour of white blood" (Boxer 1965b: 147).

As such, patterns of local govenance across the Portuguese colonies follow the general pattern observed for other European colonies. Where significant numbers of Europeans congregated (relative to the size of the indigenous population), some form of democracy generally eventuated, even if it was limited to local levels.

Democracy and Oppression

We have now discussed the colonial and (more briefly) the post-colonial histories of the four largest European overseas empires, British, French, Spanish, and Portuguese. Although we do not have the space to continue this tour in any detail, it is worth noting that similar patterns seem to have existed in smaller imperial realms.

The situation was similar, for example, within the German Empire (Townsend 1966: 277), where the colony with the most settlers – Southwest Africa – enjoyed the greatest measure of self-governance (Albertini, Wirz 1982: 411–12; Smith 1978: 205).

In the Dutch Empire, New Amsterdam – where Europeans formed the vast majority of the inhabitants – was governed in much the same way as its namesake, and seemed destined for self-government were it not for the English takeover in 1664 (Jacobs 2005: 127–9, 187–9). Meanwhile, the Dutch East Indies, where Europeans were vastly outnumbered, was much slower to introduce representative institutions, and they never

---

[26] See Boxer (1969: ch. 12), Newitt (2004: 171–4).

attained sovereignty vis-à-vis appointed colonial administrators.[27] *Urban governance* in the East Indies, by contrast, enjoyed considerable autonomy and was largely elective. Naturally, it was dominated by Dutch settlers.

> The Urban Council, as noticed above, is predominantly Dutch in its constitution and character. The revenue comes mainly from a cess on Government taxes, mostly paid by Europeans, and from municipal services, such as housing, the supply of electricity, water, trams and buses. The varied range of municipal activities is very striking; even in a small town one may find a theatre and a swimming bath. It is hardly too much to say that the towns are run by Europeans for Europeans, though of course the other communities benefit by the amenities. (Furnivall 1948: 251)

This description offers an excellent example of representative democracy as a "European club."

Across the colonial and post-colonial eras one finds few signs of democracy anywhere except in the presence of European colonists.[28] This was a product of directives from the metropole as well as pressure from the colonies. Although these two forces sometimes came into conflict with each other with respect to the appropriate treatment of non-whites, there was general agreement on the question of democracy. Whites (Europeans) were considered capable of it while non-whites were not. Consequently, the metropole's perspective hinged upon demographic realities on the ground, just as it did for settlers. The logic of empire was not so different whether Europeans occupied offices in London, Paris, Madrid, Lisbon, or colonial outposts somewhere on the periphery.[29] Fieldhouse (1966: 261–2) comments: "The greater part of the new British Empire has been excluded from 'responsible government' on the principle that non-Europeans could not run a parliamentary system, partly because they were uneducated, partly because they were not European." If based on the demography of a colony London viewed

---

[27] The Volksraad, or People's Council, formed in 1918, was a flawed vehicle for popular representation. Furnivall (1948: 248) explains "The Chairman of the Volksraad is appointed by the Crown; of the other members some are elected and the rest nominated by the Governor-General. Representation is based on the communal principle. Only Dutch subjects are eligible for the franchise or for membership. Three communities are recognized: natives, Dutch and 'others' (preponderantly Chinese); until 1927 the two last categories formed one constituency." The most important limitation was that the powers of the Volksraad were advisory. Any prospect of further democratic development was halted when the Japanese took command of the colony in 1942. See Furnivall (2010[1939]), Klaveren (2013).

[28] See Fieldhouse (1966), Reinsch (1902: chs. 11–12), Ward (1976), Wight (1946).

[29] See Albertini, Wirz (1982), Lester, Boehme, Mitchell (2021), Lewis (1968: 108), Swinfen (1970: 100), Ward (1976), Wight (1946).

it as "white man's country," the colony was likely to be granted a legislature and a high degree of self-governance. If, on the other hand, there were few white settlers London was likely to maintain direct control. Southern Rhodesia, with a sizeable white settler community, followed the first route while Kenya, with a much smaller settler community, followed the second (Albertini, Wirz 1982: 454, 467).

Our argument is consistent with ongoing work on the intersection of race and liberalism.[30] Indeed, we have shown that the spread of democratic norms coincided with, and to some extent reinforced, norms of racial exclusion and exploitation. Where Europeans were a majority, the majoritarian thrust of democracy served them well. Here, elections were often comparatively free and fair. Where Europeans were a minority, they structured the institutions of democracy so that the majority was excluded, either by segregating them in "homelands," by drawing lines around colonies in a selective fashion (declaring a colony in areas controlled by Europeans), by discriminatory suffrage laws, by ballot fraud, or by the exercise of patronage and clientelism (Evans et al. 2003: 186). The *quality* of democracy thus varied with the share of Europeans in the population.

It seems clear that in most cases democracy was utilized as a weapon to monopolize power in the hands of European settlers and thereby to control property (including slaves), to dispossess indigenous peoples, and to repress rebellion and dissent. The importance of land in this calculation can hardly be overestimated (Adhikari 2015, 2021). With respect to British colonialism, Evans et al. (2003: 184) write,

In all the colonies of settlement, the primary aim of the settlers was to get possession of the land by dispossessing the Indigenous peoples, whether by sale and treaty, as in Canada and New Zealand, by conquest and treaty, as in South Africa and New Zealand, or, as in Australia, by declaring the land to be *terra nullius* and therefore automatically the property of the British Crown. Whatever political powers were to be allowed to Indigenes, they could not be such as would be capable of blocking or interfering with the continuation of the process of acquiring the land and bringing in White settlers.

Europeans had to be included in democratic institutions so that their claims to property could be ensured, and if possible extended. Indigenes had to be excluded so they had no legal recourse to complain about expropriation.

As observed by Douglass North (1990), there is an intimate relationship between democracy and property rights. Where we depart from North and his many collaborators and followers in the New

---

[30] See Centeno (2007), FitzGerald, Cook-Martin (2014), Horton (2005), Rana (2011), Smith (1997).

Institutionalist tradition is in recognizing the racial underpinnings of how democracy was defined.

Another major concern for fledgling parliaments composed of embattled Europeans was potential unrest. Consider the tiny English colony on the Cayman Islands. In 1831, acting on their own initiative (but probably anticipating support from the Crown), colonists formed their first legislature. The founders of this new initiative declared that two representatives would be elected for each of five districts. Following the election, ten representatives assembled in George Town along with eight appointed magistrates. The two bodies met in adjacent rooms, "preserving the classic British form of a bicameral legislative," Craton (2003: 98) notes. Protocol counted for quite a lot, even in a tiny society on the distant fringes of the British Empire. The first session of the legislature was occupied, most importantly, by the formation of a militia. Craton (2003: 98) explains,

Each free male between sixteen and sixty capable of bearing arms was compelled to serve in the militia and to provide himself with a serviceable musket, bayonet, and ammunition pouch ... Stiff fines were enacted for neglect of duty ... to be enforced by a marshall within each company.

One might suppose that the tiny colony was preparing to defend its shores, except that no threats from abroad were imminent and none were likely to arise given British dominance in the Caribbean. In fact, the sole purpose of the militia appears to have been as a police force, and the main threat was the possibility of a slave revolt. There was no provision to enroll slaves in the militia, Craton (2003: 98) notes pointedly.

Legislatures, where they existed, were often hostile to the interests of non-Europeans. Lewis (1968: 96) remarks,

Again and again the history of colonization has shown that the safeguard of coloured races consists in a strong Home government outside and beyond local influences, and that Home rule for a dependency, where the white men are few and the coloured many, has in past times meant for the majority of its inhabitants not so much the gift of freedom as the withdrawal of Imperial protection.

That is why slaves and indigenes routinely appealed to colonial governors, to colonial or parliamentary offices in the metropole, or to the queen or king, for relief. More favorable treatment was expected from unelected officials far away than from elected officials close to home. Swinfen (1970: 124) comments,

Immigrants, poor persons, even criminals, had to be defended against discrimination and outright cruelty. In very many of these cases the Colonial Office showed itself prepared to maintain its principles, even at the risk of friction with the colonies concerned.

This was a world in which democratic assemblies were instruments of oppression, and in which unelected officials and missionary and abolition societies in a faraway land offered the only respite (and it was, of course, only occasional) against abuse.[31]

For their part, Europeans preferred to establish representative institutions, allowing them some degree of independence from the metropole, wherever they had the demographic muscle to control political outcomes. Elections were preferred, but only where the outcome was assured, i.e., only in situations where power would remain in the hands of Europeans.

This juxtaposition corroborates our central thesis: non-whites were accorded rights in inverse proportion to their numbers. They could vote and qualify for public office where they posed little threat but were excluded wherever political representation threatened white supremacy. Accordingly, we conclude that the primary drivers of democracy throughout the European empires were demographic. More precisely, racial ideology and attitudes toward democracy were formed on the basis of demographic realities. White supremacy was a rallying cry when it was needed; liberalism was a rallying cry where it was not. This also fits the circumstances of reformers in the metropole, who had little to lose from freeing slaves or improving conditions for indigenous peoples far from home.

Statistical Tests

To examine a large set of cases simultaneously we need a measure of democracy applicable across European colonies. Fortuitously, one such measure has recently been coded by Jack Paine (2019). The sample begins in 1600, incorporating 144 former Western European colonies, a phenomenal data collection effort and a significant advance over existing data sources.

To grapple with the question of democracy in this context Paine codes the existence of an elective assembly in each year of a colony's life. The variable is coded 1 if there was an assembly that performed legislative or advisory functions and at least one member was elected. This is a permissive definition including assemblies (e.g., legislative councils) whose role was clearly subordinate to the executive, assemblies where only a small minority of members were elected, and assemblies whose elections were limited to a small elite. It excludes local assemblies such as

---

[31] See Evans et al. (2003), Lester, Dussart (2014), Vickery (1974: 319).

Table 10.3 *Elective colonial assemblies*

Sample	All colonies	All colonies	All colonies	British colonies	Non-British colonies
	1	2	3	4	5
European ancestry (%)	0.006***	0.005***	0.005***	0.010***	0.001*
	(3.832)	(3.410)	(3.807)	(4.966)	(1.968)
Year (trend)	✓	✓	✓	✓	✓
Century dummies	✓	✓	✓	✓	✓
Harbor distance		✓	✓		
Equator distance		✓	✓		
English colony			✓		
Colonies	126	121	121	62	65
Years	400	398	398	398	400
Observations	39 827	37 945	37 945	20 585	19 242
R^2	0.183	0.203	0.224	0.208	0.223

Outcome: elective colonial assembly, coded 0 or 1 (Paine 2019). *Not shown:* Constant. *Estimator:* ordinary least squares, standard errors clustered by colony, t statistics in parentheses. ***p<.01 **p<.05 *p<.10

the *cabildo*, discussed above in the context of Spanish and Portuguese colonies. Even so, the difference between having a colony-wide assembly and not having one at all was consequential at the time and probably even more consequential over the long haul, as early experiences with elective government seem to have informed later political developments, with assemblies becoming the institutional linchpins of democracies in the post-independence era.

In Table 10.3, this outcome is regressed against European ancestry along with a trend variable and century dummies (annual dummies are too numerous for the model to handle). Model 1 is the benchmark specification. Model 2 adds harbor distance and equator distance. Model 3 adds a dummy for English colony. Model 4 restricts the sample to British colonies and Model 5 to non-British colonies.

It will be seen that European ancestry has a positive impact on the outcome in all tests. However, the impact is greatest among British colonies, validating a central argument in Paine (2019). There was much more scope for democratic experimentation in British colonies than in other colonies, as discussed. Even so, within British colonies – and to some extent in non-British colonies – those with a higher share of European colonists (or descendants of European colonists) were more likely to possess an elective assembly.

Table 10.4 *The legacy of European ancestry within empires*

Sample	British Empire	Spanish Empire
	1	2
European ancestry (%)	0.715***	0.296***
	(7.287)	(2.863)
States	66	22
Years	229	229
Observations	10,306	4,072
R^2 *(pseudo-likelihood)*	0.629	0.608

Outcome: Polyarchy index of electoral democracy, augmented. *Not shown:* Harbor distance, Equator distance, Year dummies, Constant. *Estimator:* ordinary least squares, standard errors clustered by state, t statistics in parentheses. ***$p<.01$ **$p<.05$ *$p<.10$

We suspect that this relationship would be stronger if more discriminating indicators of democracy were available, e.g., pertaining to the share of members on each assembly that were elected, the degree of competition and extent of suffrage in those elections, and the prevalence of elective local assemblies, as suggested in our discussion.

The legacy of European ancestry in the *post*-independence era can be viewed by enlisting our standard measure of democracy, the Polyarchy index, to compare former colonies within the same empire. Our analysis, shown in Table 10.4, is limited to the British and Spanish empires because these contained the most colonies (and hence, offer the largest samples) and because they demonstrated the greatest cross-colony variation in European ancestry. Model 1 is limited to the British Empire and Model 2 to the Spanish Empire.

Analyses contained in Table 10.4 demonstrate that European ancestry is associated with more democratic outcomes in each sample, bolstering our main argument. Although there were important differences across empires in their tolerance for democracy, *within* each imperial realm the factor that seems to have conditioned the development of electoral and representative institutions was demographic. The higher the share of Europeans, the greater was the likelihood of democratic institutions.

It should be stressed that this sample is weighted heavily toward post-independence years. At that point, freed from the shackles of colonialism, countries were allowed to develop in a more autonomous fashion. Accordingly, we should expect greater variance in regime types and we should also expect the full impact of European demography to be manifested. Subjects were now citizens, and the metropole had limited impact on the development of political institutions.

Our analysis suggests that the impact of European ancestry is still greater within the British Empire than the Spanish Empire. This may reflect greater variance in European ancestry across British colonies as well as the more decentralized nature of the British Empire. Or, it may simply reflect the larger sample of states that arose from the detritus of the British Empire (nearly three times as many contemporary countries as the Spanish Empire).

In any case, a key finding of these analyses is that the influence of European ancestry is not solely a product of English colonialism. Indeed, a sub-sample test conducted in the following chapter shows that the main result is robust even when all former colonies of the British Empire are removed from the sample (see Table 11.4).

A final legacy effect concerns the *timing* of independence. This is by no means incidental to the topic of democracy, as sovereignty is usually regarded as a defining feature of a fully democratic polity. Moreover, there is plenty of historical evidence, reviewed above, to suggest that European settlers regarded the question of independence strategically.

In colonies where they composed a majority of the population or a minority sizeable enough to control domestic politics in the foreseeable future (using the various instruments we have discussed including franchise restrictions, homelands, vote-buying, and outright fraud), Europeans agitated for independence at an early date (even if they sometimes remained as part of a larger Commonwealth, owing nominal allegiance to the British Crown). They saw little point in paying taxes to the metropole while having limited control over their colonial policies.

By contrast, where Europeans were a small minority they often prevaricated, clinging to the metropole and, wherever there was an option, to institutions of direct rule ("Crown colony" status, in the British system). In this fashion, they avoided possible loss of power, privilege, and property in a fully independent country where the indigenous majority was bound to control government policy. The issue was seen similarly by the metropole, at least in the British case, where "dominion status [was] the accepted goal for the white colonies and ... Crown Colony system for the Negro colonies" (Lewis 1968: 108).

To explore this thesis, we offer two tests in Table 10.5. In Model 1, we regress year of independence for all states that were once colonies against European ancestry, along with colony dummies and region dummies. This is a single cross-section where all variables are measured in 2000. We expect a negative relationship between European ancestry and year of independence.

Table 10.5 *Independence*

Outcome	Year of independence	Independence
Estimator	OLS	Cox proportional hazards model
	1	2
European ancestry (%)	−0.781***	1.025***
	(−3.557)	(2.769)
States	94	103
Years	1	229
Observations	94	12 395
Failures		102
R^2 (pseudo-likelihood)	0.842	(−362)

Sample: former colonies of a European power. *Not shown:* Colony dummies (British, French, Spanish), Region dummies, Constant. *Estimator:* as indicated, standard errors clustered by state, t statistics in parentheses. ***p<.01 **p<.05 *p<.10

In Model 2, we construct an event history model in which the probability of a transition to independence is modeled as a product of European ancestry along with the same background covariates. Here, we employ a Cox proportional hazard model, where the coefficients indicate the hazard ratio – specifically, the ratio of the hazards (risk of failure) between two units whose values of $x1$ differ by one unit when all other covariates are held constant. If the hazard ratio > 1, this indicates a positive relationship, while hazard ratio below 1 indicates a negative relationship. We expect to find a positive relationship between European ancestry and probability of independence.

Both models indicate that European ancestry is a strong predictor of independence. The higher the proportion of Europeans, the earlier a colony is likely to achieve independent status. We believe that this effect is correctly interpreted as a product of the varying attitudes of European settlers. After all, imperial powers were loath to part with territory – especially profitable territories, as "little Europes" usually were. And indigenous people – the unenfranchised subjects of empire – were usually in favor of independence, or were (as in the case of Latin America) largely uninvolved. The factor that varied considerably from colony to colony, and that might reasonably account for variation on the outcome, was the attitudes and interests of European settlers, who saw which way the wind was likely to blow if they agitated for independence.

Over time, this led to a curious dynamic in which the British colonies with the highest European ancestry, who shared a political and cultural legacy with the metropole, were most likely to declare independence from the metropole. New England separated from England in 1776, Canada became self-governing in 1867, Australia declared independence in 1901, New Zealand gained effective autonomy in 1907, and South Africa became independent in 1910. Meanwhile, British colonies with predominantly indigenous populations in the Caribbean, Asia, and Africa were generally compelled to retain their subordinate status until the mid-twentieth century. A few – such as Anguilla, Bermuda, the Cayman Islands, the British Virgin Islands, the Falkland Islands, Montserrat, and Turks & Caicos Islands – remain dependencies today. (Of these, only the Falkland Islands can claim majority European descent, and this is a very recent development, occurring in the late twentieth century.)

Likewise, Spain lost its European-dominated colonies in the Americas in the early nineteenth century. Meanwhile, it retained a grip on the Philippines, Cuba, and Puerto Rico until 1898, Equatorial Guinea until 1968, and Western Sahara until 1975. Were it not for American intervention, its holdings in the Caribbean and the Pacific might have endured for another half-century or more.

Portugal was forced to recognize the independence of Brazil, which had the largest number of European settlers (by far), in 1822. It managed to hold on to other major colonies – with fewer European immigrants – such as Angola, Cape Verde, Goa, Macao, Mozambique, Sao Tome, and Timor until the late twentieth century.

This pattern is less marked within other empires only because there were so few European-dominated colonies. This may help to explain why independence came late for most Dutch and French colonies – excepting those that were captured by another European power or by the United States, and thus forcibly separated. There were few European-led movements for independence in these colonies because European settlers and their descendants would have faced a difficult demographic situation had they achieved independence. Their interests tied them to the empire. Consequently, movements for independence were led by indigenous groups and it generally took a good deal of time before they gained traction (Haiti being the obvious exception).

11   Global Analyses

> Just as none of us is outside or beyond geography, none of us is
> completely free from the struggle over geography. That struggle is
> complex and interesting because it is not only about soldiers and
> cannons but also about ideas, about forms, about images and imaginings.
>
> A whole range of people in the so-called Western or metropolitan
> world, as well as their counterparts in the Third or formerly colonized
> world, share a sense that the era of high or classical imperialism, which
> came to a climax in ... "the age of empire" and more or less formally
> ended with the dismantling of the great colonial structures after World
> War Two, has in one way or another continued to exert considerable
> cultural influence in the present. For all sorts of reasons, they feel a new
> urgency about understanding the pastness *or not* of the past, and this
> urgency is carried over into perceptions of the present and
> the future.   Edward Said (1994: 7)

Having explored the relationship between European ancestry and democracy in the colonial and post-colonial eras, we proceed to a series of
wide-ranging tests that encompass the world from 1789 to the present.

Demonstrating the plausibility of a distal causal connection on a global
scale is not easy. A great many assumptions are required in order to make a
convincing case. Fortunately, many of these assumptions are empirically
testable. Consequently, this chapter is filled with diverse tests intended to
show robustness in the face of different assumptions. Subsequent sections
focus on (a) different model specifications, (b) alternate measures of
democracy, (c) alternate measures and temporal configurations of
"Europe," (d) sub-sample analyses, (e) replications of previous work, (f)
instrumental variable analyses, and (g) estimates of causal impact (including variations in impact through time). The final section summarizes the
evidence and discusses challenges to causal inference.

Specification Tests

Table 11.1 presents an initial set of specification tests. In Model 1,
democracy is regressed against European ancestry along with year

287

Table 11.1 *Specification tests*

	1	2	3	4	5
European ancestry (%)	0.252***	0.289***	0.284***	0.493***	0.244***
	(9.692)	(7.670)	(7.389)	(8.534)	(7.417)
Natural harbor distance		✓	✓	✓	✓
Equator distance		✓	✓	✓	✓
Tropical			✓		
Temperature			✓		
Frost days			✓		
Island			✓		
Landlock			✓		
River distance			✓		
Ruggedness			✓		
Mountains			✓		
Precipitation + precipitation^2			✓		
Irrigation potential			✓		
Agricultural suitability			✓		
Desert			✓		
Headman				✓	✓
Protestant (%)				✓	✓
Muslim (%)				✓	✓
English colonial duration				✓	✓
State history				✓	
Years since independence (log)				✓	
Ethnic fractionalization				✓	
Linguistic fractionalization				✓	
Religious fractionalization				✓	
Oil resources				✓	
Population density, 1500				✓	
Settler mortality				✓	
Malaria ecology				✓	
Agricultural transition				✓	
Region dummies				✓	
States	220	195	142	66	183
Years	229	229	229	222	222
Observations	34 142	31 762	23 258	11 429	28 967
R^2 *(within)*	0.523	0.564	0.638	0.733	0.616

Outcome: Polyarchy index of electoral democracy, augmented. *Not shown:* Year dummies, Constant. *Estimator:* ordinary least squares, standard errors clustered by state, t statistics in parentheses. ***p<.01 **p<.05 *p<.10

dummies. In Model 2, we add natural harbor distance and equator distance, the two strongest and most robust geographic predictors of democracy in the modern era (see Chapter 12). In Model 3 we include additional geographic factors that might influence long-run development (discussed in Chapter 12). In Model 4, we return to the core geographic covariates, this time with some additional non-geographic factors that may have long-run implications for democracy. (Since coverage is not great for some of these covariates, the sample is considerably reduced.) In Model 5, we offer what might be regarded as a "full" specification, including all factors that offer broad coverage and seem to be theoretically and empirically justifiable.

Coefficient estimates for European ancestry are fairly stable across these specifications, and all models reveal t statistics for European ancestry that are well above usual thresholds of statistical significance. We regard Model 2 as the benchmark, as it avoids any possibility of post-treatment bias and preserves a nearly complete sample.

Measures of Democracy

In Table 11.2, we test alternate measures of democracy, introduced in Chapter 2. Outcomes are transformed to a 0–100 scale so as to be comparable to benchmark estimates. For each outcome, we employ the spare benchmark specification including geographic covariates and year (or decade) dummies. Estimation is by ordinary least squares except Model 5, which utilizes a Tobit model that is appropriate for outcomes that are bounded at zero.

Model 1 employs the usual democracy measure, the Polyarchy index of electoral democracy, with missing data interpolated. Model 2 substitutes the Polyarchy index without any interpolated data. Model 3 employs the Lexical index of electoral democracy. Model 4 employs the Polity2 index. Model 5 employs an index of electoral contestation. Model 6 examines male suffrage, the approximate percentage of enfranchised male adults older than the minimal voting age. This analysis is restricted to years prior to 1920, when there was considerable variation in suffrage laws.

All these tests show a strong and robust relationship between European ancestry and democracy. Across the six outcomes, our benchmark measure of democracy shows the weakest relationship with European ancestry, judging by estimated coefficients. (This does not appear to be a sample effect.)

Measures of European Ancestry

In Table 11.3 we test different approaches to the measurement of European ancestry, as discussed in Chapter 9, and different temporal relationships to democracy.

Table 11.2 Democracy indices

Outcome	Polyarchy augmented	Polyarchy	Lexical index	Polity2	Contestation	Male suffrage
Estimator	OLS	OLS	OLS	OLS	Tobit	OLS
	1	2	3	4	5	6
European ancestry (%)	0.289***	0.295***	0.362***	0.336***	0.518***	0.399***
	(7.670)	(7.610)	(7.006)	(5.359)	(7.382)	(7.581)
Year dummies	✓	✓	✓	✓		✓
Decade dummies					✓	
States	195	178	192	168	194	146
Years	229	229	229	218	227	131
N	31 762	23 626	18 436	16 518	34 554	5254
R^2 (pseudo-likelihood)	0.564	0.567	0.406	0.316	(−56917)	0.386

Outcome: democracy, measured in various ways and transformed to a 0–100 scale. *Not shown:* Natural harbor distance, Equator distance, Constant. *Estimator:* OLS (ordinary least squares), Tobit regression, standard errors clustered by state, t statistics in parentheses. ***p<.01 **p<.05 *p<.10

Table 11.3 Measures of European ancestry

	1789–2019	1789–2019	1789–2019	1789–2019	1789–2019	2000	1789–2019	1789–2019	1789–2000
Years									
Right-side lag	0	0	0	100	200	100	0	10	10
States	All	All	Europe	All	All	All	All	All	All
	1	2	3	4	5	6	7	8	9
European ancestry									
Benchmark	0.289***		0.455***	0.239***	0.185***	0.419***		0.298**	0.485***
	(7.670)		(3.267)	(6.229)	(4.024)	(5.656)		(2.279)	(4.219)
Quadratic			0.001						
			(0.411)						
Narrow definition		0.313***							
		(8.678)							
Stock							0.031***		
							(8.044)		
Harbor distance	✓	✓	✓	✓	✓	✓	✓		
Equator distance	✓	✓	✓	✓	✓	✓	✓		
Year dummies	✓	✓	✓	✓	✓		✓	✓	✓
State dummies							✓	✓	✓
Countries	195	194	156	195	195	192	194	220	219
Years	229	229	229	231	220	1	229	231	211
Observations	31 762	31 688	26 076	32 144	31 206	192	31 688	34 544	30 592
R^2 (within)	0.564	0.575	0.574	0.543	0.516	0.341	0.579	0.573	0.457

Outcome: Polyarchy index of electoral democracy, augmented. *European ancestry, narrow definition:* includes countries whose language is Latinate or Germanic. *Stock:* calculated from benchmark measure of European ancestry from 1600 to the present with a 10% annual depreciation rate. *Estimator:* ordinary least squares, standard errors clustered by state, t statistics in parentheses. ***p<.01 **p<.05 *p<.10

The benchmark measure of European ancestry, which defines Europe based on the proximity of territories to natural harbors, is employed in Model 1. In Model 2, European ancestry is recalculated with a narrower definition of Europe focusing on states whose primary language is Latinate or Germanic (also described in Chapter 9). Estimates from these models are extremely close, as one might expect. Changing the "European" coding of a handful of states located on the fringes of Europe scarcely affects the European heritage of the rest of the world.

In Model 3, we test for non-monotonicity in the relationship between European ancestry and democracy by including a quadratic term. (The sample for this analysis excludes Europe, as we do not want that region to unduly influence the results.) No evidence of nonlinearity is apparent.

The variable of theoretical interest, European ancestry, changes slowly through time for most states and is unlikely to be affected by the outcome (democracy). Nonetheless, it is important to establish that the findings are robust to different lags of the predictor. In Model 4, right-side variables are lagged 100 years behind the outcome and in Model 5 they are lagged by 200 years. In Model 6, we return to the 100-year lag while restricting the outcome to a single year (2000 CE). Note that because data on European ancestry stretches back to 1600 (see Chapter 9), lagging this variable results in minimal data loss; samples are comparable.

If European identity was more clearly defined and operationalized in previous historical eras (when race was a less permeable concept), one may have more confidence in lagged models than in models where right and left sides of the model are measured contemporaneously. One might also regard this as a stronger result given that it mitigates problems of simultaneity. In any case, estimates are very similar to the benchmark.

One might imagine that the impact of European ancestry on regimes is a cumulative affair, one that builds on a state's entire historical experience. To test this hypothesis, we measure European ancestry with a "stock" index.[1] Recall that our dataset measuring European ancestry extends back to 1600. A stock measure is therefore constructed across the 1600–2019 period with a 10 percent annual depreciation rate. This is tested in the benchmark specification in Model 7. Results are robust, though model-fit is not improved so there is no empirical justification for adopting a more complex functional form.

The final models in Table 11.3 enlist a fixed-effect estimator, essentially identical to including a dummy for each state. This focuses the analysis exclusively on change through time in right- and left-side

---

[1] For discussion of the stock concept see Gerring, Bond, Barndt, Moreno (2005).

variables. We do not believe this is the most appropriate test for sluggish, highly trended variables, and we do not include a model with a lagged dependent variable. Nonetheless, the fixed-effect format is a helpful robustness test since it obviates confounders like geography and culture that are largely static through time.

Model 8 enlists all the data, lagging right-side variables by ten years to avoid potential problems of simultaneity. Model 9 focuses on the years prior to 2000, when the relationship should be strongest. (The impact of European demography is expected to attenuate in the very end of our period, as Europeans lose influence in the world and racial distinctions lose their potency, as argued in Chapter 8 and shown empirically in Figure 11.2.)

Remarkably, despite all of these alterations in our definition and measurement of European ancestry and in the temporal dynamics between inputs and outputs, all the tests shown in Table 11.3 are robust.

Sub-sample Analyses

In Table 11.4 we explore various sample restrictions, building on the benchmark specification.

The benchmark analysis, reproduced as Model 1, includes all available states, whether located in Europe or outside Europe. The assumption is that whatever factors might be at work elsewhere ought to apply to Europe as well. If the presence of Europeans enhances prospects for democracy in the Americas it ought to do so in Europe, which means that excluding this region – the centerpiece of our theory – would introduce bias.

By the same token, Europe constitutes a potentially influential region in our analysis, having a high score on European ancestry (by construction), so it is important to know whether results are robust when this region is excluded. In Model 2, focused on the non-European world, the causal factor of interest can operate *only* by diffusion. As it happens, the estimate for European ancestry is higher in this sub-sample than in the full-sample analysis.

One might also wonder whether the British Empire plays an influential role in our global analysis. Note that most of the world's settler colonies (which provide much of the variation in European ancestry) were planted within the British Empire. To see how influential this group of states might be we restrict the sample in Model 3 to states that fall outside the British Empire, which is to say they were never (or only briefly) colonized by Great Britain. The estimate for European ancestry is very slightly attenuated relative to the benchmark.

Table 11.4 *Sample restrictions*

Sample	Full (benchmark)	Non-Europe	Non-British Empire	European ancestry <80%	European ancestry >5%	Non-sovereign states
	1	2	3	4	5	6
European ancestry (%)	0.289***	0.504***	0.251***	0.476***	0.121*	0.098***
	(7.670)	(7.809)	(6.548)	(5.707)	(1.750)	(2.798)
States	195	156	128	161	85	155
Years	229	229	229	229	229	229
Observations	31 762	26 076	21 127	25 658	11 728	12 639
R^2	0.564	0.574	0.586	0.546	0.573	0.274

Sample	Sovereign states	Europe, Russia, Central Asia	Americas	MENA	Sub-Saharan Africa	Asia-Pacific
	7	8	9	10	11	12
European ancestry (%)	0.300***	0.319***	0.226**	1.364***	0.736**	0.863***
	(7.380)	(3.588)	(2.540)	(14.842)	(2.358)	(15.312)
States	192	51	35	22	49	38
Years	229	229	229	229	229	229
Observations	19 123	6 773	6 840	3 571	7 733	6 845
R^2	0.510	0.599	0.684	0.561	0.614	0.644

Outcome: Polyarchy index of electoral democracy, augmented. *Not shown:* Harbor distance, Equator distance, Year dummies, Constant. *Estimator:* ordinary least squares, standard errors clustered by state, t statistics in parentheses. ***p<.01 **p<.05 *p<.10

Next, we focus on the key independent variable. Recall that the distribution of European ancestry is bimodal (Figure 9.2), so it is important to establish that our results are not contingent upon a subset of extreme cases. Model 4 is restricted to cases where Europeans compose less than 80 percent of the population, dropping Europe as well as neo-Europes in the New World. Model 5 is restricted to cases where Europeans compose greater than 5 percent of the population, eliminating cases (mostly in Asia and Africa) where Europeans are a slight presence. Estimates for European ancestry are augmented in Model 4 and attenuated in Model 5, relative to the benchmark. The latter is no surprise given the huge impact this restriction has on the sample, which shrinks from 195 states (Model 1) to 85 states (Model 5).

In Models 6 and 7 we distinguish between non-sovereign and sovereign states. Sovereignty is defined here in a formal (de jure) sense – recognition by European states, membership in international bodies, and treaty-signing powers. The non-sovereign sample thus includes colonies and dependencies. We find that the estimated coefficient for European ancestry is stronger for the sample of sovereign countries, presumably because there is greater variance in the outcome and the sample is tilted toward the contemporary era (where subsequent tests show the relationship is strongest).

The final set of tests focus on specific regions of the world: Model 8 on Europe, Russia, and Central Asia, Model 9 on the Americas, Model 10 on the Middle East and North Africa, Model 11 on sub-Saharan Africa, and Model 12 on Asia-Pacific (East Asia, Southeast Asia, South Asia, and the Pacific). Estimates for all of these tests are robust, though coefficients jump around a bit as one might expect given the changing samples, which are extremely diverse and quite small (22–51 states).

Replications

Replicability is a perennial problem for science, and especially for social science (Elman, Gerring, Mahoney 2020). Authors enjoy so much leeway to pick and choose their variables, specifications, estimators, samples, and other features of an analysis that it is easy to cherry-pick those that render the desired results.

One way around this problem is to standardize one's approach with other studies that examine the same question. In this section, we replicate three recent studies that we regard as leading exemplars of work on the long-term diffusion of democracy from Europe to the world. In the first study, Hariri (2012) argues that the diffusion of democracy was impeded in territories with a long history of state-ness, sufficient to provide resistance to the incursion of Europeans and European ideas. In the second study, Woodberry (2012) argues that the spread of conversionary Protestants fostered education and democratic norms. In the third study, Olsson (2009) argues that the duration of English colonial rule affected the propensity of societies to democratize.

We begin by replicating these studies as closely as we can. To do so, we employ data made available by the authors and focus on what appear to be their benchmark models, as noted in Table 11.5, making sure to adopt the author's preferred measure of democracy, specification, sample, and estimator. These render estimates for the key variable(s) of interest that are extremely close to those found in the published work.

The next model in each cluster adds our key variable of theoretical interest, European ancestry. This is measured in the first year of the observed outcome. For example, since Hariri measures democracy (with Polity2) across the 1991–2007 period, we measure European ancestry in 1991. (Increasing the lag to 100 years has virtually no effect on the estimated coefficient for European ancestry.)

Results from these tests show that the impact of European ancestry persists even when controlling for these alternate pathways of diffusion and even when adopting these authors' preferred modes of analysis (which may not be ideal for our theory). Because the chosen measures of democracy vary, one cannot compare estimates for European ancestry across these models. Nonetheless, t statistics suggest that it is highly robust.

One apparent exception bears notice. Woodberry includes a measure of European ancestry in his benchmark model, which is positively correlated with democracy but not statistically significant (Model 3). Evidently, our measure (shown in Model 4) suggests a stronger relationship between European ancestry and democracy than Woodberry's, even though the two variables are correlated (Pearson's r = 0.67). This is not a product of the year in which European ancestry is measured; additional tests (not shown), in which our variable is measured in 1980, reveal the same disparity in results.

Looking further, we find that Woodberry's data is drawn entirely from the *World Christian Encyclopedia* (Barrett 1982, and subsequent editions, e.g., Barrett, Kurian, Johnson 2000), a source that we also employ. However, as the reader will recall, we have a wealth of additional data sources for most states, and it appears that these additional sources disagree with Barrett in the coding of several regions of the world. For example, Barrett assigns a higher share of Europeans in Central Asian states, and a lower share of Europeans in most Latin American states, than our other sources. Since our estimates are based on multiple sources

Table 11.5 Replications

Source	Hariri 2012 (table 1, model 6)		Woodberry 2012 (table 6, model 3)		Olsson 2009 (table 6, model 3)	
Estimator	OLS, robust SEs		Robust OLS		OLS, robust SEs	
Outcome period	1991–2007 (mean)		1950–1994 (mean)		2007	
Democracy index	Polity2		Bollen, Paxton (2000)		Polity2	
	1	**2**	**3**	**4**	**5**	**6**
European ancestry (%) (beginning of period)		5.52*** (4.62)		35.91** (2.10)		5.17** (2.59)
Early state development	−4.33** (−2.04)	−4.23** (−2.07)				
Years exposure to Protestant missions			0.13** (2.60)	0.14** (2.58)		
Protestant missionaries per 10k pop			3.75** (2.36)	4.10** (2.63)		
Percent evangelized			0.17** (2.13)	0.14* (1.88)		
European ancestry (1982)			0.12 (1.12)			
English colonial duration					1.65*** (3.52)	1.79*** (3.84)
Other covariates	(see below)		(see below)		(see below)	
Observations	141	141	142	142	70	70
R²	0.3333	0.4022	.518	.5330	.4994	.5251

Additional covariates for Models 1–2: equator distance, population density, region dummies (Africa, Latin America, Asia, Middle East). *Additional covariates for Models 3–4:* British colonialism (dummy), other religious liberty colonies (dummy), Dutch colony (dummy), never significantly colonized (dummy), equator distance, island (dummy), landlocked (dummy), percent Muslim in 1970, major oil producer (dummy), literacy prior to missionary contact (dummy), year in which first democratic data available, democracy data available only after 1976 (dummy), years exposure to Catholic missions, foreign Catholic priests per 10,000 (in 1923). *Additional covariates for Models 5–6:* island (dummy), area (log), mortality (log), landlocked (dummy), year of political independence, years independent. t statistics in parentheses. ***p<.01 **p<.05 *p<.10

we have greater faith in the resulting index, which can plausibly be regarded as representing a consensus view among demographers and historians. The *World Christian Encyclopedia*, while an authoritative source with respect to religion, is not an authoritative source with respect to European demography.

Instrumental Variables

In this section we take a different approach to the problem of causal identification, modeling assignment to treatment with exogenous instruments. These analyses, shown in Table 11.6, are limited to non-European cases as the instruments attempt to model the spread of Europeans beyond Europe.

As a principal instrument we rely on indigenous population density in 1500, which served as a barrier to European migration and, more importantly, to demographic dominance, as discussed in Chapter 9. Model 1 offers a minimal specification with only the IV and decade dummies. Model 2 adds geographic covariates. Model 3 adds additional covariates, following the full specification in Table 11.1. Estimates for European ancestry are robust across all three models and consistent with the corresponding benchmark models.

In common with all non-randomized instruments, it is impossible to verify the assumptions underlying our IV analysis. Nonetheless, it is plausible to suppose that the exclusion restriction has been satisfied conditional on observed covariates.

Reassuringly, other possible instruments show similar results. In the latter columns of Table 11.6, we replicate Model 2 with a variety of other geographic or premodern historical variables commonly viewed as influences on European settlement: temperature, distance from London (squared), settler mortality, malaria transmission, years since agricultural transition, and state history.[2] The final analysis employs all instruments together in the same model.

The relationship with European ancestry is uniformly robust. No matter what instrument is chosen, European ancestry predicts higher levels of democracy. While assumptions required for any single model may be questioned, the aggregate results offer strong support for our thesis.

Individually, these factors provide weak instruments for European ancestry, as revealed in F-statistics from first-stage models. Weak

---

[2] See Acemoglu, Johnson, Robinson (2001, 2002), Easterly, Levine (2016), Ertan, Fiszbein, Putterman (2016), Hariri (2012).

Table 11.6 *Instrumental variable analyses*

Instrument(s)	Population density, 1500 (ln)			Temp-erature	London distance (ln, sq)	Settler mortality	Malaria trans-mission	Agric. transition (1000s of years since)	State history	All
	1	2	3	4	5	6	7	8	9	10
European ancestry (%)	0.461***	0.465***	0.260***	0.579**	0.896***	0.869***	0.480**	0.595***	0.586***	0.542***
	(4.633)	(4.581)	(2.933)	(2.115)	(6.060)	(5.343)	(2.319)	(4.351)	(5.608)	(7.809)
Natural harbor distance		✓	✓	✓	✓	✓	✓	✓	✓	✓
Equator distance		✓	✓	✓	✓	✓	✓	✓	✓	✓
Headman			✓							
Protestant (%)			✓							
Muslim (%)			✓							
English colonial duration			✓							
States	113	113	112	150	152	81	115	113	125	68
Years	227	227	222	227	227	227	227	227	227	227
Observations	18 664	18 664	17 835	24 830	25 436	14 292	20 113	18 749	20 799	12 289
F-statistic (first stage)	2.37	2.70	3.50	1.15	1.88	2.51	1.40	2.33	1.58	11.26
R^2	0.543	0.549	0.593	0.519	0.421	0.526	0.534	0.546	0.538	0.630

Outcome: Polyarchy index of electoral democracy, augmented. *Sample:* non-European cases. *Not shown:* Decade dummies, Constant. *Estimator:* two-stage least squares, standard errors clustered by state, t statistics in parentheses. Second-stage results only. ***p<.01 **p<.05 *p<.10

instruments should pull our results towards the OLS results, a bias that should reduce with increased F-values. When we combine the different instruments, they unsurprisingly provide a much stronger first stage fit, as shown in Model 10 (where the F-statistic is 11.26). Here, the coefficient for European ancestry is very similar to the ones in the models with weaker first stages. This does not mean that Model 10 is preferable to the other models, as there is greater potential for violating the exclusion restriction with many instruments. However, it is reassuring that the same general result is obtained whether the chosen instruments are weak or strong.

Impact

If European ancestry is a cause of democracy, one must wonder about the magnitude of this relationship. To get a better sense for what the coefficient estimates for European ancestry in the previous tables might mean, we estimate predicted values for democracy as the share of Europeans changes based on the benchmark specification (Model 2, Table 11.1). The sample is limited to the postwar era so as to grasp the contemporary relevance of this historical factor.

These estimates, surrounded by 95 percent confidence intervals, are shown in Figure 11.1. From this, we can speculate that a state whose share of Europeans increases from 0 to 100 should gain about 40 points on this 100-point index of democracy.

To explore how the relationship between European ancestry and democracy changes over time we execute a series of rolling regressions building on the benchmark specification. Here, the sample is restricted to a 30-year moving window starting in 1789 and continuing to the end of the period.

Figure 11.2 graphs the coefficients for European ancestry over these time intervals. This graph suggests that the relationship with democracy increases in a mostly monotonic fashion but with a momentary reversal in postwar years. At the end of the twentieth century there is another inflection point, after which the relationship between European ancestry and democracy appears to decline – although it is too early to say whether this decline will become a long-term trend.

The patterns shown in Figure 11.2 are for the most part consistent with our theoretical expectations, set forth in Chapter 8. Though we would have expected the modal point to arrive a little earlier in the twentieth century, it makes sense that the strength of this relationship would begin to decline as European influence in the world declines, as notions of "European-ness" (inevitably tinged with racial identities)

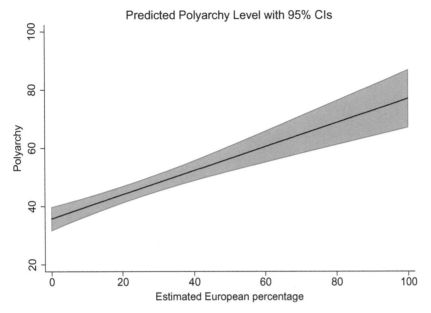

Figure 11.1 **Predicted values from benchmark model, 1960–2019**
Predicted values of the Polyarchy index of electoral democracy
(augmented) surrounded by 95% confidence intervals. Based on
estimates from Model 2, Table 11.1, with covariates set at sample
means. *Sample:* 1960–2019.

decline, and as ideas about democracy diffuse further, ceasing to be a
European monopoly. If the trend noted for the twenty-first century
continues, regime outcomes will have less and less to do with European
demography in the coming decades.

Conclusions

The problem of causal identification with observational data rests, in
large part, on the possibility of unmeasured confounders. In this
instance, we must be concerned about factors that might have affected
both European ancestry and regime type. Let us consider some of
the possibilities.

Following a large body of historical work, we theorized that Europeans
were more likely to settle where the ground was flat and fertile, the
climate salubrious, infectious disease minimal, and the ocean accessible.
They were more likely to establish plantation agriculture, and its attendant system of chattel slavery, in the tropics, leading to a situation where

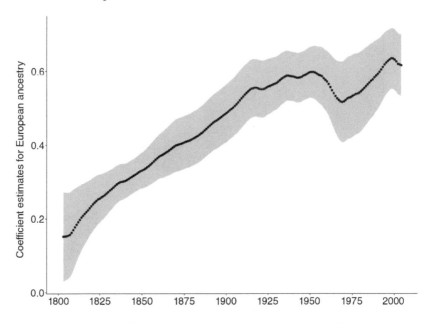

Figure 11.2 **The impact of European ancestry on democracy through time**
Rolling regressions in which the Polyarchy index (augmented) is regressed against European ancestry, geographic covariates (equator distance and harbor distance), and annual dummies in a moving 30-year window from 1789 to 2019. Sample excludes Europe. Coefficients for European ancestry, flanked by 95% confidence intervals, are graphed for the midpoint of each 30-year window.

Europeans might comprise a small minority of the population (e.g., the Caribbean). Europeans were more likely to become dominant demographically in areas that were thinly settled and highly susceptible to European diseases (e.g., the Americas away from the equator). They were (possibly) less likely to establish long-standing colonies and settlements in areas with strong states or Islamic religious traditions. These factors are reviewed at length in Chapter 9 and summarized in Figure 9.1. Since these factors might also affect the prospect of democracy (through channels other than European ancestry), any failure to include them as covariates in our analyses may generate a spurious correlation between European ancestry and democracy. Fortuitously, they are fairly easy to measure on a global scale and thus are included in specification tests shown in Table 11.1.

We can also measure the democratic-ness of preexisting political traditions using the Headman variable from the Ethnographic Atlas. And we can distinguish the demographic imprint of Europeans from other European influences such as religion (Protestantism, Catholicism), language (Latinate, German), and colonialism (e.g., the identity of the colonizer, the duration of colonial control, and direct or indirect style of rule). These factors are introduced briefly in Table 11.1 and explored further in Chapter 13.

As an additional strategy, we include region dummies (Table 11.1), as well as examining the history of English and Spanish colonial worlds in separate samples (Table 10.4). Table 11.4 provides tests in which the sample is restricted to (a) states outside Europe, (b) states outside the British Empire (current and former), (c) states with populations registering less than 80 percent European ancestry, (d) states with populations registering more than 10 percent European ancestry, (e) sovereign states, (f) non-sovereign states (colonies, dependencies), (g) Europe, North Asia, and Central Asia, (h) the Americas, (i) the Middle East and North Africa, (j) sub-Saharan Africa, and (k) Asia-Pacific. All subsample tests show robust results.

In Table 11.3, we offer a number of tests centered on measurement and functional form of the key concept, European ancestry. Here, European ancestry is lagged several centuries prior to the outcome. It is also variously operationalized – as a historical stock, as a quadratic, and according to a narrower definition of "Europe." Finally, we offer a series of fixed-effect estimations in which attention is focused on changes in European ancestry and regime type. Although both right- and left-side variables are sluggish, and therefore not ideal for a temporal design, it is reassuring to find the same relationship, and similar coefficient estimates, in this austere format, which obviates any static factors (cultural, geographic, etc.) that might otherwise serve as confounders.

Replication analyses based on benchmark models from Hariri (2012), Woodberry (2012), and Olsson (2009) show that when European ancestry is introduced into these specifications it is a strong predictor of democracy.

A different approach to causal identification attempts to identify antecedent conditions that influenced the European diaspora and subsequent demographic trajectories of states around the world outside Europe without directly affecting regime type, thus satisfying the exclusion restriction. This sort of assumption is impossible to prove empirically, which is why we cannot regard any of the instrumental variable analyses presented in Table 11.6 as pristine and why we offer a large number of instruments, each of which comprises the basis for a separate analysis. This includes population density in 1500, temperature, distance to London (log, squared), settler mortality, malaria transmission, agricultural transition, and state history. Note that some of these factors were also introduced as covariates in Table 11.1, indicating our uncertainty about the data-generating process. (We do not know for sure whether temperature has a direct effect on regimes, other than through European ancestry.) Although results resting on a single instrument might be doubted, the fact that all instruments lead to the same finding is reassuring.

These wide-ranging empirical findings, taken together, reinforce our sense that the relationship between European ancestry and democracy is causal rather than merely correlational.

IV

Alternate Explanations

> The nations in cold regions, particularly Europe, are full of spirit but somewhat deficient in intelligence and craft knowledge. That is precisely why they remain comparatively free, but are apolitical and incapable of ruling their neighbors. Those in Asia, on the other hand, have souls endowed with intelligence and craft knowledge, but they lack spirit. That is precisely why they are ruled and enslaved.
>
> Aristotle, *Politics*, Book VII, Chapter 6 (1998: 202)

Writers have been speculating on the sources of democracy since the concept arose, as the epigraph (above) attests. This book has focused thus far on just two distal causes: natural harbors (Part II) and European ancestry (Part III). Other factors have played a supporting role, e.g., as covariates or instruments. It is now time to give them more forthright consideration.

Naturally, we do not have space to elucidate these theories in great detail. Our presentation will be scandalously brief, offering a concise statement of the main argument along with citations to the literature, to which readers can repair for further details.

Nor can we offer a detailed consideration of specific cases (along the lines of Chapters 5 and 10) or hundreds of empirical tests (along the lines of Chapters 6 and 11). Our empirical analyses will be limited to one or several measures of the key concept and a few specifications, all of which focus on the modern era.

Nonetheless, we believe there is much to be gained from this endeavor. We need to gauge how well our explanations stack up against alternative explanations. This is not just an empirical matter, ascertainable from regression tests. It also requires a careful consideration of the assumptions required for causal inference.

We divide this vast subject into three chapters. Chapter 12 discusses alternate geographic factors – including climate, irrigation, agriculture, mountains, and islands – which are considered in tandem with natural harbors. As such, this chapter relates closely to Part II of the book.

Chapter 13 discusses alternate modes of diffusion from Europe to the rest of the world – including colonialism, religion, and language – which are considered in tandem with European ancestry. This chapter relates closely to Part III of the book.

Chapter 14 considers additional factors that might be classified as economics, institutions, or culture. This includes agricultural transitions, modernization, inequality, labor scarcity, marriage and family patterns, feudalism, parliaments, Christianity, Catholicism, state size, state–society relations, and ideas. This chapter relates in a more diffuse fashion to both parts of the book.

12   Modalities of Geography

> If it is true that the character of the spirit and the passions of the heart
> are extremely different in the various climates, *laws* should be relative
> to the differences in these passions and to the differences in these
> characters.   Montesquieu (1989 [1748]: 231)

A tradition of work stretching back to Herodotus offers innumerable
conjectures about how natural features of the landscape may have
affected civilizations (Dikshit 2011; Elliott 1979). Many of these arguments are surely false, and some are downright noxious (e.g., May 1877:
xxxii–xxxiv).

Fanciful, often racist, arguments eventually discredited the enterprise.
By the mid-twentieth century, work that sought to link the climate, soil,
or topography of an area with its culture, economics, or politics was
regarded with suspicion. Where these arguments were tolerated it was
only in delimited settings – with respect to a particular time and place.
Broad generalizations were eschewed.

More recently, geography has come back into vogue as a general
explanatory framework. A starring role in this revival may be accorded
to Jared Diamond's masterful synthesis, *Guns, Germs, and Steel*
(Diamond 1992), which inspired a corpus of work in the social sciences.
Reflecting on this corpus, Barry Cunliffe (2015: 451) asserts, "History is
the result of the interaction between human agency and the constraints
and opportunities imposed by geography."

In Part II, we made the case for natural harbors as a long-run influence
on democracy. In this chapter, we review alternate geographic explanations. We divide this subject into five broad categories: (a) climate, (b)
irrigation, (c) agriculture, (d) mountains, and (e) islands.

For each argument, we shall consider potential weaknesses or limitations. Since our principal theoretical concern is with the deep roots of
modern democracy, we consider whether the argument has enduring
relevance for regimes today.

In the final section of the chapter we subject these alternate theories to several empirical tests, following the same general approach used to test our own theory. Previously, these factors were employed as background variables. Now, our focus shifts. We wish to see how robust these factors are and – if causal – how much regime variability they might explain, and how their impact compares with natural harbors. A short conclusion summarizes the main takeaways from our theoretical discussion and empirical forays.

Climate

A number of factors may conspire (individually or collectively) to diminish prospects for democracy in tropical areas, i.e., in low-lying areas close to the equator that receive abundant rainfall. Most of these factors also affect economic development, which one may view as a proximal cause of democracy (see discussion of modernization theory in Chapter 14).

Tropical climates affect the epidemiological environment. Specifically, malaria and many other communicable diseases are fostered by hot, humid climates. This limits human capital and economic productivity at large (Mellinger, Sachs, Gallup 2000).

Where disease vectors were rampant, European settlers were less likely to tread – or at least less likely to settle in large numbers (Curtin 1989, 1998). This, in turn, may have had important repercussions for economic development (Easterly, Levine 2016) and for the sort of regimes that developed in the modern world, as discussed in Part III of the book.

Tropical climates also condition the sort of crops that can be grown. Crops requiring massive labor inputs – and therefore suitable for a plantation mode of production – are often viable in hot, humid climates. This includes coffee, cotton, rubber, sugar cane, tobacco, and other highly profitable cash crops, which formed – and to a large extent still form – the basis of economies in the tropics. Labor extraction of this sort fostered the slave trade, vast inequalities in landholding and wealth, and poor institutions in subsequent centuries (Engerman, Sokoloff 2012).

By contrast, too *little* rainfall – or unpredictable rainfall – may be an invitation for centralized control, as farmers need the state to assist them in times of drought and may also need a centralized political organization to develop and maintain irrigation systems, as discussed below.

It follows that the sort of climate most conducive to democracy is one featuring regular rainfall – neither scarce nor torrential and occurring at predictable intervals. Regular rainfall is likely to generate a trajectory of economic development based on independent family farms (as opposed to large plantations), which are often viewed as a social foundation of democracy.[1] This, in turn, obviates the need for state intervention and impedes consolidation of power in the capital.[2]

A similar set of arguments has been made about agricultural potential – which of course rests crucially upon rainfall and is therefore closely related (Ang, Fredriksson, Gupta 2020).

In these various respects, climate may affect prospects for democratization and democratic consolidation. Of course, it is possible that the nexus between climate and institutions was tighter in the premodern era than it is today – when technology compensates for some of the adversities of climate, when tropical disease is less prevalent and less deadly, when most economies have shifted away from agriculture towards industry and services, and when populations have shifted from the countryside to cities. Even so, the weight of the past may hang over the present insofar as institutions endure.

Irrigation

One may trace the notion of "hydraulic" autocracy as far back as Adam Smith, Karl Marx, and various followers of the latter (Wittfogel 1957: ch. 9). For Marxists, the idea was wedded to the theory of an "Asiatic" mode of production (Sawer 2012). Max Weber also identified irrigation as a potential source of despotism. In *The Agrarian Sociology of Ancient Civilizations*, he describes Mesopotamia as follows:

> The basis of the economy was irrigation, for this was the crucial factor in all exploitation of land resources. Every new settlement demanded construction of a canal, so that the land was essentially a man-made product. Now canal construction is necessarily a large-scale operation, demanding some sort of collective social organization; it is very different from the relatively individualistic activity of clearing virgin forest. Here then is the fundamental economic cause for the overwhelmingly dominant position of the monarchy in Mesopotamia (and also in Egypt). (Weber 2013 [1909]: 84)

Evidently, the notion that irrigation might foster autocracy was by no means new when Karl Wittfogel (1957) turned his attention to the thesis in a lengthy book that has become a classic reference point. For Wittfogel, areas where there was a strong need for irrigation and flood control would also see a consequent need for the development of centralized states to provide those public goods. Because there were no mechanisms of popular accountability operable at large scale in

---

[1] See Ansell, Samuels (2010, 2014), Blinkhorn, Gibson (1991), Griswold (1946), Huber, Safford (1995), B. Moore (1966), Russett (1964), Vanhanen (2003), Ziblatt (2008).
[2] See Elis, Haber, Horrillo (2017), Midlarsky (1995), Welzel (2013, 2014).

premodern societies this led to the formation of authoritarian states, whose legacies extend to the present day.

More recently, Bentzen, Kaarsen, and Wingender (2016) build on this thesis, offering a subtle twist – that irrigation required major investments and as such gave crucial advantages to local elites who were in a position to build and maintain those systems. This led to greater inequality and, in turn, encouraged the formation of autocratic governments.

The literature on irrigation and autocracy is now sizeable, as every author concerned with politics in the premodern age is compelled to address it. Although we cannot summarize this large body of work it is worth pointing out several weaknesses in the irrigation–autocracy theory that this scholarship has revealed. In particular, it seems that most traditional irrigation systems did *not* require centralized planning and were often implemented and maintained at local levels without a significant role for the state. In Europe, for example, local-level irrigation was widespread in areas brought under sedentary agriculture from the medieval era. This was true throughout the continent, even as far north as Iceland and Greenland (Leibundgut, Kohn 2014).[3] Insofar as this public good could be provided at local levels one may doubt whether there is any connection to despotic rule – though it does not rule out the possibility that this institutional feature might bolster the power of local elites charged with maintaining irrigation works (per Bentzen et al. 2016).

Agriculture

Early states were generally situated on a rich agricultural base. Surplus from the land provided revenue for the state, and sedentary, densely settled areas provided fodder for armies and bureaucracies. Thus, where geographic conditions – soil, climate, topography – are conducive to a single, dominant crop, serving as the staple diet in a community, this may have encouraged the rise of highly centralized, agrarian states.

Cereals, in particular, seem to be susceptible to hierarchy and centralized control.[4] To begin with, they offer a predictable source of revenue. They are also highly transparent – visible to the tax collector and hard to hide, whether in the field or in the silo. Accordingly, cereals offer a rich harvest for the state, one that can be collected cheaply in a coercive fashion, without need for consent.

---

[3] Studies of irrigation and political organization bearing on this theme focus on Egypt (Butzer 1976; 1996), Java (Christie 1986: 78), Southeast Asia (Stargardt 1986: 32), South India (Mosse 2003), and Europe (referenced in the text). For general treatments, see Bonneau (1993), Butzer (1996), Hunt (1988, 1989).

[4] See Mayshar, Moav, Neeman (2017), Scott (2017), Stasavage (2020).

By contrast, where the environment is unpropitious for agriculture – excessively dry, cold, or hot – states are likely to develop much later and will be weaker and less prone to authoritarian rule. Likewise, where the climate is wet and humid, nature provides an abundance of food which can be gathered easily but is difficult to preserve. In this fashion, a geography of perishable plenty discourages the adoption of sedentary agriculture, urbanization, and state formation. Here, we can expect power to be exercised in a more diffuse fashion.

A closely related approach to this subject examines agricultural *variability* as a key to political development. Where the geographic conditions of an area encourage the development of a wide array of agricultural products strong states may develop but their structure is likely to differ from the prototypical agrarian state. This is because in a situation of agricultural diversity it is more difficult for elites to appropriate surplus revenue. In this vein, Mayshar, Moav, and Neeman (2017) contrast the monoculture of Egypt with the more diverse agricultural portfolio of Northern Mesopotamia, arguing that the former provided easy revenue – revenue that could be garnered without negotiation or consent – while the latter made it difficult for statemakers to extract revenue at a distance, leading to nucleated settlements and decentralized political control. Ahmed and Stasavage (2020) build on this idea, showing that variability in agricultural potential is correlated with early democracy.

In addition to a territory's own agricultural fertility one might also consider the surrounding environment. If a fertile region is surrounded by less fertile regions (e.g., mountains, deserts, or dense tropical forests), the latter may serve to *circumscribe* the fertile territory.[5] This, in turn, may enhance the power of statebuilders, as they can more easily define and control the fertile territory, within which citizens are effectively "caged" (Mann 1986). From this perspective, it is the environmental differential between adjacent regions that leads to authoritarian outcomes. Egypt, once again, serves as a point of reference.[6]

A final agricultural argument about long-term economic development concerns aquaculture. Dalgaard, Knudsen and Selaya (2020) argue that countries bordering on fertile shoreline offered a bounty of the sea, which served as a source of nutrition and agricultural surplus, leading to long-term economic development. They do not make a case for the impact of fish on political development but one can easily imagine that economic development might have spillover effects on politics.

---

[5] See Carneiro (1970, 1988, 2012), Schönholzer (2020).
[6] See Jones (1981: 10–11), Stasavage (2020).

As with other theories, one may question whether patterns of agriculture have enduring consequences for regime types in the modern era, when agriculture plays a much smaller role in the economy and when a much larger share of the population is living in cities and engaged in non-agricultural pursuits. Even so, it is easy to imagine that state institutions and accompanying political cultures, once established, have a long shelf life.

Mountains

Mountains are often regarded as a redoubt of democracy.[7] Plutarch remarked upon "the Men of the Hills, who were the most democratic party, the Men of the Plain, who were the most oligarchic, and thirdly the Men of the Coast, who favored an intermediate, mixed kind of system."[8] Much later, Fernand Braudel (1972 [1949]: 38–9) draws quotations from early modern writers, who also commented on the vigor and liberty of mountain folk:

Loys Le Roy ... writes, "A country covered with mountains, rocks, and forests, fit only for pasture, where there are many poor men, as is most of Switzerland, is best suited for democracy ... The lands of the plain, where there are greater numbers of rich and noble men, are better suited to an aristocratic form of government". Jean Bodin ... reports that Leo Africanus was astonished by the robust physique of the mountain folk of Mount Megeza, while the plain-dwellers were smaller men. "This force and vigour doth cause the mountaineers to love popular liberty, as we have said of the Swissers and Grisons", The Middle Ages in Corsica, says Lorenzi de Bradi, ... were a great period for liberty. "The Corsican would not suffer any man to rob him of the product of his labour. The milk from his goat and the harvest from his field were his alone." And H. Taine ... says "freedom took root here deep in the past, a gruff and wild sort of freedom".

In a more recent study, Andrey Korotayev (1995: 61–3) writes,

The first thing that draws one's attention when studying their political organization is the surprising uniformity of some basic characteristics among most of the mountain polities in the various parts of the Old World Oecumene. Indeed, if we take the ancient highlanders of Yemen or Greece, the Medieval Swiss and Basques, Medieval or Early Modern mountain communities of Albania and Montenegro, *volnye obshchestva* of the Caucasus, some highlanders of Afghanistan, the Apa Tanis of the Assam Mountains, *gumlao* communities of the Highland Burma Kachins, the Berbers of the Atlas, or the Ifugao of the Philippines etc., almost everywhere, notwithstanding the natural diversity of the political forms we find some highland "common denominator."

---

[7] Braudel (1972[1949]: 38–9), Hechter (1975: 50–1), Korotayev (1995), Leach (1960), Matloff (2017), Peattie (1936), Scott (2009), Wolf (1982: 57, 221–2).
[8] Quoted in Acemoglu, Robinson (2019: ch. 2).

The main characteristic of this "demoninator" could be described as the relative "delay" of the processes of the political centralization in comparison with the processes of the general cultural evolution. In other words, the mountain societies with the same level of general cultural and economic development as the "lowland" ones are usually characterized by a considerably lower level of political centralization. That is to say, they are usually characterized by a significantly higher level of communal autonomy ... Simple and complex chiefdoms or even early states of the lowlands often correspond to "highland" sovereign communities with developed internal structures (frequently incorporated into various loose confederations).

Another important characteristic ... is the relative "democracy" of mountain polities. Political evolution ... here is often not towards supra-communal government (which usually becomes more and more "autocratic", less and less accountable), the system of centralized redistribution etc., in the course of which the masses of commoners normally lose any effective control over the political centre, being transformed into "subjects." In the highlands the political evolution often goes in a rather different way: the primitive democracy does not decline or disappear, but develops further, moving beyond the limits of "primitivity." The mass of commoners does not lose control over the political centre, but improve this control, transforming themselves into "citizens."

Mountain communities, Korotayev (1995: 63) concludes, are more likely to sustain political structures "reminiscent of those of the Classical polis."

All of these arguments are highly plausible. And yet, there is no comprehensive study of mountain communities that we are aware of. Moreover, one may question the assumption that democracy in non-state communities such as these would influence political institutions in the modern state. Isolated communities in the highlands may have little effect on the structure of government in the capital. And forms of democracy operative in the highlands – which are, we suppose, primarily "direct" rather than "representative" – may have little relevance for governing a large nation-state. Worse, they may provide hideouts for bandits and rebels who foster unrest and destabilize democratic institutions (Carter, Shaver, Wright 2019; Jimenez-Ayora, Ulubaşoğlu 2015). The thesis of "mountain freedom" is therefore open to debate.

Islands

Many writers regard island status as a force in favor of democratic outcomes.[9] A number of reasons have been (or might be) offered.

[9] See Anckar (2008), Baldacchino (2012), Congdon Fors (2014), Dommen (1980), Doumenge (1985), Srebrnik (2004), Sutton, Payne (1993).

First, island states are exposed to oceans and this may influence the propensity of a state to democratize, as argued in Part II of this book.

Second, islands offered appealing ports of call and colonies of settlement for Europeans (Anckar 2008; Hadenius 1992: 126–7). Because they are generally small, their populations were overshadowed by European settlers to a greater extent than continental polities. Indeed, some island-states like Mauritius and Seychelles had no native populations at all; others, like many Caribbean islands, experienced a dramatic fall in indigenous population due to a combination of disease, expropriation, and exploitation during the colonial period. Thus, islands may have served as an invitation to high levels of European ancestry, a feature explored in Part III of the book.

Relatedly, islands were often subjected to a lengthy colonial relationship with a European power, culminating in many years' experience with electoral politics and semi-autonomous governance prior to independence. For a variety of reasons, one may suppose that the colonial experience was more transformative for island states than for other states (Caldwell et al. 1980; Srebrnik 2004). Insofar as colonialism fosters democracy (a thesis explored in Chapter 13), islands may be especially subject to that pathway.

Fourth, most islands depend upon international trade or tourism for a large share of their national income. This may encourage a more open attitude toward democracy, though the point is disputed (Milner, Mukherjee 2009).

Fifth, islands tend to be small, limiting the population. And with natural borders provided by the sea, island living may foster a greater sense of national community than one finds in land-based states.[10] These features are often regarded as conducive to democracy.

Finally, being geographically isolated, island states may be less militarist because their sovereignty is more secure than land-based states and because expansionist policies are more difficult to pursue (Clague et al. 2001: 22–3).

Evidently, there are many reasons to expect islands to be more democratic than their mainland cousins. On the flip side, the same features of smallness, consensus, and isolation may make it easier for a single clique to monopolize power, resisting democratic rule. Where there are few viable contenders for a state's top office, and few social or economic bases upon which an opposition can organize, democratization could be impeded (Veenendaal 2014b).

---

[10] Anckar, Anckar (1995: 213, 220–2), Congdon Fors (2014), Royle (2001).

Tests

To provide adequate empirical tests for each of the myriad geographic factors vetted above would be a monumental endeavor. Nonetheless, it is possible to measure many of these factors in a provisional fashion drawing on extant work or on readily available datasets.

As measures of climate, we include (a) distance from the equator (absolute latitude), (b) tropical (share of territory classified as tropical), (c) temperature (annual mean temperature), (d) frost days (number of days per annum when the temperature dips below freezing), and (e) precipitation (annual rainfall plus its quadratic, allowing for a non-monotonic functional form).[11]

As a measure of irrigation potential, we adopt a variable developed by Bentzen and associates (2016) that identifies areas where irrigation could make a big impact on agricultural productivity. Specifically, the authors calculate the share of land suitable for agriculture where irrigation can more than double agricultural production.

As measures of agriculture, we include (a) soil quality, (b) overall agricultural suitability, (c) caloric suitability (the calories an area would yield if farmed to its potential), (d) caloric variability (the standard deviation of caloric suitability across a grid-cell, averaged across grid-cells in a state), and (e) fish (the Bounty of the Sea index developed by Dalgaard, Knudsen, Selaya 2020).

As measures of mountains, we employ a coding of territory classified as mountainous as a share of all territory within a grid-cell (Tollefsen et al. 2012), aggregated up to state levels. We also employ a ruggedness variable from Nunn and Puga (2012) that calculates differences in elevation across grid-cells, aggregated to states.

To code islands, we examine whether a state is attached to a continental landmass or not. Typically, states that conform to one or several small plots of land surrounded by sea or ocean are classified as islands.

Finally, we include natural harbor distance, the key variable from Part II of the book. (Further details on all of these variables can be found in Appendix A.)

We do *not* include a measure of mineral resource wealth, often regarded as having a negative impact on democracy and development (Ross 2012). This factor is employed as a control variable in various specification tests (see Tables 6.3 and 12.1). However, since its impact

---

[11] Measuring rainfall and its quadratic achieves much the same thing as measuring potential crop yield and its quadratic (Ang, Fredriksson, Gupta 2020), and is more robust according to our measure of the latter.

seems to be limited to the postwar era, or perhaps to the era following the Organization of Petroleum-Exporting Countries (OPEC) oil embargo in 1973 (Andersen, Ross 2014), it does not qualify as a distal cause.

In Table 12.1, we depict intercorrelations among these many factors. Measures of similar concepts tend to cluster, as one might expect. Other correlations are modest. Tellingly, natural harbor distance is not highly correlated with any other geographic predictor, which helps to account for why it is so stable in specification tests shown in Chapter 6. A principal components analysis (not shown) confirms that there are multiple dimensions represented among these fifteen variables. By all appearances, they are not measuring the same latent variable.

In Table 12.2, we examine the possible impact of these predictors on democracy in the modern era, enlisting our usual approach. In column 2, we indicate the expected relationship between each of these geographic factors and democracy. This is based on the discussion above and on literature cited therein.

In the next column, we show the results of bivariate models in which democracy is regressed against each of these variables individually, along with year dummies.

In Model 16, we test all factors together in a single specification. Our assumption is that they are all exogenous (or mostly so), and therefore independent of each other. There is little risk of post-treatment bias.

Several factors survive this packed specification test, as judged by t statistics and conventional thresholds of statistical significance. These are included in Model 17. In Model 18, we continue the winnowing process, dropping factors that do not perform well in the preceding test. In Model 19, we repeat the same specification with the addition of a vector of regional dummies. In Model 20, the specification is restricted to variables that pass all previous tests.

Most of the theories vetted in this chapter do not receive much empirical support from the tests shown in Table 12.2. To be clear, it is not our intention to reject these alternate arguments about the imprint of geography on the long-run development of political institutions. Stronger relationships might appear if we had chosen different model specifications, different indicators, or different temporal or spatial contexts. Note that our measure of regimes begins in 1789, limiting our analysis to the modern era, while some of the theories seem more suited to the premodern era. All we can report is that this particular set of tests, focused on the modern era and on a global sample, does not offer strong corroboration for most geographically based theories of democracy.

Table 12.1 *Geographic factors, intercorrelations*

	1.	2.	3.	4.	5.	6.	7.	8.	9.	10.	11.	12.	13.	14.
1. Equator distance	1.00													
2. Tropical	-0.75	1.00												
3. Temperature	-0.85	0.67	1.00											
4. Frost days	0.88	-0.70	-0.94	1.00										
5. Precipitation	-0.48	0.78	0.41	-0.49	1.00									
6. Irrigation potential	0.07	-0.43	0.10	0.07	-0.58	1.00								
7. Soil quality	0.11	0.14	-0.10	0.15	0.29	-0.49	1.00							
8. Agric. suitability	0.04	0.15	-0.10	0.03	0.16	-0.55	0.48	1.00						
9. Caloric suitability	0.00	0.26	-0.05	-0.01	0.22	-0.67	0.56	0.80	1.00					
10. Caloric variability	0.35	-0.43	-0.52	0.40	-0.26	-0.10	0.15	0.24	0.21	1.00				
11. Fish	0.33	-0.21	-0.30	0.27	-0.06	-0.17	0.11	0.16	0.14	-0.01	1.00			
12. Mountains	0.19	-0.24	-0.42	0.28	-0.05	-0.17	0.10	0.23	0.11	0.78	-0.04	1.00		
13. Rugged	0.10	-0.20	-0.29	0.25	0.02	-0.15	0.12	0.16	0.08	0.66	-0.13	0.81	1.00	
14. Island	-0.24	0.37	0.31	-0.21	0.42	-0.15	0.25	-0.09	0.05	-0.27	-0.13	-0.19	0.05	1.00
15. Natural harbor distance	0.00	-0.26	-0.14	0.17	-0.29	0.32	-0.31	-0.19	-0.21	0.09	-0.25	0.03	0.03	-0.24

Correlation table (Pearson's r).

Table 12.2 *Geographic factors, specification tests*

	E			16.	17.	18.	19.	20.
Equator	↑	1.	0.415***	0.319**	0.549***	0.600***	0.481***	0.448***
distance			(6.891)	(2.321)	(3.686)	(9.729)	(4.608)	(8.011)
Tropical	↓	2.	−0.084***	−0.158***	−0.068			
			(−3.137)	(−2.989)	(−1.132)			
Temperature	↓	3.	−0.898***	−0.930*	−0.056			
			(−5.361)	(−1.900)	(−0.171)			
Frost days	↑	4.	0.653***	−0.622*				
			(4.285)	(−1.707)				
Precipitation	↑	5.	0.035***	0.121***	0.105***	0.060***	0.021	
			(2.733)	(3.121)	(4.176)	(5.331)	(1.446)	
Precipitation^2	↓		−0.000***	−0.000**	−0.000***	−0.000***	−0.000	
			(−2.695)	(−2.154)	(−3.482)	(−3.676)	(−1.017)	
Irrigation	↓	6.	−17.594***	−2.848				
potential			(−5.070)	(−0.546)				
Soil quality	↓	7.	0.136***	0.090*				
			(2.676)	(1.881)				
Agricultural	↓	8.	8.553*	8.482				
suitability			(1.694)	(1.359)				
Caloric	↓	9.	0.003	−0.010***	−0.002			
suitability			(1.229)	(−3.979)	(−1.257)			
Caloric	↑	10.	0.008	0.027				
variability			(0.631)	(1.450)				
Fish	↑	11.	66.311***	14.352				
			(4.545)	(1.487)				
Mountains	↑	12.	−3.910	−16.223*				
			(−0.736)	(−1.819)				
Rugged	↑	13.	−0.568	−2.235				
			(−0.500)	(−1.080)				
Island	↑	14.	4.077	5.926				
			(1.539)	(1.490)				
Natural harbor	↓	15.	−1.275***	−0.821***	−0.995***	−0.661***	−0.761***	−1.184***
distance			(−5.198)	(−3.226)	(−4.045)	(−2.899)	(−3.260)	(−5.424)
Region							✓	✓
dummies								
States				142	173	196	196	196
Years				231	231	231	231	231
Observations				23 543	29 013	32 322	32 322	32 324
R^2				0.592	0.548	0.521	0.551	0.487

Outcome: Polyarchy index of electoral democracy, augmented. *E:* expected direction of the relationship. Models 1–15 are shown in a single column (model-fit statistics omitted). *Not shown:* Year dummies, Constant. Ordinary least squares, standard errors clustered by state, t statistics in parentheses. ***$p<.01$ **$p<.05$ *$p<.10$

Precipitation is a partial exception – showing the expected curvilinear relationship to democracy in all specifications except where a vector of regional dummies is included, which means the impact of precipitation may be proxying for regional effects.

Two predictors are robust in all specification tests: equator distance (+) and natural harbor distance (−). Importantly, equator distance is highly correlated with other measures of climate including temperature, tropical, and frost days (see Table 12.1). All show the expected relationship to democracy in bivariate tests (Models 1–4, Table 12.2), though equator distance is somewhat more robust in the "horse-race" tests that follow. We regard these four variables as alternate measures of the traditional geographic narrative, which may stretch back in time to the earliest days of human civilization (Diamond 1992), to the colonial conquest (Acemoglu, Johnson, Robinson 2001, 2002), or may be rooted in the contemporary era (Mellinger, Sachs, Gallup 2000). Despite important differences among these narratives, they all stress the influence of climate on long-term development. We regard equator distance as a suitable proxy for this set of factors.

Impact

If there are two "winners" in the horse-race tests depicted in Table 12.2, a separate question concerns what sort of power these two geographic factors have as predictors of democracy. We focus on the contemporary era (1960–2019) since this is of greatest relevance.

To gauge impact, Table 12.3 presents standardized coefficients (the impact of a one-standard-deviation change in the independent variable on the outcome) and model-fit statistics in a series of specifications. Model-fit statistics may be judged relative to each other and relative to a baseline model including only year dummies (Model 1). These tests suggest that equator distance has a slightly stronger impact on regime type in the contemporary era than natural harbor distance.

Table 12.3 *Geographic factors, predictive power in the contemporary era*

	1	2	3	4	5
Equator distance		0.340		0.331	−0.007
Natural harbor distance			−0.228	−0.214	−0.111
European ancestry					✓
Observations	11 051	11 051	11 051	11 051	10 609
R^2	0.134	0.249	0.186	0.295	0.414

Outcome: Polyarchy index of electoral democracy, augmented. *Sample years:* 1960–2019. *Not shown:* Year dummies, Constant. Ordinary least squares, standardized coefficients. ***p<.01 **p<.05 *p<.10

Model 5 in Table 12.3 indicates something important about the causal mechanisms that may be at work. When European ancestry is included in the specification the impact of natural harbor distance is attenuated, though still highly significant, corroborating our theoretical framework (see Figure 1.1). However, the impact of equator distance reduces to something very close to zero. We conclude that equator distance matters but its impact is mediated entirely by European settlement. This story is addressed in Part III of the book so there is no need to repeat it here.

Conclusions

Arguments grounded in geography offer several intrinsic advantages with respect to causal inference. They can be measured in a fairly precise fashion based on contemporary geography – so long as it is reasonable to assume that the factor has changed little over the centuries or that such changes are unlikely to affect the outcome of theoretical interest.

Geographic factors are also exogenous, or largely so. Of course, humans can alter their environment – cutting down (or burning) forests, exterminating species, constructing canals, burning fossil fuels, and so forth. What is natural and human-made is sometimes hard to distinguish. Even so, most of the geographic factors reviewed in this chapter have not been affected by humans in ways that could have significantly altered their impact on democracy. Geography is thus a plausible prime mover.

Among geographic factors, we find fairly strong evidence for equator distance, which bears a positive relationship to democracy. However, this effect is entirely mediated by European ancestry. Other geographic factors have a more tenuous relationship to democracy when tested in a global sample. Accordingly, we conclude that the case for natural harbors is quite strong relative to alternate geographic explanations that might apply to the long-run development of democracy.

At the same time, we must bear in mind some of the problems involved in ascertaining the causal effect of geography on political institutions. The causal factor of interest does not (usually) change over time, so available evidence is spatial rather than temporal. Likewise, there is no point in time that might be regarded as the onset of treatment. Geography exerts its influence on human affairs over extremely long periods of time and in ways that are virtually impossible to directly observe. Inferences are accordingly more difficult. One must reconstruct plausible accounts from traces that remain from actions and events long ago.

Relatedly, geographic factors are not randomly assigned and tend to cluster in ways that may generate spurious correlations. For example, natural harbor distance or equator distance could be proxying for some other factor that is causing political institutions to develop in democratic or autocratic ways. That is why we have included so many geographic factors in our canvas of causes in this chapter and in Chapter 6.

With these caveats, we turn to factors that are closer to the outcome of interest and easier to observe – but also less exogenous, and thus prone to a different sort of confounding.

13   Modalities of European Diffusion

In Part III of the book we put forth a demographic argument about the diffusion of modern democracy from Europe to other regions of the world. Now, we consider other potential pathways from Europe.

The most overt attempt by Europeans to control the world was of course the creation of formal colonies, ruled directly or indirectly from the metropole. We begin by looking at the potential influence of different colonists and different ways of measuring colonial intervention. Europeans also spread their religious ideas and institutions throughout the world, aspiring to convert the heathen. In the second section we explore the two dominant branches of Christianity in Europe: Catholicism and Protestantism. Finally, one must consider European languages, which may also have served as mechanisms of cultural diffusion and identity.

For each topic – colonialism, religion, and language – we provide several empirical tests. In the penultimate section of the chapter we include them together, along with our measure of European ancestry, in a series of "horse-race" tests. The final section offers an interpretation of the results.

Colonialism

The most obvious way in which Europeans influenced the world was through their overt control of territory and peoples, i.e., *colonialism*. Colonies often modeled their political institutions after the metropole, and these institutions often survived long into the post-colonial era. This includes the form of the executive (e.g., parliamentary or presidential), the electoral system (e.g., proportional or majoritarian), the judiciary, the legal system (e.g., common law or civil law), the regulatory system (e.g., mercantilist or liberal), and so forth.[1] In this light, it would not be surprising to find a legacy effect of colonialism on regimes.

It is now well documented that English colonies offered greater scope for the development of democratic institutions than other European colonies (Paine 2019). With respect to the post-independence legacy of colonial rule the verdict is less clear. Some studies find that colonial heritage – and especially British colonial heritage – is associated with greater democracy.[2] Other studies report weaker relationships, relationships that attenuate over time, or no relationship at all.[3]

The question is complicated by the fact that European colonialism was a complex phenomenon and consequently can be operationalized in a variety of ways. In tests reported in Table 13.1 we settle on five measures, drawing on recent work and on what we surmise are the strongest versions of the colonialism argument.

Models 1–2 explore English colonialism, measured by a dummy variable (coded 1 if a state was or is a dependency of the United Kingdom). Models 3–4 measure English colonial duration, the number of years England controlled a colony (Olsson 2009). Models 5–6 employ European colonial duration, the number of years a colony was controlled by *any* European power (Olsson 2009). Models 7–8 employ a measure of indirect rule constructed by Lange (2004) and extended by Hariri (2012).[4]

Models 9–10 focus on a measure of Forced settlement constructed by Owolabi (2015) which identifies colonies where a majority of the population consisted of imported slaves. Owolabi reasons that these colonies may be more likely to democratize in the post-colonial era because they experienced an extensive tutelary relationship with a European power and were integrated into the metropole's legal institutions. (As such, this is similar in spirit to Lange's argument about direct rule.) We extend Owolabi's coding to include additional cases so there is no artificial truncation of the sample. All such cases are assigned a zero code (no forced settlement), which seems consistent with Owolabi's discussion.

---

[1] See De Juan, Pierskalla (2017), Fieldhouse (1966), Go (2003), Klerman, Mahoney, Spamann, Weinstein (2011), Krieckhaus (2006), La Porta, Lopez-de-Silanes, Shleifer, Vishny (1998), Mahoney (2010).

[2] See Bernhard et al. (2004), Hariri (2012), Lange, Mahoney, Vom Hau (2006), Narizny (2012), Olsson (2009), Paine (2019).

[3] See Goldring, Greitens (2019), Gunitsky (2014: table 14), Houle, Kayser, Xiang (2016), Lee, Paine (2019), Miller (2012), Przeworski et al. (2000), Woodberry (2012).

[4] Lange (2004) finds that direct rule is associated with greater democracy in the postwar era, as European institutional practices are more likely to be grafted onto the colony and less power is devolved to traditional authorities, who often played an obstructive role.

Table 13.1 Colonialism

	1	2	3	4	5	6	7	8	9	10	11	12	13
English colony	3.725*	4.996***									−0.140		
	(1.708)	(2.915)									(−0.043)		
English colonial duration			0.024***	0.013**							0.024**	0.015	0.017**
			(3.175)	(2.125)							(2.040)	(1.624)	(2.341)
European colonial duration					0.014**	0.006***						0.012**	0.004*
					(2.080)	(2.709)						(2.098)	(1.702)
Indirect rule							−16.716***	−16.621***					
							(−6.937)	(−4.101)					
Forced settlement									6.637***	−1.331		2.619	−4.640*
									(3.210)	(−0.570)		(0.981)	(−1.707)
Natural harbor distance	✓	✓	✓	✓	✓	✓	✓	✓	✓	✓	✓	✓	✓
Equator distance	✓	✓	✓	✓	✓	✓	✓	✓	✓	✓	✓	✓	✓
Headman		✓		✓		✓		✓		✓			✓
Muslim (%)		✓		✓		✓		✓		✓			✓
Region dummies		✓		✓		✓		✓		✓			✓
States	156	150	156	150	156	150	88	87	156	150	156	156	150
Years	230	230	230	230	230	230	230	230	230	230	230	230	230
Observations	26,231	25,468	26,231	25,468	26,079	25,320	15,534	15,318	26,231	25,468	26,231	26,079	25,320
R^2	0.430	0.550	0.437	0.543	0.439	0.540	0.580	0.610	0.432	0.540	0.437	0.448	0.545

Outcome: Polyarchy index of electoral democracy, augmented. Sample: excludes Europe. Not shown: Year dummies, Constant. Estimator: ordinary least squares, standard errors clustered by state, t statistics in parentheses. ***$p<.01$ **$p<.05$ *$p<.10$

For each measure, we conduct two tests. The first includes our usual geographic covariates. The second offers a fuller specification including regional dummies. All samples exclude Europe.

We expect that measures of colonial intervention will be positively correlated with democracy and indirect rule negatively correlated with democracy. Results posted in Models 1–10 corroborate these expectations.

In the final models of Table 13.1 we run horse-race tests among the four variables with strong coverage (excluding indirect rule, which is coded only for a subset of mostly English colonies). These tests show that the duration of British rule and of European rule is associated with greater democracy in the post-colonial era. Dummies measuring English colony and Forced settlement do not perform consistently and are therefore dropped from subsequent tests.

Religion

Many studies have explored possible links between religion and democracy.[5] Since our interest is in influences emanating from Europe we focus on Christianity, the region's dominant religion.

Religion establishes a sense of community around a shared set of practices and (usually) membership in a formal organization. If the religion is global, as is the case for Christianity, it provides a ready-made transnational civil society (Rudolph 1997). There are many examples of Christian activists defending the rights of indigenous peoples, most prominently the antislavery movement (Stamatov 2010). With this in mind, it is plausible to suppose that religion might serve as a mechanism of global diffusion with respect to a wide range of values and beliefs (Beyer 2001). Since Europe was the leading exemplar of representative democracy, it is plausible to suppose that churches and missionaries might have instilled democratic values wherever they spread the Christian faith (Anckar 2011).

The influence of Protestantism on democracy is a long-standing hypothesis.[6] In addition to serving as a platform for diffusion of the idea of democracy, Woodberry (2012: 244–5) argues that "conversionary

---

[5] See Anderson (2004, 2006), Cheng, Brown (2006), Diamond, Plattner, Costopoulos (2005), Driessen (2014), Gerring, Hoffman, Zarecki (2018), Gifford (1995), Haynes (2015), Huntington (1991: 73), Ozzano, Cavatorta (2013), Ranger (2008).

[6] See Anderson (2004), Bollen, Jackman (1985), Brown (1944), Bruce (2004), Hadenius (1992), Lankina, Getachew (2012), Tusalem (2009), Woodberry (2012). Lee, Paine (2019) find that the influence of Protestantism on democracy attenuates in the late twentieth century.

Protestants ... were a crucial catalyst initiating the development and spread of religious liberty, mass education, mass printing, newspapers, voluntary organizations, most major colonial reforms, and the codification of legal protections for nonwhites in the nineteenth and early twentieth centuries." Others, following Weber, have noted Protestantism's effect on overarching values such as individualism and universalism (Eisenstadt 1968), which may have spillover effects on democracy.

A few studies explore a possible relationship between Catholicism and modern democracy.[7] Originally, the Catholic Church, i.e., the papacy and church officialdom, was no friend to democracy. Troy (2009) reports, "the Church opposed the first attempts to establish the 'rights of man' and democracy as a political system as this very process threatened the Church's unity and questioned its claim of holding absolute truths such as moral values as well as political convictions such as its claims of regulating political and social life." However, over the course of the twentieth century – and at an accelerated pace after Vatican II – the church embraced democratic institutions in Eastern Europe (where this tendency was bolstered by the church's historic animosity to communism), in Latin America, and in other regions with significant Catholic populations. The "third wave" of democratization centered on predominantly Catholic societies in Europe (Portugal, Spain) and beyond.[8]

Thus, there are strong grounds for supposing that Protestantism, and perhaps Catholicism, advanced the cause of democracy in the modern era. To test these propositions, we adopt two indices that attempt to measure the share of Protestants and Catholics (respectively) in states throughout the world in the modern era.

Woodberry (2012) offers several measures of Protestantism: (a) years of exposure to Protestant missions, (b) Protestant missionaries per 10,000 in 1923, and (c) percent evangelized by 1900. Unfortunately, these are available for only single points in time and offer incomplete coverage of states around the world. Moreover, a recent replication finds that these predictors of democracy are not robust with a larger sample, different measures of democracy, or a different choice of instruments (Nikolova, Polansky 2020).

For these reasons, and to remain consistent with our approach to other variables measuring European influence, we elect to focus on the

---

[7] A much longer-range view of Catholicism, discussed in Chapter 12, argues that by changing family structures and fertility rates it paved the way for Europe's *Sonderweg*. Here, we are concerned with Catholicism as a global factor.

[8] See Anderson (2007), Chu (2011), Corrin (2010), Huntington (1991), Mantilla (2010), Philpott (2004), Troy (2009).

share of the population that belongs to a Protestant sect or shares a Protestant heritage. For present purposes, Protestantism is defined as Christian denominations that are neither Catholic nor Orthodox. This includes Anglican, Baptist, Congregational, Lutheran, Methodist, Mormon, Presbyterian, and Quaker sects, as well as myriad smaller groups – some as small as a single church – that do not align with an international body.

To generate a time series, we assign a value of 0 to each state in the year prior to the arrival of the first Christian missionary, as dated by Woodberry (2012) and supplemented by other sources including Barrett (1982), Hillerbrand (2004), Moreau et al. (2000), Neill (1991), and Tucker (2004). The Correlates of War Project (COW; Maoz, Henderson 2013) provides estimates for all states at 5-year increments from 1945–2010, and Woodberry (2012) provides estimates for 1900. We complete the time series for each state by linear interpolation.

Admittedly, this procedure is not ideal, and leaves open the possibility that different sources may interpret religious identity differently. We assume that for most sources it is understood as an inheritance: one is Protestant if one's parents are Protestant unless one explicitly disavows the faith. In any case, we believe our data offers the most complete account currently available of the historical diffusion of Protestantism throughout the modern world.

Unfortunately, we have not been able to uncover estimates of the number of Catholics in states around the world prior to the contemporary era. Consequently, we extrapolate contemporary values back into the past in order to achieve full coverage of the 1789–2019 period. This is, evidently, a much cruder measure.

Table 13.2 offers a series of tests in which democracy is regressed on the two measures just described. (Since they are not highly correlated, there is no reason not to test them in the same model.) Model 1 includes only the variables of theoretical interest along with year dummies. Model 2 adds geographic covariates. Model 3 measures right-side variables 100 years prior to the outcome – though readers should recall that because we do not have historical data for Catholicism there is no change in this static variable. Model 4 adds covariates measuring Headman, Muslim, and major regions of the world. Model 5 excludes Europe from the sample.

These tests corroborate the conventional finding. Protestantism is robustly associated with democracy while Catholicism has a weaker relationship. Bear in mind that because these variables are measured with the same scale (adherents as a percent of the general population), coefficients are comparable.

Table 13.2 *Religion*

Lag (years)	0	0	100	0	0
Sample	Full 1	Full 2	Full 3	Full 4	~~Europe~~ 5
Protestant (%)	0.476***	0.344***	0.617***	0.305***	0.351***
	(10.012)	(7.812)	(9.408)	(6.369)	(3.440)
Catholic (%)	0.141***	0.159***	0.206***	0.113***	0.083**
	(6.340)	(8.007)	(7.756)	(3.848)	(2.077)
Harbor distance		✓	✓	✓	✓
Equator distance		✓	✓	✓	✓
Headman				✓	✓
Muslim (%)				✓	✓
Region dummies				✓	✓
States	196	190	189	184	149
Years	231	222	131	222	222
Observations	31 022	29 929	21 653	29 139	24 004
R^2	0.492	0.558	0.576	0.598	0.549

Outcome: Polyarchy index of electoral democracy, augmented. *Not shown:* Year dummies, Constant. *Estimator:* ordinary least squares, standard errors clustered by state, t statistics in parentheses. ***p<.01 **p<.05 *p<.10

Language

Ideas encoded in a text, a recording, or a film are most likely to reach those fluent in the language in which that artifact was produced (Weyland 2007). Language also plays a critical role in establishing and maintaining a sense of community.[9] Speakers of the same language find it easier to establish friendships and professional bonds, while those with different native tongues must struggle to communicate, and are hence excluded (Marquardt 2018).

In this fashion, learning a European language may open an enduring link to an international network, centered – at least initially – on Europe. Francophones were connected to France, Lusophones to Portugal, Hispanics to Spain, Anglophones to England, and so forth. By virtue of speaking a European language, individuals around the world were presumably drawn into a social network centered on Europe and its offshoots, aka "the West." Although these polyglot individuals were initially elites, they probably served as transmission belts for ideas and practices that diffused broadly throughout societies in the non-European world. Thus, in states where significant numbers of citizens are conversant with

[9] See Barbour, Carmichael (2000), De Swaan (2001), Joseph (2004).

Table 13.3 *Language*

Sample	Full	Full	Full	~~Europe~~
	1	2	3	4
European language (%)	0.257***	0.215***	0.171***	0.191***
	(9.106)	(9.070)	(4.893)	(6.763)
Harbor distance		✓	✓	✓
Equator distance		✓	✓	✓
Headman			✓	✓
Muslim (%)			✓	✓
Region dummies			✓	
States	172	172	168	134
Years	231	231	231	230
Observations	28 783	28 783	28 146	22 742
R^2	0.497	0.578	0.614	0.549

Outcome: Polyarchy index of electoral democracy, augmented. *Not shown:* Year dummies, Constant. *Estimator:* ordinary least squares, standard errors clustered by state, t statistics in parentheses. ***p<.01 **p<.05 *p<.10

a European language they are more likely to feel connected to Europe – to travel there, to be educated there, to have business contacts there, and to absorb ideas from there. Accordingly, one may conjecture that democracy, as an idea and an institution, diffused through linguistic networks across the world.

In parallel to our measures of European religion, we measure the share of populations in states around the world that speak (as a first or second tongue) a European language.[10] Unfortunately, we are not able to obtain historical estimates of this quantity. Consequently, current values are extrapolated into the past to obtain historical coverage. All due caveats obtain.

In Table 13.3, we regress democracy against this variable in a battery of tests, following the protocol in previous tables. It will be seen that European language is a strong predictor of democracy in all four tests, with some attenuation in the final models.

Importantly, the adoption of a European language is likely to be endogenous to many factors that might also influence the adoption of democracy. Africa and the New World were colonized linguistically, while Asia was not. This had a lot to do with the lack of written languages in the former territories and the heterogeneity of their linguistic heritage

---

[10] This approach follows Hariri (2015), although he regards language as a proxy for European settlement.

(Laitin, Ramachandrany 2022; Liu 2015). It may also have resulted from the strength or weakness of states, the varying resistance of indigenous peoples to European diseases, and so forth. So, it is conceivable that our measure of European language is proxying for some underlying confounder.

All Together Now

We have now explored multiple modalities of European influence including European ancestry (in Part III of the book), English colonialism, English colonial duration, European colonial duration, Indirect rule, Forced settlement, Protestants, Catholics, and European language.

All of these factors are emanations of Europe. The fact that there is a strong empirical association between these factors and modern democracy bolsters our general claim about the central role of Europeans.

How are these pathways related to each other? Which factors show the strongest relationship to democracy? In the remainder of the chapter we try to come to grips with these questions.

To simplify our task, we limit our attention to variables that offer extensive coverage and perform reasonably well in previous tests. This narrows the field to six indicators: English colonial duration, European colonial duration, Protestants, Catholics, European language, and European ancestry.

A correlation table, shown in Table 13.4, demonstrates that these pathways from Europe are only weakly correlated with each other, suggesting that Europe's presence throughout the world was not all of a piece. As an example, Etherington (2005: 2) considers the disjuncture between British missionaries and British colonial occupation.

Plantation owners in the West Indies and officials of the East India Company put up stubborn resistance to missionaries seeking admission to lands already under imperial control. Colonial administrators barred Christian missionaries from parts of Nigeria and Sudan. Elsewhere, missionaries worked for decades in lands that never came under imperial control. They pointedly resisted colonization schemes for New Zealand, South Africa, Malawi, and other regions.

In this light, it is not surprising to find a modest correlation between Protestantism and colonialism. Similar contrasts can be found along most other dimensions. Indeed, a principal component analysis (not shown) demonstrates that there are as many components as variables, and the first component explains only 45 percent of the variance. As befits a fragmented continent with fragmented institutions it is no surprise that there were multiple channels from Europe.

Table 13.4 *Intercorrelations among European pathways*

	1.	2.	3.	4.	5.
1. English colonial duration	1.00				
2. European colonial duration	0.13	1.00			
3. Protestants (%)	0.24	0.36	1.00		
4. Catholics (%)	−0.04	0.30	−0.11	1.00	
5. European language (%)	0.10	0.56	0.34	0.61	1.00
6. European ancestry (%)	0.05	0.73	0.36	0.33	0.60

Pearson's r correlation.

Another example of this is provided by the replication tests in Table 11.5, where we introduce European ancestry to benchmark analyses provided by three recent studies: Hariri (2012), Woodberry (2012), and Olsson (2009). Strikingly, the addition of European ancestry has virtually no impact on estimates for the key variables in these studies: State history, Protestantism, and British colonial duration. Evidently, quite different mechanisms are at work.

Which Mattered Most?

There remains an important question about which of these pathways were (and are) most influential. In this section we test these factors in a series of horse-race regression models, intended to illuminate which factors bear the strongest relationship to democracy in the modern era. Samples in Table 13.5 are restricted to the non-European world, except where noted.

In Model 1 all six variables are included on the right side, along with year dummies. Model 2 is limited to variables that have received considerable support in the literature or are highly robust in Model 1. The remaining models focus on variables that are robust in Model 2, which narrows the field to English colonial duration, Protestants, and European ancestry.

Model 3 broadens the sample to include Europe, and thus provides a global sample. Model 4 is restricted to the postwar era (1950–). Model 5 adds geographic covariates to the specification. Model 6 adds Muslim (the share of populations with an Islamic heritage) and a vector of regional dummies. Model 7 is a one-period cross-section, centered on the year 2000.

Tests depicted in Table 13.5 demonstrate that among a wide variety of indicators intended to measure European influence throughout the

Table 13.5 "Horse races"

States	Europe	Europe	Full	Europe	Europe	Europe	Full
Time period	Full	Full	Full	1950–	Full	Full	2000
Lag (years)	0	0	0	0	0	0	0
	1	2	3	4	5	6	7
English colonial duration	0.012	0.017**	0.024***	0.047***	0.012**	0.011*	0.019
	(1.363)	(2.519)	(4.486)	(3.955)	(2.115)	(1.970)	(1.479)
European colonial duration	0.003**	−0.004					
	(2.035)	(−0.518)					
Protestants (%)	0.309***	0.298***	0.157***	0.297***	0.285***	0.261***	0.186**
	(3.563)	(4.995)	(3.419)	(4.816)	(5.090)	(3.996)	(1.991)
Catholics (%)	−0.014						
	(−0.454)						
European language (%)	0.047						
	(1.649)						
European ancestry (%)	0.404***	0.401***	0.220***	0.504***	0.461***	0.441***	0.504***
	(7.537)	(6.911)	(9.156)	(6.095)	(9.085)	(6.269)	(5.390)
Natural harbor distance					✓	✓	✓
Equator distance					✓	✓	✓
Muslim						✓	✓
Region dummies						✓	✓
States	134	157	217	157	154	152	151
Years	222	229	229	67	229	229	1
Observations	21 613	25 014	32 323	8899	24 572	24 246	151
R²	0.602	0.572	0.539	0.426	0.603	0.612	0.409

Outcome: Polyarchy index of electoral democracy, augmented. *Not shown:* Year dummies (except Model 7), Constant. *Estimator:* ordinary least squares, standard errors clustered by state, t statistics in parentheses. ***p<.01 **p<.05 *p<.10

Table 13.6 *Major pathways from Europe, predictive power*

	1	2	3	4
English colonial duration	0.119			0.065
Protestants (%)		0.297		0.200
European ancestry (%)			0.413	0.397
Observations	26 231	24 575	26 076	24 572
R^2	0.437	0.467	0.574	0.603

Outcome: Polyarchy index of electoral democracy, augmented. *Not shown:* Natural harbor distance, Equator distance, Year dummies, Constant. *Estimator:* ordinary least squares, showing standardized coefficients. *Sample:* non-European states.

world there are three plausible "winners." Judging by t statistics, European ancestry is the best predictor of democracy, followed by Protestantism and English colonial duration.

For a more focused look at predictive power we regress democracy on these three factors along with two geographic covariates and year dummies, which we regard as a suitable benchmark model. In Table 13.6, we report *standardized* coefficients – the impact of a one-standard-deviation change in X on the outcome. In this fashion, we can directly compare impact across variables measured on different scales. Results confirm that European ancestry is the strongest predictor, followed by Protestantism and finally (a distant third) English colonial duration.

Thus, on empirical grounds the case for European ancestry as a cause of democracy is somewhat stronger than for other pathways from Europe. In the following sections, we discuss several additional issues of causal inference related to (a) measurement, (b) causal order, and (c) selection and proxy effects. Here, too, we find somewhat stronger reasons for accepting demography as a cause.

Measurement

Measurement error is a potential problem for all indicators of European influence. However, it is more problematic for some than for others.

Demographic data is captured in countless surveys and censuses, extending back several centuries for many states. Frequently, these data sources distinguish persons by their race or country/region of origin, allowing us to generate a measure of European ancestry through time, as described in Chapter 9.

By contrast, there are few historical sources allowing us to count the number of Protestant and Catholic adherents or the number of

Europhones. We see no easy way to solve this data problem. Accordingly, it is very difficult to test these factors in a panel analysis. In the case of Catholicism and European language, we have simply extrapolated contemporary values backward in time – not a very satisfactory solution. In the case of Protestantism, we have managed to cobble together a time-series measure with a good deal of interpolation. However, it is based on very few "real" data points, and these are of varying sorts – in some cases, a count of adherents, in others, a count of missionaries. It is difficult to anticipate what sort of bias the errors in measurement introduce.

Causal Order

Up to now, we have treated each pathway from Europe as if it was entirely independent of the others. We know that this cannot be true. In all likelihood, these pathways reinforce each other. European colonialism abets European religion abets European language abets Europeans. It is virtually impossible to sort out which came first, as their order of appearance varied. Moreover, they are all matters of degree so it would be impossible to construct a determinate sequence even for a single colony.

Even so, a few arguments can be hazarded.

Language is probably the most endogenous of the lot. It is the product, we assume, of all the other factors, and scarcely affects the others. As such, the association between European language and democracy may be regarded as downstream from the other factors.

The style of colonial rule – whether "direct" or "indirect" – is to some extent endogenous to European ancestry. Although colonizing powers had different ideologies of rule – the Dutch and British being more inclined to delegate power to local potentates than the Spanish, French, and Portuguese – what took shape in the colonies had more to do with the demographic components of the territory than with a preconceived, formal plan of conquest and governance. British colonies were ruled directly in places where Europeans predominated (e.g., New England), and indirectly where they composed a small minority (e.g., India). Likewise, for other colonizers. New Amsterdam was ruled directly while the Dutch East Indies was ruled indirectly. Algeria was ruled in a more direct fashion than the French Congo. Because Europeans tended to enjoy majorities in the New World these territories tended to be ruled directly. Because they tended to be small minorities in Europe and Africa, these territories were more likely to be ruled indirectly. So, indirect rule may be viewed as downstream from European ancestry.

Other possible interrelationships are more difficult to sort out. For example, the establishment of a formal colony certainly facilitated European settlement. However, colonization was often preceded by settlement, and indeed was often a response to settler demands for protection. So, these two factors bear a complex relationship to each other. Likewise, Protestant missionary societies encouraged settlement, but settlements also provided a base for missionary activity. There is not much that can be said about causal priority in the general case.

Selection Effects and Proxy Effects

There are, finally, potential selection and proxy effects to consider. Where did Europeans (colonists, missionaries, traders, etc.) choose to go, and to remain (for long periods of time), and to invest resources? How might measures of European influence proxy for the characteristics of native populations?

It seems plausible to try to reconstruct the selection effect for European settlers, which were largely a response to geographic factors such as the propensity for infectious disease (common in tropical climates), the availability of arable land, and ocean access, as discussed in Chapter 9. There was little choice involved on the part of indigenous peoples, although there was some resistance to European penetration – modeled in our analyses with a control for state history prior to European contact (following Hariri 2012) and share of the population practicing Islam. Here, instrumental variables are useful, though one must be wary of instruments that may violate the exclusion restriction. Discussion and empirical tests, including a wide variety of instruments, can be found in Chapter 11.

Other measures of European penetration are also subject to geographic conditions that influenced where European colonists settled (Oto-Peralías, Romero-Ávila 2017). In the case of missionaries, Jedwab et al. (2018: 1) show that in sub-Saharan Africa, "locational decisions were driven by economic factors, as missionaries went to healthier, safer, and more accessible and developed areas, privileging the best locations first." These geographic factors can be modeled, either through controls or instrumental variables.

However, many measures of European penetration are often difficult to separate from selection effects on the part of the subject population (non-Europeans). When one measures the prevalence of European religions or languages one is also measuring take-up by slaves and indigenes. Note that although the decision to adopt a new religion or a language is not entirely voluntary, it involves greater choice than is encountered with the spread of Europeans. European religions were resisted in areas with "universalizing creeds and sacred written texts" (Etherington 2005: 8). The reception of European languages was affected by preexisting linguistic heterogeneity and the preexistence of a written language, as noted. Some of these factors can be measured and accounted for; others are difficult to measure and condition, leaving open the possibility of confounding. Specifically, one might suppose that the spread of European religion or language is indicative of a society's general receptiveness to European ideas and institutions. If so, any empirical association between Christianity and democracy is likely to be spurious, the product of an underlying confounder – "receptiveness" – that is impossible to measure.

For Protestantism, one might get around the problem of endogeneity by counting only European missionaries, as Woodberry (2012) does in some of his tests. However, this does not solve the selection problem as the receptiveness of native populations to European religion may have affected the propensity of missionary societies (and individual missionaries) to invest time and resources, and to risk their lives. Areas open to conversion were apt to receive more missionaries than areas that resisted the proselytizing urge. Moreover, the missionary movement itself was fairly quickly indigenized in many parts of the world. Dana Robert (2009: 1–2) notes,

The term "missionary" is caricatured as representing a white Anglo-Saxon man in a pith helmet, preaching to unwilling "natives" in a steamy jungle. Yet over the 2,000 years of Christianity, the "missionary" is likely to have been a Korean couple working among university students in China, or an Indian medical doctor tending to refugees, or a Tongan family living peaceably in a Fijian village, or a Nestorian trader making his living along the Silk Road.

In Africa, a "majority of missionaries involved in mission schools were of African origin and were maintained by African resources" (Frankema, Green, Hillbom 2016: 246).

It is plausible to suppose that the same factors that cause receptiveness to European religion might also predispose native populations to adopt European political institutions, e.g., democracy. Unless we can measure and condition on that factor(s), there is an omitted confounder.

Even more worrying is the possibility of circularity between the outcome and the purported cause. Authoritarian states may prohibit, or harass, adherents of "foreign" religions, or may outlaw religion of any sort, as in communist states. This makes sense if one considers religion a threat to the authority of autocratic regimes. It is no accident that there are lots of Protestants in South Korea today and vanishingly few in North Korea, China, the former USSR, or the Middle East. By contrast, where states were weaker, or less authoritarian, Christianity was allowed to spread. There is no simple cure for circularity between the right and left side of a causal model, especially when data is sparse.

We recognize that states also erected barriers to the influx of Europeans, which might pose a problem of confounding for our key variable, European ancestry. However, the impact of states is minimal compared to other factors reviewed in Chapter 9 – principally, geography and indigenous population density. In the New World, areas with the strongest states in Mesoamerica and South America attracted the most European migrants initially, but their eventual demographic dominance was greatest in areas with the weakest pre-colonial structures. This had nothing to do with states or cultural resistance.

Conclusions

In Part III of the book we offered a great deal of argumentation and evidence pertaining to the role of European ancestry in promoting, and limiting, democracy throughout the world. In this chapter, we have introduced and tested a variety of alternative pathways from Europe including colonialism, religion, and language.

All of these pathways are correlated with democracy when tested singly (see Tables 13.1–13.3). However, European ancestry is more strongly correlated with democracy than the alternative mechanisms (Tables 13.5–13.6), and there are additional reasons pertaining to problems of measurement, causal order, and selection/proxy effects that give us greater confidence in reaching causal inference with respect to demography's influence on regime development over the course of modern history.

That said, in an ideal empirical test (e.g., an experimental or quasi-experimental design with a very large sample) we expect that *all* of these modalities of European influence would demonstrate positive effects on the outcome. Insofar as Europe mattered, its influence probably flowed through multiple pathways.

Suppose we wish to obtain a summary glimpse of that impact over the course of modern history. To do so, let us assume that English colonial duration, Protestantism, and European ancestry all contributed to the shaping of political institutions around the world, albeit in varying degrees. With this assumption, we regress democracy against these three variables in a series of rolling regressions focused on a moving 30-year window beginning in 1789 and ending in 2019. Figure 13.1 plots the R^2 (a model-fit statistic) from these regressions against time.

Rising from a low point in the early nineteenth century, Europe's influence on regime types appears to have peaked in the early twentieth

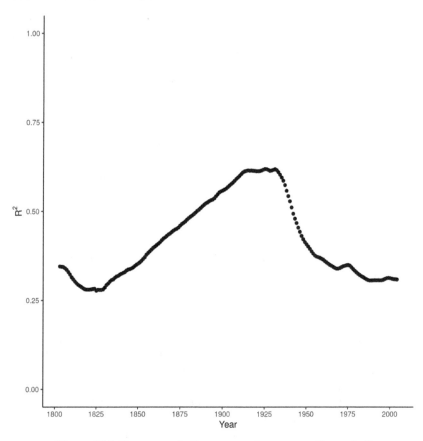

Figure 13.1 **European influence on democracy through time**
Model fit statistics (R^2) from a series of rolling regressions centered on a
moving 30-year window from 1789 to 2019. Results are reported for the
middle year. In this model, the Polyarchy index of electoral democracy
(augmented) is regressed against Protestants (%), English colonial
duration (years), and European ancestry (%). Sample restricted to
states outside Europe.

century. At that point, European colonizers, settlers, and missionaries
exerted influence over the vast majority of the world's territory and
(arguably) enjoyed a moment of enormous power and prestige. At this
point, roughly *two-thirds* of the variability in regime types appears to be
"explained" by these emanations of Europe. As the twentieth century
progresses, European influence wanes. By the turn of the twenty-first
century, only one-third of the variability in regimes may be accounted for
by English colonial duration, Protestantism, and European ancestry.

Of course, these are probably exaggerated estimates since we have not attempted to control for many potential confounders – some of which, as the foregoing discussion suggests, are probably impossible to eliminate. Our point is that Europe's influence on regimes is not constant through the ages. Currently, it appears to be in demise. This makes sense if one considers that the global influence of Europe is weakening (by most measures) and that democracy has become a universal ideal, which can no longer be regarded as the exclusive property of Europeans.

Before concluding, we must take notice of the interconnections between European diffusion and maritime geography. Note that European ancestry, Protestantism, and British colonialism could all be regarded as adaptations to Europe's aqueous natural environment. The first European migrants – those who established most of the European colonies around the world and established a path for future migrations (through chain migration) – came from the most oceanic portions of the continent. Among the European countries with overseas empires, Britain is the most aqueous and its political culture is often said to exemplify that of a seafaring people.[11] Protestantism was born in Northern Germany and from thence spread primarily northward – to Scandinavia, the Lowlands, and to Britain, the most oceanic regions (aside from Ireland) of an aqueous continent. And in the modern era, the spread of Christianity across the non-European world was achieved via the ocean, generating a strong link between creed and tide (Cabantous 2014; Fernandez-Armesto 2016).

The probable interconnections among these various elements are revealed in a comment by Edmund Burke, who described a global community of Britons that was "Protestant, commercial, maritime and free."[12] As such, this chapter may be viewed as an elaboration of the geographic arguments vetted in Part II of the book.

---

[11] See Bryant (1985), Friel (2003), Lavery (2005), Scott (2011), Sobecki (2011).
[12] Quoted in Travers (2007: 2). See also Pestana (2009).

14 Economics, Institutions, Culture

Having considered alternate geographic factors (Chapter 12) and alternate pathways from Europe (Chapter 13), we turn to a grab-bag of residual factors that might be described as economic, institutional, or cultural. For greater tractability, we divide these factors into twelve more specific categories: (a) agricultural transitions, (b) modernization, (c) inequality, (d) labor scarcity, (e) marriage and family, (f) feudalism, (g) parliaments, (h) Christianity, (i) Catholicism, (j) state size, (k) state–society relations, and (l) ideas.

Many of these arguments center on the European experience. That is, they seek to identify what was unique about this subcontinent that might account for its central role in the development of representative democracy. (Readers will recall from our discussion in Chapter 2 that lots of places exhibited elements of direct democracy prior to the modern era, but only Europe – and European colonies abroad – developed representative institutions and constitutional constraints on the exercise of power.)

For those explanations that can be operationalized on a global scale we offer a limited series of tests, intended to subject these alternate hypotheses to the same research design we applied to our own hypotheses. In the concluding section, we offer thoughts on problems of causal inference faced by this set of predictors. Our general conclusion is that most of these factors are best considered as proximal causes of democracy. As such, they are not necessarily at odds with the framework provided in Parts II and III; indeed, we cite many of these factors as potential causal mechanisms.

Agricultural Transitions

The transition from hunting and foraging to sedentary agriculture is widely viewed as a critical step in civilizational development, stimulating greater population densities, state formation, and further technological change. According to a now-standard view, societies that experienced an early agricultural transition are wealthier today.[1]

Olsson and Paik (2016, 2020) dispute this view, arguing that within regions initial advantages enjoyed by areas with advanced agriculture attenuated over time, eventually reversing themselves. In their words, "early farming states were eventually overcome by younger states that tended to be characterized by less extractive capacity and more inclusive political institutions. These institutions, in turn, would gradually become of key importance for modern era innovation-led economic growth and for countries' ability to attain superior productivity levels." Accordingly, one should observe a negative relationship (within regions) between time elapsed since the agricultural transition and indicators of development today.

Our interest, of course, is in democracy – one of several outcomes explored in an adventurous series of studies by Olsson and Paik. To measure democratic norms at a subnational level, the authors employ responses from the World Values Survey, aggregated within grid-cells across the European continent. There is also one bivariate regression analysis with democracy as the outcome, which shows the expected negative correlation – though with no covariates and a limited sample of sixty-four countries.

To provide a more comprehensive test of the thesis, we employ a measure of agricultural transitions from Putterman (2006) that offers coverage for 146 contemporary countries. As with Olsson and Paik, the index counts the number of years (in thousands) since an agricultural transition occurred within the present-day borders of these countries.

We regress democracy against this index in a series of tests displayed in Table 14.1. The first specification includes only the variable of theoretical interest. Model 2 includes two geographic variables used in benchmark models throughout this book. Model 3 adds a panel of regional dummies. This last test is especially important in light of Olsson and Paik's argument that within-region relationships are different from cross-region relationships.

All three tests show the expected negative relationship. Time since agricultural transition is associated with lower levels of democracy. However, the relationship is not especially strong or robust. On this basis, we conclude that agricultural transitions may have a small effect on democracy in the modern era, but that effect is underwhelming.

---

[1] See Ashraf, Özak, Galor (2010), Bleaney, Dimico (2011), Putterman (2008), Putterman, Weil (2010).

Table 14.1 *Agricultural transition*

	1	2	3
Agricultural transition, years since (1000s)	−0.226	−1.662***	−1.327
	(−0.336)	(−2.617)	(−1.251)
Harbor distance		✓	✓
Equator distance		✓	✓
Regional dummies			✓
States	146	146	146
Years	231	231	231
Observations	24 321	24 321	24 321
R^2	0.334	0.495	0.545

Outcome: Polyarchy index of electoral democracy, augmented. *Not shown:* Year dummies, Constant. *Estimator:* ordinary least squares, standard errors clustered by state, t statistics in parentheses. ***p<.01 **p<.05 *p<.10

Modernization

For many writers, the key to political development is to be found in economic development. Specifically, the rise of cities, trade, the middle classes, education, and wealth – or some subset of these factors – is thought to facilitate the rise of democracy (Lipset 1959). The thesis is intuitive and grounded in a large literature known generically as modernization theory (Levy 1966). Empirical studies generally support the idea, whether focused on European history,[2] American history (Brown 1969), or globally in the modern era.[3]

We find no reason to quarrel with the proposition that economic development has positive short-term effects on democracy, at least in the modern era. However, economic development is pretty clearly endogenous to geography[4] and to European-led globalization.[5] That is why we have approached this topic as a causal mechanism rather than a prime mover in our theoretical framework.

[2] See Abramson, Boix (2019), Bates, Lien (1985), Blickle (1997), Ertman (1997), Guizot (1877[1838]), Harriss (1993), Pirenne (1963), Reynolds (1984), Sabetti (2004).
[3] See Boix, Stokes (2003), Inglehart, Welzel (2005), Knutsen et al. (2019), Lipset (1959), Murtin, Wacziarg (2014), Przeworski, Limongi 1997), Treisman (2020b). Debates about whether economic development has a symmetric or asymmetric effect on democratization and autocratization are not relevant here.
[4] See Diamond (1992), Mellinger, Sachs & Gallup (2000).
[5] See Acemoglu, Johnson, Robinson (2001, 2002), Easterly, Levine (2016), Feyrer, Sacerdote (2009), Grier (1999), Mahoney (2010).

By the same token, there are reasons to doubt whether economic development has played a *distal* role in the development of democratic institutions.[6]

Suppose we accept conventional wisdom that the first turning-points toward democracy in Europe occurred in antiquity or in the Middle Ages. Modernization theory must reckon with the fact that these societies were extremely poor by today's standards. Even by the standards of the time they were not especially wealthy. One cannot argue that the Magna Carta occurred in England rather than China because England was wealthier or more developed than China. If anything, historical records suggest the reverse.

Granted, within Europe, beginning sometime in the Middle Ages, wealth and democracy appear to correlate. Polities in northern Italy, Germany, the Lowlands, and Britain were richer *and* more democratic than the rest of Europe. However, it is exceedingly challenging to differentiate cause and effect. While some studies assign causal priority to wealth (Abramson, Boix 2019), others accord priority to institutions.[7] We see no way to prise apart these factors so as to convincingly solve problems of causal identification.

In any case, prior to the industrial revolution there was little difference in living standards or other measures of economic progress between the eastern and western edges of Asia. All societies were predominantly rural and agrarian. At various points in time, China, Japan, India, the Ottoman Empire, or some shifting portion of Western Europe may have had the edge,[8] but the edge was not so great. If economic development mattered to democracy one would expect to find inklings of it in other developed parts of the world. Yet, economic development and *autocracy* went together more often than not. Outside Europe, areas with the densest populations, largest cities, and most advanced technology and infrastructure were rarely governed democratically.[9] Thus, there are reasons to

---

[6] Similar doubts are raised in Doucette, Møller (2020) and Stasavage (2020).

[7] See Acemoglu, Johnson, Robinson (2005), De Long, Shleifer (1993), Wahl (2018).

[8] See Broadberry, Gupta (2006), Morris (2013b: 240–3, tables 7.1–7.2), Pomeranz (2000), Wong (1997).

[9] An early nineteenth century observer of the world concludes on a Rousseauian note: "the more abject the state of man in the scale of social improvement, the freer the form of his government; and in proportion as he advances in civilization, is that freedom abridged, until, at the top of the scale, he is subjected to a tyranny where not a vestige of liberty is discoverable. In short, he enjoys freedom when he has nothing else worth enjoying; and when the comforts of civil life accumulate around him he is deprived of the liberty of benefiting by them" (Crawfurd 1820, v.3: 3–4).

Table 14.2 *Economic development*

	1	2	3
Per capita GDP (log), t − 200	−3.030 (−0.453)		
Per capita GDP (log), t − 100		4.900*** (2.669)	−0.189 (−0.095)
European ancestry (%), t − 100			✓
States	67	99	99
Years	31	131	131
Observations	1628	10733	10733
R^2	0.020	0.228	0.453

Outcome: Polyarchy index of electoral democracy, augmented. Per capita GDP comes from Fariss et al. (2017), which draws on Bolt, van Zanden (2014). *Not shown:* Year dummies, Constant. *Estimator:* ordinary least squares, standard errors clustered by state, t statistics in parentheses. ***p<.01 **p<.05 *p<.10

doubt whether economic development per se had a positive influence on democracy in the premodern era.

Unfortunately, we cannot test the relationship empirically as there are no global indicators of democracy prior to 1789 (a problem discussed in Chapter 2). However, we can probe the validity of modernization theory in the modern era. Since our interest is in distal causes, we offer a series of tests in which democracy is regressed against per capita GDP with a very long lag.

Tests reproduced in Table 14.2 show that when GDP is lagged two centuries behind the outcome (Model 1) there is no relationship or possibly a negative relationship – signaling a "reversal of fortune" (Acemoglu, Johnson, Robinson 2002) – between economic development and democracy. When GDP is lagged one century behind the outcome (Model 2) there is a modest positive relationship, seeming to corroborate the tenets of modernization theory. However, when we add a measure of European ancestry (Model 3), this effect disappears. Since European ancestry is presumably exogenous to GDP,[10] not much support can be found for modernization as a distal cause of democracy. This conclusion is reinforced when we examine other proxies for economic development such as population density, which also has no distal relationship to the outcome, as shown in Table 14.3 (below).

[10] It is much more likely that Europeans caused growth (Easterly, Levine 2016; Krieckhaus 2006) than the reverse.

Table 14.3 *Labor scarcity*

	1	2
Population density (1500)	0.077	−1.057
	(0.055)	(−1.000)
Harbor distance		✓
Equator distance		✓
States	147	147
Years	231	231
Observations	24 411	24 411
R^2	0.323	0.485

Outcome: Polyarchy index of electoral democracy, augmented. *Not shown:* Year dummies, Constant. *Estimator:* ordinary least squares, standard errors clustered by state, t statistics in parentheses. ***p<.01 **p<.05 *p<.10

Inequality

A third economic perspective on the sources of democracy rests not on aggregate wealth but rather on its distribution, i.e., relative (in)equality within a society.

The oldest and still the most common argument is that inequality fosters autocracy in a monotonic fashion. When elites are greatly privileged over the masses they have the motive and the means to monopolize power. The disadvantaged masses have a motive to fight for democracy but they do not have the means, as they are (relatively) poor, uneducated, and lacking in other resources that might help them seize political power. Typically, this is understood as a redistributional struggle, with elites aiming to maintain their wealth by forestalling democracy and masses aiming to redistribute wealth through the ballot box (Boix 2003).

Variants of this argument are legion. If democratic transitions are primarily about wealth redistribution, then as inequality in a society increases elites should be more resistant and masses should be more eager. This might result in a stalemate, which would suggest that inequality has no explanatory power. Alternatively, Acemoglu and Robinson (2005) envision a sweet-spot somewhere in the middle – at a moderate level of inequality – at which masses are sufficiently motivated to push for a transition and elites are sufficiently indifferent to accept it. If so, there should be a curvilinear relationship between inequality and the probability of a regime transition.

Other authors have attempted to get beneath the surface of the abstract concept of inequality to discover *which* social groups are most likely to push for, or resist, a democratic transition. Among privileged classes, members of the bourgeoisie may be more inclined to accept democracy than agricultural elites (B. Moore 1966). Among less privileged classes, members of the working class may be in a better position to push for democracy than peasants or the rural proletariat (Rueschemeyer, Stephens, Stephens 1992). Another view rejects the notion that democratic transitions are primarily about social classes, instead focusing on the motivations of insurgent elites (Ansell, Samuels 2010, 2014).

These are complex theories and we have certainly not done them justice. Ideally, we could test them in our usual regression framework. Unfortunately, inequality is hard to measure on a global scale in the contemporary era and virtually impossible to measure in prior historical eras.

In any case, inequality is usually treated as a proximal cause of regime transition. That is, the level of inequality in a society is measured a few years or decades prior to the outcome.[11] Since inequality is clearly endogenous to geography and European colonialism,[12] we regard it as a potential mechanism but not a distal cause in our framework.

Labor Scarcity

Yet another economic theory about politics rests on the nature of the labor market. In societies where labor is abundant and land is scarce, rulers have no incentive to cater to workers as there are plenty of them and their exit options are limited. This situation may have obtained in East Asia, along the Nile, and in other areas of early population growth. By contrast, where labor is scarce and land abundant, rulers have an incentive to attract migrants and prevent their departure. To do so, they may be forced to cede civil and political rights. Likewise, landowners may need to offer enhanced wages, which in turn empowers workers. Or workers may be granted property rights, allowing them to establish small farms, which should enhance their economic independence and political power. This dynamic seems to have obtained in Western Europe after the Black Death and perhaps in the New World (where labor has always been scarce) through the present day. From this perspective, labor scarcity should foster democracy.[13]

Of course, labor scarcity does not always lead to outcomes that are beneficial for workers. It may also be met with schemes of forced

---

[11] See Ansell, Samuels (2010, 2014), Boix (2003), Houle (2009), Ziblatt (2008).
[12] See Angeles (2007), Engerman, Sokoloff (2000).
[13] See Engerman, Sokoloff (2012: ch. 4), Stasavage (2020).

migration and restrictions on labor mobility such as serfdom or slavery (Domar 1970). Divergent paths appeared in Europe after the Black Death, when Western Europe followed a liberalizing strategy and Eastern Europe a coercive strategy.[14] Divergent experiences can also be found in the Americas during the early modern and modern eras, when labor-poor areas away from the equator followed a liberalizing strategy while labor-poor areas near the equator (e.g., the Caribbean) followed a coercive strategy. Arguably, this is a case of extreme causal heterogeneity, where – due to some unidentified moderator – a single causal factor has contrary effects.[15]

To test this relationship in the modern era, we regress democracy against population density, understood as a proxy for labor scarcity. Population density is measured in 1500, prior to European globalization, a period when arguments about labor scarcity are commonly vetted. Results are shown in Table 14.3.

Model 1 includes only the regressor of theoretical interest along with year dummies. Model 2 includes our familiar geographic controls. Neither of these estimates is very strong, and the sign switches. Evidently, this is not a very robust relationship. Perhaps it is not causal, or its impact is registered only under certain scope-conditions, yet to be determined.

Marriage and Family

Europe may have experienced a distinctive demographic pattern. For John Hajnal (1965), the key features were celibacy prior to marriage, delayed age of marriage contingent on securing gainful employment, and monogamy within marriage. This has become known as the European Marriage Pattern, or "EMP" (Reher 1998; Wrigley et al. 1997), and may be regarded as a distal cause of labor scarcity in Europe, discussed above.

Scholars debate the causes of the EMP. Possible sources include (a) relatively egalitarian gender norms, allowing women to work outside the home and choose a marriage partner (arguably, the product of the Catholic doctrine of consent), (b) limited parental authority, (c) neolocality, (d) urbanization (De Moor, van Zanden 2010), and (e) the Black Death, which instituted a severe labor shortage, as discussed (Voigtländer, Voth 2013).

---

[14] See Brenner (1976), Engerman (2014: 37).
[15] Acemoglu and Wolitzky (2011) offer a formal model attempting to resolve this conundrum but do not supply an easily testable proposition.

Whatever its causes, the potential implications of the EMP are considerable. By placing normative constraints on reproduction, it is argued that Europeans established a low fertility/low mortality regime organized around the nuclear family. This, in turn, is viewed as the cradle of English individualism (Macfarlane 1978), a trait that extended over time to the rest of the continent, in varying degrees. Meanwhile, other regions of the world were mired in a Malthusian demographic pattern of high fertility, high mortality, and collective forms of social organization. It is a short step to imagine the potential impact of these diverging demographic patterns for economic development and democracy.

Some aspects of the EMP have been challenged. Fertility rates in early modern China were also low, perhaps even lower than Europe due to "abortion, female infanticide, adoption, low rates of male marriage, chaste widowhood, and greater spacing between births" (Lieberman 2009: 5; see also Lee, Campbell, Feng 2002). Lieberman (2009: 5) argues that "whereas the European family system limited fertility by controlling access to marriage, China achieved the same result by controlling fertility within marriage."

In this light, the defining feature of European demography may not be low fertility per se but rather *family structure* (Dilli 2016; Todd 1985). While there are many ways of classifying family structure, a simplified version of the usual argument is that European families evolved in the direction of nuclear families while in other parts of the world extended families remained the norm. This, too, may have important implications for democracy. Bondarenko and Korotayev (2000: 157) reason,

The extended family community, in which social ties are markedly vertical and have the shape of kinship relations (elder–younger), is more characteristic of hierarchical societies. The territorial community (composed of nuclear families), in which social ties are horizontal and understood as those of neighborhood (and the neighbors are regarded to be equal in their rights), is basically peculiar to nonhierarchical societies. As supralocal sociopolitical structures and institutions arise out of a communal substratum ..., the type of community determines to a significant extent the character of an evolving complex society, the basic principle of its organization ... Hence, we hypothesize that family size and communal democracy will be negatively correlated.

Schulz et al. (2019) argue that family structures in Europe generate a distinctive personality type, which they describe as "individualistic, independent, and impersonally prosocial (e.g., trusting of strangers) while revealing less conformity and in-group loyalty."

Empirically, these relationships have been explored in a number of settings. Bondarenko and Korotayev employ data from the Ethnographic

Table 14.4 *Kinship intensity*

Outcome	Polyarchy	Polyarchy	Polity2
	1	2	3
Kinship intensity index	−8.837***	−0.730	−5.259
	(−7.794)	(−0.682)	(−1.522)
European ancestry		✓	✓
Region dummies		✓	✓
States	194	193	164
Years	231	229	218
Observations	32 585	32 023	16 379
R^2	0.475	0.579	0.372

Not shown: Year dummies, Constant. *Estimator:* ordinary least squares, standard errors clustered by state, t statistics in parentheses. ***p<.01 **p<.05 *p<.10

Atlas, where local democracy is measured by examining selection procedures for the local headman (discussed in Chapter 2) and family structure is measured in a variety of ways, including size and polygyny/monogamy. They find a (weak) negative correlation between these aspects of family structure and local democracy among ethnic groups around the world.[16]

Building on earlier work by Woodley and Bell (2013), Schulz et al. (2019: 3) produce a Kinship Intensity Index, "an omnibus measure for kinship intensity that captures the presence of cousin-marriage preferences, polygamy, co-residence of extended families, clan organization, and community endogamy." Their data also draws on the Ethnographic Atlas with some supplementary coding by the authors. One outcome (among many) explored in this wide-ranging set of studies is democracy in the contemporary era, where Schulz (2019) finds a strong negative correlation between kinship intensity and democracy as measured by the Polity2 index.

Our test of the thesis follows the same format with a few variations, shown in Table 14.4. Model 1 regresses democracy (measured by the Polyarchy index) against the Kinship Intensity Index along with year dummies. In Model 2, we add European ancestry along with a panel of regional dummies. Model 3 repeats this specification with Polity2 as the outcome measure, as in Schulz (2019).

It will be seen that there is a negative relationship between kinship intensity and democracy in all three tests, corroborating the thesis.

---

[16] See Bondarenko, Korotayev (2000), Korotayev, Bondarenko (2000).

However, this relationship passes standard thresholds of statistical significance only in the first model. Since the right-side covariates – European ancestry and region dummies – are almost certainly exogenous, it is hard to argue against their inclusion in the model. Accordingly, we conclude that the relationship between kinship and democracy is highly sensitive to choices in specification.

The relationship is also sensitive to period effects. It turns out that the Kinship Intensity Index is a strong predictor of democracy around the turn of the twenty-first century. A cross-sectional analysis centered on year 2000 is strongly significant. However, as one moves away from this watershed year (in either direction), the relationship attenuates. (It is not clear what year, or set of years, is employed in analyses shown in Schulz 2019 but we infer that it is 2000, or thereabouts.) We cannot envision a reason why the relationship between kinship intensity and democracy would peak at the end of the twentieth century, so we do not explore this option.

Since kinship is likely to be endogenous to many factors, we are also led to consider antecedent causes. Woodley and Bell (2013: 273) identify pathogens, economic freedom, power resources, and Islam as exogenous factors. Other writers focus on the role of the Christian church, which regulated marriage norms, prohibiting cousin marriage.[17]

To make the case for Christianity, Schulz and collaborators (Schulz 2019; Schulz et al. 2019) measure exposure to the Eastern and Western church (measured separately) in European cities (i.e., distance from nearest bishopric) from the birth of Christ to 1500, showing that areas with greater exposure were more likely to develop communes – forms of government in which power was constrained. Of course, the spread of bishoprics throughout Europe may have been induced by factors that were also conducive to communal political organization. Modernization theory (discussed above) would suggest that growing wealth attracts both a bishopric and a communal form of organization, for example. Likewise, the impact of the Christian church on the development of communes may have occurred for other reasons, as discussed below.

Feudalism

Narrowly defined, feudalism describes a formal bond in which a lord acknowledges rights of ownership or use of land (fief) by a vassal in exchange for military service or labor. However, when the concept is

---

[17] See Greif (2006a, 2006b), Greif, Tabellini (2017), Korotayev, Bondarenko (2000), Mitterauer (2010), Schulz et al. (2019).

employed as a factor in the rise of democracy authors usually adopt a broader understanding centered on political institutions, i.e., a system in which authority is generated by a series of reciprocal arrangements between hierarchs and lowerarchs. This sort of authority is loose because lords and vassals were enmeshed in webs of mutual dependence, and relationships were open to continual negotiation. Kings may have claimed absolute power, but if they ruled through a feudal system of power their orders would be filtered through a diaphanous prism in which each vassal could maneuver across various allegiances and agreements.

Feudalism is thus sometimes regarded as the social basis of weak, decentralized governance in which landed aristocrats served as a counterweight to a reigning monarch. It is also seen as the social basis for the rise of the *Standestaat*, in which each social class has its own rights and channels of political influence, ensconced in different estates with representation in regional or national parliaments.[18]

One might also credit feudalism, and the fragmented institutional field it created, with the rise of other organizational forms including communes, guilds, corporations, churches, and universities.[19] Perhaps these were the wellsprings of communal democracy, a story consistent with a social capital model of political development (Putnam et al. 1994).

And yet, several doubts arise about this feudalism-to-democracy story.

To begin with, the concept of feudalism is devilishly hard to define and to measure. Narrowly interpreted, it seems to have existed only in Europe and perhaps Japan. More expansive definitions recognize shades of feudalism in ancient Mesopotamia, Iran and Egypt, the Byzantine Empire, India, China, and Russia (Coulborn 1956). Beyond the core distinction between economic and political definitions, numerous definitional traits have been attached to the concept. None are very amenable to measurement.[20] Evidently, if we do not know when and where feudalism existed, we cannot begin to evaluate its possible causal effects. Nor can we construct a systematic test, either within Europe or globally.

Second, with respect to the role of parliaments it must be noted that they arose in virtually every corner of Europe, including areas where feudalism was (by all accounts) weakest such as the Celtic fringe of Iceland, Scandinavia, and Ireland. So, feudalism cannot effectively

---

[18] See Anderson (1974), Blaydes, Chaney (2013), Bloch (1971[1939]), Downing (1989), Duby (1978), Hintze (1975), Löwenthal (1977), Mitterauer (2010), Poggi (1978: ch. 2), Stasavage (2016), Strayer (1970).

[19] See Black (1984), Ciepley (2017), De Moor (2008), Epstein (1991), Greif (2006b), Maitland (2003).

[20] For further discussion see Brown (1974), Brunner (1975), Møller (2015), Reynolds (1994), Ward (1985).

differentiate the strength, or timing, of democracy across the European continent.

Finally, the key sub-state institution of the merchant or craft guild, although common in Europe (Ogilvie 2019), was by no means unique to that region of the world (Lucassen, De Moor, Van Zanden 2008). Indeed, it was common throughout the urbanized regions of the Eurasian continent including China (Moll-Murata 2008), Japan (Nagata 2008), the Byzantine and Ottoman Empires (Yildirim 2008), and South Asia (Bayly 1988). If the guild played a different role in the development of European society than elsewhere it must have been due to some other factor that moderated its varying influence across different regions.

Parliaments

Modern democracy is often viewed as the end-product of a long historical process that began with medieval assemblies and parliaments. To many writers, therefore, the development of an assembly performing representative functions is the critical juncture upon which the subsequent fate of democracy depends.[21] This is why we feel justified in treating parliaments as a measure of democracy in the premodern era in Chapter 5 (see Table 5.2).

Parliaments presumably grew out of assemblies, whose history can be traced back within Germanic ("barbarian") peoples to Roman times (Mouritsen 2017) and back to the city-states of Ancient Greece. Tacitus provides one of the first descriptions, though it is short on detail and probably not entirely reliable. By the medieval age, assemblies could be found in most regions of Europe. These early parliaments allowed a small stratum of elites the opportunity of congregating in one place, presenting demands to the executive, extracting political concessions for new taxes, and approving the line of succession when a reigning monarch passed, or even selecting the new ruler. Their power was enhanced by kings' need for revenue during times of war, which was much of the time.[22]

---

[21] See Congleton (2010), Maddicott (2010), Poggi (1978: ch. 3), Selinger (2019), Van Zanden, Buringh, Bosker (2012). For surveys of representative assemblies in medieval and early modern Europe see Albareda, Sánchez (2018), Barnwell, Mostert (2003), Bass (1995), Bisson (1966, 2001), Graves (2001), Hébert (2014), Jansson (2007), Jones (2012), Lord (1930), Maddicott (2010), Marongiu (1968), Meyers (1975), Monahan (1987), Van Zanden, Buringh, Bosker (2012).
[22] See Bates, Lien (1985), Bisson (1966), Hintze (1975), Kiser, Barzel (1991), Møller (2017), Moore (2004), Poggi (1978).

The tug of war between executive and parliament was continual, sometimes inclining in the assembly's favor (as it often did when the monarch was desperate for fighting men, taxes, and materiel), and sometimes in the executive's favor (as it did for most European states during the so-called Age of Absolutism). Occasionally, parliament was prorogued for an extended period, as it was in France in the seventeenth and eighteenth centuries (though regional parliaments continued to function). The movement toward democracy was not steady and certainly not monotonic.

Nonetheless, once an assembly existed it often proved difficult to dislodge, and parliaments bounced back in every European state, generating a long record of parliamentary rule. Likewise, the development of parliaments in the New World, especially within English colonies, is often viewed as critical to the political evolution of those polities (Greene 1986). Thus, it is easy to see a connection between parliamentarism in the medieval and early modern periods and mass democracy in the modern era.

However, it is difficult to assess the claim that one *caused* the other since they are so closely connected. At best, the claim that parliamentarism causes democracy identifies a proximal factor associated with the rise of democracy. One is left wondering why some polities developed parliaments in the premodern era, while others did not.

Christianity

In some respects, the Christian tradition seems to accord greater respect for the individual, greater scope for human rights, and greater separation between the world of man and the world of god than other religious traditions. On these accounts, societies imbued with Christianity – even if they no longer adhere to the strictures of organized religion – may be more inclined to a democratic form of rule in the modern era.[23]

This is a difficult argument to assess because a religion is not a clearly defined treatment. Accordingly, one is hard put to envision the appropriate counterfactual. One can imagine a world in which Jesus was never born; but we know that Christianity was the work of more than one man. Indeed, a wide variety of mystical religious frameworks circulated around the time of Christ, sharing some properties with Christianity (Bremmer 2014). From this perspective, Christianity was not sui generis and it is possible to imagine that one of these other religions might have been

---

[23] See de Gruchy (1995), Maddox (1996), Siedentop (2014).

enshrined as the house religion of the Roman Empire, and subsequently become the hegemonic religion of Europe. Would this have had a bearing on the course of democracy? It is difficult to say because we don't know much about these alternatives to Christianity, or how they might have developed through time. It is not even clear that we can differentiate religion from society in the premodern world (Price 1999). As such, it is hard to construct a plausible counterfactual and to identify the ceteris paribus conditions of the argument. If Christianity is viewed as a product of the times and of the region, it is inseparable from these background factors and cannot be considered a cause.

Now let us move beyond the point of origin to the development of religions through time. After all, they are not static entities. One must be concerned not only with founding documents (which are, for many religions, difficult to identify) but also with how those documents are interpreted over time – interpretations that may be endogenous to other (non-religious) factors. What *is* Judaism, Hinduism, Buddhism, and Islam? The problem becomes even more acute as one grapples with innumerable indigenous folkways and belief systems that do not have the formally articulated aspects of a "religion."

The idea that Christianity offers a democratic advantage may be assessed empirically in the modern era by examining the correlation between faiths and regimes. In Chapter 13, we found a strong correlation between one branch of western Christianity – Protestantism – and democracy. However, the main branch of Western Christianity, and the one with the longest continuous history – now known as Catholicism – does not seem to be robustly associated with democracy in the modern era. Nor, for that matter, are other variants of Christianity such as Eastern Orthodox or Oriental Orthodox. Indeed, non-Protestant branches of Christianity are sometimes regarded as fodder for authoritarian rule (Grigoriadis 2016).

This poses a problem for those who view Christianity as a doctrine peculiarly suited to democratic rule. If it is only *one sect* of Christianity that is predisposed to democracy one must wonder about the evolution, and potential endogeneity, of that sect.

Note also that Christianity was not founded in Europe or by Europeans. It arose in Judea, on the fringes of the Roman Empire, from which it migrated into Europe. By the end of the Middle Ages most of Europe had been Christianized, at least to some degree. But the process of conversion to Roman Catholicism was accompanied by some considerable transformation of religious practices and understandings. "In almost every case, these non-Roman peoples maintained and advanced a significant portion of their inherited cultural identities and traditions, even while they adopted the new Christian faith. In so doing, they also profoundly transformed the Early Christianity of the Roman Empire, so that previous expression of this faith gave way to something distinctly new: medieval Christianity," observes O'Sullivan (2016: 55). After the rise of Islam, Christianity declined in its natal region. Eventually the faith fragmented – into Orthodox, Catholic, and myriad Protestant sects.

It is implausible to suppose that this pattern of Christian migration, schism, and eventual retrenchment was entirely random. If Luther had been born in Madrid, Naples, or Lublin it is unlikely he would have led a Reformation of the Western church, for example. Thus, we are led to consider factors that might account for the different Christian practices that arose across Europe and its periphery.

Various answers to this classic question have been offered. The victory of Catholicism in the south and Protestantism in the north might have been a response to cultural and economic features of these regions (Akçomak, Webbink, ter Weel 2016; Tawney 1936), differing levels of urbanization (Blickle 1992; Ozment 1975), varying agricultural institutions in the countryside (Hopcroft 1997), or political institutions (Swanson 1967). *Many* features distinguished northern and southern Europe by the time Luther (so the story goes) nailed his theses to the door, each of which might be regarded as an exogenous cause and each of which might also impact the development of political institutions.[24]

Did Christianity change Europe, or did Europe change Christianity?

In this light, one may consider the geographic thesis launched in Part II of the book. After the fall of Byzantium, orthodoxy migrated to the southern and eastern fringes of the European landmass – to what is now Egypt, Ethiopia, Greece, Armenia, Ukraine, and Russia. With the notable exception of Greece, these are the least aqueous regions. Catholicism retained its hold over the central European landmass, encompassing polities with varying degrees of ocean access. Protestantism, the upstart faith, was ascendant in northern Europe, the most harbor-rich region of the continent (perhaps, of the world). Insofar as religious practices are shaped by geography, one might view the historical development of Christianity as adaptive, rather than generative. Perhaps it is not coincidental that a number of the Apostles were fishermen and others lived by the sea. We can only speculate.

Catholicism

Let us now shift gears to examine a more specific thesis connected with the largest and (arguably) the oldest sect of Christianity. By the high

[24] This literature is reviewed in Becker, Pfaff, Rubin (2016).

Middle Ages, Catholicism had developed into a centralized, hierarchical religious organization. At its head was the pope, who bore all the markings of a monarch. As such, the Catholic Church did not appear very democratic, either to its supporters or its detractors.

However, the pontiff was selected by a vote of the college of cardinals, and many features of the church embodied ideals of consultation, deliberation, and (canon) law. The Dominican order, building on Roman precedents, incorporated many features that we would today recognize as characteristic of political representation (Doucette 2020). In these respects, the church may have served as an inspiration to secular leaders crafting representative constitutions for cities and city-states on the model of conciliar rule.

In addition to being a centralized organization, the Catholic Church was also unique insofar as it achieved a near-monopoly on religious practice within Europe and considerable independence from secular rulers. No other major religion has ever achieved this set of accomplishments, and there are good reasons to suppose this peculiar feature of Europe may have figured in the rise of democracy on that subcontinent. According to a well-worn argument, the church created and sustained the fragmented institutional field that was characteristic of Europe after the fall of the Roman Empire, offering succor to dissenters and occasionally constraining the behavior of kings, and also taking a gigantic cut of the agricultural surplus that otherwise would have gone into the king's coffers. Kings were dependent upon popes to bless their marriages, sanction their wars, and sanctify their successors. Jurists were often drawn from ecclesiastical offices, clergy served as formal and informal bureaucrats, and canon law served as a model for secular law. Clergy were also represented in parliaments. Early cities required a charter in order to secure their legal position; often, the chartering institution was the papacy. Insofar as cities played a central role in the development of European institutions, the church may be credited with a causal role.

In these two respects – as an institutional model and a fragmenting force – the Catholic Church may have served as a handmaiden for the development of democratic institutions in Europe.[25]

---

[25] Elements of this thesis can be traced back to David Hume, Immanuel Kant, and Max Weber (Karayalcin 2008; Mokyr 2006), as well as to Lord Acton (1919: ch. 2), and are found in many recent studies, e.g., Berman (1983), Black (1992), Doucette (2020), Doucette, Hall (1985), Jones (1981), Landes (1998), Mitterauer (2010), Møller (2018a), Monahan (1987, 130), Morris (1989), Oakley (2003; 2010; 2012; 2015), Scheidel (2019), Siedentop (2014), Southern (1970: 22), Tierney (1966, 1982, 1988), along with works cited in Scheidel (2019: 538, fn. 19).

At the same time, one must wonder about the exogeneity of this remarkable institution. Recall that Christianity was a minor religion until adopted by Constantine as the state religion of the Roman Empire. We do not know whether it would have been able to establish hegemony across Europe, and achieve a highly centralized organization centered on the papacy, without this institutional support. Likewise, had the empire survived it seems likely that the church would have been its handmaiden, not its rival. And had subsequent statebuilders succeeded in uniting the continent there is little doubt that they would have gained control of the papacy, shackling it to the new empire.[26]

Arguably, the centralization and independence of the papacy were a product of the initial success and subsequent failure of European state-builders' efforts to unite the continent under a single secular power. Thus, we return to the conundrum of causal order. The unique role of the church was both a cause, and an effect, of state fragmentation, an issue to which we now turn.

State Size

The size of polities is often regarded as a causal factor in politics (Gerring, Veenendaal 2020), and Europe since the demise of the Roman Empire has been credited for its diminutive polities. Montesquieu (1989 [1748]: 283–4) observes:

In Asia one has always seen great empires; in Europe they were never able to continue to exist. This is because the Asia we know has broader plains; it is cut into larger parts by seas; and, as it is more to the south, its streams dry up more easily, its mountains are less covered with snow, and its smaller rivers form slighter barriers. Therefore, power should always be despotic in Asia. For if servitude there were not extreme, there would immediately be a division that the nature of the country cannot endure. In Europe, the natural divisions form many medium-sized states in which the government of laws is not incompatible with the maintenance of the state; on the other hand, they are so favorable to this that without laws this state falls into decadence and becomes inferior to all the others. This is what has formed a genius for liberty, which makes it very difficult to subjugate each part and to put it under a foreign force other than by laws and by what is useful to its commerce. By contrast in Asia there reigns a spirit of servitude that has never left it, and in all the histories of this country it is not possible to find a single trait marking a free soul; one will never see there anything but the heroism of servitude.

---

[26] Similar conclusions are reached by Scheidel (2019: 316).

Leaving aside the invidious language, one may infer that when governing units are small, citizens have a better chance of solving collective action problems that underlie a democratic system of rule. This line of argument seems especially compelling in the premodern era, when transport and communications infrastructure was crude and it was logistically challenging for large groups to come together. In city-states, leading citizens could assemble in a forum, square, or hall. And in mid-sized states such as England and the Netherlands it was possible for elites to gather in one place on a semi-regular schedule without imposing undue travel burdens on the participants. This was a significant advantage for those attempting to craft representative institutions.

Another consequence of smallness is that multiple states cluster together in the same region. As such, they will jostle for power and engage in continual wars, as there is no hegemon in the region to keep the peace. This describes Europe through most of its history (Howard 2009). By contrast, in East Asia conflict was infrequent, due in no small part to the fact that there were few statelike adversaries capable of fighting a full-on war and one of them (China) was so much bigger and more powerful than its neighbors that it kept the peace. Neighbors were regarded as subordinate tributary states, not as equals or rivals (Fairbank 1968; Kang 2010). If war makes states, and states make war (Tilly 1992), it follows that the more states one has in a region, and the closer they are to geopolitical parity, the more frequent war will be, and the more it will stimulate statemaking.

It is sometimes argued that this dynamic of frequent warfare – and continual threat of war – fosters a diffusion of political power, as rulers depend upon citizens to pay for their wars and, on occasion, to sacrifice their lives to protect territory (Ferejohn, Rosenbluth 2016). In this respect, war makes rulers dependent upon the common people, or at least the monied classes (the bourgeoisie and the aristocracy).

Whatever the precise dynamic, a number of studies suggest that the diminutive size of polities in Europe was critical to the development of representative institutions.[27] More broadly, one may observe that smallness seems to have been a feature of democratic polities everywhere in the premodern world. This may help to explain why republics were common in Europe and in ancient India and unknown in China.

We embrace this general argument in Chapter 3. However, we view it as a by-product of geography, in particular of natural harbors. One is hard put to envision polity size as an exogenous distal cause, as the

---

[27] Blockmans (1978, 1994), Cox (2017), Hansen (2000: 611–12), Stasavage (2010, 2011).

borders of most states were ill-defined, porous, and in continual flux throughout the premodern era (Bartlett 1994; Watts 2009).

State–Society Relationships

Plausibly, democracy is a product of the relationship between state and society. One version of this argument rests on *sequencing*. Some writers regard state-ness – specifically, the existence of a "Weberian" state, with a defined territory and set of people who belong in it (citizens) – as a prerequisite of stable democracy.[28] Running a democracy is a complicated task – arguably, a lot more complicated than running an autocracy. In particular, it requires coordinating the demands of the great mass of citizens, who number in the thousands or millions. To do so, the state must organize elections that allow each citizen to cast a ballot under circumstances that are free and fair. State institutions must also have the capacity, and independence, to carry out tasks of economic management, criminal justice, social welfare, and defense without undue intervention from the executive or political parties (which would subvert the ideal of a level playing field). The role of an independent judiciary is especially important. All of these tasks may be regarded as components, or offshoots, of state-ness, and all presumably support the democratic ideal.

Other writers regard state-ness as an *obstacle* to democratization. Where statebuilding precedes popular mobilization it may be more difficult for democracy to establish itself, for there is a powerful and canny adversary and a political culture sanctioning centralized political authority. Bureaucratic structures, including the institution of writing (Wang 2014), once established, often endure (Crooks, Parsons 2016; Gibson, Biggs 1991). In this fashion, ancient patterns of governance may be exploited by modern dictators. China, with its early adoption of a meritocratic exam system for selection into bureaucratic service offers one example.[29] The Ottoman Empire, with its mamluk (slave) system of administration, offers another,[30] a template that may apply across the Middle East (Blaydes 2017). The argument is reminiscent of Tocqueville's (2010) view that elements of the Old Regime persisted after the French Revolution; the constitution changed (from monarchy to republic) but the highly centralized structure of power did not, he argued.

---

[28] See Fukuyama (2007), Linz, Stepan (1996: 17), Møller, Skaaning (2011: ch. 6), Rose, Shin (2001), Tilly (2007).
[29] See Balazs (1964), Bielenstein (1980), Elman (2013), Feng (2008).
[30] See Blaydes, Chaney (2013), Crone (1980), Imber (2002).

Where state formation occurs later, or is unsuccessful, societies are strong and states correspondingly weak. Accordingly, it is difficult for would-be statebuilders to achieve a thorough centralization of power. This leaves the way open for eventual democratization. Europe through the medieval and early modern eras offers one example; sub-Saharan Africa and Southeast Asia offer others.

Another version of the argument leaves questions of sequencing aside, preferring to focus on the *balance of power* between state and society at each point in time. In a recent formulation, Acemoglu and Robinson (2019: xv–xvi) argue,

for liberty to emerge and flourish, both state and society must be strong. A strong state is needed to control violence, enforce laws, and provide public services that are critical for a life in which people are empowered to make and pursue their choices. A strong, mobilized society is needed to control and shackle the strong state. Doppelgänger solutions and checks and balances don't solve the Gilgamesh problem because, without society's vigilance, constitutions and guarantees are not worth much more than the parchment they are written on. Squeezed between the fear and repression wrought by despotic states and the violence and lawlessness that emerge in their absence is a narrow corridor to liberty. It is in this corridor that the state and society balance each other out. This balance is not about a revolutionary moment. It's a constant, day-in, day-out struggle between the two. This struggle brings benefits. In the corridor the state and society do not just compete, they also cooperate. This cooperation engenders greater capacity for the state to deliver the things that society wants and foments greater societal mobilization to monitor this capacity.[31]

This model of institutional development envisions a contest between state and society. Where society predominates, or where the two are well balanced, democracy is the likely outcome. Where the state predominates, its domination is likely to continue.[32]

While sequencing and balancing models of political development are intuitively appealing, they do not translate easily into testable causal models. In particular, one is hard put to conceptualize state and society as independent causal factors. Everything we know about politics suggests that they are mutually constitutive: the structure of the state affects the structure of society, and vice versa. So, to say that one has a long-term effect on the other – or that the sequence of development between these factors has a long-term effect – is difficult to wrap one's mind around, causally.

---

[31] For a formal version of the argument see Acemoglu, Robinson (2017).

[32] See also Hui (2005), Møller (2018b), Stasavage (2020). For Hariri (2012), state strength affects democracy through the intermediary of European influence. Where states are strong they are able to resist European colonization and hegemony, and thus maintain autocratic forms of rule. He does not attribute direct causal force to state strength.

Relatedly, there is no obvious way to operationalize these concepts, especially as one moves back in time. Accordingly, it is difficult to envision what a theory based on state–society sequencing or balancing means and how it might be tested. In particular, one struggles to understand how a factor like societal strength could be measured – now or historically. What was the strength of society at the time of state formation in Mesopotamia, China, or Egypt? Likewise, the timing of state formation is an eternal question that resists precise dates. One is hard put to classify sequences, as neither element in the sequence seems amenable to binary coding.[33]

Fortunately, one side of the equation – state strength – can be measured if one adopts a non-dichotomous view of the concept. For this, we rely on the State Antiquity Index (Borcan, Olsson, Putterman 2018), which codes territories conforming to the present-day boundaries of 159 countries at regular intervals from 2900 BCE to 2000 CE. Scoring of the State history variable reflects (a) the existence of a government, (b) the proportion of the territory covered by that government, and (c) whether it was indigenous or externally imposed. Our chosen variable measures state history up to 1500, just prior to the age of European imperialism, with a 1 percent annual depreciation rate. If state histories matter, these histories should be in place prior to the modern era.[34]

In Table 14.5, we regress modern democracy against this variable in a series of tests. Model 1 includes only the regressor of theoretical interest along with year dummies. Model 2 adds several geographic covariates. Model 3 adds a variable measuring the share of contemporary populations that have a Muslim heritage.

These models show that older states are negatively associated with democracy in the modern era, as predicted. However, the relationship is not outstandingly robust. Although one may quibble over our choices of specification one must conclude that the relationship, if causal, is delicate.[35]

Ideas

We end our discussion with the most commonsensical of explanations – *ideas*. Ostensibly, political institutions are designed to promote what

---

[33] Studies that attempt to operationalize and test the impact of sequencing such as Gjerløw et al. (2022) – who look at growth – often find little support for sequencing theories.

[34] Other variables drawn from the Putterman dataset, which employ different time periods and depreciation rates, show very similar results.

[35] This does not preclude the possibility that state history may have served as a deterrent to European influence, thus affecting the diffusion of democracy in the modern era, as argued by Hariri (2012).

Table 14.5 *State history*

	1	2	3
State history, pre-1500	−10.393*	−20.560***	−7.414
	(−1.657)	(−3.503)	(−1.116)
Harbor distance		✓	✓
Equator distance		✓	✓
Muslim			✓
States	159	159	157
Years	231	231	231
Observations	26 595	26 595	26 188
R^2	0.358	0.526	0.551

Outcome: Polyarchy index of electoral democracy, augmented. *Not shown:* Year dummies, Constant. *Estimator:* ordinary least squares, standard errors clustered by state, t statistics in parentheses. ***p<.01 **p<.05 *p<.10

societies hold near and dear, their vision of the good life. Whatever standards a society regards as just should be reflected in its political institutions, and those institutions should uphold its ideals of justice. From this perspective, ideas are central to political institutions. Likewise, the spread of ideas about politics clearly affects the formation of political institutions through history. Founders and reformers look to neighboring states or to especially influential states, and they consult ideas that are current at the time. It is hard to imagine monarchy without the *idea* of monarchy, or democracy without the *idea* of democracy.

Commonly, the history of democracy is traced back to a set of ideas that were born in Greece, perpetuated by Rome, preserved by the church, rediscovered in the Renaissance, shaped by the Enlightenment and the Age of Revolution, and applied on a broad scale during the age of mass democracy. At some point in the twentieth century democracy became irresistible, a juggernaut of an ideal, sweeping everything in its path. John Dunn (2005: 14) remarks, "Within the last three-quarters of a century democracy has become the political core of the civilization which the West offers to the rest of the world."[36]

---

[36] The role of ideas features prominently in most narrative works dealing with democracy and adjacent concepts (republicanism, representation, liberty etc.). See Acton (1919), Canfora (2006), Cartledge (2016), Clayton (1911), DeWiel (2000), Dunn (1992, 2005), Eliot (1853), Gierke 1900[1881], Guizot (2002[1851]), Israel (2010, 2013), Kloppenberg (2016), Meier (2011), Miller (2018), Morgan (1989), Muller (1966), Osborne (2012), Pitkin (1967), Pocock (1975; 1980), Siedentop (2014), Sidgwick (1903), Skinner (1978), Stromberg (1996), Tuck (2016).

Despite the obviousness of the thesis, a number of difficulties arise. Most importantly, this narrative has nothing to say about the moment of discovery. Where did the idea of democracy come from?

If the idea of democracy owes its origins to another idea then the chain of ideas is never-ending and we face the philosophical problem of what it means to explain a phenomenon in a causal fashion (discussed at the end of the chapter). If the idea of democracy owes its origins to something else (other than ideas) then it is that something else that deserves to be identified as the cause.

It should be acknowledged that histories of democracy featuring the role of ideas do not usually adopt a rigorously "idealist" vision of history, one in which ideas – floating freely from material constraints – determine outcomes. The typical approach combines a history of ideas with a history of events. Accordingly, there is no identifiable treatment that one could regard as the primary cause. Histories of this sort are perhaps better classified as narrative or descriptive rather than idealist. However, it seems important to mention them here because they are commonly regarded as telling a history of ideas.

Diffusion

In our view, the idealist vision of democracy's history is more compelling as an explanation of *diffusion* than of invention.[37] But even here, difficulties arise.

If direct democracy was not unique to the Greek city-states, as we argued in Chapter 2, then Europe was not in a privileged position with respect to democratic institutions. Other parts of the world also had precedents they could turn to. Accordingly, democracy should have diffused everywhere, not just across Europe. But it did not, at least not until the modern era. The failures of diffusion must be accounted for, along with the successes.

With respect to the purported rediscovery of Aristotle – sometimes viewed as key to the reawakening of democracy in Europe in the Middle Ages and Renaissance (Hanson 1989: 71; Pocock 1975) – Stasavage (2020) points out that Aristotle's *Politics* was translated into Latin about AD 1260, by which time Italian communes were already in full bloom. So, it must have been the case that they discovered this idea on their own, or never lost it. Stasavage also points out that the legacy of Greece was

---

[37] For work on the diffusion of ideas about political institutions through history see Anderson (1991), Elkins (2010), Elkins, Simmons (2005), Lieberman (2003, 2009), Meyer, Boli, George, Ramirez (1997), Renfrew, Cherry (1986).

preserved in the Muslim world, so they presumably had examples they could draw upon.

Another note of skepticism arises from a close study of the concept of democracy. In Chapter 2, we noted that democracy has no widely recognized founding figures and no recognized canon, and that its verbal manifestations varied from place to place and time to time. Most of the time, it was a term of abuse. Accordingly, one cannot argue that the rise of democracy was owed to the popularity of the term. This does not mean that ideas were irrelevant; their semantic freight may have been carried by other terms that varied from place to place and time to time (e.g., representation, rights, the avoidance of tyranny). But it calls into question a simple story of diffusion according to which democracy is self-evidently superior to other forms of government.

In the modern era, things change. Over the course of the nineteenth and twentieth centuries, "democracy" becomes a universally valorized concept and its meaning – centered on representative bodies and elections – comes to be widely shared across the world. In this setting, diffusion by example seems plausible.

Empirical studies of diffusion in the modern era are legion, and most show a substantial correlation in regime status among countries situated in the same geographic region or sharing some characteristic (e.g., colonial history, religion, language). For the most part, these studies focus on proximal relationships, e.g., how Country A at time t is related to Country B at $t - 1$. Diffusion is rarely studied as a distal force; arguably, the concept is inappropriate to describe relationships across centuries. Consequently, we shall not attempt to conduct an empirical test of the diffusion idea.

Yet, even in the modern era the process of diffusion seems to have been structured by cultures and institutions; its spread was neither smooth nor inexorable. Witness the many countries – roughly one-third of humanity – who resist its pull, and the sizeable number of voters who embrace patently anti-democratic parties.

In short, diffusion is a very persuasive explanation for the proximal dynamics of democracy, especially in the modern age. But any distal explanation must offer an account for why democracy was adopted here, and not (or only much later) there.

Conclusions

We have now introduced a wide variety of arguments – based on economics, institutions, or culture – about the origins of democracy. Some of these hypotheses have been tested to see how well they predict regimes in the modern era. We adopt lags of at least one century to ensure we are identifying distal causal relationships.

These tests are exploratory, not definitive. We do not delve into possible interaction effects, contextual effects, or temporal effects. We do not explore potential instruments for variables that might not be entirely exogenous. Just a few specifications are offered. (More extensive tests can sometimes be found in work published elsewhere, cited in the text.) Even so, we believe that applying a standardized set of tests to alternate explanations is a useful exercise, for reasons set forth in Chapter 1.

These analyses show little evidence for economic development (prox-ied by per capita GDP) or labor scarcity (proxied by population density) as distal predictors of democracy. There is some evidence in favor of agricultural transitions, kinship intensity, and state history, though these relationships are sensitive to choices in specification and not always statistically significant (at standard thresholds).

In this final section, we pause to consider potential problems of causal inference from a more general perspective.

We begin with the challenge of measurement. Arguments centered on economics, institutions, and culture are difficult to operationalize as one moves back in time. Sometimes, it is possible to measure a limited subset of factors in a single region, especially regions like Europe and East Asia where historical records are more complete. Unfortunately, it is difficult to generalize from these results since the samples are small (meaning that results are likely to be unstable) and obviously unrepresentative. Most of the arguments vetted in this chapter have never been measured on a global scale. Some are probably too abstract to operationalize. Others are measurable only in recent years, foreclosing the possibility of testing distal effects.

Problems of measurement do not imply that an argument is wrong. But they do mean that it is, as yet, unfalsifiable (in the strong sense of the term).

Another set of concerns arise from the formal desiderata of a causal explanation. Within the potential-outcomes framework a cause is under-stood as a factor that could be altered – at least, in some imaginable thought-experiment – without affecting background factors that might serve as confounders (Holland 1986). Very abstract factors such as modernization cannot easily satisfy this desideratum. It is difficult to imagine a country that is the same on all background factors *except* its level of economic development. As such, it is difficult to conceptualize economic development as a cause. The same might be said for most of the other factors reviewed in this chapter. What does medieval France look like without feudalism? If we cannot answer this question it is doubtful whether we should regard feudalism as a cause.

Finally, one must consider interconnections that may exist among the various factors discussed in this chapter. A confusing aspect of the literature on the origins of democracy is that causal factors intermingle. Indeed, we are often hard put to assign specific arguments to specific authors in the foregoing sections as most accounts enlist multifarious causal factors – some, explicitly so.[38]

The intermingling of causal factors would not be a problem if one could distinguish which are exogenous and which are endogenous. However, authors often disagree. Some regard conflicts among states as primary, others regard them as secondary. Some regard class relations as primary, others regard them as secondary. And so forth.

Since tracking these developments through time is difficult and perhaps impossible (except in a very crude fashion), we may never know which factors came first or if there is even a common sequence. Accordingly, these factors are difficult to prize apart. We are hard put to test one against the other because they are highly correlated and (presumably) mutually constitutive.

The problem of causal regress looms large. If feudalism was stronger in Europe than elsewhere, why was this so? If towns and cities were more independent in Europe than elsewhere, why was this so? And so forth. Each potential causal factor raises further questions, and none seems to offer a secure resting point.

Hence, the same recitation of historical events – or regression analysis – is often consistent with several conflicting explanations. Problems of causal identification persist even where plausible instruments are utilized in a two-stage analysis as such analyses usually rest on assumptions that are untested and (probably) untestable.

Problems are compounded when multiple causal factors are combined into a single explanation. Brian Downing (1989: 214) declares the rise of liberal democracy in Europe to be a product of four factors: "a rough balance between crown and nobility, decentralized military systems, the preservation in some regions of Germanic tribal customs, and peasant property rights with reciprocal ties to the landlord." While plausible, there is no way the conjunction of these factors can be tested in a systematic fashion. Even if they were all measurable, one would quickly exhaust the available degrees of freedom.

---

[38] See Bendix (1978), Chirot (1985), Mitterauer (2010), Stasavage (2020).

Like Downing, many writers focus on what made Europe distinct from other regions of the world. Unfortunately, *many* factors set Europe apart, offering fodder for an extensive literature on European exceptionalism (e.g., Jones 1981; Mitterauer 2010). Virtually all of these factors are also candidates for explaining why representative democracy arose in Europe and not elsewhere, leading to a serious problem of causal inference. Anything that differentiates Europe from other regions of the world is a possible cause, and all such causes are collinear.

We do not wish to discourage scholarship on these subjects. It is possible that future research will overcome these difficulties, revealing strong empirical patterns that can be understood as causal. To this point, however, scholarship focused on the economic, institutional, and cultural origins of democracy has thrown up a great many hypotheses and few conclusive tests.

We should acknowledge that some of the problems of measurement and causal inference raised in this section are generic to macro-level historical work and thus also apply to our own arguments, set forth in Parts II and III of the book. Even so, causal factors grounded in geography and European influence are more tractable in several respects.

Geographic factors can be measured globally and usually with a fair degree of precision if historic geography can be inferred from contemporary geography. Some arguments about European influence are also measurable with a high degree of precision and comprehensiveness, as there are records of European travel and engagement in the world. (Colonial and post-colonial history was often scrupulously recorded.) Arguments based on geography and European influence are also easier to distinguish from potential confounders, as those confounders are generally measurable and are not perfectly collinear. Finally, geographic factors are exogenous, for the most part, and thus do not face the problem of infinite causal regress. European influence is certainly not exogenous. However, the diffusion of Europeans and European ideas throughout the world is a factor that can be modeled with instrumental variables that, plausibly, satisfy the requisite assumptions.

In these respects, we regard our empirical results as sturdier than distal claims about the role of economic, institutional, and cultural factors. Further discussion of these vexing issues is offered in the next chapter, which begins with a summary and review of the evidence.

V

Conclusions

Centuries after the arrival of the world's first mass democracy (the United States), and millennia after the invention of the concept of democracy (commonly credited to ancient Greece), the world is still divided. Ultra-democracies like Estonia and Costa Rica coexist with autocracies like Saudi Arabia. Sometimes, as in the case of South and North Korea, they are neighbors.

By some measures, this age-old division is deeper than ever before.

In the premodern era, politics in large states assumed some form of "high politics," a rarefied sphere where ordinary citizens had little voice. In this respect, there was not much difference between England (arguably, the most democratic state) and China (one of the least democratic). Additionally, central governments did not have very much power over people's lives. They simply did not have the tools – fiscal, military, bureaucratic, technological – to intervene. Nor did they have the ambition to do so. Thus, for those living in the countryside – which is to say, for the great mass of humanity – governments were a distant force, to be reckoned with only rarely, and usually through intermediaries. Everyday life had much more to do with local structures of power.

In the contemporary era, by contrast, national governments intervene in virtually every aspect of our lives. They have the capacity to do great good and great evil. One of the greatest die-outs in recorded history occurred at the behest of the Chinese government, who – following Mao's instructions – instituted the radically flawed program known as the Great Leap Forward (Thaxton 2008). In the ensuing years, an estimated 36 million people died of famine, disease, and other avoidable hardships (Yang 2012: 430). It is no accident that the Chinese government was autocratic. Amartya Sen (1994) reckons that no democratic country has succumbed to famine in the modern era.[1]

The divergence between democracies and autocracies is increasing in other ways, as well.

In democracies, the Internet has opened up new vehicles of citizen expression and accountability (though also of polarization). In autocracies, by contrast, these new media are often suppressed, manipulated, or used for surveillance.[2] The arrival of advanced information technology means that governments can enlist cameras fitted with facial recognition technology, computerized records that include all facets of an individual's life from cradle to grave, relatively comprehensive social networks that can track citizens' relationship to family, friends, acquaintances, and co-workers, and techniques to mold public opinion that are more subtle, and by most accounts more effective, than ever before.[3]

The prospect of totalitarian rule along lines envisioned decades ago by George Orwell now seems quite real, technologically speaking. And since autocracies have every incentive to secure their hold by deploying these new technologies, a country's regime type may become even more consequential in the coming years, as more autocrats study China's example and invest in mechanized surveillance and control.

To be sure, the long-term trend over the past two centuries has been toward greater democracy (Coppedge, Gerring, Glynn et al. 2020). If this trend continues it will culminate in convergence at the democratic end of the spectrum. Unfortunately, recent trends are not encouraging. Over the past two decades, many democracies have slipped back in an authoritarian direction (Lührmann et al. 2019). As we progress through the twenty-first century the regime question remains as important, and mysterious, as ever.

In this final section of the book we summarize the evidence presented in Parts II and III (Chapter 15) and then offer a theoretical synthesis that attempts to tie together the many strands of our arguments (Chapter 16).

---

[1] We do not mean to imply that democracies always produce better outcomes for their citizens. In some instances, regime type appears not to have much impact on governance, and along a few dimensions autocratic forms of government may be superior. But, on balance, democracy seems to bring more favorable outcomes than autocracy (Gerring, Knutsen 2022).

[2] See Gunitsky (2015), Tucker et al. (2017), Wilson (2017).

[3] See Dukalskis (2017), Feldstein (2019), Guriev, Treisman (2019), Kendall-Taylor, Frantz, Wright (2020).

15   A Summary View

In this book, we have put forth a concise argument about long-run forces affecting regime types in the modern era.

Part II centers on coastal geography. We argue that by virtue of enhancing connections to the wider world natural harbors fostered economic development, naval power, small states, and openness. Through these pathways, operative over centuries, geography placed its imprint on political institutions. As a consequence, areas blessed with natural harbors were more likely to develop democratic forms of government in the modern era.

Part III centers on the long-run impact of European-led globalization. Beginning about 1500, with the advent of sailing vessels capable of circumnavigating the globe, Europeans began to populate the distant abroad. We argue that the resulting ratio of Europeans to non-Europeans structured the fate of democracy around the world. Where Europeans were numerous they established some form of representative democracy, though often with restrictions limiting suffrage or officeholding to those of European heritage. Where they were in the minority they were more reticent about popular rule and often actively resisted democratization. And where Europeans were entirely absent, the concept of representative democracy was unfamiliar and the practice undeveloped.

These two arguments are intimately conjoined. Natural harbors have a direct effect on democracy as well as an indirect effect, through the European diaspora. The implicit causal diagram is illustrated in Figure 1.1.

We begin this chapter by reviewing evidence presented in preceding chapters. Next, we discuss an issue that has been lurking on the back burner: the extent to which our arguments might be considered "deterministic."

The Evidence Reviewed

Any attempt to piece together distal, macro-level causal relationships extending across the world over several centuries encounters a good deal of ambiguity.

To begin with, there is the problem of ascertaining causal mechanisms. Although the nodes in Figure 1.1 are specific, measurable, and testable, the arrows connecting these nodes are quite complex. We have done our best to identify the most plausible mechanisms in Chapters 3 and 8. But, try as we might, we are unable to integrate these multifarious mechanisms into a parsimonious model. History, in this case, seems quite complex, and we are loath to ignore this complexity in the interest of theoretical reduction. Doing so would obscure much of the action, making the arguments clearer and simpler but also less tenable.

Because these mechanisms are multiple, and often difficult to disentangle or to measure, we cannot make confident assessments about which factors are carrying what portion of the causal weight. We do our best to test mechanisms associated with natural harbors in Chapter 7, but these tests are subject to quite a few caveats. Accordingly, most of our attention in previous chapters centers on inputs and outputs rather than on mechanisms.

With respect to the main causal effects it must be admitted that they are neither precise nor "well identified" by standards set by randomized control trials. Error is expected. One can hope that it is randomly distributed (nonsystematic), or, if systematic, that it is not great enough to alter our substantive conclusions. This hope rests on assumptions that are not easily tested. As such, some readers may conclude that the attempt to understand the deep roots of democracy is a doomed enterprise.

Yet, for any research question that has important ramifications for society the relevant methodological standard must be a relative one – relative to the state of current research and the evidence that is available (Gerring 2011). Can we advance current understandings of a question? Can we get a few paces closer to the truth? These are the important questions.

Having presented an array of evidence for our claims about harbors and European ancestry in preceding chapters, it is time to take stock.

Qualitative evidence is drawn from the historical literature, arrayed in a most-similar design framework. In Chapter 5, we compared polities within and across various regions of the world: Europe, North Eurasia, MENA, sub-Saharan Africa, East Asia, Southeast Asia, and South Asia. In Chapter 10, we compared the colonial and post-colonial histories of states within the English, French, Spanish, and Portuguese empires. These are dense and lengthy chapters so we will not attempt to regurgitate the evidence.

Quantitative evidence on a global scale is enlisted in Chapters 6 and 11.[1] This involved the collection of original data across a period of nearly two and a half centuries – four centuries in the case of European ancestry – allowing for a historical view of the relationships of theoretical interest. Both formally sovereign states and semisovereign colonies and dependencies are included, along with micro-states and now-defunct states. This inclusive approach to data collection generates a sample with 218 state-level units, offering considerable empirical leverage on our questions. It is more of a census than a sample, mitigating the problem of inference from sample to population.

Our geographic theory about harbors and democracy is tested at the grid-cell level and the state level, while our theory about European ancestry is tested only at the state level since we do not have finely grained locational measures of where Europeans settled. For both theories, we utilize a wide array of specifications and employ multiple measures of key predictors and outcomes (indicators of democracy). Most analyses are cross-sectionally dominated – though for European ancestry, which changes over time, we also employ time-series models with state fixed effects.

Instrumental variables attempt to model assignment to treatment. Although any choice of instruments may be questioned, it is reassuring that results are stable across a variety of possible instruments. (It seems unlikely that *all* of these instruments fail the exclusion restriction.)

We also test for causal heterogeneity across regions and periods. We find that although the impact of natural harbors and European ancestry increases in a fairly monotonic fashion through most of the modern era, there is a noticeable reversal at the very end of the period, suggesting that the influence of these factors may have peaked in the late twentieth century (see Figures 6.3 and 11.2). Time will tell.

We are acutely aware that geographic features often cluster together. Where there are natural harbors there may be other features that also affect the development of political institutions. Unless identified, these factors serve as unmeasured confounders. Reassuringly, tests show that natural harbors are not strongly correlated with widely used measures of climate, soil, location, and topography that might explain long-run economic and institutional development (see Table 12.1). Consequently, the addition of these controls – singly or together – has little effect on estimates for harbor distance (Tables 6.2–6.3). We also address the problem of spatial correlation by assessing the consistency of our results

---

[1] The rise of parliaments within premodern Europe is analyzed quantitatively in Chapter 5, but this analysis cannot be extended to other parts of the world.

across different spatial units including countries and a range of differently sized grid-cells. Our results remain robust across these various tests.

With respect to the influence of Europe on the world, we worried about the same possibility: that factors such as colonialism, religion, and language would correlate. That is why we spend a good deal of time trying to measure and test these alternate pathways from Europe (Chapter 13). As it happens, these factors are not highly correlated and their inclusion in the same specification scarcely attenuates the impact of European ancestry (Table 13.5).

Amidst all these empirical tests we want to highlight a persistent feature: benchmark models generally show weaker estimates than robustness tests. In Chapter 6 the benchmark model shows weaker estimates for harbor distance than additional tests with different specifications (Tables 6.2–6.3), alternate measures of harbor distance (Table 6.4), alternate measures of democracy (Table 6.5), and different samples (Table 6.6). In Chapter 11, the benchmark model generally shows weaker estimates for European ancestry than additional tests with different specifications (Table 11.1), alternate measures of democracy (Table 11.2), alternate measures and temporal configurations of European ancestry (Table 11.3), and instrumental variables (Table 11.6). In light of this, we regard estimates from benchmark models as a *conservative* estimate of the true causal effect.

We conclude that natural harbors and European demography, considered together, explain a good deal of the variability in regime type in the modern era. That said, many other distal factors also come into play, along with innumerable proximal factors, as discussed in Part IV of the book. A two-factor theory cannot be regarded as a complete explanation of a phenomenon as complex as democracy – a point we address in the next section.

Determinism?

While most work on democracy focuses on proximal causes, this book examines the distal forces behind contemporary outcomes. We are, in effect, privileging the static or sluggish causes of democracy over the dynamic causes. That means that we are explaining why some polities are democratic and others autocratic, rather than how polities *become* democratic or autocratic at specific points in time.

In these respects, we are bucking established practice in social science, which tends to focus on causes and effects that change quickly and whose causal connection to an outcome is proximal (Pierson 2011). It also generates an impression that we are putting forth a "deterministic" vision of world history. To answer this charge we must inquire: what, exactly, is determinism? And why is it so unpopular?

Against Free Will?

According to one interpretation, determinism refers to a causal argument in which the causal factor of theoretical interest is exogenous (unaffected by other factors) and explains a high portion (perhaps even *all*) of the variance in an outcome. In set-theoretic terms, such a cause is necessary and sufficient.

This, of course, is what any causal theory aims to achieve. To the extent that it succeeds, we can say that a causal model is triumphant. It fully explains the phenomena. From this perspective, determinism is the goal of all scientific ventures.

At the same time, the idea of a fully determined outcome seems objectionable if the outcome in question is human action. If our behavior is determined by forces beyond our control this would seem to contradict a defining characteristic of our species, namely, free will.[2]

In our context, the juxtaposition of determinism and democracy is especially jarring. Why would a book on democracy – a system where people govern themselves – focus on deep-rooted structural factors like geography and demography that individuals have little control over (leaving little room for agency)? Is freedom produced by processes outside of human control?

To a certain degree, we argue that the answer is, *yes*. Environments shape the space for agency. Opportunities to exercise democratic rights are not randomly distributed throughout the world. By virtue of being born in a particular place, at a particular time, and by virtue of having certain ascriptive characteristics, one was more or less likely to enjoy political rights. That is the deterministic part of our story. However, it is not the whole story.

Fortunately – for fans of free will – social science theories are never entirely successful. Even natural science theories require certain assumptions (e.g., the absence of friction) to achieve necessary and sufficient causal effects, assumptions that are rarely attained in the real world. In social science, the caveats multiply. We speak of "variation explained" and "ceteris paribus" conditions, acknowledging that other

---

[2] It should be noted that many conceptualizations of free will are fully compatible with causal determinism (e.g., Dennett 2015), a category of views known as "free-will compatibilism".

factors – including "stochastic" factors that cannot be measured or modeled – are at work.

To our knowledge, the fields of economics, political science, sociology, and their allied subfields have never identified a causal relationship that is fully explained by one cause. There ain't no such thing. Social science is focused on decisional behavior under uncertainty in complex systems. Our theoretical framework is no exception.

A Failed Theory?

This brings us to another meaning of "determinism," which is sometimes used in a pejorative sense for a theory that aims high but does not deliver. It explains little of the variance in the outcome it purports to explain or the claimed scope-conditions are overly broad, neglecting heterogeneity in the relationship of interest. Here, determinism is a marker for theories that are insufficiently nuanced, bordering on the naïve. A deterministic theory in this sense is a *failed* theory. It doesn't determine anything, or not as much as is claimed by the author.

We have tried to lay out clear scope-conditions for our theorizing. While littoral geography may have some causal ramifications for the premodern world (Chapter 5), this impact increased over time – in tandem with the growth of seaborne travel and transport – reaching full blossom in the twentieth century (Figure 6.3). European ancestry is a product of the age of globalization and thus has no relevance for the premodern era. It also reaches an apogee in the late twentieth century (Figure 11.2). Both factors appear to attenuate at the turn of the twenty-first century. Our framework is, ultimately, a historical framework not a universal framework, and we have endeavored to carefully define its temporal boundaries.

Even for the claimed time period (1789 to the present), let us state clearly that however successful our arguments about geography and globalization might be they cannot explain more than about a third of the variability in regime types across the modern world. (This is what the model-fit statistics suggest from a simple cross-sectional model centered on 2000.) There is a lot of room for proximal causes, not to mention other distal causes. No state is preordained to adopt a particular regime or to maintain it indefinitely. Regime change is "on the table" for all countries, now and probably forever. Countries that currently score high on global indices may slide back. And countries that currently score low may improve.

So, as much as we have aimed for a complete explanation we have surely not succeeded. The nature of the problem suggests that no parsimonious theory will ever explain all of the variability in regime types.

Prospects for democracy are probably affected – at least marginally – by everything going on in a society, now and at previous points in history. If so, there are an infinite number of causes and no explanation can hope for comprehensiveness.

Humility is in order for those of us in the business of explaining macro-level social phenomena. There are surely aspects of our argument that are frustratingly opaque, or just plain wrong. We trust that future research will refine our theoretical framework, establishing clearer scope-conditions, revising our provisional view of the causal mechanisms, and offering greater precision about the treatments. This is a fast-moving frontier, as social scientists have only recently begun to take an interest in the distant past.

Does It Matter?

"Determinism" can refer, finally, to a misguided focus on structure when we should instead be focused on contingency. After all, contingency is what we can change. And if we want to make the world a better place it would seem that this is where we ought to concentrate our energy. At worst, an obsessive focus on structure deprives actors of their sense of agency, fostering what existentialists call "bad faith" (Sartre 2001). Determinism, in this view, inculcates fatalism.

Our focus on deep causes means that no obvious policy recommendations flow from this book. In this respect, our work is less useful than work focused on proximal causes such as electoral systems, foreign aid, and constitutional structures that are in our power to alter.

However, a structural perspective is sometimes essential for *evaluating* proximal factors. Consider the following questions of institutional reform. What impact (if any) would a shift from presidentialism to parliamentarism have on prospects for democratization or democratic consolidation? What sort of electoral system is most propitious for democracy in an ethnically divided society? Is it possible to enhance the independence of the judiciary by offering terms of service with extended tenure? Does an investment in secondary education enhance the stability of democracy? Does the provision of public finance for election campaigns generate a more competitive playing field?

These questions are not amenable to randomized control trials (RCTs) – at least, not at national levels, and subnational RCTs are difficult to generalize from if the object of interest lies at national levels. Natural experiments that might provide as-if randomization are exceedingly rare, and usually require strong assumptions about the data-generating process.

Consequently, scholars evaluate these questions by recourse to what-ever observational data is available. Whether the analysis is qualitative (e.g., most-similar) or quantitative (e.g., crossnational regression), this sort of causal inference presupposes lots of things about background causes – causes that, if not adequately measured and controlled, are apt to confound the analysis. For example, in comparing the possible impact of presidential and parliamentary systems on democracy we need to know about any background factors that might serve as confounders – affecting both the treatment of theoretical interest (parliamentarism/presidentialism) and the outcome (democracy).

We never know for sure what these confounders might be. Hence, the usual approach is to measure and condition on all factors that are known to affect the outcome and are upstream from the predictor of theoretical interest. Natural harbors and European ancestry are two such factors. Consequently, any (non-fixed effect) analysis that does not control for these factors is subject to a potentially serious problem of bias. Reported results may be entirely spurious. In this very practical sense, an understanding of structural causes enhances our ability to evaluate proximal causes.

More generally, we trust that our attention to structure will not divert attention from aspects of the world that are within our capacity to change. Indeed, it is our hope that by paying attention to structural features impinging upon regimes in the modern era this book will help identify those institutions that are reformable. Note that agency is a largely residual concept; it is what general causal factors *cannot* explain. So, in studying the structural – "deterministic" – aspects of politics we are also shedding light on what is in flux.

16   Connectedness

> Travel is fatal to prejudice, bigotry, and narrow-mindedness, and many of our people need it sorely on these accounts. Broad, wholesome, charitable views of men and things cannot be acquired by vegetating in one little corner of the earth all one's lifetime.   Mark Twain (2007 [1869])

The roles of natural harbors and European-led globalization are of more than historical interest, as they continue to influence the course of regimes in the twenty-first century. However, they are also part of a larger story extending forward and backward in time, which we label *connectedness* (or connectivity).

The connectedness of a society refers to the ease with which people, goods, capital, and ideas pass back and forth between that society and the rest of the world. A connected area has a high pass-through rate; an isolated area is largely self-contained.[1]

Connectedness is an abstract feature of human societies that is contingently determined by physical geography. It is also a product of transport and communications technologies, which have served to enhance connectedness through every epoch of human history, with accelerating effects in the modern era.

In this final chapter we consider the possible impact of connectedness on democracy.[2] Our treatment will be schematic, as befits an epilogue. While some empirical material is presented it is offered by way of illustration rather than proof. Our goal is to introduce a rather new idea in a synoptic fashion in the hopes that others (perhaps, we ourselves) will pick up the thread at a later date in a more systematic fashion. This chapter is more like a beginning than an ending.

---

[1] In the case of a grid-cell, connectedness refers to other regions of the state as well as other states. In the case of a state, connectedness refers to other states or to interconnectedness *within* the state.

[2] Wide-ranging studies of human evolution (McNeill, McNeill 2003), globalization (Rosenberg 2012), openness (Norberg 2020), and the diffusion of democracy (Schwartzman 1998) echo some of the themes raised in this chapter.

Much of what we have to say fits within the rubric of *diffusion*.[3] However, rather than simply pointing to the fact that ideas and institutions spread we hope to understand the reasons why they spread more quickly at certain historical moments and why some areas are more susceptible to diffusion than others. And, in contrast to most work on diffusion, our focus is on long-term patterns rather than period-to-period change. Connectedness signals a *distal* causal relationship.

The Changing Relevance of Connectedness

Once upon a time, remoteness may have served the cause of democracy. This claim is often made about mountainous areas such as the famous cantons of Switzerland, discussed in Chapter 12. In the premodern era, prior to the development of advanced military and infrastructure technology, mountains offered zones of relative independence, meaning that small communities could govern themselves in relative safety from external threats. Whether the threat came from a local hegemon, marauding nomads, or an expanding empire, interlopers had trouble projecting power into the highlands. For much of human history, James Scott (1998) observes, states couldn't climb hills. In the contemporary era, despite advanced transport technology, mountainous areas remain harder to reach than lowland areas. Accordingly, the association between mountains and regimes should offer a glimpse into the relationship between connectedness and democracy as it has evolved over time.

To explore this theme, we regress democracy on mountainous terrain (the geographic share of each polity classified as mountainous) along with region dummies in a thirty-year moving window from 1789 to 2019. The coefficients from these rolling regressions are graphed in Figure 16.1. They show that in the eighteenth and early nineteenth centuries there was little correlation between mountainous zones and regime type. By the mid-nineteenth century, however, this was starting to change and by the end of the twentieth century mountainous areas were considerably less likely to possess democratic institutions than areas located on flat terrain.

This simple exercise is not intended to estimate a precise causal relationship.[4] Our purpose, rather, is to explore *changes* in the mountains/democracy relationship. Note that estimates in the early part of the modern era lie outside the confidence intervals of estimates from the

---

[3] See Coppedge, Denison, Friesen, Tiscornia (2022), Elkins (2010), Elkins, Simmons (2005).

[4] Previous tests shown in Table 12.2 indicate that the relationship between mountains and democracy is contingent upon choices in specification.

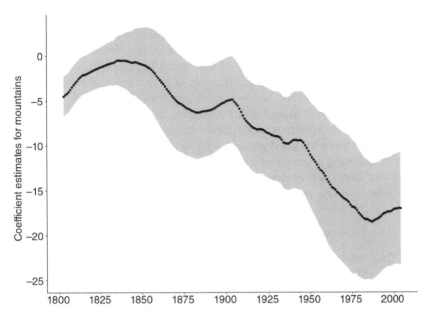

Figure 16.1 **Mountains and democracy through the modern era**
Rolling regressions in which the Polyarchy index of electoral democracy
(augmented) is regressed against mountainous terrain (percent of a
state's territory characterized as mountainous) and region dummies in a
moving 30-year window from 1789 to 2019. Estimated coefficients,
flanked by 95% confidence intervals, are graphed for the midpoint of
each 30-year window.

latter part of the era. Mountains become more negatively associated with
democracy as the modern era progresses. This finding dovetails with the
major arguments of the book, which might also be viewed as examples
of connectedness.

In Part II we discussed the role of oceans as mediums of transport and
communication, which enhanced the connectedness of areas blessed
with natural harbors. Due to developments in shipping, the world was
interconnected for the first time around 1500. As time went on, those
areas with greater access to the ocean were more likely to develop
democratic systems of rule (see Figure 6.3).

In Part III, we chronicled the European diaspora. Employing the latest
developments in maritime technology, European migrants traveled the
oceans, settling the world (in varying proportions), and serving as connecting points between cultures. By diffusing technology, fostering

infrastructure and education, and imposing European languages (which began to function as international languages), they also promoted greater connectedness in the modern world (Parker 2010). While there is much to decry in the brutal process of European imperialism, one positive result seems to have been the diffusion of representative institutions, a trend culminating in the late twentieth century (Figure 11.2).

Whether we look at mountains, harbors, or Europeans the impact of connectedness on democracy appears to have increased over time. We shall argue there are good reasons for this increasingly tight relationship. In the following sections we explore four general factors: (a) the obsolescence of direct democracy, (b) economic development, (c) the search for political equality, and (d) the scope of conflict.

The Obsolescence of Direct Democracy

In the premodern era, isolated regions were well suited for direct democracy. Most communities were very small, so leading members could assemble in one place to deliberate on matters of importance. Being small, and located in sparsely populated territories, exit was a viable option for groups unhappy with their treatment or their status. Since accumulation of wealth and power in a state depended upon human capital – which was scarce in the premodern era – leaders had strong incentives to canvass widely for support and to establish cooperative systems of decisionmaking, lest they lose their constituents.

In this light, we should not be surprised if isolated communities were more democratic than neighboring empires in the premodern era. Anecdotally, one might contrast the Roman Empire with the Germanic tribes at its fringes, the Chinese Empire with tribal groups at its periphery, or the Mughal Empire with the tribal villages located in hilly regions along its edges. In each case, systems of governance in isolated regions on the periphery were probably more democratic than those in the core region. One explanation is that small communities on the periphery were able to incorporate a good deal of citizen input, a feat impossible to replicate on an imperial scale.

In the modern era, direct democracy is difficult to sustain. The size of human populations has grown, making it impractical for citizens to assemble in one place, to deliberate, and to reach consensus – even within a single city (Gerring, Veenendaal 2020: ch. 7; Ladner 2002). Of course, one could diffuse political authority to ever smaller units, e.g., to neighborhoods within cities. However, these communities would not be sovereign in any meaningful sense. (What matters of importance would a neighborhood be able to resolve?)

The growth of global markets and the extraordinary mobility of capital make it difficult to raise revenue and legislate at local levels. Neighborhoods cannot establish their own fuel efficiency standards, corporate tax rates, labor standards, or immigration law – much less, their own foreign policy.

If globalization and modernization attenuate the feasibility of direct democracy, we should not expect isolation to foster democracy in the contemporary era. A community nestled in a remote valley of Afghanistan may be governed by consultative bodies; but the community's loss of political and economic autonomy means that democratic decisionmaking at local levels doesn't matter as much as it used to. And the isolation of each community from other communities within Afghanistan makes it extremely difficult to operate a nation-state on *representative* democratic principles. For that, greater connectivity is required.

Economic Development

In a world with global markets, connectivity drives prosperity. Territories that are well connected to the world are primed for economic development. Isolated territories are hard put to attract technology, capital, and human capital, and they have immense difficulty bringing their goods to market.

Connectivity probably mattered to economic development in the premodern era (Bakker et al. 2020), and it certainly matters in the modern era (Pascali 2017; Redding, Venables 2004). The further globalization proceeds, the more important connectivity becomes to economic success. The ingredients of economic growth tend to flow to the most connected areas, generating highly productive regions that spur further development. Isolated areas tend to fall further and further behind. This is one reason for the growing dislocation between urban and rural settings around the world.

In Chapter 14, we reviewed the proximal relationship between economic development (proxied by per capita GDP) and democracy, which is generally considered to be positive – at least in the modern era. If connectivity fosters economic development, it follows that it should have secondary effects on regimes.

The case becomes even more persuasive when one considers the type of economic development generated in areas with high connectivity. Connected regions tend to develop economies grounded in trade (Feyrer 2019), a sector often viewed as "progressive" relative to industries producing for a primarily domestic market. Industries that depend upon trade have an incentive to promote the mobility of capital, goods, and labor – and, in a more general sense, to foster closer ties with the world. Accordingly, traders tend to be cosmopolitan in orientation. Typically, the cause of free trade is linked to liberal parties and liberal causes (e.g., free speech, civil liberty, antislavery, anti-imperialism), a pattern that stretches back to the nineteenth century, and perhaps beyond.[5] In these respects, we can expect those who profit from trade to be supportive of democratic norms.

Granted, attempts to demonstrate a causal connection between trade and democracy are not always successful. However, most studies, whether focused on medieval Europe or the contemporary world, suggest a positive relationship.[6] We suspect that the impact of openness on democracy builds over time as global economic ties mature. Proximal correlations (from year to year or even decade to decade) may be driven by short-term adjustments – which in the case of globalization might be turbulent and dislocating. Longer-term trends should be more robust.

The Search for Equality

Having discussed the economic ramifications of connectedness, we turn to mechanisms of a sociological nature. Over the course of recorded history, invidious distinctions based on ascriptive characteristics (gender, race, ethnicity, caste, religion) served to limit participation in politics. In the modern era, many of the formal barriers have lifted. However, informal barriers remain in varying degrees. The development of democracy is thus linked historically, and in the present and future, to the search for political equality (Hanagan, Tilly 1999). In this section, we consider how this search may be related to a region's isolation or connectedness.

Premodern patterns of interaction were largely local, though elites usually enjoyed a somewhat wider ambit (Crone 1989). For centuries, European elites interacted with each other – intermarrying, vacationing, educating, engaging in wars and diplomacy, and distinguishing themselves from peasants and other riffraff, whose geographic purview was restricted (de facto and sometimes de jure). For millennia, similar patterns of interaction occurred on the South Asian continent, leading to an even more rigid system of caste hierarchy. In both settings, clergy,

---

[5] See Gerring (1998), Macdonagh (1962), Palen (2015, 2016).

[6] See, e.g., López-Córdova, Meissner (2008). A few studies find a weak, or null, relationship (e.g., Milner, Mukherjee 2009). In one of the more comprehensive studies of this question the authors report a bidirectional relationship between democracy and globalization (Eichengreen, Leblang 2008).

warriors, and landowners interacted on a fairly regular basis, while lower classes and castes were tied to the land where they were born.

We surmise that where there is limited trans-local communication, and where that communication is monopolized by elites, this is likely to entrench invidious vertical distinctions, e.g., between aristocrats and commoners, between different castes, or between rich and poor. Those in the privileged group are likely to feel that they have more in common with each other than with those in less privileged situations living in their midst.

Isolated groups are weak, almost by definition. They have fewer economic and political resources, little human capital, and are often socially fragmented. Thus circumscribed, there may be little they can do to enhance their power and status. Nor is it clear where they would come upon the idea that they have legitimate rights beyond those enshrined by custom. Tradition is all-encompassing if there are no alternatives in sight.

If patterns of interaction are larger in ambit and involve more than elites, these distinctions may break down in the face of the immense diversities – of religion, dress, language, cuisine, family structure, comportment – that characterize peoples around the world. When interconnected, a single system of hierarchy is confronted with multiple hierarchies, which crosscut each other in strange and unpredictable ways. Local patterns are robbed of their naturalness and lose any sense of determinacy. The "constructed" nature of society becomes apparent, or at least more apparent than it would otherwise be. There are options.

Exposure to the wider world reveals that in some societies slaves have gained their freedom, women have achieved great heights, and people from modest backgrounds have risen to positions of wealth and authority. Awareness of these examples may instill a sense of possibility and hope.[7]

It also serves as a battering ram against discrimination. If people like you enjoy rights over there, why not here? Accordingly, challenges to political inequality often come from, or are inspired by, what is going on elsewhere.

It is not only the downtrodden whose perceptions are affected by contact with the wider world. Foreign travel, whether by elites or non-elites, seems likely to promote a broader vision of oneself and one's place in the world, as suggested by Mark Twain in the epigraph to this chapter.

---

[7] In this vein, a survey experiment situated in several impoverished South African townships finds that informing participants about inequality in other countries leads to a sizeable drop in those characterizing inequality in South Africa as "inevitable" and an increase in support for government-led redistribution (Pellicer, Piraino, Wegner 2019).

This sort of moral transformation may be glimpsed in the rise of transcendental world religions such as Buddhism, Christianity, and Islam, whose founders and early proselytizers were usually traders or itinerant preachers. In the case of Judaism, the origin of the religion is associated with exile and subsequent diaspora, which made Jews a stateless and effectively itinerant people. The experience of venturing far from home is replicated in many religions by ritual pilgrimages and proselytizing missions, animating the metaphor of spiritual discovery as a voyage. The effect of this journey may be broadening across many dimensions (Clingingsmith, Khwaja, Kremer 2009).

Contact with the outside world may also assume a secular form. The well-worn genre of the travel narrative traces back to Herodotus in the ancient era, Marco Polo and Ibn Battuta in the late medieval era, Christopher Columbus in the early modern era, and Captain James Cook, Alexis de Tocqueville, Alexander von Humboldt, and Charles Darwin in the modern era (Adams 1988). Sankar Muthu (2003: 270) notes that "travel narratives played a central role in contemplating what it might mean to be, in some fundamental sense, a human being." Although scholarship often focuses on derogatory stereotypes and misperceptions arising from these foreign encounters one must also consider the role of the exotic in changing the way people thought of themselves and others in their midst. Amidst racism and orientalism, there was a genuine attempt to understand (Osterhammel 2018). Some contemporary research, including both observational and experimental evidence, suggests that foreign travel leads to greater generalized trust (Cao et al. 2014).

A third factor pushing diverse people into contact with one another is the perennial search to expand control over foreign lands. The concept of imperialism is defined by invidious hierarchies separating ruling classes in the metropole from subject classes inhabiting the periphery. However, empires also aspire to world dominion. Like world religions, they seek to embrace all peoples. As such, empires set in motion antithetical impulses – toward distinction but also equality, toward nationalism but also cosmopolitanism.[8]

In the case of European imperialism, contact with indigenous people outside Europe stimulated a good deal of racial theorizing. Initially, Europeans were apostles of inequality. At the same time, European imperialism stimulated a broader view of the human race, beginning with the writings of the sixteenth-century Spanish missionary, Bartolomé de

---

[8] These themes are explored in recent work on imperial history, e.g., Bang, Kolodziejczyk (2012), Burbank, Cooper (2010), Chua (2009), Lavan, Payne, Weisweiler (2016).

las Casas (Clayton, Lantigua 2020), and extending through Diderot, Kant, and other writers of the European Enlightenment.[9]

Arguably, there is a fit between the scope of an empire and the scope of its ideals. In this light, it is no coincidence that the most extensive European empire (the British) was also the most cosmopolitan. Land empires, with a more restricted scope and more homogeneous membership, such as the Egyptian, Chinese, Persian, Mughal, and Russian empires, tended to be more parochial.

One might look, finally, at the proponents of equality and democracy. Those at the forefront of these various movements often led lives that transcended their natal land. As exemplars, one might cite Diogenes, Seneca, Simon de Montfort, Erasmus, Jean-Jacques Rousseau, Mary Wollstonecraft, Jean-Paul Marat, Thomas Paine, Alexander Hamilton, Thomas Jefferson, Marquis de Lafayette, Simón Bolívar, William Duane, Alexis de Tocqueville, Giuseppe Mazzini, Giuseppe Garibaldi, Richard Cobden, Adam Mickiewitz, James Mill, John Stuart Mill, Lajos Kossuth, Alexander Herzen, Peter Kropotkin, Karl Marx, Sun Yat-Sen, Rabindranath Tagore, B. R. Ambekdar, Mohandas Gandhi, and Albert Einstein. All of these visionaries traveled or lived abroad for critical periods – or, in the case of the Mills, served as administrators in the East India Company (Zastoupil 1988). Many regarded themselves as citizens of the world. These cosmopolitan experiences presumably motivated their thinking about the rights of ordinary people and their capacity to fulfill the obligations of citizenship.[10]

In Part III of this book we saw how democracy was used as a mechanism of exclusion – a system of government by Europeans and for Europeans. However, over the longer term we saw how institutions of incomplete democracy served as the foundation for later democratic developments – extensions of the franchise, a liberalization of restrictions on who could stand for election, and the increasing preeminence of elective over nonelective positions. Little by little, exclusive democracies became inclusive democracies.

Winning this fight, and achieving a more fulsome democracy, was not just a matter of force against force. It was also a battle of ideas. And that battle was won by those who saw democracy in an inclusive fashion. Europeans with jaundiced views of the capacities of non-Europeans changed their views. And this transformation of perspectives grew

---

[9] See Jacob (2006), Muthu (2003), O'Brien (1997), Schlereth (1977), Scrivener (2015).

[10] Of course, we don't mean to suggest that their views were enlightened by today's standards; but they were surely enlightened by the standards of their day.

directly out of the global encounter. As such, it offers a good example of cosmopolitan ideals emerging from interconnections among diverse peoples.

In these respects, one might think of democracy as the product of an encompassing vision of humanity. As that vision takes in more of the world, becoming more heterogeneous (racially, ethnically, religiously, linguistically), it is harder to sustain invidious distinctions. Despite our differences, or perhaps because of them (what other species contains such diversity?), there is something that we share, qua humans, that endows each of us with equal moral value.

Some have argued that global contact is the foundation of our understanding of humanity (Abulafia 2008), of global justice (Singer 1981), and of human cooperation (Buchan et al. 2009; 2012). If so, it is not much of a stretch to imagine that cosmopolitan experiences might also foster greater support for the ideal of democracy. Of course, democracy, as currently constituted, is based on national rather than international identity. But the idea that every person – regardless of race, religion, sex, education, property, or condition of servitude – is deserving of political power and capable of exercising it is surely a cosmopolitan vision.[11]

The Scope of Conflict

Years ago, E. E. Schattschneider (1960) proposed that politics follows a dynamic of expansion or containment. He explains,

Every fight consists of two parts: (1) the few individuals who are actively engaged at the centre and (2) the audience that is irresistibly attracted to the scene. The spectators are as much a part of the over-all situation as are the overt combatants. The spectators are an integral part of the situation, for, as likely as not, the audience determines the outcome of the fight. The crowd is loaded with portentousness because it is apt to be a hundred times as large as the fighting minority, and the relations of the audience and the combatants are highly unstable. (Schattschneider 1960: 2)

The weaker party in any local conflict has an incentive to broaden the scope of conflict for it is only in this fashion that it has any hope of emerging victorious. Losers therefore usually try to engage onlookers; it is your fight too, they say. With a larger number of players, the balance of power is less predictable, and losers may form a winning coalition.

---

[11] For further thoughts on the interplay between democracy and cosmopolitanism see Benhabib (2009).

Whether the scope of conflict remains contained, or expands, is thus a key ingredient of politics (Brown 2002).[12]

In a highly connected community, the whole world is watching (as the phrase goes). Accordingly, losers have many opportunities to appeal to onlookers. Local struggles may be regionalized, regional struggles may be nationalized, and national struggles may be internationalized.

Consider the struggle for civil rights in the American South. For centuries, white elites managed to maintain a system of racial supremacy – first through slavery, then through Jim Crow, and finally through the white primary that effectively disenfranchised blacks in the South (Mickey 2015). Throughout, white leaders did their best to insulate the region, insisting on the principle of "states' rights." Occasionally, they failed, and these failures led to significant advances toward equal rights, including the abolition of slavery (through the instrument of the Civil War) and, much later, the passage of civil rights and voting rights laws. In these moments, a local conflict was nationalized; it was no longer a Southern problem but an American problem.

To a certain extent, these conflicts were also international. By 1865, most of the world's settled states had abolished slavery or had few enslaved persons to begin with. The prevalence of slavery in the US, and its official, constitutional embrace, seemed strange to many international observers – though some had pecuniary reasons to root for Dixie (Doyle 2014). By the 1960s, the apartheid-style system in the American South seemed even stranger. A world interconnected by television looked on with dismay as white cops turned fire hoses onto peaceful (mostly black) protestors (Gitlin 1980). Things did not look good for American elites attempting to style themselves leaders of the free world (Layton 2000). In this sense, the struggle for civil rights was internationalized.

The global dynamic was even more apparent in the struggle against the South African system of apartheid. While the (white) leaders of that nation defended the principle of national sovereignty, protesters around

---

[12] To be clear, when the scope of conflict expands elites usually play a key role. To be a "loser" in a local fight means that one is identified with the losing side, not that one is personally in a bad way. Leaders of peasant movements often appealed to the king, and kings attempted to mobilize the peasantry; both had an interest in restraining the aristocratic classes. In India, Muslims and out-castes have been wooed by elites in the Congress party attempting to stave off challenges from the Hindu middle classes, led by the Bharatiya Janata party (BJP). In the US, leaders in the civil rights movement generally came from the educated strata. They were black as well as white, and many pursued successful political careers within the Democratic party. These examples follow the logic of a "sandwich" coalition, in which top and bottom strata unite against the middle (Swamy 2003).

the world insisted that it was an international problem. The anti-apartheid movement that eventually enlisted supporters throughout the world offers a good example of international action motivated by universalist norms (Thorn 2006).

It follows that groups that are well connected to the outside world are likely to have an easier time making their case and enlisting assistance. Bosnians were more favorably positioned than Tutsis, which helps to account for why the international community responded to the siege of Sarajevo but not to an impending genocide in Central Africa. Because of the international diaspora of Armenians, and because Armenians have long been active in international trade networks, they are in a better position to advocate for their rights in the international court of public opinion than neighboring Kurds. For similar reasons, Jews are in a better position than Palestinians.

Even within the same country, different groups often have differential access to the international community. Consider the contrasting cases of Hong Kong and Xinjiang within China today. While both regions are resentful of Beijing's authority, Beijing has deployed its overwhelming power more gently in the former than in the latter case. We surmise that this has something to do with the greater connectedness – and hence, visibility – of Hong Kong. One can incarcerate a million (or so) Uighurs without the world taking much notice. But it would be much more noticeable if the incarcerated are located in an international city like Hong Kong. Hong Kongers are globally networked. If a million were rounded up and placed in detention camps it is almost certain they would have friends, business associates, and family members across the world who, caring deeply about their fate, would do whatever they could to protest the situation. This infringement of human rights would not escape notice.

Of course, appeals to outsiders do not always result in a more democratic outcome. Violent groups with no commitment to democracy may also appeal for assistance. Nationalist forces allied with Franco received support from the fascist powers during the Spanish Civil War. Bashar Assad received support from Russia and Iran in his bloody repression of the Syrian rebellion. Some global powers in the modern era – including Nazi Germany, the Soviet Union/Russia, and Communist China – have little interest in achieving democratic outcomes.

However, it is harder to craft an appeal to outsiders if the appeal is blatantly undemocratic or goes against the wishes of the great majority of the populace. This calls attention to an important feature of the international domain. In the modern era, democracy has had the upper hand, rhetorically speaking, for virtually all international actors claim to stand for democracy.

Consider the foreign policies of countries around the world. Democratic governments often seek to promote democratic outcomes in foreign countries. They do so openly and proudly, even though the goal is sometimes compromised for other policy objectives of a more realist nature. "Democracy promotion" is a well-established goal (Carothers 2011). By contrast, authoritarian regimes do not explicitly promote autocracy. They may do so implicitly, behind the scenes, but they would never state such a policy publicly. There is no such thing as "autocracy promotion." Actions that degrade democracy must be justified along other lines, e.g., as an ideological conflict (e.g., communism/anti-communism, fascism/anti-fascism), a religious conflict (e.g., Christian/Muslim, Sunni/Shi'a), or a national conflict (defending the homeland against foreign intrusion). This means that when the scope of a conflict is broadened it is more likely to play into the hands of democracy advocates than the enemies of democracy.

In the modern era, a key role in conflict expansion is often played by transnational social movements and non-governmental organizations (NGOs).[13] The early history of this phenomenon encompasses movements against slavery (beginning in the late eighteenth century), against Chinese footbinding (late nineteenth century), against imperialism (late nineteenth century), against female circumcision (early twentieth century), and against hunger (early twentieth century). Today, transnational NGOs embrace a wide range of issues and constituencies (Risse 2000), of which those categorized as democracy or human rights are most relevant to our theme (Guilhot 2005; Risse et al. 1999).

Likewise, international institutions such as the United Nations, the International Court of Justice, the International Criminal Court, the World Health Organization, the World Bank, the International Monetary Fund, and regional bodies such as the European Union and the African Union have also played a key role in broadening the scope of conflict. They are the most visible manifestations of global connectedness in the contemporary era, and their increasing prominence suggests that the acceleration of globalization is by no means complete (Cogan et al. 2016).

Of course, the hegemony of liberal institutions is not unchallenged, and it is much too early to declare victory (Ikenberry 2020). Even so, we anticipate that an expansion of conflict is more likely to encounter international actors who favor a democratic system than those who do not. The spectators watching the fight – returning to Schattschneider's metaphor – are likely to be on the people's side.

---

[13] See Florini (2012), Keck, Sikkink (2014), Markoff (1996).

Globalization and Democracy

We have now presented four complementary explanations for why connected territories, and connected peoples, are more likely to develop democratic institutions than isolated territories in the modern era (and especially in the contemporary era).

First, in premodern times, democracy was usually implemented in a direct fashion, which meant that isolated territories with small populations could run their own affairs with maximum popular input. In modern times, increasing interdependence across the world means that small communities can no longer govern themselves in any meaningful sense. Accordingly, isolation is not a democratic virtue.

Second, connectedness fosters economic development, and economic development probably fosters (representative) democracy. This is especially true when one considers the sort of economic development that depends on global markets.

Third, the search for equality, a foundation of democracy, is assisted when people are connected to the world. This connection broadens perspectives on local arrangements, calling into question the naturalness of ascriptive categories and invidious distinctions and offering alternative models by which society might be governed.

Fourth, those without power may receive assistance from outsiders if the scope of conflict is broadened. In the modern era, onlookers in the international community are more likely to support democracy than to oppose it. Connectedness makes it easier to expand the scope of conflict, thereby enlisting outside allies.

In light of these arguments, one would expect to find a strong association between democracy and various measures of "globalization" such as trade, media, migration, travel, and membership in international organizations. To evaluate this issue in a concise fashion we enlist a globalization index produced by the KOF Swiss Economic Institute, which integrates economic, social and political dimensions of globalization into a single variable (Gygli et al. 2019). This is placed on the X axis of Figure 16.2, with democracy on the Y axis. A few outliers can be seen in the bottom right corner, composed of countries like Singapore that score high on globalization but low on democracy. However, the overall pattern is one of covariation. Countries with more global connections tend to be more democratic.[14]

---

[14] See also Norris, Inglehart (2009).

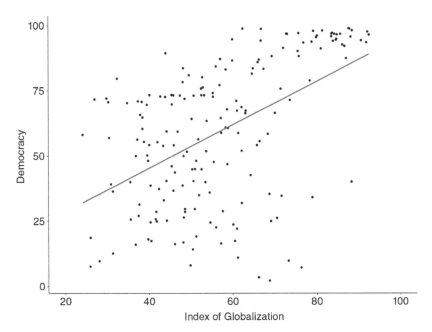

Figure 16.2 **Globalization and democracy**
Scatterplot, along with best-fit regression line, of democracy (Polyarchy index, augmented) and the KoF index of globalization (Dreher 2006). Sample includes 182 countries measured in 2010.

Three interpretations of this relationship are possible. One is that globalization fosters democracy, as suggested by our previous arguments.

A second interpretation is that unmeasured factors (confounders) affect both dimensions. While plausible, this seems likely to explain only a portion of the covariance. Indeed, the relationship between globalization and democracy is scarcely affected when potential confounders such as per capita GDP and population are included in a regression model.

A third interpretation is that democracies foster globalization. This might seem to vitiate our argument. However, we see it as corroborating in the following sense. When autocrats act to close off their borders they often seem to be motivated by political anxieties. (There is certainly no economic rationale for doing so.) Consider states behind the Iron Curtain during the Cold War; China under Mao; Belarus, the Central Asian republics, the mountain states of Bhutan and Nepal in the contemporary era; Paraguay under Stroessner; and North Korea since its formation. In all these cases, one could argue that isolationism was pursued as a strategy of authoritarian control. Autocrats feared the destabilizing effects of outside influences.

Generally speaking, isolationism serves to centralize power, depriving opponents of ideas, information, revenue, allies, and escape routes. Connectedness, by contrast, undermines autocracy, and for this reason autocrats usually attempt to prevent the free flow of ideas, goods, and persons. Margaret Jacob (2006: 10) remarks on this interplay in Europe during the early modern era.

The defenders of orthodoxy and the power of churches and kings thought that border crossing might threaten their authority. They believed that opposition politics could arise more easily when social experience spilled beyond the confines of confessional community, or kith and kin. They had been right to worry ... By the 1770s a cosmopolitan affect did indeed knit together the many participants who made up a growing, international and republican conversation. It spelled trouble for empires, monarchs, and their states or colonies throughout the Atlantic world.

Happily, the world is becoming a more connected place. Although the importance of factors discussed in this book – natural harbors and European ancestry – may have attenuated in recent years, other forces working toward greater connectedness (e.g., motorized transport, electronic communications, increased travel and work mobility) have more than compensated. If one could measure global connectedness in a comprehensive fashion it would surely be growing. (We assume that the interruption generated by the coronavirus outbreak will prove to be a hiccup rather than a fundamental reversal of historic patterns.)

Advances in communications and transport infrastructure make the world smaller, metaphorically speaking. Distance poses less and less of a barrier. Even remote areas such as those located in mountainous terrain are not so remote as they once were, and they will be even less isolated in the coming decades (Cairncross 1997). If our reasoning is correct, this augurs well for democratic forms of governance.

Of course, technological advances that would normally connect people to one another can be subverted by tyrannical states. The Internet can be shut down, censored, or closely monitored so as to prevent the free flow of ideas. It is not clear how the technological arms race between rulers and the ruled will end – with totalitarian control (Feldstein 2019; Gunitsky 2015) or tools for conviviality (Illich 1973). Moreover, connectivity is not the only factor affecting the fate of regimes around the world. So, we cannot make strong predictions about what the future might hold.

Even so, our theory offers a peek into the future. The relationship between connectivity and democracy has a long history, stretching back to the beginning of the modern era and perhaps further. Unless some fundamental feature of the world changes, we expect it to endure for some time to come.

From National to International Democracy?

Thus far, we have treated democracy as a governance mechanism for states. This may seem highly arbitrary in the contemporary era, when the increasing connectivity of economies and societies poses a challenge to state sovereignty. Consider the ever-growing list of problems that surpasses the boundaries of nation-states. This includes environmental protection, international trade, peace, and health (witnessed by the current Covid-19 pandemic). These are properly classified as global public goods. As such, it is not surprising that they are under-provided in the current international system, where political authority is parceled out to a few hundred formally sovereign nation-states, each looking after its own affairs.

Helpfully, international institutions such as the United Nations, the International Court of Justice, the World Bank, the International Monetary Fund, and the World Trade Organization play a growing role. However, these organizations are not fully empowered to achieve the goals they are tasked with. Moreover, they do not properly represent the eight billion or so people living on earth. Their membership is broad; but citizens from different countries do not possess equal power, and lines of accountability are vanishingly weak. The world's global hegemon (the United States) and various regional hegemons (China, India, Russia, and the European Union) exert disproportionate power. Not surprisingly, the rise of globalization is often regarded as a threat to democracy, as it seems to displace the power of states – many of whose leaders are democratically elected – with unelected international organizations and hegemonic powers.

Rather than recoil from globalization – which is probably impossible and would in any case eliminate any possibility of providing global public goods – there is another option. This involves democratizing institutions that operate internationally (Archibugi 2008; Held 1995).

We recognize that there is considerable resistance to the idea of democracy on a global scale. One might have thought that the larger the purview, and the greater the potential impact on our lives, the greater the need for democracy. But this is not the perspective of most commentators. Their position appears to be that democracy is well and good for national governments but inappropriate for international bodies.

Opponents of world democracy in the West are surely cognizant that they would wield considerably less power if international institutions were equally responsive to all peoples everywhere. The principle of one-person one-vote, which seems so self-evident when applied to countries, has less appeal when applied to international institutions.

Parallels to our story about the role of Europeans in the diffusion of democracy around the world in the modern era are inescapable. In Part III of the book we showed that Europeans were fond of the democratic ideal in situations where they constituted a majority. Elsewhere, they engineered limitations on democracy – via suffrage laws, vote-buying, coercion and intimidation, or gerrymandering – to ensure that they retained control. And where these expedients failed, or seemed destined to fail, Europeans were fierce opponents of independence, clinging to their status as colonial appendages of the metropole.

This sort of strategic positioning is familiar to those who follow debates about world government. Archibugi (2008: 6) remarks,

The West has preached the lofty principle of the sovereignty of the people, at the same time applying this principle with suspicious parsimony. The West has often declared its intention to promote democracy in other people's back yard but is by no means willing to share the management of global affairs with others.

Democracy sounds great when applied to "our" people, but is not so enticing when it entails a sacrifice of power to "other" people. Evidently, any system of world government with a legitimate claim to the concept of democracy would not be controlled by Europeans and their descendants, who compose a shrinking portion of the global populace.

We do not want to suggest that opposition to democracy on a global scale is motivated solely by racism and self-interest. After all, there are formidable problems to be worked out and nontrivial dangers to be concerned about.

By the same token, one should not assume that because the path to global democracy is murky the ideal is unachievable. Recall that *all* democratic innovations initially met with skepticism. The idea of extending full membership rights in the body politic to slaves, women, non-propertied men, non-Christians, non-whites, and to the uneducated masses was regarded by more privileged citizens – who previously enjoyed a monopoly on those rights – as unrealistic and utopian. Only after these extensions of membership occurred did they come to seem natural, obvious, and incontrovertible.

The American Declaration of Independence declared "We hold these truths to be self-evident, that all men are created equal ..." Implicit in this bold declaration is that women – not to mention slaves – were not equal. This was obvious to the signers. But just a few decades later it was not obvious to those who began agitating for female suffrage. And by the mid-twentieth century it seemed self-evident to most people throughout the world that women were as deserving of political rights as men.

Through most of its history, democracy was viewed as a form of government feasible only in very small communities such as the Greek polis. When representative institutions were proposed for the territories of the newly independent United States there were many skeptics, both within the US and abroad, as no one had attempted this feat across such a vast area of land and such a vast diversity of peoples. Similar doubts were voiced about the prospect of extending democracy among non-European peoples, who were not initially viewed as capable of self-government. Doubts were magnified in large and diverse countries such as India. Who would have thought that democracy would flourish in a community of a billion inhabitants with no majority language, a central religious cleavage, and extreme poverty? Who would have thought that the subcontinent of Europe, equally diverse and equally fractious – the site of two world wars – could unite (mostly) within a single confederation?

Like any instance of foundational change, democratic innovations are difficult to conceive until they are realized, at which point they become the warp and woof of lived reality. Just two centuries ago democracy was regarded as a pipe dream. Now, it is regarded as the only morally defensible way to run a country.

In this light, it does not seem inconceivable that democracy on a global scale lies just over the horizon. The more connected we are, the greater the challenge – as well as the opportunity – of global democracy. In this fashion, we may be forced to reconceptualize democratic theory once again.

Appendix A: Variables

This appendix is divided into three sections. Table A.1 includes state-level variables. Table A.2 includes grid-cell level variables. Table A.3 includes bespoke datasets that pertain to a single data table in the text. Descriptive statistics are located in Appendix B (online at Dataverse). "Authors" refers to Gerring et al.

Table A.1 *State-level variables*

DEMOCRACY

Colonial election. An elective assembly, coded 1 if there is a colony-wide assembly that performs legislative or advisory functions and at least one member was elected. Observed from 1600 to independence. For further discussion see Chapter 10. *Source:* Paine (2019)

Contestation. Incumbent–challenger formula of electoral contestation, calculated as the incumbent (the party with the largest share of votes in the previous election) share of votes in a national legislative or presidential election minus the share of the largest challenger, subtracted from 100. For further discussion see Chapter 2. *Source:* Gerring, Hicken, Weitzel, Cojocaru (2018)

Headman. A measure of traditional (premodern) democratic characteristics. Coded 1 if headman chosen by "election or other formal consensus" or "informal consensus." 0 otherwise. Aggregated up to state levels, weighting each ethnic group by its size. For further discussion see Chapter 2. *Source:* Giuliano, Nunn (2013), drawing on Murdock (1967)

Lexical index. The electoral components of democracy measured in a cumulative fashion, transformed to 0–100 scale. For further discussion see Chapter 2. *Source:* Skaaning, Gerring, Bartusevičius (2015)

Male suffrage. Share (percent) of adult males who are enfranchised as a share of total number of adult male citizens. Coding unaffected by electoral regime interruptions. *Source:* V-Dem (Coppedge, Gerring, Glynn et al. 2020), supplemented by Bilinski (2015)

Polity2. A weighted additive aggregation procedure across five sub-components: competitiveness and openness of executive recruitment, competitiveness and regulation of political participation, and constraints on the chief executive. Transformed to 0–100 scale. Observed from 1800 to 2018. *Source:* Polity IV (Marshall, Jaggers 2016)

Polyarchy, augmented. Electoral democracy index, missing data interpolated using Lexical index and Contestation, transformed to 0–100 scale. For further discussion see Chapter 2. *Source:* As above

Table A.1 (*cont.*)

Polyarchy. Electoral democracy index, transformed to 0–100 scale. For further discussion see Chapter 2. *Source:* V-Dem (Coppedge, Gerring, Glynn et al. 2020; Teorell et al. 2018)

PORTS, HARBORS

Natural harbor distance (1953). The distance (100 km) from each grid-cell to the nearest port classified as a natural harbor in the WPI (1953). This score is aggregated across all grid-cells to generate a mean value for each territory-year. For further discussion see Chapter 4. *Source:* Authors

Natural harbor distance (2017). The distance (100 km) from each grid-cell to the nearest port classified as a natural harbor in the WPI (2017). This score is aggregated across all grid-cells to generate a mean value for each territory-year. For further discussion see Chapter 4. *Source:* Authors

Natural harbor distance (benchmark). Geomorphic characteristics of coastlines are used to predict the existence of ports listed in the WPI (1953). We then calculate the distance (100 km) from each grid-cell across the world to the nearest predicted port. This score is aggregated across all grid-cells to generate a mean value for each territory-year. For further discussion see Chapter 4. *Source:* Authors

Natural harbor distance, ln. Geomorphic characteristics of coastlines are used to predict the existence of ports listed in the WPI (1953). We then calculate the distance (100 km) from each grid-cell across the world to the nearest predicted port. This score is aggregated across all grid-cells to generate a mean value for each territory-year. For further discussion see Chapter 4. *Source:* Authors

Port distance (1953). The distance (100 km) from each grid-cell to the nearest port in the WPI (1953). This score is aggregated across all grid-cells to generate a mean value for each territory-year. For further discussion see Chapter 4. *Source:* Authors

Port distance (2017). The distance (100 km) from each grid-cell to the nearest port in the WPI (2017). This score is aggregated across all grid-cells to generate a mean value for each territory-year. For further discussion see Chapter 4. *Source:* Authors

Port distance (Lloyd's). The distance (100 km) from each grid-cell to the nearest port in *Lloyd's List* (Ducruet 2018), observed from 1890 to 2009. This score is aggregated across all grid-cells to generate a mean value for each territory-year. For further discussion see Chapter 4. *Source:* Authors

AGRICULTURAL ZONES

Barren. Share of territory classified as barren. Aggregated from grid-cells (see Table A.2). *Source:* Tollefsen et al. (2012), drawing on Meiyappan, Jain (2012)

Crop. Share of territory classified as crop. Aggregated from grid-cells (see Table A.2). *Source:* Tollefsen et al. (2012), drawing on Meiyappan, Jain (2012)

Forest. Share of territory classified as forest. Aggregated from grid-cells (see Table A.2). *Source:* Tollefsen et al. (2012), drawing on Meiyappan, Jain (2012)

Grass. Share of territory classified as grass. Aggregated from grid-cells (see Table A.2). *Source:* Tollefsen et al. (2012), drawing on Meiyappan, Jain (2012)

Mountains. Share of territory classified as mountains. Aggregated from grid-cells (see Table A.2). *Source:* Tollefsen et al. (2012), drawing on Meiyappan, Jain (2012)

Pasture. Share of territory classified as pasture. Aggregated from grid-cells (see Table A.2). *Source:* Tollefsen et al. (2012), drawing on Meiyappan, Jain (2012)

Savanna. Share of territory classified as savanna. Aggregated from grid-cells (see Table A.2). *Source:* Tollefsen et al. (2012), drawing on Meiyappan, Jain (2012)

Table A.1 (*cont.*)

===

Shrub. Share of territory classified as shrub. Aggregated from grid-cells (see Table A.2). *Source:* Tollefsen et al. (2012), drawing on Meiyappan, Jain (2012)

Water. Share of territory classified as water. Aggregated from grid-cells (see Table A.2). *Source:* Tollefsen et al. (2012), drawing on Meiyappan, Jain (2012)

GEOGRAPHY (Misc)

Agricultural suitability. Geographic endowments favoring agricultural production including climate, soil, and terrain. *Source:* Ashraf, Michalopoulos (2015)

Area. Area (km). *Source:* Authors

Caloric suitability. Calories a grid-cell would yield if farmed to its potential, aggregated across grid-cells in a state. *Source:* Galor, Özak (2016)

Caloric variability. Standard deviation of caloric suitability across a grid-cell, averaged across grid-cells in a state. *Source:* Galor, Özak (2016)

Desert. Share of territory classified as desert. *Source:* Tollefsen et al. (2012)

Elevation. Mean elevation. *Source:* Nunn, Puga (2012)

Equator distance. Distance from equator measured as the absolute value of a state's mean latitude. *Source:* La Porta et al. (1999)

Fish. The Bounty of the Sea (BoS) index is a measure of the potential abundance of marine fish resources in the oceans. Its construction is a two-step procedure. First, the relevant marine fish species are identified using global fish landings statistics from the US Food and Agriculture Organization (FAO), and second, the unweighted average habitat suitability of these species is calculated using gridded data from *AquaMaps*. The chosen variable represents the mean suitability of the top fifteen species of fish in the 1950s. Landlocked countries are assigned a zero score. *Source:* Dalgaard, Knudsen, Selaya (2020)

Frost days. Number of frost days per annum (mean). *Source:* Authors

Irrigation potential. Areas where irrigation could make a big impact on agricultural productivity. Specifically, the share of land suitable for agriculture where irrigation can more than double agricultural production (land in Impact Class 5 as a share of land in Impact Classes 1–5). *Source:* Bentzen et al. (2016), drawing on FAO Global Agro-Ecological Zones (GAEZ) 2002 database

Island. Indicates whether a state is attached to a continental landmass or not. For further discussion see Chapter 12. *Source:* Authors

Landlock. Coded 1 if a territory does not border an ocean or sea; 0 otherwise. *Source:* Authors

London distance. Distance (km) from state capital to London. *Source:* Gleditsch (2002)

Malaria ecology. Measure of the stability of malarial transmission in a given territory. *Source:* Easterly, Levine (2016), drawing on Kiszewski et al. (2004)

Ocean distance. Distance from ocean (km), averaged across all grid-cells in a state. *Source:* Authors

Oil income per capita. The aggregated real value of a state's petroleum production as a share of total population. Interpolated forward and extended backward for cases of presumed zero or near-zero oil income (authors). *Source:* Haber, Menaldo (2011)

Precipitation. Average annual rainfall. *Source:* Tollefsen et al. (2012), drawing on Schneider et al. (2015)

Regions. A vector of dummies: 1 = Europe, Russia, Central Asia, 2 = Americas, 3 = MENA, 4 = Sub-Saharan Africa, 5 = East, Southeast, South Asia, Pacific. *Source:* Authors

Table A.1 (*cont.*)

River distance. Distance from nearest navigable river (km), averaged across all grid-cells in a state. *Source:* Authors

Rugged. Differences in elevation across grid-cells, aggregated to states. *Source:* Nunn, Puga (2012)

Soil. Share of territory with fertile soil. *Source:* Nunn, Puga (2012)

Temperature. Mean temperature. *Source:* Tollefsen et al. (2012), drawing on Fan, van den Dool (2008)

Tropical. Share of territory classified as tropical. *Source:* Nunn, Puga (2012)

STATE & SOCIETY

Agricultural transition. Estimated years (in thousands) since the transition to an agricultural society. *Source:* Putterman (2006)

Corruption. The V-Dem corruption index includes measures of six distinct types of corruption that cover both different areas and levels of the polity realm, distinguishing between executive, legislative and judicial corruption. Within the executive realm, the measures also distinguish between corruption mostly pertaining to bribery and corruption due to embezzlement. Finally, they differentiate between corruption in the highest echelons of the executive at the level of the rulers/cabinet on the one hand, and in the public sector at large on the other. The measures thus tap into several distinguished types of corruption: both "petty" and "grand"; both bribery and theft; both corruption aimed at influencing lawmaking and that affecting implementation. *Source:* V-Dem (Coppedge, Gerring, Glynn et al. 2020), McMann et al. (2019)

Ethnic fractionalization. Uses Herfindahl index to calculate the probability of two randomly chosen individuals being members of the same ethnic group. Base year: 2001, extrapolated backward and forward by the authors. *Source:* Alesina et al. (2003), drawing on *Encyclopedia Britannica*

GDP per cap. Gross domestic product per capita in constant 1990 dollars, based on data from the Maddison Project (Bolt, van Zanden 2014), supplemented by estimates from Bairoch (1976), Broadberry (2015), Broadberry, Klein (2012), Gleditsch (2002), and the World Development Indicators (WDI; World Bank 2016), which are combined in a dynamic, three-dimensional latent trait model. *Source:* Fariss et al. (2017)

Governance. Five variables from the Worldwide Governance Indicators – political stability and absence of violence/terrorism, government effectiveness, regulatory quality, rule of law, and control of corruption – are combined into a single index which represents the first component from a principal component analysis. Observed from 1997 to 2010. For further discussion see Appendix D (online at Dataverse). *Source:* Authors, drawing on Kaufmann, Kraay, Mastruzzi (2010)

Kinship intensity index. "An omnibus measure for kinship intensity that captures the presence of cousin-marriage preferences, polygamy, co-residence of extended families, clan organization, and community endogamy." *Source:* Schulz et al. (2019: 3), drawing on Ethnographic Atlas (Murdock 1967)

Linguistic fractionalization. Uses Herfindahl index to calculate the probability of two randomly chosen individuals being members of the same linguistic group (sharing mother tongue). Base year: 2001, extrapolated backward and forward by the authors. *Source:* Alesina et al. (2003), drawing on *Encyclopedia Britannica*

Muslim. Share of population that is Muslim by heritage (%). *Source:* Authors

Naval/land forces. The relative strength of naval-to-land forces. Naval strength proxied by naval tonnage. Land forces proxied by total military personnel. Step 1: missing values

Table A.1 (*cont.*)

replaced by minimum values. Step 2: variables transformed by the natural logarithm. Step 3: ratio variable calculated as naval forces index/land forces index. For further discussion see Chapter 7. *Source:* naval tonnage (Crisher, Souva 2014), military personnel (National Material Capabilities, COW v 5.0 [Singer 1987])

Population density, 1500. Population density in 1500. *Source:* Acemoglu, Johnson, Robinson (2001, 2002)

Religious fractionalization. Uses Herfindahl index to calculate the probability of two randomly chosen individuals being members of the same religious group. Base year: 2001, extrapolated backward and forward by the authors. *Source:* Alesina et al. (2003), drawing on *Encyclopedia Britannica*

Sovereignty. Sovereignty, coded 1 if a territory is recognized as sovereign by European powers or exercises de facto sovereignty. *Source:* Authors

State history. State Antiquity Index, which codes territories conforming to the present-day boundaries of 159 countries at 50-year intervals from 2900 BCE to 2000 CE. Scoring reflects (a) existence of a government, (b) the proportion of the territory covered by that government, and (c) whether it was indigenous or externally imposed. Our variable applies a 1 percent depreciation rate to each score. *Source:* Borcan, Olsson, Putterman (2018)

Trade openness. Imports as a share of GDP. Observed from 1800 to 2009. *Source:* COW (Barbieri, Keshk 2016)

University distance. We mark the location (lat./long.) of all extant universities across the world along with their year of founding, beginning with the University of Bologna in, or about, 1088. "University" refers broadly to any institution of higher education that grants at least one bachelor's degree or its equivalent. This excludes two-year universities, universities that grant only associates' degrees, as well as technical schools, military schools, theological training centers, police academies, social work schools, and yoga schools. This definition is consonant with institutions that fit the International Standard Classification of Education (ISCED) levels 6–8 (UNESCO 2019). Because universities of this sort rarely expire, it is possible to construct a fairly comprehensive panel dataset of universities through time by marking the founding date of each extant university. Note, however, that this dataset does not track universities that no longer exist. Next, for each grid-cell across the world the authors calculate the distance to the nearest university (which may or may not be in the same state) annually from 1789 to the present. This statistic is logged and then calculated as a historical stock with a 1 percent annual depreciation rate. *Source:* Apfeld (2019)

Year of independence. Year in which state gains international recognition. *Source:* Authors

Years since independence. Number of years since independence (de facto or de jure) or 1000 (whichever comes later). *Source:* Authors

EUROPE

Catholic. Percentage of the population that was Catholic in 1980, extrapolated forward and backward by the authors. *Source:* La Porta et al (1999)

English colonial duration. Number of years of English colonial rule. Original coding extended by the authors. *Source:* Olsson (2009)

English colony. Current or former English colony/dependency. *Source:* Authors

Europe. Those states within the European continent that lie closest to a natural harbor, namely: Albania, Andorra, Austria, Baden, Bavaria, Belgium, Bosnia, Brunswick,

Table A.1 *(cont.)*

Bulgaria, Croatia, Czech Republic, Denmark, East Germany, Estonia, Finland, France, Germany, Greece, Hamburg, Hanover, Hesse-Darmstadt, Hesse-Kassel, Hungary, Iceland, Ireland, Italy, Latvia, Liechtenstein, Lithuania, Luxembourg, Macedonia, Mecklenburg Schwerin, Modena, Moldova, Montenegro, Nassau, Netherlands, Norway, Oldenburg, Papal States, Parma, Piedmont-Sardinia, Poland, Portugal, Romania, San Marino, Saxe-Weimar-Eisenach, Saxony, Serbia, Slovenia, Spain, Sweden, Switzerland, Tuscany, Two Sicilies, Ukraine, United Kingdom, Vatican City, and Württemberg. For further discussion see Chapter 9. *Source:* Authors

European ancestry (benchmark). Share of population of European descent, with Europe defined by distance from natural harbors (as above). For territories outside Europe, we mark the date of the first recorded European settlement or (if the latter is unknown) the first European contact (discovery). This is coded as zero (no Europeans), forming the first data point in the series. For territories within continental Europe, we record the number of Europeans as 100% in 1950. This estimate is extended back to 1600. For the remaining time period (after the point of first European contact for non-European territories and after 1950 for European territories), we use a quadratic function to estimate yearly data points across available data points. Observed from 1600 to 2019. For further discussion see Chapter 9 and Appendix E (online at Dataverse). *Source:* Authors

European ancestry, Latin or Germanic. Share of population of European descent, with Europe defined by states with a Latin or Germanic language. For states outside Europe, we mark the date of the first recorded European settlement or (if the latter is unknown) the first European contact (discovery). This is coded as zero (no Europeans), forming the first data point in the series. For territories within continental Europe, we record the number of Europeans as 100% in 1950. This estimate is extended back to 1789. For the remaining time period (after the point of first European contact for non-European territories and after 1950 for European territories), we use a quadratic function to estimate yearly data points across available data points. For further discussion see Chapter 9. *Source:* Authors

European ancestry, stock. European ancestry (distance from natural harbors) calculated as a stock variable, computed by adding up scores from 1600 to the present with a 10% annual depreciation rate. For further discussion see Chapter 9. *Source:* Authors

European colonial duration. Number of years of European colonial rule. Original coding extended by the authors. *Source:* Olsson (2009)

European language. Share of population (%) speaking a European language. Procedure: (1) Using Alesina et al. (2003), identify European languages: Bajan (English-Creole), Basque, Belgian, Bislama (English Creole), Castilian Spanish, Catalan (Andorran), Catalan (Catala), Catalan, Crioulo (Portuguese Creole), Danish, Dutch (Flemish; Netherlandic), Dutch (lingua franca), Dutch, English (lingua franca), English Creole (lingua franca), English Creole, English Creoles, English Creole, English/Creole, English/English Creole (lingua franca), English/English Creole, English/English Creoles, English/French Creole, Finnish, French (Haitian) Creole, French (Walloon), French (lingua franca), French Creole (mostly Haitian), French Creole, French, French/French Creole, French/French Creoles, Galician, German, Greek, Haitian (French) Creole, Icelandic, Irish, Italian (Romagnolo), Italian, Krio (English Creole), Krio (English Creole) (lingua franca), Luxemburgian, Maltese, Monegasque, Norman French, Norwegian, Polish, Portuguese (lingua franca), Portuguese, Rhaetian, Sami (Lapp),

Table A.1 *(cont.)*

Sardinian, Scots-Gaelic, Seselwa (French Creole), Solomon Island Pidgin (English Creole), Spanish (lingua franca), Spanish, Swedish, Tok Pisin (English Creole), Trinidad English, Welsh. (2) For each state, add up the percentages for each of these languages. (3) If a state exceeds 100% (which occasionally happens), assign a value of 100. For further discussion see Chapter 11. *Source:* Authors

Forced settlement. Coded 1 if a European colony was composed predominantly of slaves, experienced at least 25 years of colonial control, and colonial period ended after 1800 (or did not end at all). The list of forced settlement colonies is drawn from sources listed in the adjacent column. Original coding extended by the authors, assigning 0 to uncoded cases. *Source:* Owolabi (2015: appendix I)

Former colony. Former European colony. *Source:* Easterly, Levine (2016)

French colony. Current or former French colony/dependency. *Source:* Authors

Indirect rule. Ratio of colonially recognized court cases to all court cases in 1955. Original coding extended by Hariri (2012). *Source:* Lange (2004)

Protestant. Percentage of population belonging to a Protestant denomination – defined as Christian denominations that are neither Catholic nor Orthodox (e.g., Anglican, Baptist, Congregational, Lutheran, Methodist, Mormon, Presbyterian, Quaker). We assign a value of 0 to each state in the year prior to the arrival of the first Christian missionary, as dated by Woodberry (2012) and supplemented by other sources including Barrett (1982), Hillerbrand (2004), Moreau et al. (2000), Neill (1991), and Tucker (2004). The Correlates of War Project (Maoz, Henderson 2013) provides estimates for all states at 5-year increments from 1945 to 2010, and Woodberry (2012) provides estimates for 1900. We complete the time series for each state by linear interpolation. *Source:* Authors, drawing on multiple sources, as indicated

Settler mortality. Historical deaths per 1000 European settlers per year. *Source:* Easterly, Levine (2016), drawing on Acemoglu, Johnson, Robinson (2001, 2002)

Spanish colony. Current or former Spanish colony/dependency. *Source:* Authors

Table A.2 *Grid-cell level variables*

DEMOCRACY

Headman. A measure of traditional (premodern) democratic characteristics. Coded 1 if headman chosen by "election or other formal consensus" or "informal consensus." 0 otherwise. Measured for a single year (although actual data may refer to any period in the early modern or modern era). For further discussion see Chapter 2. *Source:* Ethnographic Atlas (Murdock 1967)

Polyarchy, augmented. Electoral democracy index, missing data interpolated, transformed to 0–100 scale. For further discussion see Chapter 2. *Source:* see Table A.1

PORTS, HARBORS

Natural harbor distance (benchmark). Geomorphic characteristics of coastlines are used to predict the existence of ports listed in the WPI (1953). We then calculate the distance (100 km) from each grid-cell across the world to the nearest predicted port. For further discussion see Chapter 4. *Source:* Authors

Table A.2 (*cont.*)

AGRICULTURAL ZONES

Barren. The percentage barren areas in a cell extracted from the ISAM-HYDE historical landuse dataset. To compute barren_ih we aggregate using the following landuse classes: "Tundra", "Desert", "PdRI". In PRIO-GRID, this indicator is available for the years 1950, 1960, 1970, 1980, 1990, 2000, and 2010. *Source:* Tollefsen et al. (2012)

Crop. The percentage area of the cell covered by agricultural area, based on ISAM-HYDE landuse data. To compute agri_ih we follow the land cover classification system used by ISAM-HYDE and aggregate to the category "Total cropland" (landuse classes "C3crop", "C4crop"). In PRIO-GRID, this indicator is available for the years 1950, 1960, 1970, 1980, 1990, 2000, and 2010. *Source:* Tollefsen et al. (2012)

Forest. The percentage area of the cell covered by forest area, based on ISAM-HYDE landuse data. Source: Tollefsen et al. (2012)

Grass. The percentage area of the cell covered by grasslands, based on ISAM-HYDE landuse data. To compute grass_ih we follow the land cover classification system used by ISAM-HYDE and aggregate to the category "Total grassland" (landuse classes "C3grass", "C4grass"). In PRIO-GRID, this indicator is available for the years 1950, 1960, 1970, 1980, 1990, 2000, and 2010. *Source:* Tollefsen et al. (2012)

Mountains. The proportion of mountainous terrain within the cell based on elevation, slope and local elevation range, taken from a high-resolution mountain raster developed for the United Nations Environment Program (UNEP)'s Mountain Watch Report. The original pixel values are binary, capturing whether the pixel is a mountain pixel or not, based on the seven different categories of mountainous terrain in the report. *Source:* Tollefsen et al. (2012)

Pasture. The percentage area of a grid-cell covered by pasture area, based on ISAM-HYDE landuse data. To compute pasture_ih we follow the land cover classification system used by ISAM-HYDE and aggregate to the category "Total pastureland" (landuse classes "C3past", "C4past"). In PRIO-GRID, this indicator is available for the years 1950, 1960, 1970, 1980, 1990, 2000, and 2010. *Source:* Tollefsen et al. (2012)

Savanna. Area (percentage) of a grid-cell covered by grasslands, based on ISAM-HYDE landuse data. To compute savanna_ih we follow the land cover classification system used by ISAM-HYDE and aggregate to the category "Savanna" (landuse class "Savanna"). Data available for 1950, 1960, 1970, 1980, 1990, 2000, and 2010. *Source:* Tollefsen et al. (2012)

Shrub. The percentage area of the cell covered by grasslands, based on ISAM-HYDE landuse data. *Source*: Tollefsen et al. (2012)

Water. The coverage of water areas in each cell, extracted from the Globcover 2009 dataset v.2.3. To compute water_gc we follow but deviate slightly from the FAO land cover classification system used by Globcover and aggregate only to the "Natural/Artificial water bodies" class excluding the "Permanent snow and ice" class (landuse class 2010). The value indicates the percentage area of the cell covered by water area. This indicator is a snapshot for the year 2009. *Source:* Tollefsen et al. (2012)

GEOGRAPHY (Misc)

Equator distance. Distance (km) from grid-cell centroid to equator. *Source:* Authors

Irrigation potential. The area equipped for irrigation within each cell (in hectares). The data is taken from the Historical Irrigation dataset v.1, which indicates pixelated data on

Table A.2 (*cont.*)

areas equipped for irrigation across time. Specifically we used the AEI_EARTHSTAT_IR dataset, which reports irrigation based on subnational sources and Earthstat historical landuse data. In PRIO-GRID, this indicator is only available for the years 1950, 1960, 1970, 1980, 1985, 1990, 1995, 2000, and 2005. *Source:* Authors

Ocean distance. Distance from grid-cell centroid to nearest ocean (km). *Source:* Authors

Precipitation. Yearly total amount of precipitation (millimeters) in a grid-cell, based on monthly meteorological statistics from 1946 to 2013, as maintained by the Global Precipitation Climatology Centre. *Source:* Tollefsen et al. (2012)

Regions. A vector of dummies: 1 = Europe, Russia, Central Asia, 2 = Americas, 3 = MENA, 4 = Sub-Saharan Africa, 5 = East, Southeast, South Asia, Pacific. *Source:* Authors

River distance. Distance from grid-cell centroid to nearest river. Rivers are identified from the Aquastat database, developed by the Land and Water Division of the FAO, which includes information about rivers' hydrological regime indicating its rank based on connectivity and hierarchy, ranging from 1 to 7, where 1 is a small stream (a leaf without children), while 7 indicates a major navigable river. We use rivers with Strahler Stream order 3 to 7. *Source:* FAO (2016)

Temperature. The yearly mean temperature (in degrees Celsius) in the cell, based on monthly meteorological statistics from GHCN/CAMS, developed at the Climate Prediction Center, US National Oceanic and Atmospheric Administration (NOAA)/ National Weather Service. This indicator contains data for the years 1948–2014. *Source:* Tollefsen et al. (2012)

STATE & SOCIETY

Gross cell product. Gross cell product, measured in USD (PPP). Available at five-year intervals since1990. *Source:* Tollefsen et al. (2012), drawing on G-Econ dataset v4.0 (Nordhaus 2006)

Jurisdictional hierarchy. 0 = Missing data, 1 = No political authority beyond the local community, 2 = One level above the local community (e.g., petty chiefdoms), 3 = Two levels above the local community (e.g., larger chiefdoms), 4 = Three levels above the local community (e.g., states), 5 = Four levels above the local community (e.g., large states). *Source:* Ethnographic Atlas (Murdock 1967)

Population. Population located within a grid-cell. *Source:* Hyde (Klein Goldewijk et al. 2011)

State size. For each grid-cell, we measure the territorial size of the state it is a part of. Units: log square kilometers. *Source:* Authors

Urbanization. The percentage area of a cell covered by urban area, based on ISAM-HYDE landuse data. Available for 1950, 1960, 1970, 1980, 1990, 2000, and 2010. *Source:* Tollefsen et al. (2012), drawing on Meiyappan, Jain (2012)

Table A.3 *Bespoke datasets*

TABLE 5.2: EUROPEAN PARLIAMENTS, 1200–1700

Democratic values index. Index based on questions from the World Values Survey (WVS) registering respondents' approval or disapproval of the following regimes: (a) democracy, (b) army rule, (c) rule by experts, (d) theocracy, and (e) rule by a strong leader. Each is on a 0–5 Likert scale. For the purposes of the index, the items are scaled such that positive scores indicate more democratic attitudes; then they are summed together into a composite index. Source: Haerpfer, Inglehart et al. (2020)

Parliaments. Presence of a parliament at the city-level, adopted to grid-cells. We use EuroAtlas (also used by Abramson and Boix) to circumscribe "Europe." So defined, this source yields 11,756 grid-cells, each of which is measured at century intervals between 1200 and 1700. *Source:* Abramson, Boix (2019)

TABLE 7.4: DIVERSITY IN INLAND AND COASTAL CITIES

Coastal. Coded 1 if located on or very near the coast, 0 otherwise. *Source:* Authors

Ethnic fractionalization. Herfindahl index of ethnic heterogeneity, understood as the probability that two randomly chosen persons living in a city are members of different ethnic groups. Calculated by the authors from information on ethnic populations contained in Wikipedia articles on each city, using most recent data available. *Source:* Authors

Population. Population of a city, most recent year available. Garnered from Wikipedia articles on each city. *Source:* Authors

TABLE 10.1: LEGISLATIVE ACTIVITY ACROSS BRITISH COLONIES IN THE AMERICAS

Bills per annum. The number of bills passed in colonial assemblies across the Americas from 1692 to 1800, observed at decadal intervals (with varying coverage). *Source:* Graham (2018)

European ancestry. Share of population of European heritage. For further discussion see Table A.1 and Chapter 9. *Source:* Authors

Population. Population of colony. *Source:* Various

Glossary

Democracy	Rule by the people. Understood across two dimensions: *Membership* (number of people who are granted citizenship rights) and *Accountability* (citizen control over policymaking).
Direct democracy	Governance by popular assembly or consultative bodies.
Representative democracy	Governance by elected representatives.

SPATIAL UNITS

State	Territory with a capital (a single locus of power), sovereignty or semisovereignty, and a governmental apparatus that persists from one ruler to the next. E.g., city-state, country, empire, or colony.
Colony	Semisovereign territory governed by an overseas metropole.
Country	Sovereign state.
Empire	Sovereign state that controls territories containing subjects that do not enjoy full citizenship, are not fully integrated into the metropole, and have no right to secede.
Sovereignty	In the modern era, recognition by European powers. In the premodern era, de facto control of a territory by a state.
Semisovereignty	A form of political organization that obtains when a state claims formal sovereignty but the territory is governed separately from the metropole (e.g., a colony or dependency) and may enjoy a high degree of autonomy (at least over domestic policies).

Grid-cell	Generally, a division of the earth's surface into uniformly sized squares. Specifically, grid-cells from the PRIO database, which divides the world into cells, each of which is 0.5 × 0.5 decimal degrees, i.e., approximately 50 × 50 km at the equator (Tollefsen et al. 2012). There are 259,200 grid-cells across the entire world and 64,818 across the terrestrial world, excluding the Antarctic. (All maps and analyses in the book exclude the Antarctic.)

PERIODIZATION (SEE CHAPTER 1)

Premodern	From the first civilizations until 1789 or first European contact.
Ancient	From the first civilizations to 800.
Medieval	From 800 to 1500.
Early modern	From 1500 to 1789 or first European contact.
Modern	From 1789 (or first European contact) to the present.
Contemporary	From 1960 to the present.

MARITIME GEOGRAPHY (SEE CHAPTER 4)

Port	Location where boats dock. Assumed to offer ocean access (perhaps via a navigable river), unless otherwise indicated.
Harbor	Port constructed on a location with natural features that facilitate docking.
Natural harbor	Coastline with geomorphic conditions that facilitate the creation of a working port.

EUROPE (SEE CHAPTERS 9, 13)

European ancestry	Share of persons with European heritage, however that category is understood in a particular time and place.
Colonialism	A formal arrangement in which a European power claims sovereignty over an overseas territory that is not completely integrated (on equal terms) with the metropole and in which the indigenous people are neither consulted on their incorporation into the empire nor given the option of leaving the empire.
Protestantism	Share of persons of Protestant heritage – Christian but not Catholic or Orthodox.

Bibliography

Abernethy, David B. 2000. *The Dynamics of Global Dominance: European Overseas Empires, 1415–1980*. New Haven: Yale University Press.

Abramson, Scott F., Carles Boix. 2019. "Endogenous Parliaments: The Domestic and International Roots of Long-Term Economic Growth and Executive Constraints in Europe." *International Organization* 73:4, 793–837.

Abu-Hakima, Ahmad Mustafa. 1972. "The Development of the Gulf States." In Derek Hopwood (ed.), *The Arabian Peninsula: Society and Politics* (London: George Allen & Unwin), 31–53.

Abulafia, David (ed.). 2003. *The Mediterranean in History*. London: Thames and Hudson.

2008. *The Discovery of Mankind: Atlantic Encounters in the Age of Columbus*. New Haven: Yale University Press.

2010. *The Great Sea: A Human History of the Mediterranean*. London: Allan Lane.

2014. "Thalassocracies." In Peregrine Horden and Sharon Kinoshita (eds.), *A Companion to Mediterranean History* (Oxford: Wiley-Blackwell), 137–53.

2019. *The Boundless Sea: A Human History of the Oceans*. Oxford: Oxford University Press.

Abu-Lughod, Janet L. 1989. *Before European Hegemony: The World System AD 1250–1350*. Oxford: Oxford University Press.

à Campo, Joseph Norbert Frans Marie. 2002. *Engines of Empire: Steamshipping and State Formation in Colonial Indonesia*. Hilversum: Uitgeverij Verloren.

Acemoglu, Daron, James A. Robinson. 2005. *Economic Origins of Dictatorship and Democracy*. Cambridge: Cambridge University Press.

2012. *Why Nations Fail: The Origins of Power, Prosperity, and Poverty*. New York: Crown Books.

2017. "The Emergence of Weak, Despotic and Inclusive States." NBER Working Paper No. w23657. Cambridge, MA: National Bureau of Economic Research.

2019. *The Narrow Corridor: States, Societies, and the Fate of Liberty*. New York: Penguin Press.

Acemoglu, Daron, Alexander Wolitzky. 2011. "The Economics of Labor Coercion." *Econometrica* 79:2, 555–600.

Acemoglu, Daron, Simon Johnson, James A. Robinson. 2001. "Colonial Origins of Comparative Development: An Empirical Investigation." *American Economic Review* 91:5, 1369–401.

2002. "Reversal of Fortune: Geography and Institutions in the Making of the Modern World Income Distribution." *Quarterly Journal of Economics* 117:4, 1231–94.

2005. "The Rise of Europe: Atlantic Trade, Institutional Change and Economic Growth." *American Economic Review* 95:3, 546–79.

Acemoglu, Daron, Simon Johnson, James A. Robinson, Pierre Yared. 2008. "Income and Democracy." *American Economic Review* 98:3, 808–42

Acemoglu, Daron, Suresh Naidu, Pascual Restrepo, James A. Robinson. 2019. "Democracy Does Cause Growth." *Journal of Political Economy* 127:1, 47–100.

Acharya, Avidit, Alexander Lee. 2019. "Path Dependence in European Development: Medieval Politics, Conflict, and State Building." *Comparative Political Studies* 52:13–14, 2171–206.

Acharya, Avidit, Matthew Blackwell, Maya Sen. 2018. *Deep Roots: How Slavery Still Shapes Southern Politics*. Princeton: Princeton University Press.

Acton, Emerich Edward Dalberg. 1919. *The History of Freedom and Other Essays*. London: Macmillan.

Adams, Percy G. (ed.). 1988. *Travel Literature through the Ages: An Anthology*. New York: Garland.

Adas, Michael. 1981. "From Avoidance to Confrontation: Peasant Protest in Precolonial and Colonial Southeast Asia." *Comparative Studies in Society and History* 23:2, 217–47.

Adelman, Jeremy. 1994. *Frontier Development: Land, Labour, and Capital on the Wheatlands of Argentina and Canada, 1890–1914*. Oxford: Oxford University Press.

Adhikari, Mohamed (ed.). 2015. *Genocide on Settler Frontiers: When Hunter-Gatherers and Commercial Stock Farmers Clash*. New York: Bergahn.

(ed.). 2021. *Civilian-Driven Violence and the Genocide of Indigenous Peoples in Settler Societies*. London: Routledge.

Adsera Alicia, Carles Boix. 2002. "Trade, Democracy, and the Size of the Public Sector: The Political Underpinnings of Openness." *International Organization* 56, 229–62.

Ahmed, Ali T., David Stasavage. 2020. "Origins of Early Democracy." *American Political Science Review* 114:2, 502–18.

Akçomak, İ., Dinand Semih Webbink, Bas ter Weel. 2016. "Why Did the Netherlands Develop So Early? The Legacy of the Brethren of the Common Life." *Economic Journal* 126:593, 821–60.

Alagoa, Ebiegberi Joe. 1970. "Long-Distance Trade and States in the Niger Delta." *Journal of African History* 11:3, 319–29.

Alavi, Seema. 2015. *Muslim Cosmopolitanism in the Age of Empire*. Cambridge, MA: Harvard University Press.

Albareda, Joaquim, Manuel Herrero Sánchez (eds.). 2018. *Political Representation in the Ancien Régime*. London: Routledge.

Albertini, Rudolf con, Albert Wirz. 1982. *European Colonial Rule, 1880–1940: The Impact of the West on India, Southeast Asia, and Africa*. Westport, CT: Greenwood.

Albertus, Michael. 2017. "Landowners and Democracy: The Social Origins of Democracy Reconsidered." *World Politics* 69:2, 233–76.

Alcock, Susan E., John Bodel, Richard J. A. Talbert (eds.). 2012. *Highways, Byways, and Road Systems in the Pre-modern World*. New York: John Wiley & Sons.

Alef, Gustave. 1970. *The Crisis of the Muscovite Aristocracy: A Factor in the Growth of Monarchical Power*. Berlin: Osteuropa-Institut an der Freien Univ. Berlin, Historische Veröffentlichungen.

Alesina, Alberto Romain Wacziarg. 1998. "Openness, Country Size and the Government." *Journal of Public Economics* 69, 305–22.

Alesina, Alberto, Arnaud Devleeschauwer, William Easterly, Sergio Kurlat, Romain Wacziarg. 2003. "Fractionalization." *Journal of Economic Growth* 8:2, 155–94.

Alexanderson, Kris. 2019. *Subversive Seas: Anticolonial Networks across the Twentieth-Century Dutch Empire*. Cambridge: Cambridge University Press.

Alexandersson, Gunnar, Göran Norström. 1963. *World Shipping: An Economic Geography of Ports and Seaborne Trade*. New York: Wiley.

Alktekar, A. S. 1984. *State and Government in Ancient India*. Delhi: Motilal Banarsidass Publishers.

Allen, David Grayson. 1981. *In English Ways: The Movement of Societies and the Transfer of English Local Law and Custom to Massachusetts Bay in the Seventeenth Century*. Chapel Hill: University of North Carolina Press.

Allen, Theodore W. 1994. *The Invention of the White Race*. London: Verso.

Allin, Lawrence C. 1981. "The Integrated Inland Waterways of the USSR." *Naval War College Review* 34:3, 88–96.

Al-Nakib, Farah. 2014. "Inside a Gulf Port: The Dynamics of Urban Life in Pre-oil Kuwait." In Lawrence Potter (ed.), *The Persian Gulf in Modern Times: People, Ports, and History* (Boston: Springer), 199–228.

Alonso, Paula. 1996. "Voting in Buenos Aires (Argentina) before 1912." In Eduardo Posada-Carbo (ed.), *Elections before Democracy: The History of Elections in Europe and Latin America* (London: Palgrave Macmillan), 181–99.

Alpers, Edward A. 2014. *The Indian Ocean in World History*. Oxford: Oxford University Press.

Altman, David. 2010. *Direct Democracy Worldwide*. Cambridge: Cambridge University Press.

Alvarez-Villa, Daphne, Jenny Guardado. 2020. "The Long-Run Influence of Institutions Governing Trade: Evidence from Smuggling Ports in Colonial Mexico." *Journal of Development Economics* 102453.

Amirell, Stefan Eklöf, Leos Müller (eds.). 2014. *Persistent Piracy: Maritime Violence and State-Formation in Global Historical Perspective*. Berlin: Springer.

Anckar, Carsten. 2008. "Size, Islandness, and Democracy: A Global Comparison." *International Political Science Review*, 29:4, 440–1.

2011. *Religion and Democracy: A Worldwide Comparison*. London: Routledge.

Anckar, Dag, Carsten Anckar. 1995. "Size, Insularity and Democracy." *Scandinavian Political Studies*, 18:4, 211–29.

Andaya, Barbara Watson. 1992. "Political Development between the Sixteenth and Eighteenth Centuries." In Nicholas Tarling (ed.), *The Cambridge History of Southeast Asia. Volume 2: From c. 1500 to c. 1800* (Cambridge: Cambridge University Press), 402–59.

Andaya, Barbara Watson, Leonard Y. Andaya. 2015. *A History of Early Modern Southeast Asia, 1400–1830*. Cambridge: Cambridge University Press.

Andaya, Leonard Y. 1975. *The Kingdom of Johor, 1641–1728*. Oxford: Oxford University Press.

1981. *The Heritage of Arung Palakka: A History of South Sulawesi (Celebes) in the Seventeenth Century*. Boston: Springer Science & Business Media.

Andersen, David, Jørgen Møller, Lasse Lykke Rørbæk, Svend-Erik Skaaning. 2014. "State Capacity and Political Regime Stability." *Democratization* 21:7, 1305–25.

Andersen, Jørgen J., Michael L. Ross. 2014. "The Big Oil Change: A Closer Look at the Haber–Menaldo Analysis." *Comparative Political Studies* 47:7, 993–1021.

Anderson, Atholl. 2010. "The Origins and Development of Seafaring: Towards a Global Approach." In Atholl Anderson, James H. Barrett, Katherine V. Boyle (eds.), *The Global Origins and Development of Seafaring*, McDonald Institute for Archaeological Research (Cambridge: Cambridge University Press), 3–16.

Anderson, Benedict. 1991. *Imagined Communities: Reflections on the Origin and Spread of Nationalism*, revised ed. London: Verso.

Anderson, Clare, Niklas Frykman, Lex Heerma van Voss, Marcus Rediker (eds.). 2013. *Mutiny and Maritime Radicalism in the Age of Revolution*. Cambridge: Cambridge University Press.

Anderson, John. 2004. "Does God Matter, and If So Whose God? Religion and Democratization." *Democratization* 11, 192–217.

(ed.). 2006. *Religion, Democracy and Democratization*. London: Routledge.

2007. "The Catholic Contribution to Democratization's 'Third Wave': Altruism, Hegemony or Self-Interest?" *Cambridge Review of International Affairs* 20:3, 383–99.

Anderson, John L. 1995. "Piracy and World History: An Economic Perspective on Maritime Predation." *Journal of World History* 6:2, 175–99.

Anderson, Jon, Kimberley Peters (eds.). 2014. *Water Worlds: Human Geographies of the Ocean*. Farnham: Ashgate.

Anderson, Lisa. 1991. "Absolutism and the Resilience of Monarchy in the Middle East." *Political Science Quarterly* 106:1, 1–15.

2000. "Dynasts and Nationalists: Why Monarchies Survive." In Joseph Kostiner (ed.), *Middle East Monarchies* (London: Westview), 53–69.

Anderson, Perry. 1974. *Lineages of the Absolutist State*. London: New Left Books.

Andrade, Tonio. 2010. "Beyond Guns, Germs, and Steel: European Expansion and Maritime Asia, 1400–1750." *Journal of Early Modern History* 14:1–2, 165–86.

2011. "Was the European Sailing Ship a Key Technology of European Expansion? Evidence from East Asia." *International Journal of Maritime History* 23:2, 17–40.

2014. "Asian States and Overseas Expansion, 1500–1700: An Approach to the Problem of European Exceptionalism." In Geoff Wade (ed.), *Asian Expansions: The Historical Experiences of Polity Expansion in Asia* (London: Routledge), 64–80.

Andrade, Tonio, Xing Hang, Anand A. Yang, Kieko Matteson. 2016. *Sea Rovers, Silver, and Samurai: Maritime East Asia in Global History, 1550–1700*. Honolulu: University of Hawaii Press.

Andrews, George Reid. 2016. *Afro-Latin America: Black Lives, 1600–2000*. Cambridge, MA: Harvard University Press.

Andrews, Kenneth R. 1978. *The Spanish Caribbean: Trade and Plunder, 1530–1630*. New Haven: Yale University Press.

——— 1984. *Trade, Plunder and Settlement: Maritime Enterprise and the Genesis of the British Empire, 1480–1630*. Cambridge: Cambridge University Press.

Ang, James B., Per G. Fredriksson, Satyendra Kumar Gupta. 2020. "Crop Yield and Democracy." *Land Economics* 96:2, 265–90.

Angeles, Luis. 2007. "Income Inequality and Colonialism." *European Economic Review* 51:5, 1155–76.

Angelucci, Charles, Simone Meraglia, Nico Voigtländer. 2017. "How Merchant Towns Shaped Parliaments: From the Norman Conquest of England to the Great Reform Act." NBER Working Paper No. w23606. Cambridge, MA: National Bureau of Economic Research.

Ansell, Ben W., David J. Samuels. 2010. "Inequality and Democratization: A Contractarian Approach." *Comparative Political Studies* 43:12, 1543–74.

——— 2014. *Inequality and Democratization*. Cambridge: Cambridge University Press.

Anwar, Muhammad. 2001. "The Participation of Ethnic Minorities in British Politics." *Journal of Ethnic and Migration Studies* 27:3, 533–49.

Apfeld, Brendan. 2019. "Spatial and Temporal University Database." Working Paper. https://brendanapfeld.com/files/univ_database.pdf.

Appelbaum, Nancy P., Anne S. Macpherson, Karin Alejandra Rosemblatt (eds.). 2003. *Race and Nation in Modern Latin America*. Chapel Hill: University of North Carolina Press.

Aquinas, St. Thomas. 2012. *De Regno: On Kingship to the King of Cyprus*, trans. Gerald B. Phelan, rev. I. Th. Eschmann, Lexington: O.P. Veritatis Splendor Publications. Kindle edition.

Arasaratnam, Sinnappah. 1986. *Merchants, Companies and Commerce on the Coromandel Coast 1650–1740*. New Delhi: Oxford University Press.

——— 1994. *Maritime India in the Seventeenth Century*. Delhi: Oxford University Press.

Archibugi, Daniele. 2008. *The Global Commonwealth of Citizens: Toward Cosmopolitan Democracy*. Princeton: Princeton University Press.

Aristotle. 1932. *The Politics*, trans. H. Rackham. Cambridge, MA: Harvard University Press.

——— 1998. *The Politics*, trans. C. D. C. Reeve. Indianapolis: Hackett.

Armit, Ian, Chris Knüsel, John Robb, Rick Schulting. 2006. "Warfare and Violence in Prehistoric Europe: An Introduction." *Journal of Conflict Archaeology* 2:1, 1–11.

Armitage, David. 2007. "The Elephant and the Whale: Empires of Land and Sea." *Journal for Maritime Research* 9:1, 23–36.

Armitage, David, Alison Bashford (eds.). 2014. *Pacific Histories: Ocean, Land, People*. London: Palgrave Macmillan.

Armitage, David, Alison Bashford, Sujit Sivasundaram (eds.). 2017. *Oceanic Histories*. Cambridge: Cambridge University Press.

Armitage, David, Sanjay Subrahmanyam (eds.). 2009. *The Age of Revolutions in Global Context, c. 1760–1840*. London: Palgrave Macmillan.

Arnaud, Pascal. 2007. "Diocletian's Prices Edict: The Prices of Seaborne Transport and the Average Duration of Maritime Travel." *Journal of Roman Archaeology* 20: 321–36.

Arnheim, M. T. W. 1972. *The Senatorial Aristocracy in the Later Roman Empire*. Oxford: Clarendon Press.

Arnold, Rosemary. 1957. "A Port of Trade: Whydah on the Guinea Coast." In Karl Polanyi, Conrad M. Arensberg, Harry W. Pearson (eds.), *Trade and Market in the Early Empires: Economies in History and Theory* (New York: Free Press), 154–76.

Ashdown, P. 1979. *Caribbean History in Maps*. London: Addison-Wesley Longman Ltd.

Ashraf, Quamrul, Stelios Michalopoulos. 2015. "Climatic Fluctuations and the Diffusion of Agriculture." *Review of Economics and Statistics* 97:3, 589–609.

Ashraf, Quamrul, Ömer Özak, Oded Galor. 2010. "Isolation and Development." *Journal of the European Economic Association* 8:2–3, 401–12.

Audretsch, David B., Maryann P. Feldman. 1996. "Knowledge Spillovers and the Geography of Innovation and Production." *American Economic Review* 86, 630–40.

Aung-Thwin, Michael A. 1985. *Pagan: The Origins of Modern Burma*. Honolulu: University of Hawaii Press.

Avari, Burjor. 2007. *India: The Ancient Past: A History of the Indian Sub-continent from c. 7000 BC to AD 1200*. London: Routledge.

Avelino, George, David S. Brown, Wendy Hunter. 2005. "The Effects of Capital Mobility, Trade Openness, and Democracy on Social Spending in Latin America, 1980–1999." *American Journal of Political Science* 49, 625–41.

Ayalon, Ami. 2000. "Post-Ottoman Arab Monarchies: Old Bottles, New Labels?" In Joseph Kostiner (ed.), *Middle East Monarchies* (London: Westview), 159–77.

Ayittey, George. 2006. *Indigenous African Institutions*, 2nd ed. Ardsley, NY: Transnational Publishers.

Ayres, Alex. 2010. *The Wit and Wisdom of Mark Twain*. New York: HarperCollins.

Bączkowski, Włodzimierz. 1958. *Russian Colonialism: The Tsarist and Soviet Empires*. New York: Frederick A. Praeger.

Bagehot, Walter. 1872. *The English Constitution: By Walter Bagehot*. Garden City, NY: Doubleday.

Bagwell, Philip S. 1974. *The Transport Revolution from 1770*. London: B.T. Batsford.

Bailyn, Bernard. 1967. *The Ideological Origins of the American Revolution*. Cambridge, MA: Harvard University Press.

Baines, John, Norman Yoffee. 1998. "Order, Legitimacy, and Wealth in Ancient Egypt and Mesopotamia." In Gary M. Feinman and Joyce Marcus (eds.), *Archaic States* (Santa Fe, NM: School of American Research Press), 199–260.

Bairoch, Paul. 1976. "Europe's Gross National Product, 1800–1975." *Journal of European Economic History* 5:2, 273–340.

Baker, Chris, Pasuk Phongpaichit. 2017. *A History of Ayutthaya: Siam in the Early Modern World*. Cambridge: Cambridge University Press.

Bakker, Jan David, Stephan Maurer, Jörn-Steffen Pischke, Ferdinand Rauch. 2020. "Of Mice and Merchants: Connectedness and the Location of Economic Activity in the Iron Age." *Review of Economics and Statistics* 103:4, 652–65.

Balard, Michel (ed.). 2017. *The Sea in History: The Medieval World*. Woodbridge, Suffolk: Boydell.

Balázs, Étienne. 1964. *Chinese Civilization and Bureaucracy*. New Haven: Yale University Press.

Baldacchino, Godfrey. 2012. "Islands and Despots." *Commonwealth and Comparative Politics*, 50:1, 103–20.

Baldwin, Kate. 2016. *The Paradox of Traditional Chiefs in Democratic Africa*. Cambridge: Cambridge University Press.

Ball, Philip. 2017. *The Water Kingdom: A Secret History of China*. Chicago: University of Chicago Press.

Banaji, Jairus. 2009. "Aristocracies, Peasantries and the Framing of the Early Middle Ages." *Journal of Agrarian Change* 9:1, 59–91.

Bang, Peter Fibiger, Christopher Bayly (eds.). 2011. *Tributary Empires in Global History*. London: Palgrave Macmillan.

Bang, Peter Fibiger, Dariusz Kolodziejczyk (eds.). 2012. *Universal Empire: A Comparative Approach to Imperial Culture and Representation in Eurasian History*. Cambridge: Cambridge University Press.

Bang, Peter Fibiger, Walter Scheidel (eds.). 2013. *The Oxford Handbook of the State in the Ancient Near East and Mediterranean*. Oxford: Oxford University Press.

Banga, Indu (ed.). 1992. *Ports and Their Hinterlands in India, 1700–1950*. New Delhi: South Asia Books.

Bankoff, Greg. 2017. "Aeolian Empires: The Influence of Winds and Currents on European Maritime Expansion in the Days of Sail." *Environment and History* 23:2, 163–96.

Barber, Benjamin. 1974. *The Death of Communal Liberty: The History of Freedom in a Swiss Mountain Canton*. Princeton: Princeton University Press.

2000. "Can Democracy Survive Globalization?" *Government and Opposition* 35:3, 275–301.

2003. *Strong Democracy: Participatory Politics for a New Age*. Berkeley: University of California Press.

Barbieri, Katherine, Omar M. G. Keshk. 2016. "Correlates of War Project Trade Data Set Codebook, Version 4.0." https://correlatesofwar.org/data-sets/bilateral-trade.

Barbosa, Duarte. 1866 [1519]. *A Description of the Coasts of East Africa and Malabar in the Beginning of the Sixteenth Century*, trans. Henry E. J. Stanley. London: Hakluyt Society.

Barbour, Stephen, Cathie Carmichael. 2000. *Language and Nationalism in Europe*. New York: Oxford University Press.

Barendse, Rene J. 2000. "Trade and State in the Arabian Seas: A Survey from the Fifteenth to the Eighteenth Century." *Journal of World History* 11:2, 173–225.
2016. *The Arabian Seas: The Indian Ocean World of the Seventeenth Century.* London: Routledge.
Barfield, Thomas. 1989. *Perilous Frontier: Nomadic Empires and China.* Oxford: Blackwell.
1993. *The Nomadic Alternative.* Englewood Cliffs: Prentice Hall.
2010. *Afghanistan: A Cultural and Political History.* Princeton: Princeton University Press.
Barkey, Karen. 2008. *Empire of Difference: The Ottomans in Comparative Perspective.* Cambridge: Cambridge University Press.
Barkey, Karen, Rudi Batzell. 2011. "Comparisons across Empires: The Critical Social Structures of the Ottomans, Russians and Habsburgs during the Seventeenth Century." In Peter Bang and Christopher Bayly (eds.), *Tributary Empires in Global History* (London: Palgrave Macmillan), 226–61.
Barnwell, P. S., Marco Mostert. 2003. *Political Assemblies in the Earlier Middle Ages.* Leiden: Brepols.
Barrett, David B. 1982. *World Christian Encyclopedia.* New York: Oxford University Press.
Barrett, David B., George T. Kurian, Todd M. Johnson. 2000. *World Christian Encyclopedia. Volume 3.* Oxford: Oxford University Press.
Bartlett, Richard H. 1979–80. "Citizens Minus: Indians and the Right to Vote." *Saskatchewan Law Review* 44:2, 163–94.
Bartlett, Robert. 1994. *The Making of Europe: Conquest, Colonization, and Cultural Change, 950–1350.* Princeton: Princeton University Press.
Basham, Arthur Llewellyn. 1967. *The Wonder That Was India,* 3rd ed. London: Sidgwick & Jackson.
Bass, Allen M. 1995. "Early Germanic Experience and the Origins of Representation." *Parliaments, Estates and Representation* 15:1, 1–11.
Bassin, Mark. 1991. "Russia between Europe and Asia: The Ideological Construction of Geographical Space." *Slavic Review* 50:1, 1–17.
Basu, Dilip K. (ed.). 1985. *The Rise and Growth of the Colonial Port Cities in Asia.* Berkeley: University of California Press.
Bateman, Fiona, Lionel Pilkington (eds.). 2011. *Studies in Settler Colonialism: Politics, Identity and Culture.* Boston: Springer.
Bates, Robert H., Da-Hsiang Donald Lien. 1985. "A Note on Taxation, Development, and Representative Government." *Politics and Society* 14:1, 53–70.
Bathurst, R. D. 1972. "Maritime Trade and Imamate Government: Two Principal Themes in the History of Oman to 1728." In Derek Hopwood (ed.), *The Arabian Peninsula: Society and Politics* (London: George Allen & Unwin), 89–106.
Bayly, Christopher Alan. 1988. *Rulers, Townsmen and Bazaars: North Indian Society in the Age of British Expansion, 1770–1870.* Cambridge: Cambridge University Press.
2012. *Recovering Liberties: Indian Thought in the Age of Liberalism and Empire.* Cambridge: Cambridge University Press.

2016. *Imperial Meridian: The British Empire and the World 1780–1830*. London: Routledge.

Bayly, Christopher Alan, Eugenio F. Biagini (eds.). 2008. *Giuseppe Mazzini and the Globalisation of Democratic Nationalism (1830–1920)*. Oxford: Oxford University Press.

Beattie, John. 1960. *Bunyoro: An African Kingdom*. New York: Wadsworth.

1967. "Checks on the Abuse of Political Power in Some African States: A Preliminary Framework for Analysis." In Ronald Cohen and John Middleton (eds.), *Comparative Political Systems: Studies in the Politics of Pre-industrial Societies* (Garden City, NY: Natural History Press), 355–73.

Beaven, Brad, Karl Bell, Robert James (eds.). 2016. *Port Towns and Urban Cultures: International Histories of the Waterfront, c. 1700–2000*. Boston: Springer.

Becker, Gary S. 1971. *The Economics of Discrimination*. Chicago: University of Chicago Press.

Becker, Sascha O., Steven Pfaff, Jared Rubin. 2016. "Causes and Consequences of the Protestant Reformation." *Explorations in Economic History* 62, 1–25.

Beckles, Hilary. 1990. *A History of Barbados: From Amerindian Settlement to Nation-State*. Cambridge: Cambridge University Press.

Bednarik, Robert G. 2014. "The Beginnings of Maritime Travel." *Advances in Anthropology* 4:4, 209–21.

Beerbühl, Margrit Schulte, Jörg Vögele (eds.). 2004. *Spinning the Commercial Web. International Trade, Merchants and Commercial Cities, c. 1640–1939*. Frankfurt am Main: Peter Lang.

Begley, Vimala, Richard Daniel De Puma (eds.). 1991. *Rome and India: The Ancient Sea Trade*. Madison: University of Wisconsin Press.

Beik, William. 1985. *Absolutism and Society in Seventeenth-Century France: State Power and Provincial Aristocracy in Languedoc*. Cambridge: Cambridge University Press.

Belich, James. 2009. *Replenishing the Earth: The Settler Revolution and the Rise of the Angloworld*. Oxford: Oxford University Press.

2010. "How Much Did Institutions Matter? Cloning Britain in New Zealand." In Jack P. Greene (ed.), *Exclusionary Empire: English Liberty Overseas: 1600–1900* (Cambridge: Cambridge University Press), 248–68.

Bellwood, Peter. 2005. *First Farmers: The Origins of Agricultural Societies*. Malden, MA: Blackwell.

Benda, Harry J. 1962. "The Structure of Southeast Asian History: Some Preliminary Observations." *Journal of Southeast Asian History* 3:1, 106–38.

Bender, Gerald Jacob. 1978. *Angola under the Portuguese: The Myth and the Reality*. Berkeley: University of California Press.

Bendix, Reinhard. 1978. *Kings or People: Power and the Mandate to Rule*. Berkeley: University of California Press.

Benhabib, Seyla. 2009. "Cosmopolitanism and Democracy: Affinities and Tensions." *The Hedgehog Review* 11:3, 30–42.

Bentley, Jerry H. 1993. *Old World Encounters: Cross-cultural Contacts and Exchanges in Premodern Times*. New York: Oxford University Press.

1999. "Sea and Ocean Basins as Frameworks of Historical Analysis." *Geographical Review* 89:2, 215–24.

Bentley, Jerry H., Renate Bridenthal, Kären Wigen (eds.). 2007. *Seascapes: Maritime Histories, Littoral Cultures, and Transoceanic Exchanges*. Honolulu: University of Hawaii Press.

Benton, Lauren, Nathan Perl-Rosenthal (eds.). 2020. *A World at Sea: Maritime Practices and Global History*. Philadelphia: University of Pennsylvania Press.

Bentzen, Jeanet Sinding, Nicolai Kaarsen, Asger Moll Wingender. 2016. "Irrigation and Autocracy." *Journal of the European Economic Association* 15:1, 1–53.

Bentzen, Jeanet Sinding, Jacob Gerner Hariri, James A. Robinson. 2019. "Power and Persistence: The Indigenous Roots of Representative Democracy." *The Economic Journal* 129:618, 678–714.

Benzell, Seth G., Kevin Cooke. 2018. "A Network of Thrones: Kinship and Conflict in Europe, 1495–1918." Working Paper. https://ide.mit.edu/wp-content/uploads/2018/05/Network-of-Thrones-Benzell-and-Cooke-5-19-2018.pdf.

Berce, Yves-Marie. 1987. *Revolt and Revolution in Early Modern Europe: An Essay on the History of Political Violence*. New York: Saint Martin's Press.

Berend, Nora, Przemysław Urbańczyk, Przemysław Wiszewski. 2013. *Central Europe in the High Middle Ages: Bohemia, Hungary and Poland, c. 900–c. 1300*. Cambridge: Cambridge University Press.

Berman, Harold J. 1983. *Law and Revolution: The Formation of the Western Legal Tradition*. Cambridge, MA: Harvard University Press.

Berman, Sheri. 2007. "How Democracies Emerge: Lessons from Europe." *Journal of Democracy* 18:1, 28–41.

Bernhard, Michael, Christopher Reenock, Timothy Nordstrom. 2004. "The Legacy of Western Overseas Colonialism on Democratic Survival." *International Studies Quarterly* 48, 225–50.

Berry, Mary Elizabeth. 1986. "Public Peace and Private Attachment: The Goals and Conduct of Power in Early Modern Japan." *Journal of Japanese Studies* 12:2, 237–71.

Bethencourt, Francisco. 2007. "Political Configurations and Local Powers." In Francisco Bethencourt and Diogo Ramada Curto (eds.), *Portuguese Oceanic Expansion, 1400–1800* (Cambridge: Cambridge University Press), 197–254. 2015. *Racisms: From the Crusades to the Twentieth Century*. Princeton: Princeton University Press.

Bethencourt, Francisco, Diogo Ramada Curto (eds.). 2007. *Portuguese Oceanic Expansion, 1400–1800*. Cambridge: Cambridge University Press.

Beyer, Peter (ed.). 2001. *Religion in the Process of Globalization*. Würzburg: Ergon Verlag.

Bhandar, Brenna. 2018. *Colonial Lives of Property: Law, Land, and Racial Regimes of Ownership*. Durham, NC: Duke University Press.

Bicchieri, Marco Giuseppe (ed.). 1972. *Hunters and Gatherers Today: Socioeconomic Study of Eleven Such Cultures in the Twentieth Century*. Long Grove, IL: Waveland Press.

Bickers, Robert. 1998. "Shanghailanders: The Formation and Identity of the British Settler Community in Shanghai, 1843–1937." *Past & Present* 159, 161–211.

Bickers, Robert, Isabella Jackson (eds.). 2016. *Treaty Ports in Modern China: Law, Land and Power*. London: Routledge.

Bielenstein, Hans. 1980. *The Bureaucracy of Han Times*. Cambridge: Cambridge University Press.

Bilder, Mary Sarah. 2006. "The Corporate Origins of Judicial Review." *Yale Law Journal* 116, 502–66.

Bilinski, Adam. 2015. "Paths to Success, Paths to Failure: Historical Trajectories to Democratic Stability." PhD dissertation, University of Florida.

Birnbaum, Henrik. 1981. *Lord Novgorod the Great: Essays in the History and Culture of a Medieval City-State*. Columbus, OH: Slavica Publishers.

Bisson, Thomas N. 1964. *Assemblies and Representation in Languedoc in the Thirteenth Century*. Princeton: Princeton University Press.

1966. "The Military Origins of Medieval Representation." *American Historical Review* 71:4, 1199–218.

2001. "Medieval Parliamentarianism: Review of Work." *Parliaments, Estates and Representation* 21:1, 1–14.

Black, Antony. 1984. *Guilds and Civil Society in European Political Thought from the Twelfth Century to the Present*. Ithaca: Cornell University Press.

1992. *Political Thought in Europe 1250–1450*. Cambridge: Cambridge University Press.

Black, Jeremy. 2004. *The British Seaborne Empire*. New Haven: Yale University Press.

Blackman, David J. 2008. "Sea Transport, Part 2: Harbors." *The Oxford Handbook of Engineering and Technology in the Classical World* (Oxford: Oxford University Press), 638–72.

Blain, Neil, Hugh O'Donnell (eds.). 2001. *Media, Monarchy and Power: The Postmodern Culture in Europe*. Bristol: Intellect.

Blake, Stephen P. 2011. "Returning the Household to the Patrimonial-Bureaucratic Empire: Gender, Succession, and Ritual in the Mughal, Safavid and Ottoman Empires." In Peter Fibiger Bang and C. A. Bayly (eds.), *Tributary Empires in Global History* (London: Palgrave Macmillan), 214–26.

Blanton, Richard E. 1998. "Beyond Centralization: Steps toward a Theory of Egalitarian Behavior in Archaic States." In Gary M. Feinman and Joyce Marcus (eds.), *Archaic States* (Santa Fe, NM: School of American Research Press), 199–260.

2016. *How Humans Cooperate: Confronting the Challenges of Collective Action*. Boulder: University Press of Colorado.

Blanton, Richard, Lane Fargher. 2008. *Collective Action in the Formation of Premodern States*. Boston: Springer.

Blaydes, Lisa. 2017. "State Building in the Middle East." *Annual Review of Political Science* 20, 487–504.

Blaydes, Lisa, Eric Chaney. 2013. "The Feudal Revolution and Europe's Rise: Political Divergence of the Christian West and the Muslim World before 1500 CE." *American Political Science Review* 107:1, 16–34.

Blaydes, Lisa, Justin Grimmer, Alison McQueen. 2018. "Mirrors for Princes and Sultans: Advice on the Art of Governance in the Medieval Christian and Islamic Worlds." *Journal of Politics* 80:4, 1150–67.

Bleakley, Hoyt, Jeffrey Lin. 2012. "Portage and Path Dependence." *Quarterly Journal of Economics* 127, 587–644.

Bleaney, Michael, Arcangelo Dimico. 2011. "Biogeographical Conditions, the Transition to Agriculture, and Long-Run Growth." *European Economic Review* 55:7, 943–54.

Blickle, Peter. 1992. *Communal Reformation: The Quest for Salvation in Sixteenth-Century Germany*. Leiden: Brill.

(ed.). 1997. *Resistance, Representation, and Community*. Oxford: Oxford University Press.

Blinkhorn, Martin, Ralph Gibson (eds.). 1991. *Landownership and Power in Modern Europe*. London: Routledge.

Bloch, Marc. 1971 [1939]. *Feudal Society. Volume I. The Growth of Ties of Dependence*. London: Routledge and Kegan Paul.

Blockmans, Willem Pieter. 1978. "A Typology of Representative Institutions in Late Medieval Europe." *Journal of Medieval History* 4, 189–215.

1994. "Voracious States and Obstructing Cities: An Aspect of State Formation in Preindustrial Europe." In Charles Tilly and Wim P. Blockmans (eds.), *Cities and the Rise of States in Europe, A.D. 1000 to 1800* (Boulder: Westview Press), 218–50.

2009. "Citizens and Their Rulers." In Willem Pieter Blockmans, André Holenstein, Jon Mathieu (eds.), *Empowering Interactions: Political Cultures and the Emergence of the State in Europe: 1300–1900* (Farnham: Ashgate), 281–91.

Blockmans, Willem Pieter, Marjolein 't Hart. 2013. "Power." In Peter Clark (ed.), *The Oxford Handbook of Cities in World History* (Oxford: Oxford University Press), 421–37.

Blockmans, Willem Pieter, Mikhail Krom, Justyna Wubs-Mrozewicz (eds.). 2017. *The Routledge Handbook of Maritime Trade around Europe 1300–1600: Commercial Networks and Urban Autonomy*. London: Taylor & Francis.

Blondé, Bruno, Marc Boone, Anne-Laure Van Bruaene (eds.). 2018. *City and Society in the Low Countries, 1100–1600*. Cambridge: Cambridge University Press.

Blum, Jerome. 1961. *Lord and Peasant in Russia: From the Ninth to the Nineteenth Century*. Princeton: Princeton University Press.

Blussé, Leonard. 2013. "Port Cities of South East Asia: 1400–1800." In Peter Clark (ed.), *The Oxford Handbook of Cities in World History* (Oxford: Oxford University Press), 345–63.

Bockstette, Valerie, Areendam Chanda, Louis Putterman. 2002. "States and Markets: The Advantage of an Early Start." *Journal of Economic Growth* 7:4, 347–69.

Bodin, Jean. 1955. *Six Books of the Commonwealth*, trans. M. J. Tooley. Oxford: Basil Blackwell.

Boehm, Christopher. 1984. *Blood Revenge: The Anthropology of Feuding in Montenegro and Other Tribal Societies*. Lawrence: University Press of Kansas.

2009. *Hierarchy in the Forest: The Evolution of Egalitarian Behavior*. Cambridge, MA: Harvard University Press.

Bogaards, Matthijs. 2019. "Case-Based Research on Democratization." *Democratization* 26:1, 61–77.

Böhmelt, Tobias, Ulrich Pilster, Atsushi Tago. 2017. "Naval Forces and Civil–Military Relations." *Journal of Global Security Studies* 2:4, 346–63.

Boix, Carles. 2003. *Democracy and Redistribution*. New York: Cambridge University Press.

2015. *Political Order and Inequality: Their Foundations and Their Consequences for Human Welfare*. Cambridge: Cambridge University Press.

Boix, Carles, Susan C. Stokes. 2003. "Endogenous Democratization." *World Politics* 55:4, 517–49.

Boix, Carles, Michael Miller, Sebastian Rosato. 2013. "A Complete Dataset of Political Regimes, 1800–2007." *Comparative Political Studies* 46:12, 1523–54.

Bol, Peter K. 2008. *Neo-Confucianism in History*. Cambridge, MA: Harvard University Asia Center.

Bollen, Kenneth A., Robert W. Jackman. 1985. "Political Democracy and the Size Distribution of Income." *American Sociological Review* 50, 438–57.

Bollen, Kenneth A., Pamela Paxton. 2000. "Subjective Measures of Liberal Democracy." *Comparative Political Studies* 33, 58–86.

Bolt, Jutta, Jan Luiten van Zanden. 2014. "The Maddison Project: Collaborative Research on Historical National Accounts." *Economic History Review* 67:3, 627–51.

Bondarenko, Dmitri, Andrey Korotayev. 2000. "Family Size and Community Organization: A Cross-cultural Comparison." *Cross-cultural Research* 34:2, 152–89.

Bonneau, Danielle. 1993. *Le Régime administratif de l'eau du Nil dans l'Égypte Grecque, Romaine et Byzantine*. Leiden: Brill.

Bonnett, Alastair. 1998. "Who Was White? The Disappearance of Non-European White Identities and the Formation of European Racial Whiteness." *Ethnic and Racial Studies* 21:6, 1029–55.

Bonvini, Alessandro, Stephen Jacobson. 2022. "Democratic Imperialism and Risorgimento Colonialism: European Legionnaires on the Argentine Pampa in the 1850s." *Journal of Global History* 17:1, 89–108.

Boomgaard, Peter (ed.). 2007. *A World of Water: Rain, Rivers and Seas in Southeast Asian Histories*. Leiden: Brill.

Borcan, Oana, Ola Olsson, Louis Putterman. 2018. "State History and Economic Development: Evidence from Six Millennia." *Journal of Economic Growth* 23:1, 1–40.

Bordo, Michael D., Alan M. Taylor, Jeffrey G. Williamson (eds.). 2003. *Globalization in Historical Perspective* Chicago: University of Chicago Press.

Bosa, Miguel Suarez (ed.). 2014. *Atlantic Ports and the First Globalisation c. 1850–1930*. London: Macmillan.

Bose, Sugata. 2006. *A Hundred Horizons: The Indian Ocean in the Age of Global Empire*. Cambridge, MA: Harvard University Press.

Boserup, Ester. 1965. *The Conditions of Agricultural Growth: The Economics of Agrarian Change under Population Pressure*. Chicago: Aldine.

Bosker, Maarten, Eltjo Buringh. 2017. "City Seeds: Geography and the Origins of the European City System." *Journal of Urban Economics* 98, 139–57.

Bosker, Maarten, Eltjo Buringh, Jan Luiten van Zanden. 2013. "From Baghdad to London: Unravelling Urban Development in Europe, the Middle East and North Africa, 800–1800." *Review of Economics and Statistics* 95:4, 1418–37.

Boussac, Marie-Françoise, Jean-François Salles, Jean-Baptiste Yon (eds.). 2016. *Ports of the Ancient Indian Ocean.* Delhi: Primus Books.

Bowen, Huw, John McAleer, Robert J. Blyth. 2011. *Monsoon Traders: The Maritime World of the East India Company.* London: Scala.

Bowen, Huw Vaughan, Elizabeth Mancke, John G. Reid (eds.). 2012. *Britain's Oceanic Empire: Atlantic and Indian Ocean Worlds, c. 1550–1850.* Cambridge: Cambridge University Press.

Boxer, Charles Robbins. 1965a. *The Dutch Seaborne Empire.* London: Hutchinson.

1965b. *Portuguese Society in the Tropics: The Municipal Councils of Goa, Macao, Bahia, and Luanda, 1510–1800.* Madison: University of Wisconsin Press.

1969. *The Portuguese Seaborne Empire, 1415–1825.* London: Hutchinson.

Boyle, Katherine V., Atholl Anderson (eds.). 2010. *The Global Origins and Development of Seafaring.* McDonald Institute for Archaeological Research. Cambridge: Cambridge University Press.

Brady, Thomas A. 1985. *Turning Swiss: Cities and Empire, 1450–1550.* Cambridge: Cambridge University Press.

Brakel, L. F., Anthony Reid, Lauce Castles. 1975. *Precolonial State Systems in Southeast Asia.* Kuala Lumpur: Malaysian Branch of the Royal Asiatic Society.

Branch, Jordan. 2014. *The Cartographic State: Maps, Territory, and the Origins of Sovereignty.* Cambridge: Cambridge University Press.

Braudel, Fernand. 1972 [1949]. *The Mediterranean and the Mediterranean World in the Age of Philip II,* 2 vols. New York: Harper & Row.

Bray, Francesca. 1986. *The Rice Economies: Technology and Development in Asian Societies.* Berkeley: University of California Press.

Bremer, Stuart A. 1992. "Dangerous Dyads: Conditions Affecting the Likelihood of Interstate War, 1816–1965." *Journal of Conflict Resolution* 36:2, 309–41.

Bremmer, Jan N. 2014. *Initiation into the Mysteries of the Ancient World.* Berlin: Walter de Gruyter.

Brenner, Robert. 1976. "Agrarian Class Structure and Economic Development in Pre-industrial Europe." *Past & Present* 70:1, 30–75.

2003. *Merchants and Revolution: Commercial Change, Political Conflict, and London's Overseas Traders, 1550–1653.* London: Verso.

Bretagnolle, Anne. 2016. "City-Systems and Maritime Transport in the Long Term." In César Ducruet (ed.), *Maritime Networks: Spatial Structures and Time Dynamics* (London: Routledge), 51–60.

Breuilly, John. 1993. *Nationalism and the State.* Chicago: University of Chicago Press.

Breunig, Christian, Xun Cao, Adam Luedtke. 2012. "Global Migration and Political Regime Type: A Democratic Disadvantage." *British Journal of Political Science* 42:4, 825–54.

Brinks, Daniel, Michael Coppedge. 2006. "Diffusion Is No Illusion: Neighbor Emulation in the Third Wave of Democracy." *Comparative Political Studies* 39, 463–89.

Broadberry, Stephen. 2015. "Accounting for the Great Divergence." www
.nuffield.ox.ac.uk/users/Broadberry/AccountingGreatDivergence6.pdf.
Broadberry, Stephen, Bishnupriya Gupta. 2006. "The Early Modern Great
Divergence: Wages, Prices and Economic Development in Europe and
Asia, 1500–1800." *Economic History Review* 59:1, 2–31.
Broadberry, Stephen, A. Klein. 2012. "Aggregate and per Capita GDP in
Europe, 1870–2000: Continental, Regional and National Data with
Changing Boundaries." *Scandinavian Economic History Review* 60:1,
79–107.
Broeze, Frank (ed.). 1989. *Brides of the Sea: Port Cities of Asia from the Sixteenth to
the Twentieth Centuries.* Honolulu: University of Hawaii Press.
    1996. "The Ports and Port System of the Asian Seas: An Overview with
Historical Perspective from c. 1750." *The Great Circle* 18:2, 73–96.
    (ed.). 1997a. *Gateways of Asia: Port Cities of Asia in the 13th–20th Centuries.*
London: Routledge.
    1997b. "Kuwait before Oil: The Dynamics and Morphology of an Arab Port
City." In Frank Broeze (ed.), *Gateways of Asia: Port Cities of Asia in the 13th–
20th Centuries* (London: Routledge), 149–90.
    2002. *The Globalisation of the Oceans: Containerisation from the 1950s to the
Present.* St. John's: International Maritime Economic History Association.
Broeze, Frank, Peter Reeves, Kenneth McPherson. 1986. "Imperial Ports and
the Modern World Economy: The Case of the Indian Ocean." *Journal of
Transport History,* 1st Ser., 7:2, 1–20.
Broodbank, Cyprian. 2006. "The Origins and Early Development of
Mediterranean Maritime Activity." *Journal of Mediterranean Archaeology*
19:2, 199–230.
    2013. *The Making of the Middle Sea: A History of the Mediterranean from the
Beginning to the Emergence of the Classical World.* London: Thames and
Hudson.
Brooks, George E. 2003. *Eurafricans in Western Africa: Commerce, Social Status,
Gender, and Religious Observance from the Sixteenth to the Eighteenth Century.*
Athens, OH: Ohio University Press.
Brooks, Sarah M., Marcus J. Kurtz. 2016. "Oil and Democracy: Endogenous
Natural Resources and the Political 'Resource Curse.'" *International
Organization* 70:2, 279–311.
Brown, Delmer M. (ed.). 1993. *The Cambridge History of Japan: Ancient Japan.*
Cambridge: Cambridge University Press.
Brown, Elizabeth A. R. 1974. "The Tyranny of a Construct: Feudalism and
Historians of Medieval Europe." *American Historical Review* 79:4,
1063–88.
Brown, G. Gordon. 1944. "Missions and Cultural Diffusion." *American Journal
of Sociology* 50:3, 214–19.
Brown, Robert E. 1969. *Middle-Class Democracy and the Revolution in
Massachusetts, 1691–1780.* New York: Harper.
Brown, Robin. 2002. "The Contagiousness of Conflict: E.E. Schattschneider as
a Theorist of the Information Society." *Information, Communication and
Society* 5:2, 258–75.

Bruce, Steve. 2004. "Did Protestantism Create Democracy?" *Democratization* 11:4, 3–20.

Bruijn, Jaap R., Femme S. Gaastra (eds.). 1993. *Ships, Sailors and Spices: East India Companies and Their Shipping in the 16th, 17th and 18th Centuries*. Amsterdam: Amsterdam University Press.

Brunner, O. 1975. "Feudalism: The History of a Concept." In F.-L. Cheyette (ed.), *Lordship and Community in Medieval Europe: Selected Readings*. New York: Holt, Rinehart and Winston.

Bryan, Frank M. 2010. *Real Democracy: The New England Town Meeting and How It Works*. Chicago: University of Chicago Press.

Bryant, Arthur. 1985. *Set in a Silver Sea: The Island Peoples from Earliest Times to the Fifteenth Century. Volume 1*. London: Panther.

Buchan, Nancy R., Gianluca Grimalda, Rick Wilson, Marilynn Brewer, Enrique Fatas, Margaret Foddy. 2009. "Globalization and Human Cooperation." *Proceedings of the National Academy of Sciences* 106:11, 4138–42.

Buchan, Nancy R., Enrique Fatas, Gianluca Grimalda. 2012. "Connectivity and Cooperation." In Gary E. Bolton and Rachel T. A. Croson (eds.), *The Oxford Handbook of Economic Conflict Resolution* (Oxford: Oxford University Press), 151–81.

Buchanan, James M. 1965. "An Economic Theory of Clubs." *Economica* 32:125, 1–14.

Buchet, Christian, Gérard Le Bouëdec (eds.). 2017. *The Sea in History: The Early Modern World*. Woodbridge, Suffolk: Boydell Press.

Bueno de Mesquita, Bruce, Alastair Smith, James D. Morrow, Randolph M. Siverson. 2003. *The Logic of Political Survival*. Cambridge, MA: MIT Press.

Buhaug, Halvard, Scott Gates, Päivi Lujala. 2009. "Geography, Rebel Capability, and the Duration of Civil Conflict." *Journal of Conflict Resolution* 53:4, 544–69.

Bulliet, Richard W. 1975. *The Camel and the Wheel*. Cambridge, MA: Harvard University Press.

Burbank, Jane, Frederick Cooper. 2010. *Empires in World History: Power and the Politics of Difference*. Princeton: Princeton University Press.

Burkholder, Mark A., Dewitt Samuel Chandler. 1977. *From Impotence to Authority: The Spanish Crown and the American Audiencias, 1687–1808*. Columbia: University of Missouri Press.

Burling, Robbins. 1974. *The Passage of Power: Studies in Political Succession*. New York: Academic Press.

Butel, Paul. 1999. *The Atlantic*. London: Routledge.

Butler, Lee A. 2002. *Emperor and Aristocracy in Japan, 1467–1680: Resilience and Renewal*. Cambridge, MA: Harvard University Press.

Butzer, Karl W. 1976. *Early Hydraulic Civilization in Egypt: A Study in Cultural Ecology*. Chicago: Chicago University Press.

——— 1996. "Irrigation, Raised Fields and State Management: Wittfogel Redux?" *Antiquity* 70:267, 200–4.

Cabantous, Alain. 2014. *Le Ciel dans la mer: Christianisme et civilisation maritime (XVIe–XIXe siècle)*. Paris: Fayard.

Cahall, Raymond Du Bois. 1915. "The Sovereign Council of New France: A Study in Canadian Constitutional History." PhD dissertation, Columbia University.

Cain, Philip J., Anthony G. Hopkins. 1993. *British Imperialism: Innovation and Expansion 1688–1914*. New York: Longman.

Cairncross, Frances. 1997. *The Death of Distance: How the Communications Revolution Will Change Our Lives*. Boston: Harvard Business School Press.

Caldwell, John C., Graham E. Harrison, Pat Quiggin. 1980. "The Demography of Micro-states." *World Development*, 8:12, 953–62.

Cameron, David R. 1978. "The Expansion of the Public Economy: A Comparative Analysis." *American Political Science Review* 72, 1243–61.

Campbell, Brian. 2012. *Rivers and the Power of Ancient Rome*. Chapel Hill: University of North Carolina Press.

Canfora, Luciano. 2006. *Democracy in Europe: A History of an Ideology*. Chichester: John Wiley & Sons.

Cañizares-Esguerra, Jorge, Erik R. Seeman. 2016. *The Atlantic in Global History: 1500–2000*. London: Routledge.

Cannadine, David (ed.). 2007. *Empire, the Sea and Global History: Britain's Maritime World, c. 1760–c. 1840*. New York: Palgrave Macmillan.

Canny, Nicholas (ed.). 1994. *Europeans on the Move: Studies on European Migration 1500–1800*. Oxford: Clarendon Press.

Cao, Jiyin, Adam D. Galinsky, William W. Maddux. 2014. "Does Travel Broaden the Mind? Breadth of Foreign Experiences Increases Generalized Trust." *Social Psychological and Personality Science* 5:5, 517–25.

Capen, Nahum. 1875. *The History of Democracy: Or, Political Progress, Historically Illustrated, from the Earliest to the Latest Periods*. New York: American Publishing Co.

Capoccia, Giovanni, Daniel Ziblatt. 2010. "The Historical Turn in Democratization Studies: A New Research Agenda for Europe and Beyond." *Comparative Political Studies* 43, 931–68.

Carneiro, Robert L. 1970. "A Theory of the Origin of the State." *Science* 169: 3947, 733–8.

    1988. "The Circumscription Theory: Challenge and Response." *American Behavioral Scientist* 31:4, 497–511.

    2012. "The Circumscription Theory: A Clarification, Amplification, and Reformulation." *Social Evolution and History* 11:2, 5–30.

Carothers, Thomas. 2011. *Aiding Democracy Abroad: The Learning Curve*. Washington, DC: Carnegie Endowment.

Carter, David B., Curtis S. Signorino. 2010. "Back to the Future: Modeling Time Dependence in Binary Data." *Political Analysis* 18:3, 271–92.

Carter, Susan B., Richard Sutch. 2013. "Why the Settlers Soared: The Dynamics of Immigration and Economic Growth in the 'Golden Age' for Settler Societies." In Christopher Lloyd, Jacob Metzer, Richard Sutch (eds.), *Settler Economies in World History* (Leiden: Brill), 37–64.

Carter, David B., Andrew C. Shaver, Austin L. Wright. 2019. "Places to Hide: Terrain, Ethnicity, and Civil Conflict." *Journal of Politics* 81:4, 1446–65.

Cartledge, Paul. 2016. *Democracy: A Life*. Oxford: Oxford University Press.

Carvalho, Jean-Paul, Christian Dippel. 2020. "Elite Identity and Political Accountability: A Tale of 14 Islands." *Economic Journal* 130:631, 1995–2029.

Carvalho, Jose Alberto Magno de, Charles H. Wood, Flavia Cristina Drumond Andrade. 2004. "Estimating the Stability of Census-Based Racial Classifications: The Case of Brazil." *Population Studies* 58, 331–43.

Cashdan, Elizabeth A. 1980. "Egalitarianism among Hunters and Gatherers." *American Anthropologist* 82, 116–20.

Cassidy, Vincent H. 1968. *The Sea around Them: The Atlantic Ocean, AD 1250.* Baton Rouge: Louisiana State University Press.

Casson, Lionel. 1984. *Ancient Trade and Society.* Detroit: Wayne State University Press.

1991. *The Ancient Mariners: Seafarers and Sea Fighters of the Mediterranean in Ancient Times.* Princeton: Princeton University Press.

1994a. *Ships and Seafaring in Ancient Times.* Austin: University of Texas Press.

1994b. *Travel in the Ancient World.* Baltimore: Johns Hopkins University Press.

1995. *Ships and Seamanship in the Ancient World.* Baltimore: Johns Hopkins University Press.

Castillo, Daniel, Jesus M. Valdaliso. 2017. "Path Dependence and Change in the Spanish Port System in the Long Run (1880–2014): A Historical Perspective." *International Journal of Maritime History* 29:3, 569–96.

Castro, Joseph Justin. 2013. *Wireless: Radio, Revolution, and the Mexican State, 1897–1938.* Norman: University of Oklahoma Press.

Catsambis, Alexis, Ben Ford (eds.). 2011. *The Oxford Handbook of Maritime Archaeology.* Oxford: Oxford University Press.

Cavanagh, Edward, Lorenzo Veracini (eds.). 2017. *The Routledge Handbook of the History of Settler Colonialism.* London: Taylor & Francis.

Centeno, Miguel Angel. 2007. "Liberalism and the Good Society in the Iberian World." *Annals of the American Academy of Political and Social Science* 610:1, 45–72.

Chandler, Tertius. 1987. *Four Thousand Years of Urban Growth: An Historical Census.* Lewiston, NY: Edwin Mellen Press.

Chandra, Satish. 2007. *History of Medieval India (800–1700).* Hyderabad: Orient Black Swan.

Chaney, Eric. 2012. "Democratic Change in the Arab World, Past and Present," *Brookings Papers on Economic Activity,* Spring, 363–414.

Chapman, Anne C. 1957. "Port of Trade Enclaves in Aztec and Maya Civilizations." In Karl Polanyi, Conrad M. Arensberg, Harry W. Pearson (eds.), *Trade and Market in the Early Empires: Economies in History and Theory* (New York: Free Press), 114–53.

Charlton-Stevens, Uther. 2020. "Anglo-Indians in Colonial India: Historical Demography, Categorization, and Identity." In Zarine L. Rocha and Peter Aspinall (eds.), *The Palgrave International Handbook of Mixed Racial and Ethnic Classification* (London: Palgrave Macmillan), 669–92.

Chaudhuri, K. N. 1978. *The Trading World of Asia and the English East India Company: 1660–1760.* Cambridge: Cambridge University Press.

1985. *Trade and Civilisation in the Indian Ocean: An Economic History from the Rise of Islam to 1750.* Cambridge: Cambridge University Press.

1991. *Asia before Europe: Economy and Civilization of the Indian Ocean from the Rise of Islam to 1750.* Cambridge: Cambridge University Press.

Cheibub, Jose Antonio, Jennifer Gandhi, James Raymond Vreeland. 2010. "Democracy and Dictatorship Revisited." *Public Choice* 143:1–2, 67–101.

Cheng, Tun-Jen, Deborah A. Brown (eds.). 2006. *Religious Organizations and Democratization: Case Studies from Contemporary Asia*. Armonk, NY: M.E. Sharpe.

Chirot, Daniel. 1985. "The Rise of the West." *American Sociological Review* 50:2, 181–95.

Chittick, Neville. 1980. "East Africa and the Orient: Ports and Trade before the Arrival of the Portuguese." In *Historical Relations across the Indian Ocean: Report and Papers of the Meeting of Experts Organized by Unesco at Port Louis, Mauritius, from 15 to 19 July 1974* (United Nations Educational), 13–22.

Choi, Sung. 2017. "French Algeria, 1830–1962." In Edward Cavanagh and Lorenzo Veracini (eds.), *The Routledge Handbook of the History of Settler Colonialism* (London: Taylor & Francis), 201–14.

Choi, Sze Hang. 2017. *The Remarkable Hybrid Maritime World of Hong Kong and the West River Region in the Late Qing Period*. Leiden: Brill.

Choudhuri, Keshab. 1973. *Calcutta: Story of Its Government*. Bombay: Orient Longman.

Christie, Jan Wisseman. 1986. "Negara, Mandala, and Despotic State: Images of Early Java." In David G. Marr and Anthony Crothers Milner (eds.), *Southeast Asia in the 9th to 14th Centuries* (Singapore: Institute of Southeast Asian Studies), 65–93.

   1995. "State Formation in Early Maritime Southeast Asia: A Consideration of the Theories and the Data." *Bijdragen tot de taal-, land-en volkenkunde* 151:2, 235–88.

Christophersen, Jens Andreas. 1966. *The Meaning of "Democracy" as Used in European Ideologies from the French to the Russian Revolution: An Historical Study in Political Language*. Atlantic Highlands, NJ: Humanities Press.

Chu, Lan T. 2011. "Unfinished Business: The Catholic Church, Communism, and Democratization." *Democratization* 18:3, 631–54.

Chua, Amy. 2009. *Day of Empire: How Hyperpowers Rise to Global Dominance – and Why They Fall*. New York: Anchor.

Chust, Manuel. 2017. "The National Road of the Cádiz Cortes: Anticolonialism, Liberalism, Nation and State." In Paul Garner and Ángel Smith (eds.), *Nationalism and Transnationalism in Spain and Latin America, 1808–1923* (Cardiff: University of Wales Press), 18–44.

Ciepley, David. 2017. "Is the US Government a Corporation? The Corporate Origins of Modern Constitutionalism." *American Political Science Review* 111:2, 418–35.

Cipolla, Carlo M. 1965. *Guns, Sails and Empires: Technological Innovation and the Early Phases of European Expansion, 1400–1700*. New York: Thomas Y. Crowell.

Claessen, Henri J. M., Peter Skalník (eds.). 1978. *The Early State*. The Hague: Mouton.

Clague, Christopher, Suzanne Gleason, Stephen Knack. 2001. "Determinants of Lasting Democracy in Poor Countries: Culture, Development, and Institutions." *Annals of the American Academy of Political and Social Science* 773, 16–41.

Clark, Hugh R. 1991. *Community, Trade, and Networks: Southern Fujian Province from the Third to the Thirteenth Century*. Cambridge: Cambridge University Press.

Clark, Peter. 2000. *British Clubs and Societies 1580–1800: The Origins of an Associational World*. Oxford: Oxford University Press.

2009. *European Cities and Towns 400– 2000*. Oxford: Oxford University Press.

Clark, Samuel. 1995. *State and Status: The Rise of the State and Aristocratic Power in Western Europe*. Montreal: McGill-Queen's University Press.

Clayton, Joseph. 1911. *The Rise of the Democracy*. London: Cassell, Limited.

Clayton, Lawrence A., David M. Lantigua. 2020. *Bartolomé de Las Casas and the Defense of Amerindian Rights: A Brief History with Documents*. Atlantic Crossings. Tuscaloosa: University of Alabama Press.

Clingingsmith, David, Asim Ijaz Khwaja, Michael Kremer. 2009. "Estimating the Impact of the Hajj: Religion and Tolerance in Islam's Global Gathering." *Quarterly Journal of Economics* 124:3, 1133–70.

Clulow, Adam. 2010. "A Fake Embassy, the Lord of Taiwan and Tokugawa Japan." *Japanese Studies* 30:1, 23–41.

2016. "The Art of Claiming: Possession and Resistance in Early Modern Asia." *American Historical Review* 121:1, 17–38.

Coe, Michael D. 2003. *Angkor and the Khmer Civilization*. New York: Thames and Hudson.

Cœdès, George. 1975. *The Indianized States of Southeast Asia*. Canberra: Australian National University Press.

Cogan, Jacob Katz, Ian Hurd, Ian Johnstone (eds.). 2016. *The Oxford Handbook of International Organizations*. Oxford: Oxford University Press.

Cohen, Abner. 1971. "Cultural Strategies in the Organization of Trading Diasporas." In Claude Meillassoux (ed.), *The Development of Indigenous Trade and Markets in West Africa* (London: Oxford University Press), 266–81.

Cohen, J. M. (ed.). 1969. *The Four Voyages of Christopher Columbus*. London: Penguin.

Cohen, Mark Nathan. 1977. *The Food Crisis in Prehistory: Overpopulation and the Origins of Agriculture*. New Haven: Yale University Press.

Cohen, Ronald, Elman R. Service (eds.). 1978. *Origins of the State: The Anthropology of Political Evolution*. Philadelphia: Institute for the Study of Human Issues.

Collier, Simon, William F. Sater. 2004. *A History of Chile, 1808–2002*. Cambridge: Cambridge University Press.

Colson, Elizabeth, Max Gluckman (eds.). 1951. *Seven Tribes of British Central Africa*. Manchester: Manchester University Press.

Congdon Fors, Heather. 2014. "Do Island States Have Better Institutions?" *Journal of Comparative Economics*, 42:1, 34–60.

Congleton, Roger D. 2010. *Perfecting Parliament: Constitutional Reform, Liberalism, and the Rise of Western Democracy*. Cambridge: Cambridge University Press.

Connah, Graham. 1981. *Three Thousand Years in Africa: Man and His Environment in the Lake Chad Region of Nigeria*. Cambridge: Cambridge University Press.

1987. *African Civilizations: An Archaeological Perspective*. Cambridge: Cambridge University Press.

Cooper, Frederick. 2014. *Citizenship between Empire and Nation: Remaking France and French Africa, 1945–1960*. Princeton: Princeton University Press.

Coppedge, Michael. 2012. *Democratization and Research Methods*. Cambridge: Cambridge University Press.

Coppedge, Michael, Wolfgang H. Reinicke. 1990. "Measuring Polyarchy." *Studies in Comparative International Development* 25:1, 51–72.

Coppedge, Michael, Benjamin Denison, Paul Friesen, Lucía Tiscornia. 2022a. "International Factors." In Michael Coppedge, Amanda Edgell, Carl Henrik Knutsen, and Staffan I. Lindberg (eds.), *Why Democracies Develop and Decline* (Cambridge: Cambridge University Press).

Coppedge, Michael, Amanda Edgell, Carl Henrik Knutsen, Staffan I. Lindberg (eds.). 2022b. *Why Democracies Develop and Decline*. Cambridge: Cambridge University Press.

Coppedge, Michael, John Gerring, with David Altman, Michael Bernhard, Steven Fish, Allen Hicken, Matthew Kroenig, Staffan I. Lindberg, Kelly McMann, Pamela Paxton, Holli A. Semetko, Svend-Erik Skaaning, Jeffrey Staton, Jan Teorell. 2011. "Conceptualizing and Measuring Democracy: A New Approach." *Perspectives on Politics* 9:1, 247–67.

Coppedge, Michael, John Gerring, Adam Glynn, Carl Henrik Knutsen, Staffan I. Lindberg, Daniel Pemstein, Brigitte Seim, Svend-Erik Skaaning, Jan Teorell. 2020. *Varieties of Democracy: Measuring Two Centuries of Political Change*. Cambridge: Cambridge University Press.

Coppedge, Michael, John Gerring, Carl Henrik Knutsen, Staffan I. Lindberg, Jan Teorell, David Altman, Michael Bernhard, M. Steven Fish, Adam Glynn, Allen Hicken, Anna Lührmann, Kyle L. Marquardt, Kelly McMann, Pamela Paxton, Daniel Pemstein, Brigitte Seim, Rachel Sigman, Svend-Erik Skaaning, Jeffrey Staton, Agnes Cornell, Lisa Gastaldi, Haakon Gjerløw, Valeriya Mechkova, Johannes von Römer, Aksel Sundtröm, Eitan Tzelgov, Luca Uberti, Yi-ting Wang, Tore Wig, and Daniel Ziblatt. 2020. "V-Dem Codebook v10." Varieties of Democracy (V-Dem) Project. Gothenburg: V-Dem Institute, University of Gothenburg.

Corrin, Jay P. 2010. *Catholic Intellectuals and the Challenge of Democracy*. Notre Dame: University of Notre Dame Press.

Coulborn, Rushton (ed.). 1956. *Feudalism in History*. Princeton: Princeton University Press.

Couper, Alastair D. 2009. *Sailors and Traders: A Maritime History of the Pacific Peoples*. Honolulu: University of Hawaii Press.

Cox, Gary W. 2017. "Political Institutions, Economic Liberty, and the Great Divergence." *Journal of Economic History* 77:3, 724–55.

Cox, Gary W., Mark Dincecco, Massimiliano Gaetano Onorato. 2020. "War, Trade, and the Origins of Representative Governance." Social Science Research Network. file:///C:/Users/jg29775/Downloads/SSRN-id3616438.pdf.

Crafts, Nicholas, Anthony Venables. 2003. "Globalization in History: A Geographical Perspective." In Michael D. Bordo, Alan M. Taylor, Jeffrey G. Williamson (eds.), *Globalization in Historical Perspective* (Chicago: University of Chicago Press), 323–70.

Crais, Clifton C. 1992. *White Supremacy and Black Resistance in Pre-industrial South Africa: The Making of the Colonial Order in the Eastern Cape, 1770–1865.* Cambridge: Cambridge University Press.

Craton, Michael. 2003. *Founded upon the Seas: A History of the Cayman Islands and Their People. I.* Kingston, Jamaica: Randle Publishers.

Crawfurd, John. 1820. *History of the Indian Archipelago: Containing an Account of the Manners, Art, Languages, Religions, Institutions, and Commerce of Its Inhabitants,* 3 vols. Edinburgh: Archibald Constable and Company.

Crisher, Brian Benjamin, Mark Souva. 2014. "Power at Sea: A Naval Power Dataset, 1865–2011." *International Interactions* 40:4, 602–29.

Crone, Patricia. 1980. *Slaves on Horses: The Evolution of the Islamic Polity.* Cambridge: Cambridge University Press

1989. *Pre-industrial Societies: Anatomy of the Premodern World.* Oxford: Oxford University Press.

Crook, John A. 1996. "Augustus: Power, Authority, Achievement." In Alan K. Bowman, Edward Champlin, Andrew Lintott (eds.), *The Cambridge Ancient History. Volume 10. The Augustan Empire, 43 BC–AD 69* (Cambridge: Cambridge University Press), 113–46.

Crooks, Peter, Timothy H. Parsons (eds.). 2016. *Empires and Bureaucracy in World History: From Late Antiquity to the Twentieth Century.* Cambridge: Cambridge University Press.

Crosby, Alfred W. 1972. *The Columbian Exchange: Biological and Cultural Consequences of 1492.* Westport, CT: Greenwood Publishing Group.

1986. *Ecological Imperialism: The Biological Expansion of Europe, 900–1900.* New York: Cambridge University Press.

Crowder, Michael, Obaro Ikime (eds.). 1970. *West African Chiefs: Their Changing Status under Colonial Rule and Independence.* Ile-Ife, Nigeria: University of Ife Press.

Crummey, Robert O. 1987. *The Formation of Muscovy 1300–1613.* London: Routledge.

Crystal, Jill. 1990. *Oil and Politics in the Gulf: Rulers and Merchants in Kuwait and Qatar.* Cambridge: Cambridge University Press.

Cunliffe, Barry W. 2001. *Facing the Ocean: The Atlantic and Its Peoples, 8000 BC–AD 1500.* New York: Oxford University Press.

2008. *Europe between the Oceans: 9000 BC to AD 1000.* New Haven: Yale University Press.

2015. *By Steppe, Desert, and Ocean: The Birth of Eurasia.* New York: Oxford University Press.

Curtin, Philip D. 1984. *Cross-cultural Trade in World History.* Cambridge: Cambridge University Press.

1989. *Death by Migration: Europe's Encounter with the Tropical World in the Nineteenth Century.* Cambridge: Cambridge University Press.

1998. *Disease and Empire: The Health of European Troops in the Conquest of Africa.* Cambridge: Cambridge University Press.

2002. *The World and the West: The European Challenge and the Overseas Response in the Age of Empire.* Cambridge: Cambridge University Press.

Curtin, Philip D., Steven Feierman, Leonard Thompson, Jan Vansina. 1978. *African History.* London: Longman.

1995. *African History: From Earliest Times to Independence*, 2nd ed. London: Longman.

Curtis, Michael. 2009. *Orientalism and Islam: European Thinkers on Oriental Despotism in the Middle East and India*. Cambridge: Cambridge University Press.

Dahl, Robert A. 1971. *Polyarchy: Participation and Opposition*. New Haven: Yale University Press.

Dahlum, Sirianne, and Tore Wig. 2021. "Chaos on Campus: Universities and Mass Political Protest." *Comparative Political Studies* 54:1, 3–32.

Dale, Stephen F. 2010. *The Muslim Empires of the Ottomans, Safavids, and Mughals*. Cambridge: Cambridge University Press.

Dalgaard, Carl-Johan, Anne Sofie B. Knudsen, Pablo Selaya. 2020. "The Bounty of the Sea and Long-Run Development." *Journal of Economic Growth* 25:3, 259–95.

D'Arcy, Paul. 2006. *The People of the Sea: Environment, Identity, and History in Oceania*. Honolulu: University of Hawaii Press.

Darwin, John. 2020. *Unlocking the World: Port Cities and Globalization in the Age of Steam, 1830–1930*. London: Penguin.

Das Gupta, Ashin. 1994. *Merchants of Maritime India, 1500–1800*. Aldershot: Variorum.

2004. *India and the Indian Ocean World: Trade and Politics*. Oxford: Oxford University Press.

Das Gupta, Ashin, Michael N. Pearson (eds.). 1987. *India and the Indian Ocean, 1500–1800*. New Delhi: Oxford University Press.

Daudin, Guillaume. 2017. "Le Commerce maritime et la croissance européenne au XVIIe siècle." In Christian Buchet, Gérard Le Bouëdec (eds.), *The Sea in History: The Early Modern World* (Woodbridge, Suffolk: Boydell Press), 9–18.

Davis, Colin John. 2003. *Waterfront Revolts: New York and London Dockworkers, 1946–61*. Champaign: University of Illinois Press.

Davis, Eric. 1991. "Theorizing Statecraft and Social Change in Arab Oil-Producing Countries." In Eric Davis and Nicolas Gavrielides (eds.), *Statecraft in the Middle East: Oil, Historical Memory, and Popular Culture* (Miami: Florida International University Press), 1–35.

Davison, Walter Phillips. 1965. *International Political Communication*. Washington, DC: Council on Foreign Relations.

Dawkins, Richard. 1978. *The Selfish Gene*. Oxford: Oxford University Press.

Deasy, George F. 1942. "The Harbors of Africa." *Economic Geography* 18:4, 325–42.

de Casparis, J. G. 1986. "Some Notes on Relations between Central and Local Government in Ancient Java." In David G. Marr and Anthony Crothers Milner (eds.), *Southeast Asia in the 9th to 14th Centuries* (Singapore: Institute of Southeast Asian Studies), 49–63.

Dedieu, Jean Pierre, Silvia Marzagalli, Pierrick Pourchasse, Werner Scheltjens. 2011. "Navigocorpus, a Database for Shipping Information: A Methodological and Technical Introduction." *International Journal of Maritime History* 18:2, 241–62.

de Graauw, Arthur. 2017. *The Catalogue of Ancient Ports and Harbours*, 6th ed., Grenoble. www.ancientportsantiques.com/docs-pdf.

de Gruchy, John Wesley. 1995. *Christianity and Democracy: A Theology for a Just World Order*. Cambridge: Cambridge University Press.

de Hartog, Leo. 1996. *Russia and the Mongol Yoke: The History of the Russian Principalities and the Golden Horde, 1221–1502*. London: Tauris Academic Studies.

De Juan, Alexander, Jan Henryk Pierskalla. 2017. "The Comparative Politics of Colonialism and Its Legacies: An Introduction." *Politics and Society* 45:2, 159–72.

Deloche, Jean. 1983. "Geographical Considerations in the Localisation of Ancient Sea-ports of India." *The Indian Economic, Social History Review* 20:4, 439–48.

de Long, J. Bradford, Andrei Shleifer. 1993. "Princes and Merchants: European City Growth before the Industrial Revolution." *Journal of Law and Economics* 36:2, 671–702.

De Madariaga, Isabel. 2006. "Tsar into Emperor: The Title of Peter the Great." In Robert Oresko, G. C. Gibbs, H. M. Scott (eds.), *Royal and Republican Sovereignty in Early Modern Europe: Essays in Memory of Ragnhild Hatton* (Cambridge: Cambridge University Press), 351–81.

Demélas-Bohy, M. D., François-Xavier Guerra. 1996. "The Hispanic Revolutions: The Adoption of Modern Forms of Representation in Spain and America, 1808–1810." In Eduardo Posada Carbó (ed.), *Elections before Democracy: The History of Elections in Europe and Latin America* (London: Macmillan), 33–60.

De Moor, Tine. 2008. "The Silent Revolution: A New Perspective on the Emergence of Commons, Guilds, and Other Forms of Corporate Collective Action in Western Europe." *International Review of Social History* 53:16, 179–212.

De Moor, Tine, Jan Luiten van Zanden. 2010. "Girl Power: The European Marriage Pattern and Labour Markets in the North Sea Region in the Late Medieval and Early Modern Period." *Economic History Review* 63:1, 1–33.

Deng, Gang. 1997. *Chinese Maritime Activities and Socioeconomic Development, c. 2100 BC–1900 AD*. Westport, CT: Greenwood Publishing Group.

1999. *Maritime Sector, Institutions, and Sea Power of Premodern China*. Westport, CT: Greenwood Publishing Group.

Deng, Kent. 2011. "Why Shipping 'Declined' in China from the Middle Ages to the Nineteenth Century." In Richard W. Unger (ed.), *Shipping and Economic Growth 1350–1850* (Leiden: Brill), 207–22.

Dennett, Daniel. C. 2015. *Elbow Room: The Varieties of Free Will Worth Wanting*. Cambridge, MA: MIT Press.

Denoon, Donald. 1983. *Settler Capitalism: The Dynamics of Dependent Development in the Southern Hemisphere*. Oxford: Clarendon Press.

Denoon, Donald, Malama Meleisea (eds.). 1997. *The Cambridge History of the Pacific Islanders*. Cambridge: Cambridge University Press.

De Ruggiero, Guido. 1927. *The History of European Liberalism*. London: Oxford University Press.

De Souza, Philip. 2002. *Seafaring and Civilization: Maritime Perspectives on World History*. London: Profile.

De Souza, Philip, Pascal Arnaud (eds.). 2017. *The Sea in History: The Ancient World*. Woodbridge, Suffolk: Boydell.

De Swaan, Abram. 2001. *Words of the World: The Global Language System*. Cambridge: Polity.

Deutsch, Karl Wolfgang. 1966. *The Nerves of Government: Models of Communication and Control*. New York: Free Press.

De Vries, Jan. 2010. "The Limits of Globalization in the Early Modern World." *Economic History Review* 63:3, 710–33.

DeWiel, Boris. 2000. *Democracy: A History of Ideas*. Vancouver: University of British Columbia Press.

Diamond, Jared. 1992. *Guns, Germs, and Steel: The Fates of Human Societies*. New York: W.W. Norton.

1998. "Peeling the Chinese Onion." *Nature* 391, 433–4.

2005. *Collapse: How Societies Choose to Fail or Succeed*. London: Penguin.

Diamond, Larry, Marc F. Plattner, Philip J. Costopoulos (eds.). 2005. *World Religions and Democracy*. Baltimore: Johns Hopkins University Press.

Diffie, Bailey W., George D. Winius. 1977. *Foundations of the Portuguese Empire: 1415–1580*. Minneapolis: University of Minnesota Press.

Dike, Kenneth Onwuka. 1956. *Trade and Politics in the Niger Delta, 1830–1885: An Introduction to the Economic and Political History of Nigeria*. Oxford: Clarendon Press.

Dikshit, Ramesh Dutta. 2011. *Geographical Thought: A Contextual History of Ideas*. New Delhi: PHI Learning Pvt.

Dilli, Selin. 2016. "Family Systems and the Historical Roots of Global Gaps in Democracy." *Economic History of Developing Regions* 31:1, 82–135.

Dincecco, Mark. 2009. "Fiscal Centralization, Limited Government, and Public Revenues in Europe, 1650–1913." *Journal of Economic History* 69, 48–103.

2010. "Fragmented Authority from Ancien Régime to Modernity: A Quantitative Analysis." *Journal of Institutional Economics* 6:3, 305–28.

2011. *Political Transformations and Public Finances*. Cambridge: Cambridge University Press.

Dincecco, Mark, Massimiliano Gaetano Onorato. 2018. *From Warfare to Wealth: The Military Origins of Urban Prosperity in Europe*. Cambridge: Cambridge University Press.

Disney, Anthony R. 2009. *A History of Portugal and the Portuguese Empire. Volume 2. The Portuguese Empire*. Cambridge: Cambridge University Press.

Djuve, Vilde, Carl Henrik Knutsen, Tore Wig. 2019. "Patterns of Regime Breakdown since the French Revolution." *Comparative Political Studies* 53:6, 923–58.

Domar, E. D. 1970. "The Causes of Slavery or Serfdom: A Hypothesis." *Journal of Economic History*, 30, 18–32.

Domingos, Nuno, Miguel Bandeira Jerónimo, Ricardo Roque (eds.). 2019. *Resistance and Colonialism: Insurgent Peoples in World History*. Boston: Springer.

Dommen, Edward. 1980. "Some Distinguishing Characteristics of Island States." *World Development* 8:12, 931–43.

Donaldson, Dave. 2018. "Railroads of the Raj: Estimating the Impact of Transportation Infrastructure." *American Economic Review* 108:4–5, 899–934.

Doucette, Jonathan Stavnskær. 2020. "The Diffusion of Urban Medieval Representation: The Dominican Order as an Engine of Regime Change." *Perspectives on Politics* 19:3, 1–16.

Doucette, Jonathan Stavnskær, Jørgen Møller. 2020. "The Collapse of State Power, the Cluniac Reform Movement, and the Origins of Urban Self-Government in Medieval Europe." *International Organization* 75:1, 1–20.

Doumenge, François. 1985. "The Viability of Small Intertropical Islands." In Edward Dommen and Patrick Hein (eds.), *States, Microstates, and Islands* (Dover, NH: Croom Helm), 70–118.

Downing, Brian M. 1989. "Medieval Origins of Constitutional Government in the West." *Theory and Society* 18:2, 213–47.

1992. *The Military Revolution and Political Change: Origins of Democracy and Autocracy in Early Modern Europe*. Princeton: Princeton University Press.

Doyle, Don H. 2014. *The Cause of All Nations: An International History of the American Civil War*. New York: Basic Books.

Doyle, Michael W. 1986. *Empires*. Ithaca: Cornell University Press.

Drake, Paul W. 2009. *Between Tyranny and Anarchy: A History of Democracy in Latin America, 1800–2006*. Stanford: Stanford University Press.

Dreher, Axel. 2006. "Does Globalization Affect Growth? Evidence from a New Index of Globalization." *Applied Economics*, 38:10, 1091–110.

Drekmeier, Charles. 1962. *Kingship and Community in Early India*. Stanford: Stanford University Press.

Driessen, Henk. 2005. "Mediterranean Port Cities: Cosmopolitanism Reconsidered." *History and Anthropology* 16:1, 129–41.

Driessen, Michael D. 2014. *Religion and Democratization: Framing Religious and Political Identities in Muslim and Catholic Societies*. Oxford: Oxford University Press.

Dubois, Laurent. 2004. *Avengers of the New World*. Cambridge, MA: Harvard University Press.

Duby, Georges. 1978. *The Early Growth of the European Economy: Warriors and Peasants from the 7th to the 12th Century*. Ithaca: Cornell University Press.

Ducruet, César. 2006. "Port–City Relationships in Europe and Asia." *Journal of International Logistics and Trade* 4:2, 13–35.

(ed.). 2016. *Maritime Networks: Spatial Structures and Time Dynamics*. London: Routledge.

Ducruet, César, Sung-Woo Lee, Adolf KY Ng. 2010. "Centrality and Vulnerability in Liner Shipping Networks: Revisiting the Northeast Asian Port Hierarchy." *Maritime Policy and Management* 37:1, 17–36.

Ducruet, César, Sylvain Cuyala, Ali El Hosni. 2018. "Maritime Networks as Systems of Cities: The Long-Term Interdependencies between Global Shipping Flows and Urban Development (1890–2010)." *Journal of Transport Geography* 66, 340–55.

Duindam, Jeroen. 2016. *Dynasties: A Global History of Power, 1300–1800.* Cambridge: Cambridge University Press.

Duindam, Jeroen, Tülay Artan, Metin Kunt (eds.). 2011. *Royal Courts in Dynastic States and Empires: A Global Perspective.* Leiden: Brill.

Du Jourdin, Michel Mollat. 1993. *Europe and the Sea.* Oxford: Blackwell.

Dukalskis, Alexander. 2017. *The Authoritarian Public Sphere: Legitimation and Autocratic Power in North Korea, Burma, and China.* New York: Routledge.

Duncan, John B. 2000. *The Origins of the Choson Dynasty.* Seattle: University of Washington Press.

Dunn, John (ed.). 1992. *Democracy: The Unfinished Journey, 508 BC to AD 1993.* Oxford: Oxford University Press.

2005. *Democracy: A History.* Boston: Atlantic Monthly Press.

Duus, Peter. 1976. *Feudalism in Japan.* New York: Alfred A. Knopf.

Easterly, William. 2007. "Inequality Does Cause Underdevelopment." *Journal of Development Economics* 84:2, 755–76.

Easterly, William, Ross Levine. 2016. "The European Origins of Economic Development." *Journal of Economic Growth* 21:3, 225–57.

Eckert, Carter J. 1990. *Korea, Old and New: A History.* Cambridge, MA: Harvard University Press.

Edgecombe, D. R. 1978. "The Non-racial Franchise in Cape Politics, 1853–1910." *Kleio* 10:1–2, 21–37.

Edwards, R., S. Ali, C. Caballero, M. Song (eds.). 2012. *International Perspectives on Racial and Ethnic Mixedness and Mixing.* London: Routledge.

Eichengreen, Barry, David Leblang. 2008. "Democracy and Globalization." *Economics and Politics* 20:3, 289–334.

Einhorn, Robin L. 2001. *Property Rules: Political Economy in Chicago, 1833–1872.* Chicago: University of Chicago Press.

Eisenstadt, Shmuel Noah (ed.). 1968. *The Protestant Ethic and Modernization: A Comparative View.* New York: Basic Books.

Eisenstein, Elizabeth. 1979. *The Printing Press as an Agent of Change.* Cambridge: Cambridge University Press.

Eisner, Manuel. 2001. "Modernization, Self-Control and Lethal Violence: The Long-Term Dynamics of European Homicide Rates in Theoretical Perspective." *British Journal of Criminology* 41:4, 618–38.

Ejiofor, Lambert U. 1981. *Dynamics of Igbo Democracy: A Behavioural Analysis of Igbo Politics in Aguinyi Clan.* Ibadan: University Press.

Eklof, Stefan. 2006. *Pirates in Paradise: A Modern History of Southeast Asia's Maritime Marauders.* Copenhagen: Nias Press.

Elections Canada. 2007. *A History of the Vote in Canada.* Ottawa: Chief Electoral Officer of Canada.

Elias, Norbert. 1983. *The Court Society.* Oxford: Basil Blackwell.

Eliav-Feldon, Miriam, Benjamin H. Isaac, Joseph Ziegler (eds.). 2009. *The Origins of Racism in the West.* Cambridge: Cambridge University Press.

Eliot, Samuel. 1853. *History of Liberty,* 2 vols. Boston: Little, Brown.

Elis, Roy, Stephen Haber, Jordan Horrillo. 2017. "The Ecological Origins of Economic and Political Systems." Stanford University. chrome-extension:// efaidnbmnnnibpcajpcglclefindmkaj/viewer.html?pdfurl=https%3A%2F%2F.

Elkins, Caroline, Susan Pedersen (eds.). 2005. *Settler Colonialism in the Twentieth Century: Projects, Practices, Legacies*. New York: Routledge.

Elkins, Zachary. 2010. "Diffusion and the Constitutionalization of Europe." *Comparative Political Studies* 43:8–9, 969–99.

Elkins, Zachary, Beth Simmons. 2005. "On Waves, Clusters, and Diffusion: A Conceptual Framework." *Annals of the American Academy of Political and Social Science* 598:1, 33–51.

Elkins, Zachary, Tom Ginsburg, James Melton. 2009. *The Endurance of National Constitutions*. Cambridge: Cambridge University Press.

Elliott, Harold M. 1979. "Mental Maps and Ethnocentrism: Geographic Characterizations in the Past." *Journal of Geography* 78:7, 250–65.

Elliott, John Huxtable. 1992. "A Europe of Composite Monarchies." *Past & Present* 137, 48–71.

Elman, Benjamin A. 2013. *Civil Examinations and Meritocracy in Late Imperial China*. Cambridge, MA: Harvard University Press.

Elman, Colin, John Gerring, James Mahoney (eds.). 2020. *The Production of Knowledge: Enhancing Progress in Social Science*. Cambridge: Cambridge University Press.

Eltis, David. 1993. "Europeans and the Rise and Fall of African Slavery in the Americas: An Interpretation." *American Historical Review* 98:5, 1399–1423.

Eltis, David, Stephen D. Behrendt, David Richardson, Herbert S. Klein. 1999. *The Trans-Atlantic Slave Trade: A Database on CD-Rom*. New York: Cambridge University Press.

Emmer, Pieter Cornelis, Femme S. Gaastra (eds.). 1996. *The Organization of Interoceanic Trade in European Expansion, 1450–1800*. Aldershot: Variorum.

Emmer, Pieter Cornelis, Magnus Morner (eds.). 1992. *European Expansion and Migration: Essays on the Intercontinental Migration from Africa Asia and Europe*. London: Bloomsbury.

Emmerson, Donald K. 1980. "The Case for a Maritime Perspective on Southeast Asia." *Journal of Southeast Asian Studies* 11:1, 139–45.

Engerman, Stanley L. 1981. "Notes on the Patterns of Economic Growth in the British North American Colonies in the Seventeenth, Eighteenth, and Nineteenth Centuries." In Paul Bairoch and Maurice Levy-Leboyer (eds.), *Disparities in Economic Development since the Industrial Revolution* (New York: Saint Martin's Press), 44–57.

2014. "Slavery, Serfdom and Other Forms of Coerced Labour: Similarities and Differences." In Michael Laccohee Bush (ed.), *Serfdom and Slavery: Studies in Legal Bondage* (London: Routledge), 18–41.

Engerman, Stanley L., Kenneth L. Sokoloff. 1997. "Factor Endowments, Institutions, and Differential Paths of Growth among New World Economics." In Samuel H. Haber (ed.), *How Latin America Fell Behind* (Stanford: Stanford University Press), 261–91.

2000. "Factor Endowments, Inequality, and Paths of Development among New World Economies." *Journal of Economic Perspectives* 14:3, 217–32.

2005. "The Evolution of Suffrage Institutions in the New World." *Journal of Economic History* 65:4, 891–921.

2012. *Economic Development in the Americas since 1500: Endowments and Institutions*. Cambridge: Cambridge University Press.

Epstein, Stephan R. 2002. *Freedom and Growth: The Rise of States and Markets in Europe, 1300–1750*. London: Routledge.

Epstein, Steven A. 1991. *Wage Labor and Guilds in Medieval Europe*. Chapel Hill: University of North Carolina Press.

Erie, Steven P. 1990. *Rainbow's End: Irish-Americans and the Dilemmas of Urban Machine Politics, 1840–1985*. Berkeley: University of California Press.

Erlandson, Jon M. 2010. "Ancient Immigrants: Archaeology and Maritime Migrations." In Jan Lucassen, Leo Lucassen, and Patrick Manning (eds.), *Migration History in World History: Multidisciplinary Approaches* (Leiden: Brill), 191–214.

Ertan, Arhan, Martin Fiszbein, Louis Putterman. 2016. "Who Was Colonized and When? A Cross-country Analysis of Determinants." *European Economic Review* 83, 165–84.

Ertman, Thomas. 1997. *Birth of the Leviathan: Building States and Regimes in Medieval and Early Modern Europe*. Cambridge: Cambridge University Press.

Eser, Thomas et al. 2018. *Harbours as Objects of Interdisciplinary Research: Archaeology + History + Geosciences*. Berlin: Romisch Germanisches Zentralmuseum.

Espinosa, Aurelio. 2009. *The Empire of the Cities: Emperor Charles V, the Comunero Revolt, and the Transformation of the Spanish System*. Leiden: Brill.

Etemad, Bouda. 2007. *Possessing the World: Taking the Measurements of Colonisation from the 18th to the 20th Century*. New York: Berghahn Books.

Etherington, Norman (ed.). 2005. *Missions and Empire*. London: Oxford University Press.

Evans, Geoffrey. 1958. "Ancient Mesopotamian Assemblies." *Journal of the American Oriental Societies* 78, 1–11.

Evans, Julie, Patricia Grimshaw, David Phillips, Shurlee Swain. 2003. *Equal Subjects, Unequal Rights: Indigenous Peoples in British Settler Colonies, 1830–1910*. Oxford: Oxford University Press.

Evans-Pritchard, E. E. 1940. *The Nuer: A Description of the Modes of Livelihood and Political Institutions of a Nilotic People*. Oxford: Clarendon Press.

Ezrow, Natasha M., Erica Frantz. 2011. *Dictators and Dictatorships: Understanding Authoritarian Regimes and Their Leaders*. London: Bloomsbury.

Fairbank, John K. 1968. "A Preliminary Framework." In John K. Fairbank (ed.), *The Chinese World Order* (Cambridge, MA: Harvard University Press), 1–19.

Fan, Yun, Huug van den Dool. 2008. "A Global Monthly Land Surface Air Temperature Analysis for 1948–Present." *Journal of Geophysical Research* 113, D01103.

Fanon, Frantz. 1970. *Black Skin, White Masks*. London: Paladin.

FAO. 2016. AQUASTAT Main Database. Food and Agriculture Organization (FAO) of the United Nations. www.fao.org/aquastat/en.

Farhadi, Minoo. 2015. "Transport Infrastructure and Long-run Economic Growth in OECD Countries." *Transportation Research Part A: Policy and Practice* 74, 73–90.

Fariss, Christopher J., Charles D. Crabtree, Therese Anders, Zachary M. Jones, Fridolin J. Linder, Jonathan N. Markowitz. 2017. "Latent Estimation of

GDP, GDP per Capita, and Population from Historic and Contemporary Sources." chrome-extension://efaidnbmnnnibpcajpcglclefindmkaj/viewer.html?pdfurl=https%3A%2F%2Farxiv.org%2Fpdf%2F1706.01099.pdf&clen=4176818&chunk=true.

Farrar, Cynthia. 1988. *The Origins of Democratic Thinking: The Invention of Politics in Classical Athens*. Cambridge: Cambridge University Press.

Faulkner, William. 2011 [1951]. *Requiem for a Nun*. New York: Vintage.

Fawaz, Leila Tarazi, Chris Bayly (eds.). 2002. *Modernity and Culture: From the Mediterranean to the Indian Ocean*. New York: Columbia University Press.

Fawtier, Robert. 1960. *The Capetian Kings of France*. New York: Saint Martin's Press.

Fayle, C. E., C. Wright. 1928. *A History of Lloyd's from the Founding of Lloyd's Coffee House to the Present Day*. London: Macmillan and Company Limited.

Fearon, James D., David D. Laitin. 2003. "Ethnicity, Insurgency, and Civil War." *American Political Science Review* 97:1, 75–90.

Fedorowicz, J. K. (ed.). 1982. *A Republic of Nobles: Studies in Polish History to 1864*. Cambridge: Cambridge University Press.

Feinberg, Richard (ed.). 1995. *Seafaring in the Contemporary Pacific Islands: Studies in Continuity and Change*. DeKalb: Northern Illinois University Press.

Feinman, Gary M. 2017. "Re-visioning Classic Maya Polities." *Latin American Research Review* 52:3, 458–68.

Feinman, Gary M., Joyce Marcus (eds.). 1999. *Archaic States*. Oxford: James Currey.

Feldstein, Steven. 2019. "The Road to Digital Unfreedom: How Artificial Intelligence is Reshaping Repression." *Journal of Democracy* 30:1, 40–52.

Feng, Li. 2008. *Bureaucracy and the State in Early China*. Cambridge: Cambridge University Press.

Ferejohn, John, Frances McCall Rosenbluth. 2016. *Forged through Fire: War, Peace, and the Democratic Bargain*. New York: W.W. Norton.

Fernandez-Armesto, Felipe. 2016. "Early Modern Missions and Maritime Expansion." In Lamin Sanneh and Michael McClymond (eds.), *The Wiley Blackwell Companion to World Christianity* (New York: Wiley), 96–106.

Feyrer, James. 2019. "Trade and Income – Exploiting Time Series in Geography." *American Economic Journal: Applied Economics* 11:4, 1–35.

Feyrer, James, Bruce Sacerdote. 2009. "Colonialism and Modern Income: Islands as Natural Experiments." *Review of Economics and Statistics* 91:2, 245–62.

Feys, Torsten. 2012. *The Battle for the Migrants: The Introduction of Steamshipping on the North Atlantic and Its Impact on the European Exodus*. Oxford: Oxford University Press.

Feys, Torsten, Lewis R. Fischer, Stephane Hoste, Stephen Vanfraechem. 2007. *Maritime Transport and Migration: The Connections between Maritime and Migration Networks*. St. John's: International Maritime Economic History Association.

Fichtner, Paula Sutter. 1976. "Dynastic Marriage in Sixteenth Century Habsburg Diplomacy and Statecraft: An Interdisciplinary Approach." *American Historical Review* 81, 243–65.

1989. *Protestantism and Primogeniture in Early Modern Germany*. New Haven: Yale University Press.

2003. *The Habsburg Monarchy 1490–1848: Attributes of Empire*. London: Palgrave Macmillan.

Fieldhouse, D. K. 1966. *The Colonial Empires: A Comparative Study from the Eighteenth Century*. London: Macmillan.

Filmer, Robert. 1991. *Patriarcha and other Writings*, ed. Johann P. Sommerville. Cambridge: Cambridge University Press.

Finamore, Daniel (ed.). 2004. *Maritime History as World History*. Gainesville: University Press of Florida.

Findlay, Ronald, Mats Lundahl (eds.). 2017. *The Economics of the Frontier: Conquest and Settlement*. London: Palgrave Macmillan.

Finer, Samuel E. 1997. *The History of Government*, 3 vols. Cambridge: Cambridge University Press.

Fisher, Andrew B., Matthew D. O'Hara (eds.). 2009. *Imperial Subjects: Race and Identity in Colonial Spanish America*. Durham, NC: Duke University Press.

Fisher, H. J. 1975. "The Central Sahara and Sudan." In Richard Gray and Roland Anthony Oliver (eds.), *The Cambridge History of Africa. Volume 4* (Cambridge: Cambridge University Press), 58–141.

Fisher, Lewis, Adrian Jarvis (eds.). 1999. *Harbours and Havens: Essays in Port History in Honour of Gordon Jackson*. Research in Maritime History 16. St. John's: International Maritime Economic Association.

FitzGerald, David Scott, David Cook-Martin. 2014. *Culling the Masses*. Cambridge, MA: Harvard University Press.

Flannery, Kent, Joyce Marcus. 2012. *The Creation of Inequality: How Our Prehistoric Ancestors Set the Stage for Monarchy, Slavery, and Empire*. Cambridge, MA: Harvard University Press.

Fleck, Robert K., F. Andrew Hanssen. 2006. "The Origins of Democracy: A Model with Application to Ancient Greece." *Journal of Law and Economics* 49:1, 115–46.

Fleming, Patricia H. 1973. "The Politics of Marriage among Non-Catholic European Royalty." *Current Anthropology* 14:3, 231–49.

Fletcher, Joseph. 1986. "The Mongols: Ecological and Social Perspectives." *Harvard Journal of Asiatic Studies* 46:1, 11–50.

Floor, Willem M. 2006. *The Persian Gulf: A Political and Economic History of Five Port Cities, 1500–1730*. Washington, DC: Mage Publications.

Florini, Ann M. (ed.). 2012. *The Third Force: The Rise of Transnational Civil Society*. Washington, DC: Brookings Institution Press.

Foner, Eric. 1994. "Slavery and Freedom in Nineteenth-Century America." *Anos* 90, 7–11.

Ford, Daryll, P. M. Kaberry (eds.). 1967. *West African Kingdoms in the Nineteenth Century*. Oxford: Oxford University Press.

Fortes, Meyer. 1953. "The Structure of Unilineal Descent Groups." *American Anthropologist* 55:1, 17–41.

Fortes, Meyer, E. E. Evans-Pritchard. 1940. *African Political Systems*. Oxford: Oxford University Press.

Foucault, Michel. 1986. "Of Other Spaces." *Diacritics* 16:1, 22–7.

Fox, Edward Whiting. 1971. *History in Geographical Perspective: The Other France*. New York: W.W. Norton.

Fox, Richard Gabriel. 1977. *Urban Anthropology: Cities in Their Cultural Settings*. Englewood Cliffs: Prentice Hall.

Fradera, Josep. 2018. *The Imperial Nation: Citizens and Subjects in the British, French, Spanish, and American Empires*. Princeton: Princeton University Press.

François, Pieter, Joseph Manning, Harvey Whitehouse, Rob Brennan, Thomas Currie, Kevin Feeney, Peter Turchin. 2016. "A Macroscope for Global History: Seshat Global History Databank, a Methodological Overview." *Digital Humanities Quarterly* 10:4.

Frankel, J., David Romer. 1999. "Does Trade Cause Growth?" *American Economic Review* 27:3, 379–99.

Frankema, Ewout. 2012. "The Origins of Formal Education in Sub-Saharan Africa: Was British Rule More Benign?" *European Review of Economic History* 16:4, 335–55.

Frankema, Ewout, Erik Green, Ellen Hillbom. 2016. "Endogenous Processes of Colonial Settlement: The Success and Failure of European Settler Farming in Sub-Saharan Africa." *Revista de Historia Economica* 34:2, 237–65.

Franklin, Simon, Jonathan Shepard. 1996. *The Emergence of Rus, 750–1200*. London: Longman.

Frantz, Erica, Natasha M. Ezrow. 2011. *The Politics of Dictatorship: Institutions and Outcomes in Authoritarian Regimes*. Boulder: Lynne Rienner Publishers.

Fredrickson, George M. 1971. *The Black Image in the White Mind: The Debate on Afro-American Character and Destiny, 1817–1914*. New York: Harper & Row. 2002. *Racism: A Short History*. Princeton: Princeton University Press.

Freedom House. 2015. "Methodology. Freedom in the World 2015." New York. https://freedomhouse.org/sites/default/files/Methodology_FIW_2015.pdf.

Freeman, Donald B. 2010. *The Pacific*. London: Routledge.

Fried, Morton H. 1967. *The Evolution of Political Society*. New York: Random House.

Friedrichs, Christopher R. 2000. *Urban Politics in Early Modern Europe*. London: Routledge.

Friel, Ian. 1995. *The Good Ship: Ships, Shipbuilding and Technology in England, 1200–1520*. London: British Museum Press. 2003. *Maritime History of Britain and Ireland, c. 400–2001*. London: British Museum Publications Limited.

Frost, Peter, Henry C. Harpending. 2015. "Western Europe, State Formation, and Genetic Pacification." *Evolutionary Psychology* 13, 230–43.

Froude, James Anthony. 1888. *The English in the West Indies: Or, the Bow of Ulysses*. New York: Charles Scribner's Sons.

Fuhrmann, Malte. 2020. *Port Cities of the Eastern Mediterranean: Urban Culture in the Late Ottoman Empire*. Cambridge: Cambridge University Press.

Fujita, Masahisa, Tomoya Mori. 1996. "The Role of Ports in the Making of Major Cities: Self-Agglomeration and Hub-Effect." *Journal of Development Economics* 49, 93–120.

Fukuyama, Francis. 2007. "Liberalism versus State-Building." *Journal of Democracy* 18:3, 10–13.

2011. *The Origins of Political Order: From Prehuman Times to the French Revolution*. New York: Farrar, Straus, Giroux.

2014. *Political Order and Political Decay: From the Industrial Revolution to the Globalization of Democracy*. New York: Macmillan.

Fung, Archon, Erik Olin Wright (eds.). 2003. *Deepening Democracy: Institutional Innovations in Empowered Participatory Governance*. London: Verso.

Furnivall, John Sydenham. 1948. *Colonial Policy and Practice*. Cambridge: Cambridge University Press.

2010 [1939]. *Netherlands India: A Study of Plural Economy*. Cambridge: Cambridge University Press.

Gaikwad, Nikhar. 2014. "East India Companies and Long-Term Economic Change in India." American Political Science Association, Princeton. //efaidnbmnnnibp cajpcglclefindmkaj/viewer.html?pdfurl=https%3A%2F%2Fwww.nikhargaik wad.com%2Fresources%2FGaikwad_EICs_2014.pdf&clen=4129863&chunk= true.

Gallie, Walter Bryce. 1955. "Essentially Contested Concepts." *Proceedings of the Aristotelian Society* 56, 167–98.

Galor, Oded, Ömer Özak. 2015. "Land Productivity and Economic Development: Caloric Suitability vs. Agricultural Suitability." Brown University, Working Paper No. 2015-5. //efaidnbmnnnibpcajpcglclefindm kaj/viewer.html?pdfurl=https%3A%2F%2Fwww.econstor.eu%2Fbitstream %2F10419%2F145428%2F1%2F829208674.pdf.

2016. "The Agricultural Origins of Time Preference." *American Economic Review* 106, 3064–103.

Gandhi, Jennifer. 2010. *Political Institutions under Dictatorship*. Cambridge: Cambridge University Press.

Gann, Lewis H., Peter Duignan. 1962. *White Settlers in Tropical Africa*. London: Penguin Books.

Garcia, Ana Catarina Abrantes. 2017. "New Ports of the New World: Angra, Funchal, Port Royal and Bridgetown." *International Journal of Maritime History* 29:1, 155–74.

Garlake, P. S. G. 1973. *Great Zimbabwe*. London: Thames and Hudson.

Garner, Paul, Ángel Smith. 2017. *Nationalism and Transnationalism in Spain and Latin America, 1808–1923*. Cardiff: University of Wales Press.

Garson, Noel. 1986. "The Cape Franchise after Union: The Queenstown By-election of December 1921." *African Studies* 45:1, 61–89.

Gauci, Perry. 2001. *The Politics of Trade: The Overseas Merchant in State and Society, 1660–1720*. Oxford: Oxford University Press.

Gause, E. Gregory. 1994. *Oil Monarchies: Domestic and Security Challenges in the Arab Gulf States*. New York: Council on Foreign Relations.

2000. "The Persistence of Monarchy in the Arabian Peninsula: A Comparative Analysis." In Joseph Kostiner, (ed.), *Middle East Monarchies* (London: Westview), 167–86.

Geddes, Barbara, Erica Frantz, Joseph Wright. 2014. "Autocratic Breakdown and Regime Transitions: A New Data Set." *Perspectives on Politics* 12:2, 313–31.

Geertz, Clifford. 1980. *Negara: The Theatre State in Nineteenth-Century Bali*. Princeton: Princeton University Press.

Geiss, Paul Georg. 2004. *Pre-Tsarist and Tsarist Central Asia: Communal Commitment and Political Order in Change*. London: Routledge.

Geler, Lea Natalia, Mariela Eva Rodríguez. 2020. "Mixed Race in Argentina: Concealing Mixture in the 'White' Nation." In Zarine L. Rocha and Peter Aspinall (eds.), *The Palgrave International Handbook of Mixed Racial and Ethnic Classification* (London: Palgrave Macmillan), 179–94.

Gellner, Ernest. 1983. *Nations and Nationalism*. Ithaca: Cornell University Press.

Gelman, Andrew, Eric Loken. 2014. "The Statistical Crisis in Science: Data-Dependent Analysis – A Garden of Forking Paths – Explains Why Many Statistically Significant Comparisons Don't Hold Up." *American Scientist* 102:6, 460–6.

Gerring, John. 1998. *Party Ideologies in America, 1828–1996*. Cambridge: Cambridge University Press.

2011. "How Good Is Good Enough? A Multidimensional, Best-Possible Standard for Research Design." *Political Research Quarterly* 64:3, 625–36.

2012. *Social Science Methodology: A Unified Framework*, 2nd ed. Cambridge: Cambridge University Press.

2017. *Case Study Research: Principles and Practices*, 2nd ed. Cambridge: Cambridge University Press.

Gerring, John, Carl Henrik Knutsen, Jonas Berge. 2022. "Democracy's Effects." *Annual Review of Political Science* 25 (May), 357–75.

Gerring, John, Wouter Veenendaal. 2020. *Population and Politics: The Impact of Scale*. Cambridge: Cambridge University Press.

Gerring, John, Philip Bond, William T. Barndt, Carola Moreno. 2005. "Democracy and Economic Growth: A Historical Perspective." *World Politics* 57:3, 323–64.

Gerring, John, Daniel Ziblatt, Johan Van Gorp, Julian Arevalo. 2011. "An Institutional Theory of Direct and Indirect Rule." *World Politics* 63:3, 377–433.

Gerring, John, Allen Hicken, Daniel Weitzel, Lee Cojocaru. 2018. "Electoral Contestation: A Comprehensive Polity-Level Analysis." University of Gothenburg, Varieties of Democracy Institute: Working Paper No. 73.

Gerring, John, Michael Hoffman, Dominic Zarecki. 2018. "The Diverse Effects of Diversity on Democracy." *British Journal of Political Science* 48:2, 283–314.

Gerring, John, Matthew Maguire, Jillian Jaeger. 2018. "A General Theory of Power Concentration: Demographic Influences on Political Organization." *European Political Science Review* 10:4, 491–513.

Gerring, John, Tore Wig, Wouter Veenendaal, Daniel Weitzel, Jan Teorell, Kyosuke Kikuta. 2020. "Why Monarchy? The Rise and Demise of a Regime Type." *Comparative Political Studies* 54, 585–622.

Giavazzi, Francesco, Guido Tabellini. 2005. "Economic and Political Liberalizations." *Journal of Monetary Economics* 52, 1297–330.

Gibler, Douglas M. 2007. "Bordering on Peace: Democracy, Territorial Issues, and Conflict." *International Studies Quarterly* 51:3, 509–32.

2012. *The Territorial Peace: Borders, State Development, and International Conflict*. Cambridge: Cambridge University Press.

Gibson, McGuire, Robert D. Biggs (eds.). 1991. *The Organization of Power: Aspects of Bureaucracy in the Ancient Near East*. Chicago: Oriental Institute of the University of Chicago.

Giddens, Anthony. 1985. *The Nation State and Violence*. Cambridge: Polity Press.

Gierke, Otto von. 1900 [1881]. *Political Theories of the Middle Ages*. Cambridge: Cambridge University Press.

Gifford, Paul (ed.). 1995. *The Christian Churches and the Democratisation of Africa*. Leiden: Brill.

Gilbert, Jérémie. 2014. *Nomadic Peoples and Human Rights*. London: Routledge.

Gilchrist, David T. (ed.). 1967. *The Growth of the Seaport Cities, 1790–1825*. Charlottesville: University Press of Virginia.

Giliomee, Hermann, Richard Elphick. 1979. "The Structure of European Domination at the Cape, 1652–1820." *The Shaping of South African Society, 1652–1820* (Cape Town: Longman), 359–90.

Gilje, Paul A. 2007. *Liberty on the Waterfront: American Maritime Culture in the Age of Revolution*. College Station: University of Pennsylvania Press.

Gillis, John. 2012. *The Human Shore: Seacoasts in History*. Chicago: University of Chicago Press.

Gipouloux, François. 2011. *The Asian Mediterranean: Port Cities and Trading Networks in China, Japan and Southeast Asia, 13th–21st Century*. Cheltenham: Edward Elgar.

Gitlin, Todd. 1980. *The Whole World Is Watching: Mass Media in the Making and Unmaking of the New Left*. Berkeley: University of California Press.

Giuliano, Paola, Nathan Nunn. 2013. "The Transmission of Democracy: From the Village to the Nation-State." *American Economic Review* 103:3, 86–92.

Gjerløw, Haakon, Carl Henrik Knutsen, Tore Wig and Matt Wilson. 2022. *One Road to Riches? How State Building and Democratization Affect Economic Development*. Cambridge: Cambridge University Press.

Glaeser, Edward L. 2000. "The New Economics of Urban and Regional Growth." In Gordon L. Clark, Maryann P. Feldman, Meric S. Gertler (eds.), *The Oxford Handbook of Economic Geography* (Oxford: Oxford University Press), 83–98.

Glassman, Ronald M. 2017. *The Origins of Democracy in Tribes, City-States and Nation-States*. Boston: Springer.

Gleditsch, Kristian Skrede. 2002. "Expanded Trade and GDP Data." *Journal of Conflict Resolution* 46:5, 712–24.

   2009. *All International Politics Is Local: The Diffusion of Conflict, Integration, and Democratization*. Ann Arbor: University of Michigan Press.

Gleditsch, Kristian Skrede, Michael D. Ward. 1999. "A Revised List of Independent States since the Congress of Vienna." *International Interactions* 25:4, 393–413.

   2006. "Diffusion and the International Context of Democratization." *International Organization* 60:4, 911–33.

Glete, Jan. 1993. *Navies and Nations: Warships, Navies and State Building in Europe and America, 1500–1860*, 2 vols. Almqvist: Wiksell International.

   2002. *War and the State in Early Modern Europe: Spain, the Dutch Republic and Sweden as Fiscal-Military States*. London: Routledge.

Gluckman, Max. 1959. *Custom and Conflict in Africa*. Glencoe, IL: Free Press. 1963. *Order and Rebellion in Tribal Africa*. London: Cohen and West.

Go, Julian. 2003. "A Globalizing Constitutionalism? Views from the Postcolony, 1945–2000." *International Sociology* 18:1, 71–95.

Gøbel, E. 2010. "The Sound Toll Registers Online Project, 1497–1857." *International Journal of Maritime History* XXII, 2: 305–24.

Golden, Peter B. 1992. *An Introduction to the History of the Turkic Peoples: Ethno-genesis and State-Formation in Medieval and Early Modern Eurasia and the Middle East*. Turcologica Bd. 9. Wiesbaden: Otto Harrassowitz.

Goldring, Edward, Sheena Chestnut Greitens. 2019. "Rethinking Democratic Diffusion: Bringing Regime Type Back In." *Comparative Political Studies* 53:2, 319–53.

Goldstein, Robert Justin. 2013. *Political Repression in 19th Century Europe*. London: Routledge.

Gommans, Jos, Jacques Leider (eds.). 2002. *The Maritime Frontier of Burma: Exploring Political, Cultural and Commercial Interaction in the Indian Ocean World, 1200–1800*. Leiden: Brill.

Goodliffe, Jay, Darren Hawkins. 2015. "Dependence Networks and the Diffusion of Domestic Political Institutions." *Journal of Conflict Resolution* 61:4, 903–29.

Goodman, D. 1997. *Spanish Naval Power, 1589–1665: Reconstruction and Development*. Cambridge: Cambridge University Press.

Goodwyn, Lawrence. 1976. *Democratic Promise: The Populist Movement in America*. New York: Oxford University Press.

Goody, Jack, Joan Thirsk, E. P. Thompson (eds.). 1979. *Family and Inheritance: Rural Society in Western Europe, 1200–1800*. Cambridge: Cambridge University Press.

Gora, Anna, Pieter de Wilde. 2020. "The Essence of Democratic Backsliding in the European Union: Deliberation and Rule of Law." *Journal of European Public Policy* 27:12, 1–21.

Gordon, April A. 2003. *Nigeria's Diverse Peoples: A Reference Sourcebook*. Santa Barbara: ABC-CLIO.

Gordon, Scott. 1999. *Controlling the State: Constitutionalism from Ancient Athens to Today*. Cambridge, MA: Harvard University Press.

Gottmann, Felicia. 2016. *Global Trade, Smuggling, and the Making of Economic Liberalism: Asian Textiles in France 1680–1760*. Boston: Springer.

Gould, Richard A. 2011. *Archaeology and the Social History of Ships*. Cambridge: Cambridge University Press.

Graf, Arndt, Chua Beng Huat (eds.). 2008. *Port Cities in Asia and Europe*. London: Routledge.

Gragg, Larry Dale. 2003. *Englishmen Transplanted: The English Colonization of Barbados, 1627–1660*. Oxford: Oxford University Press.

Graham, Aaron. 2018. "Legislatures, Legislation and Legislating in the British Atlantic, 1692–1800." *Parliamentary History* 37:3, 369–88.

Graham, Gerald Sandford. 1956. "The Ascendancy of the Sailing Ship, 1850–85." *Economic History Review* 9, 74–88.

Graham, Richard. 1994. *Patronage and Politics in Nineteenth-Century Brazil.* Stanford: Stanford University Press.

(ed.). 2010. *The Idea of Race in Latin America, 1870–1940.* Austin: University of Texas Press.

Graves, Michael A. R. 2001. *The Parliaments of Early Modern Europe.* New York: Routledge.

Gray, Richard, Roland Anthony Oliver (eds.). 1975. *The Cambridge History of Africa. Volume 4.* Cambridge: Cambridge University Press.

Gray, Thomas R., Daniel S. Smith. 2019. "Vox Populi: Popular Politics before Liberal Democracy." *Journal of Politics* 82:2, 21–6.

Greenbaum, Lenora. 1977. "Cross-cultural Study of the Use of Elections for Selection of the Village Headman." *Behavior Science Research* 12.1: 45–53.

Greene, Jack P. 1986. *Peripheries and Center: Constitutional Development in the Extended Polities of the British Empire and the United States, 1607–1788.* Athens, GA: University of Georgia Press.

1988. *Pursuits of Happiness: The Social Development of Early Modern British Colonies and the Formation of American Culture.* Chapel Hill: University of North Carolina Press.

(ed.). 2010. *Exclusionary Empire: English Liberty Overseas, 1600–1900.* Cambridge: Cambridge University Press.

Greif, Avner. 2006a. "Family Structure, Institutions, and Growth: The Origins and Implications of Western Corporations." *American Economic Review* 96:2, 308–12.

2006b. *Institutions and the Path to the Modern Economy: Lessons from Medieval Trade.* Cambridge: Cambridge University Press.

Greif, Avner, Guido Tabellini. 2017. "The Clan and the City: Sustaining Cooperation in China and Europe." *Journal of Comparative Economics* 45, 1–35.

Grewal, Jagtar Singh (ed.). 2005. *The State and Society in Medieval India.* Oxford: Oxford University Press.

Grier, Robin M. 1999. "Colonial Legacies and Economic Growth." *Public Choice* 98:3–4, 317–35.

Griffeth, Robert, Carol G. Thomas (eds.). 1981. *The City-State in Five Cultures.* Santa Barbara: ABC-CLIO Incorporated.

Griffin, Larry J. 1995. "How Is Sociology Informed by History?" *Social Forces* 73:4, 1245–54.

Griffiths, D. 1997. *Steam at Sea: Two Centuries of Steam-Powered Ships.* London: Conway Maritime Press.

Grigoriadis, Theocharis. 2016. "Religious Origins of Democracy & Dictatorship." *Journal of Policy Modeling* 38:5, 785–809.

Griswold, A. Whitney. 1946. "The Agrarian Democracy of Thomas Jefferson." *American Political Science Review* 40:4, 657–81.

Gross, Leo. 1948. "The Peace of Westphalia, 1648–1948." *American Journal of International Law* 42:1, 20–41.

Grossman, H. I., 2002. "Make Us a King: Anarchy, Predation, and the State." *European Journal of Political Economy* 18, 31–46.

Grotius, Hugo. 2012 [1609]. *The Free Sea.* Indianapolis: Liberty Fund.

Guerra, François-Xavier. 1994. "The Spanish-American Tradition of Representation and Its European Roots." *Journal of Latin American Studies* 26:1, 1–35.

Gugliuzzo, Elina. 2015. *Economic and Social Systems in the Early Modern Age Seaports: Malta, Messina, Barcelona, and Ottoman Maritime Policy.* Lewiston, NY: Edwin Mellen Press.

Guilhot, Nicolas. 2005. *The Democracy Makers: Human Rights and the Politics of Global Order.* New York: Columbia University Press.

Guillaume, X. 1985. "Saigon, or the Failure of an Ambition (1858–1945)." In Robert Ross and Gerard J. Telkamp (eds.), *Colonial Cities* (Dordrecht: Martinus Nijhoff), 181–92.

Guizot, François. 1877 [1838]. *General History of Civilization in Europe: From the Fall of the Roman Empire to the French Revolution.* New York: D. Appleton.
  2002 [1851]. *The History of the Origins of Representative Government in Europe,* trans. Andrew R. Scoble. Indianapolis: Liberty Fund.

Gullick, J. M. 1958. *Indigenous Political Systems of Western Malaya.* London: Athlone Press.

Gunda, Bela. 1984. *The Fishing Culture of the World: Studies in Ethnology, Cultural Ecology and Folklore,* Budapest, Akademiai Kiado.

Gunitsky, Seva. 2014. "From Shocks to Waves: Hegemonic Transitions and Democratization in the Twentieth Century." *International Organization* 68, 561–97.
  2015. "Corrupting the Cyber-Commons: Social Media as a Tool of Autocratic Stability." *Perspectives on Politics* 13:1, 42–54.

Gunn, Geoffrey C. 2003. *First Globalization: The Eurasian Exchange, 1500–1800.* Lanham: Rowman & Littlefield.

Guriev, Sergei, Daniel Treisman. 2019. "Informational Autocrats." *Journal of Economic Perspectives* 33:4, 100–27.

Gustafsson, Harald. 1998. "The Conglomerate State: A Perspective on State Formation in Early Modern Europe." *Scandinavian Journal of History* 23:3–4, 189–213.

Gygli, Savina, Florian Haelg, Niklas Potrafke, Jan-Egbert Sturm. 2019. "The KOF Globalisation Index – Revisited." *Review of International Organizations* 14:3, 543–74.

Haas, Ernst B. 2008. *Beyond the Nation State: Functionalism and International Organization.* Colchester: ECPR Press.

Haber, Stephen, Victor Menaldo. 2011. "Do Natural Resources Fuel Authoritarianism? A Reappraisal of the Resource Curse." *American Political Science Review* 105:1, 1–26.

Habermas, Jurgen. 1991. *The Structural Transformation of the Public Sphere: An Inquiry into a Category of Bourgeois Society.* Cambridge, MA: MIT Press.

Hadenius, Axel. 1992. *Democracy and Development.* Cambridge: Cambridge University Press.

Haerpfer, C., Ronald Inglehart, A. Moreno, Christian Welzel, K. Kizilova, J. Diez-Medrano, M. Lagos, P. Norris, E. Ponarin, B. Puranen, et al. (eds.). 2020. *World Values Survey: Round Seven – Country-Pooled Datafile.* Madrid and Vienna: JD Systems Institute & WVSA Secretariat. www .worldvaluessurvey.org/WVSDocumentationWV7.jsp.

Hajnal, John. 1965. "European Marriage Patterns in Perspective." In D. V. Glass and D. E. Eversley (eds.), *Population in History: Essays in Historical Demography* (Chicago: Aldine Publishing Company), 101–40.

Hale, Julian Anthony Stuart. 1975. *Radio Power: Propaganda and International Broadcasting*. London: Paul Elek.

Halecki, Oskar. 1952. *Borderlands of Western Civilization: A History of East Central Europe*. New York: Ronald Press Company.

Hall, John A. 1985. *Powers and Liberties: The Causes and Consequences of the Rise of the West*. Berkeley: University of California Press.

(ed.). 1986. *States in History*. Oxford: Basil Blackwell.

Hall, John Whitney. 1955. "The Castle Town and Japan's Modern Urbanization." *Far Eastern Quarterly*, 15:1, 37–56.

(ed.). 1991. *The Cambridge History of Japan. Volume 4. Early Modern Japan*. Cambridge: Cambridge University Press.

Hall, John Whitney, Toyoda Takeshi (eds.). 1977. *Japan in the Muromachi Age*. Berkeley: University of California Press.

Hall, Kenneth R. 1980. *Trade and Statecraft in the Age of Colas, 850–1279*. New Delhi: Abhinav Publications.

1985. *Maritime Trade and State Development in Early Southeast Asia*. Honolulu: University of Hawaii Press

2011. *A History of Early Southeast Asia: Maritime Trade and Societal Development, 100–1500*. Lanham: Rowman & Littlefield.

Hall, Robert E., Charles I. Jones. 1999. "Why Do Some Countries Produce So Much More Output per Worker Than Others?" *Quarterly Journal of Economics* 114:1, 83–116.

Halperin Donghi, Tulio. 1981. *Historia Contemporanea de America Latina*, 9th ed. Madrid: Alianza Editorial.

Hamilton-Paterson, James. 2011. *Seven-Tenths: The Sea and Its Thresholds*. London: Faber and Faber.

Hanagan, Michael, Charles Tilly (eds.). 1999. *Extending Citizenship, Reconfiguring States*. Lanham: Rowman & Littlefield.

Hang, Xing. 2015. *Conflict and Commerce in Maritime East Asia: The Zheng Family and the Shaping of the Modern World, c. 1620–1720*. Cambridge: Cambridge University Press.

Hanioğlu, M. Şükrü. 2010. *A Brief History of the Late Ottoman Empire*. Princeton: Princeton University Press.

Hansen, Mogens Herman. 1999. *The Athenian Democracy in the Age of Demosthenes: Structure, Principles, and Ideology*. Norman: University of Oklahoma Press.

(ed.). 2000. *A Comparative Study of Thirty City-State Cultures: An Investigation*. Copenhagen: Royal Danish Academy of Sciences and Letters.

Hanson, Elizabeth C. 2008. *The Information Revolution and World Politics*. Lanham: Rowman & Littlefield.

Hanson, Mark. 1974. "Organizational Bureaucracy in Latin America and the Legacy of Spanish Colonialism." *Journal of Interamerican Studies and World Affairs* 16:2, 199–219.

Hanson, R. L. 1989. "Democracy." In T. Ball, J. Farr and R. L. Hanson (eds.), *Political Innovation and Conceptual Change* (Cambridge: Cambridge University Press), 68–89.

Haring, Clarence H. 1999. "The Cabildo." In Anthony J. R. Russell-Wood (ed.), *Local Government in European Overseas Empires, 1450–1800* (Aldershot: Ashgate), 1–20.

Hariri, Jacob Gerner. 2012. "The Autocratic Legacy of Early Statehood." *American Political Science Review* 106:3, 471–94.

2015. "A Contribution to the Understanding of Middle Eastern and Muslim Exceptionalism." *Journal of Politics* 77:2, 477–90.

Harlaftis, Gelina, Jesús Valdaliso, Stig Tenold (eds.). 2012. *The World's Key Industry: History and Economics of International Shipping*. London: Palgrave Macmillan.

Harper, Marjory, Stephen Constantine. 2010. *Migration and Empire*. London: Oxford University Press.

Harris, Lynn (ed.). 2016. *Sea Ports and Sea Power: African Maritime Cultural Landscapes*. Boston: Springer.

Harriss, Gerald L. 1993. "Political Society and the Growth of Government in Late Medieval England." *Past & Present* 138:1, 28–57.

Hartley, Janet M. 2021. *The Volga: A History*. New Haven: Yale University Press.

Hartz, Louis. 1955. *The Liberal Tradition in America: An Interpretation of American Political Thought since the Revolution*. New York: Houghton Mifflin Harcourt.

(ed.). 1969. *The Founding of New Societies: Studies in the History of the United States, Latin America, South Africa, Canada, and Australia*. New York: Houghton Mifflin Harcourt.

Hasan, Farhat. 2004. *State and Locality in Mughal India: Power Relations in Western India, c. 1572–1730*. Cambridge: Cambridge University Press.

Hattendorf, John B. (ed.). 2007. *The Oxford Encyclopedia of Maritime History*, 4 vols. Oxford: Oxford University Press.

Hattersley, Alan Frederick. 1930. *A Short History of Democracy*. Cambridge: Cambridge University Press.

Hatton, Timothy J., Jeffrey G. Williamson. 2005. *Global Migration and the World Economy: Two Centuries of Policy and Performance*. Cambridge, MA: MIT Press.

Havrylyshyn, Oleh, Nora Srzentiæ. 2014. *Institutions Always Mattered: Explaining Prosperity in Medieval Ragusa (Dubrovnik)*. London: Palgrave Macmillan.

Haws, Duncan, Alexander Anthony Hurst. 1985. *The Maritime History of the World: A Chronological Survey of Maritime Events from 5,000 BC until the Present Day. Volume 1*. Peekskill, NY: National Maritime Historical Society.

Hay, Denys. 1966. *Europe: The Emergence of an Idea*. New York: Harper.

Haynes, Jeffrey (ed.). 2015. *Religion and Political Change in the Modern World*. London: Routledge.

Head, Randolph C. 2002. *Early Modern Democracy in the Grisons: Social Order and Political Language in a Swiss Mountain Canton, 1470–1620*. Cambridge: Cambridge University Press.

Headrick, Daniel R. 1981. *The Tools of Empire: Technology and European Imperialism in the Nineteenth Century*. New York: Oxford University Press.

2000. *When Information Came of Age: Technologies of Knowledge in the Age of Reason and Revolution, 1700–1850*. Oxford: Oxford University Press.

Hearnshaw, Fossey John Cobb. 1940. *Sea-Power and Empire*. London: G. G. Harrap.

Hebblewhite, Mark. 2016. *The Emperor and the Army in the Later Roman Empire, AD 235–395*. London: Taylor & Francis.

Hébert, Michel (ed.). 2014. *Parliamenter: Assemblées représentatives et échange politique en Europe occidentale à la fin du Moyen Age*. Paris: Ed. De Boccard.

Hechter, Michael. 1975. *Internal Colonialism: The Celtic Fringe in British National Development*. New Brunswick: Transaction Publishers.

2013. *Alien Rule*. Cambridge: Cambridge University Press.

Heginbotham, Eric. 2002. "The Fall and Rise of Navies in East Asia: Military Organizations, Domestic Politics, and Grand Strategy." *International Security* 27:2, 86–125.

2004. "Crossed Swords: Divided Militaries and Politics in East Asia." PhD dissertation, Massachusetts Institute of Technology.

Hein, Carola (ed.). 2011. *Port Cities: Dynamic Landscapes and Global Networks*. London: Routledge.

Held, David. 1995. *Democracy and the Global Order: From the Modern State to Cosmopolitan Governance*. Stanford: Stanford University Press.

2006. *Models of Democracy*. Stanford: Stanford University Press.

Hellyer, Robert I. 2009. *Defining Engagement: Japan and Global Contexts, 1640–1868*. Cambridge, MA: Harvard University Press.

Henderson, J. Vernon, Tim Squires, Adam Storeygard, David Weil. 2016. *The Global Spatial Distribution of Economic Activity: Nature, History, and the Role of Trade*. Cambridge, MA: National Bureau of Economic Research.

Henshall, Nicholas. 1992. *The Myth of Absolutism*. London: Routledge.

Herb, Michael. 1999. *All in the Family: Absolutism, Revolution, and Democracy in the Middle Eastern Monarchies*. Albany: SUNY Press.

2014. *The Wages of Oil: Parliaments and Economic Development in Kuwait and the UAE*. Ithaca: Cornell University Press.

Herbst, Jeffrey. 2000. *States and Power in Africa: Comparative Lessons in Authority and Control*. Princeton: Princeton University Press.

Hérubel, Marcel. 1936. *L'Homme et la côte*. Paris: Gallimard.

Herzog, Tamar. 2003. *Defining Nations: Immigrants and Citizens in Early Modern Spain and Spanish America*. New Haven: Yale University Press.

Heyerdahl, Thor. 1950. *Kon-Tiki: Across the Pacific by Raft*. Chicago: Rand McNally.

Hibbert, Christopher. 1968. *Charles I*. London: Weidenfeld & Nicolson.

Hibbs, Douglas A., Jr., Ola Olsson. 2004. "Geography, Biogeography, and Why Some Countries Are Rich and Others Are Poor." *Proceedings of the National Academy of Sciences*, 101:10, 3715–25.

Hidalgo, Daniel Castillo, César Ducruet. 2020. "Port Systems and Regional Hierarchies in Africa in the Long Term." In Ayodeji Olukoju and Daniel Castillo Hidalgo (eds.), *African Seaports and Maritime Economics in Historical Perspective*. London: Palgrave Macmillan, 45–80.

Hillerbrand, Hans J. 2004. *Encyclopedia of Protestantism*, 4 vols. London: Routledge.

Hilling, David. 1969. "The Evolution of the Major Ports of West Africa." *Geographical Journal* 135, 365–78.

Hilling, David, Brian Stewart Hoyle (eds.). 1970. *Seaports and Development in Tropical Africa*. London: Palgrave Macmillan.

Hintze, Otto. 1975. "The Pre-conditions of Representative Government in the Context of World History." In F. Gilbert (ed.), *The Historical Essays of Otto Hintze* (New York: Oxford University Press), 302–56.

Hirschman, Albert O. 1970. *Exit, Voice, Loyalty: Responses to Decline in Firms, Organizations, and States*. Cambridge, MA: Harvard University Press.

1977. *The Passions and the Interests*. Princeton: Princeton University Press.

Hirst, John Bradley. 2008. *Freedom on the Fatal Shore: Australia's First Colony*. Melbourne: Black Inc.

Hitchins, Keith. 2014. *A Concise History of Romania*. Cambridge: Cambridge University Press.

Hittle, J. Michael. 1979. *The Service City: State and Townsmen in Russia, 1600–1800*. Cambridge, MA: Harvard University Press.

Ho, Dahpon David. 2011. "Sealords Live in Vain: Fujian and the Making of a Maritime Frontier in Seventeenth-Century China." PhD dissertation, University of California at San Diego.

Hoare. J. E. 1995. *Japan's Treaty Ports and Foreign Settlements: The Uninvited Guests, 1858–1899*. London: Routledge.

Hobsbawm, Eric. 1981. *Bandits*, rev. ed. New York: Pantheon.

Hobsbawm, Eric, Terence Ranger (eds.). 1983. *The Invention of Tradition*. Cambridge: Cambridge University Press.

Hobson, John M. 2004. *The Eastern Origins of Western Civilisation*. Cambridge: Cambridge University Press.

Hoerder, Dirk, Leslie Page Moch (eds.). 1996. *European Migrants: Global and Local Perspectives*. Boston: Northeastern University Press.

Hoffman, Philip T. 2015. *Why Did Europe Conquer the World?* Princeton: Princeton University Press.

Hoffman, Philip T., Kathryn Norberg. 1994. "Conclusion." In Philip T. Hoffman and Kathryn Norberg (eds.), *Fiscal Crises, Liberty, and Representative Government, 1450–1789* (Stanford: Stanford University Press), 299–312.

Hofstadter, Richard. 1944. *Social Darwinism in American Thought*. Philadelphia: University of Pennsylvania Press.

Hogben, Sidney John, Anthony H. M. Kirk-Greene. 1966. *The Emirates of Northern Nigeria: A Preliminary Survey of Their Historical Traditions*. London: Oxford University Press.

Höghammer, Kerstin. 2017. *Ancient Ports: The Geography of Connections*. Uppsala: Acta Universitatis Upsaliensis.

Hohlfelder, Robert L. (ed.). 2008. *The Maritime World of Ancient Rome*. Ann Arbor: University of Michigan Press.

Holland, Paul W. 1986. "Statistics and Causal Inference." *Journal of the American Statistical Association* 81:396, 945–60.

Holt, James Clarke. 2016. *Magna Carta*. Cambridge: Cambridge University Press.

Hopcroft, Rosemary L. 1997. "Rural Organization and Receptivity to Protestantism in Sixteenth-Century Europe." *Journal for the Scientific Study of Religion* 36:2, 158–81.

Horden, Peregrine, Nicholas Purcell. 2000. *The Corrupting Sea: A Study of Mediterranean History*. Oxford: Blackwell.

Hornell, James. 2015 [1946]. *Water Transport*. Cambridge: Cambridge University Press.

Horowitz, Dan, Moshe Lissak. 1979. *Origins of the Israeli Polity: Palestine under the Mandate*. Chicago: University of Chicago Press.

Horowitz, Richard S. 2004. "International Law and State Transformation in China, Siam, and the Ottoman Empire during the Nineteenth Century." *Journal of World History* 15:4, 445–86.

Horton, Carol A. 2005. *Race and the Making of American Liberalism*. Oxford: Oxford University Press.

Horton, Mark, John Middleton. 2000. *The Swahili: The Social Landscape of a Mercantile Society*. Oxford: Wiley-Blackwell.

Houle, Christian. 2009. "Inequality and Democracy: Why Inequality Harms Consolidation but Does Not Affect Democratization." *World Politics* 61, 589–622.

Houle, Christian, Mark A. Kayser, Jun Xiang. 2016. "Diffusion or Confusion? Clustered Shocks and the Conditional Diffusion of Democracy." *International Organization* 70, 687–726.

Hourani, George Fadlo. 1975. *Arab Seafaring in the Indian Ocean in Ancient and Early Medieval Times*. Princeton: Princeton University Press.

Howard, Michael. 2009. *War in European History*. New York: Oxford University Press.

Howe, Kerry R. 1984. *Where the Waves Fall: A New South Sea Islands History from First Settlement to Colonial Rule*. Honolulu: University of Hawaii Press.

Howell, Colin D., Richard J. Twomey (eds.). 1991. *Jack Tar in History: Essays in the History of Maritime Life and Labour*. New Brunswick: Acadiensis Press.

Hoyle, Brian Stewart. 1967a. "Early Port Development in East Africa: An Illustration of the Concept of Changing Port Hierarchies." *Tijdschrift voor Economische en Sociale Geografie* 58, 94–102.

1967b. *The Seaports of East Africa: A Geographical Study*. Nairobi: East African Publishing House.

1968. "East African Seaports: An Application of the Concept of 'Anyport.'" *Transactions of the Institute of British Geographers* 44:May, 163–83.

1989. "The Port–City Interface: Trends, Problems, and Examples." *Geoforum* 20:4, 429–35.

Hoyle, Brian Stewart, D. A. Pinder. 1992. *European Port Cities in Transition*. London: Belhaven Press.

Huber, Evelyne, Frank Safford (eds.). 1995. *Agrarian Structure and Political Power: Landlord and Peasant in the Making of Latin America*. Pittsburgh, PA: University of Pittsburgh Press.

Hughes, Robert. 1988. *The Fatal Shore*. New York: Random House.

Hugill, Peter J. 1995. *World Trade since 1431: Geography, Technology, and Capitalism*. Baltimore: Johns Hopkins University Press.

Hui, Victoria Tin-bor. 2005. *War and State Formation in Ancient China and Early Modern Europe*. Cambridge: Cambridge University Press.

Hull, Richard W. 1976. *African Cities and Towns before the European Conquest*. New York: W.W. Norton.

Hummels, David. 2007. "Transportation Costs and International Trade in the Second Era of Globalization." *Journal of Economic Perspectives* 21:3, 131–54.

Humphrey, Shawn, Bradley A. Hansen. 2010. "Constraining the State's Ability to Employ Force: The Standing Army Debates, 1697–99." *Journal of Institutional Economics* 6:2, 243–59.

Humphreys, Sarah C. 1978. *Anthropology and the Greeks*. London: Routledge.

Hunt, Robert C. 1988. "Size and the Structure of Authority in Canal Irrigation Systems." *Journal of Anthropological Research* 44:4, 335–55.

1989. "Appropriate Social Organization? Water User Associations in Bureaucratic Canal Irrigation Systems." *Human Organization* 48:1, 79–90.

Huntington, Samuel P. 1966. "The Political Modernization of Traditional Monarchies." *Daedalus* 95:3, 763–88.

1968. *Political Order in Changing Societies*. New Haven: Yale University Press.

1991. *The Third Wave: Democratization in the Late Twentieth Century*. Norman: University of Oklahoma Press.

Hurst, G. Cameron III. 1999. "Insei." In Donald H. Shively and William H. McCullough (eds.), *The Cambridge History of Japan. Volume 2. Heian Japan* (Cambridge: Cambridge University Press), 576–643.

Hutchinson, Gillian. 1994. *Medieval Ships and Shipping*. London: Leicester University Press.

Huttenback, Robert A. 1976. *Racism and Empire: White Settlers and Colored Immigrants in the British Self-Governing Colonies, 1830–1910*. Ithaca: Cornell University Press.

Ignatiev, Noel. 2012. *How the Irish Became White*. London: Routledge.

Ikenberry, G. John. 2020. *A World Safe for Democracy: Liberal Internationalism and the Crises of Global Order*. New Haven: Yale University Press.

Illich, Ivan. 1973. *Tools for Conviviality*. New York: Harper & Row.

Imai, Kosuke, Luke Keele, Dustin Tingley, Teppei Yamamoto. 2011. "Unpacking the Black Box of Causality: Learning about Causal Mechanisms from Experimental and Observational Studies." *American Political Science Review* 105:4, 765–89.

Imber, Colin. 2002. *The Ottoman Empire, 1300–1650: The Structure of Power*. London: Palgrave Macmillan.

Inglehart, Ronald, Christian Welzel. 2005. *Modernization, Cultural Change, and Democracy: The Human Development Sequence*. Cambridge: Cambridge University Press.

Inman, Douglas L. 1975. "Ancient and Modern Harbors: A Repeating Phylogeny." *Coastal Engineering* 1974, 2048–67.

Irwin, Geoffrey. 1994. *The Prehistoric Exploration and Colonisation of the Pacific*. Cambridge: Cambridge University Press.

Isaacs, Ann Katherine, Maarten Prak. 1996. "Cities, Bourgeoisies and States." In Wolfgang Reinhard (ed.), *Power Elites and State Building* (Oxford: Clarendon Press), 207–35.

Isakhan, Benjamin, Stephen Stockwell (eds.). 2011. *The Secret History of Democracy.* London: Palgrave Macmillan.

(eds.). 2015. *Edinburgh Companion to the History of Democracy.* Edinburgh: Edinburgh University Press.

Israel, Jonathan I. 1995. *The Dutch Republic: Its Rise, Greatness and Fall 1477–1806.* New York: Oxford University Press.

2010. *A Revolution of the Mind: Radical Enlightenment and the Intellectual Origins of Modern Democracy.* Princeton: Princeton University Press. Kindle edition.

2013. *Democratic Enlightenment: Philosophy, Revolution and Human Rights 1750–1790.* Oxford: Oxford University Press.

Ittmann, Karl. 2013. *A Problem of Great Importance.* Berkeley: University of California Press.

Jacks, David S., Krishna Pendakur. 2010. "Global Trade and the Maritime Transport Revolution." *Review of Economics and Statistics* 92:4, 745–55.

Jackson, Gordon. 1983. *The History and Archaeology of Ports.* Tadworth, Surrey: World's Work.

Jacob, Margaret C. 2006. *Strangers Nowhere in the World: The Rise of Cosmopolitanism in Early Modern Europe.* Philadelphia: University of Pennsylvania Press.

Jacobs, Jaap. 2005. *The Colony of New Netherland: A Dutch Settlement in Seventeenth-Century America.* Leiden: Brill.

Jacobsen, Thorkild. 1943. "Primitive Democracy in Ancient Mesopotamia." *Journal of Near Eastern Studies* 2:3, 159–72.

Jae-Woo, Park. 2011. "Consultative Politics and Royal Authority in the Goryeo Period." *Seoul Journal of Korean Studies* 24:2, 203–18.

James, Daniel. 1995. "Uncertain Legitimacy: The Social and Political Restraints Underlying the Emergence of Democracy in Argentina, 1890–1930." In George Reid Andrews, Herrick Chapman (eds.), *The Social Construction of Democracy, 1870–1990* (London: Palgrave Macmillan), 56–70.

Jansson, Maija (ed.). 2007. *Realities of Representation.* New York: Palgrave Macmillan.

Jarvis, Adrian (ed.). 1998. *Port and Harbour Engineering.* London: Taylor & Francis.

Jarvis, Adrian, W. Robert Lee (eds.). 2008. *Trade, Migration and Urban Networks in Port Cities, c. 1640–1940.* St. John's: International Maritime Economic History Association.

Jedruch, Jacek. 1998. *Constitutions, Elections and Legislatures of Poland, 1493–1993: A Guide to Their History.* New York: Ejj Books.

Jedwab, Remi, Felix Meier zu Selhausen, Alexander Moradi. 2018. "The Economics of Missionary Expansion: Evidence from Africa and Implications for Development." CSAE Working Paper WPS/2018-07. Oxford: Centre for the Study of African Economies.

Jelavich, Barbara. 1983. *History of the Balkans. Volume I. Eighteenth and Nineteenth Centuries.* Cambridge: Cambridge University Press.

Jha, Saumitra. 2013. "Trade, Institutions, and Ethnic Tolerance: Evidence from South Asia." *American Political Science Review* 107:4, 806–32.

Jia, Ruixie. 2014. "The Legacies of Forced Freedom: China's Treaty Ports." *Review of Economics and Statistics* 4:96, 596–608.

Jimenez-Ayora, Pablo, Mehmet Ali Ulubaşoğlu. 2015. "What Underlies Weak States? The Role of Terrain Ruggedness." *European Journal of Political Economy* 39, 167–83.

Johnson, Allen W., Timothy Earle. 2000. *The Evolution of Human Societies*, 2nd ed. Stanford: Stanford University Press.

Johnson, G. Wesley. 1971. *The Emergence of Black Politics in Senegal: The Struggle for Power in the Four Communes, 1900–1920*. Stanford: Stanford University Press.

Johnson, Gordon. 2005. *Provincial Politics and Indian Nationalism: Bombay and the Indian National Congress 1880–1915*. Cambridge: Cambridge University Press.

Johnston, Hugh Anthony Stephens. 1967. *The Fulani Empire of Sokoto*. London: Oxford University Press.

Johnstone, Paul. 1980. *The Seacraft of Prehistory*. Cambridge, MA: Harvard University Press.

Jones, Arnold Hugh Martin. 1964. *The Later Roman Empire, 284–602: A Social Economic and Administrative Survey*, 3 vols. Norman: University of Oklahoma Press.

Jones, Clyve (ed.). 2012. *A Short History of Parliament: England, Great Britain, the United Kingdom, Ireland and Scotland*. Woodbridge, Suffolk: Boydell Press.

Jones, Dan. 2013. *The Plantagenets: The Warrior Kings and Queens Who Made England*. London: Penguin.

Jones, E. L. 1981. *The European Miracle: Environments, Economies and Geopolitics in the History of Europe and Asia*, 2nd ed. Cambridge: Cambridge University Press.

Jones, Evan T. 2000. "River Navigation in Medieval England." *Journal of Historical Geography* 26:1, 60–75.

Jones, Gwilym Iwan. 1956. "The Political Organization of Old Calabar." In Daryll Forde (ed.), *Efik Traders of Old Calabar* (London: Oxford University Press), 116–57.

  1963. *The Trading States of the Oil Rivers: A Study of Political Development in Eastern Nigeria*. London: Oxford University Press.

Jordan, David William. 2002. *Foundations of Representative Government in Maryland, 1632–1715*. Cambridge: Cambridge University Press.

Jorgensen, Joseph. 1980. *Western Indians: Comparative Environments, Languages, and Cultures of 172 Western American Indian Tribes*. San Francisco: W.H. Freeman and Company.

Jorrin, Miguel, John D. Martz. 1970. *Latin-American Political Thought and Ideology*. Chapel Hill: University of North Carolina Press.

Joseph, John. 2004. *Language and Identity: National, Ethnic, Religious*. Boston: Springer.

Jowitt, Claire, Craig Lambert, Steve Mentz (eds.). 2020. *The Routledge Companion to Marine and Maritime Worlds 1400–1800*. Oxford: Routledge.

Kagan, Richard L., Philip D. Morgan (eds.). 2009. *Atlantic Diasporas: Jews, Conversos, and Crypto-Jews in the Age of Mercantilism, 1500–1800*. Baltimore: Johns Hopkins University Press.

Kaifu, Y., T.H. Kuo, Y. Kubota, et al. 2020. "Palaeolithic Voyage for Invisible Islands beyond the Horizon." *Scientific Reports* 10, 19785.

Kaldellis, Anthony. 2015. *The Byzantine Republic*. Cambridge, MA: Harvard University Press.

Kammen, Michael G. 1969. *Deputyes, Libertyes: The Origins of Representative Government in Colonial America*. New York: Knopf.

Kang, David C. 2010. *East Asia before the West: Five Centuries of Trade and Tribute*. New York: Columbia University Press.

Kantorowicz, Ernst. 1957. *The King's Two Bodies: A Study in Medieval Political Theology*. Princeton: Princeton University Press.

Karashima, Noboru (ed.). 2014. *A Concise History of South India: Issues and Interpretations*. Oxford: Oxford University Press.

Karawan, Ibrahim A. 1992. "Monarchs, Mullas, and Marshals: Islamic Regimes?" *Annals of the American Academy of Political and Social Science* 524, 103–19.

Karayalcin, Cem. 2008. "Divided We Stand, United We Fall: The Hume–Weber–Jones Mechanism for the Rise of Europe." *International Economic Review* 49, 973–97.

Karlen, A. 1995. *Man and Microbes: Disease and Plagues in History and Modern Times*. New York: Simon and Schuster.

Karras, Alan L., John Robert McNeill (eds.). 1992. *Atlantic American Societies: From Columbus through Abolition, 1492–1888*. London: Routledge.

Kaṣetṛśiri, Jāñvidya. 1976. *The Rise of Ayudhya: A History of Siam in the Fourteenth and Fifteenth Centuries*. Oxford: Oxford University Press.

Kathirithamby-Wells, Jaya, John Villiers (eds.). 1990. *The Southeast Asian Port and Polity: Rise and Demise*. Singapore: Singapore University Press.

Kaufmann, Daniel, Aart Kraay, Massimo Mastruzzi. 2010. "The Worldwide Governance Indicators: Methodology and Analytical Issues." World Bank Policy Research Working Paper No. 5430. Washington, DC: World Bank.

Kaukiainen, Yrjö. 2012. "The Advantages of Water Carriage: Scale Economies and Shipping Technology, c. 1870–2000." In Harlaftis, Gelina, Jesús Valdaliso, Stig Tenold (eds.), *The World's Key Industry* (London: Palgrave Macmillan), 64–87.

Kautsky, John H. 1982. *The Politics of Aristocratic Empires*. New Brunswick: Transaction Publishers.

Kaviraj, Sudipta, Sunil Khilnani (eds.). 2001. *Civil Society: History and Possibilities*. Cambridge: Cambridge University Press.

Kayali, Hasan. 1995. "Elections and the Electoral Process in the Ottoman Empire, 1876–1919." *International Journal of Middle East Studies* 27:3, 265–86.

Kea, Ray A. 1982. *Settlements, Trade, and Polities in the Seventeenth-Century Gold Coast*. Baltimore: Johns Hopkins University Press.

Keane, John. 2009. *The Life and Death of Democracy*. New York: Simon and Schuster.

Keay, John. 2010. *India: A History*. New York: HarperCollins.

Kechichian, Joseph A. 2001. *Succession in Saudi Arabia*. London: Palgrave Macmillan.

Keck, Margaret E., Kathryn Sikkink. 2014. *Activists beyond Borders: Advocacy Networks in International Politics*. Ithaca: Cornell University Press.

Kedourie, Elie. 1960. *Nationalism*. London: Hutchinson.

Keeley, Lawrence H. 1996. *War before Civilization: The Myth of the Peaceful Savage*. Oxford: Oxford University Press.

Kellam, Marisa. 2013. "Suffrage Extensions and Voting Patterns in Latin America: Is Mobilization a Source of Decay?" *Latin American Politics and Society* 55:4, 23–46.

Kelley, Liam. 2020. "Srivijaya 00: Un-imagining 'Srivijaya.'" Blog post. https://leminhkhai.blog/imagining-srivijaya-a-series/?fbclid=IwAR21qT3hhT_IQiVprSKHTII_B_YyQ9_tyhIph_x0GSPN9Q-xqACsh-cNWJc.

Kelly, David, Anthony Reid (eds.). 1998. *Asian Freedoms: The Idea of Freedom in East and Southeast Asia*. Cambridge: Cambridge University Press.

Kelly, Morgan, Cormac Ó Gráda. 2019. "Speed under Sail during the Early Industrial Revolution (c. 1750–1830)." *Economic History Review* 72:2, 459–80.

Kelly, Morgan, Cormac Ó Gráda, Peter M. Solar. 2021. "Safety at Sea during the Industrial Revolution." *Journal of Economic History* 81:1, 239–75.

Kelly, Robert L. 2013. *The Lifeways of Hunter-Gatherers: The Foraging Spectrum*. Cambridge: Cambridge University Press.

Kendall-Taylor, Andrea, Erica Frantz, Joseph Wright. 2020. "The Digital Dictators: How Technology Strengthens Autocracy." *Foreign Affairs* 99, 103–15.

Kenkel, Brenton, Jack Paine. 2020. "International Warfare, Cooperative Statebuilding, and European Parliaments." Vanderbilt University. https://bkenkel.com/files/external-threats.pdf.

Kennedy, Dane Keith. 1987. *Islands of White: Settler Society and Culture in Kenya and Southern Rhodesia, 1890–1939*. Durham, NC: Duke University Press.

Kennedy, Hugh. 2013. *The Armies of the Caliphs: Military and Society in the Early Islamic State*. London: Routledge.

Kennedy, Paul. 1987. *The Rise and Fall of the Great Powers*. New York: Vintage.

Kerner, Robert Joseph. 1942. *The Urge to the Sea: The Course of Russian History*. Berkeley: University of California Press.

Kertzer, David I., Dominique Arel (eds.). 2002. *Census and Identity: The Politics of Race, Ethnicity, and Language in National Censuses*. Cambridge: Cambridge University Press.

Key, Valdimer Orlando. 1949. *Southern Politics in State and Nation*. New York: Vintage Books.

Keyder, Çağlar, Y. Eyüp Özveren, Donald Quataert. 1993. "Port-Cities in the Ottoman Empire: Some Theoretical and Historical Perspectives." *Historical Review (Fernand Braudel Center)* 16:4, 519–58.

Khaldun, Ibn. 2015. *The Muqaddimah: An Introduction to History*, trans. Danyal Nicholson. Istanbul: The Olive Press. Kindle edition.

Khazanov, Anatoly Michailovich. 1994. *Nomads and the Outside World*. Madison: University of Wisconsin Press.

Khodarkovsky, Michael. 2002. *Russia's Steppe Frontier: The Making of a Colonial Empire, 1500–1800*. Bloomington: Indiana University Press.

Khoury, Philip S., Joseph Kostiner (eds.). 1990. *Tribes and State Formation in the Middle East*. Berkeley: University of California Press.

Kiaupa, Zigmantas. 2002. *The History of Lithuania: Before 1795*. Vilnius: Arturas Braziunas.

Kim, Djun Kil. 2012. *The History of Korea*. Bloomington: Indiana University Press.

Kindleberger, Charles P. 1975. "The Rise of Free Trade in Western Europe, 1820–1875." *Journal of Economic History* 35:1, 20–55.

King, Gary, James Honaker, Anne Joseph, Kenneth Scheve. 2001. "Analyzing Incomplete Political Science Data: An Alternative Algorithm for Multiple Imputation." *American Political Science Review* 95:1, 49–69.

King, Preston T. 1974. *The Ideology of Order: A Comparative Analysis of Jean Bodin and Thomas Hobbes*. London: Barnes, Noble.

Kingsley, Sean A. 2004. *Barbarian Seas: Late Rome to Islam*. London: Periplus.

Kinkel, Sarah. 2018. *Disciplining the Empire: Politics, Governance, and the Rise of the British Navy*. Cambridge, MA: Harvard University Press.

Kirby, David. 2014. *Northern Europe in the Early Modern Period: The Baltic World 1492–1772*. London: Routledge.

Kirby, David Gordon, Merja-Liisa Hinkkanen. 2000. *The Baltic and the North Seas*. London: Routledge.

Kirch, Patrick Vinton. 1988. "Circumscription Theory and Sociopolitical Evolution in Polynesia." *American Behavioral Scientist* 31:4, 416–27.

    2017. *On the Road of the Winds: An Archaeological History of the Pacific Islands before European Contact*, 2nd ed. Berkeley: University of California Press.

Kiser, Edgar, Yoram Barzel. 1991. "The Origins of Democracy in England." *Rationality and Society* 3:4, 396–422.

Kiser, Edgar, April Linton. 2002. "The Hinges of History: State-Making and Revolt in Early Modern France." *American Sociological Review* 67:6, 889–910.

Kiszewski, A., A. Mellinger, A. Spielman, P. Malaney, S. E. Sachs, Jeffrey Sachs. 2004. "A Global Index Representing the Stability of Malaria Transmission." *American Journal of Tropical Medicine and Hygiene* 70:5, 486–98.

Kitamura, Shuhei, Nils-Petter Lagerlöf. 2015. "Natural Borders." *IIES Seminar Paper*, No. 773. Institute for International Economic Studies, Stockholm University.

Kivelson, Valerie Ann. 1996. *Autocracy in the Provinces: The Muscovite Gentry and Political Culture in the Seventeenth Century*. Stanford: Stanford University Press.

Klaveren, N. 2013. *The Dutch Colonial System in the East Indies*. Boston: Springer.

Klein, Bernhard, Gesa Mackenthun (eds.). 2004. *Sea Changes: Historicizing the Ocean*. New York: Routledge.

Klein Goldewijk, Kees, Arthur Beusen, Peter Janssen. 2010. "Long-Term Dynamic Modeling of Global Population and Built-up Area in a Spatially Explicit Way: HYDE 3.1." *The Holocene* 20:4, 565–73.

Klein Goldewijk, Kees, Arthur Beusen, Gerard Van Drecht, Martine De Vos. 2011. "The HYDE 3.1 Spatially Explicit Database of Human-Induced

Global Land-Use Change over the Past 12,000 Years." *Global Ecology and Biogeography* 20:1, 73–86.

Klerman, Daniel M., Paul G. Mahoney, Holger Spamann, Mark I. Weinstein. 2011. "Legal Origin or Colonial History?" *Journal of Legal Analysis* 3:2, 379–409.

Klinkner, Philip A., Rogers M. Smith. 1999. *The Unsteady March: The Rise and Decline of Racial Equality in America*. Chicago: University of Chicago Press.

Kloppenberg, James T. 2016. *Toward Democracy: The Struggle for Self-Rule in European and American Thought*. Oxford: Oxford University Press.

Kloppenborg, John S., Stephen G. Wilson (eds.). 1996. *Voluntary Associations in the Graeco-Roman World*. London: Routledge.

Knauft, Bruce B. 1991. "Violence and Sociality in Human Evolution." *Current Anthropology* 32, 391–428.

Knight, Franklin W., Peggy K. Liss (eds.). 1991. *Atlantic Port Cities: Economy, Culture, and Society in the Atlantic World, 1650–1850*. Knoxville: University of Tennessee Press.

Knutsen, Carl Henrik, Jørgen Møller, Svend-Erik Skaaning. 2016. "Going Historical: Measuring Democraticness before the Age of Mass Democracy." *International Political Science Review* 37:5, 679–89.

Knutsen, Carl Henrik, John Gerring, Svend-Erik Skaaning, Jan Teorell, Matthew Maguire, Michael Coppedge, Staffan Lindberg. 2019. "Economic Development and Democracy: An Electoral Connection." *European Journal of Political Research* 58:1, 292–314.

Knutsen, Carl Henrik, Jan Teorell, Tore Wig, Agnes Cornell, John Gerring, Haakon Gjerløw, Svend-Erik Skaaning, Daniel Ziblatt, Kyle L. Marquardt, Dan Pemstein, Brigitte Seim. 2019. "Introducing the Historical Varieties of Democracy Dataset: Political Institutions in the Long 19th Century." *Journal of Peace Research* 56:3, 440–51.

Koenig, William J. 1990. *The Burmese Polity, 1752–1819: Politics, Administration, and Social Organization in the Early Kon-baung Period*. Ann Arbor: University of Michigan Press.

Koenigsberger, Helmut Georg. 1989. "Composite States, Representative Institutions and the American Revolution." *Historical Research* 62:148, 135–53.

2001. *Monarchies, States Generals and Parliaments: The Netherlands in the Fifteenth and Sixteenth Centuries*. Cambridge: Cambridge University Press.

Kohli, Atul. 2020. *Imperialism and the Developing World: How Britain and the United States Shaped the Global Periphery*. Oxford: Oxford University Press.

Kohn, Hans. 1944. *The Idea of Nationalism*. New York: Macmillan.

Kohut, Zenon E. 1988. *Russian Centralism and Ukrainian Autonomy: Imperial Absorption of the Hetmanate, 1760s–1830s*. Cambridge, MA: Harvard Ukrainian Research Institute.

Kojiro, Naoki. 1993. "The Nara State." In Delmer M. Brown (ed.), *The Cambridge History of Japan. Volume I. Ancient Japan* (Cambridge: Cambridge University Press), 221–67.

Kokkonen, Andrej, Jørgen Møller. 2020. "Succession, Power-Sharing and the Development of Representative Institutions in Medieval Europe." *European Journal of Political Research* 59:4, 954–75.

Kokkonen, Andrej, Anders Sundell. 2014. "Delivering Stability: Primogeniture and Autocratic Survival in European Monarchies 1000–1800." *American Political Science Review* 108:2, 438–53.

Kolb, Robert. 2013. *The International Court of Justice*. London: Bloomsbury Publishing.

Kollmann, Nancy Shields. 1987. *Kinship and Politics: The Making of the Muscovite Political System, 1345–1547*. Stanford: Stanford University Press.

Konvitz, Josef W. 1978. *Cities and the Sea: Port City Planning in Early Modern Europe*. Baltimore: Johns Hopkins University Press.

Korotayev, Andrey V. 1995. "Mountains and Democracy: An Introduction." In N. N. Kradin and V. A. Lynsha (eds.), *Alternative Pathways to Early State* (Vladivostok: Dal'nauka), 60–74.

2000. "Parallel-Cousin (FBD) Marriage, Islamization, and Arabization." *Ethnology* 395–407.

Korotayev, Andrey, Dmitri Bondarenko. 2000. "Polygyny and Democracy: A Cross-cultural Comparison." *Cross-cultural Research* 34:2, 190–208.

Kosambi, M., J. Brush. 1988. "Three Colonial Port Cities in India." *Geographical Review* 78, 32–47.

Kottak, Conrad P. 1972. "Ecological Variables in the Origin and Evolution of African States: The Buganda Example." *Comparative Studies in Society and History* 14:3, 351–80.

Kovietz, J. W. 1978. *Cities and the Sea: Port Cities Planning in Early Modern Europe*. Lanham, MD: Johns Hopkins University Press.

Krieckhaus, Jonathan Tabor. 2006. *Dictating Development: How Europe Shaped the Global Periphery*. Pittsburgh, PA: University of Pittsburgh Press.

Krieger, Leonard. 1970. *Kings and Philosophers 1689–1789*. New York: W.W. Norton.

Krugman, Paul. 1991. "Increasing Returns and Economic Geography." *Journal of Political Economy*, 99: 483–99.

1993. "On the Number and Location of Cities." *European Economic Review*, 37:2–3, 293–8.

Kulke, Hermann. 1986. "The Early and the Imperial Kingdom in Southeast Asian History." In David G. Marr and Anthony Crothers Milner (eds.), *Southeast Asia in the 9th to 14th Centuries* (Singapore: Institute of Southeast Asian Studies), 1–22.

2016. "Śrīvijaya Revisited: Reflections on State Formation of a Southeast Asian Thalassocracy." *Bulletin de l'École française d'Extrême-Orient* 102, 45–96.

Kuper, Adam. 1970. *Kalahari Village Politics: An African Democracy*. Cambridge: Cambridge University Press.

1982. "Lineage Theory: A Critical Retrospect." *Annual Review of Anthropology* 11:1, 71–95.

Kuper, Hilda. 1986. *The Swazi: A South African Kingdom*. New York: Holt, Rinehart, Winston.

Kupperman, Karen Ordahl. 2012. *The Atlantic in World History*. Oxford: Oxford University Press.

Kuran, Timur. 2012. *The Long Divergence: How Islamic Law Held Back the Middle East*. Princeton: Princeton University Press.

Kuru, Ahmet T. 2019. *Islam, Authoritarianism, and Underdevelopment: A Global and Historical Comparison.* Cambridge: Cambridge University Press.

Kurunmäki, Jussi, Jeppe Nevers, Henk Te Velde (eds.). 2018. *Democracy in Modern Europe: A Conceptual History.* New York: Berghahn Books.

Kurzman, Charles, Erin Leahey. 2004. "Intellectuals and Democratization, 1905–1912 and 1989–1996." *American Journal of Sociology* 109:4, 937–86.

LaBianca, Oystein S., Sandra Arnold Scham. 2016. *Connectivity in Antiquity: Globalization as a Long-term Historical Process.* London: Routledge.

Lachaud, Frédérique, Michael Penman (eds.). 2008. *Making and Breaking the Rules: Succession in Medieval Europe, c. 1000–c. 1600.* Turnhout: Brepols.

Ladner, Andreas (2002). "Size and Direct Democracy at the Local Level: The Case of Switzerland." *Environment and Planning C: Government and Policy* 20:6, 813–28.

Lagerlof, Nils-Petter. 2014. "Population, Technology and Fragmentation: The European Miracle Revisited." *Journal of Development Economics* 108, 87–105.

Laidlaw, Zoë, Alan Lester (eds.). 2015. *Indigenous Communities and Settler Colonialism: Land Holding, Loss and Survival in an Interconnected World.* Boston: Springer.

Laitin, David D., Rajesh Ramachandrany. 2022. "Linguistic Diversity, Official Language Choice and Human Capital." *Journal of Development Economics* 156.

Lake, Marilyn. 2012. "The Gendered and Racialised Self Who Claimed the Right to Self-Government." *Journal of Colonialism and Colonial History* 13:1.

Lamar, Howard Roberts, Leonard Thompson (eds.). 1981. *The Frontier in History: North America and Southern Africa Compared.* New Haven: Yale University Press.

Lambert, Andrew. 2018. *Seapower States: Maritime Culture, Continental Empires and the Conflict That Made the Modern World.* New Haven: Yale University Press.

Lambert, D., L. Martins, M. Ogborn. 2006. "Current Visions and Voyages: Historical Geographies of the Sea." *Journal of Historical Geography* 32, 479–93.

Lanctot, Gustove. 1934. "The Elective Council of Quebec of 1657." *Canadian Historical Review* 15:2, 123–32.

Land, Aubrey C. 1981. *Colonial Maryland, a History.* Millwood, NY: Kto Press.

Landen, Robert Geran. 1967. *Oman since 1856.* Princeton: Princeton University Press.

Landes, David S. 1969. *The Unbound Prometheus: Technological Change and Industrial Development in Western Europe from 1750 to the Present.* Cambridge: Cambridge University Press.

1998. *The Wealth and Poverty of Nations: Why Some Are so Rich and Some so Poor.* New York: W.W. Norton.

Lane, Frederic C. 1964. "Tonnages, Medieval and Modern." *Economic History Review* 17:2, 213–33.

1973. *Venice, a Maritime Republic.* Baltimore, MD: Johns Hopkins University Press.

1979. *Profits from Power: Readings in Protection Rent and Violence-Controlling Enterprises.* Albany: State University of New York Press.

Lane, Tony. 1997. *Liverpool: City of the Sea*. Liverpool: Liverpool University Press.

Lange, Matthew. 2004. "British Colonial Legacies and Political Development." *World Development* 32:6, 905–22.

Lange, Matthew, James Mahoney, Matthias Vom Hau. 2006. "Colonialism and Development: A Comparative Analysis of Spanish and British Colonies." *American Journal of Sociology* 111:5, 1412–62.

Lankina, Tomila, Lullit Getachew. 2012. "Mission or Empire, Word or Sword? The Human Capital Legacy in Post-colonial Democratic Development." *American Journal of Political Science* 56:2, 465–83.

Lape, Peter Vanderford. 2000. "Contact and Conflict in the Banda Island: Eastern Indonesia 11th–17th centuries." PhD dissertation, Brown University.

Lapidus, Ira M. 1984. *Muslim Cities in the Later Middle Ages*. Cambridge: Cambridge University Press.

La Porta, Rafael, Florencio Lopez-de-Silanes, Andrei Shleifer, Robert W. Vishny. 1998. "Law and Finance." *Journal of Political Economy* 106:6, 1113–55.

1999. "The Quality of Government." *Journal of Law, Economics, and Organization*, 15:1, 222–79.

La Porta, Rafael, Florencio Lopez-de-Silanes, Andrei Shleifer. 2008. "The Economic Consequences of Legal Origins." *Journal of Economic Literature* 46:2, 285–332

Lattimore, Owen. 1963. "Chingis Khan and the Mongol Conquests." *Scientific American* 209:2, 54–71.

Lavan, Myles, Richard E. Payne, John Weisweiler (eds.). 2016. *Cosmopolitanism and Empire: Universal Rulers, Local Elites, and Cultural Integration in the Ancient Near East and Mediterranean*. Cambridge: Cambridge University Press.

Lavery, Brian. 2005. *The Island Nation: A History of Britain and the Sea*. London: Anova Books.

LaViolette, Adria. 2008. "Swahili Cosmopolitanism in Africa and the Indian Ocean World, AD 600–1500." *Archaeologies* 4:1, 24–49.

Lawson, Stephanie. 1996. *Tradition versus Democracy in the South Pacific: Fiji, Tonga and Western Samoa*. Cambridge: Cambridge University Press.

Lawton, Richard, Robert Lee (ed.). 2002. *Population and Society in Western European Port Cities, c. 1650–1939*. Liverpool: Liverpool University Press.

Layton, Azza Salama. 2000. *International Politics and Civil Rights Policies in the United States, 1941–1960*. Cambridge: Cambridge University Press.

Leach, Edmund R. 1960. "The Frontiers of 'Burma.'" *Comparative Studies in Society and History* 3:1, 49–68.

Lee, Alexander, Jack Paine. 2019. "British Colonialism and Democracy: Divergent Inheritances and Diminishing Legacies." *Journal of Comparative Economics* 47:3, 487–503.

Lee, James, Cameron Campbell, Wang Feng. 2002. "Positive Check or Chinese Checks?" *Journal of Asian Studies* 61, 591–607.

Lee, Richard Borshay. 1979. *The !Kung San: Men, Women and Work in a Foraging Society*. Cambridge: Cambridge University Press.

Lee, Richard Borshay, Irven DeVore. 1968. *Man the Hunter*. Berlin: Aldine de Gruyter.

Lee, Robert. 1998. "The Socio-economic and Demographic Characteristics of Port Cities: A Typology for Comparative Analysis?" *Urban History* 25:2, 147–72.

Lee, S. W., D. W. Song, Cesar Ducruet. 2008. "A Tale of Asia's World Ports: The Spatial Evolution in Global Hub Port Cities." *Geoforum* 39, 372–85.

Leeson, Peter T., Andrea M. Dean. 2009. "The Democratic Domino Theory: An Empirical Investigation." *American Journal of Political Science* 53:3, 533–51.

Legesse, Asmarom. 2000. *Oromo Democracy: An Indigenous African Political System*. Lawrenceville: Red Sea Press.

Leibundgut, Christian, Irene Kohn. 2014. "European Traditional Irrigation in Transition, Part I: Irrigation in Times Past – A Historic Land Use Practice across Europe." *Irrigation and Drainage* 63:3, 273–93.

Leidwanger, Justin. 2013. "Modeling Distance with Time in Ancient Mediterranean Seafaring: A GIS Application for the Interpretation of Maritime Connectivity." *Journal of Archaeological Science* 40:8, 3302–8.

Leighton, Albert C. 1972. *Transport and Communication in Early Medieval Europe AD 500–1100*. Newton Abbot: David & Charles Publishers.

Lemarchand, Rene (ed.). 1970. *African Kingships in Perspective: Political Change and Modernisation in Monarchical Settings*. London: Routledge.

Lemisch, Jesse. 2015. *Jack Tar vs. John Bull: The Role of New York's Seamen in Precipitating the Revolution*. London: Routledge.

Lendvai, Paul. 2014. *The Hungarians: A Thousand Years of Victory in Defeat*. Princeton: Princeton University Press.

Lenski, Gerhard. 1966. *Power and Privilege: A Theory of Social Stratification*. Chapel Hill: University of North Carolina Press.

Lerner, Daniel. 1958. *The Passing of Traditional Society*. New York: Free Press.

Lester, Alan, Fae Dussart. 2014. *Colonization and the Origins of Humanitarian Governance: Protecting Aborigines across the Nineteenth-Century British Empire*. Cambridge: Cambridge University Press.

Lester, Alan, Kate Boehme, Peter Mitchell. 2021. *Ruling the World: Freedom, Civilisation and Liberalism in the Nineteenth-Century British Empire*. Cambridge: Cambridge University Press.

Leur, Jacob Cornelis van. 1955. *Indonesian Trade and Society: Essays in Asian Social and Economic History*. The Hague: W. van Hoeve.

Levathes, Louise. 1994. *When China Ruled the Seas: The Treasure Fleet of the Dragon Throne, 1405–1433*. New York: Simon and Schuster.

Levi, Margaret. 1989. *Of Rule and Revenue*. Berkeley: University of California Press.

Levinson, Marc. 2016. *The Box: How the Shipping Container Made the World Smaller and the World Economy Bigger*. Princeton: Princeton University Press.

Levitsky, Steven, Lucan A. Way. 2010. *Competitive Authoritarianism: Hybrid Regimes after the Cold War*. Cambridge: Cambridge University Press.

Levtzion, Nehemia. 1973. *Ancient Ghana and Mali*. New York: Methuen.

Levy, Marion J. 1966. *Modernization and the Structure of Societies*. New York: Transaction.

Lewer, Joshua J., Hendrik Van den Berg. 2003. "How Large Is International Trade's Effect on Economic Growth?" *Journal of Economic Surveys* 17:3, 363–96.

Lewis, Archibald Ross. 1951. *Naval Power and Trade in the Mediterranean, AD 500–1100*. Princeton: Princeton University Press.

1953. *The Sea and Medieval Civilizations*. London: Variorum Reprints.

1958. *The Northern Seas: Shipping and Commerce in Northern Europe, AD 300–1100*. Princeton: Princeton University Press.

Lewis, Archibald Ross, Timothy J. Runyan. 1985. *European Naval and Maritime History, 300–1500*. Bloomington: Indiana University Press.

Lewis, Bernard. 2000. "Monarchy in the Middle East." In Joseph Kostiner, (ed.), *Middle East Monarchies* (London: Westview), 167–86.

2001. *The Multiple Identities of the Middle East*. New York: Schocken Books.

Lewis, Gordon K. 1968. *Growth of Modern West Indies*. New York: New York University Press.

Lewis, Herbert S. 1974. "Neighbors, Friends, and Kinsmen: Principles of Social Organization among the Cushitic-Speaking Peoples of Ethiopia." *Ethnology* 13.2: 145–57.

Lewis, Ioan M. 1961. *A Pastoral Democracy*. New York: Oxford University Press.

Lewis, Mark Edward. 2007. *The Early Chinese Empires: Qin and Han*. Cambridge, MA: Harvard University Press.

Li, Quan, Rafael Reuveny. 2003. "Economic Globalization and Democracy: An Empirical Analysis." *British Journal of Political Science* 33:1, 29–54.

Lieberman, Evan S., Prerna Singh. 2012. "Conceptualizing and Measuring Ethnic Politics: An Institutional Complement to Demographic, Behavioral, and Cognitive Approaches." *Studies in Comparative Political Development* 47, 255–86.

Lieberman, Victor B. 1984. *Burmese Administrative Cycles: Anarchy and Conquest, c. 1580–1760*. Princeton: Princeton University Press.

2003. *Strange Parallels: Southeast Asia in Global Context, c. 800–1830. Volume 1. Integration on the Mainland*. Cambridge: Cambridge University Press.

2009. *Strange Parallels: Southeast Asia in Global Context, c. 800–1830. Volume 2. Mainland Mirrors: Europe, Japan, China, South Asia, and the Islands*. Cambridge: Cambridge University Press.

Lindholm, Charles. 1986. "Kinship Structure and Political Authority: The Middle East and Central Asia." *Comparative Studies in Society and History* 28:2, 334–55.

1996. "Despotism and Democracy: State and Society in the Premodern Middle East." *Poznan Studies in the Philosophy of the Sciences and the Humanities* 48, 329–56.

Lindsay, William Schaw. 2013 [1874–6]. *History of Merchant Shipping and Ancient Commerce*, 4 vols. Cambridge: Cambridge University Press.

Linebaugh, Peter, Marcus Rediker. 2000. *The Many-Headed Hydra: Sailors, Slaves, Commoners and the Hidden History of the Revolutionary Atlantic*. Boston: Beacon Press.

Linz, Juan J., Alfred Stepan. 1996. *Problems of Democratic Transition and Consolidation: Southern Europe, South America, and Post-communist Societies.* Baltimore: Johns Hopkins University Press.

Lipset, Seymour Martin. 1959. "Some Social Requisites of Democracy: Economic Development and Political Legitimacy." *American Political Science Review* 53:1, 69–105.

Liu, Amy H. 2015. *Standardizing Diversity: The Political Economy of Language Regimes.* Philadelphia: University of Pennsylvania Press.

Liu, Xuepeng, Emanuel Ornelas. 2014. "Free Trade Agreements and the Consolidation of Democracy." *American Economic Journal: Macroeconomics* 6:2, 29–70.

Lloyd, Christopher, Jacob Metzer, Richard Sutch (eds.). 2013. *Settler Economies in World History.* Leiden: Brill.

Lo Jung-Pang. 2012. *China as a Sea Power, 1127–1368: A Preliminary Survey of the Maritime Expansion and Naval Exploits of the Chinese People during the Southern Song and Yuan Periods.* Singapore: NUS Press.

Loades, David. 2000. *England's Maritime Empire: Seapower, Commerce, and Policy, 1490–1690.* Harlow: Longman.

Lockard, Craig A. 2010. "'The Sea Common to All': Maritime Frontiers, Port Cities, and Chinese Traders in the Southeast Asian Age of Commerce, ca. 1400–1750." *Journal of World History* 21:2, 219–47.

Lombard, D., J. Aubin (eds.). 2000. *Asian Merchants and Businessmen in the Indian Ocean and the China Sea.* New Delhi: Oxford University Press.

London, Jennifer. 2016. "Re-imagining the Cambridge School in the Age of Digital Humanities." *Annual Review of Political Science* 19, 351–73.

Longworth, Philip. 1990. "The Emergence of Absolutism in Russia." In John Miller (ed.), *Absolutism in Seventeenth-Century Europe* (London: Palgrave), 175–94.

Lopez, R. S. 1956. "The Evolution of Land Transport in the Middle Ages." *Past & Present* 9, 17–29.

López-Alves, Fernando. 2000. *State Formation and Democracy in Latin America, 1810–1900.* Durham, NC: Duke University Press.

López-Córdova, Ernesto, Christopher Meissner. 2008. "The Impact of International Trade on Democracy: A Long-Run Perspective." *World Politics* 60:4, 539–75.

Lord, Robert Howard. 1930. "The Parliaments of the Middle Ages and the Early Modern Period." *Catholic Historical Review* 16:2, 125–44.

Lorenzi, Rossella. 2013. "Most Ancient Port, Hieroglyphic Papyri Found." *Discovery News.* www.seeker.com/most-ancient-port-hieroglyphic-papyri-found-1767404864.html.

Loveman, Mara. 2009. "Whiteness in Latin America: Measurement and Meaning in National Censuses (1850–1950)." *Journal de la Société des Américanistes* 95:2, 207–34.

  2014. *National Colors: Racial Classification and the State in Latin America.* Oxford: Oxford University Press.

Löwenthal, Richard. 1977. "Kontinuität und Diskontinuität." In Karl Bosl (ed.), *Der moderne Parlamentarismus und seine Grundlagen in der ständischen Repräsentation* (Berlin: Drucker & Hamblot), 341–56.

Lowry, Heath W. 2009. *The Islamization and Turkification of the City of Trabzon (Trebizond), 1461–1583*. Istanbul: Isis Press.

Lucas, Russell E. 2012. "Rules and Tools of Succession in the Gulf Monarchies." *Journal of Arabian Studies* 2:1, 75–91.

Lucassen, Jan, Leo Lucassen. 2009. "The Mobility Transition Revisited, 1500–1900: What the Case of Europe Can Offer to Global History." *Journal of Global History* 4:3, 347–77.

Lucassen, Jan, Richard W. Unger. 2000. "Labour Productivity in Ocean Shipping, 1450–1875." *International Journal of Maritime History* 12:2, 127–41.

Lucassen, Jan, Tine De Moor, Jan Luiten Van Zanden. 2008. "The Return of the Guilds: Towards a Global History of the Guilds in Pre-industrial Times." *International Review of Social History* 53:S16, 5–18.

Lührmann, Anna, Lisa Gastaldi, Sandra Grahn, Staffan I. Lindberg, Laura Maxwell, Valeriya Mechkova, Richard Morgan, Natalia Stepanova, Shreeya Pillai. 2019. *V-Dem Annual Democracy Report 2019. Democracy Facing Global Challenges*. Gothenburg: V-Dem Institute, University of Gothenburg.

Lukin, Pavel V. 2017. "Novgorod: Trade, Politics and Mentalities in the Time of Independence." In Willem Pieter Blockmans, Mikhail Krom, and Justyna Wubs-Mrozewicz (eds.), *The Routledge Handbook of Maritime Trade around Europe 1300–1600: Commercial Networks and Urban Autonomy* (London: Taylor & Francis).

Lustick, Ian S. 2019. "The Red Thread of Israel's 'Demographic Problem.'" *Middle East Policy* 26:1, 141–9.

Lutz, Donald. 1998. *Colonial Origins of the American Constitution: A Documentary History*. Indianapolis: Liberty Press.

Lützelschwab, Claude. 2013. "Settler Colonialism in Africa." In Christopher Lloyd, Jacob Metzer, Richard Sutch (eds.), *Settler Economies in World History* (Leiden: Brill), 141–68.

Lynch, John. 1973. *The Spanish American Revolution, 1808–1826*. New York: W.W. Norton.

    1992. "The Institutional Framework of Colonial Spanish America." *Journal of Latin American Studies* 24, 69–81.

Lynn, Martin. 1999. "British Policy, Trade, and Informal Empire in the Mid-nineteenth Century." *The Oxford History of the British Empire. Volume III*, 101–21.

MacDonagh, Oliver. 1962. "The Anti-imperialism of Free Trade." *Economic History Review* 14, 489–501.

MacElwee, Roy Samuel. 1925. *Port Development*. New York: McGraw-Hill.

Macfarlane, Alan. 1978. *The Origins of English Individualism: The Family, Property and Social Transition*. Oxford: Basil Blackwell.

Machado, Pedro. 2014. *Ocean of Trade: South Asian Merchants, Africa and the Indian Ocean, c.1750–1850*. Cambridge: Cambridge University Press.

MacKay, Angus. 1977. *Spain in the Middle Ages: From Frontier to Empire, 1000–1500*. London: Macmillan.

Mackay, Ruth. 1999. *Limits of Royal Authority: Resistance and Obedience in Seventeenth-Century Castile*. Cambridge: Cambridge University Press.

Mackinder, Halford John. 1919. *Democratic Ideals and Reality: A Study in the Politics of Reconstruction*. New York: Henry Holt.

Macmillan, Allister (ed.). 1926. *Seaports of the Far East: Historical and Descriptive, Commercial and Industrial, Facts, Figures, Resources*. London: Collingridge.

1928. *Seaports of India, Ceylon: Historical and Descriptive, Commercial and Industrial, Facts, Figures, Resources*. London: Collingridge.

Macpherson, Crawford Brough. 1977. *The Life and Times of Liberal Democracy*. Oxford: Oxford University Press.

Madariaga, I. D. 1995. "The Russian Nobility in the Seventeenth and Eighteenth Centuries." In Hamish M. Scott (ed.), *The European Nobilities in the Seventeenth and Eighteenth Centuries. Volume II* (London: Addison-Wesley Longman), 223–73.

Maddicott, John R. 2010. *The Origins of the English Parliament, 924–1327*. Oxford: Oxford University Press.

Maddison, Angus. 1995. *Monitoring the World Economy 1820–1992*. Paris: Development Centre Studies, Organisation for Economic Co-operation and Development.

2001. *The World Economy*, 2 vols.: *I. A Millennial Perspective; II. Historical Statistics*. Paris: Organisation for Economic Co-operation and Development.

Maddox, Graham. 1996. *Religion and the Rise of Democracy*. London: Routledge.

Maddox, Gregory (ed.). 1993. *Conquest and Resistance to Colonialism in Africa*. New York: Garland.

Madrid, Raúl. 2020. "The Emergence of Democracy in Colombia." Kellogg Working Paper 441. Kellogg Institute for International Studies, Notre Dame, IN. https://keough.nd.edu/publications/the-emergence-of-democracy-in-colombia.

Magaloni, Beatriz. 2008. "Credible Power-Sharing and the Longevity of Authoritarian Rule." *Comparative Political Studies* 41:4–5, 715–41.

Magra, Christopher P. 2009. *The Fisherman's Cause: Atlantic Commerce and Maritime Dimensions of the American Revolution*. Cambridge: Cambridge University Press.

Mah, Alice. 2014. *Port Cities and Global Legacies: Urban Identity, Waterfront Work, and Radicalism*. Boston: Springer.

Mahan, Alfred Thayer. 1890. *The Influence of Sea Power upon History, 1660–1783*, 2nd ed. Boston: Little, Brown.

Mahoney, James. 2010. *Colonialism and Postcolonial Development: Spanish America in Comparative Perspective*. Cambridge: Cambridge University Press.

Maine, Henry Sumner. 1886. *Popular Government: Four Essays*. New York: Henry Holt.

Maitland, F. W. 2003. *State, Trust and Corporation*, Cambridge: Cambridge University Press.

Major, J. Russell. 1980. *Representative Government in Early Modern France*. New Haven: Yale University Press.

Malekandathil, Pius. 2010. "Coastal Polity and the Changing Port-Hierarchy of Kerala." In Yogesh Sharma (ed.), *Coastal Histories: Society and Ecology in Pre-modern India* (Delhi: Primus Books), 75–90.

Malkin, Irad. 2011. *A Small Greek World: Networks in the Ancient Mediterranean.* Oxford: Oxford University Press.

Mancall, Peter C., Carole Shammas. 2015. *Governing the Sea in the Early Modern Era: Essays in Honor of Robert C. Ritchie.* San Marino, CA: Huntington Library Press.

Mance, Harry Osborne, J. E. Wheeler. 1945. *International Sea Transport.* Oxford: Oxford University Press.

Mancke, Elizabeth. 1999. "Early Modern Expansion and the Politicization of Oceanic Space." *Geographical Review* 89:2, 225–36.

Manent, Pierre. 1996. *An Intellectual History of Liberalism.* Princeton: Princeton University Press.

Manglapus, Raul S. 1987. *Will of the People: Original Democracy in Non-western Societies.* Westport, CT: Greenwood Press.

Manguin, Pierre-Yves. 1986. "Shipshape Societies: Boat Symbolism and Political Systems in Insular Southeast Asia." In David G. Marr and Anthony Crothers Milner (eds.), *Southeast Asia in the 9th to 14th Centuries* (Singapore: Institute of Southeast Asian Studies), 187–214.

1991. "The Merchant and the King: Political Myths of Southeast Asian Coastal Polities." *Indonesia* 52, 41–54.

2004. "The Archaeology of Early Maritime Polities of Southeast Asia." In Ian Glover and Peter S. Bellwood (eds.), *Southeast Asia: From Prehistory to History* (Abingdon, Oxon: Routledge), 282–313.

Mann, Michael. 1986. *The Sources of Social Power. Volume I. A History of Power from the Beginnings to 1760 AD.* Cambridge: Cambridge University Press.

Manning, Joseph Gilbert. 2013. "Egypt." In Peter Fibiger Bang and Walter Scheidel (eds.), *The Oxford Handbook of the State in the Ancient Near East and Mediterranean* (Oxford: Oxford University Press), 61–93.

2018. *The Open Sea: The Economic Life of the Ancient Mediterranean World from the Iron Age to the Rise of Rome.* Princeton: Princeton University Press.

Manning, Patrick. 1990. *Slavery and African Life.* Cambridge: Cambridge University Press.

2003. *Navigating World History: Historians Create a Global Past.* Boston: Springer.

2005. *Migration in World History.* London: Routledge.

2015. "Locating Africans on the World Stage: A Problem in World History." *Journal of World History* 26:3, 605–37.

Manning, Patrick, Jamie Miller. 2019. "Historical Writing in Postcolonial Africa: The Institutional Context." *International Journal of African Historical Studies* 52:2, 191–216.

Mansbridge, Jane J. 1983. *Beyond Adversary Democracy.* Chicago: University of Chicago Press.

Mantilla, Luis Felipe. 2010. "Mobilizing Religion for Democracy: Explaining Catholic Church Support for Democratization in South America." *Politics and Religion* 3:3, 553–79.

Manz, Beatrice Forbes. 1989. *The Rise and Rule of Tamerlane.* Cambridge: Cambridge University Press.

Manzanilla, Linda. 2001. "State Formation in the New World." In Gary M. Feinman and T. Douglas Price (eds.), *Archaeology at the Millennium* (Boston: Springer), 381–413.

Maoz, Zeev, Errol A. Henderson. 2013. "The World Religion Dataset, 1945–2010: Logic, Estimates, and Trends." *International Interactions* 39, 265–91.

Marciano, Alain. 2021. "James Buchanan: Clubs and Alternative Welfare Economics." *Journal of Economic Perspectives* 35:3, 243–56.

Marcus, Harold G. 2002. *A History of Ethiopia*, 2nd ed. Berkeley: University of California Press.

Margariti, Roxani Eleni. 2008. "Mercantile Networks, Port Cities, and 'Pirate' States: Conflict and Competition in the Indian Ocean World of Trade before the Sixteenth Century." *Journal of the Economic and Social History of the Orient* 51:4, 543–77.

Markoff, John. 1996. *Waves of Democracy*. Thousand Oaks, CA: Pine Forge.
1999. "Where and When Was Democracy Invented?" *Comparative Studies in Society and History* 41:4, 660–90.

Marnot, Brunot. 2011. *Les Grands Ports de commerce français et la mondialisation au XIXe siècle*. Paris: Librairie des Presses de l'Université Paris-Sorbonne.

Marongiu, Antonio (ed.). 1968. *Medieval Parliaments: A Comparative Study*. London: Eyre & Spottiswoode.

Marquardt, Kyle L. 2018. "Identity, Social Mobility, and Ethnic Mobilization: Language and the Disintegration of the Soviet Union." *Comparative Political Studies* 51:7, 831–67.

Marr, David G., Anthony Crothers Milner (eds.). 1986. *Southeast Asia in the 9th to 14th Centuries*. Singapore: Institute of Southeast Asian Studies.

Marsh, Zoe, G. W. Kingsnorth. 1972. *A History of East Africa: An Introductory Survey*. Cambridge: Cambridge University Press.

Marshall, Monty G., Keith Jaggers. 2016. "Polity IV Project: Political Regime Characteristics and Transitions, 1800–2015." Center for Systemic Peace, College Park, MD. www.systemicpeace.org/inscrdata.html.

Marshall, Monty G., Ted Gurr, Keith Jaggers. 2014. *Polity IV Project: Dataset Users' Manual*. College Park, MD: Center for Systemic Peace.

Marshall, Peter J. 1990. "The Whites of British India, 1780–1830: A Failed Colonial Society?" *International History Review* 12:1, 26–44.

Martin, Frederick. 1876. *The History of Lloyd's and of Marine Insurance in Great Britain: With an Appendix Containing Statistics Relating to Marine Insurance*. London: Macmillan and Company.

Martin, Janet. 2007. *Medieval Russia, 980–1584*. Cambridge: Cambridge University Press.

Marx, Karl, Friedrich Engels. 1967 [1948]. *The Communist Manifesto. 1848*, trans. Samuel Moore. London: Penguin.

Masi, Tania, Roberto Ricciuti. 2019. "The Heterogeneous Effect of Oil Discoveries on Democracy." *Economics and Politics* 31:3, 374–402.

Mathew, Gervase. 1956. "The Culture of the East African Coast: In the Seventeenth and Eighteenth Centuries in the Light of Recent Archaeological Discoveries." *Man* 56, 65–8.

Mathew, Kuzhippalli Skaria (ed.). 1995. *Mariners, Merchants, and Oceans: Studies in Maritime History.* New Delhi: Manohar.

Mathieson, Charlotte (ed.). 2016. *Sea Narratives: Cultural Responses to the Sea, 1600–Present.* Basingstoke: Palgrave Macmillan.

Matloff, Judith. 2017. *No Friends but the Mountains: Dispatches from the World's Violent Highlands.* New York: Basic Books.

Matsuda, Matt K. 2012. *Pacific Worlds: A History of Seas, Peoples, and Cultures.* Cambridge: Cambridge University Press.

Matthews, John Frederick. 1975. *Western Aristocracies and Imperial Court, AD 364–425.* Oxford: Clarendon Press.

Mauro, Frederic. 1990. "Merchant Communities, 1350–1750." In James D. Tracy (ed.), *Rise of Merchant Empires: Long-Distance Trade in the Early Modern World 1350–1750* (Cambridge: Cambridge University Press), 55–86.

May, Thomas Erskine. 1877. *Democracy in Europe: A History*, 2 vols. London: Longmans, Green, and Company.

Mayers, William Frederick, Nicholas Belfield Dennys. 1867. *The Treaty Ports of China and Japan: A Complete Guide to the Open Ports of Those Countries, Together with Peking, Yedo, Hongkong and Macao.* New York: A. Shortrede and Company.

Mayshar, Joram, Omer Moav, Zvika Neeman. 2017. "Geography, Transparency, and Institutions." *American Political Science Review* 111:3, 622–36.

Mazzuca, Sebastián L., Gerardo L. Munck. 2014. "State or Democracy First? Alternative Perspectives on the State–Democracy Nexus." *Democratization* 21:7, 1221–43.

McCabe, Ina Baghdiantz, Gelina Harlaftis, Ioanna Pepelasis Minoglou (eds.). 2005. *Diaspora Entrepreneurial Networks: Four Centuries of History.* Oxford: Berg.

McCormick, Michael. 2001. *Origins of the European Economy: Communications and Commerce AD 300–900.* Cambridge: Cambridge University Press.

McCracken, John Leslie. 1967. *The Cape Parliament 1854–1910.* Oxford: Clarendon Press.

McCusker, John J. 1991. "The Early History of 'Lloyd's List.'" *Historical Research* 64:155, 427–31.

McDonagh, Eileen. 2015. "Ripples from the First Wave: The Monarchical Origins of the Welfare State." *Perspectives on Politics* 13:4, 992–1016.

McDonald, Kevin P. 2015. *Pirates, Merchants, Settlers, and Slaves: Colonial America and the Indo-Atlantic World.* Berkeley: University of California Press.

McEvedy, Colin, Richard Jones. 1978. *Atlas of World Population History.* New York: Facts on File.

McGowan, Alan Patrick. 1980. *The Century before Steam: The Development of the Sailing Ship 1700–1820.* London: HM Stationery Office.

McGrail, Sean. 2004. *Boats of the World: From the Stone Age to Medieval Times.* Oxford: Oxford University Press.

McGrail, Seán. 2014. *Ancient Boats in North-West Europe: The Archaeology of Water Transport to AD 1500.* London: Routledge.

  2015. *Early Ships and Seafaring: Water Transport beyond Europe.* Barnsley: Pen and Sword.

McIntosh, Susan Keech (ed.). 2005a. *Beyond Chiefdoms: Pathways to Complexity in Africa*. Cambridge: Cambridge University Press.

2005b. "Modeling Political Organization in Large-Scale Settlement Clusters: A Case Study from the Inland Niger Delta." In Susan Keech McIntosh (ed.), *Beyond Chiefdoms: Pathways to Complexity in Africa* (Cambridge: Cambridge University Press), 66–79.

McLaren, John, Andrew Richard Buck, Nancy E. Wright (eds.). 2005. *Despotic Dominion: Property Rights in British Settler Societies*. Vancouver: University of British Columbia Press.

McLaughlin, Andrew C. 1932. *The Foundations of American Constitutionalism*. New York: New York University Press.

McMann, Kelly M., Brigitte Seim, Jan Teorell, Staffan I. Lindberg. 2019. "Why Low Levels of Democracy Promote Corruption and High Levels Diminish It." *Political Research Quarterly* 73:4, 893–907.

McNamee, Lachlan. 2020. "Colonial Legacies and Comparative Racial Identification in the Americas." *American Journal of Sociology* 126:2, 1–36.

2023 In press. *Settling for Less: Why States Colonize and Why They Stop*. Princeton: Princeton University Press.

McNeill, John Robert, William Hardy McNeill. 2003. *The Human Web: A Bird's-Eye View of World History*. New York: W.W. Norton.

McNeill, William Hardy. 1976. *Plagues and Peoples*. New York: Anchor Press.

1991. *The Rise of the West: A History of the Human Community*. Chicago: University of Chicago Press.

McPherson, Kenneth. 1993. *The Indian Ocean: A History of People and the Sea*. New York: Oxford University Press.

2002. "Port Cities as Nodal Points of Change: The Indian Ocean, 1890s–1920s." In Leila Tarazi Fawaz and Chris Bayly (eds.), *Modernity and Culture: From the Mediterranean to the Indian Ocean* (New York: Columbia University Press), 75–95.

Mearsheimer, John J. 2001. *The Tragedy of Great Power Politics*. New York: W.W. Norton.

Mehlum, H., K. Moene, R. Torvik. 2006. "Institutions and the Resource Curse." *Economic Journal* 116, 1–20.

Meier, Christian. 2011. *A Culture of Freedom: Ancient Greece and the Origins of Europe*. Oxford: Oxford University Press.

Meilink-Roelofsz, Marie Antoinette Petronella. 1962. *Asian Trade and European Influence in the Indonesian Archipelago between 1500 and about 1630*. Boston: Springer.

Meinhard, Stephanie, Niklas Potrafke. 2012. "The Globalization–Welfare State Nexus Reconsidered." *Review of International Economics* 20:2, 271–87.

Meiyappan, Prasanth, Atul K. Jain. 2012. "Three Distinct Global Estimates of Historical Land-Cover Change and Land-Use Conversions for over 200 Years." *Frontiers of Earth Science* 6:2, 122–39.

Mellinger, Andrew D., Jeffrey D. Sachs, John Gallup. 2000. "Climate, Coastal Proximity, and Development." In Gordon L. Clark, Meric S. Gertler, Maryann P. Feldman (eds.), *The Oxford Handbook of Economic Geography* (Oxford: Oxford University Press), 169–94.

Melville, Herman. 1850. *White Jacket; or, the World in a Man-of-War*. London: Richard Bentley.

Menaldo, Victor. 2012. "The Middle East and North Africa's Resilient Monarchs." *Journal of Politics* 74, 707–22.

Menon, A. Sreedhara. 2007. *A Survey of Kerala History*. Washington: DC Books.

Metcalf, Thomas R. 2008. *Imperial Connections: India in the Indian Ocean Arena, 1860–1920*. Berkeley: University of California Press.

Meyer, John W., John Boli, Thomas M. George, Francisco O. Ramirez. 1997. "World Society and the Nation-State." *American Journal of Sociology* 103:1, 144–81.

Meyers, Alec R. 1975. *Parliaments and Estates in Europe to 1789*. London: Thames and Hudson.

Michalopoulos, Stelios. 2012. "The Origins of Ethnolinguistic Diversity." *American Economic Review*, 102:4, 1508–39.

Michel, Jean-Baptiste et al. 2011. "Quantitative Analysis of Culture Using Millions of Digitized Books." *Science* 331:6014, 176–82.

Mickey, Robert. 2015. *Paths out of Dixie: The Democratization of Authoritarian Enclaves in America's Deep South, 1944–1972*. Princeton: Princeton University Press.

Middleton, John. 2004. *African Merchants of the Indian Ocean: Swahili of the East African Coast*. Long Grove, IL: Waveland Press.

Middleton, John, David Tait. 2013. *Tribes without Rulers: Studies in African Segmentary Systems*. London: Routledge.

Midlarsky, Manus I. 1995. "Environmental Influences on Democracy: Aridity, Warfare, and a Reversal of the Causal Arrow." *Journal of Conflict Resolution* 39:2, 224–62.

Migdal, Joel S. 1988. *Strong Societies and Weak States: State–Society Relations and State Capabilities in the Third World*. Princeton: Princeton University Press.

2012. *Through the Lens of Israel: Explorations in State and Society*. Albany: SUNY Press.

Miksic, John N. 2000. "Heterogenetic Cities in Premodern Southeast Asia." *World Archaeology* 32:1, 106–20.

Milanovic, Branko, Peter Lindert, Jeffrey Williamson. 2011. "Pre-industrial Inequality." *Economic Journal* 121, 255–72.

Mill, John Stuart. 1862. "On the Government of Dependencies by a Free State." In *Considerations on Representative Government* (New York: Harper & Brothers), 322–3.

Miller, James. 2018. *Can Democracy Work? A Short History of a Radical Idea, from Ancient Athens to Our World*. New York: Simon and Schuster.

Miller, Michael B. 2012. *Europe and the Maritime World: A Twentieth Century History*. Cambridge: Cambridge University Press.

Miller, Michael K. 2012. "Economic Development, Violent Leader Removal, and Democratization." *American Journal of Political Science* 56: 4, 1002–20.

2016. "Democracy by Example? Why Democracy Spreads When the World's Democracies Prosper." *Comparative Politics* 49:1, 83–116.

Mills, Charles Wade. 1997. *The Racial Contract*. Ithaca: Cornell University Press.

Milner, Helen V., Bumba Mukherjee. 2009. "Democratization and Economic Globalization." *Annual Review of Political Science* 12, 163–81.
Misra, Bankey Bihari. 1970. *The Administrative History of India, 1834–1947: General Administration.* London: Oxford University Press.
Mitchell, Harold. 1973. *Europe in the Caribbean: The Policies of Great Britain, France and the Netherlands toward Their West Indian Territories.* New York: Coper Square Publishers.
Mitterauer, Michael. 2010. *Why Europe? The Medieval Origins of Its Special Path.* Chicago: University of Chicago Press.
Moch, Leslie Page. 2003. *Moving Europeans: Migration in Western Europe since 1650.* Bloomington: Indiana University Press.
Modelski, George. 2003. *World Cities: −3000 to 2000.* Washington, DC: FAROS.
Modelski, George, William R. Thompson. 1988. *Seapower in Global Politics, 1494–1993.* Boston: Springer.
Moertono, Soemarsaid. 1963. *State and Statecraft in Old Java: A Study of the Later Mataram Period, 16th to 19th Century.* Ithaca: Cornell University Press.
Mohanram, Radhika. 2007. *Imperial White: Race, Diaspora, and the British Empire.* Minneapolis: University of Minnesota Press.
Mokyr, Joel. 2006. "Mobility, Creativity, and Technological Development: David Hume, Immanuel Kant and the Economic Development of Europe." In Günter Abel (ed.), *Kreativität. Tagungsband: XX. Deutscher Kongreß für Philosophie* (Hamburg: Felix Meiner Verlag), 1129–60.
Molho, Anthony, Kurt Raaflaub, Julia Emlen (eds.). 1991. *City States in Classical Antiquity and Medieval Italy.* Ann Arbor: University of Michigan Press.
Møller, Jørgen. 2015. "Mapping Definitions of Feudalism: A Conceptual Analysis." In Ferdinand Müller-Rommel and Fernando Casal Bértoa (eds.), *Party Politics and Democracy in Europe: Essays in Honor of Peter Mair* (London: Routledge), 19–33.
2017. "The Birth of Representative Institutions: The Case of the Crown of Aragón." *Social Science History* 41:2, 175–200.
2018a. "The Ecclesiastical Roots of Representation and Consent." *Perspectives on Politics* 16:4, 1075–84.
2018b. "Medieval Roots of the Modern State: The Conditional Effects of Geopolitical Pressure on Early Modern State Building." *Social Science History* 42:2, 295–316.
Møller, Jørgen, Svend-Erik Skaaning. 2011. *Requisites of Democracy: Conceptualization, Measurement, and Explanation.* London: Routledge.
2013. *Democracy and Democratization in Comparative Perspective: Conceptions, Conjunctures, Causes, and Consequences.* London: Macmillan.
Moll-Murata, Christine. 2008. "Chinese Guilds from the Seventeenth to the Twentieth Centuries: An Overview." *International Review of Social History* 53:S16, 213–47.
Monahan, Arthur P. 1987. *Consent, Coercion, and Limit: The Medieval Origins of Parliamentary Democracy.* Leiden: E.J. Brill.
Montesquieu, Charles-Louis de Secondat. 1989 [1748]. *The Spirit of the Laws.* Cambridge: Cambridge University Press.

Mookerji, Radhakumud. 1919. *Local Government in Ancient India*. Oxford: Clarendon Press.

Moore, Barrington. 1966. *Social Origins of Dictatorship and Democracy: Lord and Peasant in the Making of the Modern World*. Boston: Beacon Press.

Moore, John Preston. 1954. *The Cabildo in Peru under the Hapsburgs: A Study in the Origins and Powers of the Town Council in the Viceroyalty of Peru, 1530–1700*. Durham, NC: Duke University Press.

1966. *The Cabildo in Peru under the Bourbons: A Study in the Decline and Resurgence of Local Government in the Audiencia of Lima, 1700–1824*. Durham, NC: Duke University Press.

Moore, Mick. 2004. "Revenues, State Formation, and the Quality of Governance in Developing Countries." *International Political Science Review* 25:3, 297–319.

Moreau, A. Scott, Harold A. Netland, Charles Edward Van Engen, David Burnett. 2000. *Evangelical Dictionary of World Missions*. Carlisle: Paternoster.

Morgan, Edmund S. 1975. *American Slavery, American Freedom*. New York: W.W. Norton.

1989. *Inventing the People: The Rise of Popular Sovereignty in England and America*. New York: W.W. Norton.

Morgan, Frederick Wallace. 1952. *Ports and Harbours*. London: Hutchinson's University Library.

Morgan, Kenneth. 2017. "Port Location and Development in the British Atlantic World in the Seventeenth and Eighteenth Centuries." In Christian Buchet and Gérard Le Bouëdec (eds.), *The Sea in History: The Early Modern World* (Woodbridge, Suffolk: Boydell Press), 158–67.

Morrill, John. 2004. "Conclusion: King-Killing in Perspective." In Robert von Friedeburg (ed.), *Murder and Monarchy: Regicide in European History, 1300–1800* (London: Palgrave Macmillan), 293–9.

Morris, Colin. 1989. *The Papal Monarchy: The Western Church from 1050 to 1250*. Oxford: Clarendon Press.

Morris, Ian. 1996. "The Strong Principle of Equality and the Archaic Origins of Greek Democracy." In Josiah Ober and Charles W. Hedrick (eds.), *Demokratia: A Conversation on Democracies, Ancient and Modern* (Princeton: Princeton University Press), 19–48.

2013a. "Greek Multicity States." In Peter Fibiger Bang and Walter Scheidel (eds.), *The Oxford Handbook of the State in the Ancient Near East and Mediterranean* (Oxford: Oxford University Press), 279–303.

2013b. *The Measure of Civilization: How Social Development Decides the Fate of Nations*. Princeton: Princeton University Press.

Morris, Roger. 1992. *Atlantic Seafaring: Ten Centuries of Exploration and Trade in the North Atlantic*. New York: International Marine.

Morris, V. Dixon. 1981. "The City of Sakai and Urban Autonomy." In *Warlords, Artists, and Commoners: Japan in the Sixteenth Century* (Honolulu: University Press of Hawaii), 23–54.

Morrison, Kathleen D., Laura L. Junker (eds.). 2002. *Forager-Traders in South and Southeast Asia: Long-Term Histories*. Cambridge: Cambridge University Press.

Moscona, Jacob, Nathan Nunn, James A. Robinson. 2017. "Keeping It in the Family: Lineage Organization and the Scope of Trust in Sub-Saharan Africa." *American Economic Review* 107:5, 565–71.

Mosse, David. 2003. *The Rule of Water: Statecraft, Ecology and Collective Action in South India.* Oxford: Oxford University Press.

Most, Benjamin A., Harvey Starr. 1980. "Diffusion, Reinforcement, Geopolitics, and the Spread of War." *American Political Science Review* 74:4, 932–46.

Mouritsen, Henrik. 2017. *Politics in the Roman Republic.* Cambridge: Cambridge University Press.

Moya, Jose C. 1998. *Cousins and Strangers: Spanish Immigrants in Buenos Aires, 1850–1930.* Berkeley: University of California Press.

Muhlberger, Steven, Phil Paine. 1993. "Democracy's Place in World History." *Journal of World History* 4:1, 23–45.

Mukherjee, Rila (ed.). 2013. *Oceans Connect: Reflections on Water Worlds across Time and Space.* Delhi: Primus Books.

(ed.). 2014. *Vanguards of Globalization: Port-Cities from the Classical to the Modern.* Delhi: Primus Books.

Mukherjee, Rudrangshu, Lakshmi Subramanian (eds.). 1998. *Politics and Trade in the Indian Ocean World: Essays in Honour of Ashin Das Gupta.* Oxford: Oxford University Press.

Mukherjee, Tilottama. 2010. "Of Rivers and Roads: Transport Networks and Economy in Eighteenth-Century Bengal." In Yogesh Sharma (ed.), *Coastal Histories: Society and Ecology in Pre-modern India* (Delhi: Primus Books), 15–42.

Muller, Herbert J. 1966. *Freedom in the Modern World.* New York: Harper & Row.

Munoz, Paul Michel. 2006. *Early Kingdoms of the Indonesian Archipelago and the Malay Peninsula.* Singapore: Editions Didier Millet.

Murdock, George Peter. 1959. *Africa: Its Peoples and Their Culture History.* New York: McGraw-Hill.

1967. *Ethnographic Atlas.* Pittsburgh, PA: University of Pittsburgh Press.

Murdock, George Peter, D. R. White. 1969. "Standard Cross-cultural Sample." *Ethnology* 8:4, 329–69.

Murphey, Rhoads. 1969. "Traditionalism and Colonialism: Changing Urban Roles in Asia." *Journal of Asian Studies* 29:1, 67–84.

1989. "On the Evolution of the Port City." In Frank Broeze (ed.), *Brides of the Sea: Port Cities of Asia from the 16th – 20th Centuries* (Honolulu: University of Hawaii Press), 223–45.

Murphy, M. N. 2007. *Contemporary Piracy and Maritime Terrorism: The Threat to International Security.* Adelphi Paper No. 338. London: International Institute for Strategic Studies.

Murray, Augustus Taber (ed. and trans.). 1919. *The Odyssey.* Cambridge, MA: Harvard University Press.

Murtin, Fabrice, Romain Wacziarg. 2014. "The Democratic Transition." *Journal of Economic Growth* 19:2, 141–81.

Muthu, Sankar. 2003. *Enlightenment against Empire.* Princeton: Princeton University Press.

Myers, Henry Allen. 1982. *Medieval Kingship.* Chicago: Nelson-Hall.

Myrdal, Gunnar. 1944. *An American Dilemma; The Negro Problem and Modern Democracy.* New York: Harper, Bros.

1972. *Asian Drama: An Inquiry into the Poverty of Nations.* New York: Pantheon.

Nader, Helen. 1990. *Liberty in Absolutist Spain: The Habsburg Sale of Towns, 1516–1700.* Baltimore: Johns Hopkins University Press.

Naess, Arne. 1956. *Democracy, Ideology, and Objectivity: Studies in the Semantics and Cognitive Analysis of Ideological Controversy.* Oslo: Norwegian Research Council for Science and the Humanities Press.

Nagata, Mary Louise. 2008. "Brotherhoods and Stock Societies: Guilds in Pre-modern Japan." *International Review of Social History* 53:S16, 121–42.

Najemy, John. 1979. "Guild Republicanism in Trecento Florence: The Successes and Ultimate Failure of Corporate Politics." *American Historical Review* 84, 53–71.

Nandi, R. N. 2000. *State Formation, Agrarian Growth and Social Change in Feudal South India, c. AD 600–1200.* New Delhi: Manohar.

Narayanan, M. G. S. 1996. *Perumals of Kerala: Political and Social Conditions of Kerala under the Cèra Perumals of Makotai (c. 800 AD–1124 AD).* Calicut: Kerala University, Thiruvananthapuram.

Narizny, Kevin. 2012. "Anglo-American Primacy and the Global Spread of Democracy: An International Genealogy." *World Politics* 64:2, 341–73.

Nash, Gary B. 1986. *The Urban Crucible: The Northern Seaports and the Origins of the American Revolution.* Cambridge, MA: Harvard University Press.

National Geospatial-Intelligence Agency (NGIA). 2017. *World Port Index 2017*, 26th ed. Springfield, VA: United States Government.

Neill, Stephen. 1991. *A History of Christian Missions.* London: Penguin.

Nelson, Janet. 1995. "Kingship and Royal Government." In Rosamond McKitterick (ed.), *The New Cambridge Medieval History. Volume II. c.700–c.900* (Cambridge: Cambridge University Press), 381–430.

Newitt, Malyn. 2004. *A History of Portuguese Overseas Expansion 1400–1668.* London: Routledge.

Newton, Arthur Percival. 1924. *The Universities and Educational Systems of the British Empire.* New York: Henry Holt.

Ng, Adolf Koi Yu, César Ducruet. 2014. "The Changing Tides of Port Geography (1950–2012)." *Progress in Human Geography* 38:6, 785–823.

Ng, Chin-Keong. 2017. *Boundaries and Beyond: China's Maritime Southeast in Late Imperial Times.* Singapore: National University of Singapore Press.

Nicholas, David. 1999. *The Transformation of Europe 1300–1600.* London: Arnold.

Nicholls, Christine Stephanie. 1971. *The Swahili Coast: Politics, Diplomacy and Trade on the East African Littoral, 1798–1856.* New York: Holmes & Meier.

Nichols, Deborah L., Thomas H. Charlton (eds.). 1997. *The Archaeology of City-States: Cross-cultural Approaches.* Washington, DC: Smithsonian Institution Press.

Nield, Robert. 2015. *China's Foreign Places: The Foreign Presence in China in the Treaty Port Era, 1840–1943.* Hong Kong: Hong Kong University Press.

Nik Hassan Shuhaimi, bin Nik Abd. Rahman. 1990. "The Kingdom of Srivijaya as Socio-political and Cultural Entity." In Jaya Kathirithamby-Wells and

John Villiers (eds.), *The Southeast Asian Port and Polity: Rise and Demise* (Singapore: Singapore University Press), 61–82.

Nikolova, Elena, Jakub Polansky. 2020. "Conversionary Protestants Do Not Cause Democracy." *British Journal of Political Science* 51:4, 1–11.

Nilsson, Klas. 2017. "The Money of Monarchs: The Importance of Non-tax Revenue for Autocratic Rule in Early Modern Sweden." PhD dissertation, Lund University.

Nobles, Melissa. 2000. *Shades of Citizenship*. Stanford: Stanford University Press.

Norberg, Johan. 2020. *Open: The Story of Human Progress*. London: Atlantic Books.

Norcross, Jonathan. 1883. *The History of Democracy: Considered as a Party Name and as a Political Organization*. New York: G. P. Putnam.

Nordhaus, William D. 2006. "Geography and Macroeconomics: New Data and New Findings." *Proceedings of the National Academy of Sciences* 103:10, 3510–17.

Nordholt, H. G. C. Schulte. 2010. *The Spell of Power: A History of Balinese Politics, 1650–1940*. Leiden: Brill.

Norena, Carlos F. 2015. "Urban Systems in the Han and Roman Empires: State Power and Social Control." In Walter Scheidel (ed.), *State Power in Ancient China and Rome* (Oxford: Oxford University Press), 181–203.

Norris, Pippa, Ronald Inglehart. 2009. *Cosmopolitan Communications: Cultural Diversity in a Globalized World*. Cambridge: Cambridge University Press.

North, Douglass C. 1958. "Ocean Freight Rates and Economic Development 1750–1913." *Journal of Economic History* 18:4, 537–55.

1965. "The Role of Transportation in the Economic Development of North America." In *Les Grandes Voies maritime dans le monde, XV–XIX siècles* (Paris: SEVPEN), 209–46.

1968. "Sources of Productivity Change in Ocean Shipping, 1600–1850." *Journal of Political Economy* 76:5, 953–70.

1990. *Institutions, Institutional Change and Economic Performance*. Cambridge: Cambridge University Press.

North, Douglass C., Robert P. Thomas. 1973. *The Rise of the Western World: A New Economic History*. New York: Cambridge University Press.

North, Douglass C., Barry R. Weingast. 1989. "Constitutions and Commitment: The Evolution of Institutions Governing Public Choice in Seventeenth-Century England." *Journal of Economic History* 49, 803–32.

North, Douglass C., John J. Wallis, Barry R. Weingast. 2009. *Violence and Social Orders: A Conceptual Framework for Interpreting Recorded Human History*. New York: Cambridge University Press.

North, Michael. 2015. *The Baltic*. Cambridge, MA: Harvard University Press.

Norwich, John Julius. 2007. *The Middle Sea: A History of the Mediterranean*. New York: Vintage.

Nosov, Evgenij. 1996. "The River Systems of Eastern Europe and Their Role in the Formation of Towns and the Russian State." In Gian Pietro Brogiolo (ed.), *Early Medieval Towns in the Western Mediterranean* (Ravello: Centro Universitario Europeo per i Beni Culturali), 175–9.

Nugent, Walter. 1989. "Frontiers and Empires in the Late Nineteenth Century." *Western Historical Quarterly* 20:4, 393–408.

   1995. *Crossings: The Great Transatlantic Migrations, 1870–1914.* Indianapolis: Indiana University Press.

Nunn, Nathan. 2008. "The Long-Term Effects of Africa's Slave Trades." *Quarterly Journal of Economics* 123:1, 139–76.

   2009. "The Importance of History for Economic Development." *Annual Review of Economics* 1:1, 65–92.

Nunn, Nathan, Diego Puga. 2012. "Ruggedness: The Blessing of Bad Geography in Africa." *Review of Economics and Statistics* 94:1, 20–36.

Nussli, Christos. 2017. "Euratlas Historical Atlas and Gazetteer of Europe." www.euratlas.net/history/europe/index.html.

Nwabara, Samuel N. 1977. *Iboland: A Century of Contact with Britain, 1860–1960.* Atlantic Highlands, NJ: Humanities Press.

Oakley, Francis. 2003. *The Conciliarist Tradition: Constitutionalism in the Catholic Church, 1300–1870.* Oxford: Oxford University Press.

   2010. *Empty Bottles of Gentilism: Kingship and the Divine in Late Antiquity and the Early Middle Ages (to 1050).* New Haven and London: Yale University Press.

   2012. *The Mortgage of the Past: Reshaping the Ancient Political Inheritance (1050–1300).* New Haven and London: Yale University Press.

   2015. *The Watershed of Modern Politics: Law, Virtue, Kingship, and Consent (1300–1650).* New Haven and London: Yale University Press.

O'Brien, Karen. 1997. *Narratives of Enlightenment: Cosmopolitan History from Voltaire to Gibbon.* Cambridge: Cambridge University Press.

O'Callaghan, Joseph. 1989. *The Cortes of Castile-Leon, 1188–1350.* Philadelphia: University of Pennsylvania.

O'Connor, Sue, Peter Veth (eds.). 2000. *East of Wallace's Line: Studies of Past and Present Maritime Cultures in the Indo-Pacific Region.* Boca Raton: CRC Press.

O'Flanagan, Patrick. 2008. *Port Cities of Atlantic Iberia, c. 1500–1900.* Burlington: Ashgate.

Ogilvie, Sheilagh. 2019. *The European Guilds: An Economic Analysis.* Princeton: Princeton University Press.

Ojala, Jari. 2011. "Productivity Change Eighteenth Century Finnish Shipping." In Richard W. Unger (ed.), *Shipping and Economic Growth 1350–1850* (Leiden: Brill), 167–88.

Oldstone, M. 1998. *Viruses, Plagues, and History.* New York: Oxford University Press.

Oleson, John Peter, Robert L. Hohlfelder. 2011. "Ancient Harbors in the Mediterranean." *The Oxford Handbook of Maritime Archaeology* (Oxford: Oxford University Press).

Oliver, Roland, Anthony Atmore. 1981. *The African Middle Ages, 1400–1800.* Cambridge: Cambridge University Press.

Olson, Mancur. 1993. "Dictatorship, Democracy, and Development." *American Political Science Review* 87:3, 567–76.

Olsson, Ola. 2009. "On the Democratic Legacy of Colonialism." *Journal of Comparative Economics* 37:4, 534–51.

Olsson, Ola, Christopher Paik. 2016. "Long-Run Cultural Divergence: Evidence from the Neolithic Revolution." *Journal of Development Economics* 122, 197–213.

2020. "A Western Reversal since the Neolithic? The Long-Run Impact of Early Agriculture." *Journal of Economic History* 80:1, 100–35.

Openshaw, Stan. 1984. "Ecological Fallacies and the Analysis of Areal Census Data." *Environment and Planning* 16:1, 17–31.

Oppenheimer, Franz. 1975 [1914]. *The State*, trans. John M. Gitterman. New York: Free Life.

O'Rourke, Kevin H., Jeffrey G. Williamson. 1999. *Globalization and History: The Evolution of a Nineteenth-Century Atlantic Economy*. Cambridge, MA: MIT Press.

Osafo-Kwaako, Philip, James A. Robinson. 2013. "Political Centralization in Pre-colonial Africa." *Journal of Comparative Economics* 41:1, 6–21.

Osborne, Roger. 2012. *Of the People, by the People: A New History of Democracy*. New York: Random House.

Osterhammel, Jürgen. 2014. *The Transformation of the World*. Princeton: Princeton University Press.

2018. *Unfabling the East: The Enlightenment's Encounter with Asia*. Princeton: Princeton University Press.

Ostrowski, Donald. 2002. *Muscovy and the Mongols: Cross-cultural Influences on the Steppe Frontier, 1304–1589*. Cambridge: Cambridge University Press.

O'Sullivan, Tomás. 2016. "Christianity and the European Conversions." In Lamin Sanneh and Michael McClymond (eds.), *The Wiley-Blackwell Companion to World Christianity* (New York: Wiley-Blackwell), 54–66.

Oto-Peralías, Daniel, Diego Romero-Ávila. 2017. *Colonial Theories of Institutional Development*. Boston: Springer.

Outhwaite, L. 1957. *The Atlantic: A History of an Ocean*. New York: Coward-McCann.

Owen, John M., IV. 2010. *The Clash of Ideas in World Politics: Transnational Networks, States, and Regime Change, 1510–2010*. Princeton: Princeton University Press.

Owolabi, Olukunle P. 2015. "Literacy and Democracy despite Slavery: Forced Settlement and Postcolonial Outcomes in the Developing World." *Comparative Politics* 48:1, 43–78.

Ozment, Steven E. 1975. *The Reformation in the Cities: The Appeal of Protestantism to Sixteenth-Century Germany and Switzerland*. New Haven: Yale University Press.

Ozzano, Luca, Francesco Cavatorta. 2013. "Introduction: Religiously Oriented Parties and Democratization." *Democratization* 20:5, 799–806.

Padfield, Peter. 2000. *Maritime Supremacy and the Opening of the Western Mind: Naval Campaigns That Shaped the Modern World*. Woodstock: Overlook Press.

Pagden, Anthony (ed.). 2002. *The Idea of Europe: From Antiquity to the European Union*. Cambridge: Cambridge University Press.

Pagden, Anthony. 2009. "The Peopling of the New World: Ethnos, Race and Empire in the Early-Modern World." In Miriam Eliav-Feldon, Benjamin H.

Isaac, Joseph Ziegler (eds.), *The Origins of Racism in the West* (Cambridge: Cambridge University Press), 292–312.

Paine, Jack. 2019. "Democratic Contradictions in European Settler Colonies." *World Politics* 71:3, 542–85.

Paine, Lincoln. 2013. *The Sea and Civilization: A Maritime History of the World.* New York: Alfred A. Knopf.

Palais, James B. 1991. *Politics and Policy in Traditional Korea.* Cambridge, MA: Harvard University Asia Center.

Palen, Marc-William. 2015. "Free-Trade Ideology and Transatlantic Abolitionism: A Historiography." *Journal of the History of Economic Thought* 37:2, 291–304.

2016. *The 'Conspiracy' of Free Trade: The Anglo-American Struggle over Empire and Economic Globalisation, 1846–1896.* Cambridge: Cambridge University Press.

Palmer, Robert R. 1953. "Notes on the Use of the Word 'Democracy,' 1789–1799." *Political Science Quarterly* 68, 203–26.

2014. *The Age of the Democratic Revolution.* Princeton: Princeton University Press.

Panikkar, Kavalam Madhava. 1945. *India and the Indian Ocean.* London: George Allen & Unwin.

Papaioannou, Elias, Gregorios Siourounis. 2008. "Economic and Social Factors Driving the Third Wave of Democratization." *Journal of Comparative Economics* 36:3, 365–87.

Paquette, Gabriel. 2019. *The European Seaborne Empires: From the Thirty Years War to the Age of Revolutions.* New Haven: Yale University Press.

Parker, Bradley J. 2011. "The Construction and Performance of Kingship in the Neo-Assyrian Empire." *Journal of Anthropological Research* 67:3, 357–86.

Parker, Charles H. 2010. *Global Interactions in the Early Modern Age, 1400–1800.* Cambridge: Cambridge University Press.

Parker, Geoffrey. 2004. *Sovereign City: The City-State through History.* London: Reaktion Books.

Parkins, Helen M., Christopher J. Smith (eds.). 1998. *Trade, Traders and the Ancient City.* London: Routledge.

Parry, John Horace. 1971. *Trade and Dominion: The European Overseas Empires in the Eighteenth Century.* New York: Praeger.

1981. *The Discovery of the Sea.* Berkeley: University of California Press.

Parthesius, Robert. 2009. *Dutch Ships in Tropical Waters: The Development of the Dutch East India Company (VOC) Shipping Network in Asia 1595–1660.* Amsterdam: Amsterdam University Press.

Pascali, Luigi. 2017. "The Wind of Change: Maritime Technology, Trade and Economic Development." *American Economic Review* 107, 2821–54.

Pateman, Carole. 1970. *Participation and Democratic Theory.* Cambridge: Cambridge University Press.

Patterson, Orlando. 1991. *Freedom in the Making of Western Culture.* New York: HarperCollins.

Payne, Stanley G. 1973. *A History of Spain and Portugal. volume I.* Madison: University of Wisconsin Press.

Pearson, Michael Naylor. 1976. *Merchants and Rulers in Gujarat: The Response to the Portuguese in the Sixteenth Century*. Berkeley: University of California Press.

1991. "Merchants and States." In James D. Tracy (ed.), *The Political Economy of Merchant Empires: State Power and World Trade 1350–1750* (Cambridge: Cambridge University Press), 41–116.

1998. *Port Cities and Intruders: The Swahili Coast, India, and Portugal in the Early Modern Era*. Baltimore: Johns Hopkins University Press.

2003. *The Indian Ocean*. London: Routledge.

2005. *The World of the Indian Ocean, 1500–1800: Studies in Economic, Social, and Cultural History*. Burlington: Ashgate.

Peattie, Roderick. 1936. *Mountain Geography*. Cambridge, MA: Harvard University Press.

Peers, Douglas M. 2013. *India under Colonial Rule: 1700–1885*. London: Routledge.

Pellicer, Miquel, Patrizio Piraino, Eva Wegner. 2019. "Perceptions of Inevitability and Demand for Redistribution: Evidence from a Survey Experiment." *Journal of Economic Behavior and Organization* 159, 274–88.

Pemstein, Daniel, Stephen A. Meserve, James Melton. 2010. "Democratic Compromise: A Latent Variable Analysis of Ten Measures of Regime Type." *Political Analysis* 18:4, 426–49.

Pennell, C. R. (ed.). 2001. *Bandits at Sea: A Pirates Reader*. New York: New York University Press.

Peregrine, Peter N. 2003. "Atlas of Cultural Evolution." In J. P. Gray (ed.), *World Cultures: Journal of Comparative and Cross-cultural Research* 14:1, 1–96.

Peregrine, Peter N., Melvin Ember (eds.). 2001. *Encyclopedia of Prehistory. Volume 6. North America*. Boston: Springer.

Perrie, Maureen, D. C. B. Lieven, Ronald Grigor Suny (eds.). 2006. *The Cambridge History of Russia. Volume I: From Early Rus' to 1689*. Cambridge: Cambridge University Press.

Pestana, Carla. 2009. *Protestant Empire: Religion and the Making of the British Atlantic World*. Philadelphia: University of Pennsylvania Press.

Peters, Kimberley, Jon Anderson (eds.). 2016. *Water Worlds: Human Geographies of the Ocean*. London: Routledge.

Petersen, Andrew. 2005. *The Towns of Palestine under Muslim Rule, AD 600–1600*. BAR International Series. Oxford: Archaeopress.

Petersen, Michael Bang, Svend-Erik Skaaning. 2010. "Ultimate Causes of State Formation: The Significance of Biogeography, Diffusion, and Neolithic Revolutions." *Historical Social Research* 35:3, 200–26.

Pétré-Grenouilleau, Olivier. 2009. "Maritime Powers, Colonial Powers: The Role of Migration (c. 1492–1792)." In *Migration, Trade, and Slavery in an Expanding World* (Leiden: Brill), 45–72.

Pettegree, Andrew (ed.). 1992. *The Early Reformation in Europe*. Cambridge: Cambridge University Press.

Phillips, Andrew, J. C. Sharman. 2020. *Outsourcing Empire: How Company-States Made the Modern World*. Princeton: Princeton University Press.

Phillips, Earl. 1969. "The Egba at Abeokuta: Acculturation and Political Change, 1830–1870." *Journal of African History* 10:1, 117–31.

Phillips, John Roland Seymour. 1998. *The Medieval Expansion of Europe*. Oxford: Oxford University Press.

Phillips, Seymour. 1994. "The Outer World in the European Middle Ages." In Stuart B. Schwartz (ed.), *Implicit Understandings: Observing, Reporting and Reflecting on the Encounters between Europeans and Other Peoples in the Early Modern Era* (Cambridge: Cambridge University Press), 23–63.

Philpott, Daniel. 2004. "Christianity and Democracy: The Catholic Wave." *Journal of Democracy* 15:2, 32–46.

Pierson, Paul. 2011. *Politics in Time: History, Institutions, and Social Analysis*. Princeton: Princeton University Press.

Pilster, Ulrich, Tobias Bohmelt. 2012. "Do Democracies Engage Less in Coup-Proofing? On the Relationship between Regime Type and Civil–Military Relations." *Foreign Policy Analysis* 8:4, 355–72.

Pincus, Steve. 2009. *1688: The First Modern Revolution*. New Haven: Yale University Press.

Pincus, Steve, James A. Robinson. 2011. *What Really Happened during the Glorious Revolution?* NBER Working Paper No. w17206. Cambridge, MA: National Bureau of Economic Research.

Pines, Yuri, Michal Biran, Jörg Rüpke (eds.). 2021. *The Limits of Universal Rule: Eurasian Empires Compared*. Cambridge: Cambridge University Press.

Pinker, Steven. 2011. *The Better Angels of Our Nature: Why Violence Has Declined*. New York: Viking.

Pipes, Richard. 1974. *Russia under the Old Regime*. New York: C. Scribner's Sons.

Pirenne, Henri. 1925. *Medieval Cities, Their Origins and the Revival of Trade*. Princeton: Princeton University Press.

1963. *Early Democracies in the Low Countries: Urban Society and Political Conflict in the Middle Ages and the Renaissance*. New York: Harper & Row.

2013. *Mohammed and Charlemagne*. London: Routledge.

Pitkin, Hanna Fenichel. 1967. *The Concept of Representation*. Berkeley: University of California Press.

Pitts, Forrest R. 1978. "The Medieval River Trade Network of Russia Revisited." *Social Networks* 1:3, 285–92.

Plutarch. 1957. *Moralia. Volume XII*, trans. Harold Cherniss and William C. Helmbold. Cambridge, MA: Harvard University Press.

Po, Ronald C. 2018. *The Blue Frontier: Maritime Vision and Power in the Qing Empire*. Cambridge: Cambridge University Press.

Pocock, J. G. A. 1975. *The Machiavellian Moment: Florentine Political Thought and the Atlantic Republican Tradition*. Princeton: Princeton University Press.

1980. *Three British Revolutions: 1641, 1688, 1776*. Princeton: Princeton University Press.

Poettering, Jorun. 2018. *Migrating Merchants: Trade, Nation, and Religion in Seventeenth-Century Hamburg and Portugal*. Berlin: Walter de Gruyter GmbH & Co KG.

Poggi, Gianfranco. 1978. *The Development of the Modern State*. Stanford: Stanford University Press.

Polanyi, Karl. 1963. "Ports of Trade in Early Societies." *Journal of Economic History* 23:1, 30–45.

1968. *Primitive, Archaic and Modern Economies*. Boston: Beacon Press.

Polasky, Janet. 2015. *Revolutions without Borders*. New Haven: Yale University Press.

Pole, Jack Richon. 1966. *Political Representation in England and the Origins of the American Republic*. London: Macmillan.

Pollard, Edward, Elgidius B. Ichumbaki. 2017. "Why Land Here? Ports and Harbors in Southeast Tanzania in the Early Second Millennium AD." *Journal of Island and Coastal Archaeology* 12:4, 459–89.

Pomeranz, Kenneth. 2000. *The Great Divergence: Europe, China, and the Making of the Modern World Economy*. Princeton: Princeton University Press.

Pomeranz, Kenneth, Steven Topik. 2014. *The World That Trade Created: Society, Culture and the World Economy, 1400 to the Present*. London: Routledge.

Porter, Andrew. 2004. *Religion versus Empire? British Protestant Missionaries and Overseas Expansion, 1700–1914*. Manchester: Manchester University Press.

Posada-Carbó, Eduardo (ed.). 2016. *Elections before Democracy: The History of Elections in Europe and Latin America*. Berlin: Springer.

Post, Gaines. 1943. "Plena Potestas and Consent in Medieval Assemblies: A Study in Romano-Canonical Procedure and the Rise of Representation, 1150–1325." *Traditio* 1, 355–408.

1964. *Studies in Medieval Legal Thought: Public Law and the State 1100–1322*. Princeton: Princeton University Press.

Postan, Michael. 1987. "The Trade of Medieval Europe: The North." In Michael Postan and Edward Miller (eds.), *The Cambridge Economic History of Europe. Volume II. Trade and Industry in the Middle Ages* (Cambridge: Cambridge University Press), 168–305.

Potter, Lawrence G. (ed.). 2009. *The Persian Gulf in History*. Boston: Springer.

(ed.). 2014a. *The Persian Gulf in Modern Times: People, Ports, and History*. Boston: Springer.

2014b. "Rise and Fall of Port Cities in the Persian Gulf." In Lawrence Potter (ed.), *The Persian Gulf in Modern Times: People, Ports, and History* (Boston: Springer), 131–52.

Pounds, Norman J. G. 1973. *An Historical Geography of Europe 450 BC–AD 1330*. Cambridge: Cambridge University Press.

Pounds, Norman J. G., Sue S. Ball. 1964. "Core-Areas and the Development of the European States System." *Annals of the Association of American Geographers* 54, 24–64.

Powelson, John P. 1988. *The Story of Land: A World History of Land Tenure and Agrarian Reform*. Lincoln, NE: Lincoln Institute of Land Policy.

Preiser-Kapeller, Johannes, Falko Daim (eds.). 2015. *Harbours and Maritime Networks as Complex Adaptive Systems*. Berlin: Verlag des Römisch-Germanischen Zentralmuseums.

Price, Simon. 1999. *Religions of the Ancient Greeks*. Cambridge: Cambridge University Press.

Price, T. Douglas, Gary M. Feinman (eds.). 2010. *Pathways to Power: New Perspectives on the Emergence of Social Inequality*. New York: Springer.

Princewill, Kingta Irene. 2000. "The City-States of the Eastern Niger Delta." In Mogens Herman Hansen (ed.), *A Comparative Study of Thirty City-State*

Cultures (Copenhagen: Royal Danish Academy of Sciences and Letters), 533–45.

Pritchard, James S. 2004. *In Search of Empire: The French in the Americas, 1670–1730*. Cambridge: Cambridge University Press.

Prochaska, David. 1990. *Making Algeria French: Colonialism in Bône, 1870–1920*. Cambridge: Cambridge University Press.

Pryor, John H. 1992. *Geography, Technology, and War: Studies in the Maritime History of the Mediterranean, 649–1571*. Cambridge: Cambridge University Press.

Przeworski, Adam, Fernando Limongi. 1997. "Modernization: Theories and Facts." *World Politics* 49:2, 155–83.

Przeworski, Adam, Michael Alvarez, Jose Cheibub, Fernando Limongi. 2000. *Democracy and Development: Political Institutions and Well-being in the World, 1950–1990*. New York: Cambridge University Press.

Ptak, Roderich, Dietmar Rothermund (eds.). 1991. *Emporia, Commodities and Entrepreneurs in Asian Maritime Trade, c. 1400–1750*. Stuttgart: Steiner.

Putnam, Robert D., Robert Leonardi, Raffaella Y. Nanetti. 1994. *Making Democracy Work: Civic Traditions in Modern Italy*. Princeton: Princeton University Press.

Putterman, Louis. 2006. "Agricultural Transition Year Dataset." Department of Economics, Brown University. https://sites.google.com/brown.edu/louis-put terman/agricultural-transition-data-set.

2008. "Agriculture, Diffusion and Development: Ripple Effects of the Neolithic Revolution." *Economica* 75:300, 729–48.

Putterman, Louis, David Weil. 2010. "Post-1500 Population Flows and the Long Run Determinants of Economic Growth and Inequality." *Quarterly Journal of Economics* 125:4, 1627–82.

Pye, Lucian W. (ed.). 1963. *Communications and Political Development*. Princeton: Princeton University Press.

Raaflaub, Kurt A., Josiah Ober, Robert Wallace. 2007. *Origins of Democracy in Ancient Greece*. Berkeley: University of California Press.

Raccagni, Gianluca. 2010. *The Lombard League, 1167–1225*. Oxford: Oxford University Press.

Radvan, Laurentiu. 2010. *At Europe's Borders: Medieval Towns in the Romanian Principalities*. Leiden: Brill.

Rady, Martyn. 2000. *Nobility, Land and Service in Medieval Hungary*. Boston: Springer.

Radziwill, Catherine. 1915. *The Royal Marriage Market of Europe*. New York and London: Funk and Wagnalls Co.

Ramseyer, J. Mark, Frances Rosenbluth. 1995. *The Politics of Oligarchy*. Cambridge: Cambridge University Press.

Rana, Aziz. 2011. *The Two Faces of American Freedom*. Cambridge, MA: Harvard University Press.

Ranger, Terence O. (ed.). 2008. *Evangelical Christianity and Democracy in Africa*. London: Oxford University Press.

Raudzens, George. 1999. "Military Revolution or Maritime Evolution? Military Superiorities or Transportation Advantages as Main Causes of European Colonial Conquests to 1788." *Journal of Military History* 63:3, 631.

Ravina, Mark. 1995. "State-Building and Political Economy in Early-Modern Japan." *Journal of Asian Studies* 54:4, 997–1022.

Ray, Himanshu Prabha (ed.). 1999. *Archaeology of Seafaring: The Indian Ocean in the Ancient Period*. Delhi: Pragati.

    2003. *The Archaeology of Seafaring in Ancient South Asia*. Cambridge: Cambridge University Press.

Reade, Julian (ed.). 1996. *The Indian Ocean in Antiquity*. London and New York: Kegan Paul International.

Reader, John. 1997. *Africa: A Biography of the Continent*. New York: Vintage.

Reba, Meredith, Femke Reitsma, Karen C. Seto. 2016. "Spatializing 6,000 Years of Global Urbanization from 3700 BC to AD 2000." *Scientific Data* 3:160034.

Redding, Stephen, Anthony J. Venables. 2004. "Economic Geography and International Inequality." *Journal of International Economics* 62:1, 53–82.

Redford, Duncan (ed.). 2013. *Maritime History and Identity: The Sea and Culture in the Modern World*. London: I.B. Tauris.

Rediker, M. 1987. *Between the Devil and the Deep Blue Sea: Merchant Seamen, Pirates and the Anglo American World, 1700–1750*. Cambridge: Cambridge University Press.

Reher, David Sven. 1998. "Family Ties in Western Europe: Persistent Contrasts." *Population and Development Review* 24:2, 203–34.

Reid, Anthony. 1980. "The Structure of Cities in Southeast Asia, Fifteenth to Seventeenth Centuries." *Journal of Southeast Asian Studies* 11:2, 235–50.

    1988. *Southeast Asia in the Age of Commerce, 1450–1680. Volume I. The Lands below the Winds*. New Haven: Yale University Press.

    1989. "The Organization of Production in the Pre-colonial Southeast Asian Port City." In Frank Broeze (ed.), *Brides of the Sea: Port Cities of Asia from the Sixteenth to the Twentieth Centuries* (Honolulu: University of Hawaii Press), 54–74.

    1993a. *Southeast Asia in the Age of Commerce, 1450–1680. Volume II. Expansion and Crisis*. New Haven: Yale University Press.

    (ed.). 1993b. *Southeast Asia in the Early Modern Era: Trade, Power, and Belief*. Ithaca: Cornell University Press.

    (ed.). 1997. *The Last Stand of Asian Autonomies: Responses to Modernity in the Diverse States of Southeast Asia and Korea, 1750–1900*. Boston: Springer.

    1999. *Charting the Shape of Early Modern Southeast Asia*. Bangkok: Silkworm Books.

    2000. "Negeri: The Culture of Malay-Speaking City-States of the Fifteenth and Sixteenth Centuries." In Mogens Herman Hansen (ed.), *A Comparative Study of Thirty City-State Cultures* (Copenhagen: Royal Danish Academy of Sciences and Letters), 417–29.

    2004. "Global and Local in Southeast Asian History." *International Journal of Asian Studies* 1:1, 5–21.

Reid, Anthony, Lance Castles (eds.). 1975. *Pre-colonial State Systems in Southeast Asia: The Malay Peninsula, Sumatra, Bali-Lombok, South Celebes*. Kuala Lumpur: Malaysian Branch of the Royal Asiatic Society.

Reid, John Phillip. 1988. *The Concept of Liberty in the Age of the American Revolution*. Chicago: University of Chicago Press.

Reid, Richard. 2002. *Political Power in Pre-colonial Buganda: Economy, Society and Warfare in the Nineteenth Century*. Oxford: James Currey.

Reinsch, Paul Samuel. 1901. "French Experience with Representative Government in the West Indies." *American Historical Review* 6:3, 475–97.

1902. *Colonial Government: An Introduction to the Study of Colonial Institutions*. London: Macmillan.

Renfrew, Colin, John F. Cherry (eds.). 1986. *Peer Polity Interaction and Socio-Political Change*. Cambridge: Cambridge University Press.

Revere, Robert B. 1957. "'No Man's Coast': Ports of Trade in the Eastern Mediterranean." In Karl Polanyi, Conrad M. Arensberg, Harry W. Pearson (eds.), *Trade and Market in the Early Empires: Economies in History and Theory* (New York: Free Press), 38–63.

Reynolds, Clark G. 1974. *Command of the Sea: The History and Strategy of Maritime Empires*. New York: William Morrow & Company.

Reynolds, Susan. 1984. *Kingdoms and Communities in Western Europe, 900–1300*. Oxford: Oxford University Press.

1994. *Fiefs and Vassals*. Oxford: Clarendon Press.

1999. "Government and Community." In D. Luscombe and J. Riley-Smith (eds.), *The New Cambridge Medieval History. Volume IV. c.1024–c.1198, Part I* (Cambridge: Cambridge University Press), 86–112.

Riasanovsky, Nicholas Valentine. 1963. *A History of Russia*. New York: Oxford University Press.

Ricart-Huguet, Joan. 2021. "The Origins of Colonial Investments in Former British and French Africa." *British Journal of Political Science* 1, 1–22.

Richards, Audrey (ed.). 1959. *East African Chiefs: A Study of Political Development in Some Uganda and Tanganyika Tribes*. London: Faber and Faber.

Richards, Audrey, Adam Kuper (eds.). 1971. *Councils in Action*. Cambridge: Cambridge University Press.

Ricklefs, M. C. 2008. *A History of Modern Indonesia since c. 1200*, 4th ed. Stanford: Stanford University Press.

Ringrose, David. 1989. "Towns, Transport and Crown: Geography and the Decline of Spain." In Eugene D. Genovese and Leonard Hochberg (eds.), *Geographic Perspectives in History* (Oxford: Wiley-Blackwell), 57–94.

Ringrose, David R. 1996. "Capital Cities and Their Hinterlands: Europe and the Colonial Dimension." In Peter Clark & Bernard Lepetit (eds.), *Capital Cities and Their Hinterlands in Early Modern Europe* (Farnham: Ashgate), 217–40.

2018. *Europeans Abroad, 1450–1750*. Lanham: Rowman & Littlefield.

Risse, Thomas. 2000. "The Power of Norms versus the Norms of Power: Transnational Civil Society and Human Rights." In A. Florini (ed.), *The Third Force: The Rise of Transnational Civil Society* (Washington, DC: Carnegie Endowment for International Peace), 177–209.

Risse, Thomas, Thomas Risse, Stephen C. Ropp, Kathryn Sikkink (eds.). 1999. *The Power of Human Rights: International Norms and Domestic Change*. Cambridge: Cambridge University Press.

Robert, Dana L. 2009. *Christian Mission: How Christianity Became a World Religion*. New York: John Wiley & Sons.

Roberts, Hugh. 2014. *Berber Government: The Kabyle Polity in Pre-colonial Algeria.* London: I.B. Tauris.

Roberts, Stephen H. 1967 [1929]. *The History of French Colonial Policy, 1870–1925.* London: Frank Cass.

Robinson, E. W. 2011. *Democracy beyond Athens: Popular Government in the Greek Classical Age.* Cambridge: Cambridge University Press.

Robinson, Glenn E. 1997. *Building a Palestinian State: The Incomplete Revolution.* Bloomington: Indiana University Press.

Robinson, J., R. Torvik, T. Verdier. 2006. "Political Foundations of the Resource Curse." *Journal of Development Economics* 79, 447–68.

Rocha, Zarine L., Peter Aspinall (eds.). 2020. *The Palgrave International Handbook of Mixed Racial and Ethnic Classification.* Basingstoke: Palgrave-Macmillan.

Rodger, N. A. M. 2017. "Social Structure and Naval Power: Britain and the Netherlands." In Christian Buchet and Gérard Le Bouëdec (eds.), *The Sea in History: The Early Modern World* (Woodbridge, Suffolk: Boydell Press), 158–67.

Rodger, N. A. M., Christian Buchet (eds.). 2017. *The Sea in History: The Modern World.* Woodbridge, Suffolk: Boydell Press.

Rodney, Walter. 1975. "The Guinea Coast." In Richard Gray and Roland Anthony Oliver (eds.), *The Cambridge History of Africa. Volume IV* (Cambridge: Cambridge University Press), 223–324.

Rodriguez, Francisco, Dani Rodrik. 2000. "Trade Policy and Economic Growth: A Skeptic's Guide to the Cross-national Evidence." *NBER Macroeconomics Annual* 15, 261–325.

Rodríguez O., Jaime E. 1998. *The Independence of Spanish America.* Cambridge: Cambridge University Press.

Roehner, Bertrand M. 1995. *Theory of Markets: Trade and Space-Time Patterns of Price Fluctuations: A Study in Analytical Economics.* Boston: Springer Science & Business Media.

Rogers, Adam. 2013. "Social Archaeological Approaches in Port and Harbour Studies." *Journal of Maritime Archaeology* 8, 181–96.

Rogers, Clifford J. (ed.). 2018. *The Military Revolution Debate: Readings on the Military Transformation of Early Modern Europe.* London: Routledge.

Rogers, Everett M. 1995. *Diffusion of Innovations,* 4th ed. New York: Simon and Schuster.

Rogers, Howard Aston. 1970. "The Fall of the Old Representative System in the Leeward and Windward Islands, 1854–1877." PhD dissertation, University of Southern California.

Rogin, Michael Paul. 1975. *Fathers and Children: Andrew Jackson and the Subjugation of the American Indian.* New York: Alfred Knopf.

Rogowski, Jon, John Gerring, Lee Cojocaru, Matthew Maguire. 2021. "Institutions and Development: A Postal Story." *American Journal of Political Science* (forthcoming).

Rommelse, Gijs, Roger Downing. 2015. "The Fleet as an Ideological Pillar of Dutch Radical Republicanism, 1650–1672." *International Journal of Maritime History* 27:3, 387–410.

Ronnback, Klas. 2012. "The Speed of Ships and Shipping Productivity in the Age of Sail." *European Review of Economic History* 16:4, 469–89.

Rosanvallon, Pierre. 1995. "The History of the Word Democracy in France." *Journal of Democracy* 6, 140–54.

Rose, Richard, Doh Chull Shin. 2001. "Democratization Backwards: The Problem of Third-Wave Democracies." *British Journal of Political Science* 31:2, 331–54.

Rose, Susan. 2020. "Why the Medieval Sea Mattered." In Claire Jowitt, Craig Lambert, Steve Mentz (eds.), *The Routledge Companion to Marine and Maritime Worlds 1400–1800* (Oxford: Routledge), 33–49.

Rosecrance, Richard N. 1986. *The Rise of the Trading State: Commerce and Conquest in the Modern World.* New York: Basic Books.

Rosenberg, Emily S. (ed.). 2012. *A World Connecting, 1870–1945.* Cambridge: Belknap Press of Harvard University Press.

Rosenblatt, Helena. 2018. *The Lost History of Liberalism: From Ancient Rome to the Twenty-First Century.* Princeton: Princeton University Press.

Ross, Michael. 2012. *The Oil Curse: How Petroleum Wealth Shapes the Development of Nations.* Princeton: Princeton University Press.

Ross, Robert (ed.). 1982. *Racism and Colonialism.* Leiden: Leiden University Press.

   1985. "Cape Town (1750–1850): Synthesis in the Dialectic of Continents." In Robert Ross and Gerard J. Telkamp (eds.), *Colonial Cities* (Dordrecht: Martinus Nijhoff), 105–21.

Ross, Robert, Gerard J. Telkamp (eds.). 1985. *Colonial Cities.* Dordrecht: Martinus Nijhoff.

Rossabi, Morris. 1998. "The Legacy of the Mongols." In Beatrice F. Manz (ed.), *Central Asia in Historical Perspective* (Boulder: Westview), 27–44.

Rousseau, Jean-Jacques. 1994. *Discourse on Political Economy and the Social Contract,* trans. Christopher Betts. Oxford: Oxford University Press.

Royle, Stephen A. 2001. *A Geography of Islands: Small Island Insularity.* London: Routledge.

Rozman, Gilbert. 1976. *Urban Networks in Russia, 1750–1800, and Pre-modern Periodization.* Princeton: Princeton University Press.

Rubiés, Joan-Pau. 2005. "Oriental Despotism and European Orientalism: Botero to Montesquieu." *Journal of Early Modern History* 9:1, 109–80.

Rubin, Donald B. 1986. "Comment: Which If's Have Causal Answers." *Journal of the American Statistical Association* 81:396, 961–2.

Rudolf, Wolfgang. 1980. *Harbour and Town: A Maritime Cultural History.* Leipzig: Editions Leipzig.

Rudolph, Susanne Hoeber. 1997. "Introduction: Religion, States, and Transnational Civil Society." In Susanne Hoeber Rudolph and James Piscatori (eds.), *Transnational Religion and Fading States* (Boulder: Westview Press).

Rudra, Nita. 2005. "Globalization and the Strengthening of Democracy in the Developing World." *American Journal of Political Science* 49, 704–30.

Rueschemeyer, Dietrich, Evelyne Huber Stephens, John D. Stephens. 1992. *Capitalist Development and Democracy.* Chicago: University of Chicago Press.

Ruff, Julius R. 2001. *Violence in Early Modern Europe 1500–1800.* Cambridge: Cambridge University Press.

Runciman, David. 2000. "Is the State a Corporation?" *Government and Opposition* 35:1, 90–104.

Runyan, Timothy (ed.). 1987. *Ships, Seafaring, and Society: Essays in Maritime History.* Detroit: Wayne State University Press.

Russell, Lynette (ed.). 2001. *Colonial Frontiers: Indigenous–European Encounters in Settler Societies.* Manchester: Manchester University Press.

Russell-Wood, Anthony J. R. (ed.). 1999. *Local Government in European Overseas Empires, 1450–1800.* Aldershot: Ashgate.

Russett, Bruce. 1964. "Inequality and Instability: The Relation of Land Tenure to Politics." *World Politics* 16:3, 442–54.

Russett, Bruce, William Antholis. 1993. "The Imperfect Democratic Peace of Ancient Greece." In Bruce Russett (ed.), *Grasping the Democratic Peace* (Princeton: Princeton University Press), 43–71.

Sabato, Hilda. 2001. *The Many and the Few: Political Participation in Republican Buenos Aires.* Stanford: Stanford University Press.

2018. *Republics of the New World: The Revolutionary Political Experiment in Nineteenth-Century Latin America.* Princeton: Princeton University Press.

Sabetti, Filippo. 2004. "Local Roots of Constitutionalism." *Perspectives on Political Science* 33:2, 70–8.

Sager, Samuel. 1985. *The Parliamentary System of Israel.* Syracuse: Syracuse University Press.

Sahlins, Marshall D. 1961. "The Segmentary Lineage: An Organization of Predatory Expansion." *American Anthropologist* 63:2, 322–45.

Sahlins, Peter. 1989. *Boundaries: The Making of France and Spain in the Pyrenees.* Berkeley: University of California Press.

Said, Edward W. 1978. *Orientalism.* New York: Vintage.

1994. *Culture and Imperialism.* New York: Vintage.

Sajima, Naoko, Kyōichi Tachikawa. 2009. *Japanese Sea Power: A Maritime Nation's Struggle for Identity.* Canberra: Sea Power Centre-Australia.

Salomon, Ferreol, Simon Keay, Nicolas Carayon, Jean-Philippe Goiran. 2016. "The Development and Characteristics of Ancient Harbours: Applying the PADM Chart to the Case Studies of Ostia and Portus." *PLoS ONE* 11:9, e0170140.

Salter, Alexander William, Andrew T. Young. 2018. "Medieval Representative Assemblies: Collective Action and Antecedents of Limited Government." *Constitutional Political Economy* 29:2, 171–92.

Salzman, P. C. 2004. *Pastoralists: Equality, Hierarchy, and the State.* Boulder: Westview Press.

Santos, A. M. P., R. Salvador, C. Guedes Soares. 2018. "A Dynamic View of the Socioeconomic Significance of Ports." *Maritime Economics and Logistics* 20:2, 169–89.

Sargent, Arthur John. 1938. *Seaports and Hinterlands.* London: A. and C. Black.

Sargent, Mark L. 1988. "The Conservative Covenant: The Rise of the Mayflower Compact in American Myth." *New England Quarterly* 61:2, 233–51.

Sarkar, Sumit. 1983. *Modern India 1885–1947.* Chennai: Macmillan.

Sartori, Andrew. 2006. "The British Empire and Its Liberal Mission." *Journal of Modern History* 78:3, 623–42.

Sartre, Jean-Paul. 2001. *Being and Nothingness: An Essay in Phenomenological Ontology*. New York: Citadel Press.

Sastri, Kallidaikurichi Aiyah Nilakanta. 1975. *A History of South India from Prehistoric Times to the Fall of Vijayanagar*, 4th ed. New Delhi: Oxford University Press.

Sastri, Kallidaikurichi Aiyah Nilakanta. 1955 [1935]. *The Colas*. Madras: University of Madras.

Satz, Ronald N. 1975. *American Indian Policy in the Jacksonian Era*. Norman: University of Oklahoma Press.

Sawer, Marian. 2012. *Marxism and the Question of the Asiatic Mode of Production. Volume III*. Boston: Springer Science & Business Media.

Scammell, Geoffrey Vaughn. 1981. *The World Encompassed: The First European Maritime Empires, c. 800–1650*. Berkeley: University of California Press.

    1995. *Ships, Oceans, and Empire: Studies in European Maritime and Colonial History, 1400–1750*. Aldershot: Variorum Publishing.

    2003. *Seafaring, Sailors and Trade, 1450–1750: Studies in British and European Maritime and Imperial History*. Aldershot: Ashgate Publishing.

Schapera, Isaac. 1956. *Government and Politics in Tribal Societies*. New York: Schocken.

Scharfe, Hartmut. 1989. *The State in Indian Tradition*. Leiden: E.J. Brill.

Schattschneider, E. E. 1960. *The Semisovereign People: A Realist's View of Democracy in America*. London: Wadsworth.

Schedler, Andreas. 2002. "Elections without Democracy: The Menu of Manipulation." *Journal of Democracy* 13:2, 36–50.

    (ed.). 2006. *Electoral Authoritarianism: The Dynamics of Unfree Competition*. Boulder: Lynne Rienner.

Scheidel, Walter (ed.). 2009. *Rome and China: Comparative Perspectives on Ancient World Empires*. Oxford: Oxford University Press.

    (ed.). 2015. *State Power in Ancient China and Rome*. Oxford: Oxford University Press.

    2017. *The Great Leveler*. Princeton: Princeton University Press.

    2019. *Escape from Rome: The Failure of Empire and the Road to Prosperity*. Princeton: Princeton University Press.

Schlereth, Thomas J. 1977. *The Cosmopolitan Ideal in Enlightenment Thought: Its Form and Function in the Ideas of Franklin, Hume, and Voltaire, 1694–1790*. Notre Dame: University of Notre Dame Press.

Schmidtz, David, Jason Brennan. 2010. *A Brief History of Liberty*. New York: John Wiley & Sons.

Schmitt, Carl. 1997 [1954]. *Land and Sea*. Washington, DC: Plutarch Press.

    2003 [1950]. *The Nomos of the Earth*, trans. G. L. Ulmen. New York: Telos Press.

Schneider, Udo, Andreas Becker, Peter Finger, Anja Meyer-Christoffer, Bruno Rudolf, Markus Ziese. 2015. "GPCC Full Data Reanalysis Version 7.0 at 0.5°: Monthly Land-Surface Precipitation from Rain-Gauges built on GTS-Based and Historic Data." https://opendata.dwd.de/climate_environment/ GPCC/html/fulldata_v7_doi_download.html.

Schönholzer, David. 2020. "The Origin of the Incentive Compatible State: Environmental Circumscription." Working paper. Institute for International Economic Studies, Stockholm University, Frescativägen 6, Stockholm. www.dropbox.com/s/7rv2po5ek53el75/circumscription_paper_ 191207.pdf?dl=0.

Schottenhammer, Angela. 2005. *Trade and Transfer across the East Asian "Mediterranean". Volume I.* Wiesbaden: Otto Harrassowitz Verlag.

(ed.). 2008. *The East Asian Mediterranean: Maritime Crossroads of Culture, Commerce and Human Migration.* Wiesbaden: Otto Harrassowitz Verlag.

2019. "China's Rise and Retreat as a Maritime Power." In Robert J. Antony and Angela Schottenhammer (eds.), *Beyond the Silk Roads: New Discourses on China's Role in East Asian Maritime History* (Wiesbaden: Harrassowitz), 189–212.

Schrikker, Alicia. 2007. *Dutch and British Colonial Intervention in Sri Lanka, 1780–1815: Expansion and Reform.* Leiden: Brill.

Schulz, Jonathan F. 2019. *Kin Networks and Institutional Development.* SSRN Working Paper. Social Science Research Network.

Schulz, Jonathan F., Duman Bahrami-Rad, Jonathan P. Beauchamp, Joseph Henrich. 2019. "The Church, Intensive Kinship, and Global Psychological Variation." *Science* 366:6466.

Schumpeter, Joseph A. 1942. *Capitalism, Socialism, and Democracy.* New York: Harper & Brothers.

Schwartz, Stuart B. (ed.). 1994. *Implicit Understandings: Observing, Reporting and Reflecting on the Encounters between Europeans and Other Peoples in the Early Modern Era.* Cambridge: Cambridge University Press.

Schwartzman, Kathleen C. 1998. "Globalization and Democracy." *Annual Review of Sociology* 24:1, 159–81.

Schwoerer, Lois G. 1974. *'No Standing Armies!': The Antiarmy Ideology in Seventeenth-Century England.* Baltimore: Johns Hopkins University Press.

Scott, James C. 1998. *Seeing Like a State: How Certain Schemes to Improve the Human Condition Have Failed.* New Haven: Yale University Press.

2009. *The Art of Not Being Governed: An Anarchist History of Upland Southeast Asia.* New Haven: Yale University Press.

2017. *Against the Grain: A Deep History of the Earliest States.* New Haven: Yale University Press.

Scott, Jonathan. 2011. *When the Waves Ruled Britannia: Geography and Political Identities, 1500–1800.* Cambridge: Cambridge University Press.

Scott, Tom. 2012. *The City–State in Europe, 1000–1600: Hinterland, Territory, Region.* Oxford: Oxford University Press.

Scrivener, Michael. 2015. *The Cosmopolitan Ideal.* London: Routledge.

Scully, Timothy R. 1992. *Rethinking the Center: Party Politics in Nineteenth- and Twentieth-Century Chile.* Stanford: Stanford University Press.

Seal, Anil. 1971. *The Emergence of Indian Nationalism: Competition and Collaboration in the Later Nineteenth Century.* Cambridge: Cambridge University Press.

Seawright, Jason. 2019. "Statistical Analysis of Democratization: A Constructive Critique." *Democratization* 26:1, 21–39.

Sedlar, Jean W. 1994. *East Central Europe in the Middle Ages, 1000–1500.* Seattle: University of Washington Press.

Selinger, William. 2019. *Parliamentarism, From Burke to Weber.* Cambridge: Cambridge University Press.

Semple, Ellen Churchill. 1931. *Geography of the Mediterranean Region.* New York: Henry Holt.

Sen, Amartya. 1994. "Liberty and Poverty: Political Rights and Economics." *New Republic* 210:10, 31–7.

2003. "Democracy and Its Global Roots." *New Republic* (October 6), 228–35.

Sengupta, Nitish. 2011. *Land of Two Rivers: A History of Bengal from the Mahabharata to Mujib.* London: Penguin UK.

Serulnikov, Sergio. 2013. *Revolution in the Andes: The Age of Túpac Amaru.* Durham, NC: Duke University Press.

Service, Elman. 1975. *Origins of the State and Civilization.* New York: W.W. Norton.

Seshan, Radhika. 2012. *Trade and Politics on the Coromandel Coast: Seventeenth and Early Eighteenth Centuries.* Delhi: Primus Books.

2017. "Intersections: Peoples, Ports and Trade in Seventeenth-Century Surat and Madras." *International Journal of Maritime History* 29:1, 111–22.

Seth, Michael J. 2010. *A History of Korea: From Antiquity to the Present.* Lanham: Rowman & Littlefield.

Seymour, M. J. 2004. *The Transformation of the North Atlantic World.* London: Praeger.

Shaffer, Lynda Norene. 1995. *Maritime Southeast Asia, 300 BC to AD 1528.* London: Routledge.

Shafir, Gershon. 1996. *Land, Labor, and the Origins of the Israeli–Palestinian Conflict 1882–1914.* Berkeley: University of California Press.

2017. "Theorizing Zionist Settler Colonialism in Palestine." In Edward Cavanagh and Lorenzo Veracini (eds.), *The Routledge Handbook of the History of Settler Colonialism* (London: Taylor & Francis), 339–52.

Shaler, Nathaniel Southgate. 1894. *The Geological History of Harbors.* Washington, DC: Department of the Interior, US Geological Survey.

Sharma, Jagdish P. 1968. *Republics in Ancient India: c. 1500 BC–500 BC.* Leiden: E.J. Brill.

Sharma, Ram Sharan. 2005. *Aspects of Political Ideas and Institutions in Ancient India.* Delhi: Motilal Banarsidass Publishers.

Sharman, Jason. 2019. *Empires of the Weak: The Real Story of European Expansion and the Creation of the New World Order.* Princeton: Princeton University Press.

Shennan, J. H. 1968. *Parlement of Paris.* Ithaca: Cornell University Press.

Sheriff, Abdul. 2010. *Dhow Cultures of the Indian Ocean: Cosmopolitanism, Commerce and Islam.* New York: Columbia University Press.

Sheriff, Abdul, Engseng Ho (eds.). 2014. *The Indian Ocean: Oceanic Connections and the Creation of New Societies.* London: Hurst.

Shively, Donald H., William H. McCullough (eds.). 1993. *The Cambridge History of Japan. Volume II. Heian Japan.* Cambridge: Cambridge University Press.

Shoemaker, Robert W. 1966. "'Democracy' and 'Republic' as Understood in Late Eighteenth Century America." *American Speech* 41, 83–95.

Shon, James. 1998. "Traditional Korean Consensus Policy-making: The Hwabaek Syndrome as a Universal Model." *Asian Journal of Political Science* 6:2, 118–31.

Sidgwick, Henry. 1903. *The Development of European Polity.* New York: Macmillan.

Siedentop, Larry. 2014. *Inventing the Individual.* Cambridge, MA: Harvard University Press.

Simmons, A. H. 2014. *Stone Age Sailors: Paleolithic Seafaring in the Mediterranean.* Walnut Creek, CA: Left Coast Press.

Simon, Joshua. 2017. *The Ideology of Creole Revolution.* Cambridge: Cambridge University Press.

Simon, P., V. Piché, A. A. Gagnon (eds.). 2015. *Social Statistics and Ethnic Diversity: Cross-national Perspectives in Classifications and Identity Politics.* London: Springer.

Sinclair, Paul, Thomas Håkansson. 2000. "The Swahili City-State Culture." In Mogens Herman Hansen (ed.), *A Comparative Study of Thirty City-State Cultures* (Copenhagen: Royal Danish Academy of Sciences and Letters), 463–82.

Singer, J. David. 1987. "Reconstructing the Correlates of War Dataset on Material Capabilities of States, 1816–1985." *International Interactions* 14, 115–32.

Singer, Peter. 1981. *The Expanding Circle.* Oxford: Clarendon Press.

Singh, G. P. 2003. *Republics, Kingdoms, Towns and Cities in Ancient India.* New Delhi: D.K. Printworld.

Singh, Naunihal. 2014. *Seizing Power: The Strategic Logic of Military Coups.* Baltimore: Johns Hopkins University Press.

Sinha, Surajit (ed.). 1987. *Tribal Polities and State Systems in Pre-colonial Eastern and North Eastern India.* Calcutta: K.P. Bagchi & Co.

Sinopoli, Carla M. 2003. *The Political Economy of Craft Production: Crafting Empire in South India, c. 1350–1650.* Cambridge: Cambridge University Press.

Sircar, Dinesh Chandra. 1989. *Studies in the Political and Administrative Systems in Ancient and Medieval India.* New Delhi: Motilal Banarsidass Publishers.

Skaaning, Svend-Erik. 2011. "Democratic Survival or Autocratic Revival in Interwar Europe: A Comparative Examination of Structural Explanations." In Gero Erdmann and Marianne Kneuer (eds.), *Regression of Democracy?* (Boston: Springer Science & Business Media), 247–65.

Skaaning, Svend-Erik, John Gerring, Henrikas Bartusevičius. 2015. "A Lexical Index of Electoral Democracy." *Comparative Political Studies* 48, 1491–1525.

Skempton, A. W. 1953. "The Engineers of the English River Navigations, 1620–1760." *Transactions of the Newcomen Society* 29:1, 25–54.

Skinner, G. William (ed.). 1977. *The City in Late Imperial China.* Stanford: Stanford University Press.

Skinner, Quentin. 1978. *The Foundations of Modern Political Thought,* 2 vols. Cambridge: Cambridge University Press.

2012. *Liberty before Liberalism*. Cambridge: Cambridge University Press.

Smaldone, Joseph P. 1976. *Warfare in the Sokoto Caliphate: Historical and Sociological Perspectives*. Cambridge: Cambridge University Press.

Small, Christopher, Robert J. Nicholls. 2003. "A Global Analysis of Human Settlement in Coastal Zones." *Journal of Coastal Research* 19:3, 584–599.

Smith, Adam. 1976 [1776]. *The Wealth of Nations*. Chicago: University of Chicago Press.

Smith, Anthony D. 1978. "The Diffusion of Nationalism: Some Historical and Sociological Perspectives." *The British Journal of Sociology* 29:2, 234–48.

1988. *The Ethnic Origins of Nations*. Oxford: Blackwell.

Smith, Crosbie. 2018. *Coal, Steam and Ships: Engineering, Enterprise and Empire on the Nineteenth-Century Seas*. Cambridge: Cambridge University Press.

Smith, Laurence C. 2020. *Rivers of Power: How a Natural Force Raised Kingdoms, Destroyed Civilizations, and Shapes Our World*. New York: Little, Brown.

Smith, Maurice Greer. 1925. *Political Organization of the Plains Indians*. Lincoln: University of Nebraska Press.

Smith, Michael G. 1956. "On Segmentary Lineage Systems." *Journal of the Royal Anthropological Institute of Great Britain and Ireland* 86:2, 39–80.

Smith, Robert Sydney. 1988. *Kingdoms of the Yoruba*, 3rd ed. Madison: University of Wisconsin Press.

Smith, Rogers M. 1997. *Civic Ideals: Conflicting Visions of Citizenship in U.S. History*. New Haven: Yale University Press.

Smith, Woodruff D. 1978. *The German Colonial Empire*. Chapel Hill: University of North Carolina Press.

Smooha, Sammy. 2002. "The Model of Ethnic Democracy: Israel as a Jewish and Democratic State." *Nations and Nationalism* 8:4, 475–503.

Snell, Daniel C. 2001. *Flight and Freedom in the Ancient Near East*. Leiden: Brill.

So, Billy K. L.. 2000. *Prosperity, Region, and Institutions in Maritime China: The South Fukien Pattern, 946–1368*. Cambridge, MA: Harvard University Asia Center.

Sobecki, Sebastian I. (ed.). 2011. *The Sea and Englishness in the Middle Ages: Maritime Narratives, Identity and Culture*. Woodbridge, Suffolk: Boydell & Brewer Ltd.

Socolow, Susan M. 1982. "Buenos Aires at the Time of Independence." In Stanley R. Ross and Thomas F. McGann (eds.), *Buenos Aires: 400 Years* (Austin: University of Texas Press), 18–39.

Solar, Peter M., Luc Hens. 2016. "Ship Speeds during the Industrial Revolution: East India Company Ships, 1770–1828." *European Review of Economic History* 20:1, 66–78.

Solorzano y Pereira, Juan de (1575–1655). 1776. *Obras posthumas*. Madrid: Abe Books.

Sommers, Lawrence M. 1960. "Distribution and Significance of the Foreign Trade Ports of Norway." *Economic Geography* 36, 306–12.

Soucek, Svat. 2008. "The Ottoman Merchant Marine." In Svat Soucek (ed.), *Studies in Ottoman Naval History and Maritime Geography* (Istanbul: Isis Press), 171–80.

Southall, Aidan. 1988. "The Segmentary State in Africa and Asia." *Comparative Studies in Society and History* 30:1, 52–82.

Southern, Richard W. 1970. *Western Society and the Church in the Middle Ages.* New York: Penguin Books.

Southworth, Constant. 1931. *The French Colonial Venture.* London: P.S. King & Son.

Spence, Daniel Owen. 2015. *A History of the Royal Navy: Empire and Imperialism.* London: Bloomsbury Publishing.

Spooner, Brian. 1971. "Towards a Generative Model of Nomadism." *Anthropological Quarterly* 44:3, 198–210.

Spring, David (ed.). 1977. *European Landed Elites in the Nineteenth Century.* Baltimore: Johns Hopkins University Press.

Spruyt, Hendrik. 2007. "War, Trade, and State Formation." In Carles Boix and Susan Stokes (eds.), *Oxford Handbook of Comparative Politics* (Oxford: Oxford University Press), 211–36.

　　1994. *The Sovereign State and Its Competitors: An Analysis of Systems Change.* Princeton: Princeton University Press.

　　2020. *The World Imagined: Collective Beliefs and Political Order in the Sinocentric, Islamic and Southeast Asian International Societies.* Cambridge: Cambridge University Press.

Spufford, Peter. 2002. *Power and Profit: The Merchant in Medieval Europe.* London: Thames & Hudson.

Spurdle, Frederick G. 1962. *Early West Indian Government: Showing the Progress of Government in Barbados, Jamaica, and the Leeward Islands, 1660–1783.* Christchurch, NZ: Whitcombe and Tombs.

Srebrnik, Henry. 2004. "Small Island Nations and Democratic Values." *World Development* 32:2, 329–41.

Stamatov, Peter. 2010. "Activist Religion, Empire, and the Emergence of Modern Long-Distance Advocacy Networks." *American Sociological Review* 75:4, 607–28.

Stargardt, Janice. 1986. "Hydraulic Works and South East Asian Polities." In David G. Marr and Anthony Crothers Milner (eds.), *Southeast Asia in the 9th to 14th Centuries* (Singapore: Institute of Southeast Asian Studies), 23–48.

Starr, Chester G. 1989. *The Influence of Sea Power on Ancient History.* Oxford: Oxford University Press.

Stasavage, David. 2010. "When Distance Mattered: Geographic Scale and the Development of European Representative Assemblies." *American Political Science Review* 104:4, 625–43.

　　2011. *States of Credit: Size, Power, and the Development of European Polities.* Princeton: Princeton University Press.

　　2016. "Representation and Consent: Why They Arose in Europe and Not Elsewhere." *Annual Review of Political Science* 19, 145–62.

　　2020. *The Decline and Rise of Democracy: A Global History from Antiquity to Today.* Princeton: Princeton University Press.

Steel, Frances. 2011. *Oceania under Steam: Sea Transport and the Cultures of Colonialism, c. 1870–1914.* Manchester: Manchester University Press.

Steensgaard, Niels. 1975. *The Asian Trade Revolution: The East India Companies and the Decline of the Caravan Trade.* Chicago: University of Chicago Press.

Stein, Burton. 1980. *Peasant State and Society in Medieval South India*. Delhi: Oxford University Press.

1989. *The New Cambridge History of India*. Volume II. *Vijayanagara*. Cambridge: Cambridge University Press.

Stein, Stephen K. (ed.) 2017. *The Sea in World History: Exploration, Travel, and Trade*, 2 vols. Santa Barbara: ABC-CLIO.

Steinberg, Jonathan. 1996. *Why Switzerland?* 2nd ed. Cambridge: Cambridge University Press.

Steinberg, Philip E. 2001. *The Social Construction of the Ocean*. Cambridge: Cambridge University Press.

Stone, Daniel Z. 2014. *The Polish-Lithuanian State, 1386–1795*. Seattle: University of Washington Press.

Stone, Elizabeth. 1997. "City-States and Their Centers." In Deborah L. Nichols and Thomas H. Charlton (eds.), *The Archaeology of City-States: Cross-cultural Approaches* (Washington, DC: Smithsonian Institution Press), 15–26.

Strahler, Alan H., Arthur N. Strahler. 1992. *Modern Physical Geography*, 4th ed. New York: John Wiley and Sons, Inc.

Strang, David, John W. Meyer. 1993. "Institutional Conditions for Diffusion." *Theory and Society* 22:4, 487–511.

Strayer, Joseph R. 1970. *On the Medieval Origins of the Modern State*. Princeton: Princeton University Press.

Stromberg, R. N. 1996. *Democracy: A Short, Analytical History*. London: Routledge.

Strootman, Rolf. 2020. "Introduction: Maritime Empires in World History." In Rolf Strootman, Floris van den Eijnde, and Roy van Wijk (eds.), *Empires of the Sea: Maritime Power Networks in World History* (Leiden: Brill), 1–38.

Strootman, Rolf, Miguel John Versluys (eds.). 2017. *Persianism in Antiquity*. Stuttgart: Franz Steiner Verlag.

Strootman, Rolf, Floris van den Eijnde, Roy van Wijk (eds.). 2020. *Empires of the Sea: Maritime Power Networks in World History*. Leiden: Brill.

Studnicki-Gizbert, Daviken. 2007. *A Nation upon the Ocean Sea: Portugal's Atlantic Diaspora and the Crisis of the Spanish Empire, 1492–1640*. Oxford: Oxford University Press.

Subrahmanyam, Sanjay. 1986. "Aspects of State Formation in South India and Southeast Asia, 1500–1650." *Indian Economic and Social History Review* 23:4, 357–77.

(ed.). 1996. *Merchant Networks in the Early Modern World*. Aldershot: Variorum.

1990. *The Political Economy of Commerce: Southern India, 1500–1650*. Cambridge: Cambridge University Press.

Subramanian, Ajantha. 2009. *Shorelines: Space and Rights in South Asia*. Stanford: Stanford University Press.

Subramanian, Lakshmi (ed.). 2008. *Ports, Towns, Cities: A Historical Tour of the Indian Littoral*. Mumbai: Marg Publications.

Subtelny, Orest. 1986. *Domination of Eastern Europe: Native Nobilities and Foreign Absolutism 1500–1715*. McGill-Queen's University Press.

Sugar, Peter F., Peter Hanak, Tibor Frank. 1994. *A History of Hungary*. Indianapolis: Indiana University Press.

Suryadinata, Leo (ed.). 2005. *Admiral Zheng He and Southeast Asia.* Singapore: Institute of Southeast Asian Studies.

Sutherland, Heather. 2003. "Southeast Asian History and the Mediterranean Analogy." *Journal of Southeast Asian Studies* 34:1, 1–20.

2007. "Geography as Destiny? The Role of Water in Southeast Asian History." In Peter Boomgaard (ed.), *A World of Water: Rain, Rivers and Seas in Southeast Asian Histories* (Leiden: Brill).

Sutherland, Ingeborg. 2001. "From Warlords to Kings, C.E. 1–752: In Search of Military and Political Legitimacy in Germanic Societies." PhD dissertation, Concordia University.

Sutton, John E. G. 1993. "The Antecedents of the Interlacustrine Kingdoms." *Journal of African History* 34:1, 33–64.

Sutton, Paul, Anthony Payne. 1993. "Lilliput under Threat: The Security Problems of Small Island and Enclave Developing States." *Political Studies* 41:4, 579–93.

Swamy, Arun. 2003. "Consolidating Democracy by Containing Distribution: 'Sandwich Tactics' in Indian Political Development, 1936–96." *India Review* 2:2, 1–34.

Swanson, Guy E. 1967. *Religion and Regime: A Sociological Account of the Reformation.* Ann Arbor: University of Michigan Press.

Swinfen, David B. 1970. *Imperial Control of Colonial Legislation, 1813–1865: A Study of British Policy towards Colonial Legislative Powers.* Oxford: Clarendon Press.

Szűcs, Jenő, Julianna Parti. 1983. "The Three Historical Regions of Europe: An Outline." *Acta Historica Academiae Scientiarum Hungaricae* 29:2/4, 131–84.

Tackett, Nicolas. 2017. *The Origins of the Chinese Nation: Song China and the Forging of an East Asian World Order.* Cambridge: Cambridge University Press.

2018. "Spatial Organization of Chinese Imperial Government and Society." *Oxford Research Encyclopedia of Asian History* (Oxford: Oxford University Press), 1–22.

Tai, Hue-Tam Ho. 1984. "The Politics of Compromise: The Constitutionalist Party and the Electoral Reforms of 1922 in French Cochinchina." *Modern Asian Studies* 18:3, 371–91.

Talbert, Richard J. A. 1984. *The Senate of Imperial Rome.* Princeton: Princeton University Press.

Talbot, Cynthia. 2001. *Precolonial India in Practice: Society, Region, and Identity in Medieval Andhra.* Oxford: Oxford University Press.

Tambiah, S. J. 1976. *World Conqueror and World Renouncer.* Cambridge: Cambridge University Press.

Tan, Tai-Yong. 2007. "Port Cities and Hinterlands: A Comparative Study of Singapore and Calcutta." *Political Geography* 26:7, 851–65.

Tartaron, Thomas F. 2013. *Maritime Networks in the Mycenaean World.* Cambridge: Cambridge University Press.

Tawney, R. H. 1936. *Religion and the Rise of Capitalism*, 2nd ed. London: John Murray.

Taylor, Robert H. (ed.). 2002. *The Idea of Freedom in Asia and Africa.* Stanford: Stanford University Press.

Telles, Edward. 2014. *Pigmentocracies: Ethnicity, Race, and Color in Latin America.* Chapel Hill: University of North Carolina Press.

Teorell, Jan. 2010. *Determinants of Democratization: Explaining Regime Change in the World, 1972–2006.* Cambridge: Cambridge University Press.

Teorell, Jan, Staffan I. Lindberg. 2015. "The Structure of the Executive in Authoritarian and Democratic Regimes: Regime Dimensions across the Globe, 1900–2014." University of Gothenburg, Varieties of Democracy Institute, Working Paper No. 5.

Teorell, Jan, Nicholas Charron, Marcus Samanni, Sören Holmberg, Bo Rothstein. 2011. "The Quality of Government Dataset." University of Gothenburg: The Quality of Government Institute.

Teorell, Jan, Stefan Dahlberg, Sören Holmberg, Bo Rothstein, Felix Hartmann, Richard Svensson. 2015. "The Quality of Government Standard Dataset." University of Gothenburg: The Quality of Government Institute.

Teorell, Jan, Michael Coppedge, Staffan Lindberg, Svend-Erik Skaaning. 2018. "Measuring Polyarchy across the Globe, 1900–2017." *Studies in Comparative International Development* 54, 71–95.

Thaden, Edward C. 1984. *Russia's Western Borderlands, 1710–1870.* Princeton: Princeton University Press.

Thapar, Romila. 2002. *The Penguin History of Early India.* London: Penguin Books.

2012. *Aśoka and the Decline of the Mauryas.* Oxford: Oxford University Press.

Thaxton, Ralph. 2008. *Catastrophe and Contention in Rural China: Mao's Great Leap Forward Famine and the Origins of Righteous Resistance in Da Fo Village.* Cambridge: Cambridge University Press.

Thoreau, Henry David. 1906. "Cape Cod." In *The Writings of Henry David Thoreau. Volume IV* (Boston: Houghton Mifflin).

Thorn, H. 2006. *Anti-Apartheid and the Emergence of a Global Civil Society.* London: Palgrave Macmillan.

Tiebout, Charles M. 1956. "A Pure Theory of Local Expenditures." *Journal of Political Economy* 64:5, 416–24.

Tierney, Brian. 1966. "Medieval Canon Law and Western Constitutionalism." *Catholic Historical Review* 52, 1–17.

1982. *Religion, Law, and the Growth of Constitutional Thought, 1150–1650.* Cambridge: Cambridge University Press.

1988. *The Crisis of Church and State, 1050–1300.* Toronto: University of Toronto Press.

Tilley, Alec F. 2004. *Seafaring on the Ancient Mediterranean: New Thoughts on Triremes and Other Ancient Ships.* Oxford: British Archaeological Reports.

Tilly, Charles (ed.). 1975. *The Formation of National States in Western Europe.* Princeton: Princeton University Press.

1985. "War Making and State Making as Organized Crime." In Peter B. Evans, Dietrich Rueschemeyer, Theda Skocpol (eds.), *Bringing the State Back In* (Cambridge: Cambridge University Press), 169–91.

1992. *Coercion, Capital, and European States, 990–1992,* rev. ed. Oxford: Blackwell.

2007. *Democracy.* Cambridge: Cambridge University Press.

Tilly, Charles, Willem Pieter Blockmans (eds.). 1994. *Cities and the Rise of States in Europe, A.D. 1000–1800.* Oxford: Westview.

Tobacco, Giovanni. 1989. *The Struggle for Power in Medieval Italy: Structures of Political Rule, 400–1400,* trans. Rosalind Brown Jensen. Cambridge: Cambridge University Press.

Tocqueville, Alexis de. 2010. *The Old Regime and the French Revolution.* New York: Anchor.

Todd, Emmanuel. 1985. *The Explanation of Ideology: Family Structures and Social System.* Oxford: Basil Blackwell.

Tollefsen, Andreas Forø, Havard Buhaug. 2015. "Insurgency and Inaccessibility." *International Studies Review* 17:1, 6–25.

Tollefsen, Andreas Forø, Håvard Strand, Halvard Buhaug. 2012. "PRIO-GRID: A Unified Spatial Data Structure." *Journal of Peace Research* 49:2, 363–74.

Townsend, Mary Evelyn. 1966 [1930]. *The Rise and Fall of Germany's Colonial Empire, 1884–1918.* New York: Howard Fertig.

Tracy, James D. (ed.). 1990. *Rise of Merchant Empires: Long-Distance Trade in the Early Modern World 1350–1750.* Cambridge: Cambridge University Press.

(ed.). 1991. *The Political Economy of Merchant Empires: State Power and World Trade 1350–1750.* Cambridge: Cambridge University Press.

Trapido, Stanley. 1963. "Natal's Non-racial Franchise, 1856." *African Studies* 22:1, 22–32.

1964. "The Origins of the Cape Franchise Qualifications of 1853." *Journal of African History* 5:1, 37–54.

1990. "From Paternalism to Liberalism: The Cape Colony, 1800–1834." *The International History Review* 12:1, 76–104.

Travers, Robert. 2007. *Ideology and Empire in Eighteenth-Century India: The British in Bengal.* Cambridge: Cambridge University Press.

Treadgold, Donald W. 1990. *Freedom: A History.* New York: New York University Press.

Treisman, Daniel. 2020a. "Democracy by Mistake." *American Political Science Review* 114:3, 792–810.

2020b. "Economic Development and Democracy: Predispositions and Triggers." *Annual Review of Political Science* 23, 241–57.

Trenchard, John, Walter Moyle. 1697. *An Argument Shewing, that a Standing Army Is Inconsistent with a Free Government, and Absolutely Destructive to the Constitution of the English Monarchy.* London.

Trigger, Bruce. 1998. *Sociocultural Evolution.* Oxford: Blackwell.

Trigger, Bruce G. 2003. *Understanding Early Civilizations: A Comparative Study.* Cambridge: Cambridge University Press.

Troy, Jodok. 2009. "'Catholic Waves' of Democratization? Roman Catholicism and Its Potential for Democratization." *Democratization* 16:6, 1093–114.

Truhart, Peter. 1996. *Historical Dictionary of States: States and State-like Communities from Their Origins to the Present.* Munich: KG Saur Verlag.

Tuck, Richard. 2016. *The Sleeping Sovereign: The Invention of Modern Democracy.* Cambridge: Cambridge University Press.

Tucker, Joshua A., Yannis Theocharis, Margaret E. Roberts, Pablo Barberá. 2017. "From Liberation to Turmoil: Social Media and Democracy." *Journal of Democracy* 28:4, 46–59.

Tucker, Ruth, 2004. *From Jerusalem to Irian Jaya: A Biographical History of Christian Missions*. London: Zondervan.

Turchin, Peter, R. Brennan, T. E. Currie, K. C. Feeney, P. François, D. Hoyer. 2015. "Seshat: The Global History Databank." *Cliodynamics: The Journal of Quantitative History and Cultural Evolution* 6:1, 77–107.

Tusalem, Rollin F. 2009. "The Role of Protestantism in Democratic Consolidation among Transitional States." *Comparative Political Studies* 42:7, 882–915.

Tussman, Joseph. 1968. *Obligation and the Body Politic*. Oxford: Oxford University Press.

Tvedt, Terje. 2015. *Water and Society: Changing Perceptions of Societal and Historical Development*. London: I.B. Tauris.

Tvedt, Terje, Richard Coopey (eds.). 2010. *A History of Water. Series II, Volume 2. Rivers and Society: From Early Civilizations to Modern Times*. London: I.B. Tauris.

Twain, Mark. 2007 [1869]. *The Innocents Abroad*. London: Penguin.

Twinam, Ann. 2015. *Purchasing Whiteness: Pardos, Mulattos, and the Quest for Social Mobility in the Spanish Indies*. Stanford, Stanford University Press.

Tymowski, Michal. 2009. *The Origins and Structures of Political Institutions in Pre-colonial Black Africa: Dynastic Monarchy, Taxes and Tributes, War and Slavery, Kinship and Territory*. Lewiston, NY: Edwin Mellen Press.

Udovitch, Abraham L. 1977. "A Tale of Two Cities: Commercial Relations between Cairo and Alexandria during the Second Half of the Eleventh Century." In Harry A. Miskimin, David Herlihy, Abraham L. Udovitch (eds.), *The Medieval City* (New Haven: Yale University Press), 143–62.

UNESCO 2019. "International Standard Classification of Education: ISCED 2011." Montreal: UNESCO Institute for Statistics.

Unger, Richard W. 1980. *The Ship in the Medieval Economy, 600–1600*. London: McGill-Queen's University Press.

1997. *Ships and Shipping in the North Sea and Atlantic, 1400–1800*. Aldershot: Variorum.

2006. "Shipping and Western European Economic Growth in the Late Renaissance: Potential Connections." *International Journal of Maritime History* 18:2, 85–104.

(ed.). 2011. *Shipping and Economic Growth 1350–1850*. Leiden: Brill.

UNU-WIDER. 2017. "World Income Inequality Database" WIID3.4. www.wider.unu.edu/database/world-income-inequality-database-wiid34.

Usher, A. P. 1928. "Growth of English Shipping, 1572 to 1922." *Quarterly Journal of Economics* 42:2, 465–78.

US Navy. 1953. *World Port Index 1953*. Washington, DC: Hydrographic Office, US Navy.

Valenzuela, J. Samuel. 1996. "Building Aspects of Democracy before Democracy: Electoral Practices in Nineteenth Century Chile." In Eduardo

Posada-Carbó (ed.), *Elections before Democracy: The History of Elections in Europe and Latin America* (London: Macmillan), 223–57.

Van der Walt, Lucien. 2011. "Anarchism and Syndicalism in an African Port City: The Revolutionary Traditions of Cape Town's Multiracial Working Class, 1904–1931." *Labor History* 52:2, 137–71.

Van Dommelen, Peter. 2012. "Colonialism and Migration in the Ancient Mediterranean." *Annual Review of Anthropology* 41, 393–409.

Van Evera, Stephen. 1998. "Offense, Defense, and the Causes of War." *International Security* 22:4, 5–43.

van Gelderen, Martin, Quentin Skinner (eds.). 2002. *Republicanism: A Shared European Heritage*, 2 vols. Cambridge: Cambridge University Press.

Vanhanen, Tatu. 2003. *Democratization: A Comparative Analysis of 170 Countries*. London: Routledge.

Van Oss, Adriaan C. 1985. "Central America's Autarkic Colonial Cities (1600–1800)." In Robert Ross and Gerard J. Telkamp (eds.), *Colonial Cities* (Dordrecht: Martinus Nijhoff), 33–50.

Vansina, Jan M. 1962. "A Comparison of African Kingdoms." *Africa* 32:4, 324–35.

1966. *Kingdoms of the Savanna*. Madison: University of Wisconsin Press.

1990. *Paths in the Rainforests: Toward a History of Political Tradition in Equatorial Africa*. Madison: University of Wisconsin Press.

2004. *How Societies Are Born: Governance in West Central Africa before 1600*. Charlottesville: University of Virginia Press.

2005. *Antecedents to Modern Rwanda: The Nyiginya Kingdom*. Madison: University of Wisconsin Press.

Van Zanden, Jan Luiten, Eeltjo Buringh, Maarten Bosker. 2012. "The Rise and Decline of European Parliaments, 1188–1789." *Economic History Review* 65:3, 835–61.

Veenendaal, Wouter P. 2013. "Political Representation in Microstates: St. Kitts and Nevis, Seychelles, and Palau." *Comparative Politics* 45:4, 437–56.

2014a. "A Big Prince in a Tiny Realm: Smallness, Monarchy, and Political Legitimacy in the Principality of Liechtenstein." *Swiss Political Science Review* 21:2, 333–49.

2014b. *Politics and Democracy in Microstates*. London: Routledge.

Veikou, Myrtou. 2015. "Mediterranean Byzantine Ports and Harbours in the Complex Interplay between Environment and Society: Spatial, Socio-economic and Cultural Considerations Based on Archaeological Evidence from Greece, Cyprus and Asia Minor." In Johannes Preiser-Kapeller and Falko Daim (eds.), *Harbours and Maritime Networks as Complex Adaptive Systems* (Mainz: Verlag des Romisch-Germanischen Zentralmuseums), 39–60.

Veliz, Claudio. 1980. *The Centralist Tradition of Latin America*. Princeton: Princeton University Press.

Veluthat, Kesavan. 1993. *The Political Structure of Early Medieval South India*. New Delhi: Orient Longman.

2009. *The Early Medieval in South India*. Oxford: Oxford University Press.

Veracini, Lorenzo. 2006. *Israel and Settler Society*. London: Pluto Press.

2010. *Settler Colonialism*. London: Springer.

Vernadsky, George. 1948. *Kievan Russia*. New Haven: Yale University Press.

Vernon-Harcourt, Leveson Francis. 1885. *Harbours and Docks*. Oxford: Clarendon Press.

Vickery, Kenneth P. 1974. "'Herrenvolk' Democracy and Egalitarianism in South Africa and the US South." *Comparative Studies in Society and History* 16.3: 309–28.

Villiers, Alan. 1952. *Monsoon Seas: The Story of the Indian Ocean*. New York: McGraw-Hill.

Villiers, John. 1981. "Trade and Society in the Banda Islands in the Sixteenth Century." *Modern Asian Studies* 15:4, 723–50.

1990a. "The Cash-Crop Economy and State Formation in the Spice Islands in the Fifteenth and Sixteenth Centuries." In Jaya Kathirithamby-Wells and John Villiers (eds.), *The Southeast Asian Port and Polity: Rise and Demise* (Singapore: Singapore University Press), 83–105.

1990b. "Makassar: The Rise and Fall of an East Indonesian Maritime Trading State, 1512–1669." In Jaya Kathirithamby-Wells and John Villiers (eds.), *The Southeast Asian Port and Polity: Rise and Demise* (Singapore: Singapore University Press), 143–59.

Vlassopoulos, Kostas. 2007. *Unthinking the Greek Polis: Ancient Greek History beyond Eurocentrism*. Cambridge: Cambridge University Press.

Voigtländer, Nico, Hans-Joachim Voth. 2013. "How the West 'Invented' Fertility Restriction." *American Economic Review* 103:6, 2227–64.

Voltaire. 2007. *Philosophical Letters: Or, Letters Regarding the English Nation*, ed. John Leigh. Indianapolis: Hackett Publishing.

von Rueden, Christopher, Mark van Vugt. 2015. "Leadership in Small-Scale Societies: Some Implications for Theory, Research, and Practice." *Leadership Quarterly* 26:6, 978–90.

Wacziarg, Romain, Enrico Spolaore. 2018. "Ancestry and Development: New Evidence." *Journal of Applied Econometrics* 33:5, 748–62.

Wade, Peter. 2017. *Degrees of Mixture, Degrees of Freedom: Genomics, Multiculturalism, and Race in Latin America*. Durham, NC: Duke University Press.

Wahl, Fabian. 2018. "Political Participation and Economic Development: Evidence from the Rise of Participative Political Institutions in the Late Medieval German Lands." *European Review of Economic History* 23:2, 193–213.

Wahman, Michael, Jan Teorell, Axel Hadenius. 2013. "Authoritarian Regime Types Revisited: Updated Data in Comparative Perspective." *Contemporary Politics* 19:1, 19–34.

Wakita, Haruko. 1999. "Ports, Markets, and Medieval Urbanism in the Osaka Region." In James L. McClain and Wakita Osamu (eds.), *Osaka: The Merchants' Capital of Early Modern Japan* (Ithaca: Cornell University Press), 22–43.

Waldner, David. 1999. *State Building and Late Development*. Ithaca: Cornell University Press.

Wandycz, Piotr S. 2001. *The Price of Freedom: A History of East Central Europe from the Middle Ages to the Present*. London: Routledge.

Wang, C., Cesar Ducruet. 2013. "Regional Resilience and Spatial Cycles: Long-Term Evolution of the Chinese Port System (221BC–2010AD)." *Tijdschrift voor Economische en Sociale Geografie*, 104:5, 524–38.

Wang, Haicheng. 2014. *Writing and the Ancient State: Early China in Comparative Perspective*. Cambridge: Cambridge University Press.

Ward, J. O. 1985. "Feudalism: Interpretative Category or Framework of Life in the Medieval West?" In E. Leach, S. N. Mukherjee, J. O. Ward (eds.), *Feudalism: Comparative Studies* (Sydney: Sydney Association for Studies in Society and Culture), 40–67.

Ward, John Manning. 1976. *Colonial Self-Government: The British Experience, 1759–1856*. Boston: Springer.

Ward, Michael D., Brian D. Greenhill, and Kristin M. Bakke. 2010. "The Perils of Policy by P-value: Predicting Civil Conflicts." *Journal of Peace Research* 47:4, 363–75.

Waterhouse, Richard. 2010. "Liberty and Representative Government in Australia, 1788–1901." In Jack P. Greene (ed.), *Exclusionary Empire: English Liberty Overseas: 1600–1900* (Cambridge: Cambridge University Press), 220–47.

Watts, John. 2009. *The Making of Polities: Europe, 1300–1500*. Cambridge: Cambridge University Press.

Weaver, John C. 2003. *The Great Land Rush and the Making of the Modern World, 1650–1900*. Montreal: McGill-Queen's University Press.

Webb, Herschel. 1968. *The Japanese Imperial Institution in the Tokugawa Period*. New York: East Asian Institute, Columbia University.

Webb, Walter Prescott. 1986. *The Great Frontier*. Lincoln: University of Nebraska Press.

Weber, Max. 1922. *The City*, trans. and ed. Don Martindale and Gertrud Neuwirth. New York: The Free Press.

1958 [1904–5]. *The Protestant Ethic and the Spirit of Capitalism*. New York: Charles Scribner's.

1978. *Economy and Society: An Outline of Interpretive Sociology*, 2 vols., ed. Guenther Roth and Claus Wittich. Berkeley: University of California Press.

2013 [1909]. *The Agrarian Sociology of Ancient Civilizations*. London: Verso.

Webster's. 2014. *Webster's New World College Dictionary*, 5th ed. New York: Houghton Mifflin Harcourt.

Weidmann, Nils B., Doreen Kuse, Kristian Skrede Gleditsch. 2010. "The Geography of the International System: The CShapes Dataset." *International Interactions* 36:1, 86–106.

Weigend, Guido G. 1958. "Some Elements in the Study of Port Geography." *Geographical Review* 48:2, 185–200.

Weinbaum, Martin (ed.). 2010. *British Borough Charters 1307–1660*. Cambridge: Cambridge University Press.

Weir, Shelagh. 2007. *A Tribal Order: Politics and Law in the Mountains of Yemen*. Austin: University of Texas Press.

Welzel, Christian. 2013. *Freedom Rising: Human Empowerment and the Quest for Emancipation*. Cambridge: Cambridge University Press.

2014. "Evolution, Empowerment, and Emancipation: How Societies Climb the Freedom Ladder." *World Development* 64, 33–51.

Wenzlhuemer, Roland. 2013. *Connecting the Nineteenth-Century World: The Telegraph and Globalization*. Cambridge: Cambridge University Press.

Westerdahl, Christer. N. 2015. "Boats, Portages and Texts Comments on Society and Water Transport in Inland Russia during the Viking Age." *Årbok Norsk Maritimt Museum* 14, 71–109.

Weyland, Kurt G. 2007. *Bounded Rationality and Policy Diffusion: Social Sector Reform in Latin America*. Princeton: Princeton University Press.

White, H. P. 1970. "The Morphological Development of West African Seaports." In David Hilling and Brian Stewart Hoyle (eds.), *Seaports and Development in Tropical Africa* (London: Palgrave Macmillan), 11–25.

Whitehouse, Harvey, Pieter François, Patrick E. Savage, Thomas E. Currie, Kevin C. Feeney, Enrico Cioni, Rosalind Purcell, Robert M. Ross, Jennifer Larson, John Baines, Barend ter Haar, Alan Covey, Peter Turchin. 2019. "Complex Societies Precede Moralizing Gods throughout World History." *Nature* 568:7751, 226–9.

Wickham, Chris. 2009. *The Inheritance of Rome: A History of Europe from 400 to 1000*. London: Allen Lane.

Wight, Martin. 1946. *The Development of the Legislative Council, 1606–1945*. London: Faber and Faber.

   1952. *British Colonial Constitutions, 1947*. Oxford: Clarendon Press.

Wilkinson, J. C. 1972. "The Origins of the Omani State." In Derek Hopwood (ed.), *The Arabian Peninsula: Society and Politics* (London: George Allen & Unwin), 67–88.

Williams, Eric Eustace. 1970. *From Columbus to Castro: The History of the Caribbean, 1492–1969*. New York: Vintage.

Williams, Stephen, Gerard Friell. 1999. *The Rome That Did Not Fall: The Survival of the East in the Fifth Century*. London: Routledge.

Wills, John E., Jr. 1993. "Maritime Asia, 1500–1800: The Interactive Emergence of European Domination." *American Historical Review* 98:1, 83–105.

   2011. "Maritime Europe and the Ming." In John E. Wills, Jr. (ed.), *China and Maritime Europe, 1500–1800: Trade, Settlement, Diplomacy, and Missions* (Cambridge: Cambridge University Press), 24–77.

Wilson, Kevin, Jan van der Dussen (eds.). 2005. *The History of the Idea of Europe*. London: Routledge.

Wilson, Peter H. 2016. *Holy Roman Empire*. John Wiley & Sons.

Wilson, Steven Lloyd. 2017. "Information and Revolution." University of Gothenburg, Varieties of Democracy working paper series 2017:50.

Wink, André. 2002. "From the Mediterranean to the Indian Ocean: Medieval History in Geographic Perspective." *Comparative Studies in Society and History* 44, 416–45.

   2004. *Al-Hind: The Making of the Indo-Islamic World. Volume III. Indo-Islamic Society: 14th–15th Centuries*. Leiden: Brill.

   2011. "Post-nomadic Empires: From the Mongols to the Mughals." In Peter Bang and Christopher Bayly (eds.), *Tributary Empires in Global History* (London: Palgrave Macmillan), 120–31.

   2020. *The Making of the Indo-Islamic World c.700–1800 CE*. Cambridge: Cambridge University Press. Kindle edition.

Winnacker, Rudolph A. 1938. "Elections in Algeria and the French Colonies under the Third Republic." *American Political Science Review* 32:2, 261–77.

Winters, Christopher. 1983. "The Classification of Traditional African Cities." *Journal of Urban History* 10:1, 3–31.

Wittfogel, Karl August. 1957. *Oriental Despotism: A Study of Total Power*. New Haven: Yale University Press.

Wolf, Armin. 1991. "The Family of Dynasties in Medieval Europe: Dynasties, Kingdoms and Tochterstamme." *Studies in Medieval and Renaissance History* 12, 185–260.

Wolf, Eric. 1982. *Europe and the People without History*. Berkeley: University of California Press.

Wolfe, Patrick. 2006. "Settler Colonialism and the Elimination of the Native." *Journal of Genocide Research* 8:4, 387–409.

Wolff, Larry. 1994. *Inventing Eastern Europe: The Map of Civilization on the Mind of the Enlightenment*. Stanford: Stanford University Press.

Wolters, Oliver William. 1967. *Early Indonesian Commerce*. Ithaca: Cornell University Press.

1982. *History, Culture, and Religion in Southeast Asian Perspectives*. New York: SEAP Publications.

Wong, R. Bin. 1997. *China Transformed: Historical Change and the Limits of European Experience*. Ithaca: Cornell University Press.

Wood, Gordon S. 2011. *The Radicalism of the American Revolution*. New York: Vintage.

Woodberry, Robert D. 2012. "The Missionary Roots of Liberal Democracy." *American Political Science Review* 106:2, 244–74.

Woodley, Michael A., Edward Bell. 2013. "Consanguinity as a Major Predictor of Levels of Democracy: A Study of 70 Nations." *Journal of Cross-cultural Psychology* 44, 263–80.

Woodward, C. Vann. 1951. *Origins of the New South, 1877–1913*. Baton Rouge: Louisiana State University Press.

Woollacott, Angela. 2015. *Settler Society in the Australian Colonies: Self-government and Imperial Culture*. Oxford: Oxford University Press.

World Bank. 2016. *World Development Indicators 2016*. Washington, DC: World Bank.

Wright, Joseph. 2008. "To Invest or Insure? How Authoritarian Time Horizons Impact Foreign Aid Effectiveness." *Comparative Political Studies* 41:7, 971–1000.

Wrigley, Christopher. 1996. *Kingship and State: The Buganda Dynasty*. Cambridge: Cambridge University Press.

Wrigley, Edward Anthony, Ros S. Davies, James Oeppen, Roger S. Schofield. 1997. *English Population History from Family Reconstitution, 1580–1837*. Cambridge: Cambridge University Press.

Wrong, Humphrey Hume. 1923. *Government of the West Indies*. Oxford: Clarendon Press.

Yang, Jisheng. 2012. *Tombstone: The Great Chinese Famine, 1958–1962*. London: Macmillan.

Yangwen, Zheng. 2011. *China on the Sea: How the Maritime World Shaped Modern China*. Leiden: Brill.

Yazdani, Kaveh. 2017. *India, Modernity and the Great Divergence: Mysore and Gujarat (17th to 19th C.).* Leiden: Brill.

Yiftachel, Oren. 2006. *Ethnocracy: Land and Identity Politics in Israel/Palestine.* Philadelphia: University of Pennsylvania Press.

Yildirim, Onur. 2008. "Ottoman Guilds in the Early Modern Era." *International Review of Social History* 53:S16, 73–93.

Ylvisaker, Marguerite. 1979. *Lamu in the Nineteenth Century: Land, Trade, and Politics.* Boston: Boston University, African Studies Center.

Yu, Miaojie. 2010. "Trade, Democracy, and the Gravity Equation." *Journal of Development Economics* 91:2, 289–300.

Yuan, Bingling. 2000. *Chinese Democracies: A Study of the Kongsis of West Borneo (1776–1884).* Leiden: Research School of Asian, African, and Amerindian Studies, Universiteit Leiden.

Zahlan, Rosemarie Said. 2016. *The Making of the Modern Gulf States: Kuwait, Bahrain, Qatar, the United Arab Emirates and Oman.* London: Routledge.

Zastoupil, Lynn. 1988. "JS Mill and India." *Victorian Studies* 32:1, 31–54.

Zeisler-Vralsted, Dorothy. 2015. *Rivers, Memory and Nation-Building.* New York: Bergahn.

Zhao, Dingxin. 2015. *The Confucian-Legalist State: A New Theory of Chinese History.* Oxford: Oxford University Press.

Zhao, Gang. 2013. *The Qing Opening to the Ocean: Chinese Maritime Policies, 1684–1757.* Honolulu: University of Hawaii Press.

Ziblatt, Daniel. 2008. "Does Landholding Inequality Block Democratization? A Test of the 'Bread and Democracy' Thesis and the Case of Prussia." *World Politics* 60, 610–41.

Zimmermann, Andreas, Johanna Hilpert, Karl Peter Wendt. 2009. "Estimations of Population Density for Selected Periods between the Neolithic and AD 1800." *Human Biology* 81, 2–3.

Zimmermann, Eduardo. 2009. "Elections and the Origins of an Argentine Democratic Tradition, 1810–1880." Kellogg Institute Working Paper #365.

Zolberg, Aristide R. 1980. "Strategic Interactions and the Formation of Modern States: France and England." *International Social Science Journal* 32:4, 687–716.

Zumerchik, John, Steven Laurence Danver (eds.). 2010. *Seas and Waterways of the World: An Encyclopedia of History, Uses, and Issues.* Santa Barbara: ABC-CLIO.

Zürcher, Erik J. 2017. *Turkey: A Modern History.* London: Bloomsbury Publishing.

Zwart, Pim de, Jan Liuten van Zanden. 2018. *The Origins of Globalization: World Trade in the Making of the Global Economy, 1500–1800.* Cambridge: Cambridge University Press.

Index

Abramson, Scott F. 118
Africa
  democratic origins 32
  rivers and waterways 102
  sub-Saharan 132–4
agriculture 8, 310–12
  agricultural transitions 340–2
apartheid 390
aquaculture 311
Aristotle 363
Asia
  democratic origins 30–2
  East Asia 140
  South Asia 157–63
  Southeast Asia 151–7
autocracy 26–7
  fostered by economic inequality 345
  "hydraulic" 309
  technological surveilence 370

Barrett, David B. 296
Boix, Carles 118
bourgeoisie 50–2
British Empire 229, 249
  Americas 251
  Australia 256
  Canadian provinces 256
  Caribbean 252
  Cayman Islands 280
  colonial assemblies 251, 253, 258, 261
  Commonwealth Franchise Act (1902) 256
  East Asia 263
  Franchise and Ballot Act (1892) 260
  India 260
  indirect rule 57
  Middle East 264
  Native Law system 259
  Parliamentary Voters' Registration Act
    (1887) 259
  political and civil rights 250
  Southern Africa 258
Byzantine Empire 129

Catalogue of Ancient Ports and Harbours 11,
  77, 80
China 140–4, 150–1
  fertility rates 348
  Great Leap Forward 369
  Xinjiang 390
Christianity 353–5
  authoritarianism and 354
  Catholicism and democracy 324–7,
    353–5
  correlation with democracy 327–8, 333
  Protestantism and democracy 324–7
cities 184–5
  ocean and river port 188
city-states 137
climate 8
  influence on democratization 308
colonialism 243, 322–4
  correlation with democracy development
    322–4
  demographic restraints on
    democratization 211–13
  development of representative
    democracies 215
  direct and indirect rule 58, 334
  duration correlated with democracy 333
  landlocked capitals 228
  role of natural harbors 230
connectedness 380
  direct democracy and 382–3
  economic development and 383
  equality and 384–8
contestation 41
  index of electoral 176, 289
Cshapes 93

Dahl, Robert 38
democracy 14–16, 23–5
  accountability 25
  as a coordinating device for group
    interests 216
  diffusion of 363–4

democracy (cont.)
  direct *See* direct democracy
  discussion of determinism 374–8
  European origins 27–30
  evolution of 33–5
  ideas of 361–3
  intellectual history of 20–3
  membership 24, 217
  problems of causal inferences 11, 367
  proto-democracy 30
  representative *See* representative
    democracy
  values 201–2
  world democracy 396
Democracy–Dictatorship index 41
demography 184
  European family structures 348
  patterns of European 347
direct democracy 15, 34, 382–3
  Switzerland 118
Downing, Brian 366
Dutch Empire 229, 277
  Indies 157

East India Company 260
economic development 48–50, 184, 202–4,
    383–4
  and autocracy 343
  and democratization 50–2
  GDP *See* Gross Domestic Product
    (GDP)
economic inequality 344–6
elections 41
England 116
Ethnographic Atlas 12, 35–8, 166, 303, 349
Euratlas 93
Europe 108–9, 234
  geography 111
  rivers and waterways 102
  statebuilding 109–12
European ancestry 4
  constructivist definition 237–8
  correlation with democracy 287–8, 333
  correlation with elected colonial
    assemblies 283
  correlation with European colonialism
    243
  correlation with timing of colony
    independence 285
  problems of causal inferences 301–4
  various measures of 290–1
European diaspora 228–31
European diffusion 8, 380
  and democratization 211–13
European identity 235–7

feudalism 116, 350–2
France 114
Freedom House 41
French Empire 229, 267
  direct rule 267
  political and civil rights 269

GeaCron 93
geography 8, 320–1
  as condition for European settlers
    335
  geographic factors correlated with
    democracy 317–18
  "mountain freedom" 312–13
  mountainous terrain correlated with
    regime type 380
German Empire 277
globalization 6
  correlation with democracy
    392–3
grid-cells 86, 93
  as unit of analysis 100, 139
  endogeneity 168
gross domestic product (GDP)
    51, 183
  correlation with democracy 344

Hanseatic League 120
harbors 68, 87
  Arctic 121
  distance correlated with democracy
    172–6
  economic development 49
Hariri, Jacob Gerner 295, 303, 331
Hartz, Louis 250
Heritage Foundation 203
Holy Roman Empire 110
Hong Kong 390

imperialism
  European 225–6
  role of harbors 227
indigenous peoples 211, 232
international institutions 391, 395
irrigation 8
  autocracy and 310
ISAM-Hyde dataset 189
Islam 302
  Middle East and North Africa 124
  Southeast Asia 154
islands 8
  influence on democratization 314
Israel 245, 264–7

Japan 146–50

Kinship Intensity Index 349
    correlation with democracy 350
Korea 144–6, 150–1
    origins of democracy 31–2
Kuwait 131

labor scarcity 345–6
landlocked areas 66
language 324–9, 334–5
    European language correlated with
        democracy 324–9
Lexical index of electoral democracy 12, 40,
    176, 289
Lloyd's List 11, 79, 81, 98, 174
Loades, David 116

Major, Russell 114
Middle East and North Africa 124–32
migration 60
    and democratization 60–3
    European 228–31, 245
    impact of demography on 231–3
Mill, John Stuart 214
modernization theory 342–4
    causal challenges 343

natural harbor distance 94
    collinearity concerns 94
    correlation with democracy 166, 173, 177
    correlation with democratic values 201
    correlation with economic development
        202–4
    correlation with geographic factors
        315–17
    correlation with parliamentary activity
        118
    correlation with population density 190
    correlation with state size 191–5
    East Asia 139
    Europe 109
    landlocked countries 94
    Middle East and North Africa 124
    United States 94
natural harbors 47, 68, 91
    Africa 93
    Asia 93
    effect on democracy 6
    Europe 93
    exogeneity 10
    geographic features of 84–6
    indirect effect on democracy 6
    promoting military organization 52–4
naval forces 116
    economic and political impact of 116
    implications for democracy 54–5

Navigocorpus 80
North America
    indigenous peoples 33

Olsson, Ola 296, 303, 331, 341
    orientalism 28
Ottoman Empire 129–30

Paik, Christopher 341
Paine, Jack 281
Palestine 264–7
parliaments 352–3
Penn World Tables 203
Polity IV project 12
    Polity2 index 39, 176, 212, 289
population density 190
    correlation with democracy 347
ports 68, 76, 184–5
    Arctic 123
    distance correlated with democracy
        169–76
    geomorphological requirements 78
    infrastructure requirements 78, 84
    migration and 49
    modern era 79–82
    path dependency regarding the location
        of 83–4
    premodern era 76–9
Portuguese Empire 229, 276
    Brazil 274
    colonial assemblies 277
    direct rule 276
Putterman, Louis 341

religion 324–7, 335
    Christianity *See* Christianity
    Islam *See* Islam
representative democracy 4, 15
    as a "European club" 278
    European origins 35
    exclusion in 214, 279
    property rights 279
    white supremacy and 248
Russia 27, 119
    authoritarianism 120
    rivers and waterways 102, 122

Schultz, Jonathan F. 349–50
Smith, Adam 48
social diversity 200
Soundtoll Registers 79
Spanish Empire 229, 270–1
    Americas 272
    Argentina 273
    Chile 273–4

Spanish Empire (cont.)
  fear of revolts 271
  racial divisions 275–6
  self-governance 272
states 16
  as unit of analysis 101, 139
  correlation between democracy and
    history of 361
  correlation between democracy and size
    of 194–6, 357–9
  statebuilding 55–7
  state-ness as obstacle to democratization
    359
suffrage 41, 279
Switzerland 117

Tilly, Charles 115
tourism 314
trade 6, 50, 60
  barriers 64

Unified Democracy Scores 41
United States 257
  civil rights 389
  Declaration of Independence 397
urbanization 113
  near ports 185–7

V-Dem (Varieties of Democracy) 12,
    23, 38
  Polyarchy index of electoral democracy
    38, 168, 176, 179, 212, 289

Wittfogel, Karl 309
Woodberry, Robert D. 296, 303, 331
World Development Indicators
    203
World Port Index 11, 80, 86, 98, 174
World Port Source 80
World Seastems project 80
World Values Survey 11, 200, 341